DOMESDAY BOOK

THREE ESSAYS

IN THE

EARLY HISTORY OF ENGLAND.

'Why still read it? Why should scholars consult it and undergraduates study it? The plain answer is that still after ninety years *Domesday Book and Beyond* remains the greatest single book on English medieval history': thus J. C. Holt in his foreword to this new impression of one of the classic historical texts in any language.

In three extended essays Maitland exploits the information in Domesday to analyse and reconstruct the society, law, government, economy and even something of the mental and imaginative world of early medieval England. Essay I examines the nature of English society in 1066 and how, by 1086, this had changed. The second essay explores pre-Conquest England, stretching back through the Anglo-Saxon law-codes and land-books to the English settlement, its social structure and administrative geography. Essay III uses an exhaustive discussion of the hide (that 'dreary old question') to look again at methods of assessment and measurement, and their relationship to the wealth and resources of England: in this Maitland displays, in addition to his customary lucidity, subtlety and enormous powers of historical insight, very considerable statistical competence, of an order hitherto foreign to English historical writing.

In his Foreword Professor Holt looks afresh at this monument of medieval scholarship, assessing its place both within the wider context of historical study, and also, more specifically, its continued contribution to that debate on the nature of Domesday Book with which scholars have been pre-occupied for nearly one hundred years. That Maitland's hypotheses and conclusions should still be central to such a debate is not the least remarkable feature of this extraordinary book.

FREDERIC WILLIAM MAITLAND (1850–1906) was, from 1888, Downing Professor of the Laws of England in the University of Cambridge.

J. C. HOLT is Master of Fitzwilliam College and Professor of Medieval History in the University of Cambridge.

DOMESDAY BOOK AND BEYOND

THREE ESSAYS

IN THE

EARLY HISTORY OF ENGLAND

BY

FREDERIC WILLIAM MAITLAND, LL.D.

FORMERLY DOWNING PROFESSOR OF THE LAWS OF ENGLAND
IN THE UNIVERSITY OF CAMBRIDGE, OF LINCOLN'S INN, BARRISTER-AT-LAW

Foreword by J. C. Holt,

MASTER OF FITZWILLIAM COLLEGE
AND PROFESSOR OF MEDIEVAL HISTORY
IN THE UNIVERSITY OF CAMBRIDGE

Cambridge University Press

Cambridge

New York   New Rochelle

Melbourne   Sydney

Published by the Press Syndicate of the University of Cambridge
The Pitt Building, Trumpington Street, Cambridge CB2 1RP
40 West 20th Street, New York, NY 10011-4211 USA
10 Stamford Road, Oakleigh, Melbourne 3166, Australia

First published 1897
This edition, with a new Foreword, first published 1987
Reprinted 1989, 1996

British Library cataloguing in publication data
Maitland, F. W.
  Domesday book and beyond: three essays
  in the early history of England.
  1. Great Britain — History — Anglo-
  Saxon period, 449–1066. 2. Great Britain —
  History — Medieval period, 1066–1485.
  I. Title.
  942.02   DA152

Library of Congress cataloguing in publication data
Maitland, Frederic William, 1850–1906.
  Domesday book and beyond.
  1. Domesday book. 2. Great Britain — History —
  Norman period, 1066–1154. 3. Great Britain — History —
  Anglo-Saxon period, 449–1066. 4. England — Economic
  conditions — Medieval period, 1066–1485. 5. Land tenure —
  England — History. 6. Feudalism — England — History.
  I. Title.
  DA190.D7M25   1987   333.3′22′0942   87-7971

ISBN 0 521 34112 4 hard covers
ISBN 0 521 34818 4 paperback

Printed in Great Britain by
Athenæum Press Ltd, Gateshead, Tyne & Wear

FOREWORD.

Why still read it? Why should scholars consult it and undergraduates study it? The plain answer is that still after ninety years it remains the greatest single book on English medieval history. So it is a monument, an index of ultimate achievement, to be admired and scrutinized as one might Gibbon or Macaulay. Yet it is more than that. *Domesday Book and Beyond* was conceived and executed at a time of dawning opportunity when Maitland, J. H. Round and a few others were beginning to do history as it ought to be done: analytically, scientifically, with questions asked and answered. The methods Maitland followed in this book showed the way. Many, though not all, of his conclusions remain valid. Some extensive sections of the book are still the best that we have on important aspects of Norman and English government and society. No other book of such compass has so endured.

The compass is immense. Maitland decided to use Domesday Book as a kind of information centre from which he explored and reconstructed the society, the law, the government, the economy, even the vocabulary and something of the imagination of early medieval England. The first essay tells us what England was like in 1066 and what had happened by 1086. It is insular; there is little of Normandy or of Norman origins. The second asks how the circumstances of 1066 had been attained; it stretches back through the Anglo-Saxon law-codes and land-books to the English settlement, its social structure and administrative geography. The third attacks the 'dreary old question' of the hide which is seen as "pre-judicial" to all the great questions of early English history' (357). It focuses the arguments and conclusions of the first two essays on methods of assessment and measurement and their relationship to wealth and resources, carrying back once again the Domesday evidence for comparison with the earlier records of the burghal and tribal hidage. Less obviously attractive than the first two essays, it hides behind its arithmetic numerous insights into the coherence and systematization of early English government. Taken together, the three linked essays are vast in range and conception. Maitland alone had the nerve, the imagination, the flair and the learning to attempt such a scheme. This is the combination which makes the book unique. And he brings it off.

Naturally it shares many of its qualities with Maitland's other work.[1] There is the same style and gentle but incisive irony, heightened here perhaps because he was less constrained by the limitations of a lecture or essay or the encyclopaedic requirements of the *History of English Law*. He gave himself more freedom, to rich effect. Hence, on *wergelds* – 'The sons of a *villanus* who had but two oxen must have been under some temptation to wish that their father would get himself killed by a solvent thegn' (44); or, in criticising the idea of common ownership – 'Who held this manor in the past? Nine sokemen held it. Rather a large party of joint lords we say: but still families will grow' (138); or in dismissing the facile equation of the vill with the Roman *villa* – 'And so England is full of vills which are Roman and satraps who, no doubt, are Persian' (337). The lawyer would add, very reasonably, that the whole corpus of Maitland's work is stamped by a legal mind and training.[2] Here, to be sure, the lawyer in Maitland is often in the foreground: in the examination of 'private' jurisdiction (52, 269–92); in the beautifully subtle discussion of freedom (42ff.) and very obviously in the opening sections on the borough – 'What is it that makes a borough to be a borough? That is the problem that we desire to solve. It is a legal problem' (173). But, on the whole, the lawyer is less dominant than in Maitland's other work. Indeed here and there he is wary of the law – '[manerium] loses that meaning [i.e. a technical meaning connected with the geld] in the course of time because the danegeld gives way before newer forms of taxation. It never again acquires a technical meaning until the late days when retrospective lawyers find the essence of a manor in its court' (128).

[1] For a contemporary comment on Maitland's qualities see R. L. Poole's scheme for combining him and Round in one of the volumes of the *Political History of England*. This, he wrote, needed 'the criticism of Round joined to the constructive gift which he has not' (C. H. S. Fifoot, ed., *The Letters of Frederic William Maitland*, Selden Society, supplementary series, 1, 1965, p. 230 n.); the possible outcome defies the imagination. For more general and recent comment see G. R. Elton, *F. W. Maitland* (London, 1985). The standard biography is H. A. L. Fisher, *Frederic William Maitland* (Cambridge, 1910). See also H. E. Bell, *Maitland* (London, 1965).

[2] See S. F. C. Milsom, reviewing Elton, *op. cit.*, *The Times Literary Supplement*, 28 Feb. 1986.

Maitland was also a mathematician.[3] It is this which gives *Domesday Book and Beyond* its unique quality among his works. He was in the forefront not as a mathematical thinker but in the use to which he put his mathematics. He did more than engage in extended simple arithmetic, like Round: he used sampling techniques, and this long before they were in general use for social analysis. Whether this came to him by instinct, as McDonald and Snooks have recently suggested, or through the advisers available in the Cambridge of the 1890s, is far from clear.[4] The method makes its first appearance early in the book – 'We take 100 entries (four batches of 25 apiece) and see that the number of *villani* and *bordarii* has risen from 1486 to 1894, while the number of *servi* has fallen from 423 to 303. We make another experiment with a hundred entries. This gives the following result . . .' (35). Thereafter the language of experiment and the tactics of sampling, averaging and approximating recur throughout the work, culminating in the interplay of numbers in Essay III which led Maitland to a tentative argument quite different from Round's – 'No one can look along these lines of figures without fancying that some force, conscious or unconscious, has made for "One pound, one hide"' (465) – a suggestion reinforced with characteristic humour – 'We may, if we like such excursions, fancy the conservatives arguing for the good old rule "One teamland, one hide," while a party of financial reformers has raised the cry "One pound, one hide." Then "pressure was brought to bear in influential quarters," and in favour of their own districts the witan in the moots jobbed and jerrymandered and rolled the friendly log, for all the world as if they had been mere modern politicians' (471). Hence beneficial hidation of shires as well as manors.

At this point Maitland suggested that he was less than serious. In

[3] Maitland read for the Mathematical Tripos during his first year at Cambridge (1869–70) before changing, under Henry Sidgwick's influence, to the Moral and Mental Science Tripos (Fisher, pp. 6–10).

[4] One possible source may have been William Bateson. Whether Maitland enjoyed any special contact with Bateson through his daughter Mary as early as 1894–7 is uncertain. In any case Maitland encountered Bateson in general university affairs on which they were not wholly in agreement (Fifoot, no. 191 and *passim*). Bateson was certainly using sampling methods, closely similar to Maitland's, in biometrical studies in the summer of 1892 (W. Bateson, *Materials for the Study of Variation*, London, 1894, pp. 40–1).

It should also be noted that Maitland and Karl Pearson, one of the founders of modern statistics, overlapped as members of the Bar in 1882–3, after which Maitland returned to Cambridge, with Pearson going on to University College, London, in 1884 as Professor of Applied Mathematics and Mechanics. But Maitland was a Bencher of Lincoln's Inn, Pearson of the Inner Temple.

fact the work is shot through with similar comments which reveal a humorous understanding of the human condition. On gelding in the manor – 'For one reason the king can not easily tax the rich; for another he can not easily tax the poor; so he gets at the poor through the rich' (121–2). On the privileges of the church of Worcester – 'The bishop who fully understands the object of the inquest, does not mean to have his assessment raised' (424), a comment all the more pertinent because the bishop in question was the Englishman Wulfstan. On fold-soke – 'It is the manure that the lord wants; the demand for manure has played a large part in the history of the human race' (76). And on royal benefaction to the church – '[The king] obtains not only remission of his sins, but also the friendship and aid of bishops and clergy. And so large stretches of land are "booked" to the churches. It is to be feared that if England of the sixth century had been visited by modern Englishmen, the Saxon chieftains would have been awakened to a consciousness of their "booking" powers by offers of gin and rifles' (242). Thus easily did he use the present to interpret the past.

His ability to adjust his mind to the past, to imagine and rethink it as it was, is even more remarkable. Repeatedly he dwells on language and the meaning of words: *ceorl*, *sac* and *soc*, manor and hall, burgh (59, 84–7, 108–9, 183–6). Always he moves behind the static figures of his chief record to the organic growth which deposited them. So it is a book which describes what English society was like, what government was like, how men's minds worked in organizing an archaic community. He does this with marvellous dexterity and with the most intractable material. 'Men are learning to say what they really mean', he tells us (226). Then a warning – 'Against many kinds of anachronism we now guard ourselves. We are careful of costume, of armour and architecture, of words and forms of speech. But it is far easier to be careful of these things than to prevent the intrusion of untimely ideas. In particular there lies a besetting danger for us in the barbarian's use of a language which is too good for his thought' (356). Nevertheless Maitland tries to interpret it. 'The barbarian, for all his materialism, is an idealist. He is, like the child, a master in the art of make-believe. He sees things not as they are, but as they might conveniently be. Every householder has a hide; every hide has 120 acres of arable; every hide is worth one pound a year; every householder has a team, every team is of eight oxen; every team is worth one pound. If all this be not so, then it ought to be so and must be deemed to be so' (389–90). And again – 'The result is that every manor in a certain district has four hides and sixteen teamlands. It is very pretty; it was never (except for technical

purposes) very true, and every year makes it less true' (472). That is
followed immediately by a very characteristic qualification – 'That
exactly this was done, we do not say and do not think; but something
like it may have been done' (473). Maitland is not always easy to pin
down. He appreciated the difficulty of his chief source; Domesday
Book is 'taciturn', its language 'not very patient of . . . analysis' (50,
67). He responded scarcely ever with vagueness, but rather with
delicate qualification. But he never abandoned his logical attack on the
evidence: 'If a vill consists, as in Devonshire often enough it will, of
some three *villani*, some four *bordarii* and some two *servi*, the "township-moot" if such a moot there be, will be a queer little assembly, the
manorial court, if such a court there be, will not have much to do' (21).
These qualities embolden the tendentious critic, for it is easy enough to
select particular targets with no attention to their place in the whole.
Maitland is much subtler, his arguments more qualified and condi-
tioned, than his critics usually allow.

For the critic, in this book above all others, Maitland presents the
disconcerting habit of bouncing back – posthumously. The second essay
was designed in part to challenge Seebohm's *English Village Community* and the doctrine which derived the English villein from the
slave of the Roman villa.[5] It was firmly embedded, therefore, in its
contemporary setting of the conflict between Germanists and Roman-
ists, now long subsided. Yet what Maitland has to say underlies the
discussion opened by Joan Thirsk on the common fields[6] and by Trevor
Aston on the origins of the manor.[7] It is relevant to Susan Reynolds'
recent study of communities in western Europe;[8] indeed Maitland still
provides an important corrective to that work because he retains
lordship in its proper proportion – 'But then we have to notice that a
village which has to pay a provender rent or even a *tailla* or *gersuma* is
not altogether a free village. Its communal action is called out by
seignorial pressure' (147). And, most remarkably, it includes many of
the essentials of the argument of Alan Macfarlane's *The Origins of
English Individualism*.[9] Macfarlane's generous acknowledgement of
Maitland would probably have been even more enthusiastic if he had

[5] Frederic Seebohm, *The English Village Community* (London, 1883).

[6] Joan Thirsk, 'The common fields', *Past and Present*, no. 29 (1964), 3–25.

[7] T. H. Aston, 'The origins of the manor in England', *Trans. Royal Historical
Soc.*, 5th Ser. viii (1958), 59–83.

[8] Susan Reynolds, *Kingdoms and Communities in Western Europe 900–1300*
(Oxford, 1984).

[9] Alan Macfarlane, *The Origins of English Individualism* (Oxford, 1978). All the
references to Maitland which Macfarlane indexes are to the *History of English Law*.

used *Domesday Book and Beyond* as well as the *History of English Law*, for his argument is here reinforced in ringing phrases – 'the very fields themselves seemed to rebel against communities and to demand a ring-fenced severalty' (351); and also by a detailed reconstruction of the economy and organization of what he called the free villages of eastern England (352–4).

That is simply one example of Maitland revived. The recent work of McDonald and Snooks illustrates another, for they argue not simply that in his sampling method Maitland was far ahead of other Domesday scholars including Round, but also that his broad equation of £1 = 1 hide was statistically correct.[10] And there are many phrases or short sections in which Maitland anticipates later work: Postan, for example, in his comment on the development of labour services (58);[11] Lemarignier[12] in the discussion of *consuetudines* (78–9); Stenton in the association of the freedom of some of the eastern counties with the Scandinavian settlements[13] and also R. H. C. Davis's[14] criticism of Stenton in the reservation – 'But in truth we must be careful how we use our Dane' (139); and finally the continuing debate about succession and inheritance, which has exercised Thorne, Milsom and the present writer,[15] in the following comment on these intricate problems, much more emphatic than anything in the *History of English Law* – 'The noble obtains a spacious territory, perhaps a county, from the king by way of "benefaction"; *precarium* becomes the *beneficium*, the *beneficium* becomes the *feudum*. The king can not prevent the *beneficia*, the *feuda*, from becoming hereditary" (301).

This is not to say that the whole structure of the book still stands without need for addition or repair. The problem of assessment and

[10] John McDonald and G. D. Snooks, *Domesday Economy* (Oxford, 1986), especially pp. 42–9.

[11] M. M. Postan, 'The chronology of labour services', *Trans. Royal Historical Soc.*, 4th Ser. xx (1937), 169–93; also E. A. Kosminsky, *Studies in the Agrarian History of England in the Thirteenth Century* (Oxford, 1956).

[12] J.-F. Lemarignier, 'La Dislocation du "pagus" et le problème des "Consuetudines" (x^e–xie siècles)', in *Mélanges d'histoire du moyen âge dédiés à la mémoire de L. Halphen* (Paris, 1951), pp. 401–10.

[13] F. M. Stenton, 'The Danes in England', *Proc. British Academy*, xiii (1927), 203–46.

[14] R. H. C. Davis, 'East Anglia and the Danelaw', *Trans. Royal Historical Soc.*, 5th Ser. v (1955), 23–39.

[15] S. E. Thorne, 'English feudalism and estates in land', *Cambridge Law Journal* (1959), 193–209; J. C. Holt, 'Politics and property in early medieval England', *Past and Present*, no. 57 (1972), 3–52; S. F. C. Milsom, *The Legal Framework of English Feudalism* (Cambridge, 1976).

taxation dealt with in Essay III now has to be read in the light of later work, especially that of C. R. Hart,[16] and Sally Harvey.[17] H. C. Darby and his colleagues have discussed in five volumes of *The Domesday Geography*[18] matters which Maitland compressed within less than a hundred pages throughout the book, so much of what he says of the geographic distribution of wealth and the measurement of resources has been superseded. Likewise the criticism of Anglo-Saxon charters, on which part of the second essay depends, has advanced far since Maitland's day;[19] his story of the development of seignorial jurisdiction, so dependent as he saw it on the alienation of royal rights, no longer seems so clear cut. It must now be read in conjunction with the work of Helen Cam and Naomi Hurnard.[20] Certain sections of the work are plainly defective. Like Round, Maitland made only occasional use of the Exon Domesday (39, 120, 167, 479), an essential component of the survey which was given insufficient attention by all Domesday scholars until Baring's paper of 1912.[21] And from a commentary on the effects of the Norman Conquest one whole area of study – the settlement of the Norman aristocracy – is almost entirely missing. Indeed, Maitland washed his hands of it – 'The day for an artistically proportioned picture of the growth of feudalism has not yet come; the day for a quantitative analysis of the elements of feudalism may never come' (221), thus leaving the field to a whole host of scholars among whom Stenton and Le Patourel have been the leading figures.[22]

[16] C. R. Hart, 'The hidation of Huntingdonshire', *Proc. Cambridge Antiquarian Soc.*, lxi (1968), 55–66; *The Hidation of Northamptonshire* (Leicester, 1970).

[17] Sally P. J. Harvey, 'Domesday Book and Anglo-Norman governance', *Trans. Royal Historical Soc.*, 5th Ser. xxv (1975), 175–93; 'Taxation and the ploughland in Domesday Book' in P. Sawyer, ed., *Domesday Book: a Reassessment* (London, 1985), pp. 86–103; 'Taxation and the economy' in J. C. Holt, ed., *Domesday Studies* (Woodbridge, 1987), pp. 249–64.

[18] H. C. Darby and others, *The Domesday Geography of England*, 5 vols. (Cambridge, 1954–67); supplemented by H. C. Darby, *Domesday England* (Cambridge, 1977) and H. C. Darby and G. R. Versey, *Domesday Gazeteer* (Cambridge, 1975).

[19] For a useful summary of part of this see N. Brooks, 'Anglo-Saxon charters: the work of the last twenty years', *Anglo-Saxon England*, 3 (1974), 211–31.

[20] Helen M. Cam, 'The evolution of the medieval English franchise', *Speculum*, xxxii (1957), 427–42; 'The "private" hundred before the Norman conquest', in J. Conway Davies, ed., *Studies presented to Sir Hilary Jenkinson* (London, 1957), 50–60. Naomi D. Hurnard, 'The Anglo-Norman franchises', *English Historical Review*, lxiv (1949), 289–323, 433–60.

[21] F. H. Baring, 'The Exeter Domesday', *English Historical Review*, xxvii (1912), 309–18.

[22] See especially F. M. Stenton, *The First Century of English Feudalism* (Oxford, 1932), and John Le Patourel, *The Norman Empire* (Oxford, 1976).

From major controversies the book has emerged with varying and still changing fortunes. Within the year of publication it provoked a famous review by James Tait,[23] generously acknowledged by Maitland himself.[24] Tait challenged two of Maitland's arguments. The first and less important concerned the garrison theory of the origin of boroughs (172–219). Tait was right; it may be that Maitland's readiness to reconstruct systems of assessment misled him here; so the section on boroughs remains largely as a historiographical curiosity. The second was Maitland's theory that *manerium* had the technical meaning of a house against which geld was charged and that men gelded in the manor, not the vill (120ff.). This was much more central to Maitland's general theses; it extended, for example, into his lines of social classification (24, 126–7). Tait's criticism has been generally accepted, but it is by no means as convincing as his views about the borough. Some of his arguments concerning detached portions of manors are as difficult to reconcile with manorial as geld renders. Maitland was not convinced by the criticism, although he never answered it.[25] It has remained for Dr J. N. N. Palmer to revive Maitland's hypothesis.[26]

The debate about feudalism has been much more diffuse. Here Maitland certainly deserved some of the shot he has had to take. His first attempt to evaluate the English and Norman contribution is far from satisfactory – 'in the west we have already what in substance are knights' fees. The Bishop of Worcester held 300 hides over which he had sake and soke and all customs; he was bound to put 60 *milites* into the field; if he failed in this duty he had to pay 40 shillings for each deficient *miles*. At the beginning of Henry II's reign he was charged with 60 knights' fees' (160). That, surprisingly, contains a simple but crucial error: the 60 knights provided for Henry II did not come solely from the 300 hides of Oswaldslow but from the whole of the bishopric of Worcester. So the equation, 60 knights = 300 hides is false and the continuity is broken. The mistake condemned Maitland's argument.[27] However, the critics rarely note his much fuller and subtler treatment of the same problem in Essay II. Here he examined the *laen* lands of Oswaldslow and concluded – 'These men may be bound to fight at the bishop's call, but fighting is not their main business; they are not

[23] *English Historical Review*, xii (1897), 768–77.

[24] Fifoot, no. 200.

[25] *Ibid.*, and no. 264.

[26] J. J. N. Palmer, 'The Domesday manor', in J. C. Holt, ed., *Domesday Studies* (Woodbridge, 1987), pp. 139–53.

[27] For a summary of the criticism see R. Allen Brown, *Origins of English Feudalism* (London, 1973), pp. 61–2.

professional warriors. They are the predecessors not of the military
tenants of the twelfth century, but of the *radchenistres* and *radmanni*
of Domesday Book, the *rodknights* of Bracton's text, the thegns and
drengs of the northern counties who puzzle the lawyers of the Angevin
time' (308); 'Dependent tenure is here and, we may say, feudal tenure,
and even tenure by knight's service, for though the English *cniht* of the
tenth century differs much from the knight of the twelfth, still it is a
change in military tactics rather than a change in legal ideas that is
required to convert the one into the other' (309). Here, in extended
form, he still maintains a challenge to our latter-day Normanists and
Saxonists alike. He was concerned with the origins and nature of
seignorial power. He did not now pretend, as some of his followers have
done, that Norman military arrangements could be traced back to the
Anglo-Saxon period.[28] Indeed, he had already accepted in the *History
of English Law* the conclusion of Round's great paper on the Introduction of Knight-Service.[29] But he could not accept that feudalism
was to be defined in narrow military terms – 'when compared with
seignorial justice, military tenure is a superficial matter, one out of
many effects rather than a deep-seated cause. Seignorial justice is a
deep-seated cause of many effects, a principle which when once
introduced is capable of transfiguring a nation' (258); and here he saw
real continuity across the great divide of the Norman Conquest. He
deserves closer attention and better understanding than knockabout
partisanship has allowed him.

Curiously, the work is only occasionally determined by one of its
preliminary assumptions about Domesday Book – 'One great purpose
seems to mould both its form and substance; it is a geld book' (3); 'Our
record is no register of title, it is no feodary, it is no custumal, it is no
rent roll, it is a tax book, a geld book' (5). Maitland did not examine
this contention in any depth; it was perhaps sufficient that on this he
and Round were in agreement. These much quoted broad assertions are
necessarily imprecise. No-one is likely to dispute that Domesday is in
some sense a geld-book; it records geld-assessments systematically
throughout. But to move beyond this to an assertion that the prime
purpose of both the survey and the Book lay in the reassessment and/or
collection of the geld involves a logical leap. It does not follow. It

---

[28] For a critical review of such arguments see *ibid.*, pp. 34–43. A subsequent
statement of them is made by John Gillingham, 'The introduction of knight service
in England', *Proceedings of the Battle Conference on Anglo-Norman Studies*, iv
(1981), 53–64.

[29] *History of English Law*, i, 258, 259 n.

requires proof. Maitland does not provide it. It is only much later, in Essay III, and then almost incidentally, that it becomes apparent that this was indeed his view. It almost steals out – 'With an eye to future taxation, he [the king] wishes for figures expressive of the normal condition of things' (422); 'They are not asking about area; they are asking about the number of teams requisite for the tillage of the tenement. With this and its value as data, William's ministers hope to correct the antiquated assessments' (423); and most clearly of all – 'If Domesday Book is to serve its primary purpose, if it is to tell the king's officers how much geld is due, it is absolutely necessary that by some ready process they should be able to work sums in hides and acres and in carucates and acres' (475).

Now it should be obvious that an idea vividly expressed on p. 5 which does not resurface until p. 422 can scarcely be taken as determining the main structure of Maitland's great work. *Domesday Book and Beyond*, the bulk and the best of it, is concerned with much more than this plain assumption. Yet the assumption was made, and Galbraith was surely right when he pointed out that it was from Maitland, rather than Round, that it derived its main strength.[30] As Maitland came to express it, it was almost self-defeating. The king's officers were to be able to 'work sums' 'by some ready process'. At this point Maitland was concerned with the arithmetic of Domesday Book: 1 hide or carucate = 120 acres: within that his point is valid. But it is quite invalid within wider parameters. Domesday Book is a hopelessly complicated and inadequate instrument for 'working sums' 'by some ready process' concerning the geld. Such calculations are not merely difficult; the information on geld is arranged in such a way and presented in such a format that geld calculations are positively impeded. If any economic information is emphasised it is not geld-assessments, still less changes therein, but values, and these only by leaving them for the most part at the end of the manorial entries. Even then no attempt was made to rubricate them and no obstacle seems to have been envisaged against adding information after them. So the geld information is obscured. Geld-assessment is an essential component of Domesday but Domesday cannot be a geld-book in Maitland's sense. In this it stands in sharp contrast to the *Inquisitio Geldi* of the south-western counties, which fulfilled just such a purpose.

Perhaps Maitland was fascinated by his own arithmetic. His resulting misapprehension is not at all obvious. It is shared by others firmly committed even now to diagnosing immediate financial purposes

[30] V. H. Galbraith, *The Making of Domesday Book* (Oxford, 1961), p. 13.

behind the Domesday data. So let us be quite precise about what went
wrong and still goes wrong. Does Domesday contain geld-assessments
and reassessments? Yes. Can the assessment of manors, of vills, or
hundreds, or of shires, be calculated? Yes. Is the Book so arranged to
present such information readily and tidily? No; only in the case of
manors and there it is given no emphasis either by location in the text,
or capitals or rubrication. Can the total assessment of individual
tenements in hundreds, or of vills divided between tenants or of
tenements in shires be calculated? Yes; but only by inconvenient
search and summing. So could Domesday tell the King's officers 'how
much geld is due'? Yes; but only if they did what Maitland does. Can
the Book then provide the 'ready process' which Maitland required? No.
Indeed *Domesday Book and Beyond* itself, with all its splendid calculations occupying many pages, contradicts the purpose it attributes to
Domesday. It is not that it imposes on eleventh-century officials a task
beyond their competence. Their arithmetic was up to it, given time
and equipment. It is that Domesday is not the ready reckoner which
the argument requires. The *Inquisitio Geldi* fills this function much
better. The moral is that Domesday reveals its purpose as much in its
arrangement and format as in its content.[31]

Behind this there lies a real weakness. No-one has ever matched
Maitland in his ability to conjure the society of the eleventh and earlier
centuries from the aridities of Domesday. Yet Galbraith far surpasses
him in his sense that the Book was an enormous artefact made for a
purpose, to a plan, and for use in a particular way; that it was in its
time a living, working record. Half a century lay between the two, and
one highly important work intervened: *Domesday Rebound* published
for the Public Record Office in 1954, after Galbraith's first paper but
before his first book.[32] Maitland, of course, was conscious enough of a
plan, a system; but it was his, not King William's. It owed much to
nineteenth-century statistics, practically nothing at all to the study of
the manuscript. It was, as Galbraith put it, 'Victorian'.[33] The passage
of time and change in approach which lies between the two is revealed
in an almost casual footnote towards the end of Essay I – 'The one
glimpse that I have had of the manuscript suggested to me (1) that the
accounts of some of the boroughs were postscripts, and (2) that space
was left for accounts of London and Winchester. The anatomy of the

[31] This argument is further developed in J. C. Holt, '1086', in J. C. Holt, ed.,
Domesday Studies (Woodbridge, 1987), pp. 41–63.
[32] *Domesday Book Rebound* (London, HMSO, 1954).
[33] Galbraith, *op. cit.*, pp. 14–15.

book deserves examination by an expert' (178, n.1). That may well astonish the reader ninety years later.[34] It reflects not dereliction of duty on Maitland's part, but what has happened since, and in particular the achievement and consequences of Galbraith's inspired intervention.

At this point *Domesday Book and Beyond* may well be compared with Round's *Feudal England*. To some extent the two run in parallel; indeed at several points Maitland deliberately avoids duplication of Round's work, published two years previously. It may be because of this that he is somewhat hazy about how Domesday was made. It may equally be that he was not so resolved as Round on the interrelationships of the Domesday texts. Neither of them was perhaps as firm of mind as Galbraith's critique of them suggests. However, Maitland did say something. He came to it by a roundabout route in his third essay on the hide. Here he dwells on the considerable variation in the record of teamlands, arguing that the return of 'land for x teams' in some counties or hundreds was equivalent to the statement that 'there were x teams TRE' in others (420–4). In noting this varied response, he attributes the variation in Leicestershire, where it occurs within the confines of a single county, to 'a clerk's caprice' (421, n.2). Elsewhere, especially in the contrast in these matters between Great Domesday, where the teamlands appear, and Little Domesday, where the matter is covered by a threefold response stating the number of ploughs actually on the land, he suggests that the original threefold questionnaire, seeking information TRE, TRW and when King William gave the land, was 'unneccessarily cumbrous. The design of collecting the statistics of the past broke down . . . Some interrogatories were dropped' (421–2). This was entirely consistent with Round, who took the 'so-called second volume to be really a first attempt at the codification of the returns' on which the first volume, i.e. Exchequer Domesday, was 'a wonderful improvement'.[35] But Maitland's view was subtler, for his explanation depends on variations in both the questions asked by the commissioners and the responses given by the jurors (420–3). Unlike Round, he approaches, but never really attains, the modern view that the final Book retains evidence of successive layers of data-retrieval and reduction which necessarily reveal differences in method and

---

[34] Round said something very similar in comparing Great and Little Domesday (*Feudal England*, p. 140). In assessing both Maitland and Round it should be born in mind that the zincographic facsimile of both Great and Little Domesday was published in county volumes by the Ordnance Survey Office, 1861–4.

[35] *Feudal England*, p. 141.

procedure between circuits, counties and smaller units. This was genius nudging against the confines of his time. The next great leap forward was Galbraith's.

How then should we assess Maitland in this work? By his range and style, certainly. By his learning and acute intelligence, equally so. Also by his moving language: the final paragraph grips the reader like the closing sentences of *Wuthering Heights* and is as often quoted. Perhaps above all by a single phrase which embraces his mind, method and achievement, and also the Cambridge of his day: 'We make another experiment.' It was some experiment. If only all such could be both so venturesome and so rewarding.

PREFACE.

THE greater part of what is in this book was written in order that it might be included in the *History of English Law before the Time of Edward I.* which was published by Sir Frederick Pollock and me in the year 1895. Divers reasons dictated a change of plan. Of one only need I speak. I knew that Mr Round was on the eve of giving to the world his *Feudal England,* and that thereby he would teach me and others many new lessons about the scheme and meaning of Domesday Book. That I was well advised in waiting will be evident to everyone who has studied his work. In its light I have suppressed, corrected, added much. The delay has also enabled me to profit by Dr Meitzen's *Siedelung und Agrarwesen der Germanen*[1], a book which will assuredly leave a deep mark upon all our theories of old English history.

The title under which I here collect my three Essays is chosen for the purpose of indicating that I have followed that retrogressive method 'from the known to the unknown,' of which Mr Seebohm is the apostle. Domesday Book appears to me, not indeed as the known, but as the knowable. The Beyond is still very dark : but the way to it lies through the Norman record. A result is given to us : the problem is to find cause and process. That in some sort I have been endeavouring to answer Mr Seebohm, I can not conceal from myself or from others. A hearty admiration of his *English*

[1] Siedelung und Agrarwesen der Westgermanen und Ostgermanen, der Kelten, Römer, Finnen und Slawen, von August Meitzen, Berlin, 1895.

Village Community is one main source of this book. That the task of disputing his conclusions might have fallen to stronger hands than mine I well know. I had hoped that by this time Prof. Vinogradoff's *Villainage in England* would have had a sequel. When that sequel comes (and may it come soon) my provisional answer can be forgotten. One who by a few strokes of his pen has deprived the English nation of its land, its folk-land, owes us some reparation. I have been trying to show how we can best bear the loss, and abandon as little as may be of what we learnt from Dr Konrad von Maurer and Dr Stubbs.

For my hastily compiled Domesday Statistics I have apologized in the proper place. Here I will only add that I had but one long vacation to give to a piece of work that would have been better performed had it been spread over many years. Mr Corbett, of King's College, has already shown me how by a little more patience and ingenuity I might have obtained some rounder and therefore more significant figures. But of this it is for him to speak.

Among the friends whom I wish to thank for their advice and assistance I am more especially grateful to Mr Herbert Fisher, of New College, who has borne the tedious labour of reading all my sheets, and to Mr W. H. Stevenson, of Exeter College, whose unrivalled knowledge of English diplomatics has been generously placed at my service.

F. W. M.

20 *January*, 1897.

CONTENTS.

ESSAY I.

DOMESDAY BOOK.

Domesday Book and its satellites, 1. Domesday and legal history, 2. Domesday a geld book, 3. The danegeld, 3. The inquest and the geld system, 5. Importance of the geld, 7. Unstable terminology of the record, 8. The legal ideas of century xi. 9.

§ 1. *Plan of the Survey*, pp. **9—26.**

The geographical basis, 9. The vill as the unit, 10. Modern and ancient vills, 12. Omission of vills, 13. Fission of vills, 14. The nucleated village and the vill of scattered steads, 15. Illustration by maps, 16. Size of the vill, 17. Population of the vill, 19. Contrasts between east and west, 20. Small vills, 20. Importance of the east, 21. Manorial and non-manorial vills, 22. Distribution of free men and serfs, 23. The classification of men, 23. The classes of men and the geld system, 24. Our course, 25.

§ 2. *The Serfs*, pp. **26—36.**

The *servus* of Domesday, 26. Legal position of the serf, 27. Degrees of serfdom, 27. Predial element in serfdom, 28. The serf and criminal law, 29. Serf and villein, 30. The serf of the *Leges*, 30. Return to the *servus* of Domesday, 33. Disappearance of *servi*, 35.

§ 3. *The Villeins*, pp. **36—66.**

The boors or coliberts, 36. The continental colibert, 37. The English boor, 37. *Villani, bordarii, cotarii*, 38. The villein's tenement, 40. Villeins and cottiers, 41. Freedom and unfreedom of the *villani*, 41. Meaning of freedom, 42. The villein as free, 43. The villein as

ESSAY II.

ENGLAND BEFORE THE CONQUEST.

§ 1. *Book-land and the Land-book*, pp. **226—244**.

§ 2. *Book-land and Folk-land*, pp. **244—258**.

§ 3. *Sake and Soke*, pp. **258—292**.

ESSAY III.

The Hide.

§ 1. *Measures and Fields*, pp. **362—399.**

§ 2. *Domesday Statistics*, pp. **399—490.**

Statistical Tables, 400—403.

ESSAY I.

DOMESDAY BOOK.

AT midwinter in the year 1085 William the Conqueror wore his crown at Gloucester and there he had deep speech with his wise men. The outcome of that speech was the mission throughout all England of 'barons,' 'legates' or 'justices' charged with the duty of collecting from the verdicts of the shires, the hundreds and the vills a *descriptio* of his new realm. The outcome of that mission was the *descriptio* preserved for us in two manuscript volumes, which within a century after their making had already acquired the name of Domesday Book. The second of those volumes, sometimes known as Little Domesday, deals with but three counties, namely Essex, Norfolk and Suffolk, while the first volume comprehends the rest of England. Along with these we must place certain other documents that are closely connected with the grand inquest. We have in the so-called Inquisitio Comitatus Cantabrigiae, a copy, an imperfect copy, of the verdicts delivered by the Cambridgeshire jurors, and this, as we shall hereafter see, is a document of the highest value, even though in some details it is not always very trustworthy[1]. We have in the so-called Inquisitio Eliensis an account of the estates of the Abbey of Ely in Cambridgeshire, Suffolk and other counties, an account which has as its ultimate source the verdicts of the juries and which contains some

---

[1] Inquisitio Comitatus Cantabrigiae, ed. N. E. Hamilton. When, as sometimes happens, the figures in this record differ from those given in Domesday Book, the latter seem to be in general the more correct, for the arithmetic is better. Also it seems plain that the compilers of Domesday had, even for districts comprised in the Inquisitio, other materials besides those that the Inquisitio contains. For example, that document says nothing of some of the royal manors. [Since this note was written, Mr Round, Feudal England, pp. 10 ff. has published the same result after an elaborate investigation.]

particulars which were omitted from Domesday Book[1]. We have in the so-called Exon Domesday an account of Cornwall and Devonshire and of certain lands in Somerset, Dorset and Wiltshire; this also seems to have been constructed directly or indirectly out of the verdicts delivered in those counties, and it contains certain particulars about the amount of stock upon the various estates which are omitted from what, for distinction's sake, is sometimes called the Exchequer Domesday[2]. At the beginning of this Exon Domesday we have certain accounts relating to the payment of a great geld, seemingly the geld of six shillings on the hide that William levied in the winter of 1083-4, two years before the deep speech at Gloucester[3]. Lastly, in the Northamptonshire Geld Roll[4] we have some precious information about fiscal affairs as they stood some few years before the survey[5].

Domesday and legal history.

Such in brief are the documents out of which, with some small help from the Anglo-Saxon dooms and land-books, from the charters of Norman kings and from the so-called Leges of the Conqueror, the Confessor and Henry I., some future historian may be able to reconstruct the land-law which obtained in the conquered England of 1086, and (for our records frequently speak of the *tempus Regis Edwardi*) the unconquered England of 1065. The reflection that but for the deep speech at Gloucester, but for the lucky survival of two or three manuscripts, he would have known next to nothing of that law, will make him modest and cautious. At the present moment, though much has been done towards forcing Domesday Book to yield its meaning, some of the legal problems that are raised by it, especially those which concern the time of King Edward, have hardly been stated, much less solved. It is with some hope of stating, with little hope of solving them that we begin this essay. If only we can ask the right questions we shall

---

[1] This is printed in D. B. vol. iv. and given by Hamilton at the end of his Inq. Com. Cantab. As to the manner in which it was compiled see Round, Feudal England, 133 ff.

[2] The Exon Domesday is printed in D. B. vol. iv.

[3] Round, Domesday Studies, i. 91: 'I am tempted to believe that these geld rolls in the form in which we now have them were compiled at Winchester after the close of Easter 1084, by the body which was the germ of the future Exchequer.'

[4] Printed by Ellis, Introduction to Domesday, i. 184.

[5] Round, Feudal England, 147.

have done something for a good end. If English history is to
be understood, the law of Domesday Book must be mastered.
We have here an absolutely unique account of feudalism in
two different stages of its growth, the more trustworthy, though
the more puzzling, because it gives us particulars and not
generalities.

Puzzling enough it certainly is, and this for many reasons.
Our task may be the easier if we state some of those reasons at
the outset.

To say that Domesday Book is no collection of laws or Domesday
treatise on law would be needless. Very seldom does it state book.
any rule in general terms, and when it does so we shall usually
find cause for believing that this rule is itself an exception, a
local custom, a provincial privilege. Thus, if we are to come by
general rules, we must obtain them inductively by a comparison
of many thousand particular instances. But further, Domesday
Book is no register of title, no register of all those rights and
facts which constitute the system of land-holdership. One great
purpose seems to mould both its form and its substance; it is a
geld-book.

When Duke William became king of the English, he found Danegeld.
(so he might well think) among the most valuable of his newly
acquired regalia, a right to levy a land-tax under the name of
geld or danegeld. A detailed history of that tax cannot be
written. It is under the year 991 that our English chronicle
first mentions a tribute paid to the Danes[1]; £10,000 was then
paid to them. In 994 the yet larger sum of £16,000[2] was
levied. In 1002 the tribute had risen to £24,000[3], in 1007 to
£30,000[4], in 1009 East Kent paid £3,000[5]; £21,000 was raised
in 1014[6]; in 1018 Cnut when newly crowned took £72,000
besides £11,000 paid by the Londoners[7]; in 1040 Harthacnut
took £21,099 besides a sum of £11,048 that was paid for thirty-
two ships[8]. With a Dane upon the throne, this tribute seems to
have become an occasional war-tax. How often it was levied
we cannot tell; but that it was levied more than once by the
Confessor is not doubtful[9]. We are told that he abolished it

[1] Earle, Two Chronicles, 130–1.   [2] Ibid. 132–3.   [3] Ibid. 137.
[4] Ibid. 141.   [5] Ibid. 142.   [6] Ibid. 151.   [7] Ibid. 160–1.
[8] Ibid. 167.
[9] There is a valuable paper on this subject, A Short Account of Danegeld [by
P. C. Webb] published in 1756.

in or about the year 1051, some eight or nine years after his accession, some fifteen before his death. No sooner was William crowned than 'he laid on men a geld exceeding stiff.' In the next year 'he set a mickle geld' on the people. In the winter of 1083–4 he raised a geld of 72 pence (6 Norman shillings) upon the hide. That this tax was enormously heavy is plain. Taking one case with another, it would seem that the hide was frequently supposed to be worth about £1 a year and there were many hides in England that were worth far less. But grievous as was the tax which immediately preceded the making of the survey, we are not entitled to infer that it was of unprecedented severity. It brought William but £415 or thereabouts from Dorset and £510 or thereabouts from Somerset[1]. Worcestershire was deemed to contain about 1200 hides and therefore, even if none of its hides had been exempted, it would have contributed but £360. If the huge sums mentioned by the chronicler had really been exacted, and that too within the memory of men who were yet living, William might well regard the right to levy a geld as the most precious jewel in his English crown. To secure a due and punctual payment of it was worth a gigantic effort, a survey such as had never been made and a record such as had never been penned since the grandest days of the old Roman empire. But further, the assessment of the geld sadly needed reform. Owing to one cause and another, owing to privileges and immunities that had been capriciously granted, owing also, so we think, to a radically vicious method of computing the geldable areas of counties and hundreds, the old assessment was full of anomalies and iniquities. Some estates were over-rated, others were scandalously under-rated. That William intended to correct the old assessment, or rather to sweep it away and put a new assessment in its stead, seems highly probable, though it has not been proved that either he or his sons accomplished this feat[2]. For this purpose, however, materials were to be collected which would enable the royal officers to decide what changes were necessary in order that all England might be taxed in accordance with a just and uniform plan. Concerning each estate they were to know the

---

[1] D. B. iv. 26, 489.

[2] In 1194 the tax for Richard's ransom seems, at least in Wiltshire, to have been distributed in the main according to the assessment that prevailed in 1084; Rolls of the King's Court (Pipe Roll Soc.) i. Introduction, p. xxiv.

number of geldable units ('hides' or 'carucates') for which it had answered in King Edward's day, they were to know the number of plough oxen that there were upon it, they were to know its true annual value, they were to know whether that value had been rising or falling during the past twenty years. Domesday Book has well been called a rate book, and the task of spelling out a land law from the particulars that it states is not unlike the task that would lie before any one who endeavoured to construct our modern law of real property out of rate books, income tax returns and similar materials. All the lands, all the land-holders of England may be brought before us, but we are told only of such facts, such rights, such legal relationships as bear on the actual or potential payment of geld. True, that some minor purposes may be achieved by the king's commissioners, though the quest for geld is their one main object. About the rents and renders due from his own demesne manors the king may thus obtain some valuable information. Also he may learn, as it were by the way, whether any of his barons or other men have presumed to occupy, to 'invade,' lands which he has reserved for himself. Again, if several persons are in dispute about a tract of ground, the contest may be appeased by the testimony of shire and hundred, or may be reserved for the king's audience; at any rate the existence of an outstanding claim may be recorded by the royal commissioners. Here and there the peculiar customs of a shire or a borough will be stated, and incidentally the services that certain tenants owe to their lords may be noticed. But all this is done sporadically and unsystematically. Our record is no register of title, it is no feodary, it is no custumal, it is no rent roll; it is a tax book, a geld book.

We say this, not by way of vain complaint against its meagreness, but because in our belief a care for geld and for all that concerns the assessment and payment of geld colours far more deeply than commentators have usually supposed the information that is given to us about other matters. We should not be surprised if definitions and distinctions which at first sight have little enough to do with fiscal arrangements, for example the definition of a manor and the distinction between a villein and a 'free man,' involved references to the apportionment and the levy of the land-tax. Often enough it happens that legal ideas of a very general kind are defined by fiscal

The survey and the geld system.

rules; for example, our modern English idea of 'occupation' has become so much part and parcel of a system of assessment that lawyers are always ready to argue that a certain man must be an 'occupier' because such men as he are rated to the relief of the poor. It seems then a fair supposition that any line that Domesday Book draws systematically and sharply, whether it be between various classes of men or between various classes of tenements, is somehow or another connected with the main theme of that book—geldability, actual or potential.

Weight of the dane-geld.

Since we have mentioned the stories told by the chronicler about the tribute paid to the Danes, we may make a comment upon them which will become of importance hereafter. Those stories look true, and they seem to be accepted by modern historians. Had we been told just once that some large number of pounds, for example £60,000, was levied, or had the same round sum been repeated in year after year, we might well have said that such figures deserved no attention, and that by £60,000 our annalist merely meant a big sum of money. But, as will have been seen, he varies his figures from year to year and is not always content with a round number; he speaks of £21,099 and of £11,048[1]. We can hardly therefore treat his statements as mere loose talk and are reluctantly driven to suppose that they are true or near the truth. If this be so, then, unless some discovery has yet to be made in the history of money, no word but 'appalling' will adequately describe the taxation of which he speaks. We know pretty accurately the amount of money that became due when Henry I. or Henry II. imposed a danegeld of two shillings on the hide. The following table constructed from the pipe rolls will show the sum charged against each county. We arrange the shires in the order of their indebtedness, for a few of the many caprices of the allotment will thus be visible, and our table may be of use to us in other contexts[2].

---

[1] The statement in Æthelred, II. 7 (Schmid, p. 209) as to a payment of £22,000 is in a general way corroborative of the chronicler's large figures.

[2] The figures will be given more accurately on a later page.

APPROXIMATE CHARGE OF A DANEGELD OF TWO SHILLINGS ON THE
HIDE IN THE MIDDLE OF THE TWELFTH CENTURY.

	£		£
Wiltshire	389	Cambridge	114
Norfolk	330	Derby and Nottingham	110
Somerset	278	Hertford	110
Lincoln	266	Bedford	110
Dorset	248	Kent	105
Oxford	242	Devon	104
Essex	236	Worcester	101
Suffolk	235	Leicester	100
Sussex	210	Hereford	94
Bucks	205	Middlesex	85
Berks	202	Huntingdon	71
Gloucester	190	Stafford	44
S. Hants	180	Cornwall	23
Surrey	177	Rutland	12
York	160	Northumberland	100
Warwick	129	Cheshire[1]	0
N. Hants	120		
Salop	118	Total	5198

Now be it understood that these figures do not show the amount of money that Henry I. and Henry II. could obtain by a danegeld. They had to take much less. When it was last levied, the tax was not bringing in £3500, so many were the churches and great folk who had obtained temporary or permanent exemptions from it. We will cite Leicestershire for example. The total of the geld charged upon it was almost exactly or quite exactly £100. On the second roll of Henry II.'s reign we find that £25. 7s. 6d. have been paid into the treasury, that £22. 8s. 3d. have been 'pardoned' to magnates and templars, that £51. 8s. 2d. are written off in respect of waste, and that 16s. 0d. are still due. On the eighth roll the account shows that £62. 12s. 7d. have been paid and that £37. 6s. 9d. have been 'pardoned.' No, what our table displays is the amount that would be raised if all exemptions were disregarded and no penny forborne. And now let us turn back to the chronicle and (not to take an extreme example) read of £30,000 being raised. Unless we are prepared to bring

The geld of old times.

---

[1] Cheshire pays no geld to the king. This loss is compensated by a sum which is sometimes exacted from Northumberland.

against the fathers of English history a charge of repeated, wanton and circumstantial lying, we shall think of the danegeld of Æthelred's reign and of Cnut's as of an impost so heavy that it was fully capable of transmuting a whole nation. Therefore the lines that are drawn by the incidence of this tribute will be deep and permanent; but still we must remember that primarily they will be fiscal lines.

Unstable termino- logy of the survey.

Then again, we ought not to look to Domesday Book for a settled and stable scheme of technical terms. Such a scheme could not be established in a brief twenty years. About one half of the technical terms that meet us, about one half of the terms which, as we think, ought to be precisely defined, are, we may say, English terms. They are ancient English words, or they are words brought hither by the Danes, or they are Latin words which have long been in use in England and have acquired special meanings in relation to English affairs. On the other hand, about half the technical terms are French. Some of them are old Latin words which have acquired special meanings in France, some are Romance words newly coined in France, some are Teutonic words which tell of the Frankish conquest of Gaul. In the one great class we place *scira, hundredum, wapentac, hida, berewica, inland, haga, soka, saka, geldum, gablum, scotum, heregeat, gersuma, thegnus, sochemannus, burus, coscet*; in the other *comitatus, carucata, virgata, bovata, arpentum, manerium, feudum, alodium, homagium, relevium, baro, vicecomes, vavassor, villanus, bordarius, colibertus, hospes.* It is not in twenty years that a settled and stable scheme can be formed out of such elements as these. And often enough it is very difficult for us to give just the right meaning to some simple Latin word. If we translate *miles* by *soldier* or *warrior*, this may be too indefinite; if we translate it by *knight*, this may be too definite, and yet leave open the question whether we are comparing the *miles* of 1086 with the *cniht* of unconquered England or with the knight of the thirteenth century. If we render *vicecomes* by *sheriff* we are making our sheriff too little of a *vicomte*. When *comes* is before us we have to choose between giving Britanny an *earl*, giving Chester a *count*, or offending some of our *comites* by invidious distinctions. Time will show what these words shall mean. Some will perish in the struggle for existence; others have long and adventurous careers before them. At present two sets of terms are rudely intermixed; the time when they will grow into an organic whole is but beginning.

To this we must add that, unless we have mistaken the general drift of legal history, the law implied in Domesday Book ought to be for us very difficult law, far more difficult than the law of the thirteenth century, for the thirteenth century is nearer to us than is the eleventh. The grown man will find it easier to think the thoughts of the school-boy than to think the thoughts of the baby. And yet the doctrine that our remote forefathers being simple folk had simple law dies hard. Too often we allow ourselves to suppose that, could we but get back to the beginning, we should find that all was intelligible and should then be able to watch the process whereby simple ideas were smothered under subtleties and technicalities. But it is not so. Simplicity is the outcome of technical subtlety; it is the goal not the starting point. As we go backwards the familiar outlines become blurred; the ideas become fluid, and instead of the simple we find the indefinite. But difficult though our task may be, we must turn to it.

Legal ideas of cent. xi.

§ 1.   *Plan of the Survey.*

England was already mapped out into counties, hundreds or wapentakes and vills. Trithings or ridings appear in Yorkshire and Lincolnshire, lathes in Kent, rapes in Sussex, while leets appear, at least sporadically, in Norfolk[1]. These provincial peculiarities we must pass by, nor will we pause to comment at any length on the changes in the boundaries of counties and of hundreds that have taken place since the date of the survey. Though these changes have been many and some few of them have been large[2], we may still say that as a general rule the political geography of England was already stereotyped. And we see that already there are many curious anomalies, 'detached portions' of counties, discrete hundreds, places that are extra-hundredal[3], places that for one purpose are in one county

The geographical basis.

---

[1] D. B. ii. 109 b: 'Hundret de Grenehou 14 letis.' Ib. 212 b : 'Hundret et Dim. de Clakelosa de 10 leitis.'   Round, Feudal England, 101.

[2] Some of them are mentioned by Ellis, Introduction, i. 34–9.

[3] D. B. i. 184 b: 'Haec terra non geldat nec consuetudinem dat nec in aliquo hundredo iacet'; i. 157 'Haec terra nunquam geldavit nec alicui

and for another purpose in another county[1]. We see also that proprietary rights have already been making sport of arrangements which in our eyes should be fixed by public law. Earls, sheriffs and others have enjoyed a marvellous power of taking a tract of land out of one district and placing it, or 'making it lie' in another district[2]. Land is constantly spoken of as though it were the most portable of things; it can easily be taken from one vill or hundred and be added to or placed in or caused to lie in another vill or hundred. This 'notional movability' of land, if we may use such a term, will become of importance to us when we are studying the formation of manors.

The vill as the geographical unit.   For the present, however, we are concerned with the general truth that England is divided into counties, hundreds or wapentakes and vills. This is the geographical basis of the survey. That basis, however, is hidden from us by the form of our record. The plan adopted by those who fashioned Domesday Book out of the returns provided for them by the king's commissioners is a curious, compromising plan. We may say that in part it is geographical, while in part it is feudal or proprietary. It takes each county separately and thus far it is geographical; but within the boundaries of each county it arranges the lands under the names of the tenants in chief who hold them. Thus all the lands in Cambridgeshire of which Count Alan is tenant in chief are brought together, no matter that they lie scattered about in various hundreds. Therefore it is necessary for us to understand that the original returns reported by the surveyors did not reach the royal treasury in this form. At least as regards the county of Cambridge, we can be certain of this. The hundreds were taken one by one; they were taken in a geographical order, and not until the

hundredo pertinet nec pertinuit'; i. 357 b 'Hae duae carucatae non sunt in numero alicuius hundredi neque habent pares in Lincolescyra.'

[1] D. B. i. 207 b: 'Jacet in Bedefordscira set geldum dat in Huntedonscire'; i. 61 b 'Jacet et appreciata est in Gratentun quod est in Oxenefordscire et tamen dat scotum in Berchescire'; i. 132 b, the manor of Weston 'lies in' Hitchin which is in Hertfordshire, but its *wara* 'lies in' Bedfordshire, i.e. it pays geld, it 'defends itself' in the latter county; i. 189 b, the *wara* of a certain hide 'lies in' Hinxton which is in Cambridgeshire, but the land belongs to the manor of Chesterford and therefore is valued in Essex. D. B. i. 178: five hides 'geld and plead' in Worcestershire, but pay their farm in Herefordshire.

[2] D. B. i. 157 b: 'Has [terras in Oxenefordscire] coniunxit terrae suae in Glowecestrescire'; i. 209 b 'foris misit de hundredo ubi se defendebat T. R. E.'; i. 50 'et misit foras comitatum et misit in Wiltesire.' See also Ellis, i. 36.

justices had learned all that was to be known of Staplehow hundred did they call upon the jurors of Cheveley hundred for their verdict. That such was their procedure we might have guessed even had we not been fortunate enough to have a copy of the Cambridgeshire verdicts; for, though the commissioners seem to have held but one moot for each shire, still it is plain that each hundred was represented by a separate set of jurors[1]. But from these Cambridgeshire verdicts we learn what otherwise we could hardly have known. Within each hundred the survey was made by vills[2]. If we suppose the commissioners charging the jurors we must represent them as saying, not 'Tell us what tenants in chief have lands in your hundred and how much each of them holds,' but 'Tell us about each vill in your hundred, who holds land in it.' Thus, for example, the men of the Armingford hundred are called up. They make a separate report about each vill in it. They begin by stating that the vill is rated at a certain number of hides and then they proceed to distribute those hides among the tenants in chief. Thus, for example, they say that Abington was rated at 5 hides, and that those 5 hides are distributed thus[3]:

	hides	virgates
Hugh Pincerna holds of the bishop of Winchester	2½	½
The king	½	
Ralph and Robert hold of Hardouin de Eschalers	1	1½
Earl Roger		1
Picot the sheriff		½
Alwin Hamelecoc the bedel holds of the king		½
	5	0

Now in Domesday Book we must look to several different pages to get this information about the vill of Abington,—to one page for Earl Roger's land, to another page for Picot's land,

---

[1] See Round, Feudal England, p. 118. Mr Round seems to think that the commissioners made a circuit through the hundreds. I doubt they did more than their successors the justices in eyre were wont to do, that is, they held in the shire-town a moot which was attended by (1) the magnates of the shire who spoke for the shire, (2) a jury from every hundred, (3) a deputation of *villani* from every township. See the Yorkshire and Lincolnshire *Clamores* (i. 375) where we may find successive entries beginning with (*a*) *Scyra testatur*, (*b*) *Westreding testatur*, (*c*) *Testatur wapentac*. Strikingly similar entries are found on the eyre rolls. As Sir F. Pollock (Eng. Hist. Rev. xi. 213) remarks, it is misleading to speak of the Domesday 'survey'; Domesday Inquest would be better.

[2] See Round, Feudal England, p. 44.

[3] Inquis. Com. Cantab. 60.

and we may easily miss the important fact that this vill of Abington has been rated as a whole at the neat, round figure of 5 hides. And then we see that the whole hundred of Armingford has been rated at the neat, round figure of 100 hides, and has consisted of six vills rated at 10 hides apiece and eight vills rated at 5 hides apiece[1]. Thus we are brought to look upon the vill as a unit in a system of assessment. All this is concealed from us by the form of Domesday Book.

Stability of the vill.

When that book mentions the name of a place, when it says that Roger holds Sutton or that Ralph holds three hides in Norton, we regard that name as the name of a vill; it may or may not be also the name of a manor. Speaking very generally we may say that the place so named will in after times be known as a vill and in our own day will be a civil parish. No doubt in some parts of the country new vills have been created since the Conqueror's time. Some names that occur in our record fail to obtain a permanent place on the roll of English vills, become the names of hamlets or disappear altogether; on the other hand, new names come to the front. Of course we dare not say dogmatically that all the names mentioned in Domesday Book were the names of vills; very possibly (if this distinction was already known) some of them were the names of hamlets; nor, again, do we imply that the *villa* of 1086 had much organization; but a place that is mentioned in Domesday Book will probably be recognized as a vill in the thirteenth, a civil parish in the nineteenth century. Let us take Cambridgeshire by way of example. Excluding the Isle of Ely, we find that the political geography of the Conqueror's reign has endured until our own time. The boundaries of the hundreds lie almost where they lay, the number of vills has hardly been increased or diminished. The chief changes amount to this:—A small tract on the east side of the county containing Exning and Bellingham has been made over to Suffolk; four other names contained in Domesday no longer stand for parishes, while the names of five of our modern parishes—one of them is the significant name of Newton—are not found there[2]. But about a hundred and ten vills that

---

[1] See the table in Round, Feudal England, p. 50. I had already selected this beautiful specimen before Mr Round's book appeared. He has given several others that are quite as neat.

[2] Of course we take no account of urban parishes.

were vills in 1086 are vills or civil parishes at the present day,
and in all probability they then had approximately the same
boundaries that they have now.

This may be a somewhat too favourable example of
permanence and continuity. Of all counties Cambridgeshire
is the one whose ancient geography can be the most easily
examined; but wherever we have looked we have come to the
conclusion that the distribution of England into vills is in the
main as old as the Norman Conquest[1]. Two causes of difficulty
may be noticed, for they are of some interest. Owing to what
we have called the 'notional movability' of land, we never can
be quite sure that when certain hides or acres are said to be in
or lie in a certain place they are really and physically in that
place. They are really in one village, but they are spoken of
as belonging to another village, because their occupants pay
their geld or do their services in the latter. Manorial and fiscal
geography interferes with physical and villar geography. We
have lately seen how land rated at five hides was comprised, as
a matter of fact, in the vill of Abington; but of those five
hides, one virgate 'lay in' Shingay, a half-hide 'lay in'
Litlington while a half-virgate 'lay and had always lain' in
Morden[2]. This, if we mistake not, leads in some cases to an
omission of the names of small vills. A great lord has a
compact estate, perhaps the whole of one of the small southern
hundreds. He treats it as a whole, and all the land that he has
there will be ascribed to some considerable village in which he
has his hall. We should be rash in supposing that there were
no other villages on this land. For example, in Surrey there
is now-a-days a hundred called Farnham which comprises the
parish of Farnham, the parish of Frensham and some other
villages. If we mistake not, all that Domesday Book has to
say of the whole of this territory is that the Bishop of Winchester
holds Farnham, that it has been rated at 60 hides, that it has
been worth the large sum of £65 a year and that there are so
many tenants upon it[3]. We certainly must not draw the
inference that there was but one vill in this tract. If the
bishop is tenant in chief of the whole hundred and has become

[1] Eyton's laborious studies have made this plain as regards some counties
widely removed from each other; still, *e.g.* in his book on Somerset, he has now
and again to note that names which appear in D. B. are obsolete.
[2] Inq. Com. Cant. 60–1.   [3] D. B. i. 31.

responsible for all the geld that is levied therefrom, there is
no great reason why the surveyors should trouble themselves
about the vills. Thus the simple *Episcopus tenet Ferneham*
may dispose of some 25,000 acres of land. So the same bishop
has an estate at Chilcombe in Hampshire; but clearly the
name *Ciltecumbe* covers a wide territory for there are no less
than nine churches upon it[1]. We never can be very certain
about the boundaries of these large and compact estates.

Fission of
vills.   A second cause of difficulty lies in the fact that in comparatively modern times, from the twelfth century onwards, two
or three contiguous villages will often bear the same name and
be distinguished only by what we may call their surnames—
thus Guilden Morden and Steeple Morden, Stratfield Saye,
Stratfield Turgis, Stratfield Mortimer, Tolleshunt Knights,
Tolleshunt Major, Tolleshunt Darcy. Such cases are common;
in some districts they are hardly exceptional. Doubtless they
point to a time when a single village by some process of
colonization or subdivision become two villages. Now Domesday Book seldom enables us to say for certain whether the
change has already taken place. In a few instances it marks
off the little village from the great village of the same name[2].
In some other instances it will speak, for example, of *Mordune*
and *Mordune Alia*, of *Emingeforde* and *Emingeforde Alia*, or
the like, thus showing both that the change has taken place,
and also that it is so recent that it is recognized only by very
clumsy terms. In Cambridgeshire, since we have the original
verdicts, we can see that the two Mordens are already distinct;
the one is rated at ten hides, the other at five[3]. On the other
hand, we can see that our Great and Little Shelford are rated
as one vill of twenty hides[4], our Castle Camps and Shudy
Camps as one vill of five hides[5]. Elsewhere we are left to
guess whether the fission is complete, and the surnames that
many of our vills ultimately acquire, the names of families
which rose to greatness in the twelfth and thirteenth centuries,
will often suggest that the surveyors saw but one vill where we
see two[6]. However, the broad truth stands out that England

---

[1] D. B. i. 41. We shall return to this matter hereafter.
[2] A good many cases will be found in Essex and Suffolk.
[3] Inq. Com. Cantab. 51, 53.　　　[4] Ibid. 47.　　　[5] Ibid. 29.
[6] Maitland, Surnames of English Villages, Archaeological Review, iv. 233.

was divided into vills and that in general the vill of Domesday Book is still a vill in after days[1].

The 'vill' or 'town' of the later middle ages was, like the 'civil parish' of our own day, a tract of land with some houses on it, and this tract was a unit in the national system of police and finance[2]. But we are not entitled to make for ourselves any one typical picture of the English vill. We are learning from the ordnance map (that marvellous palimpsest, which under Dr Meitzen's guidance we are beginning to decipher) that in all probability we must keep at least two types before our minds. On the one hand, there is what we might call the true village or the nucleated village. In the purest form of this type there is one and only one cluster of houses. It is a fairly large cluster; it stands in the midst of its fields, of its territory, and until lately a considerable part of its territory will probably have consisted of spacious 'common fields.' In a country in which there are villages of this type the parish boundaries seem almost to draw themselves[3]. On the other hand, we may easily find a country in which there are few villages of this character. The houses which lie within the boundary of the parish are scattered about in small clusters; here two or three, there three or four. These clusters often have names of their own, and it seems a mere chance that the name borne by one of them should be also the name of the whole parish or vill[4]. We see no traces of very large fields. On the face of the map there is no reason why a particular group of cottages should be reckoned to belong to this parish rather than to the next. As our eyes grow accustomed to the work we may arrive at some extremely important conclusions such as those which Meitzen has suggested. The outlines of our nucleated villages may have been drawn for us by Germanic settlers, whereas in the land of hamlets and scattered steads old Celtic arrangements may never have been thoroughly effaced.

The nucleated village and the vill of scattered steads.

---

[1] We do not mean to imply that there were not wide stretches of waste land which were regarded as being 'extra-villar,' or common to several vills.

[2] Hist. Eng. Law, i. 547.

[3] This of course would not be true of cases in which the lands of various villages were intermixed in one large tract of common field. As to these 'discrete vills,' see Hist. Eng. Law, i. 549.

[4] This name-giving cluster will usually contain the parish church and so will enjoy a certain preeminence. But we are to speak of a time when parish churches were novelties.

Towards theories of this kind we are slowly winning our way. In the meantime let us remember that a *villa* of Domesday Book may correspond to one of at least two very different models or may be intermediate between various types. It may be a fairly large and agrarianly organic unit, or it may be a group of small agrarian units which are being held together in one whole merely by an external force, by police law and fiscal law [1].

Illustra-
tions by
maps.
Two little fragments of 'the original one inch ordnance map' will be more eloquent than would be many paragraphs of written discourse. The one pictures a district on the border between Oxfordshire and Berkshire cut by the Thames and the main line of the Great Western Railway; the other a district on the border between Devon and Somerset, north of Collumpton and south of Wiveliscombe. Neither is an extreme example. True villages we may easily find. Cambridgeshire, for instance, would have afforded some beautiful specimens, for many of the 'open fields' were still open when the ordnance map of that county was made. But throughout large tracts of England, even though there has been an 'inclosure' and there are no longer any open fields, our map often shows a land of villages. When it does so and the district that it portrays is a purely agricultural district, we may generally assume without going far wrong that the villages are ancient, for during at least the last three centuries the predominant current in our agrarian history has set against the formation of villages and towards the distribution of scattered homesteads. To find the purest specimens of a land of hamlets we ought to go to Wales or to Cornwall or to other parts of 'the Celtic fringe': very fair examples might be found throughout the west of England. Also we may perhaps find hamlets rather than villages wherever there have been within the historic period large tracts of forest land. Very often, again, the parish or township looks on our map like a hybrid. We seem to see a village with satellitic hamlets. Much more remains to be done before we shall be able to construe the testimony of our fields and walls and hedges, but at least two types of vill must be in our eyes when we are reading Domesday Book [2].

[1] See Meitzen, Siedelung und Agrarwesen der Germanen, especially ii. 119 ff.

[2] When the hamlets bear names with such ancient suffixes as *-ton, -ham, -by,*

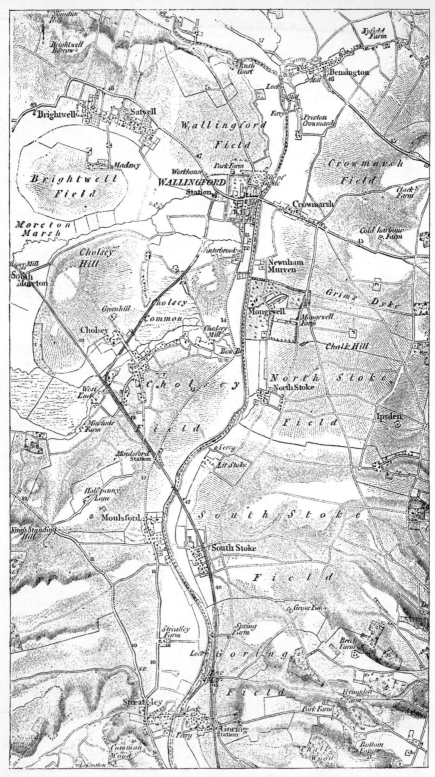

A LAND OF VILLAGES

On the border between Oxfordshire and Berkshire.

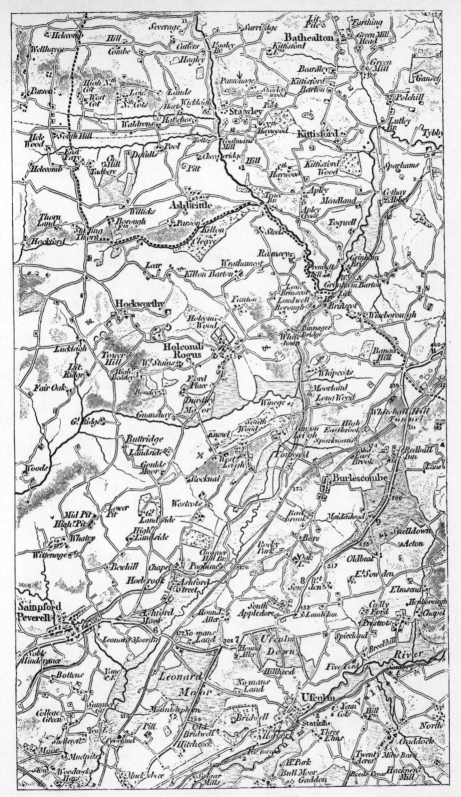

A LAND OF HAMLETS

To say that the *villa* of Domesday Book is in general the vill of the thirteenth century and the civil parish of the nineteenth is to say that the areal extent of the *villa* varied widely from case to case. More important is it for us to observe that the number of inhabitants of the *villa* varied widely from case to case. The error into which we are most likely to fall will be that of making our vill too populous. Some vills, especially some royal vills, are populous enough; a few contain a hundred households; but the average township is certainly much smaller than this[1]. Before we give any figures, it should first be observed that Domesday Book never enables us to count heads. It states the number of the tenants of various classes, *sochemanni, villani, bordarii,* and the like, and leaves us to suppose that each of these persons is, or may be, the head of a household. It also states how many *servi* there are. Whether we ought to suppose that only the heads of servile households are reckoned, or whether we ought to think of the *servi* as having no households but as living within the lord's gates and being enumerated, men, women and able-bodied children, by the head—this is a difficult question. Still we may reach some results which will enable us to compare township with township. By way of fair sample we may take the Armingford hundred of Cambridgeshire, and all persons who are above the rank of *servi* we will include under the term 'the non-servile population[2].'

ARMINGFORD HUNDRED.

	Non-servile population	Servi	Total
Abington	19	0	19
Bassingbourn	35	3	38
Clapton	19	0	19
Croydon	29	0	29

-*worth*, -*wick*, -*thorpe*, this of course is in favour of their antiquity. On the other hand, if they are known merely by family names such as *Styles's, Nokes's, Johnson's* or the like, this, though not conclusive evidence of, is compatible with their modernity. Meitzen thinks that in Kent and along the southern shore the German invaders founded but few villages. The map does not convince me that this inference is correct.

[1] When more than five-and-twenty team-lands or thereabouts are ascribed to a single place, we shall generally find reason to believe that what is being described is not a single vill. See above, p. 13.

[2] Inq. Com. Cant. 51 fol. In a few cases our figures will involve a small element of conjecture.

Hatley	18	3	21
Litlington	37	6	43
Melbourn	62	1	63
Meldreth	44	7	51
Morden	43	11	54
Morden Alia	50	0	50
Shingay	18	0	18
Tadlow	27	4	31
Wendy	12	4	16
Whaddon	44	6	50
Total	457	45	502

Here in fourteen vills we have an average of thirty-two non-servile households for every vill. Now even in our own day a parish with thirty-two houses, though small, is not extremely small. But we should form a wrong picture of the England of the eleventh century if we filled all parts of it with such vills as these. We will take at random fourteen vills in Staffordshire held by Earl Roger[1].

	Non-servile population	Servi	Total
Claverlege	45	0	45
Nordlege	9	0	9
Alvidelege	13	0	13
Halas	40	2	42
Chenistelei	11	0	11
Otne	7	1	8
Nortberie	20	1	21
Erlide	8	2	10
Gaitone	16	0	16
Cressvale	8	0	8
Dodintone	3	0	3
Modreshale	5	0	5
Almentone	8	0	8
Metford	7	1	8
Total	200	7	207

Here for fourteen vills we have an average of but fourteen non-servile households and the *servi* are so few that we may neglect them. We will next look at a page in the survey of Somersetshire which describes certain vills that have fallen to the lot of the bishop of Coutances[2].

---

[1] D. B. i. 248. We have tried to avoid vills in which it is certain or probable that some other tenant in chief had an estate.

[2] D. B. i. 88. We have tried to make sure that no tenant in chief save the

	Non-servile population	Servi	Total
Winemeresham	8	3	11
Chetenore	3	1	4
Widicumbe	21	6	27
Harpetrev	10	2	12
Hotune	11	0	11
Lilebere	6	1	7
Wintreth	4	2	6
Aisecome	11	7	18
Clutone	22	1	23
Temesbare	7	3	10
Nortone	16	3	19
Cliveham	15	1	16
Ferenberge	13	6	19
Cliveware	6	0	6
Total	153	36	189

Here we have on the average but eleven non-servile households for each village, and even if we suppose each *servus* to represent a household, we have not fourteen households. Yet smaller vills will be found in Devonshire, many vills in which the total number of the persons mentioned does not exceed ten and near half of these are *servi*. In Cornwall the townships, if townships we ought to call them, are yet smaller; often we can attribute no more than five or six families to the vill even if we include the *servi*.

Unless our calculations mislead us, the density of the population in the average vill of a given county varies somewhat directly with the density of the population in that county; at all events we can not say that where vills are populous, vills will be few. As regards this matter no precise results are attainable; our document is full of snares for arithmeticians. Still if for a moment we have recourse to the crude method of dividing the number of acres comprised in a modern county by the number of the persons who are mentioned in the survey of that county, the outcome of our calculation will be remarkable and will point to some broad truth[1]. For Suffolk the quotient

Population of the vills.

bishop had land in any of these vills, and this we think fairly certain, except as regards Harptree and Norton. There are now two Harptrees, East and West, and four or more Nortons.

[1] We take the figures from Ellis, Introduction, ii. 417 ff.

2—2

Contrast
between
east and
west.
is 46 or thereabouts; for Norfolk but little larger[1]; for Essex
61, for Lincoln 67; for Bedford, Berkshire, Northampton,
Leicester, Middlesex, Oxford, Kent and Somerset it lies between
70 and 80, for Buckingham, Warwick, Sussex, Wiltshire and
Dorset it lies between 80 and 90; Devon, Gloucester, Worcester, Hereford are thinly peopled, Cornwall, Stafford, Shropshire
very thinly.   Some particular results that we should thus attain
would be delusive.   Thus we should say that men were sparse
in Cambridgeshire, did we not remember that a large part of
our modern Cambridgeshire was then a sheet of water.   Permanent physical causes interfere with the operation of the
general rule.   Thus Surrey, with its wide heaths has, as we
might expect, but few men to the square mile.   Derbyshire has
many vills lying waste; Yorkshire is so much wasted that it
can give us no valuable result; and again, Yorkshire and
Cheshire were larger than they are now, while Rutland and
the adjacent counties had not their present boundaries.   For
all this however, we come to a very general rule :—the density
of the population decreases as we pass from east to west.   With
this we may connect another rule:—land is much more valuable
in the east than it is in the west.   This matter is indeed hedged
in by many thorny questions; still whatever hypothesis we may
adopt as to the mode in which land was valued, one general
truth comes out pretty plainly, namely, that, economic arrangements being what they were, it was far better to have a
team-land in Essex than to have an equal area of arable
land in Devon.

Small vills.   Between eastern and western England there were differences
visible to the natural eye.   With these were connected unseen
and legal differences, partly as causes, partly as effects.   But
for the moment let us dwell on the fact that many an English
vill has very few inhabitants.   We are to speak hereafter of
village communities.   Let us therefore reflect that a community
of some eight or ten householders is not likely to be a highly
organized entity.   This is not all, for these eight or ten house-

---

[1] Very possibly this figure is too low.   There is reason to think that some of
the free men and sokemen of these counties get counted twice or thrice over
because they hold land under several different lords.   On the other hand Ellis
(Introduction, ii. 491) would argue that the figure is too high.   But the words
Alii ibi tenent which occur at the end of numerous entries mean, we believe, not
that there are in this vill other unenumerated tillers of the soil, but that the vill
is divided between several tenants in chief.

holders will often belong to two, three or four different social and economic, if not legal, classes. Some may be sokemen, some *villani, bordarii, cotarii,* and besides them there will be a few *servi.* If a vill consists, as in Devonshire often enough it will, of some three *villani,* some four *bordarii* and some two *servi,* the 'township-moot' if such a moot there be, will be a queer little assembly, the manorial court, if such a court there be, will not have much to do. These men can not have many communal affairs; there will be no great scope for dooms or for by-laws; they may well take all their disputes into the hundred court, especially in Devonshire where the hundreds are small. Thus of the visible vill of the eleventh century and its material surroundings we may form a wrong notion. Often enough in the west its common fields (if common fields it had) were not wide fields; the men who had shares therein were few and belonged to various classes. Thus of two villages in Gloucestershire, Brookthorpe and Harescombe, all that we can read is that in Brostrop there were two teams, one *villanus,* three *bordarii,* four *servi,* while in Hersecome there were two teams, two *bordarii* and five *servi*[1]. Many a Devonshire township can produce but two or three teams. Often enough our 'village community' will be a heterogeneous little group whose main capital consists of some 300 acres of arable land and some 20 beasts of the plough.

On the other hand, we must be careful not to omit from our view the rich and thickly populated shires or to imagine or to speak as though we imagined that a general theory of English history can neglect the East of England. If we leave Lincolnshire, Norfolk and Suffolk out of account we are to all appearance leaving out of account not much less than a quarter of the whole nation[2]. Let us make three groups of counties: (1) a South-Western group containing Devon, Somerset, Dorset and Wiltshire: (2) a Mid-Western group containing the shires of Gloucester, Worcester, Hereford, Salop, Stafford and Warwick: (3) an Eastern group containing Lincolnshire, Norfolk and Suffolk. The first of these groups has the largest; the third the smallest acreage. In Domesday Book, however, the figures which state their population seem to be these[3]:—

Importance of the east.

---

[1] D. B. i. 162 b.

[2] Ellis's figures are: England 283,242: the three counties 72,883.

[3] We take these figures from Ellis.

South Western Group :	49,155
Mid Western Group :	33,191
Eastern Group :	72,883

These figures are so emphatic that they may cause us for a moment to doubt their value, and on details we must lay no stress. But we have materials which enable us to check the general effect. In 1297 Edward I. levied a lay subsidy of a ninth[1]. The sums borne by our three groups of counties were these :—

	£
South Western Group :	4,038
Mid Western Group :	3,514
Eastern Group :	7,329

There is a curious resemblance between these two sets of figures. Then in 1377 and 1381 returns were made for a poll-tax[2]. The number of polls returned in our three groups were these :—

	1377	1381
South Western Group :	183,842	106,086
Mid Western Group :	158,245	115,679
Eastern Group :	255,498	182,830

No doubt all inferences drawn from medieval statistics are exceedingly precarious; but, unless a good many figures have conspired to deceive us, Lincolnshire, Norfolk and Suffolk were at the time of the Conquest and for three centuries afterwards vastly richer and more populous than any tract of equal area in the West.

Manorial and non-manorial vills.

Another distinction between the eastern counties and the rest of England is apparent. In many shires we shall find that the name of each vill is mentioned once and no more. This is so because the land of each vill belongs in its entirety to some one tenant in chief. We may go further: we may say, though at present in an untechnical sense, that each vill is a manor. Such is the general rule, though there will be exceptions to it. On the other hand, in the eastern counties this rule will become the exception. For example, of the fourteen vills in the Armingford hundred of Cambridgeshire there is but one of

[1] Lay Subsidy, 25 Edw. I. (Yorkshire Archaeological Society), pp. xxxi–xxxv. Fractions of a pound are neglected.

[2] Powell, The Rising in East Anglia, 120–3. The great decrease between 1377 and 1381 in the number of persons taxed, we must not try to explain.

which it is true that the whole of its land is held by a single tenant in chief. In this county it is common to find that three or four Norman lords hold land in the same vill. This seems true not only of Cambridgeshire but also of Essex, Suffolk, Norfolk, Lincoln, Nottingham, Derby, and some parts of Yorkshire. Even in other districts of England the rule that each vill has a single lord is by no means unbroken in the Conqueror's day and we can see that there were many exceptions to it in the Confessor's. A careful examination of all England vill by vill would perhaps show that the contrast which we are noting is neither so sharp nor so ancient as at first sight it seems to be: nevertheless it exists.

A better known contrast there is. The eastern counties are the home of liberty[1]. We may divide the tillers of the soil into five great classes; these in order of dignity and freedom are (1) *liberi homines*, (2) *sochemanni*, (3) *villani*, (4) *bordarii, cotarii* etc., (5) *servi*. The two first of these classes are to be found in large numbers only in Norfolk, Suffolk, Lincolnshire, Nottinghamshire, Leicestershire and Northamptonshire. We shall hereafter see that Cambridgeshire also has been full of sokemen, though since the Conquest they have fallen from their high estate. On the other hand, the number of *servi* increases pretty steadily as we cross the country from east to west. It reaches its maximum in Cornwall and Gloucestershire; it is very low in Norfolk, Suffolk, Derby, Leicester, Middlesex, Sussex; it descends to zero in Yorkshire and Lincolnshire. This descent to zero may fairly warn us that the terms with which we are dealing may not bear precisely the same meaning in all parts of England, or that a small class is apt to be reckoned as forming part of a larger class. But still it is clear enough that some of these terms are used with care and express real and important distinctions. *The distribution of free men and serfs.*

Of this we are assured by a document which seems to reproduce the wording of the instructions which defined the duty of at least one party of royal commissioners[2]. We are about to speak of the mode in which the occupants of the soil are classified by Domesday Book, and therefore this document *The classification of men.*

---

[1] See the serviceable maps in Seebohm, Village Community, 86. But they seem to treat Yorkshire unfairly. It has 5·5 per cent. of sokemen.

[2] This is found at the beginning of the Inquisitio Eliensis; D. B. iv. 497; Hamilton, Inquisitio, 97. See Round, Feudal England. 133 ff.

deserves our best attention. It runs thus:—The King's barons inquired by the oath of the sheriff of the shire and of all the barons and of their Frenchmen and of the whole hundred, the priest, reeve and six *villani* of every vill, how the mansion (*mansio*) is called, who held it in the time of King Edward, who holds it now, how many hides, how many plough-teams on the demesne, how many plough-teams of the men, how many *villani*, how many *cotarii*, how many *servi*, how many *liberi homines*, how many *sochemanni*, how much wood, how much meadow, how much pasture, how many mills, how many fisheries, how much has been taken away therefrom, how much added thereto, and how much there is now, how much each *liber homo* and *sochemannus* had and has:—All this thrice over, to wit as regards the time of King Edward, the time when King William gave it, and the present time, and whether more can be had thence than is had now[1].

Basis of classification.

Five classes of men are mentioned and they are mentioned in an order that is extremely curious:—*villani, cotarii, servi, liberi homines, sochemanni.* It descends three steps, then it leaps from the very bottom of the scale to the very top and thence it descends one step. A parody of it might speak of the rural population of modern England as consisting of large farmers, small farmers, cottagers, great landlords, small landlords. But a little consideration will convince us that beneath this apparent caprice there lies some legal principle. We shall observe that these five species of tenants are grouped into two genera. The king wants to know how much each *liber homo*, how much each *sochemannus* holds ; he does not want to know how much each *villanus*, each *cotarius*, each *servus* holds. Connecting this with the main object of the whole survey, we shall probably be brought to the guess that between the sokeman and the villein there is some broad distinction which concerns the king as the recipient of geld. May it not be this:—the villein's lord is answerable for the geld due from the land that the villein holds, the sokeman's lord is not answerable,

---

[1] We must not hastily draw the inference that every party of commissioners received the same set of instructions. Perhaps, for example, carucates, not hides, were mentioned in the instructions given to those commissioners who were to visit the carucated counties. Perhaps the non-appearance of *servi* in Yorkshire and Lincolnshire may be due to no deeper cause.

at least he is not answerable as principal debtor for the geld
due from the land that the sokeman holds? If this be so, the
order in which the five classes of men are mentioned will not
seem unnatural. It proceeds outwards from the lord and his
mansio. First it mentions the persons seated on land for the
geld of which he is responsible, and them it arranges in an
'order of merit.' Then it turns to persons who, though in some
way or another connected with the lord and his *mansio*, are
themselves tax-payers, and concerning them the commissioners
are to inquire how much each of them holds. Of course we
can not say that this theory is proved by the statement that lies
before us; but it is suggested by that statement and may for a
while serve us as a working hypothesis. If this theory be
sound, then we have here a distinction of the utmost importance.
For one mighty purpose, the purpose that is uppermost in King
William's mind, the *villanus* is not a landowner, his lord is the
landowner; on the other hand the *sochemannus* is a landowner,
and is taxed as such. We are not saying that this is a purely
fiscal distinction. In legal logic the lord's liability for the geld
that is apportioned on the land occupied by his villeins may be
rather an effect than a cause. A lawyer might argue that the
lord must pay because the occupier is his *villanus*, not that the
occupier is a *villanus* because the lord pays. And yet, as we
may often see in legal history, there will be action and reaction
between cause and effect. The geld is no trifle. Levied at
that rate of six shillings on the hide at which King William
has just now levied it, it is a momentous force capable of de-
pressing and displacing whole classes of men. In 1086 this tax
is so much in everybody's mind that any distinction as to its
incidence will cut deeply into the body of the law.

Now this classification of men we will take as the starting Our course.
point for our enterprise. If we could define the *liber homo,
sochemannus, villanus, cotarius, servus*, we should have solved
some of the great legal problems of Domesday Book, for by the
way we should have had to define two other difficult terms,
namely *manerium* and *soca.* It would then remain that we
should say something of the higher strata of society, of earls
and sheriffs, of barons, knights, thegns and their tenures, of
such terms as *alodium* and *feudum*, of the general theory of
landownership or landholdership. We will begin with the
lowest order of men, with the *servi*, and thence work our way

upwards. But our course can not be straightforward. There
are so many terms to be explained that sometimes we shall be
compelled to leave a question but partially answered while we
are endeavouring to find a partial answer for some yet more
difficult question.

§ 2. *The Serfs.*

The serfs in Domesday Book.

The existence of some 25,000 serfs is recorded. In the
thirteenth century *servus* and *villanus* are, at least among
lawyers, equivalent words. The only unfree man is the 'serf-
villein' and the lawyers are trying to subject him to the curious
principle that he is the lord's chattel but a free man in relation
to all but his lord[1]. It is far otherwise in Domesday Book. In
entry after entry and county after county the *servi* are kept
well apart from the *villani, bordarii, cotarii.* Often they are
mentioned in quite another context to that in which the *villani*
are enumerated. As an instance we may take a manor in
Surrey[2]:—'In demesne there are 5 teams and there are 25
villani and 6 *bordarii* with 14 teams. There is one mill of
2 shillings and one fishery and one church and 4 acres of
meadow, and wood for 150 pannage pigs, and 2 stone-quarries
of 2 shillings and 2 nests of hawks in the wood and 10 *servi*.'
Often enough the *servi* are placed between two other sources of
wealth, the church and the mill. In some counties they seem
to take precedence over the *villani*; the common formula is 'In
dominio sunt *a* carucae et *b* servi et *c* villani et *d* bordarii cum
e carucis.' But this is delusive; the formula is bringing the
servi into connexion with the demesne teams and separating
them from the teams of the tenants. We must render it thus—
'On the demesne there are *a* teams and *b* servi; and there are
c villani and *d* bordarii with *e* teams.' Still we seem to see a
gently graduated scale of social classes, *villani, bordarii, cotarii,
servi,* and while the jurors of one county will arrange them in
one fashion, the jurors of another county may adopt a different
scheme. Thus in their classification of mankind the jurors will
sometimes lay great stress on the possession of plough oxen.
In Hertfordshire we read:—'There are 6 teams in demesne and

---

[1] Hist. Eng. Law, i. 398. [2] D. B. i. 34, Limenesfeld.

41 *villani* and 17 *bordarii* have 20 teams...there are 22 *cotarii* and 12 *servi*[1].'—'The priest, 13 *villani* and 4 *bordarii* have 6 teams...there are two *cotarii* and 4 *servi*[2].'—'The priest and 24 *villani* have 13 teams...there are 12 *bordarii*, 16 *cotarii* and 11 *servi*[3].' A division is in this instance made between the people who have oxen and the people who have none; *villani* have oxen, *cotarii* and *servi* have none; sometimes the *bordarii* stand above this line, sometimes below it.

Of the legal position of the *servus* Domesday Book tells us little or nothing; but earlier and later documents oblige us to think of him as a slave, one who in the main has no legal rights. He is the *theów* of the Anglo-Saxon dooms, the *servus* of the ecclesiastical canons. But though we do right in calling him a slave, still we might well be mistaken were we to think of the line which divides him from other men as being as sharp as the line which a mature jurisprudence will draw between thing and person. We may well doubt whether this principle—'The slave is a thing, not a person'—can be fully understood by a grossly barbarous age. It implies the idea of a person, and in the world of sense we find not persons but men. Legal position of the serf.

Thus degrees of servility are possible. A class may stand, as it were, half-way between the class of slaves and the class of free men. The Kentish law of the seventh century as it appears in the dooms of Æthelbert[4], like many of its continental sisters, knows a class of men who perhaps are not free men and yet are not slaves; it knows the *lœt* as well as the *theów*. From what race the Kentish *lœt* has sprung, and how, when it comes to details, the law will treat him—these are obscure questions, and the latter of them can not be answered unless we apply to him what is written about the *laeti*, *liti* and *lidi* of the continent. He is thus far a person that he has a small wergild but possibly he is bound to the soil. Only in Æthelbert's dooms do we read of him. From later days, until Domesday Book breaks the silence, we do not obtain any definite evidence of the existence of any class of men who are not slaves but none the less are tied to the land. Of men who are bound to do heavy labour services for their lords we do hear, but we do not hear that if they run away they can be Degrees of serfdom.

---

[1] D. B. i. 132 b, Hiz.   [2] D. B. i. 132 b, Waldenei.
[3] D. B. i. 136, Sandone.   [4] Æthelb. 26.

captured and brought back. As we shall see by and by,
Domesday Book bears witness to the existence of a class of
buri, burs, coliberti, who seem to be distinctly superior to the
servi, but distinctly inferior to the villeins, bordiers and cottiers.
It is by no means impossible that they, without being slaves,
are in a very proper and intelligible sense unfree men, that they
have civil rights which they can assert in courts of law, but that
they are tied to the soil. The gulf between the seventh and the
eleventh centuries is too wide to allow of our connecting them
with the *læt* of Æthelbert's laws, but still our documents are
not exhaustive enough to justify us in denying that all along
there has been a class (though it can hardly have been a large
class) of men who could not quit their tenements and yet were
no slaves. As we shall see hereafter, liberty was in certain
contexts reckoned a matter of degree; even the *villanus*, even
the *sochemannus* was not for every purpose *liber homo*. When
this is so, the *theów* or *servus* is like to appear as the unfreest of
persons rather than as no person but a thing.

Prædial
element in
serfage. In the second place, we may guess that from a remote time
there has been in the condition of the *theów* a certain element
of praediality. The slaves have not been worked in gangs nor
housed in barracks[1]. The *servus* has often been a *servus casatus*,
he has had a cottage or even a manse and yardland which *de
facto* he might call his own. There is here no legal limitation of
his master's power. Some slave trade there has been; but on the
whole it seems probable that the *theów* has been usually treated
as annexed to a tenement. The duties exacted of him from
year to year have remained constant. The consequence is that
a free man in return for a plot of land may well agree to do all
that a *theów* usually does and see in this no descent into slavery.
Thus the slave gets a chance of acquiring what will be as a
matter of fact a *peculium*. In the seventh century the church
tried to turn this matter of fact into matter of law. 'Non licet
homini,' says Theodore's Penitential, 'a servo tollere pecuniam,
quam ipse labore suo adquesierit[2].' We have no reason for
thinking that this effort was very strenuous or very successful,

---

[1] Tacitus, Germ. c. 25: 'Caeteris servis non in nostrum morem, descriptis
per familiam ministeriis, utuntur. Suam quisque sedem, suos penates regit.
Frumenti modum dominus aut pecoris aut vestis ut colono iniungit, et servus
hactenus paret.'

[2] Haddan and Stubbs, Councils, iii. 202.

or that the law of the eleventh century allowed the *servus* any proprietary rights; and yet he might often be the occupier of land and of chattels with which, so long as he did his customary services, his lord would seldom meddle.

In the third place, we may believe that for some time past police law and punitive law have been doing something to conceal, if not to obliterate, the line which separates the slave from other men. A mature jurisprudence may be able to hold fast the fundamental principle that a slave is not a person but a thing, while at the same time it both limits the master's power of abusing his human chattel and guards against those dangers which may arise from the existence of things which have wills, and sometimes bad wills, of their own. But an immature jurisprudence is incapable of this exploit. It begins to play fast and loose with its elementary notions. It begins to punish the criminous slave without being quite certain as to how far it is punishing him and how far it is punishing his master. Confusion is easy, for if the slave be punished by death or mutilation, his master will suffer, and a pecuniary mulct exacted from the slave is exacted from his master. Learned writers have come to the most opposite opinions as to the extent to which the Anglo-Saxon dooms by their distribution of penalties recognize the personality of the *theów*. But this is not all. For a long time past the law has had before it the difficult problem of dealing with crimes and delicts committed by poor and economically dependent free men, men who have no land of their own, who are here to-day and gone to-morrow, 'men from whom no right can be had.' It has been endeavouring to make the lords answerable to a certain extent for the misdeeds of their free retainers. If a slave is charged with a crime his master is bound to produce him in court. But the law requires that the lord shall in very similar fashion produce his free 'loaf eater,' his mainpast, nay, it has been endeavouring to enforce the rule that every free man who has no land of his own shall have a lord bound to produce him when he is accused. Also it has been fostering the growth of private justice. The lord's duty of producing his men, bond and free, has been becoming the duty of holding a court in which his men, free and bond, will answer for themselves. How far this process had gone in the days of the Confessor is a question to which we shall return[1].

The serf in criminal law.

[1] See on the one hand Maurer, K. U. i. 410, on the other a learned essay

Serf and
villein. For all this however, we may say with certainty that in the
eleventh century the *servi* were marked off from all other men
by definite legal lines. What is more, we may say that every
man who was not a *theów* was in some definite legal sense a
free man. This sharp contrast is put before us by the laws of
Cnut as well as by those of his predecessors. If a freeman
works on a holiday, he pays for it with his *healsfang*; if a
theówman does the like, he pays for it with his hide or his
hide-geld[1]. Equally sharp is the same distinction in the Leges
Henrici, and this too in passages which, so far as we know, are
not borrowed from Anglo-Saxon documents. For many purposes
'aut servus aut liber homo' is a perfect dilemma. There is no
confusion whatever between the *villani* and the *servi*. The
villani are 'viles et inopes personae' but clearly enough they
are *liberi homines*. So also in the Quadripartitus, the Latin
translation of the ancient dooms made in Henry I.'s reign, there
is no confusion about this matter; the *theówman* becomes a
servus, while *villanus* is the equivalent for *ceorl*. The Norman
writers still tell how according to the old law of the English
the *villanus* might become a thegn if he acquired five hides of
land[2]; at times they will put before us *villani* and *thaini* or
even *villani* and *barones* as an exhaustive classification of free
men[3].

The serf of
the Leges. Let us learn what may be learnt of the *servus* from the
Leges Henrici. Every man is either a *liber homo* or a *servus*[4].
Free men are either two-hundred-men or twelve-hundred-men;

by Jastrow, Zur strafrechtlichen Stellung der Sklaven, in Gierke's Untersuchungen zur Deutsche Geschichte, vol. i. Maurer holds that the Anglo-
Saxon slave is in the main a chattel, that *e.g.* the master must answer for the
delicts of his slave in the same way that the owner answers for damage done by
his beasts, and that this liability can be clearly marked off from the duty of the
lord of free retainers who is merely bound to produce them in court. Jastrow,
on the contrary, thinks that even at a quite early time the Anglo-Saxon slave is
treated as a person by criminal law; he has a wergild; he can be fined; his
trespasses are never compared to the trespasses of beasts; the lord's duty, if
one of his men is charged with crime, is much the same whether that man be
free or bond. Any theory involves an explanation of several passages that are
obscure and perhaps corrupt.

[1] Cnut, ii. 45-6.

[2] Schmid, Appendix v. (Of Ranks); Pseudoleges Canuti, 60 (Schmid,
p. 431).

[3] Leg. Hen. 76 § 7: 'Differentia tamen weregildi multa est in Cantia villanorum et baronum.'

[4] Leg. Hen. 76 § 2.

perhaps we ought to add that there is also a class of six-hundred-men[1]. A serf becomes such either by birth or by some event, such as a sale into slavery, that happens in his lifetime[2]. Servile blood is transmitted from father to child; some lords hold that it is also transmitted by mother to child[3]. If a slave is to be freed this should be done publicly, in court, or church or market, and lance and helmet or other the arms of free men should be given him, while he should give his lord thirty pence, that is the price of his skin, as a sign that he is henceforth 'worthy of his hide.' On the other hand, when a free man falls into slavery then also there should be a public ceremony. He should put his head between his lord's hands and should receive as the arms of slavery some bill-hook or the like[4]. Public ceremonies are requisite, for the state is endangered by the uncertain condition of accused criminals; the lords will assert at one moment that their men are free and at the next moment that these same men are slaves[5]. The descent of a free man into slavery is treated as no uncommon event; the slave may well have free kinsfolk[6]. But, to come to the fundamental rule, the *villanus*, the meanest of free men, is a two-hundred-man, that is to say, if he be slain the very substantial wergild of 200 Saxon shillings or £4 must be paid to his kinsfolk[7], while a man-bót of 30 shillings is paid to his lord[8]. But if a *servus* be slain his kinsfolk receive the comparatively trifling sum of 40 pence while the lord gets the man-bót of 20 shillings[9]. That the serf's kinsfolk should receive a small sum need not surprise us. Germanic law has

---

[1] Leg. Hen. 76 § 3.   [2] Ibid. 76 § 3.

[3] Ibid. 77; see Hist. Eng. Law, i. 405.

[4] Ibid. 78 § 2. The difficult *strublum* we leave untouched.

[5] Ibid. 78 § 2 from Cnut, ii. 20. On this see Jastrow's comment, op. cit. p. 80.

[6] Ibid. 70 § 5.   [7] Ibid. 70 § 1; 76 § 4.   [8] Ibid. 69 § 2.

[9] Ibid. 70 § 4: 'Si liber servum occidat similiter reddat parentibus 40 den. et duas mufflas et unum pullum [*al.* billum] mutilatum.' The *mufflae* are thick gloves. Compare Ancient Laws of Wales, i. 239, 511; the bondman has no *galanas* (wergild) but if injured he receives a *saraad*; 'the saraad of a bondman is twelve pence, six for a coat for him, three for trousers, one for buskins, one for a hook and one for a rope, and if he be a woodman let the hook-penny be for an axe.' If we read *billum* instead of *pullum* the English rule may remind us of the Welsh. His hedger's gloves and bill-hook are the arms appropriate to the serf, 'servitutis arma'; cf. Leg. Hen. 78 § 2. As to the *man-bót* see Liebermann, Leg. Edwardi, p. 71.

never found it easy to carry the principle that the slave is a chattel to extreme conclusions; but the payment seems trifling and half contemptuous; at any rate the life of the villein is worth the life of twenty-four serfs[1]. Then again, it is by no means certain that a lord can not kill his serf with impunity. 'If,' says our text, 'a man slay his own serf, his is the sin and his is the loss':—we may interpret this to mean that he has sinned but sinned against himself[2]. Then again, for the evil deeds of his slave the master is in some degree responsible. If my slave be guilty of a petty theft not worthy of death, I am bound to make restitution; if the crime be a capital one and he be taken handhaving, then he must 'die like a free man[3].' If my slave be guilty of homicide, my duty is to set him free and hand him over to the kindred of the slain, but apparently I may purchase his life by a sum of 40 shillings, a sum much less than the *wer* of the slain man[4]. We must not be too hard on the owners of delinquent slaves. There are cases, for example, in which, several slaves having committed a crime, one of them chosen by lot must suffer for the sins of all[5]. Our author is borrowing from the laws of several different centuries and does not arrive at any neat result; nor must we wonder at this, for the problems presented to jurisprudence by the crimes and delicts of slaves are very intricate. Then again, we have the rule that if free men and serfs join in a crime, the whole guilt is to be attributed to the free: he who joins with a slave in a theft has no companion[6]. On the whole, though the slave is likely to have as a matter of fact a *peculium* of his own, a *peculium* out of which he may be able to pay for his offences and even perhaps to purchase his liberty[7], the *servus* of our Leges seems to be in the main a rightless being. We look in vain for any trace of that idea of the relativity of servitude which becomes the core of Bracton's

---

[1] In Leg. Hen. 81 § 3 (a passage which seems to show that by his master's favour even the *servus* may sometimes sue for a wrong done to him) we have this sum :—*villanus : cothsetus : servus :: 30 : 15 : 6.*

[2] Ibid. 75 § 4: 'suum peccatum est et dampnum.' See also 70 § 10, an exceedingly obscure passage.

[3] Ibid. 59 § 23.

[4] Ibid. 70 § 5; but for this our author has to go back as far as Ine.

[5] Ibid. 59 § 25.

[6] Ibid. 59 § 24; 85 § 4 : 'solus furatur qui cum servo furatur.'

[7] Ibid. 78 § 3; 59 § 25.

doctrine¹. At the same time we observe that many, perhaps most, of the rules which mark the slavish condition of the serf are ancient rules and rules that are becoming obsolete. In the twelfth century the old system of *wer* and *bót* is already vanishing, though an antiquarian lawyer may yet try to revivify it. When it disappears altogether before the new law, which holds every grave crime to be a felony, and punishes almost every felony with death², many grand differences between the villein and the serf will have perished. The gallows is a great leveller.

If now we recur to the days of the Conquest, we cannot doubt that the law knew a definite class of slaves, and marked them off by many distinctions from the *villani* and *cotarii*, and even from the *coliberti*. Sums that seem high were being paid for men whose freedom was being purchased³. At Lewes the toll paid for the sale of an ox was a halfpenny; on the sale of a man it was fourpence⁴. In later documents we may sometimes see a distinction well drawn. Thus in the Black Book of Peterborough, compiled in 1127 or thereabouts, we may read how on one of his manors the abbot has eight herdsmen (*bovarii*), how each of them holds ten acres, has to do labour services and render loaves and poultry. And then we read that each of them must pay one penny for his head if he be a free man (*liber homo*), while he pays nothing if he be a *servus*⁵. This is a well-drawn distinction. Of two men whose economic position is precisely the same, the one may be free, the other a slave, and it is the free man, not the slave, who has to pay a head-penny. Now when the Conqueror's surveyors, or rather the jurors, call a man a *servus* they are, so it seems to us, thinking rather of his legal status than of his position in the economy of a manor. At any rate we ought to observe that the economic stratification of society may cut the legal stratification. We are accustomed perhaps to suppose that while the *villani* have lands that are in some sense their own, while they support themselves and their families by tilling those lands, the *servus* has no land that is in any sense his own, but is fed at his lord's board, is housed in his lord's court, and spends all his time in

Return to the *servus* of Domesday.

¹ Hist. Eng. Law, i. 398, 402.　　² Hist. Eng. Law, ii. 457.
³ See the Bath manumissions, Kemble, Saxons, i. 507 ff. Sometimes a pound or a half-pound is paid.
⁴ D. B. i. 26.　　⁵ Chron. Petrob. 163.

M.　　　3

the cultivation of his lord's demesne lands. Such may have
been the case in those parts of England where we hear of but
few *servi*; those few may have been inmates of the lord's house
and have had no plots of their own. But such can hardly have
been the case in the south-western counties; the *servi* are too
many to be menials. Indeed it would seem that these *servi*
sometimes had arable plots, and had oxen, which were to be
distinguished from the demesne oxen of their lords—not indeed
as a matter of law, but as a matter of economic usage[1]. It is
plain that the legal and the economic lines may intersect one
another; the menial who is fed by the lord and who must give
his whole time to the lord's work may be a free man; the slave
may have a cottage and oxen and a plot of arable land, and
labour for himself as well labouring for his lord. Hence a
perplexed and uncertain terminology:—the *servus* who has land
and oxen may be casually called a *villanus*[2], and we cannot be
sure that no one whom our record calls a *servus* has the wergild of a free man. Nor can we be sure that the enumeration
of the *servi* is always governed by one consistent principle. In
the shires of Gloucester, Hereford and Worcester we read of
numerous *ancillae*—in Worcestershire of 677 *servi* and 101
ancillae[3]—and this may make us think that in this district all
the able-bodied serfs are enumerated, whether or no they have
cottages to themselves[4]. We may strongly suspect that the
king's commissioners were not much interested in the line that
separated the *villani* from the *servi*, since the lord was as directly
answerable for the geld of any lands that were in the occupation of his villeins as he was for the geld of those plots that
were tilled for him by his slaves. That there should have been

---

[1] D. B. i. 105 b, Devon: ' Rolf tenet de B[alduino] Boslie...Terra est 8 carucis.
In dominio est 1 caruca et dimidia et 7 servi cum 1 caruca.' D. B. iv. 265:
' Balduinus habet 1 mansionem quae vocatur Bosleia...hanc possunt arare 8
carrucae et modo tenet eam Roffus de Balduino. Inde habet R. 1 ferdinum et
1 carrucam et dimidiam in dominio et villani tenent aliam terram et habent ibi
1 carrucam. Ibi habet R. 7 servos.' In the Exeter record these seven serfs seem
to get reckoned as being both *servi* and *villani*. So in the account of Rentis,
D. B. iv. 204–5, the lord is said to have one quarter of the arable in demesne
and two oxen, while the *villani* are said to have the rest of the arable and one
team; but the only *villani* are 8 *coliberti* and 4 *servi*.

[2] See last note.   [3] Ellis, Introduction, ii. 504–6.

[4] See, for example, the following Herefordshire entry, D. B. i. 180 b: ' In
dominio sunt 2 carucae et 4 villani et 8 bordarii et prepositus et bedellus. Inter
omnes habent 4 carucas. Ibi 8 inter servos et ancillas et vaccarius et daia.'

never a *theów* in all Yorkshire and Lincolnshire is hardly credible, and yet we hear of no *servi* in those counties.

This being so, we encounter some difficulty if we would put just the right interpretation on a remarkable fact that is visible in Essex. The description of that county tells us not only how many *villani*, *bordarii* and *servi* there are now, but also how many there were in King Edward's day, and thus shows what changes have taken place during the last twenty years. Now on manor after manor the number of villeins and bordiers, if of them we make one class, has increased, while the number of *servi* has fallen. We take 100 entries (four batches of 25 apiece) and see that the number of *villani* and *bordarii* has risen from 1486 to 1894, while the number of *servi* has fallen from 423 to 303. We make another experiment with a hundred entries. This gives the following result:—

	1066	1086
Villani	1273	1247
Bordarii	810	1241
Servi	384	312

This decrease in the number of *servi* seems to be pretty evenly distributed throughout the county[1]. We shall not readily ascribe the change to any mildheartedness of the lords. They are Frenchmen, and in all probability they have got the most they could out of a mass of peasantry made malleable and manageable by the Conquest. We may rather be entitled to infer that there has been a considerable change in rural economy. For the cultivation of his demesne land the lord begins to rely less and less on the labour of serfs whom he feeds, more and more upon the labour of tenants who have plots of their own and who feed themselves. From this again we may perhaps infer that the labour services of the *villani* and *bordarii* are being augmented. But at any rate it speaks ill of their fate, that under the sway of foreigners, who may fairly be suspected of some harshness and greed, their inferiors, the true

---

[1] Mr Round has drawn attention to the great increase of *bordarii*: Antiquary (1882) vi. 9. In the second of our two experiments the cases were taken from the royal demesne and the lands of the churches. The surveys of Norfolk and Suffolk profess to enumerate the various classes of peasants T. R. E.; but commonly each entry reports that there has been no change. Without saying that we disbelieve these reports, we nevertheless may say that a verdict which asserts that things have always (*semper*) been as they now are may easily be the outcome of nescience.

servi, are somewhat rapidly disappearing. However, it is by no means impossible that with a slavery so complete as that of the English *theów* the Normans were not very familiar in their own country[1].

§ 3. *The Villeins.*

The boors or coliberts. Next above the *servi* we see the small but interesting class of *buri, burs* or *coliberti*. Probably it was not mentioned in the writ which set the commissioners their task, and this may well be the reason why it appears as but a very small class. It has some 900 members; still it is represented in fourteen shires: Hampshire, Berkshire, Wiltshire, Dorset, Somerset, Devon, Cornwall, Buckingham, Oxford, Gloucester, Worcester, Hereford, Warwick, Shropshire—in short, in the shires of Wessex and western Mercia. Twice over our record explains—a piece of rare good fortune—that *buri* and *coliberti* are all one[2]. In general they are presented to us as being akin rather to the *servi* than to the *villani* or *bordarii*, as when we are told, 'In demesne there is one virgate of land and there are 3 teams and 11 *servi* and 5 *coliberti*, and there are 15 *villani* and 15 *bordarii* with 8 teams[3].' But this rule is by no means unbroken; sometimes the *coliberti* are separated from the *servi* and a precedence over the *cotarii* or even over the *bordarii* is given them. Thus of a Wiltshire manor it is written, 'In demesne there are 8 teams and 20 *servi* and 41 *villani* and 30 *bordarii* and 7 *coliberti* and 74 *cotarii* have among them all 27 teams[4].' Again of a Warwickshire manor, 'There is land for 26 teams; in demesne are 3 teams and 4 *servi* and 43 *villani* and 6 *coliberti* and 10 *bordarii* with 16 teams[5].' A classification which turns upon legal status is cut by a classification which turns upon economic condition. The *colibertus* we take to be an unfreer man (how there come to be degrees of freedom is a question to be asked by and by) than the *cotarius* or the *bordarius*, but on a given manor he may be a more important person, for he may have

---

[1] Hist. Eng. Law, i. 53–4.

[2] D. B. i. 38, Coseham: '8 burs i. coliberti.' Ib. 38 b Dene: 'et coliberti [vel bures *interlined*].'

[3] D. B. i. 65, Wintreburne. [4] D. B. i. 75, Bridetone et Bere.

[5] D. B. i. 239 b, Etone.

plough beasts while the *cotarius* has none, he may have two oxen while the *bordarius* has but an ox.

In calling him a *colibertus* the Norman clerks are giving him a foreign name, the etymological origin of which is very dark[1]; but this much seems plain, that in the France of the eleventh century a large class bearing this name had been formed out of ancient elements, Roman *coloni* and Germanic *liti*, a class which was not rightless (for it could be distinguished from the class of *servi*, and a *colibertus* might be made a *servus* by way of punishment for his crimes) but which yet was unfree, for the *colibertus* who left his lord might be pursued and recaptured[2]. As to the Englishman upon whom this name is bestowed we know him to be a *gebúr*, a boor, and we learn something of him from that mysterious document entitled 'Rectitudines Singularum Personarum[3].' His services, we are told, vary from place to place; in some districts he works for his lord two days a week and during harvest-time three days a week; he pays gafol in money, barley, sheep and poultry; also he has ploughing to do besides his week-work; he pays hearthpenny; he and one of his fellows must between them feed a dog. It is usual to provide him with an outfit of two oxen, one cow, six sheep, and seed for seven acres of his yardland, and also to provide him with household stuff; on his death all these chattels go back to his lord. Thus the boor is put before us as a tenant with a house and a yardland or virgate, and two plough oxen. He will therefore play a more important part in the manorial economy than the cottager who has no beasts. But he is a very dependent person; his beasts, even the poor furniture of his house, his pots and crocks, are provided for him by his lord. Probably it is this that marks him off from the ordinary *villanus* or 'townsman,' and brings him near the serf. In a sense he may be a free man. We have seen how the law, whether we look for it to the code of Cnut or to the Leges Henrici, is holding fast the proposition that every one who

The Continental colibert.

The English boor.

---

[1] Guérard, Cartulaire de L'Abbaye de S. Père de Chartres, vol. i. p. xlii.

[2] The position of the *coliberti* is discussed by Guérard, *loc. cit.*, and by Lamprecht, Geschichte des Französischen Wirthschaftslebens (in Schmoller's Forschungen, Bd i.), p. 81. Guérard says, 'Les coliberts peuvent se placer à peu près indifféremment ou au dernier des hommes libres, ou à la tête des hommes engagés dans les liens de la servitude.'

[3] Schmid, App. iii. c. 4.

is not a *theówman* is a free man, that every one is either a
liber homo or a *servus*. We have no warrant for denying to
the boor the full wergild of 200 shillings. He pays the hearth-
penny, or Peter's penny, and the document that tells us this
elsewhere mentions this payment as the mark of a free man[1].
And yet in a very true and accurate sense he may be unfree,
unfree to quit his lord's service. All that he has belongs to his
lord; he must be perpetually in debt to his lord; he could
hardly leave his lord without being guilty of something very
like theft, an abstraction of chattels committed to his charge.
Very probably if he flies, his lord has a right to recapture him.
On the other hand, so dependent a man will be in a very strict
sense a tenant at will. When he dies not only his tenement
but his stock will belong to the lord; like the French *colibert*
he is *mainmortable*. At the same time, to one familiar with the
cartularies of the thirteenth century the rents and services
that this boor has to pay and perform for his virgate will not
appear enormous. If we mistake not, many a *villanus* of
Henry III.'s day would have thought them light. Of course
any such comparison is beset by difficulties, for at present
we know all too little of the history of wages and prices.
Nevertheless the intermediation of this class of *buri* or *coliberti*
between the serfs and the villeins of Domesday Book must
tend to raise our estimate both of the legal freedom and of the
economic welfare of that great mass of peasants which is now to
come before us[2].

Villani,
bordarii,
cotarii.

That great mass consists of some 108,500 *villani*, some
82,600 *bordarii*, and some 6,800 *cotarii* and *coscets*[3]. Though
in manor after manor we may find representatives of each of
these three classes, we can see that for some important purpose
they form but one grand class, and that the term *villanus* may
be used to cover the whole genus as well as to designate one of

[1] Rectitudines, c. 3.

[2] Occasionally the *coliberti* of D. B. are put before us as paying rents in
money or in kind. Thus D. B. i. 38, Hants: ' In Coseham sunt 4 hidae quae
pertinent huic manerio ubi T. R. E. erant 8 burs i. coliberti cum 4 carucis
reddentes 50 sol. 8 den. minus.' D. B. i. 179 b, Heref.: 'Villani dant de
consuetudine 13 sol. et 4 den. et [sex] coliberti reddunt 3 sextarios frumenti et
ordei et 2 oves et dimidiam cum agnis et 2 den. et unum obolum.' D. B. i. 165:
'et in Glouucestre 1 burgensis reddens 5 den. et 2 coliberti reddentes 34 den.' In
a charter coming from Bishop Denewulf (K. 1079) we read of three wite-theów-
men who were boor-born and three who were theów-born.

[3] Ellis, Introduction, ii. 511–14.

its three species. In the Exon Domesday a common formula, having stated the number of hides in the manor and the number of teams for which it can find work, proceeds to divide the land and the existing teams between the demesne and the *villani*— the *villani*, it will say, have so many hides and so many teams. Then it will state how many *villani, bordarii, cotarii* there are. But it will sometimes fall out that there are no *villani* if that term is to be used in its specific sense, and so, after having been told that the *villani* have so much land and so many teams, we learn that the only *villani* on this manor are *bordarii*[1]. The lines which divide the three species are, we may be sure, much rather economic than legal lines. Of course the law may recognise them upon occasion[2], but we can not say that the *bordarius* has a different status from that of the *villanus*. In the Leges both fall under the term *villani*; indeed, as hereafter will be seen, that term has sometimes to cover all men who are not *servi* but are not noble. Nor must we suppose that the economic lines are drawn with much precision or according to any one uniform pattern. Of *villani* and *bordarii* we may read in every county; *cotarii* or *coscets* in considerable numbers are found only in Kent, Sussex, Surrey, Middlesex, Wiltshire, Dorset, Somerset, Berkshire, Hertford and Cambridge, though they are not absolutely unknown in Buckingham, in Devon, in Hereford, Worcester, Shropshire, Yorkshire. We can not tell how the English jurors would have expressed the distinction between *bordarii* and *cotarii*, for while the *cot* is English, the *borde* is French. If we are entitled to draw any inference from the distribution of the cottiers, it would be that the smallest of small tenements were to be found chiefly along the southern shore; but then there are no *cotarii* in Hampshire, plenty in Sussex, Surrey, Wiltshire and Dorset. Again, in the two shires last mentioned some distinction seems to be taken between the *coscets* and the *cotarii*, the former being superior to the latter[3]. Two centuries later we find a similar distinction among the tenants of Worcester Priory. There are *cotmanni* whose rents

[1] For examples see D. B. iv. 211 and the following pages.

[2] Leg. Hen. 81, § 3: 'Quidam villani qui sunt eiusmodi leierwitam et blodwitam et huiusmodi minora forisfacta emerunt a dominis suis, vel quomodo meruerunt de suis et in suos, quorum fletgefoth vel overseunessa est 30 den.; cothseti 15 den.; servi 6 den.'

[3] D. B. i. 71, Haseberie: '5 villani et 13 coscez et 2 cotarii.' Ibid. 80 b: Chinestanestone: '18 villani et 14 coscez et 4 cotarii.'

and services are heavier, and whose tenements are presumably larger than those of the *cotarii*, though the difference is not very great[1].

Size of the villain's tenement.

The vagueness of distinctions such as these is well illustrated by the failure of the term *bordarius* (and none is more prominent in Domesday Book) to take firm root in this country[2]. The successors of the *bordarii* seem to become in the later documents either *villani* with small or cottiers with large tenements. Distinctions which turn on the amount of land that is possessed or the amount of service that is done cannot be accurately formulated and forced upon a whole country. Perhaps in general we may endow the *villanus* of Domesday Book with a virgate or quarter of a hide, while we ascribe to the *bordarius* a less quantity and doubt whether the *cotarius* usually had arable land. But the survey of Middlesex, which is the main authority touching this matter, shows that the *villanus* may on occasion have a whole hide[3], that is four virgates, and that often he has but half a virgate; it shows us that the *bordarius*, though often he has but four or five acres, may have a half virgate, that is as much as many a *villanus*[4]; it shows us that the *cotarius* may have five acres, that is as much as many a *bordarius*[5], though he will often have no more than a croft[6]. In Essex we hear of *bordarii* who held no arable land[7]. Nor dare we lay down any stern rule about the possession of plough beasts. It would seem as if sometimes the *bordarius* had oxen, while sometimes he had none[8]. The *villanus* might have two

[1] Worcester Register, 59 b (Sedgebarrow): four *cotmanni*, each of whom pays 20*d.* or works one day a week and two in autumn; two *cottarii*, each of whom pays 12*d.* or works one day a week. Ibid. 69 b (Shipston): two *cotmanni*, each of whom pays 3*s.* or works like a virgater; two *cottarii*, each of whom pays 13*d.* Ibid. 76 a (Cropthorn): two *cotmanni*, each of whom pays 2*s.* or works like a *cottarius*; two *cottarii*, each of whom pays 18*d.* or works one day a week.

[2] Vinogradoff, Villainage, 149, gives a few instances of its occurrence; but it seems to be very rare.

[3] D. B. i. 127 b, Fuleham: 'Ibi 5 villani quisque 1 hidam.' There are a good many other instances.

[4] D. B. i. 130, Hamntone: 'et 4 bordarii quisque de dimidia virga.'

[5] D. B. i. 127, Herges: 'et 2 cotarii de 13 acris.'

[6] D. B. i. 127 b, Fuleham: 'et 22 cotarii de dimidia hida et 8 cotarii de suis hortis.'

[7] D. B. ii. 75 b: 'et 5 bordarii super aquam qui non tenent terram.'

[8] D. B. i. 163 b, Turneberie: 'et 42 villani et 18 radchenistre cum 21 carucis et 23 bordarii et 15 servi et 4 coliberti.' Ibid. 164, Hechanestede: 'et 5 villani et 8 bordarii cum 6 carucis; ibi 6 servi.'

oxen, but he might have more or less. We may find that in Cornwall a single team of eight is forthcoming where there are[1]

3	villani,	4	bordarii,	2	servi
2	„	2	„	3	„
0	„	5	„	2	„
1	„	5	„	1	„
2	„	5	„	4	„
2	„	3	„	1	„
3	„	6	„	3	„

In some Gloucestershire manors every villein seems to have a full plough team[2]. Merely economic grades are essentially indefinite. Who could have defined a ' cottage' in the eleventh century? Who can define one now[3]?

In truth the vast class of men that we are examining must have been heterogeneous to a high degree. Not only were some members of it much wealthier than others, but in all probability some were economically subject to others. So it was in later days. In the thirteenth century we may easily find a manor in which the lord is paying hardly any wages. He gets nearly all his agricultural work done for him by his villeins and his cottiers. Out of his cottiers however he will get but one day's work in the week. If then we ask what the cottiers are doing during the rest of their time, the answer surely must be that they are often working as hired labourers on the villein's virgates, for a cottier can not have spent five days in the week over the tillage of his poor little tenement. It is a remarkable feature of the manorial arrangement that the meanest of the lord's *nativi* are but rarely working for him. Thus if we were to remove the lord in order that the village community might be revealed, we should still see not only rich and poor, but employers and employed, villagers and ' undersettles.'

Villeins and cottiers.

Now all these people are in a sense unfree, while yet in some other sense they are free. Let us then spend a short while in

Freedom and unfreedom of villani.

[1] D. B. iv. 215–223 ; on p. 223 there are two *villani* with one ox.

[2] D. B. i. 164, Tedeneham : ' Ibi erant 38 villani habentes 38 carucas.' Ibid. 164 b, Nortune, '15 villani cum 15 carucis ; Stanwelle, 5 villani cum 5 carucis.'

[3] Malden, Domesday Survey of Surrey (Domesday Studies, ii.) 469, says that in Surrey ' *bordarii* and *cotarii* only occur once together upon the same manor, and very seldom in the same hundred....There are three hundreds, Godalming, Wallington and Elmbridge, where the *cotarii* are nearly universal to the exclusion of *bordarii*. In the others the *bordarii* are nearly or quite universal, to the exclusion of the *cotarii*.'

discussing the various meanings that freedom may have in a legal classification of the sorts and conditions of men. When we have put out of account the rightless slave, who is a thing, it still remains possible to say that some men are unfree, while others are free, and even that freedom is a matter of degree. But we may use various standards for the measurement of liberty.

Meaning of freedom.

Perhaps in the first place we shall think of what German writers call *Freizügigkeit*, the power to leave the master whom one has been serving. This power our ancestors would perhaps have called ' fare-worthiness[1].' If the master has the right to recapture the servant who leaves his service, or even if he has the right to call upon the officers of the state to pursue him and bring him back to his work, then we may account this servant an unfree man, albeit the relation between him and his master has been created by free contract. Such unfreedom is very distinct from rightlessness. As a freak of jurisprudence we might imagine a modern nobleman entitled to reduce by force and arms his fugitive butler to well-paid and easy duties, while all the same that butler had rights against all the world including his master, had access to all courts, and could even sue for his wages if they were not punctually paid. If we call him unfree, then freedom will look like a matter of degree, for the master's power to get back his fugitive may be defined by law in divers manners. May he go in pursuit and use force ? Must he send a constable or sheriff's officer ? Must he first go to court and obtain a judgment, ' a decree for specific performance' of the contract of service ? The right of recapture seems to shade off gradually into a right to insist that a breach of the contract of service is a criminal offence to be punished by fine or imprisonment.

Then, again, there may seem to us to be more of unfreedom in the case of one who was born a servant than in the case of one who has contracted to serve, though we should note that one may be born to serve without being born rightless.

More to the point than these obvious reflections will be the remark that in the thirteenth century we learn to think of various spheres or planes of justice. A right good in one

---

[1] Thorpe, Diplomatarium, 623. King Eadwig declares that a certain church-ward of Exeter is ' free and fare-worthy.'

sphere may have no existence in another. The rights of the
villeins in their tenements are sanctioned by manorial justice;
they are ignored by the king's courts. Here, again, the ideas of
freedom and unfreedom find a part to play. True that in the
order of legal logic freedom may precede royal protection; a
tenure is protected because it is free; still men are soon arguing
that it is free because it is protected, and this probably discloses
an idea which lies deep[1]:—the king's courts, the national courts,
are open to the free; we approach the rightlessness of the slave
if our rights are recognized only in a court of which our lord is
the president.

The thirteenth century will also supply us with the notion
that continuous agricultural service, service in which there is a
considerable element of uncertainty, is unfree service. Where
from day to day the lord's will counts for much in determining
the work that his tenants must do, such tenants, even if they
be free men, are not holding freely. But uncertainty is a
matter of degree, and therefore unfreedom may easily be regarded as a matter of degree[2].

Then, again, in the law books of the Norman age we see
distinct traces of a usage which would make *liber* or *liberalis* an
equivalent for our *noble*, or at least for our *gentle*. The common
man with the wergild of 200 shillings, though indubitably he
is no *servus*, is not *liberalis homo*[3].

Lastly, in our thirteenth century we learn that privileges
and exceptional immunities are 'liberties' and 'franchises.'
What is our definition of a liberty, a franchise? A portion of
royal power in the hands of a subject. In Henry III.'s day we
do not say that the Earl of Chester is a freer man, more of a
liber homo, than is the Earl of Gloucester, but we do say that
he has more, greater, higher liberties.

Therefore we shall not be surprised if in Domesday Book
what we read of freedom, of free men, of free land is sadly
obscure. Let us then observe that the *villanus* both is and is
not a free man.

According to the usual terminology of the Leges, everyone
who is above the rank of a *servus*, but below the rank of a
thegn, is a *villanus*. The *villanus* is the non-noble *liber homo*.

The villein
as free.

---

[1] Hist. Eng. Law, i. 341 ff.
[2] Hist. Eng. Law, i. 354–8.
[3] Liebermann, Instituta Cnuti, Transact. Roy. Hist. Soc. vii. 93.

All those numerous sokemen of the eastern counties whom Domesday ranks above the *villani*, all those numerous *liberi homines* whom it ranks above the sokemen, are, according to this scheme, *villani* if they be not thegns. And this scheme is still of great importance, for it is the scheme of *bót* and *wer*. By what have been the most vital of all the rules of law, all these men have been massed together; each of them has a *wer* of two hundred shillings[1]. This, we may remark in passing, is no trivial sum, though the shillings are the small Saxon shillings of four pence or five pence. There seems to be a good deal of evidence that for a long time past the ox had been valued at 30 pence, the sheep at 5 pence[2]. At this rate the ceorl's death must be paid for by the price of some twenty-four or thirty oxen. The sons of a *villanus* who had but two oxen must have been under some temptation to wish that their father would get himself killed by a solvent thegn. Very rarely

---

[1] Leg. Will. Conq. i. 8: 'La were del thein 20 lib. in Merchenelahe, 25 lib. in Westsexenelahe. La were del vilain 100 sol. en Merchenelahe e ensement en Westsexene.' Leg. Henr. 70, § 1: 'In Westsexa quae caput regni est et legum, twyhindi, i.e. villani, wera est 4 lib.; twelfhindi, i.e. thaini, 25 lib.' Ibid. 76, § 2: 'Omnis autem wera liberorum est aut servorum...liberi alii twyhindi, alii syxhindi, alii twelfhindi'; § 6, twihindus = cyrliscus = villanus. As to the 100 shillings in the first of these passages, see Schmid, p. 676. There is some other evidence that the equation, 1 Norman shilling = 2 English shillings, was occasionally treated as correct enough. As to the six-hynde man, see Schmid, p. 653; we may doubt whether he existed in the eleventh century, but according to the Instituta Cnuti the *radchenistres* of the west may have been six-hynde. We must not draw from Alfred's treaty with the Danes (Schmid, p. 107) the inference that the normal ceorl was seated on *gafol-land*. This international instrument is settling an exceptionally high tariff for the maintenance of the peace. Every man, whatever his rank, is to enjoy the handsome wergild of 8 half-marks of pure gold, except the Danish lysing and the English ceorl who is seated on gafol-land; these are to have but the common wer of 200 shillings. The parallel passage in Æthelred's treaty (Schmid, p. 207) sets £30 on every free man if he is killed by a man of the other race. See Schmid, p. 676.

[2] Ine, 55: a sheep with a lamb until a fortnight after Easter is worth 1 shilling. Æthelstan, vi. 6: a horse 120 pence, an ox 30 pence, a cow 20, a sheep 1 shilling (5 pence). Ibid. 8, § 5: an ox 30 pence. Schmid, App. i. c. 7: a horse 30 shillings, a mare 20 shillings, an ox 30 pence, a cow 24 pence, a swine 8 pence, a sheep 1 shilling, a goat 2 pence, a man (i.e. a slave) 1 pound. Schmid, App. iii. c. 9: a sheep or 3 pence. D. B. i. 117 b: an ox or 30 pence. D. B. i. 26: Tolls at Lewes; for a man 4 pence, an ox a halfpenny. This preserves the equation that we have already seen, namely, 1 slave = 8 oxen. Thus the full team is worth one pound. On the twelfth century Pipe Rolls the ox often costs 3 shillings (= 36 pence) or even more.

indeed do the Leges notice the sokeman or mention *liberi homines* so as to exclude the *villani* from the scope of that term[1]. Domesday Book also on occasion can divide mankind into slaves and free men. It does so when it tells us that on a Gloucestershire manor there were twelve *servi* whom the lord had made free[2]. It does so again when it tells us that in the city of Chester the bishop had eight shillings if a free man, four shillings if a serf, did work upon a festival[3]. So in a description of the manor of South Perrott in Somerset we read that a certain custom is due to it from the manor of 'Cruche' (Crewkerne), namely, that every free man must render one bloom of iron. We look for these free men at 'Cruche' and see no one on the manor but *villani, bordarii, coliberti* and *servi*[4]. Of the Count of Mortain's manor of Bickenhall it is written that every free man renders a bloom of iron at the king's manor of Curry; but at Bickenhall there is no one above the condition of a *villanus*[5]. Other passages will suggest that the *villanus* sometimes is and sometimes is not *liber homo*. On a Norfolk manor we find free villeins, *liberi villani*[6].

For all this, however, there must be some very important sense in which the *villanus* is not free. In the survey of the eastern counties he is separated from the *liberi homines* by the whole class of *sochemanni*. 'In this manor,' we are told, 'there was at that time a free man with half a hide who has now been made one of the villeins[7].' At times the word

The villein as unfree.

[1] In Leg. Will. Conq. i. 16, we hear of the *forisfacturae* (probably the 'insult fines') due to archbishops, bishops, counts, barons and sokemen; the baron has 10 shillings, the sokeman 40 pence. In the same document, c. 20, § 2, we read of the reliefs of counts, barons, vavassors and villeins. Leg. Edw. Conf. 12, § 4, speaks of the *manbót* due in the Danelaw; on the death of a *villanus* or a *socheman* 12 ores are paid, on the death of a *liber homo* 3 marks.

[2] D. B. i. 167 b, Heile: 'ibi erant 12 servi quos Willelmus liberos fecit.'

[3] D. B. i. 263: 'Si quis liber homo facit opera in die feriato inde episcopus habet 8 solidos. De servo autem vel ancilla feriatum diem infringente, habet episcopus 4 solidos.' Compare Cnut, ii. 45.

[4] D. B. i. 86: 'Huic manerio reddebatur T. R. E. de Cruche per annum consuetudo, hoc est 6 oves cum agnis totidem, et quisque liber homo i. blomam ferri.' South Perrott had belonged to the Confessor, Crewkerne to Edith, probably 'the rich and fair.' For the description of Cruche see D. B. i. 86 b. As to the 'bloom' of iron see Ellis, Introduction, i. 136.

[5] D. B. i. 92. See also p. 87 b, the account of Seveberge.

[6] D. B. ii. 145.

[7] D. B. ii. 1: 'In hoc manerio erat tunc temporis quidam liber homo de dimidia hida qui modo effectus est unus de villanis.'

francus is introduced so as to suggest for a moment that, though the villein may be *liber homo,* he is not *francus*[1]. But this suggestion, even if it be made, is not maintained, and there are hundreds of passages which implicitly deny that the villein is *liber homo.* But then these passages draw the line between freedom and unfreedom at a point high in the legal scale, a point far above the heads of the *villani.* At least for the main purposes of Domesday Book the free man is a man who holds land freely. Let us observe what is said of the men who have been holding manors. The formula will vary somewhat from county to county, but we shall often find four phrases used as equivalent, ' *X* tenuit et liber homo fuit,' ' *X* tenuit ut liber homo,' ' *X* tenuit et cum terra sua liber fuit,' ' *X* tenuit libere[2].' But this freeholding implies a high degree of freedom, freedom of a kind that would have shocked the lawyers of a later age.

Anglo-Saxon 'free-holding.'

With some regrets we must leave the peasants for a while in order that we may glance at the higher strata of society. We may take it as certain that, at least in the eyes of William's ministers, the ordinary holder of a manor in the time of the Confessor had been holding it under (*sub*) some lord, if not of (*de*) some lord. But then the closeness of the connexion between him and his lord, the character of the relation between lord, man and land, had varied much from case to case. Now these matters are often expressed in terms of a calculus of personal freedom. But let us begin with some phrases which seem intelligible enough. The man can, or he can not, ' sell or give his land '; he can, or he can not, ' sell or give it without the licence of his lord '; he can sell it if he has first offered it to his lord[4]; he can sell it on paying his lord two shillings[2]. This seems very simple :—the lord can, or (as the

[1] Thus D. B. i. 127, Mid.: ' inter francos et villanos 45 carucae'; Ibid. 70, Wilts: ' 4 villani et 3 bordarii et unus francus cum 2 carucis'; Ibid. 241, Warw.: 'Ibi sunt 3 francones homines cum 4 villanis et 3 bordariis.' Sometimes *francus* may be an equivalent for *francigena*; e.g. i. 254 b, where in one entry we have *unus francigena* and in the next *unus francus homo.* But an Englishman may be *francus*; ii. 54 b ' accepit 15 acras de uno franco teigno et misit cum terra sua.' However, it is not an insignificant fact that the very name of Frenchman (*francigena*) must have suggested free birth.

[2] For examples see the surveys of Warwick, Stafford and Shropshire.

[3] D. B. ii. 260: ' et 7 homines qui possent vendere terram suam si eam prius obtulissent domino suo.'

[4] D. B. ii. 278 b: ' si vellent recedere daret quisque 2 solidos.' Ibid. 207: ' et possent recedere si darent 2 solidos.'

case may be) can not, prevent his tenant from alienating the land; he has a right of preemption or he has a right to exact a fine when there is a change of tenants. But then come phrases that are less in harmony with our idea of feudal tenure. The man can not sell his land 'away from' his lord[1], he can not give or sell it 'outside' a certain manor belonging to his lord[2], or, being the tenant of some church, he can not 'separate' his land from the church[3], or give or sell it outside the church[4].

We have perhaps taken for granted under the influence of later law that an alienation will not impair the lord's rights, and will but give him a new instead of an old tenant. But it is not of any mere substitution such as this that these men of the eleventh century are thinking. They have it in their minds that the man may wish, may be able, utterly to withdraw his land from the sphere of his lord's rights. Therefore in many cases they note with some care that the man, though he can give or sell his land, can not altogether put an end to such relation as has existed between this land and his lord. He can sell, but some of the lord's rights will 'remain,' in particular the lord's 'soke' over the land (for the present let us say his jurisdiction over the land) will remain[5]. The purchaser will not of necessity become the 'man' of this lord, will not of necessity owe him any *servitium* or *consuetudo*, but will come under his jurisdiction[6]. Interchanging however with these phrases[7], we have others which seem to point to the same set

[1] D. B. ii. 435: 'Et super Vlnoht habuit commendationem antecessor R. Malet, teste hundredo, et non potuit vendere nec dare *de eo* terram suam.' Ibid. 397: 'viderunt eum iurare quod non poterat dare [vel] vendere terram suam *ab* antecessore Ricardi.'

[2] D. B. i. 145: 'Hoc manerium tenuit Aluuinus homo Estan, non potuit dare nec vendere extra Brichelle manerium Estani.'

[3] D. B. i. 133: 'Hanc terram tenuit Aluric Blac 2 hidas de Abbate Westmonasterii T. R. E.: non poterat separare ab aecclesia.'

[4] D. B. ii. 216 b: 'Ita est in monasterio quod nec vendere nec forisfacere potest extra ecclesia.'

[5] For example, D. B. i. 201: 'terram suam vendere potuerunt, soca vero remansit Abbati.' D. B. ii. 78: 'et poterant vendere terram set soca et saca remanebat antecessori Alberici.' Ibid. ii. 92 b: 'unus sochemannus fuit in hac terra de 15 acris quas poterat vendere, set soca iacebat in Warleia terra S. Pauli.'

[6] But the *consuetudo*, rent or the like, may 'remain': D. B. ii. 181 b: 'et possent vendere terram suam set consuetudo remanebat in manerio.' And so the *commendatio* may 'remain'; ii. 357 b: 'Hi poterant dare et vendere terram, set saca et soca et commendatio remanebant Sancto [Eadmundo].'

[7] For example, D. B. i. 201: 'Homines Abbatis de Ely fuerunt et 4 terram

of distinctions, but to express them in terms of personal freedom. The man can, or else he can not, withdraw from his lord,
go away from his lord, withdraw from his lord's manor; he can
or he can not withdraw with his land; he can or can not go to
another lord, or go wherever he pleases[1]. Some of these
phrases will, if taken literally, seem to say that the persons of
whom they are used are tied to the soil; they can not leave
the land, or the manor, or the soke. Probably in some of
these cases the bond between man and lord is a perpetual bond
of homage and fealty, and if the man breaks that bond by
refusing the due obedience or putting himself under another
lord, he is guilty of a wrong[2]. But of pursuing him and
capturing him and reducing him to servitude there can be
no talk. Many of these persons who 'can not recede' are men
of wealth and rank, of high rank that is recognized by law,
they are king's thegns or the thegns of the churches, they are
'twelve-hundred men[3].' However, it is not the man's power to
leave his lord so much as the power to leave his lord and take
his land with him, that these phrases bring to our notice;
or rather the assumption is made that no one will want to
leave his lord if he must also leave his land behind him. And
then this power of taking land from this lord and bringing it
under another lord is conceived as an index of personal freedom.
Thus we read: 'These men were so free that they could go

suam *vendere potuerunt*, soca vero remansit Abbati, et quartus 1 virgam et dimidiam habuit et *recedere non potuit.*' See the important evidence produced by
Round, Feudal England, 24, as to the equivalence of these phrases.

[1] One of the commonest terms is *recedere*—'potuit recedere'—'non potuit
recedere'; i. 41, 'non potuit cum terra *recedere ad alium dominum*'; i. 56 b, '10
liberi homines T. R. E. tenebant 12 hidas et dimidiam de terra eiusdem manerii
sed *inde recedere* non poterant'; ii. 19 b, 'non poterant *recedere a terra* sine
licentia Abbatis'; ii. 57 b, 'non poterant recedere *ab illo manerio*'; ii. 66, 'non
poterant *removere* ab illo manerio'; ii. 41, 'non poterant *recedere a soca* Wisgari';
ii. 41 b, 'nec poterant *abire* sine iussu domini'; i. 66 b, 'qui tenuit T. R. E. non
poterat ab aecclesia diverti [separari]'; ii. 116, 'unus [burgensis] erat ita dominicus ut non posset *recedere nec homagium facere* sine licentia [Stigandi]'; ii. 119,
'de istis hominibus erant 36 ita dominice Regis Edwardi ut non possent *esse
homines cuiuslibet* sed semper tamen consuetudo regis remanebat preter herigete.'
A remarkable form is, ii. 57 b, 'non potuit istam terram mittere in aliquo loco
nisi in abbatia.' Then 'potuit ire quo voluit,' 'non potuit ire quolibet' are
common enough.

[2] Ine, c. 39: He who leaves his lord without permission pays sixty shillings
to his lord.

[3] For example, D. B. i. 41: 'Tres taini tenuerunt de episcopo et non potuerunt
ire quolibet.'

where they pleased[1],' and again, ' Four sokemen held this land, of whom three were free, while the fourth held one hide but could not give or sell it[2].' Not that no one is called a *liber homo* unless he has this power of ' receding' from his lord ; far from it ; all is a matter of degree ; but the free man is freer if he can 'go to what lord he pleases,' and often enough the phrases '*X* tenuit et liber homo fuit,' '*X* tenuit libere,' '*X* tenuit ut liber homo' seem to have no other meaning than this, that the occupant of the land enjoyed the liberty of taking it with him whithersoever he would. Therefore there is no tautology in saying that the holder of the land was a thegn and a free man, though of course there is a sense, there are many senses, in which every thegn is free[3]. All this talk of the freedom that consists in choosing a lord and subjecting land to him may well puzzle us, for it puzzled the men of the twelfth century. The chronicler of Abingdon abbey had to explain that in the old days a free man could do strange things[4].

Comparisons may be instituted between the freedom of one free man and that of another :—'Five thegns held this land of Earl Edwin and could go with their land whither they would, and below them they had four soldiers, who were as free as themselves[5].' A high degree of liberty is marked when we are told that, ' The said men were so free that they could sell their land with soke and sake wherever they would[6].' But there are yet higher degrees of liberty. Of Worcestershire it is written, ' When the king goes upon a military expedition, if anyone who is summoned stays at home, then if he is so free a man that he has his sake and soke and can go whither he pleases with his land, he with all his land shall be in the king's mercy[7].' The

The scale of free-holding.

---

[1] D. B. i. 35 b, Tornecrosta.   [2] D. B. i. 212 b, Stanford.

[3] D. B. i. 249 b: ' Tres taini tenuerunt et liberi homines fuerunt'; 256, ' Ipsi taini liberi erant' ; 259 b, ' Quatuor taini tenuerunt ante eum et liberi fuerunt.'

[4] Chron. Abingd. i. 490: 'Nam quidam dives, Turkillus nomine, sub Haroldi comitis testimonio et consultu, de se cum sua terra quae Kingestun dicitur, ecclesiae Abbendonensi et abbati Ordrico homagium fecit; licitum quippe libero cuique, illo in tempore, sic agere erat.'

[5] D. B. i. 180 b : ' et poterant ire cum terra quo volebant, et habebant sub se 4 milites, ita liberos ut ipsi erant.'

[6] D. B. ii. 59.

[7] D. B. i. 172: ' si ita liber homo est ut habeat socam suam et sacam et cum terra sua possit ire quo voluerit.'

M.   4

free man is the freer if he has soke and sake, if he has jurisdiction over other men. Exceptional privileges, immunities
from common burdens, are already regarded as 'liberties.' This
is no new thing; often enough when the Anglo-Saxon land
books speak of freedom they mean privilege.

Free land   The idea of freedom is equally vague and elastic if, instead
of applying it to men, we apply it to land or the tenure of land.
Two *bordarii* are now holding a small plot; 'they themselves
held it freely in King Edward's day[1].' Here no doubt there
has been a fall; but how deep a fall we can not be sure. To
say that a man's land is free may imply far more freedom than
freehold tenure implies in later times; it may imply that the
bond between him and his lord, if indeed he has a lord, is of a
purely personal character and hardly gives the lord any hold
over the land[2]. But this is not all. Perfect freedom is not
attained so long as the land owes any single duty to the state.
Often enough—but exactly how often it were no easy task to tell
—the *libera terra* of our record is land that has been exempted
even from the danegeld; it is highly privileged land[3]. Let
us remember that at the present day, though the definition of
free land or freehold land has long ago been fixed, we still speak
as though free land might become freer if it were 'free of land-
tax and tithe rent-charge.'

The unfree-   If now we return to the *villanus* and deny that he is *liber*
dom of the *homo* and deny also that he is holding freely, we shall be saying
villein.   little and using the laxest of terms. There are half-a-dozen
questions that we would fain ask about him, and there will be
no harm in asking them, though Domesday Book is taciturn.

Can the   Is he free to quit his lord and his land, or can he be pursued
villein be
pursued?

---

[1] D. B. i. 84 b.

[2] D. B. ii. 213: 'Hanc terram calumpniatur esse liberam Vlchitel homo
Hermeri, quocunque modo iudicetur, vel bello vel iudicio, et alius est praesto
probare eo modo quod iacuit ad ecclesiam [S. Adeldredae] die quo rex Edwardus
obiit. Set totus hundretus testatur eam fuisse T. R. E. ad S. Adeldredam.'

[3] See in particular the survey of Gloucestershire; D. B. i. 165 b: 'Hoc
manerium quietum est a geldo et ab omni forensi servitio praeter aecclesiae';
Ibid. 'Haec terra libera fuit et quieta ab omni geldo et regali servitio'; 170,
'Una hida et dimidia libera a geldo.' When after reading these passages we
come upon the following (167 b), 'Isdem W. tenet Tatinton: Ulgar tenuit de
rege Edwardo: haec terra libera est,' and when we observe that the land is not
hidated, we shall probably infer that 'This land is free' means 'This land is
exempt from geld, and (perhaps) from all other royal service.'

and captured ? No one word can be obtained in answer to this question. We can only say that in Henry II.'s day the ordinary peasant was regarded by the royal officials as *ascriptitius*; the land that he occupied was said to be part of his lord's demesne; his chattels were his lord's[1]. But then this was conceived to be, at least in some degree, the result of the Norman Conquest and subsequent rebellions of the peasantry[2]. To this we may add that in one of our sets of Leges, the French Leis of William the Conqueror, there are certain clauses which would be of great importance could we suppose that they had an authoritative origin, and which in any case are remarkable enough. The *nativus* who flies from the land on which he is born, let none retain him or his chattels; if the lords will not send back these men to their land the king's officers are to do it[3]. On the other hand, the tillers of the soil are not to be worked beyond their proper rent; their lord may not remove them from their land so long as they perform their right services[4]. Whether or no we suppose that in the writer's opinion the ordinary peasant was a *nativus* (of *nativi* Domesday Book has nothing to say) we still have law more favourable to the peasant than was the common law of Bracton's age :—a tiller who does his accustomed service is not to be ejected; he is no tenant at will.

Hereafter we shall show that the English peasants did suffer by the substitution of French for English lords. But the question that we have asked, so urgent, so fundamental, as it may seem to us, is really one which, as the history of the Roman *coloni* might prove, can long remain unanswered. Men may become economically so dependent on their lords, on wealthy masters and creditors, that the legal question whether they can quit their service has no interest. Who wishes to leave his all and go forth a beggar into the world ? On the whole we can find no evidence whatever that the men of the Confessor's day who were retrospectively called *villani* were tied to the soil. Certainly in Norman times the tradition was held that

Rarity of flight.

---

[1] Dialogus, i. c. 11; ii. c. 14.   [2] Dialogus, i. c. 10.

[3] Will. Conq. I. 30, 31 : 'Si les **seignurages** ne facent altri gainurs venir a lour terre, la justise le facet.' The Latin version is ridiculous : 'Si domini terrarum non procurent *idoneos* cultores ad terras suas colendas, iustitiarii hoc faciant.' The translator seems to have been puzzled by the word *altri* or *autrui*.

[4] Ibid. 29.

according to the old law the *villanus* might acquire five hides of land and so 'thrive to thegn-right[1].'

The villein and seignorial justice. Our next question should be whether he was subject to seignorial justice. · This is part of a much wider question that we must face hereafter, for seignorial justice should be treated as a whole. We must here anticipate a conclusion, the proof of which will come by and by, namely, that the *villanus* sometimes was and sometimes was not the justiciable of a court in which his lord or his lord's steward presided. All depended on the answer to the question whether his lord had 'sake and soke.' His lord might have justiciary rights over all his tenants, or merely over his *villani*, or he might have no justiciary rights, for as yet 'sake and soke' were in the king's gift, and the mere fact that a lord had 'men' or tenants did not give him a jurisdiction over them.

The villein and national justice. With this question is connected another, namely, whether the *villani* had a *locus standi* in the national courts. We have seen six *villani* together with the priest (undoubtedly a free man) and the reeve of each vill summoned to swear in the great inquest[2]. One of the most famous scenes recorded by our book is that in which William of Chernet claimed a Hampshire manor on behalf of Hugh de Port and produced his witnesses from among the best and eldest men of the county; but Picot, the sheriff of Cambridgeshire, who was in possession, replied with the testimony of villeins and mean folk and reeves, who were willing to support his case by oath or by ordeal[3]. Again, in Norfolk, Roger the sheriff claimed a hundred acres and five *villani* and a mill as belonging to the royal manor of Branfort, and five *villani* of the said manor testified in his favour and

---

[1] Schmid, App. v.; vii., 2, §§ 9-11; Pseudoleges Canuti, 60-1 (Schmid, p. 431).

[2] D. B. iv. 497.

[3] D. B. i. 44 b: 'Istam terram calumpniatur Willelmus de Chernet, dicens pertinere ad manerium de Cerneford feudum Hugonis de Port per hereditatem sui antecessoris et de hoc suum testimonium adduxit de melioribus et antiquis hominibus totius comitatus et hundredi; et Picot contraduxit suum testimonium de villanis et vili plebe et de prepositis, qui volunt defendere per sacramentum vel dei iudicium, quod ille qui tenuit terram liber homo fuit et potuit ire cum terra sua quo voluit. Sed testes Willelmi nolunt accipere legem nisi regis Edwardi usque dum diffiniatur per regem.' It seems possible that William's witnesses wished to insist on the ancient rule that the oath of one thegn would countervail the oaths of six ceorls. This was the old English law (*lex Edwardi*) on which they relied.

offered to make whatever proof anyone might adjudge to them, but the half-hundred of Ipswich testified that the land belonged to a certain church of S^t. Peter that Wihtgar held, and he offered to deraign this[1]. Certainly this does not look as if *villani* were excluded from the national moots. But a rule which valued the oath of a single thegn as highly as the oath of six ceorls would make the ceorl but a poor witness and tend to keep him out of court[2]. The men who are active in the communal courts, who make the judgments there, are usually men of thegnly rank; but to go to court as a doomsman is one thing, to go as a litigant is another[3].

We may now approach the question whether, and if so in what sense, the land that the *villanus* occupies is his land. Throughout Domesday Book a distinction is sedulously maintained between the land of the villeins (*terra villanorum*) and the land that the lord has *in dominio*. Let us notice this phrase. Only the demesne land does the lord hold *in dominio*, in ownership. The delicate shade of difference that Bracton would see between *dominicum* and *dominium* is not as yet marked. In later times it became strictly correct to say that the lord held in demesne (*in dominico suo*) not only the lands which he occupied by himself or his servants, but also the lands held of him by villein tenure[4]. This usage appears very plainly in the Dialogue on the Exchequer. 'You shall know,' says the writer, 'that we give the name demesnes (*dominica*) to those lands that a man cultivates at his own cost or by his own labour, and also to those which are possessed in his name by his *ascriptitii*; for by the law of this kingdom not only can these *ascriptitii* be removed by their lords from the lands that they now possess and transferred to other places, but they may be sold and dispersed at will; so that rightly are both they and the lands which they cultivate for the behalf of their lords accounted to be *dominia*[5].' Far other is the normal, if not invariable, usage of Domesday Book. The *terrae villanorum*, the *silvae villanorum*,

The villein and his land.

---

[1] D. B. ii. 393: 'et 5 villani de eodem manerio testantur ei et offerunt legem qualem quis iudicaverit; set dimidium hundret de Gepeswiz testantur quod hoc iacebat ad ecclesiam T. R. E. et Wisgarus tenebat et offert derationari.'

[2] Schmid, App. vi.; Leg. Hen. 64 § 2: 'thaini iusiurandum contravalet usiurandum sex villanorum.'

[3] Leg. Hen. 29, § 1. [4] Hist. Eng. Law, i. 344.

Dialogus, i. c. 11.

the *piscariae villanorum,* the *molini villanorum*—for the villeins have woods and fisheries and mills—these the lord does not hold *in dominio*[1]. Then again the oxen of the villeins are carefully distinguished from the oxen of the demesne, while often enough they are not distinguished from the oxen of those who in every sense are free tenants[2]. Now as regards both the land and the oxen we seem put to the dilemma that either they belong to the lord or else they belong to the villeins. We cannot avoid this dilemma, as we can in later days, by saying that according to the common law the ownership of these things is with the lord, while according to the custom of the manor it is with the villeins, for we believe that a hall-moot, a manorial court, is still a somewhat exceptional institution.

On the whole we can hardly doubt that both in their land and in their oxen the villeins have had rights protected by law. Let us glance once more at the scheme of *bót* and *wer* that has been in force. A villein is slain; the *manbót* payable to his lord is marked off from the much heavier *wergild* that is payable to his kindred. If all that a villein could have belonged to his lord such a distinction would be idle.

The villein's land and the geld.

Still we take it that for one most important purpose the villein's land is the lord's land:—the lord must answer for the geld that is due from it. Not that the burden falls ultimately on the lord. On the contrary, it is not unlikely that he makes his villeins pay the geld that is due from his demesne land; it is one of their services that they must 'defend their lord's

[1] D. B. i. 67 b: 'De terra villanorum dedit abbatissa uni militi 3 hidas et dimidiam.' Ibid. 89: 'tenet Johannes de episcopo 2 hidas de terra villanorum.' Ibid. i. 169: 'unus francigena tenet terram unius villani.' Ibid. 164: 'In Sauerna 11 piscariae in dominio et 42 piscariae villanorum.' Ibid. 230: 'Silva dominica 1 leu. long. et dim. leu. lat. Silva villanorum 4 quarent. long. et 3 quarent. lat.' Ibid. 7 b: '5 molini villanorum.' We have not seen *dominicum* used as a substantive; but in the Exon. D. B. iv. 75 we have *dominicatus Regis,* for the king's demesne. There is already a slight ambiguity about the term *dominium.* We may say that a church has a manor *in dominio,* meaning thereby that the manor as a whole is held by the church itself and is not held of it by any tenant; and then we may go on to say that only one half of the land comprised in this manor is held by the church *in dominio.* Cf. Hist. Eng. Law, ii. 126.

[2] For example, D. B. i. 159: 'Nunc in dominio 3 carucae et 6 servi, et 26 villani cum 3 bordariis et 15 liberi homines habent 30 carucas.' Ibid. 165: 'In dominio 2 carucae et 9 villani et 6 bordarii et presbyter et unus rachenistre cum 10 carucis.' Ibid. 258 b: 'et 3 villani et 2 bordarii et 2 francigenae cum 2 carucis.' But such entries are common enough.

inland' against the geld. But over against the state the lord represents as well the land of his villeins as his own demesne land. From the great levy of 1084 the demesne lands of the barons had been exempted[1], but no doubt they had been responsible for the tax assessed on the lands held by their *villani*. We much doubt whether the collectors of the geld went round to the cottages of the villeins and demanded here six pence and there four pence; they presented themselves at the lord's hall and asked for a large sum. Nay, we believe that very often a perfectly free tenant paid his geld to his lord, or through his lord[2]. Hence arrangements by which some hides were made to acquit other hides; such, for example, was the arrangement at Tewkesbury; there were fifty hides which had to acquit the whole ninety-five hides from all geld and royal service[3]. And then it might be that the lord, enjoying a special privilege, was entitled to take the geld from his tenants and yet paid no geld to the king; thus did the canons of S[t]. Petroc in Cornwall[4] and the monks of S[t]. Edmund in Suffolk[5]. But as regards lands occupied by villeins, the king, so it seems to us, looks for his geld to the lord and he does not look behind the lord. This is no detail of a fiscal system. A potent force has thus been set in motion. He who pays for land,—it is but fair that he should be considered the owner of that land. We have a hint of this principle in a law of Cnut:—'He who has "defended" land with the witness of the shire, is to enjoy it without question during his life and on his death may give or sell it to whom he pleases[6].' We have another hint of this principle in a story told by Heming, the monk of Worcester:—in Cnut's time but four days of grace were given to the landowner for

---

[1] Round, Domesday Studies, i. 97.

[2] D. B. i. 28: 'Ipse Willelmus de Braiose tenet Wasingetune....De hac terra tenet Gislebertus dim. hidam, Radulfus 1 hidam, Willelmus 3 virgas, Leuuinus dim. hidam qui potuit recedere cum terra sua et dedit geldum domino suo et dominus suus nichil dedit.'

[3] D. B. i. 163, 163 b.

[4] D. B. i. 121: 'Omnes superius descriptas terras tenebant T. R. E. S. Petrocus; huius sancti terrae nunquam reddiderunt geldum nisi ipsi aecclesiae.' D. B. iv. 187: 'Terrae S. Petrochi nunquam reddiderunt gildum nisi sancto.'

[5] D. B. ii. 372: 'Et quando in hundreto solvitur ad geldum 1 libra tunc inde exeunt 60 denarii ad victum monachorum.'

[6] Cnut, ii. 79: 'And se þe land gewerod hæbbe be scire gewitnisse....' The A.-S. *werian* is just the Latin *defendere*.

the payment of the geld; when these had elapsed, anyone who paid the geld might have the land[1]. It is a principle which, if it is applied to the case of lord and villein, will attribute the ownership of the land to the lord and not to the villein.

The villein's services. And then we would ask : What services do the villeins render ? A deep silence answers us, and as will hereafter be shown, there are many reasons why we should not import the information given us by the monastic cartularies, even such early cartularies as the Black Book of Peterborough, into the days of the Confessor. No doubt the villeins usually do some labour upon the lord's demesne lands. In particular they help to plough it. A manor, we can see, is generally so arranged that the ratio borne by the demesne oxen to the demesne land will be smaller than that borne by the villeins' oxen to the villeins' land. Thus, to give one example out of a hundred, in a Somersetshire manor the lord has four hides and three teams, the villeins have two hides and three teams[2]. But then the lord gets some help in his agriculture from those who are undoubtedly free tenants. The teams of the free tenants are often covered by the same phrase that covers the teams of the villeins[3]. Radknights who are *liberi homines* plough and harrow at the lord's court[4]. The very few entries which tell us of the labour of the villeins are quite insufficient to condemn the whole class to unlimited, or even to very heavy work. On a manor in Herefordshire there are twelve bordiers who work one day in the week[5]. On the enormous manor of Leominster there are 238 *villani* and 85 *bordarii*. The *villani* plough and sow with their own seed 140 acres of their lord's land and they pay

---

[1] Heming, Cartulary, i. 278; Round, Domesday Studies, i. 89. Compare the story in D. B. i. 216 b: Osbern or Osbert the fisherman claims certain land as having belonged to his 'antecessor'; 'sed postquam rex Willelmus in Angliam venit, ille gablum de hac terra dare noluit et Radulfus Taillgebosc gablum dedit et pro forisfacto ipsam terram sumpsit et cuidam suo militi tribuit.'

[2] D. B. iv. 245, Cruca.

[3] See above p. 54, note 2.

[4] D. B. i. 163: 'Ibi erant villani 21 et 9 rachenistres habentes 26 carucas et 5 coliberti et unus bordarius cum 5 carucis. Hi rachenistres arabant et herciabant ad curiam domini.' Ibid. 'Ibi 19 liberi homines rachenistres habentes 48 carucas cum suis hominibus.' Ibid. 166: 'De terra huius manerii tenebant radchenistres, id est liberi homines, T. R. E., qui tamen omnes ad opus domini arabant et herciabant et falcabant et metebant.'

[5] D. B. i. 186, Ewias.

11 pounds and 52 pence[1]. On the manor of Marcle, which also is in Herefordshire, there are 36 *villani* and 10 *bordarii* with 40 teams. These *villani* plough and sow with their own seed 80 acres of wheat and 71 of oats[2]. At Kingston, yet another manor in the same county, 'the *villani* who dwelt there in King Edward's day carried venison to Hereford and did no other service, so says the shire[3].' On one Worcestershire manor of Westminster Abbey 10 villeins and 10 bordiers with 6 teams plough 6 acres and sow them with their own seed; on another 8 villeins and 6 bordiers with 6 teams do the like by 4 acres[4]. This is light work. Casually we are told of burgesses living at Tamworth who have to work like the other villeins of the manor of Drayton to which they are attached[5], and we are told of men on a royal manor who do such works for the king as the reeve may command[6]; but, curiously enough, it is not of any villeins but of the Bishop of Worcester's riding men (*radmanni*) that it is written 'they do whatever is commanded them[7].'

With our thirteenth century cartularies before us, we might easily underrate the amount of money that was already being paid as the rent of land at the date of the Conquest. In several counties we come across small groups of *censarii, censores, gablatores* who pay for their land in money, of *cervisarii* and *mellitarii* who bring beer and honey. Renders in kind, in herrings, eels, salmon are not uncommon, and sometimes they are 'appreciated,' valued in terms of money. The pannage pig or the grass swine, which the villeins give in return for mast and herbage, is often mentioned. Throughout Sussex it seems to be the custom that the lord should have 'for herbage' one pig from every villein who has seven pigs[8]. But money will be taken instead of swine, oxen or fish[9]. The *gersuma*, the *tailla*,

Money rents paid by villeins.

---

[1] D. B. i. 180.
[2] D. B. i. 179 b.
[3] D. B. i. 179 b.
[4] D. B. i. 174 b.

[5] D. B. i. 246 b. So the burgesses of Steyning (i. 17) 'ad curiam operabantur sicut villani T. R. E.'

[6] D. B. i. 219.

[7] D. B. i. 174 b: 'Ipsi radmans secabant una die in anno et omne servitium quod eis iubebatur faciebant.' The position of these tenants will be discussed hereafter in connexion with S[t]. Oswald's charters.

[8] D. B. i. 16 b: 'De herbagio, unus porcus de unoquoque villano qui habet septem porcos.' In the margin stands 'Similiter per totum Sussex.'

[9] D. B. i. 12 b: 'Ibi tantum silvae unde exeunt de pasnagio 40 porci aut 54 denarii et unus obolus.' Ibid. 191 b: 'De presentacione piscium 12 solidi et 9 denarii.' Ibid. 117 b: 'aut unum bovem aut 30 denarios.'

the theoretically free gifts of the tenants, are sums of money.
But often enough the *villanus* is paying a substantial money
rent. We have seen how at Leominster villeins plough and
sow 140 acres for their lord and pay a rent of more than £11 [1].
At Lewisham in Kent the Abbot of Gand has a manor valued
at £30 ; of this £2 is due to the profits of the port while two
mills with 'the gafol of the rustics' bring in £8. 12s. [2] Such
entries as the following are not uncommon—there is one villein
rendering 30d. [3]—there is one villein rendering 10s. [4]—46 *cotarii*
with one hide render 30 shillings a year [5]—the villeins give
13s. 4d. by way of *consuetudo* [6]. No doubt it would be somewhat
rare to find a villein discharging all his dues in money—this is
suggested when we are told how on the land of S[t]. Augustin one
Wadard holds a large piece 'de terra villanorum' and yet
renders no service to the abbot save 30s. a year [7]. At least
in one instance the villeins seem to be holding the manor
in farm, that is to say, they are farming the demesne land and
paying a rent in money or in provender [8]. We dare not represent
the stream of economic history as flowing uninterruptedly from a
system of labour services to a system of rents. We must remember that in the Conqueror's reign the lord very often had
numerous serfs whose whole time was given to the cultivation
of his demesne. In the south-western counties he will often
have two, three or more serfs for every team that he has on his
demesne, and, while this is so, we can not safely say that his
husbandry requires that the villeins should be labouring on his
land for three or four days in every week.

The Eng-
lish for
villanus.
    As a last question we may ask : What was the English for
villanus? It is a foreign word, one of those words which came
in with the Conqueror. Surely, we may argue, there must have
been some English equivalent for it. Yet we have the greatest
difficulty in finding the proper term. True that in the Quadripartitus and the Leges *villanus* generally represents *ceorl*; *ceorl*
when it is not rendered by *villanus* is left untranslated in some
such form as *cyrliscus homo*. But then *ceorl* must be a wider

[1] See above p. 56.
[2] D. B. i. 12 b.
[3] D. B. i. 11 b, Hamestede.
[4] D. B. i. 117 b, Colun.
[5] D. B. i. 127, Stibenhede.
[6] D. B. i. 179 b, Lene.
[7] D. B. i. 12 b, Norborne.
[8] D. B. i. 127 b : 'Wellesdone tenent canonici S. Pauli....Hoc manerium
tenent villani ad firmam canonicorum. In dominio nil habetur.'

word than the *villanus* of Domesday Book, for it has to cover
all the non-noble free men; it must comprehend the numerous
sochemanni and *liberi homines* of northern and eastern England.
This in itself is not a little remarkable; it makes us suspect
that some of the lines drawn by Domesday Book are by no
means very old; they can not be drawn by any of those
terms that have been current in the Anglo-Saxon dooms or
which still are current in the text-books that lawyers are
compiling. To suppose that *villanus* is equivalent to *gebúr*
is impossible; we have the best warrant for saying that the
Latin for *gebúr* is not *villanus* but *colibertus*[1]. Nor can we
hold that the *villanus* is a *geneat*. In the last days of the old
English kingdom the *geneat*, the 'companion,' the 'fellow,'
appears as a horseman who rides on his lord's errands; we
must seek him among the *radmanni* and *rachenistres* and
drengi of Domesday Book[2]. We shall venture the guess that
when the Norman clerks wrote down *villanus*, the English
jurors had said *túnesman*. As a matter of etymology the two
words answer to each other well enough; the *villa* is the *tún*,
and the men of the *villa* are the men of the *tún*. In the
enlarged Latin version of the laws of Cnut, known as Instituta
Cnuti, there is an important remark:—tithes are to be paid both
from the lands of the thegn and from the lands of the villeins—
'tam de dominio liberalis hominis, id est þegenes, quam de terra
villanorum, id est tuumannes (*corr.* tunmannes)[3].' Then in a
collection of dooms known as the Northumbrian Priests' Law
there is a clause which orders the payment of Peter's pence.
If a king's thegn or landlord (*landrica*) withholds his penny,
he must pay ten half-marks, half to Christ, half to the king;
but if a *túnesman* withholds it, then let the landlord pay it and
take an ox from the man[4]. A very valuable passage this is.
It shows us how the lord is becoming responsible for the man's
taxes: if the tenant will not pay them, the lord must. It is
then in connexion with this responsibility of the lord that the
term *townsman* meets us, and, if we mistake not, it is the lord's
responsibility for geld that is the chief agent in the definition

[1] See above p. 36.
[2] This matter will be discussed when we deal with S^t. Oswald's charters.
[3] Schmid, p. 263 (note). This document is Dr Liebermann's Instituta
Cnuti (Trans. Roy. Hist. Soc. vii. 77).
[4] Schmid, App. ii. 57–9.

of the class of *villani*. The pressure of taxation, civil and ecclesiastical, has been forming new social strata, and a new word, in itself a vague word, is making its way into the vocabulary of the law[1].

Summary.   The class of villeins may well be heterogeneous. It may well contain (so we think) men who, or whose ancestors, have owned the land under a political supremacy, not easily to be distinguished from landlordship, that belongs to the king; and, on the other hand, it may well contain those who have never in themselves or their predecessors been other than the tenants of another man's soil. In some counties on the Welsh march there are groups of *hospites* who in fact or theory are colonists whom the lord has invited onto his land[2]; but this word, very common in France, is not common in England. Our record is not concerned to describe the nature or the origin of the villein's tenure; it is in quest of geld and of the persons who ought to be charged with geld, and so it matters not whether the lord has let land to the villein or has acquired rights over land of which the villein was once the owner. Therefore we lay down no broad principle about the rights of the villein, but we have suggested that taken in the mass the *villani* of the Confessor's reign were far more ' law-worthy' than were the *villani* of the thirteenth century. We can not treat either the legal or the economic history of our peasantry as a continuous whole; it is divided into two parts by the red thread of the Norman Conquest. That is a catastrophe. William might do his best to make it as little of a catastrophe as was possible, to insist that each French lord should have precisely the same rights that had been enjoyed by his English *antecessor*; it may even be that he endeavoured to assure to those who were becoming *villani* the rights that they had enjoyed under King Edward[3]. Such a task, if attempted, was impossible. We hear indeed that the English 'redeemed their lands,' but probably this refers only to those English lords, those thegns or the like, who were fortunate enough to find that a ransom would be accepted[4]. We have no warrant for thinking that

---

[1] For the rest, the word *tûnesman* appears in Edgar iv. 8, 13, in connexion with provisions against the theft of cattle.

[2] D. B. i. 259, 259 b.

[3] Leg. Will. i. 29.

[4] D. B. ii. 360 b: 'Hanc terram habet Abbas in vadimonio pro duabus marcis

the peasants, the common 'townsmen,' obtained from the king any covenanted mercies. They were handed over to new lords, who were very free in fact, if not in theory, to get out of them all that could be got without gross cruelty.

We are not left to speculate about this matter. In after days those who were likely to hold a true tradition, the great financier of the twelfth, the great lawyer of the thirteenth century, believed that there had been a catastrophe. As a result of the Conquest, the peasants, at all events some of the peasants, had fallen from their free estate; free men, holding freely, they had been compelled to do unfree services[1]. But if we need not rely upon speculation, neither need we rely upon tradition. Domesday Book is full of evidence that the tillers of the soil are being depressed. Depression of the villeins.

Here we may read of a free man with half a hide who has now been made one of the villeins[2], there of the holder of a small manor who now cultivates it as the farmer of a French lord *graviter et miserabiliter*[3], and there of a sokeman who has lost his land for not paying geld, though none was due[4]; while the great Richard of Tonbridge has condescended to abstract a virgate from a villein or a villein from a virgate[5]. But, again, it is not on a few cases in which our record states that some man has suffered an injustice that we would rely. Rather we notice what it treats as a quite common event. The Normans and the peasants.

---

auri concessu Engelrici quando redimebant Anglici terras suas.' Sometimes the Englishman gets back his land as a bedesman: i. 218, 'Hanc terram tenuit pater huius hominis et vendere poterit T. R. E. Hanc rex Willelmus in elemosina eidem concessit'; i. 211, 'Hanc terram tenuit Avigi et potuit dare cui voluit T. R. E. Hanc ei postea rex Willelmus concessit et per breve R. Tallebosc commendavit ut eum servaret'; i. 218 b, a similar case.

[1] Dialogus, i. c. 10; Bracton, f. 7. On both passages see Vinogradoff, Villainage, p. 121.

[2] D. B. ii. 1: 'In hoc manerio erat tunc temporis quidam liber homo...qui modo effectus est unus de villanis.'

[3] D. B. i. 148 b: 'In Merse tenet Ailric de Willelmo 4 hidas pro uno manerio....Istemet tenuit T. R. E. sed modo tenet ad firmam de Willelmo graviter et miserabiliter.'

[4] D. B. i. 141: 'Hanc terram sumpsit Petrus vicecomes de isto sochemanno Regis Willelmi in manu eiusdem Regis pro forisfactura de gildo Regis se non reddidisse ut homines sui dicunt. Sed homines de scira non portant vicecomiti testimonium, quia semper fuit quieta de gildo et de aliis erga Regem quamdiu tenuit, testante hundret.'

[5] D. B. i. 30: 'Ricardus de Tonebrige tenet de hoc manerio unam virgatam cum silva unde abstulit rusticum qui ibi manebat.'

Free men are being 'added to' manors to which they did not belong. Thus in Suffolk a number of free men have been added to the manor of Montfort; they paid no 'custom' to it before the Conquest, but now they pay £15; Ælfric who was reeve under Roger Bigot set them this custom[1]. Hard by them were men who used to pay 20 shillings, but this same Ælfric raised their rent to 100 shillings[2]. 'A free man held this land and could sell it, but Waleran father of John has added him to this manor[3]':—Entries of this kind are common. The utmost rents are being exacted from the farmers :—this manor was let for three years at a rent of £12 and a yearly gift of an ounce of gold, but all the farmers who took it were ruined[4]—that manor was let for £3. 15s. but the men were thereby ruined and now it is valued at only 45s.[5] About these matters French and English can not agree :—this manor renders £70 by weight, but the English value it at only £60 by tale[6]—the English fix the value at £80, but the French at £100[7]—Frenchmen and Englishmen agree that it is worth £50, but Richard let it to an Englishman for £60, who thereby lost £10 a year, at the very least[8]. 'It can not pay,' 'it can hardly pay,' 'it could not stand' the rent, such are the phrases that we hear. If the lord gets the most out of the farmer to whom he has leased the manor, we may be sure that the farmer is making the most out of the villeins.

Depression of the sokemen.   But the most convincing proof of the depression of the peasantry comes to us from Cambridgeshire. The rural population of that county as it existed in 1086 has been classified thus[9] :—

sochemanni	213
villani	1902
bordarii	1428
cotarii	736
servi	548

---

[1] D. B. ii. 282 b: 'et istam consuetudinem constituit illis Aluricus prepositus in tempore R. Bigot.'

[2] D. B. ii. 284 b.   [3] D. B. ii. 84 b.

[4] D. B. ii. 353 b: 'omnes fuerunt confusi.'

[5] D. B. ii. 440 b: 'sed homines inde fuerunt confusi.'

[6] D. B. i. 65, Aldeborne.   [7] D. B. ii. 18, Berdringas.

[8] D. B. ii. 38 b, Tachesteda.

[9] Ellis, Introduction, ii. 428. We give Ellis's figures, but think that he has exaggerated the number of sokemen who were to be found in 1086.

But we also learn that the Cambridgeshire of the Confessor's day had contained at the very least 900 instead of 200 sokemen[1]. This is an enormous and a significant change. Let us look at a single village. In Meldreth there is a manor; it is now a manor of the most ordinary kind; it is rated at 3 hides and 1 virgate, but contains 5 team-lands; in demesne are half a hide and one team, and 15 *bordarii* and 3 *cotarii* have 4 teams, and there is one *servus*. But before the Conquest this land was held by 15 sokemen; 10 of them were under the soke of the Abbey of Ely and held 2 hides and half a virgate; the other 5 held 1 hide and half a virgate and were the men of Earl Ælfgar[2]. What has become of these fifteen sokemen? They are now represented by fifteen bordiers and five cottiers; and the demesne land of the manor is a new thing. The sokemen have fallen, and their fall has brought with it the consolidation of manorial husbandry and seignorial power. At Orwell Earl Roger has now a small estate; a third of it is in demesne, while the residue is held by 2 villeins and 3 bordiers, and there is a serf there. This land had belonged to six sokemen, and those six had been under no less than five different lords, two belonged to Edith the Fair, one to Archbishop Stigand, one to Robert Wimarc's son, one to the king, and one to Earl Ælfgar[3]. Displacements such as this we may see in village after village. No one can read the survey of Cambridgeshire without seeing that the freer sorts of the peasantry have been thrust out, or rather thrust down.

Evidence so cogent as this we shall hardly find in any part of the record save that which relates to Cambridgeshire and Bedfordshire. But great movements of the kind that we are examining will hardly confine themselves within the boundaries of a county. A little variation in the formula which tells us who held the land in 1066 may hide from us the true state of the case. We can not expect that men will be very accurate in stating the legal relationships that existed twenty years ago. Since the day when King Edward was alive and dead many things have happened, many new words and new forms of thought have become familiar. But taking the verdicts as we

Further illustrations of depression.

---

[1] We make considerably more than 900 by counting only those who are expressly described as sokemen and excluding the many persons who are simply described as *homines* capable of selling their land.

[2] Hamilton, Inquisitio, 65.   [3] Hamilton, Inquisitio, 77.

find them, there is still no lack of evidence. In Essex we may see the *liberi homines* disappearing[1]. But we need not look only to the eastern counties. At Bromley, in Surrey, Bishop Odo has a manor of 32 hides, 4 of which had belonged to ' free men ' who could go where they pleased, but now there are only villeins, cottiers and serfs[2]. We turn the page and find Odo holding 10 hides which had belonged to 'the alodiaries of the vill[3].' In Kent Hugh de Port is holding land that was held by 6 free men who could go whither they would ; there are now 6 villeins and 14 bordiers there, with one team between them[4]. Students of Domesday were too apt to treat the *antecessores* of the Norman lords as being in all cases lords of manors. Lords of manors, or rather holders of manors, they often were, but as we shall see more fully hereafter, when we are examining the term *manerium*, such phrases are likely to deceive us. Often enough they were very small people with very little land. For example these six free men whom Hugh de Port represents had only two and a half team-lands. We pass by a few pages and find Hugh de Montfort with a holding which comprises but one team-land and a half ; he has 4 villeins and 2 bordiers there. His *antecessores* were three free men, who could go whither they would[5]. They had need for but 12 oxen ; they had no more land than they could easily till, at all events with the help of two or three cottagers or slaves. To all appearance they were no better than peasants. They or their sons may still be tilling the land as Hugh's villeins. When we look for such instances we very easily find them. The case is not altered by the fact that the term 'manor' is given to the holdings of these *antecessores*. In Sussex an under-tenant of Earl Roger has an estate with four villeins upon it. His *antecessores* were two free men who held the land as two manors. And how much land was there to be divided between the two ? There was one team-land. Such holders of *maneria* were tillers of the soil, peasants, at best yeomen[6]. If they were of thegnly rank, this again does not alter the case. When in the survey of Dorset we read how four thegns held two

---

[1] Thus e.g. D. B. ii. 87 b : ' Hidingham tenet Garengerus de Rogero pro 25 acris quas tenuerunt 15 liberi homines T. R. E.'

[2] D. B. i. 31.

[3] D. B. i. 31 b : ' Et 10 hidas tenebant alodiarii villae.'

[4] D. B. i. 10 b.   [5] D. B. i. 13, Essella.

[6] D. B. i. 24.

team-lands, how six thegns held two team-lands, eight thegns two team-lands, nine thegns four team-lands, eleven thegns four team-lands[1], we can not of course be certain that each of these groups of co-tenants had but one holding; but thegnly rank is inherited, and if a thegn will have nine or ten sons there will soon be tillers of the soil with the wergild of twelve hundred shillings. Now if these things are being done in the middling strata of society, if the sokemen are being suppressed or depressed in Cambridgeshire, the alodiaries in Sussex, what is likely to be the fate of the poor? They will have to till their lord's demesne *graviter et miserabiliter*. He can afford to dispense with serfs, for he has villeins.

A last argument must be added. What we see in the thir- The peasants on the royal demesne. teenth century of the ancient demesne of the crown[2] might lead us to expect that in Domesday Book 'the manors of S[t]. Edward' would stand out in bold relief. Instead of a population mainly consisting of villeins shall we not find upon them large numbers of sokemen, the ancestors of the men who in after days will be protected by the little writ of right and the *Monstraverunt?* Nothing of the kind. The royal manor differs in no such mode as this from any other manor. If it lies in a county in which other manors have sokemen, then it may or may not have sokemen. If it lies in a county in which other manors have no sokemen, it will have none. Cambridgeshire is a county in which there are some, and have been many, sokemen; there is hardly a sokeman upon the ancient demesne. In after days the men of Chesterton, for example, will have all the peculiar rights attributed by lawyers to the sokemen of S[t]. Edward. But S[t]. Edward, if we trust Domesday Book, had never a sokeman there; he had two villeins and a number of bordiers and cottiers[3]. It seems fairly clear that from an early time, if not from the first days of the Conquest onwards, the king was the best of landlords. The tenants of those manors that were conceived as annexed to the crown, those tenants one and all, save the class of slaves which was disappearing, got a better, a more regular justice than that which the villeins of other lords could hope for. It was the king's justice, and there-fore—for the king's public and private capacities were hardly

[1] D. B. 83, 83 b.
[2] Vinogradoff, Villainage, 89 ff.; Hist. Engl. Law, i. 366 ff.
[3] D. B. i. 189 b.

to be distinguished—it was public justice, and so became formal justice, defined by writs, administered in the last resort by the highest court, the ablest lawyers. And so sokemen disappear from private manors. Some of them as tenants in free socage may maintain their position; many fall down into the class of tenants in villeinage. On the ancient demesne the sokemen multiply; they appear where Domesday knew them not; for those who are protected by royal justice can hardly (now that villeinage implies a precarious tenure) be called villeins, they must be 'villein sokemen' at the least. Whether or no we trust the tradition which ascribes to the Conqueror a law in favour of the tillers of the soil, we can hardly doubt that the *villani* and *bordarii* whom Domesday Book shows us on the royal manors are treated as having legal rights in their holdings. And if this be true of them, it should be true of their peers upon other manors. Yes, it should be true; the manorial courts that are arising should do impartial justice even between lord and villeins; but who is to make it true?

§ 4. *The Sokemen.*

The *sochemanni* and *liberi homines.* Now of a large part of England we may say that all the occupiers of land who are not holding 'manors[1]' will belong to some of those classes of which we have already spoken. They will be villeins, bordiers, cottiers, 'boors' or serfs. Here and there we may find a few persons who are described as *liberi homines.* In some of the western counties, Gloucester, Worcester, Hereford, Shropshire, there are *rachenistres* or *radmans;* between the Ribble and the Mersey we may find a party of *drengs.* Still it is generally true that two of those five classes that seem to have been mentioned in King William's writ[2], the *sochemanni* and the *liberi homines,* are largely represented only in certain counties. They are to be seen in Essex, yet more thickly in Suffolk and Norfolk. In Lincolnshire nearly half of the rural population consists of sokemen, though there is no class of persons described as *liberi homines.* There are some

---

[1] We shall see hereafter that some of these so-called 'manors' are but small plots and their holders small folk.

[2] See above p. 24.

sokemen in Yorkshire, but they are not very numerous and there are hardly any *liberi homines.* We have seen how in Cambridgeshire and Bedfordshire the sokemen have fared ill; but still some are left there. Traces of them may be found in Hertford and Buckingham; they are thick in Leicester, Nottingham and Northampton; there are some in Derbyshire. There have been sokemen in Middlesex[1] and in Surrey[2]; but they have been suppressed; a few remain in Kent[3]; so we should be rash were we to find anything characteristically Scandinavian in the sokemen. Even in Suffolk they are suffering ill at the hands of their new masters[4], while in Cambridgeshire, Bedfordshire, Hertfordshire they have been suppressed or displaced.

We have now to enter on a difficult task, a discussion of the relation which exists between these *sochemanni* and *liberi homines* on the one hand and their lord upon the other. The character of this relation varies from case to case. We may distinguish three different bonds by which a man may be bound to a lord, a personal bond, a tenurial bond, a jurisdictional or justiciary bond. But the language of Domesday Book is not very patient of this analysis. However in the second volume we very frequently come upon two ideas which are sharply contrasted with each other; the one is expressed by the term *commendatio,* the other by the term *soca*[5]. To these we must add the great vague term *consuetudo,* and we shall also have to consider the phrases which describe the various degrees of that freedom of 'withdrawing himself with his land' that a man may enjoy. *Lord and man.*

In order that we may become familiar with the use made of these terms and phrases we will transcribe a few typical entries: *Bonds between lord and man.*

---

[1] D. B. i. 128 b, 129, 129 b.

[2] D. B. i. 34, 35 b.   [3] D. B. i. 13.

[4] D. B. ii. 287. There are free men, apparently 120 in number, of whom it is written: 'Hii liberi homines qui tempore regis Eduardi pertinebant in soca de Bercolt, unusquisque gratis dabat preposito per annum 4 tantum denarios, et reddebat socam sicut lex ferebat, et quando Rogerius Bigot prius habuit vicecomitatum statuerunt ministri sui quod redderent 15 libras per annum, quod non faciebant T. R. E. Et quando Robertus Malet habuit vicecomitatum sui ministri creverunt illos ad 20 libras. Et quando Rogerius Bigot eos rehabuit dederunt similiter 20 libras. Et modo tenet eos Aluricus Wanz tali consuetudine qua erant T. R. E.' This is a rare instance of a reestablishment of the *status quo ante conquestum.*

[5] Compare Round, Feudal England, 33.

> Two free men, of whom Ælfwin had not even the commendation[1].
>
> Of these men Harold had not even the commendation[2].

Thus commendation seems put before us as the slightest bond that there can be between lord and man. Very often we are told that the lord had the commendation and nothing more[3]. Thus it is contrasted with the soke:—

> His predecessor had only the commendation of this, and Harold had the soke[4].
>
> Of these six free men St Benet had the soke, and of one of them the commendation[5].

And the commendation is contrasted with the 'custom,' the *consuetudo,* perhaps we might say the 'service':—

> Of the said sokeman Ralph Peverel had a custom of 3 shillings a year, but in the Confessor's time his ancestor had only the commendation[6].
>
> R. Malet claims 18 free men, 3 of them by commendation, and the rest for all custom[7].

And the soke is contrasted with the *consuetudo:*—

> To this manor belong 4 men for all custom, and other 4 for soke only[8].

In a given case all these bonds may be united:—

> There are 7 sokemen who are the Saint's men with sake and soke and all custom[9].
>
> Over this man the Saint has sake and soke and commendation with all custom[10].

Then if the man 'withdraws,' or gives or sells his land, we often

---

[1] D. B. ii. 187 b: 'Ex his non habuit Ailwinus suus antecessor etiam commendationem.'

[2] D. B. ii. 287: 'De his hominibus...non habuit Haroldus etiam commendationem.'

[3] D. B. ii. 153 b: 'Unde suus antecessor habuit commendationem tantum.' Ibid. 154 : 'Alstan liber homo Edrici commend[atione] tantum.'

[4] D. B. ii. 161 b.   [5] D. B. ii. 244.

[6] D. B. ii. 6: 'De predicto sochemano habuit Rad. Piperellus consuetudinem in unoquoque anno per 3 solidos, set in T. R. E. non habuit eius antecessor nisi tantum modo commendationem.'

[7] D. B. ii. 171 b: 'Calumpniatur R. Malet 18 liberos homines, 3 commendatione et alios de omni consuetudine.'

[8] D. B. ii. 250 b: 'Huic manerio adiacent semper 4 homines de omni consuetudine et alii 4 ad socham tantum.'

[9] D. B. ii. 356 b.   [10] D. B. ii 357.

read of the soke 'remaining'; we sometimes read of the commendation, the custom, the service 'remaining.'

> These free men could sell or give their land, but the commendation and the soke and sake would remain to St Edmund[1].
> These men could sell their land, but the soke would remain to the Saint and the service (*servitium*), whoever might be the buyer[2].
> They could give and sell their land, but the soke and the commendation and the service would remain to the Saint[3].

But after all, these distinctions are not maintained with rigour, for the soke is sometimes spoken of as though it were a species of *consuetudo*. We have a tangled skein in our hands.

The thread that looks as if it would be the easiest to unravel, is that which is styled 'mere commendation.' The same idea is expressed by other phrases—'he committed himself to bishop Herman for his defence[4]'—'they submitted themselves with their land to the abbey for defence[5]'—'he became the man of Goisfrid of his own free will[6]'—'she put herself with her land in the hand of the queen[7].' 'Homage' is not a common term in Domesday Book, but if, when speaking of the old time, it says, as it constantly does, that one person was the man of another, no doubt it is telling us of a relationship which had its origin in an oath and a symbolic ceremony[8]. 'She put herself into the hands of the queen'—we should take these words to mean just what they say. An Anglo-Saxon oath of fealty (*hyldáð*) has been preserved[9]. The swearer promises to be faithful and true to his lord, to love all that his lord loves and eschew all that his lord eschews. He makes no distinct reference to any land, but he refers to some compact

Commendation.

---

[1] D. B. ii. 353 b.

[2] D. B. ii. 362: 'set soca remaneret sancto et servitium quicunque terram emeret.'

[3] D. B. ii. 358.

[4] D. B. i. 58: 'Pater Tori tenuit T. R. E. et potuit ire quo voluit sed pro sua defensione se commisit Hermanno episcopo et Tori Osmundo episcopo similiter.'

[5] D. B. i. 32 b: ' set pro defensione se cum terra abbatiae summiserunt.'

[6] D. B. ii. 62 b: ' et T. R. W. effectus est homo Goisfridi sponte sua.'

[7] D. B. i. 36 b: ' T. R. W. femina quae hanc terram tenebat misit se cum ea in manu reginae.' Ibid. 36: ' Quidam liber homo hanc terram tenens et quo vellet abire valens commisit se in defensione Walterii pro defensione sua.'

[8] D. B. ii. 172: 'Hos calumpniatur Drogo de Befrerere pro homagio tantum.' This seems equivalent to the common ' commendatione tantum.' D. B. i. 225 b: ' fuerunt homines Burred et iccirco G. episcopus clamat hominationem eorum.'

[9] Schmid, App. x.

which exists between him and his lord:—He will be faithful and true on condition that his lord treats him according to his deserts and according to the covenant that has been established between them.

Commen- dation and protection.

To all seeming there need not be any land in the case; and, if the man has land, the act of commendation will not give the lord as a matter of course any rights in that land. Certainly Domesday Book seems to assume that in general every owner or holder of land must have had a lord. This assumption is very worthy of notice. A law of Æthelstan[1] had said that lordless men 'of whom no right could be had' were to have lords, but this command seems aimed at the landless folk, not at those whose land is a sufficient surety for their good behaviour. The law had not directly commanded the landed men to commend themselves, but it had supplied them with motives for so doing[2]. What did a man gain by this act of submission? Of advantages that might be called 'extra-legal' we will say nothing, though in the wild days of Æthelred the Unready, and even during the Confessor's reign, there was lawlessness enough to make the small proprietor wish that he had a mightier friend than the law could be. But there were distinct legal advantages to be had by commendation. In the first place, the life of the great man's man was protected not only by a *wer-gild* but by a *man-bót*:—a *man-bót* due to one who had the power to exact it; and if, as one of our authorities assures us, the amount of the *man-bót* varied with the rank of the lord[3], this would help to account for a remarkable fact disclosed by Domesday Book, namely, that the chosen lord was usually a person of the very highest rank, an earl, an archbishop, the king. Then, again, if the man got into a scrape, his lord might be of service to him. Suppose the man accused of theft: in certain cases he might escape with a single, instead of a triple ordeal, if he had a lord who would swear to his good character[4]. In yet other cases his lord would come forward as his compurgator; perhaps he was morally bound to do so; and,

[1] Æthelst. ii. 2.
[2] Also it had declared that every man must have a pledge, and probably the easiest way of fulfilling this command was to place oneself under a lord who would put one into a tithing.
[3] Leg. Edw. Conf. 12, § 5; but this is contradicted by Leg. Henr. 87, § 4.
[4] Æthelr. i. 1, § 2; compare Æthelr. iii. 3, § 4.

being a man of high rank, would swear a crushing oath. And within certain limits that we can not well define the lord might warrant the doings of his man, might take upon himself the task of defending an action to which his man was subjected[1]. What the man has sought by his submission is *defensio, tuitio*; the lord is his *defensor, tutor, protector, advocatus*, in a word, his warrantor[2].

Of warranty we are accustomed to think chiefly in connexion with the title to land:—the feoffor warrants the feoffee in his enjoyment of the tenement. But to all appearance in the eleventh century it is rather as lord than as giver, seller or lender, that the vouchee comes to the defence of his man. If the land is conceived as having once been the warrantor's land, this may be but a fiction:—the man has given up his land and then taken it again merely in order that he may be able to say with some truth that he has it by his lord's gift. But we can not be sure that as yet any such fiction is necessary. 'I will defend any action that is brought against you for this land':— as yet men see no reason why such a promise as this, if made with due ceremony, should not be enforced. A certain amount of 'maintenance' is desirable in their eyes and laudable.

Commendation and warranty.

Though we began with the statement that where there is commendation there may yet be no land in the case, we have none the less been already led to the supposition that often enough land does get involved in this nexus between man and lord. No doubt a landless man may commend himself and get no land in return for his homage; but with such an one Domesday Book is not concerned. The cases in which it takes an interest are those in which a landholder has commended himself. Now we dare not say that a landholder can never commend himself without commending his land also[3]. Howbeit, the usual practice certainly is that a man who submits or commits himself for 'defence' or 'protection' shall take his land with him; he 'goes with his land' to a lord. Very

Commendation and tenure.

---

[1] Leg. Hen. 82, § 6; 85, § 2.

[2] D. B. ii. 18 b: 'inde vocat dominum suum ad tutorem.' Ibid. 103: 'vocavit Ilbodonem ad tutorem et postea non adduxit tutorem.' Ibid. 31 b: 'revocat eam ad defensorem.' D. B. i. 141 b: 142: 'sed Harduinus reclamat Petrum vicecomitem ad protectorem.' Ibid. 227 b: 'et dicit regem suum advocatum esse.'

[3] D. B. ii. 71 b: 'Phenge tenet idem Serlo de R[anulfo Piperello] quod tenuit liber homo...qui T. R. W. effectus est homo antecessoris Ranulfi Piperelli, set terram suam sibi non dedit.' This however is not quite to the point.

curious are some of the instances which show how large a
liberty men have enjoyed of taking land wherever they please.
'Tostig bought this land from the church of Malmesbury for
three lives':—in this there is nothing strange; leases for three
lives granted by churches to thegns have been common. But
of course we should assume that during the lease the land could
have no other lord than the church of Malmesbury. Not so,
however, for during his lease Tostig 'could go with that land to
whatever lord he pleased[1].' In Essex there was before the
Conquest a man who held land; that land in some sort belonged
to the Abbey of Barking, and could not be separated from the
abbey; but the holder of it was the man ('merely the man'
say the jurors) of one Leofhild the predecessor of Geoffrey de
Mandeville[2]. In this last case we may satisfy ourselves by
saying that a purely personal relation is distinguished from a
tenurial relation; the man of Leofhild is the tenant of the
abbey. But what of Tostig's case? Land that he holds of the
church of Malmesbury, and that too by no perpetual tenure, he
can commend to another lord. From the man's point of view,
protection, defence, warranty, is the essence of commendation,
and the warranty that he chiefly needs is the warranty of his
possession, of the title by which he holds his land. It can not
but be therefore that the lord to whom he commends himself
and his land, should be in some sort his landlord.

The lord's interest in commendation.
Not that he need pay rent, or perform other services in
return for the land. The land is his land; he has not obtained
it from his lord; on the contrary he has carried it to his lord.
Mere commendation is therefore distinguished by a score of
entries from a relation that involves the payment of *consuetudines*. Doubtless however the lord obtains 'a valuable
consideration' for all that he gives. Part of this will probably
lie without the legal sphere. He has a sworn retainer who will
fight whenever he is told to fight. But even the law allows the
man to go great lengths in his lord's defence[3]. In a rough age

---

[1] D. B. i. 72: 'Toti emit eam T. R. E. de aecclesia Malmesburiensi ad
etatem trium hominum et infra hunc terminum poterat ire cum ea ad quem
vellet dominum.'

[2] D. B. ii. 57 b: 'Et haec terra quam modo tenet G. fuit in abbatia de
Berchingis sicuti hundret testatur; set ille qui tenuit hanc terram fuit tantum
modo homo [Leuild] antecessoris Goisfridi et non potuit istam terram mittere
in aliquo loco nisi in abbatia.'

[3] Leg. Hen. 82, § 3.

happy is the lord who has many sworn to defend him. When at a later time we see that the claimant of land must offer proof 'by the body of a certain free man of his,' we are taught that the lords have relied upon the testimony and the strong right arms of their vassals. That in all cases the lord got more than this we can not say, though perhaps commendation carried with it the right to the heriot, the horse and armour of the dead man[1]. The relation is often put before us as temporary. Numerous are the persons who 'can seek lords where they choose' or who can 'go with their land wherever they please.' How large a liberty these phrases accord to lord and man it were hard to tell. We can not believe that either party to the contract could dissolve it just at the moment when the other had some need to enforce it; but still at other times the man might dissolve it, and we may suppose that the lord could do so too. But the connexion might be of a more permanent kind. Perhaps in most cases in which we are told that a man can not withdraw his land from his lord the bond between them is regarded as something other than commendation—there is commendation and something more. But this is no universal truth. You might be the lord's man 'merely by commendation' and yet be unable to sell your land without the lord's leave[2]. At any rate, in one way and another 'the commendation' is considered as capable of binding the land. The commended man will be spoken of as holding the land under (*sub*) his lord, if not of (*de*) his lord[3]. In many cases if he sells the land 'the commendation will remain to his lord'—by which is meant, not that the vendor will continue to be the man of

---

[1] D. B. ii. 118 b: 'In burgo [de Tetfort] autem erant 943 burgenses T. R. E. De his habuit Rex omnem consuetudinem. De istis hominibus erant 36 ita dominice Regis E. ut non possent esse homines alicuius sine licentia Regis. Alii omnes poterant esse homines cuiuslibet set semper tamen consuetudo Regis remanebat *preter herigete*.' Compare D. B. i. 336 b, Stamford: 'In his custodiis sunt 72 mansi sochemanorum, qui habent terras suas in dominio, et qui petunt dominos ubi volunt, super quos Rex nichil aliud habet nisi emendationem forisfacturae eorum et heriete et theloneum.' In this case commendation would not carry the heriot with it.

[2] D. B. ii. 201: 'Liber homo de 80 acris terrae Almari episcopi et Alwoldi abbatis commend[atione] tantum, et hic homo erat ita in monasterio quod non potuit dare terram suam nec vendere.' See another entry of the same kind on the same page.

[3] D. B. i. 50 b: 'Hic Alwinus tenuit hanc terram T. R. E. sub Wigoto pro tuitione ; modo tenet eam sub Milone.'

that lord (for the purposes of the Domesday Inquest this would be a matter of indifference) but that the lord's rights over the land are not destroyed. The purchaser comes to the land and finds the commendation inhering in it[1].

The seignory over the commended. And so, again, the lord's rights under the commendation seem to constitute an alienable and heritable seignory. It is thus that we may best explain the case, very common in East Anglia, in which a man is commended half to one and half to another lord[2]. Thus we read of a case in which a free man was commended, as to one-third to Wulfsige, and as to the residue to Wulfsige's two brothers[3]. In this instance it seems clear that the commendation has descended to three co-heirs. In other cases a lord may have made over his rights to two religious houses; thus we hear of a man who is common to the Abbots of Ely and St. Edmund's[4]. In some cases a man may, in others he may not, be able to prevent himself being transferred from lord to lord, or from ancestor to heir. What passes by alienation or inheritance may be regarded rather as a right to his commendation than as the commendation itself[5]. Of course there is nothing to hinder one from being the man of several different lords. Ælfric Black held lands of the Abbot of Westminster which he could not separate from the church, but for other lands he was the man of Archbishop Stigand[6]. Already a lofty edifice is being constructed; B, to whom C is commended, is himself commended to A; and in this case a certain relation exists between C and A; C is 'sub-commended' to A[7].

Commendation and service. In a given case the somewhat vague obligation of the

[1] For example, D. B. ii. 353 b: 'Hii poterant dare et vendere terram suam T. R. E. set commend[atio] et soca et saca remanebat S. Edmundo.'

[2] D. B. ii. 182 b: 'Ulchetel habuit dimidiam commendationem de illo T. R. E. et de uxore ipsius totam commendationem.' Ibid. 249 b: 'Medietas istius hominis fuit antecessoris Baingnardi commendatione tantum et alia medietas S. Edmundi cum dimidia terra.' The contrast between *dimidii homines* and *integri homines* is common enough. See D. B. ii. 309: one man has a sixth and another five-sixths of a commendation.

[3] D. B. ii. 333 b.   [4] D. B. ii. 125 b.

[5] D. B. i. 58. Tori 'committed himself for defence' to Bp. Herman; Tori's son has done the same to Osmund, the successor of Herman.

[6] D. B. i. 133: 'sed pro aliis terris homo archiepiscopi Stigandi fuit.'

[7] On the whole this seems to be the meaning of 'sub-commendation.' We read a good deal of men who were sub-commended to the *antecessor* of Robert Malet. This seems to be explained by such an entry as the following (ii. 313 b): 'Eadric holds two free men who were commended to Eadric, who himself was commended to (another) Eadric, the *antecessor* of Robert Malet.'

commended man may be rendered definite by a bargain which imposes upon him the payment of rent or the performance of some specified services. When this is so, we shall often find that the land is moving, if we may so speak, not from the man but from the lord. The man is taking land from the lord to hold during good behaviour[1], or for life[2], or for lives. A form of lease or loan (*lǽn*) which gives the land to the lessee and to two or three successive heirs of his, has from of old been commonly used by some of the great churches[3]. Also we see landowners giving up their land to the churches and taking it back again as mere life tenants. During their lives the church is to have some 'service,' or at least some 'recognition' of its lordship, while after their deaths the church will have the land in demesne[4]. This is something different from mere commendation. We see here the *feuda oblata* or *beneficia oblata* which foreign jurists have contrasted with *feuda* or *beneficia data*. The land is brought into the bargain by the man, not by the lord. But often the land comes from the lord, and the tenancy is no merely temporary tenancy; it is heritable. The king has provided his thegns with lands; the earls, the churches have provided their thegns with lands, and these thegns have heritable estates, and already they are conceived as holding them of (*de*) the churches, the earls, the king. But we must not as yet be led away into any discussion about the architecture of the very highest storeys of the feudal or vassalic edifice. It must at present suffice that in humbler quarters there has been much letting and hiring of land. The leases, if we choose to call them so, the gifts, if we choose to call them so, have created heritable rights and perdurable relationships.

There is no kind of service that can not be purchased by a grant or lease of land. Godric's wife had land from the king

Land-loans and services.

---

[1] D. B. i. 45 b: 'Quidam frater Edrici tenuit tali conventione, quod quamdiu bene se haberet erga eum [Edricum] tamdiu terram de eo teneret, et si vendere vellet, non alicui nisi ei de quo tenebat vendere vel dare liceret.'

[2] Cases of life tenancies will be found in D. B. i. 47, Stantune; 67 b, Newetone; 80, Catesclive; 177 b, Witune; ii. 373, 444 b.

[3] D. B. i. 46 b, 66 b, 72, 175. We shall return to this when in the next essay we speak of *loanland*.

[4] D. B. i. 67 b: 'Hanc terram reddidit sponte sua aecclesiae Hardingus qui in vita sua per convent[ionem] debebat tenere.' See also the case in i. 177 b. Again, ii. 431: 'terram quam cepit cum uxore sua...misit in ecclesia concedente muliere tali conventione quod non potuit vendere nec dare de aecclesia.' For a 'recognitio' see i. 175, Persore.

because she fed his dogs[1]. Ælfgyfu the maiden had land from Godric the sheriff that she might teach his daughter orfrey work[2]. The monks of Pershore stipulate that their dominion shall be recognized by 'a day's farm' in every year, that is, that the lessee shall once a year furnish the convent with a day's victual[3]. The king's thegns between the Ribble and the Mersey have 'like villeins' to make lodges for the king, and fisheries and deer-hays, and must send their reapers to cut the king's crops at harvest time[4]. The radmen and radknights of the west must ride on their lord's errands and make themselves generally useful; they plough and harrow and mow, and do whatever is commanded them[5].

The man's consuetudines.

But we would here speak chiefly of the lowly 'free men' and sokemen of the eastern counties. Besides having their commendation and their soke, the lord very often has what is known as their *consuetudo* or their *consuetudines*. Often they are the lord's men *de omni consuetudine*. In all probability the word when thus employed, when contrasted with commendation on the one hand and with soke on the other, points to payments and renders to be made in money and in kind and to services of an agricultural character. Of such services only one stands out prominently; it is very frequently mentioned in the survey of East Anglia; it is fold-soke, *soca faldae*. The man must not have a fold of his own; his sheep must lie in the lord's fold. It is manure that the lord wants; the demand for manure has played a large part in the history of the human race. Often enough this is the one *consuetudo*, the one definite service, that the lord gets out of his free men[6]. And then a man who is *consuetus ad faldam*, tied to his lord's fold, is hardly to be considered as being in all respects a 'free' man. Those who are

---

[1] D. B. i. 57 b.

[2] D. B. i. 149: 'De his tenuit Aluuid puella 2 hidas...et de dominica firma Regis Edwardi habuit ipsa dimidiam hidam quam Godricus vicecomes ei concessit quamdiu vicecomes esset, ut illa doceret filiam ejus aurifrisium operari.'

[3] D. B. i. 175: 'Hanc emit quidam Godricus teinus regis Edwardi vita trium haeredum et dabat in anno monachis unam firmam pro recognitione.'

[4] D. B. i. 269 b.

[5] See above p. 56. Their tenure will be discussed hereafter in connexion with St. Oswald's land-loans.

[6] D. B. ii. 187 b: 'In Carletuna 27 liberi homines et dimidius sub Olfo commendatione tantum et soca falde...15 liberi homines sub Olfo soca falde et commendatione tantum.'

not 'fold-worthy' are to be classed with those who are not 'moot-worthy' or 'fyrd-worthy.' We are tempted to say that a man's *caput* is diminished by his having to seek his lord's fold, just as it would be diminished if he were excluded from the communal courts or the national host[1]. From the nature of this one *consuetudo* and from the prominence that is given to it, we may guess the character of the other *consuetudines*. Suit to the lord's mill would be analogous to suit to his fold[2]. Of 'mill-soke' we read nothing, but often enough a surprisingly large part of the total value of a manor is ascribed to its mill, and we may argue that the lord has not invested capital in a costly undertaking without making sure of a return. We may well suppose that like the radmen of the west the free men and sokemen of the east give their lord some help in his husbandry at harvest time. From a document which comes to us from the abbey of Ely, and which is slightly older than the Domesday Inquest, we learn that certain of S[t]. Etheldreda's sokemen in Suffolk had nothing to do but to plough and thresh whenever the abbot required this of them; others had to plough and weed and reap, to carry the victual of the monks to the minster and furnish horses whenever called upon to do so[3]. This seems to point rather to 'boon-days' than to continuous 'week-work,' and we observe that the sokemen of the east like the radmen of the west have horses. Occasionally we learn that a sokeman has to pay an annual sum of money to his lord; sometimes this looks

[1] D. B. ii. 203 b: 'In eadem villa 12 homines 6 quorum erant in soca falde et alii 6 erant liberi.' Ibid. 361 b: '70 liberi...super hos homines habet et semper habuit sacam et socam et omnem consuetudinem et ad faldam pertinent omnes preter 4.' Ibid. ii. 207: '17 liberi homines consueti ad faldam et commendati.' The term 'fold-worthy' occurs in a writ of Edward the Confessor; he gives to St. Benet of Ramsey soke over such of the men of a certain district as are moot-worthy, fyrd-worthy, and fold-worthy: Earle, Land Charters, p. 343; Kemble, iv. p. 208.

[2] In later extents of East Anglian manors the fold-soke plays an important part. Cart. Rams. iii. 267: 'R. tenuit unam carucatam terrae cum falda sua pro octo solidis. A. dabat pro terra sua quadraginta denarios et oves eius erant in falda Abbatis...H. triginta acras pro quatuor solidis et oves eius sunt in manu domini....'

[3] See the document printed by Hamilton at the end of the Inquisitio Com. Cantabr. p. 192. 'Isti solummodo arabunt et contererent messes eiusdem loci quotienscunque abbas preceperit....' 'Ita proprie sunt abbati ut quotienscunque ipse preceperit in anno arabunt suam terram, purgabunt et colligent segetes, portabunt victum monachorum ad monasterium, equos eorum in suis necessitatibus semper habebit.' For more of this matter see Round, Feudal England, 30.

like a substantial rent, sometimes like a mere 'recognition'; but the words that most nearly translate our 'rent,' *redditus, census, gablum* are seldom used in this context. All is *consuetudo.*

Nature of consuetudines. It is an interesting word. We perhaps are eager to urge the dilemma that in these cases the land must have been brought into the bargain either by the lord or by the tenant:—either the lord is conceived as having let land to the tenant, or the theory is that the tenant has commended land to the lord. But the dilemma is not perfect. It may well be that this relationship is thought of as having existed from all time; it may well be that this relationship, though under slowly varying forms, has really existed for several centuries, and has had its beginning in no contract, in no bargain. In origin the rights of the lord may be the rights of kings and ealdormen, rights over subjects rather than rights over tenants. The word *consuetudo* covers taxes as well as rents, and, if the sokeman has to do work for his lord, very often, especially in Cambridgeshire and Hertfordshire, he has to do work for the king or for the sheriff also. If he has to do carrying service for the lord, he has to do carrying service (*avera*) for the sheriff also or in lieu thereof to pay a small sum of money[1]. And another aspect of this word *consuetudo* is interesting to us. Land that is burdened with customs is customary land (*terra consuetudinaria*)[2]. As yet this term does not imply that the tenure, though protected by custom, is not protected by law; there is no opposition between law and custom; the customary tenant of Domesday Book is the tenant who renders customs, and the more customs he renders the more customary he is[3].

Justiciary consuetudines. This word *consuetudo* is the widest of words. Perhaps we find the best equivalent for *consuetudines* in our own vague 'dues[4].' It covers what we should call rents; it covers what we

[1] D. B. i. 141: there are four sokemen who are men of Æthelmær and who can not sell their land without his consent; but they are under the king's sake and soke and jointly provide the sheriff with one *avera* every year or four pence.

[2] D. B. i. 249: 'Haec terra fuit consuetudinaria solummodo de theloneo regis sed aliam socam habebat.'

[3] D. B. ii. 273 b: 'In eadem 8 consuetudinarii ad faldam sui antecessoris.' Ibid. 215: '8 homines consuetudinarios ad hoc manerium.'

[4] D. B. i. 280: 'Duae partes Regis et tercia comitis de censu et theloneo et forisfactura et de omni consuetudine.' Ibid. 42: 'Unam aecclesiam et 6 capellas cum omni consuetudine vivorum et mortuorum.'

should call rates and taxes; but further it covers what we should call the proceeds and profits of justice. Let us construe a few entries. At Romney there are burgesses who in return for the service that they do on the sea are quit of all customs except three, namely, larceny, peace-breach and ambush[1]. In Berkshire King Edward gave to one of his foresters half a hide of land free from all custom, except the king's forfeiture, such as larceny, homicide, hám-fare and peace-breach[2]. In what sense can a crime be a custom? In a fiscal sense. A crime is a source of revenue. In what sense should we wish to have our land free of crimes, free even, if this be possible, of larceny and homicide? In this sense:—we should wish that no money whatever should go out of our land, neither by way of rent, nor by way of tax, rate, toll, nor yet again by way of *forisfactura*, of payment for crime committed. We should wish also that our land with the tenants on it should be quit or quiet (*quieta*) from the incursions of royal and national officers, whether they be in search of taxes or in search of criminals and the fines due from criminals, and we should also like to put those fines in our own pockets. Justice therefore takes its place among the *consuetudines:* 'larceny' is a source of income[3]. A lord who has 'his customs,' is a lord who has among other sources of revenue, justice or the profits of justice[3]. 'Justice or the profits of justice,' we say, for our record does not care to distinguish between them. It is thinking of money while we are engaged in questioning it about the constitution and competence of tribunals. It gives us but crooked answers. However, we must make the best that can be made of them, and in particular must form some opinion about the *consuetudines* known as *sake* and *soke*.

[1] D. B. i. 10 b: 'et sunt quieti pro servitio maris ab omni consuetudine preter tribus, latrocinio, pace infracta, et forestel.'

[2] D. B. i. 61 b: 'solutam ab omni consuetudine propter forestam custodiendam excepta forisfactura Regis, sicut est latrocinium, et homicidium, et heinfara, et fracta pax.'

[3] D. B. i. 52: 'Hi infrascripti habent in Hantone consuetud[ines] domorum suarum.' Ibid. 249: 'Haec terra fuit consuetudinaria solummodo de theloneo Regis sed socam aliam habebat.'

§ 5. *Sake and soke.*

We may best begin our investigation by recalling the law of later times. In the thirteenth century seignorial justice, that is, justice in private hands, has two roots. A certain civil jurisdiction belongs to the lord as such; if he has tenants enough to form a court, he is at liberty to hold a court of and for his tenants. This kind of seignorial justice we call specifically feudal justice. But very often a lord has other and greater powers than the feudal principle would give him; in particular he has the view of frankpledge and the police justice that the view of frankpledge implies. All such powers must in theory have their origin in grants made by the king; they are franchises. With feudal justice therefore we contrast 'franchisal' justice[1].

Now if we go back to the Norman period we shall begin to doubt whether the feudal principle—the principle which as a matter of course gives the lord justiciary powers over his tenants—is of very ancient origin[2]. The state of things that then existed should be revealed to us by the Leges Henrici; for, if that book has any plan at all, it is a treatise on the law of jurisdiction, a treatise on 'soke.' To this topic the writer constantly returns after many digressions, and the leading theme of his work is found in the following sentence:—'As to the soke of pleas, there is that which belongs properly and exclusively to the royal fiscus; there is that which it participates with others; there is that which belongs to the sheriffs and royal bailiffs as comprised in their ferms; there is that which belongs to the barons who have soke and sake[3].' But, when all has been said, the picture that is left on our minds is that of a confused conflict between inconsistent and indefinite principles, and very possibly the compiler in giving us such a picture is fulfilling the duty of a faithful portrayer of facts, though he does not satisfy our demand for a rational theory.

---

[1] Hist. Eng. Law, i. 558. The terms here used were adopted when the Introduction to the Selden Society's Select Pleas in Manorial Courts (1888) was being written. M. Esmein in his Cours d'histoire du droit français, ed. 2 (1895), p. 259, has insisted on the same distinction but has used other and perhaps apter terms. According to him 'la justice rendue par les seigneurs' (my seignorial justice) is either 'la justice seigneuriale' (my franchisal justice) or 'la justice féodale' (my feudal justice).

[2] See Liebermann, Leges Edwardi, p. 88.   [3] Leg. Hen. 9, § 9.

On the one hand, it seems plain that there is a seignorial justice which is not 'franchisal.' Certain persons have a certain 'soke' apart from any regalities which may have been expressly conceded to them by the king. But it is not clear that the legal basis of this soke is the simple feudal principle stated above, namely, that jurisdiction springs from the mere fact of tenure. An element of which we hear little in later days, is prominent in the Leges, the element of rank or personal status. ' The archbishops, bishops, earls and other 'powers' (*potestates*) have sake and soke, toll, team and infangenethef in their own lands[1].' Here the principle seems to be that men of a certain rank have certain jurisdictional powers, and the vague term *potestates* may include in this class all the king's barons. But then the freeholding *vavassores* have a certain jurisdiction, they have the pleas which concern *wer* and *wíte* (that is to say ' emendable' pleas) over their own men and their own property, and sometimes over another man's men who have been arrested or attached in the act of trespass[2]. Whatever else we may think of these *vavassores*, they are not barons and probably they are not immediate tenants of the king[3]. It is clear, however, that there may be a 'lord' with 'men' who yet has no sake or soke over them[4]. We are told indeed that every lord may summon his man to stand to right in his court, and that if the man be resident in the remotest manor of the honour of which he holds, he still must go to the plea[5]. Here for a moment we seem to have a fairly clear announcement of what we call the simple feudal principle, unadulterated by any element of personal rank; still our text supposes that the lord in question is a great man, he has no mere manor but an honour or several honours. On the whole, our law seems for the time to be taking the shape that French law took. If we leave out of sight the definitely granted franchisal powers, then we may say that a baron or the holder of a grand fief has ' high justice,' or if that term be too technical, a higher justice, while the vavassor has ' low justice ' or a lower justice. But in this province, as in other provinces, of English law personal rank becomes of less and less importance. The rules which would determine it and its consequences are never allowed to become definite, and in the end a great

[1] Leg. Henr. 20 § 2.
[2] Leg. Henr. 27.
[3] Hist. Eng. Law, i. 532.
[4] Leg. Henr. 57 § 8. Cf. 59 § 19.
[5] Leg. Henr. 55.

generalization surmounts all difficulties:—every lord has a certain civil justice over his tenants; whatsoever powers go beyond this, are franchises.

As to the sort of jurisdiction that a lord of our Leges has, we can make no statement in general terms. Such categories as 'civil' and 'criminal' are too modern for use. We must of course except the pleas of the crown, of which a long and ungeneralized list is set before us[1]. We must except the pleas of the church. We must except certain pleas which belong in part to the king and in part to the church[2]. Then we observe that the justice of an archbishop, bishop or earl, probably the justice of a baron also, extends as high as *infangenethef*, while that of a vavassor goes no higher than such offences as are emendable. The whole matter however is complicated by royal grants. The king may grant away a demesne manor and retain not only 'the exclusive soke' (i.e. the soke over the pleas of the crown), but also 'the common soke' in his hand[3], and a great man may by purchase acquire soke (for example, we may suppose, the hundredal soke) over lands that are not his own[4]. Then again, we may suspect that what is said of 'soke' in general does not apply to any jurisdiction that a lord may exercise over his *servi* and *villani*. As to the *servi*, very possibly the lord's right over them is still conceived as proprietary rather than jurisdictional, while for his *villani* (*serf* and *villein* are not yet convertible terms) the lord, whatever his rank may be, will probably hold a 'hallmoot[5]' and exercise that 'common soke' which does not infringe the royal preserves. On the whole, the law of the thirteenth century seems to evolve itself somewhat easily out of the law of these Leges, the process of development being threefold: (1) the lord's rank as bishop, abbot, earl, baron, becomes unimportant; (2) the element of tenure becomes all-important; the mere fact that the man holds land of the lord makes him the lord's justiciable; thus a generalization becomes possible which permits even so lowly a person as a burgess of Dunstable to hold a court for his tenants[6]; (3) the obsolescence of the old law of *wite* and *wer*, the growth

---

[1] Leg. Henr. 10 § 1.
[2] Leg. Henr. 11 § 1.　This explains the 'participatio' of 9 § 9.
[3] Leg. Henr. 19.　　　　　　　　[4] Leg. Henr. 20 § 2.
[5] Leg. Henr. 9 § 4; 20 § 2; 57 § 8; 78 § 2.
[6] Hist. Eng. Law, i. 574.

of the new law of felony, the emergence in Glanvill's book of the distinction between criminal and civil pleas as a grand primary distinction, the introduction of the specially royal processes of presentment and inquest, bring about a new apportionment of the field of justice and a rational demarcation of feudal from franchisal powers. Still when we see the lords, especially the prelates of the church, relying upon prescription for their choicest franchises[1], we may learn (if such a lesson be needed) that new theories could not master all the ancient facts.

Whether the Conqueror or either of his sons would have admitted that any justice could be done in England that was not his justice, we may fairly doubt. They issued numerous charters which had no other object than that of giving or confirming to the donees 'their sake and soke,' and, so far as we can see, there is no jurisdiction, at least none over free men, that is not accounted to be 'sake and soke.' Occasionally it is said that the donees are to have 'their court.' However far the feudalization of justice had gone either in Normandy or in England before the Conquest, the Conquest itself was likely to conceal from view the question whether or no all seignorial jurisdiction is delegated from above; for thenceforward every lay tenant in chief, as no mere matter of theory, but as a plain matter of fact, held his land by a title derived newly and immediately from the king. Thus it would be easy for the king to maintain that, if the lords exercised jurisdictional powers, they did so by virtue of his grant, an expressed grant or an implied grant. Gradually the process of subinfeudation would make the theoretical question prominent and pressing, for certainly the Norman nobles conceived that, even if their justice was delegated to them by the king, no rule of law prevented them from appointing sub-delegates. If they claimed to give away land, they claimed also to give away justice, and no earnest effort can have been made to prevent their doing this[2].

The Norman kings and private jurisdiction.

---

[1] Hist. Eng. Law, i. 571.

[2] See e.g. Geoffrey Clinton for Kenilworth, Monast. vi. 221: 'Concedo...ut habeant curiam suam...ita libere...sicut ego meam curiam...ex concessu regis melius et firmius habeo.' Robert of Ouilly for Osney, ibid. p. 251 : 'Volo...quod habeant curiam ipsorum liberam de suis hominibus de omnimodis transgressionibus et defaltis, et quieti sint tam ipsi quam eorum tenentes de omnimodis curiae meae sectis.'

Sake and soke in Domesday Book.

Returning from this brief digression, we must consider *sake* and *soke* as they are in Domesday Book. For a moment we will attend to the words themselves[1]. Of the two *soke* is by far the commoner; indeed we hardly ever find *sake* except in connexion with *soke*, and when we do, it seems just an equivalent for *soke*. We have but an alliterative jingle like 'judgment and justice[2].' Apparently it matters little or nothing whether we say of a lord that he has *soke*, or that he has *sake*, or that he has *soke* and *sake*. But not only is *soke* the commoner, it is also the wider word; we can not substitute *sake* for it in all contexts. Thus, for example, we say that a man renders *soke* to his lord or to his lord's manor; also we say that a piece of land is a *soke* of such and such a manor; no similar use is made of *sake*.

Meaning of *sake*.

Now as a matter of etymology *sake* seems the easier of the two words. It is the Anglo-Saxon *sacu*, the German *Sache*, a thing, a matter, and hence a 'matter' or 'cause' in the lawyer's sense of these terms, a 'matter' in dispute between litigants, a 'cause' before the court. It is still in use among us, for though we do not speak of a sake between two persons, we do speak of a man acting for another's sake, or for God's sake, or for the sake of money[3]. In Latin therefore *sake* may be rendered by *placitum*:—'Roger has sake over them' will become 'Rogerius habet placita super eos[4]'; Roger has the right to hold plea over them. Thus easily enough *sake* becomes the right to have a court and to do justice.

Meaning of *soke*.

As to *soke*, this has a very similar signification, but the route by which it attains that signification is somewhat doubtful. We must start with this that *soke*, *socna*, *soca*, is the Anglo-Saxon *sócn* and has for its primary meaning a *seeking*. It may become connected with justice or jurisdiction by one or by both of two ways. One of these is explained by a passage

---

[1] See Liebermann, Leg. Edw. p. 91.

[2] Thus in D. B. ii. 409 we find two successive entries, the 'in *saca* regis et comitis' of the one, being to all seeming an equivalent for the 'in *soca* regis et comitis' of the other. D. B. ii. 416: 'de omnibus habuit antecessor Rannulfi commendationem et *sacam* excepto uno qui est in *soca* S. Edmundi.' Ibid. ii. 391 b: 'liberi homines Wisgari cum *saca*...liber homo...sub Witgaro cum *soca*.' In the Inquisitio Eliensis (e.g. Hamilton, p. 109) *saca* is sometimes used instead of *soca* in the common formula 'sed soca remansit abbati.' In D. B. ii. 264 b, a scribe having written 'sed habet sacam' has afterwards substituted an *o* for the *a*; we have noted no other instance of such care.

[3] Hist. Eng. Law, i. 566.   [4] D. B. i. 184, Ewias.

in the Leges Henrici which says that the king has certain causes or pleas 'in socna i.e. quaestione sua.' The king has certain pleas within his investigation, or his right to investigate. A later phrase may help us:—the king is entitled to 'inquire of, hear and determine' these matters[1]. But the word might journey along another path which would lead to much the same end. It means seeking, following, suing, making suit, *sequi*, *sectam facere*. The duty known as *soca faldae* is the duty of seeking the lord's fold. Thus *soca* may be the duty of seeking or suing at the lord's court and the correlative right of the lord to keep a court and exact suit. Without denying that the word has traversed the first of the two routes, the route by way of 'investigation'—in the face of the Leges Henrici we can hardly deny this—we may confidently assert that it has traversed the second, the route by way of 'suit.' There are several passages which assure us that *soke* is a genus of which *fold-soke* is a species. Thus:—'Of these men Peter's predecessor had fold-soke and commendation and Stigand had the other soke[2].' In a document which is very closely connected with the great survey we find what seems to be a Latin translation of our word. The churches of Worcester and Evesham were quarrelling about certain lands at Hamton. Under the eye of the king's commissioners they came to a compromise, which declared that the fifteen hides at Hamton belonged to the bishop of Worcester's hundred of Oswaldslaw and ought to pay the king's geld and perform the king's services along with the bishop and ought 'to seek the said hundred for pleading':—*requirere ad placitandum*, this is the main kind of 'seeking' that *soke* implies[3]. If we look back

---

[1] Leg. Henr. 20 § 1. The author of Leg. Edw. Conf., c. 22, also attempts to connect soke with seeking, but his words are exceedingly obscure: 'Soche est quod si aliquis quaerit aliquid in terra sua, etiam furtum, sua est iustitia, si inventum sit an non.' On the whole we take this nonsense to mean that my right of soke is my right to do justice in case any one seeks (by way of legal proceedings) anything in my land, even though the accusation that he brings be one of theft, and even though the stolen goods have not been found on the thief. Already the word is a prey to the etymologist.

[2] D. B. ii. 256.

[3] Heming Cart. i. 75–6: 'quod illae 15 hidae iuste pertinent ad Osuualdeslaue hundredum episcopi et debent cum ipso episcopo censum regis solvere et omnia alia servitia ad regem pertinentia et inde idem requirere ad placitandum.' Another account of the same transaction, ibid. 77, says 'et [episcopus] deraciocinavit socam et sacam de Hamtona ad suum hundred Osuualdeslauue quod ibi

far enough in the Anglo-Saxon dooms, there is indeed much to make us think that the act of seeking a lord and placing oneself under his protection, and the consequences of that act, the relation between man and lord, the fealty promised by the one, the warranty due from the other, have been known as *sócn*[1]. If so, then there may have been a time when commendation and soke were all one. But this time must be already ancient, for although we do not know what English word was represented by *commendatio*, still there is no distinction more emphatically drawn by Domesday Book than that between *commendatio* and *soca*.

Soke as jurisdiction. Now when we meet with *soca* in the Leges Henrici we naturally construe it by some such terms as 'jurisdiction,' 'justice,' 'the right to hold a court.' We have seen that the author of that treatise renders it by the Latin *quaestio*. We also meet the following phrases which seem clear enough:— 'Every cause shall be determined in the hundred, or in the county, or in the hallmoot of those who have soke, or in the courts of the lords[2]'; '...according to the soke of pleas, which some have in their own land over their own men, some over their own men and strangers, either in all causes or in some causes[3]':...'grithbrice or hámsócn or any of those matters which exceed their soke and sake[4]': 'in capital causes the soke is the king's[5].' So again our author explains that though a baron has soke this will not give him a right to justice over himself; no one, he says, can have his own forfeiture; no one has a soke of impunity:—'nullus enim socnam habet impune peccandi[6].' The use that Domesday Book makes of the word may not be quite so clear. Sometimes we are inclined to render it by *suit*, in particular when fold-soke is contrasted with 'other soke.' But very generally we must construe it by *justice* or by *justiciary*

debent placitare et geldum et expeditionem et cetera legis servitia de illis 15 hidis secum debent persolvere.'

[1] Schmid, Glossar. s. v. *sócen*. The word, it would seem, first makes its way into the vocabulary of the law as describing the act of seeking a sanctuary and the protection that a criminal gains by that act. A forged charter of Edgar for Thorney Abbey, Red Book of Thorney, Camb. Univ. Lib., f. 4, says that the word is a Danish word—'Regi vero pro consensu et eiusdem mercimonii licentia ac pro reatus emendatione quam Dani *socne* usitato nominant vocabulo, centum dedit splendidissimi auri mancusas.'

[2] Leg. Henr. 9 § 4. [3] Ibid. [4] Ibid. 22.
[5] Ibid. 20 § 3. [6] Ibid. 24.

rights, though we must be careful not to introduce the seignorial court where it does not exist, and to remember that a lord may be entitled to receive the wites or fines incurred by his criminous men without holding a court for them. Those men may be tried and condemned in a hundred court, but the wite will be paid to their lord. Then the word is applied to tracts of land. A tract over which a lord has justiciary power, or a wite-exacting power, is his *soke,* and very often his *soke* is contrasted with those other lands over which he has rights of a more definitely proprietary kind. But we must turn from words to law.

Already before the Conquest there was plenty of seignorial justice in England. The greatest of the Anglo-Saxon lords had enjoyed wide and high justiciary rights. Naturally it is of the rights of the churches that we hear most, for the rights that they had under King Edward they still claim under King William. Foremost among them we may notice the church of Canterbury. On the great day at Penenden Heath, Lanfranc proved that throughout the lands of his church in Kent the king had but three rights; all other justice was in the hands of the archbishop[1]. In Warwickshire the Archbishop of York has soke and sake, toll and team, church-scot and all other ' forfeitures' save those four which the king has throughout the whole realm[2]. These four forfeitures are probably the four reserved pleas of the crown that are mentioned in the laws of Cnut—*mundbryce, hámsócn, forsteal* and *fyrdwíte*[3]. But even these rights though usually reserved to the king may have been made over to the lord. In Yorkshire neither king nor earl has any ' custom' within the lands of S^t. Peter of York, S^t. John of Beverley, S^t. Wilfrid of Ripon, S^t. Cuthbert of Durham and the Holy Trinity. We are asked specially to note that in this region there are four royal highways, three by land and one by water where the king claims all forfeitures even when they run through the land of the archbishop or of the earl[4]. Within his immense manor of Taunton the Bishop

Seignorial justice before the Conquest.

[1] Selden's Eadmer, p. 197; Bigelow, Placita Anglo-Norman. p. 7.

[2] D. B. i. 238 b, Alvestone.

[3] Cnut, ii. 12. We may construe these terms by breach of the king's special peace, attacks on houses, ambush, neglect of the summons to the host. In Hereford, D. B. i. 179, the king is accounted to have three pleas, breach of his peace, hámfare, which is the same as hámsócn, and forsteal; and besides this he receives the penalty from a man who makes default in military service.

[4] D. B. i. 298 b.

of Winchester has pleas of the highest class, and three times a year without any summons his men must meet to hold them[1]. In Worcestershire seven of the twelve hundreds into which the county is divided are in the heads of four great churches; Worcester has three, Westminster two, Evesham one, Pershore one. Westminster holds its lands as freely as the king held them in his demesne; Pershore enjoys all the pleas of the free men; no sheriff can claim anything within the territory of S[t]. Mary of Worcester, neither in any plea, nor in any other matter[2]. In East Anglia we frequently hear of the reserved pleas of the crown. In this Danish district they are accounted to be six in number; probably they are *griðbrice, hámsócn, fihtwíte* and *fyrdwíte,* outlaw's-work and the receipt of outlaws[3]. Often we read how over the men of some lord the king and the earl have 'the six forfeitures,' or how 'the soke of the six forfeitures' lies in some royal manor[4]. But then there is a large tract in which these six forfeitures belong to S[t]. Edmund; some other lord may have sake and soke in a given parcel of that tract, but the six forfeitures belong to S[t]. Edmund; they are indeed 'the six forfeitures of S[t]. Edmund[5].' Other arrangements were possible. We hear of men over whom S[t]. Benet had three forfeitures[6]. The lawmen of Stamford had

---

[1] D. B. i. 87 b: 'Istae consuetudines pertinent ad Tantone, burgheristh, latrones, pacis infractio, hainfare, denarii de hundret, et denarii S. Petri; ter in anno teneri placita episcopi sine ammonitione; profectio in exercitum cum hominibus episcopi.' See also the English document, Kemble, Cod. Dipl. iv. p. 233. The odd word *burgheristh* looks like a corrupt form of *burhgrið* (the peace of the *burh*), or of *burhgerihta* (burh-rights, borough-dues), which word occurs in the English document.

[2] D. B. i. 172, 175.

[3] Cnut ii. 12, 13, 14. Perhaps when in other parts of England the pleas of the crown are reckoned to be but four, it is treated as self-evident that the outlaw falls into the king's hand, as also the man who harbours an outlaw. If *fihtwíte* is the right word, we must suppose with Schmid (p. 586) that a *fihtwíte* was only paid when there was homicide. A fine for mere fighting or drawing blood would not have been a reserved plea.

[4] D. B. ii. 179 b: 'Et iste Withri habebat sacham et socam super istam terram et rex et comes 6 forisfacturas.' Ibid. 223: 'In Cheiunchala soca de 6 forisfacturis.'

[5] D. B. ii. 413 b: 'socam et sacam praeter 6 forisfacturas S. Eadmundi.' Ibid. 373: 'S. Eadmundus 6 forisfacturas.' Ibid. 384 b: 'Tota hec terra iacebat in dominio Abbatiae [de Eli] T. R. E. cum omni consuetudine praeter sex forisfacturas S. Eadmundi.'

[6] D. B. ii. 244: 'sex liberi homines...ex his habet S. Benedictus socam et de uno commendationem et de 24 tres forisfacturas.'

sake and soke within their houses and over their men, save geld, heriot, larceny and forfeitures exceeding 40 ores of silver[1]. Certain burgesses of Romney serve the king on the sea, and therefore they have their own forfeitures, save larceny, peace-breach and forsteal, and these belong, not to the king, but to the archbishop[2]. Sometimes King William will be careful to limit his confirmation of a lord's sake and soke to the 'emendable forfeitures,' the offences which can be paid for with money[3].

That in the Confessor's day justiciary rights could only be claimed by virtue of royal grants, that they did not arise out of the mere relation between lord and man, lord and tenant, or lord and villein, seems to us fairly certain. In the first place, as already said, soke is frequently contrasted with com-mendation. In the second place, as we turn over the pages of our record, we shall see it remarked of some man, who held a manor in the days before the Conquest, that he had it with sake and soke, and the remark is made in such a context that thereby he is singled out from among his fellows[4]. Thus it is said of a little group of villeins and sokemen in Essex that 'their lord had sake and soke[5].' Not that we can argue that a lord has no soke unless it is expressly ascribed to him. The surveyors have no great interest in this matter. Some-times such a phrase as 'he held it freely' seems to serve as an equivalent for 'he held it with sake and soke[6].' It is said of the Countess Judith, a lady of exalted rank, that she had a manse in Lincoln without sake and soke[7]. Then we are told that throughout the city of Canterbury the king had sake and soke except in the lands of the Holy Trinity (Christ Church), S[t]. Augustin, Queen Edith, and three other lords[8]. We have a list of fifteen persons who had sake and

Soke as a regality.

---

[1] D. B. i. 336 b: 'praeter geld et heriete et forisfacturam corporum suorum de 40 oris argenti et praeter latronem.' Such a phrase as 'geld, heriot and thief' is instructive.

[2] D. B. i. 4 b.

[3] William I. for Ely, Hamilton, Inquisitio, p. xviii.: 'omnes alias forisfacturas quae emendabiles sunt.'

[4] D. B. ii. 195: 'Super hos habuit T. R. E. Episcopus 6 forisfacturas sed hundret nec vidit breve nec sigillum nec concessum Regis.'

[5] D. B. ii. 34 b.   [6] See e.g. D. B. i. 220.

[7] D. B. i. 336: 'Rogerius de Busli habet unum mansum Sueni filii Suaue cum saca et soca. Judita comitissa habet unum mansum Stori sine saca et soca.'

[8] D. B. i. 2.

soke in the two lathes of Sutton and Aylesford[1], a list of thirty-five persons who had sake and soke, toll and team in Lincolnshire (it includes the queen, a bishop, three abbots and two earls[2]), and a list of nineteen persons who had similar rights in the shires of Derby and Nottingham[3]. Such lists would have been pointless had any generalization been possible. Then in East Anglia it is common enough to find that the men who are reckoned to be the *liberi homines* of some lord are under the soke of another lord or render their soke to the king and the earl, that is to say, to the hundred court. Often enough it is said somewhat pointedly that the men over whom the king and the earl have soke are *liberi homines,* and this may for a moment suggest that the lord as a matter of course has soke over such of his men as are not ranked as 'free men'; possibly it may suggest that freedom in this context implies subjection to a national as opposed to a seignorial tribunal[4]. But on the one hand a lord often enough has soke over those who are distinctively 'free men[5],' while on the other hand, as will be explained below, he has not the soke over his sokeman[6].

Soke over villeins.

But we must go further and say that the lord has not always the soke over his villeins. This is a matter of much importance. An entry relating to a manor in Suffolk seems to put it beyond doubt:—In the hundred and a half of Sanford Auti a thegn held Wenham in King Edward's time for a manor and three carucates of land; there were then nine *villani,* four *bordarii* and one *servus* and there were two teams on the demesne; Auti had the soke over his demesne and the soke of the villeins was in Bercolt[7]. Now Bercolt, the modern Bergholt, was a royal manor, the seat of a great court, which had soke over many men in the neighbouring villages. To all seeming it was the court for the hundred, or 'hundred-and-a-half,' of

---

[1] D. B. i. 1 b.   [2] D. B. i. 337.   [3] D. B. i. 280 b.

[4] D. B. ii. 185: 'Super omnes liberos istius hundreti [de Northerpingeham] habet Rex sacam et socam.' Ibid. 188 b: 'Rex et comes de omnibus istis liberis hominibus socam.' Ibid. 203: 'Et de omnibus his liberis [Episcopi Osberni] soca in hundreto.'

[5] D. B. ii. 210: 'Super omnes istos liberos homines habuit Rex Eadwardus socam et sacam, et postea Guert accepit per vim, sed Rex Willelmus dedit [S. Eadmundo] cum manerio socam et sacam de omnibus liberis Guert sicut ipse tenebat; hoc reclamant monachi.'

[6] Below, p. 105.   [7] D. B. ii. 425 b.

Sanford[1]. Here then we seem to have villeins who are not under the soke of their lord but are the justiciables of the hundred court. In another case, also from Suffolk, it is said of the lord of a manor that he had soke ' only over the demesne of his hall,' and this seems to exclude from the scope of his justiciary rights the land held by thirty-two villeins and eight bordiers[2]. We may find the line drawn at various places. Not very unfrequently in East Anglia a lord has the soke over those men who are bound to his sheep-fold, while those who are 'fold-worthy' attend the hundred court[3]. In one case a curious and instructive distinction is taken :—'In Farwell lay in King Edward's day the sake and soke of all who had less than thirty acres, but of all who had thirty acres the soke and sake lay in the hundred[4].' In this case the line seems to be drawn just below the virgater, no matter the legal class to which the virgater belongs. To our thinking it is plain enough that many a *manerium* of the Confessor's day had no court of its own. As we shall see hereafter, the manors are often far too small to allow of our endowing each of them with a court. When of a Cheshire manor we hear that 'this manor has its pleas in its lord's hall' we are being told of something that is exceptional[5]. In the thirteenth century no one would have made such a remark. In the eleventh the *halimote* or *hall-moot* looks like a novelty.

Seignorial justice is as yet very closely connected with the general scheme of national justice. Frequently the lord

Private soke and hundredal soke.

[1] D. B. ii. 287, 287 b: 'Sanfort Hund. et dim....Supradictum manerium scilicet Bercolt...cum soca de hundreto et dimidio reddebat T. R. E. 24 lib.' On subsequent pages it is often said that the soke of certain persons or lands is in Bergholt.

[2] D. B. ii. 408 b: 'Hagala tenuit Gutmundus sub Rege Edwardo pro manerio 8 car[ucatarum] terrae cum soca et saca super dominium hallae tantum. Tunc 32 villani...8 bordarii...10 servi. Semper 4 carucae in dominio. Tunc et post 24 carucae hominum....Sex sochemanni eiusdem Gutmundi de quibus soca est in hundreto.'

[3] D. B. ii. 216: 'De Redeham habebat Abbas socam super hos qui sequebantur faldam, et de aliis soca in hundreto.' Ibid. 129 b: 'Super omnes istos qui faldam Comitis requirebant habebat Comes socam et sacam, super alios omnes Rex et Comes.' Ibid. 194 b: 'In Begetuna tenuit Episcopus Almarus per emptionem T. R. E. cum soca et saca de Comite Algaro de bor[dariis] et sequentibus faldam 3 carucatas terrae.' Ibid. 350 b: 'habebat socam et sacam super hallam et bordarios.'

[4] D. B. ii. 130 b.

[5] D. B. i. 265 b: 'Hoc manerium habet suum placitum in aula domini sui.'

who has justice has a hundred. We remember how seven
of the twelve hundreds of Worcestershire are in the hands of
four great churches[1]. S[t]. Etheldreda of Ely has the soke of
five and a half hundreds in Suffolk[2]. In Essex Swain had
the half-hundred of Clavering, and the pleas thereof brought
him in 25s. a year[3]. In Nottinghamshire the Bishop of
Lincoln had all the customs of the king and the earl throughout
the wapentake of Newark[4]. The monks of Battle Abbey
claimed that the sake and soke of twenty-two hundreds and
a half and all royal 'forfeitures' were annexed to their manor
of Wye[5]. But further—and this deserves attention—when the
hundredal jurisdiction was not in the hands of some other
lord, it was conceived as belonging to the king. The sake
and soke of a hundred or of several hundreds is described as
'lying in,' or being annexed to, some royal manor and it
is farmed by the farmer of that manor. Oxfordshire gives
us the best example of this. The soke of four and a half
hundreds belongs to the royal manor of Bensington, that of
two hundreds to Headington, that of two and a half to Kirt-
lington, that of three to Upton, that of three to Shipton, that
of two to Bampton, that of two to Bloxham and Adderbury[6].
What we see here we may see elsewhere also[7]. If then King
William gives the royal manor of Wye to his newly founded
church of S[t]. Martin in the Place of Battle, the monks will
contend that they have obtained as an appurtenance the
hundredal soke over a large part of the county of Kent[8].

Hundredal and mano- rial soke. The law seems as yet, if we may so speak, unconscious
of the fact that underneath or beside the hundredal soke a
new soke is growing up. It seems to treat *the* soke over a
man or over a piece of land as an indivisible thing that must
'lie' somewhere and can not be in two places at once. It has

---

[1] Above, p. 88. [2] D. B. ii. 385 b.
[3] D. B. ii. 46 b. [4] D. B. i. 283 b.
[5] D. B. i. 11 b; Chron. de Bello (Anglia Christiana Soc.) p. 28; Battle
Custumals (Camd. Soc.), p. 126.
[6] D. B. i. 154 b.
[7] D. B. 39 b, Hants: 'Huic manerio pertinet soca duorum hundredorum.'
Ibid. 64 b, Wilts: 'In hac firma erant placita hundretorum de Cicementone et
Sutelesberg quae regi pertinebant.' Ibid. ii. 185: 'Super omnes liberos istius
hundreti habet rex sacam et socam.' Ibid. ii. 113 b: 'Soca et sacha de
Grenehou hundreto pertinet ad Wistune manerium Regis, quicunque ibi
teneat, et habent Rex et Comes.'
[8] See above, note 5.

indeed to admit that while one lord has the soke, the king or another lord may have certain reserved and exalted 'forfeitures,' the three forfeitures or the four or the six, as the case may be[1]; but it has no classification of courts. The lord's court, if it be not the court of an ancient hundred, is conceived as the court of a half-hundred, or of a quarter of a hundred[2], or as the court of a district that has been carved out from a hundred[3]. Thus Stigand had the soke of the half-hundred of Hersham, save Thorpe which belonged to S[t]. Edmund, and Pulham which belonged to S[t]. Etheldreda[4]; thus also the king had the soke of the half-hundred of Diss, except the land of S[t]. Edmund, where he shared the soke with the saint, and except the lands of Wulfgæt and of Stigand[5]. But it is impossible to maintain this theory. The hundred is becoming full of manors, within each of which a lord is exercising or endeavouring to exercise a soke over all, or certain classes, of his men. It is possible that in Lincolnshire we see the beginnings of a differentiating process; we meet with the word *frisoca, frigsoca, frigesoca.* Whether this stands for 'free soken,' or, as seems more likely, for 'fri∂ soken,' soke in matters relating to the peace, it seems to mark off one kind of soke from other kinds[6]. We have to remember that in later days the relation of the manorial to the hundredal courts is curious. In no accurate sense can we say that the court of the manor is below the court of the hundred. No appeal, no complaint of false judgment, lies from the one to the other; and yet, unless the manor enjoys some exceptional privilege, it is not extra-hundredal and its jurisdiction in personal causes is over-lapped by the jurisdiction of the hundred court: the two courts arise from different principles[7]. In Domesday Book the feudal or tenurial principle

---

[1] Above, p. 88.

[2] D. B. ii. 379: 'Super ferting de Almeham habet W. Episcopus socam et sacam.'

[3] D. B. i. 184: 'Haec terra non pertinet...ad hundredum. De hac terra habet Rogerius 15 sextarios mellis et 15 porcos quando homines sunt ibi et placita super eos.'

[4] D. B. ii. 139 b.   [5] D. B. ii. 114.

[6] D. B. i. 340, 346, 357 b, 366, 368 b (ter). See also on f. 344, 344 b, the symbol fð in the margin. The word *friðsócn* occurs in Æthelr. viii. 1 and Cnut i. 2 § 3, where it seems to stand for a sanctuary, an asylum.

[7] If one of *A*'s tenants is sued in a personal action in the hundred court he will have to answer there unless *A* appears and 'claims his court.' This comes out plainly in certain rolls of the court of Wisbeach Hundred, which by the kind

seems still struggling for recognition. Already the Norman lords are assuming a soke which their *antecessores* did not enjoy[1]. As will be seen below, they are enlarging and consolidating their manors and thereby rendering a manorial justice possible and profitable. Whether we ought to hold that the mere shock and jar of conquest and dispossession was sufficient to set up the process which covered our land with small courts, or whether we ought to hold that an element of foreign law worked the change, is a question that will never be answered unless the Norman archives have yet many secrets to tell. The great 'honorial' courts of later days may be French; still it is hardly in this region that we should look for much foreign law. It is in English words that the French baron of the Conqueror's day must speak when he claims justiciary rights. But that the process was far from being complete in 1086 seems evident.

The seignorial court.

Many questions about the distribution and the constitution of the courts we must leave unsolved. Not only does our record tell us nothing of courts in unambiguous words, but it hardly has a word that will answer to our 'court.' The term *curia* is in use, but it seems always to signify a physical object, the lord's house or the court-yard around it, never an institution, a tribunal[2]. Almost all that we are told is conveyed to us under the cover of such words as *sake, soke, placita, forisfacturae.* We know that the Bishop of Winchester has a court at Taunton, for his tenants are bound to come together thrice

---

permission of the Bishop of Ely, I have examined. On a roll of 33 Edw. I. we find Stephen Hamond sued for a debt; 'et super hoc venit Prior Elyensis et petit curiam suam; et Thomas Doreward petit curiam suam de dicto Stephano residente suo et tenente suo.' The prior's petition is refused on the ground that Stephen is not his tenant, and Doreward's petition is refused on the ground that it is unprecedented.

[1] D. B. ii. 291: 'Et fuit in soca Regis. Postquam Briennus habuit, nullam consuetudinem reddidit in hundreto.' Ibid. 240: 'Hoc totum tenuit Lisius pro uno manerio; modo tenet Eudo successor illius et in T. R. E. soca et saca fuit in hundreto; set modo tenet Eudo.'—Ibid. 240 b: 'Soca istius terre T. R. E. iacuit in Folsa Regis; modo habet Walterius [Giffardus].'—Ibid. 285 b: the hundred testified that in truth the King and Earl had the soke and sake in the Confessor's day, but the men of the vill say that Burchard likewise (*similiter*) had the soke of his free men as well as of his villeins.

[2] D. B. i. 35 b: 'Duo fratres tenuerunt T. R. E.; unusquisque habuit domum suam et tamen manserunt in una curia.' Ibid. 103 b: 'Ibi molendinum serviens curiae.' Ibid. 163: 'arabant et herciabant ad curiam domini.'

a year to hold his pleas without being summoned[1]. This phrase—'to hold his pleas'—seems to tell us distinctly enough that the suitors are the doomsmen of the court. Then, again, we have the well-known story of what happened at Orwell in Cambridgeshire. In that village Count Roger had a small estate; he had land for a team and a half. This land had belonged to six sokemen. He had borrowed three of them from Picot the sheriff in order that they might hold his pleas, and having got them he refused to return them[2]. That the court that he wished to hold was a court merely for his land at Orwell is highly improbable, but he had other lands scattered about in the various villages of the Wetherly hundred, though in all his tenants amounted to but 14 villeins, 42 bordiers, 15 cottiers, and 4 serfs. We can not draw the inference that men of the class known as sokemen were necessary for the constitution of a court, for at the date of the survey there was no sokeman left in all Roger's land in Cambridgeshire; the three that he borrowed from Picot had disappeared or were reckoned as villeins or worse. Still he held a court and that court had doomsmen. But we can not argue that every lord who had soke, or sake and soke, had a court of his own. It may be that in some cases he was satisfied with claiming the 'forfeitures' which his men incurred in the hundred courts. This is suggested to us by what we read of the earl's third penny.

In the county court and in every hundred court that has not passed into private hands, the king is entitled to but two-thirds of the proceeds of justice and the earl gets the other third, except perhaps in certain exceptional cases in which the king has the whole profit of some specially royal plea. The soke in the hundred courts belongs to the king and the earl. And just as the king's rights as the lord of a hundredal court become bound up with, and are let to farm with, some royal manor, so the earl's third penny will be annexed to some comital manor. Thus the third penny of Dorsetshire was annexed to Earl Harold's manor of Pireton[3], and the third penny of Warwickshire to Earl Edwin's manor of Cote[4]. Harold had a manor in Herefordshire to which belonged the third penny

Soke and the earl's third penny.

---

[1] D. B. i. 87 b. Kemble, Cod. Dip., iv. p. 233: 'and þriwa secan gemot on 12 monðum.'

[2] D. B. i. 193 b; Hamilton, Inquisitio, 77–8.

[3] D. B. i. 75.   [4] D. B. i. 238.

of three hundreds[1]; Godwin had a manor in Hampshire to which belonged the third penny of six hundreds[2]; the third penny of three Devonian hundreds belonged to the manor of Blackpool[3]. Now, at least in some cases, the king could not by his grants deprive the earl of his right; the grantee of soke had to take it subject to the earl's third penny. Thus for the shires of Derby and Nottingham we have a list of nineteen persons who were entitled to the king's two-pence, but only three of them were entitled to the earl's penny[4]. The monks of Battle declared that throughout many hundreds in Kent they were entitled to 'the king's two-pence'; the earl's third penny belonged to Odo of Bayeux[5]. And so of certain 'free men' in Norfolk it is said that 'their soke is in the hundred for the third penny[6].' A man commits an offence; he incurs a *wíte*; two-thirds of it should go to his lord; one-third to the earl: in what court should he be tried? The answer that Domesday Book suggests by its silence is that this is a matter of indifference; it does not care to distinguish between the right to hold a court and the right to take the profits of justice. Just once the veil is raised for a moment. In Suffolk lies the hundred of Blything; its head is the vill of Blythburgh where there is a royal manor[7]. Within that hundred lies the considerable town of Dunwich, which Edric holds as a manor. Now in Dunwich the king has this custom that two or three men shall go to the hundred court if they be duly summoned, and if they make default they shall pay a fine of two ores, and if a thief be caught there he shall be judged there and corporeal justice shall be done in Blythburgh and the lord of Dunwich shall have the thief's chattels. Apparently in this case the lord of Dunwich will see to the trying but not to the hanging of the thief; but, at any rate, a rare effort is here made to define how justice shall be done[8]. The rarity

---

[1] D. B. i. 186.   [2] D. B. i. 38 b.   [3] D. B. i. 101.

[4] D. B. i. 280 b: 'Hic notantur qui habuerunt socam et sacam et thol et thaim et consuetudinem Regis 2 denariorum....Horum omnium nemo habere potuit tercium denarium comitis nisi eius concessu et hoc quamdiu viveret, preter Archiepiscopum et Ulf Fenisc et Godeue Comitissam.'

[5] See above, p. 92, note 5.

[6] D. B. ii. 123 b: ' De istis est soca in hundreto ad tercium denarium.'

[7] D. B. ii. 282.

[8] D. B. ii. 312: 'Rex habet in Duneuuic consuetudinem hanc quod duo vel tres ibunt ad hundret si recte moniti fuerint, et si hoc non faciunt, forisfacti

of such efforts is very significant. Of course Domesday Book is not a treatise on jurisdiction; still if there were other terms in use, we should not be for ever put off with the vague, undifferentiated *soke*. On the whole, we take it that the lord who enjoyed soke had a right to keep a court if he chose to do so, and that generally he did this, though he would be far from keeping a separate court for each of his little manors; but if his possessions were small he may have contented himself with attending the hundred court and claiming the fines incurred by his men. Sometimes a lord seems to have soke only over his own demesne lands[1]; in this case the wites that will come to him will be few. We may in later times see some curious compromises. If a thief is caught on the land of the Prior of Canterbury at Brook in Kent, the borhs-elder and frank-pledges of Brook are to take him to the court of the hundred of Wye, which belongs to the Abbot of Battle. Then, if he is not one of the Prior's men, he will be judged by the hundred. But if he is the Prior's man, then the bailiff of Brook will ' crave the Prior's court.' The Prior's folk will then go apart and judge the accused, a few of the hundredors going with them to act as assessors. If the tribunal thus constituted cannot agree, then once more the accused will be brought back into the hundred and will there be judged by the hundredors in common. In this instance we see that even in Henry II.'s day the Prior has not thoroughly extricated his court from the hundred moot[2].

It seems possible that a further hint as to the history of soke is given us by certain entries relating to the boroughs. It will already have become apparent that if there is soke over men, there is also soke over land: if men ' render soke ' so also acres ' render soke.' We can see that a very elaborate web of rules is thus woven. One man strikes another. Before

Soke and house-peace.

sunt de 2 oris, et si latro *ibi* fuerit captus *ibi* judicabitur, et corporalis iusticia in Blieburc capietur, et sua pecunia remanebit dominio de Duneuuic.' It seems to us that the first *ibi* must refer to Dunwich and therefore that the second does so likewise. Still the passage is ambiguous enough.

[1] See above, p. 91.

[2] Battle Custumals (Camden Soc.) 136. This is an interesting example, for it suggests an explanation of the common claim to hold a court ' outside' the hundred court (*petit curiam suam extra hundredum*). The claimant's men will go apart and hold a little court by themselves outside ' the four benches ' of the hundred.

M.

we can tell what the striker ought to pay and to whom he ought to pay it, we ought to know who had soke over the striker, over the stricken, over the spot where the blow was given, over the spot where the offender was attached or arrested or accused. 'The men of Southwark testify that in King Edward's time no one took toll on the strand or in the water-street save the king, and if any one in the act of committing an offence was there challenged, he paid the amends to the king, but if without being challenged he escaped under a man who had sake and soke, that man had the amends[1].' Then we read how at Wallingford certain owners of houses enjoyed 'the gafol of their houses, and blood, if blood was shed there and the man was received inside before he was challenged by the king's reeve, except on Saturday, for then the king had the forfeiture on account of the market; and for adultery and larceny they had the forfeiture in their houses, but the other forfeitures were the king's[2].' We can not hope to recover the intricate rules which governed these affairs, rules which must have been as intricate as those of our 'private international law.' But the description of Wallingford tells us of householders who enjoy the 'forfeitures' which arise from crimes committed in their own houses, and a suspicion may cross our minds that the right to these forfeitures is not in its origin a purely jurisdictional or justiciary right. However, these householders are great people (the Bishop of Salisbury, the Abbot of St Albans are among them), their town houses are considered as appurtenant to their rural manors and the soke over the manor comprehends the town house. And so when we read how the twelve lawmen of Stamford had sake and soke within their houses and over their own men 'save geld, and heriot, and corporeal forfeitures to the amount of 40 ores of silver and larceny' we may be reading of rights which can properly be described as justiciary[3].

Soke in houses.

But a much more difficult case comes before us at Warwick[4]. We first hear of the town houses that are held by great men as parts of their manors, and then we hear that 'besides these

---

[1] D. B. i. 32 : 'et si quis forisfaciens ibi calumpniatus fuisset, Regi emendabat; si vero non calumpniatus abisset sub eo qui sacam et socam habuisset, ille emendam de reo haberet.' Compare with this the account of Guildford, Ibid. 30.

[2] D. B. i. 56 b.   [3] D. B. i. 336 b.   [4] D. B. i. 238.

houses there are in the borough nineteen burgesses who have
nineteen houses with sake and soke and all customs.' Now
we can not easily believe that the burgess's house is a jurisdictional area, or that in exacting a mulct from one who
commits a crime in that house the burgess will be playing the
magistrate or exercising a right to do justice or take the
profits of justice by virtue of a grant made to him by the
king. Rather we are likely to see here a relic of the ancient
'house-peace[1].' If you commit an act of violence in a man's
house, whatever you may have to pay to the person whom
you strike and to the king, you will also have to make
amends to the owner of the house, even though he be but
a ceorl or a boor, for you have broken his peace[2]. The right
of the burgess to exact a mulct from one who has shed blood
or committed adultery within his walls may in truth be a
right of this kind, and yet, like other rights to other mulcts,
it is now conceived as an emanation of sake and soke. If
in the eleventh century we hear but little of this householder's
right, may this not be because the householder has surrendered
it to his lord, or the lord has usurped it from the householder,
and thus it has gone to swell the mass of the lord's jurisdictional rights? At Broughton in Huntingdonshire the Abbot
of Ramsey has a manor with some sokemen upon it 'and
these sokemen say that they used to have legerwite (fornication-
fine), bloodwite and larceny up to fourpence, and above fourpence the Abbot had the forfeiture of larceny[3].' Various
interpretations may be set upon this difficult passage. We
may fashion for ourselves a village court (though there are
but ten sokemen) and suppose that the commune of sokemen
enjoyed the smaller fines incurred by any of its members. But
we are inclined to connect this entry with those relating to
Wallingford and to Warwick and to believe that each sokeman
has enjoyed a right to exact a sum of money for the breach
of his peace. The law does not clearly mark off the right of
the injured housefather from the right of the offended magistrate. How could it do so? If you commit an act of violence

---

[1] The passages from the dooms are collected by Schmid s. v. *Hausfriede*,
Feohtan.

[2] Ine, 6 § 3 : 'If he fight in the house of a gavel-payer or boor, let him give
30 shillings by way of wite and 6 shillings to the boor.'

[3] D. B. i. 204.

you must pay a wite to the king. Why so? Because you
have wronged the king by breaking his peace and he requires
'amends' from you. With this thought in our minds we may
now approach an obscure problem.

Vendible soke. We have said that seignorial justice is regarded as having
its origin in royal grants, and in the main this seems true. We
hardly state an exception to this rule if we say that grantees
of justice become in their turn grantors. Not merely could
the earl who had soke grant this to one of his thegns, but
that thegn would be said to hold the soke 'under' or 'of' the
earl. Justice, we may say, was already being subinfeudated[1].
But now and again we meet with much more startling statements. Usually if a man over whom his lord has soke 'withdraws himself with his land,' or 'goes elsewhere with his land,'
the lord's soke over that land 'remains': he still has jurisdictional rights over that land though it is commended to a
new lord. We may be surprised at being very frequently told
that this is the case, for we can hardly imagine a man having
power to take his land out of one sphere of justice and to
put it into another. But that some men, and they not men
of high rank, enjoyed this power seems probable. Of a
Hertfordshire manor we read: 'In this manor there were six
sokemen, men of Archbishop Stigand, and each had one hide,
and they could sell, saving the soke, and one of them could
even sell his soke with the land[2].' This case may be exceptional; there may have been a very unusual compact
between the archbishop and this egregiously free sokeman;
but the frequency with which we are told that on a sale the
soke 'remains' does not favour this supposition.

Soke and mund. We seem driven to the conclusion that in some parts of the
country the practice of commendation had been allowed to

[1] D. B. ii. 419 b: 'Cercesfort tenuit Scapius teinnus Haroldi....Scapius
habuit socam sub Haroldo.'—Ibid. 313: 'Heroldus socam habuit et Stanuuinus
de eo....Idem Stanuuinus socam habuit de Heroldo.'
[2] D. B. i. 142 b: 'et vendere potuerunt praeter socam; unus autem eorum
etiam socam suam cum terra vendere poterat.' Comp. D. B. ii. 230: 'Huic
manerio iacent 5 liberi homines ad socam tantum commend[ati] et 2 de omni
consuetudine.'—Ibid. ii. 59: 'In Cingeham tenuit Sauinus presbyter 15 acras...
in eadem villa tenuit Etsinus 15 acras....Isti supradicti fuerunt liberi ita quod
ipsi possent vendere terram cum soca et saca ut hundretus testatur.'—Ibid. ii.
40 b: 'et iste fuit ita liber quod posset ire quo vellet cum soca et sacha set
tantum fuit homo Wisgari.'

interfere even with jurisdictional relationships : that there were men who could 'go with their land to what lord they chose' and carry with them not merely their homage, but also their suit of court and their 'forfeitures.' This may seem to us intolerable. If it be true, it tells us that the state has been very weak ; it tells us that the national scheme of justice has been torn to shreds by free contract, that men have had the utmost difficulty in distinguishing between property and political power, between personal relationships and the magistracy to which land is subject. But unless we are mistaken, the house-peace in its decay has helped to produce this confusion. In a certain sense a mere ceorl has had what is now called a soke,—it used to be called a *mund* or *griδ*—over his house and over his loaf-eaters : that is to say, he has been entitled to have money paid to him if his house-peace were broken or his loaf-eaters beaten. This right he has been able to transfer to a lord. In one way or another it has now come into the lord's hand and become mixed up with other rights. In Henry I.'s day a lawyer will be explaining that if a villein receives money when blood is shed or fornication is committed in his house, this is because he has purchased these forfeitures from his lord[1]. This reverses the order of history.

Such is the best explanation that we can give of the men who sell their soke with their land. No doubt we are accusing Domesday Book of being very obscure, of using a single word to express some three or four different ideas. In some degree the obscurity may be due to the fact that French justiciars and French clerks have become the exponents of English law. But we may gravely doubt whether Englishmen would have produced a result more intelligible to us. One cause of difficulty we may perhaps remove. In accordance with common wont we have from time to time spoken of seignorial jurisdiction. But if the word *jurisdiction* be strictly construed, then in all likelihood there never has been in this country any seignorial jurisdiction. It is not the part of the lord to declare the law (*ius dicere*); 'curia domini debet facere iudicia et non dominus[2].' From

Soke and jurisdiction.

---

[1] Leg. Henr. 81 § 3 : 'Quidam, villani qui sunt, eiusmodi leierwitam et blodwitam et huiusmodi minora forisfacta emerunt a dominis suis, vel quomodo meruerunt, de suis et in suos, quorum flet-gefoth vel overseunessa est 30 den. ; cothseti 15 den. ; servi 6 (*al.* 5) den.' The *flet-gefoth* seems to be the sum due for fighting in a man's *flet* or house.

[2] Munimenta Gildhallae, i. 66.

first to last this seems to be so, unless we take account of theories that come to us from a time when the lord's court was fast becoming an obsolete institution[1]. So it is in Domesday Book. In the hundred court the sheriff presides; it is he that appoints a day for the litigation, but the men of the hundred, the men who come together 'to give and receive right,' make the judgments[2]. The tenants of the Bishop of Winchester 'hold the bishops' pleas' at Taunton; Earl Roger borrows sokemen 'to hold his pleas[3].' Thus the erection of a new court is no very revolutionary proceeding; it passes unnoticed. If once it be granted that all the justiciary profits arising from a certain group of men or tract of land are to go to a certain lord, it is very much a matter of indifference to kings and sheriffs whether the lord holds a court of his own or exacts this money in the hundred court. Indeed, a sheriff may be inclined to say 'I am not going to do your justice for nothing; do it yourself.' So long as every lord will come to the hundred court himself or send his steward, the sheriff will have no lack of capable dooms-men. Then the men of the lord's precinct may well wish for a court at their doors; they will be spared the long journey to the hundred court; they will settle their own affairs and be a law unto themselves. Thus we ought not to say that the lax use of the word *soke* covers a confusion between 'jurisdiction' and the profits of 'jurisdiction,' and if we say that the confusion is between justice and the profits of justice, we are pointing to a distinction which the men of the Confessor's time might regard as somewhat shadowy. In any case their lord is to have their wites; in any case they will get the judgment of their peers; what is left to dispute about is mere geography, the number of the courts, the demarcation of justiciary areas. We may say, if we will, that far-sighted men would not have argued in this manner, for seignorial justice was a force mighty for good and

---

[1] Hist. Eng. Law, i. 580–2.

[2] D. B. ii. 424: 'Et dicunt etiam quod istam terram R[anulfus] calumpniavit supra Radulfum, et vicecomes Rogerius denominavit illis constitutum tempus m[odo] ut ambo adfuissent; Ranulfo adveniente defuit Radulfus et iccirco diiudicaverunt homines hundreti Rannulfum esse saisitum.'—Ibid. i. 165 b: 'Modo iacet in Bernitone hundredo iudicio hominum eiusdem hundredi.'—Ibid. i. 58 b: 'unde iudicium non dixerunt, sed ante Regem ut iudicet dimiserunt.'—Ibid. 182 b: 'In isto hundredo ad placita conveniunt qui ibi manent ut rectum faciant et accipiant.'

[3] Above, p. 95.

for ill; but it has not been proved to our satisfaction that the men who ruled England in the age before the Conquest were far-sighted. Their work ended in a stupendous failure.

To the sake and soke of the old English law we shall have to return once more in our next essay. Our discussion of the sake and soke of Domesday Book was induced by a considera-tion of the various bonds which may bind a man to a lord. And now we ought to understand that in the eastern counties it is extremely common for a man to be bound to one lord by commendation and to another lord by soke. Very often indeed a man is commended to one lord, while the soke over him and over his land 'lies in' some hundred court which belongs to another lord or is still in the hands of the king and the earl. How to draw with any exactness the line between the rights given to the one lord by the commendation and to the other lord by the soke we can not tell. For instance, we find many men who can not sell their land without the consent of a lord. This we may usually regard as the result of some term in the bargain of commendation; but in some cases it may well be the outcome of soke. Thus at Sturston in Norfolk we see a free man of St Etheldreda of Ely; his sake and soke belong to Archbishop Stigand's manor of Earsham (Sturston and Earsham lie some five miles apart); now this man if he wishes to give or sell his land must obtain the licence both of St Etheldreda and of Stigand[1]. And so as regards the forfeiture of land. We are perhaps accustomed to think of the escheat *propter delictum tenentis* as having its origin in the ideas of homage and tenure rather than in the justiciary rights of the lord. Howbeit there is much to make us think that the right to take the land of one who has forfeited that land by crime was closely con-nected with the right to other wites or *forisfacturae*. ' Of all the thegns who hold land in the Well wapentake of Lincolnshire, St Mary of Lincoln had two-thirds of every *forisfactura* and the earl the other third; and so of their heriots; and so if they forfeited their land, two-thirds went to St Mary and the re-mainder to the earl[2].' St Mary has not enfeoffed these thegns; but by some royal grant she has two-thirds of the soke over

Soke and commenda-tion.

---

[1] D. B. ii. 186: 'In Sterestuna tenuit 1 liber homo S. Aldrede T. R. E. et Stigandi erat soca et saco in Hersam, set nec dare nec vendere poterat terram suam sine licentia S. Aldrede et Stigandi.'

[2] D. B. ii. 376.

them. In Suffolk one Brungar held a small manor with soke. He was a 'free man' commended to Robert Wimarc's son; but the sake and soke over him belonged to St Edmund. Unfortunately for Brungar, stolen horses were found in his house, and we fear that he came to a bad end. At any rate he drops out of the story. Then St Edmund's Abbot, who had the sake and soke, and Robert, who had the commendation, went to law, and right gladly would we have heard the plea; but they came to some compromise and to all seeming Robert got the land[1]. If we are puzzled by this labyrinthine web of legal relationships, we may console ourselves with the reflection that the Normans also were puzzled by it. They seem to have felt the necessity of attributing the lordship of land to one lord and one only (though of course that lord might have another lord above him), of consolidating soke with commendation, homage with justice, and in the end they brought out a simple and symmetrical result, albeit to the last the relation of seignorial to hundredal justice is not to be explained by any elegant theory of feudalism.

Sokemen and free men.

Yet another problem shall be stated, though we have little hope of solving it. The writ, or rather one of the writs, which defined the scope of the survey seems to have spoken of *liberi homines* and *sochemanni* as of two classes of men that were to be distinguished from each other. In Essex, Suffolk and Norfolk this distinction is often drawn. In one and the same manor we shall find both 'free men' and sokemen[2]; we may even hear of sokemen who formerly were 'free men[3].' But the import of this distinction evades us. Sometimes it is said of sokemen that they 'hold freely[4].' We read that four sokemen held this land of whom three were free, while the fourth had one hide but could not give or sell it[5]. This may suggest

---

[1] D. B. ii. 401 b: 'Eodem tempore fuerunt furati equi inventi in domo istius Brungari, ita quod Abbas cuius fuit soca et saca et Rodbertus qui habuit commendationem super istum venerunt de hoc furto ad placitum, et sicut hundret testatur discesserunt amicabiliter sine iudicio quod vidissed (*sic*) hundret.'

[2] E.g. D. B. ii. 35 b: 'quas tenuerunt 2 sochemanni et 1 liber homo.'

[3] D. B. ii. 28 b: 'Huic manerio iacent 5 sochemanni quorum 2 occupavit Ingelricus tempore Regis Willelmi qui tunc erant liberi homines.'

[4] D. B. ii. 83: '3 sochemanni tenentes libere.'—Ibid. 88 b: 'tunc fuit 1 sochemannus qui libere tenuit 1 virgatam.'—Ibid. 58: 'in hac terra sunt 13 sochemanni qui libere tenent.'

[5] D. B. i. 212 b, Bedf.: 'Hanc terram tenuerunt 4 sochemanni quorum 3 liberi fuerunt, quartus vero unam hidam habuit, sed nec dare nec vendere potuit.'

that the principle of the division is to be found in the power
to alienate the land, to 'withdraw' with the land to another
lord[1]. There may be truth in the suggestion, but we can not
square it with all our cases[2]. Often enough the 'free man'
can not sell without the consent of his lord[3]. We have just
met with a 'free man' who had to obtain the consent both
of the lord of his commendation and of the lord of his soke[4].
On the other hand, the sokeman who can sell without his lord's
leave is no rare being[5], and it was of a sokeman that we read
how he could sell, not only his land, but also his soke[6].

Again, we dare not say that while the 'free man' is the
justiciable of a national court, the soke over the sokeman
belongs to his lord. Neither side of this proposition is true.
Very often the soke over the 'free man' belongs to a church
or to some other lord[7], who may or may not be his lord by
commendation[8]. Very often the lord has not the soke over his
sokemen. This may seem a paradox, but it is true. We make
it clearer by saying that you may have a man who is your man
and who is a sokeman, but yet you have no soke over him; his
soke 'lies' or 'is rendered' elsewhere. This is a common enough
phenomenon, but it is apt to escape attention. When we are
told that a certain English lord had a sokeman at a certain
place, we must not jump to the conclusion that he had soke
over that man of his. Thus in Hertfordshire Æthelmær held

Difference between 'free men' and sokemen.

[1] D. B. i. 35 b, 'Isti liberi homines ita liberi fuerunt quod poterant ire quo
volebant.'—Ibid. ii. 187: '5 homines...ex istis erant 4 liberi ut non possent
recedere nisi dando 2 solidos.'

[2] Round, Feudal England, 34.

[3] D. B. ii. 59 b, Essex: 'quod tenuerunt 2 liberi homines...set non poterant
recedere sine licentia illius Algari.'—Ibid. 216 b, Norf.: 'Ibi sunt 5 liberi
homines S. Benedicti commendatione tantum...et ita est in monasterio quod nec
vendere nec forisfacere pot[uerunt] extra ecclesia set soca est in hundredo.'—
Ibid. i. 137 b, Herts: 'duo teigni...vendere non potuerunt.'—Ibid. i. 30 b, Hants:
'Duo liberi homines tenuerunt de episcopo T. R. E. sed recedere cum terra non
potuerunt.'

[4] Above, p. 103, note 1.

[5] E.g. D. B. i. 129 b: 'In hac terra fuerunt 5 sochemanni de 6 hidis quas
potuerunt dare vel vendere sine licentia dominorum suorum.'

[6] Above, p. 100, note 2.

[7] E.g. D. B. ii. 358: '7 liberos homines...hi poterant dare vel vendere terram
set saca et soca et commendatio et servitium remanebant Sancto [Edmundo].'

[8] D. B. ii. 186: 'In Sterestuna tenuit unus liber homo S. Aldredae T. R. E.
et Stigandi erat soca et saco in Hersam.'—Ibid. 139 b: 'habuit socam et
sacam...de commendatis suis.'

a manor and in it there were four sokemen; they were, we
are told, his *homines*: but over two of them the king had
sake and soke[1]. Unless we are greatly mistaken, the soke of
many of the East Anglian sokemen, no matter whose men they
were, lay in the hundred courts. This prevents our saying
that a sokeman is one over whom his lord has soke, or one who
renders soke to his lord. We may doubt whether the line
between the sokemen and the 'free men' is drawn in accordance
with any one principle. Not only is freedom a matter of degree,
but freedom is measured along several different scales. At
one time it is to the power of alienation or 'withdrawal' that
attention is attracted, at another to the number or the kind
of the services and 'customs' that the man must render to
his lord. When we see that in Lincolnshire there is no class of
'free men' but that there are some eleven thousand sokemen, we
shall probably be persuaded that the distinction drawn in East
Anglia was of no very great importance to the surveyors or
the king. It may have been a matter of pure personal rank.
These *liberi homines* may have enjoyed a wergild of more than
200 shillings, for in the Norman age we see traces of a usage
which will not allow that any one is 'free' if he is not noble[2].
But perhaps when the Domesday of East Anglia has been fully
explored, hundred by hundred and vill by vill, we shall come
to the conclusion that the 'free men' of one district would have
been called sokemen in another district[3].

Holdings
of the
sokemen.

Some of these sokemen and 'free men' had very small
tenements. Let us look at a list of tenants in Norfolk. 'In
Carleton were 2 free men with 7 acres. In Kicklington were
2 free men with 2 acres. In Forncett 1 free man with 2 acres.
In Tanaton 4 free men with 4 acres. In Wacton 2 free men
with 1½ acres. In Stratton 1 free man with 4 acres. In
Moulton 3 free men with 5 acres. In Tibenham 2 free men with
7 acres. In Aslacton 1 free man with 1 acre[4].' These eighteen
free men had but sixteen oxen among them. We think it

[1] D. B. i. 141.

[2] Liebermann, Leges Edwardi, p. 72. The most important passage is Leg.
Edw. 12 § 4: 'Manbote in Danelaga de villano et de socheman 12 oras [=20
sol.]: de liberis hominibus 3 marcas [=40 sol.].'

[3] A study of the Hundred Rolls might prepare us for this result. One jury
will call *servi* those whom another jury would have called *villani*. See e.g.
R. H. ii. 688 ff.

[4] D. B. ii. 189 b, 190.

highly probable that in the survey of East Anglia one and the same free man is sometimes mentioned several times; he holds a little land under one lord, and a little under another lord; but in all he holds little. Then again, we see that these small freemen often have a few bordiers or even a few free men 'below them[1].' And then we observe that, while some of them are spoken of as having belonged to the manors of their lords, others are reported to have had manors of their own.

§ 6. *The Manor.*

This brings us face to face with a question that we have hitherto evaded. What is a manor? The word *manerium* appears on page after page of Domesday Book, but to define its meaning will task our patience. Perhaps we may have to say that sometimes the term is loosely used, that it has now a wider, now a narrower compass, but we can not say that it is not a technical term. Indeed the one statement that we can safely make about it is that, at all events in certain passages and certain contexts, it is a technical term. *What is a manor?*

We may be led to this opinion by observing that in the description of certain counties—Middlesex, Buckingham, Bedford, Cambridge, Huntingdon, Derby, Nottingham, Lincoln, York—the symbol *M* which represents a manor, is often carried out into the margin, and is sometimes contrasted with the *S* which represents a soke and the *B* which represents a berewick. This no doubt has been done—though it may not have been very consistently done—for the purpose of guiding the eye of officials who will turn over the pages in search of manors. But much clearer evidence is forthcoming. Throughout the survey of Essex it is common to find entries which take such a form as this: 'Thurkil held it for two hides and for one manor'; 'Brithmær held it for five hides and for one manor'; 'Two free men who were brothers held it for two hides and for two manors'; 'Three free men held it for three manors and for four hides and twenty-seven acres[2].' *'Manor' a technical term.*

---

[1] D. B. ii. 318: 'In Suttona tenet idem W. [de Cadomo] de R. Malet 2 liberos homines commendatos Edrico 61 acr[arum] et sub 1 ex ipsis 5 liberi [*sic*] homines.'—Ibid. 321 b: 'In Caldecota 6 liberi homines commendati Leuuino de Bachetuna 74 acr. et 7 liberi homines sub eis commend[ati] de 6 acr. et dim.'

[2] D. B. ii. 21, 26, 37 b, 59 b.

In Sussex again the statement 'X tenuit pro uno manerio[1]' frequently occurs. Such phrases as 'Four brothers held it for two manors, Hugh received it for one manor[2],'— 'These four manors are now for one manor[3],'—'Then there were two halls, now it is in one manor[4],'—'A certain thegn held four hides and it was a manor[5],'—are by no means unusual[6]. A clerk writes 'Elmer tenuit' and then is at pains to add by way of interlineation 'pro manerio[7].' 'Eight thegns held this manor, one of them, Alwin, held two hides for a manor; another, Ulf, two hides for a manor; another, Algar, one hide and a half for a manor; Elsi one hide, Turkill one hide, Lodi one hide, Osulf one hide, Elric a half-hide[8]'—when we read this we feel sure that the scribe is using his terms carefully and that he is telling us that the holdings of the five thegns last mentioned were not manors. And then Hugh de Port holds Wallop in Hampshire 'for half a manor[9].' But let us say at once that at least one rule of law, or of local custom, demands a definition of a *manerium*. In the shires of Nottingham and Derby a thegn who has more than six manors pays a relief of £8 to the king, but if he has only six manors or less, then a relief of 3 marks to the sheriff[10]. It seems clear therefore that not only did the Norman rulers treat the term *manerium* as an accurate term charged with legal meaning, but they thought that it, or rather some English equivalent for it, had been in the Confessor's day an accurate term charged with legal meaning.

The word *manerium*.   The term *manerium* seems to have come in with the Conqueror[11], though other derivatives from the Latin verb *manere*, in particular *mansa*, *mansio*, *mansiuncula* had been freely employed by the scribes of the land-books. But these had as a rule been used as representatives of the English *hide*, and just for this reason they were incapable of expressing the notion that the Normans desired to express by the word *manerium*. In its origin that word is but one more name for

---

[1] D. B. i. 21.   [2] D. B. i. 45.
[3] D. B. i. 6 b.   [4] D. B. i. 27.   [5] D. B. i. 163.
[6] So in the Exeter record, D. B. iv. 390: 'Tenuerunt 3 tegni pro 4 mansionibus, et Robertus habet illas pro 1 mansione.'
[7] D. B. i. 169 b. Similar interlineations in i. 98.
[8] D. B. i. 148; on f. 149 is a similar case.   [9] D. B. i. 45 b.
[10] D. B. i. 280 b.
[11] In several passages in D. B. the word seems to be *manerius*.

a house. Throughout the Exeter Domesday the word *mansio* is used instead of the *manerium* of the Exchequer record, and even in the Exchequer record we may find these two terms used interchangeably:—'Three free men belonged to this *manerium*; one of them had half a hide and could withdraw himself without the licence of the lord of the *mansio*[1].' If we look for the vernacular term that was rendered by *manerium*, we are likely to find it in the English *heal*. Though this is not connected with the Latin *aula*, still these two words bearing a similar meaning meet and are fused in the *aula, haula, halla* of Domesday Book.

Now this term stands in the first instance for a house and can be exchanged with *curia*. You may say that there is meadow enough for the horses of the *curia*[2], and that there are three horses in the *aula*[3]; you may speak indifferently of a mill that serves the hall[4], or of the mill that grinds the corn of the court[5]. But further, you may say that in Stonham there are 50 acres of the demesne land of the hall in Creeting, or that in Thorney there are 24 acres which belong to the hall in Stonham[6], or that Roger de Rames has lands which once were in the hall of St Edmund[7], or that in the hall of Grantham there are three carucates of land[8], or that Guthmund's sake and soke extended only over the demesne of his hall[9]. We feel that to such phrases as these we should do no great violence were we to substitute 'manor' for 'hall.' Other phrases serve to bring these two words very closely together. One and the same page tells us, first, that Hugh de Port holds as one manor what four brothers held as two manors, and then, that on another estate there is one hall though of old there were two halls[10]:—these two stories seem to have the same point. 'Four brothers held this; there was only one hall there[11].' 'Two brothers held it and each had his hall; now it is as one manor[12].' 'In these two lands there is but one hall[13].' 'Then there were two halls; now it is in one

Manor and hall.

---

[1] D. B. ii. 96 b: 'Huic manerio iacebant 3 liberi homines, unus tenuit dim. hidam et potuit abire sine licentia domini ipsius mansionis.'

[2] D. B. i. 149, Wicombe.   [3] D. B. ii. 38 b, Hersam.

[4] D. B. i. 174 b, Poiwic.   [5] D. B. i. 268, Gretford.   [6] D. B. ii. 350 b.

[7] D. B. ii. 263: 'sed fuerunt in aula S. Edmundi.'   [8] D. B. i. 337 b.

[9] D. B. ii. 408 b: 'cum soca et saca super dominium hallae tantum.'

[10] D. B. i. 45, Wicheham, Werste.   [11] D. B. i. 20, Waliland.

[12] D. B. i. 11 b, Acres.   [13] D. B. i. 26 b, Eldretune.

manor¹.' 'Ten manors; ten thegns, each had his hall².' 'In-gelric set these men to his hall......Ingelric added these men to his manor³.'

We do not contend that *manerium* and *halla* are precisely equivalent. Now and again we shall be told of a *manerium sine halla*⁴ as of some exceptional phenomenon. The term *manerium* has contracted a shade of technical meaning; it refers, so we think, to a system of taxation, and thus it is being differentiated from the term *hall*. Suppose, for example, that a hall or manor has meant a house from which taxes are collected, and that some one removes that house, houses being very portable things⁵: 'by construction of law,' as we now say, there still may be a hall or manor on the old site; or we may take advantage of the new wealth of words and say that, though the hall has gone, the manor remains: to do this is neater than to say that there is a 'constructive' hall where no hall can be seen. Then again, *manerium* is proving itself to be the more elastic of the two terms. We may indeed speak of a considerable stretch of land as belonging to or even as 'being in' a certain hall, and this stretch may include not only land that the owner of the hall occupies and cultivates by himself or his servants, but also land and houses that are occupied by his villeins⁶: still we could hardly talk of the hall being a league long and a league wide or containing a square league. Of *manerium*, however, we may use even such phrases as those just mentioned⁷. For all this, we can think of no English word for which *manerium* can stand, save *hall*; *tún*, it is clear enough, was translated by *villa*, not by *manerium*.

If now we turn from words to look at the things which those words signify, we shall soon be convinced that to describe a typical *manerium* is an impossible feat, for on the one hand there are enormous *maneria* and on the other hand there are

---

¹ D. B. i. 27, Percinges.   ² D. B. i. 284 b, Ættune.

³ D. B. ii. 29 b, 30 b.   ⁴ D. B. i. 307 b, Burghedurum ; 308, Ternusc.

⁵ D. B. i. 63: 'Ipse quoque transportavit hallam et alias domos et pecuniam in alio manerio.'

⁶ D. B. i. 338 b: 'Ad huius manerii aulam pertinent Catenai et Usun 4 car. terrae ad geldum. Terra ad 8 carucas. Ibi in dominio 2 carucae et 20 villani et 15 sochemanni et 10 bordarii habentes 9 carucas. Ibi 360 acre prati. Ad eundem manerium iacet hec soca:—In Linberge 4 car. terrae etc.'

⁷ Throughout Yorkshire the phrase is common, 'Totum manerium *x*. leu. long. et *y*. leu. lat.'

many holdings called *maneria* which are so small that we, with
our reminiscences of the law of later days, can hardly bring
ourselves to speak of them as manors. If we look in the world
of sense for the essence of the *manerium* we shall find nothing
that is common to all *maneria* save a piece of ground—very
large it may be, or very small—held (in some sense or another)
by a single person or by a group of co-tenants, for even upon a
house we shall not be able to insist very strictly. After weary
arithmetical labours we might indeed obtain an average manor;
we might come to the conclusion that the average manor
contained so many hides or acres, possibly that it included
land occupied by so many sokemen, villeins, bordiers, serfs;
but an average is not a type, and the uselessness of such calculations will soon become apparent.

We may begin by looking at a somewhat large manor. Let A large
it be that of Staines in Middlesex, which is held by St Peter of ^{manor.}
Westminster[1]. It is rated at 19 hides but contains land for
24 plough-teams. To the demesne belong 11 hides and there
are 13 teams there. The villeins have 11 teams. There are :—

> 3 villeins with a half-hide apiece.
> 4 villeins with a hide between them.
> 8 villeins with a half-virgate apiece.
> 36 bordiers with 3 hides between them.
> 1 villein with 1 virgate.
> 4 bordiers with 40 acres between them.
> 10 bordiers with 5 acres apiece.
> 5 cottiers with 4 acres.
> 8 bordiers with 1 virgate.
> 3 cottiers with 9 acres.
> 13 serfs.
> 46 burgesses paying 40 shillings a year.

There are 6 mills of 64 shillings and one fish-weir of 6*s.* 8*d.*
and one weir which renders nothing. There is pasture sufficient
for the cattle of the vill. There is meadow for the 24 teams,
and in addition to this there is meadow worth 20*s.* a year.
There is wood for 30 pigs; there are 2 arpents of vineyard. To
this manor belong four berewicks. Altogether it is worth £35
and formerly it was worth £40.—This is a handsome manor.—
The next manor that is mentioned would be a fairer specimen.
It is Sunbury held by St Peter of Westminster[2]. It is rated at
7 hides and there is land for but 6 teams. To the demesne

[1] D. B. i. 128.   [2] D. B. i. 128 b.

belong 4 hides and there is one team there. The villeins have
4 teams. There are :—

> A priest with a half-virgate.
> 8 villeins with a virgate apiece.
> 2 villeins with a virgate.
> 5 bordiers with a virgate.
> 5 cottiers.
> 1 serf.

There is meadow for 6 teams and pasture enough for the
cattle of the vill. Altogether it is worth £6 and has been
worth £7. Within this one county of Middlesex we can see
wide variations. There are manors which are worth £50 and
there are manors which are not worth as many shillings. The
archbishop's grand manor at Harrow has land for 70 teams[1];
the Westminster manor of Cowley has land for but one team
and the only tenants upon it are two villeins[2].

Enormous manors. Leominster. But far larger variations than these are to be found. Let
us look at a few gigantic manors. Leominster in Herefordshire
had been held by Queen Edith together with sixteen members[3].
The names of these members are given and we may find them
scattered about over a wide tract of Herefordshire. In this
manor with its members there were 80 hides. In the demesne
there were 30 teams. There were 8 reeves and 16 beadles and
8 radknights and 238 villeins, 75 bordiers and 82 male and
female serfs. These in all had 230 teams; so that with the
demesne teams there were no less than 260. Further there
were Norman barons paying rents to this manor. Ralph de
Mortemer for example paid 15*s.* and Hugh de Lacy 6*s.* 8*d.* It
is let to farm at a rent of £60 and besides this has to support a
house of nuns; were it freed from this duty, it might, so thinks
the county, be let at a rent of £120. It is a most interesting
manor, for we see strong traces of a neat symmetrical arrangement :—witness the 16 members, 8 reeves, 8 radknights, 16
beadles; very probably it has a Welsh basis[4]. But we have
in this place to note that it is called a manor, and for
certain purposes it is treated as a single whole. For what
purposes ? Well, for one thing, it is let to farm as a single
whole. This, however, is of no very great importance, for landlords and farmers may make what bargains they please. But

---

[1] D. B. i. 127.   [2] D. B. i. 128 b.   [3] D. B. i. 180.
[4] Compare the cases in Seebohm, Village Community, 267.

also it is taxed as a single whole. It is rated at the nice round figures of 80 hides.

No less handsome and yet more valuable is Berkeley in Berkeley. Gloucestershire[1]. It brought in a rent of £170 of refined money. It had eighteen members which were dispersed abroad over so wide a field that a straight line of thirty miles would hardly join their uttermost points[2]. 'All the aforesaid members belong to Berkeley.' There were 29 radknights, 162 villeins, 147 bordiers, 22 coliberts, 161 male and female serfs, besides some unenumerated men of the radknights; on the demesne land were 54½ teams; and the tenants had 192. Tewkesbury also is Tewkesbury. a splendid manor. 'When it was all together in King Edward's time it was worth £100,' though now but £50 at the most can be had from it and in the turmoil of the Conquest its value fell to £12[3]. It was a scattered unit, but still it was a unit for fiscal purposes. It was reckoned to contain 95 hides, but the 45 which were in demesne were quit of geld, and matters had been so arranged that all the geld on the remaining 50 hides had, as between the lord and his various tenants, been thrown on 35 of those hides. The 'head of the manor' was at Tewkesbury; the members were dispersed abroad; but 'they gelded in Tewkesbury[4].'

No list of great manors would be complete without a notice Taunton. of Taunton[5]. 'The bishop of Winchester holds Tantone or has a mansion called Tantone. Stigand held it in King Edward's day and it gelded for 54 hides and 2½ virgates. There is land for 100 teams, and besides this the bishop in his demesne has land for 20 teams which never gelded.' 'With all its appendages and customs it is worth £154. 12d.' 'Tantone' then is valued as a whole and it has gelded as a whole. But 'Tantone' in this sense covers far more than the borough which bears that name; it covers many places which have names of their own and had names of their own when the survey was made[6]. We might speak of the bishop of Exeter's manor of Crediton in Devon

---

[1] D. B. i. 163.

[2] If we mistake not, the Osleuuorde of the record is Ashleworth, which, though some miles to the north of Gloucester, either still is, or but lately was, a detached piece of the Berkeley hundred.

[3] D. B. i. 163.

[4] D. B. i. 163 b: 'Hanc terram dedit regina Rogerio de Buslei et geldabat pro 4 hidis in Tedechesberie.'

[5] D. B. i. 87 b; iv. 161.   [6] Eyton, Somerset, ii. 34.

which is worth £75 and in which are 264 villeins and 73 bordiers[1],
or of the bishop of Winchester's manor of Chilcombe in Hampshire where there are nine churches[2]; but we turn to another
part of England.

Large manors in the midlands.
        If we wish to see a midland manor with many members we
may look at Rothley in Leicestershire[3]. The vill of Rothley
itself is not very large and it is separately valued at but 62*s*.
But 'to this manor belong the following members,' and then we
read of no less than twenty-one members scattered over a large
area and containing 204 sokemen who with 157 villeins and 94
bordiers have 82 teams and who pay in all £31. 8*s*. 1*d*. Their
rents are thus reckoned as forming a single whole. In Lincolnshire Earl Edwin's manor of Kirton had 25 satellites, Earl
Morcar's manor of Caistor 16, the Queen's manor of Horncastle
15[4]. A Northamptonshire manor of 27 hides lay scattered
about in six hundreds[5].

Town-houses and berewicks attached to manors.
        It is common enough to see a town-house annexed to a
rural manor. Sometimes a considerable group of houses or
'haws' in the borough is deemed to 'lie in' or form part of
a manor remote from its walls. Thus, to give but two examples,
twelve houses in London belong to the Bishop of Durham's
manor of Waltham in Essex; twenty-eight houses in London
to the manor of Barking[6]. Not only these houses but their
occupants are deemed to belong to the manor; thus 80 burgesses
in Dunwich pertain to one of the Ely manors[7]. The berewick
(*bereuita*)[8] also frequently meets our eye. Its name seems to
signify primarily a wick, or village, in which barley is grown;
but, like the barton (*bertona*) and the grange (*grangia*) of later
days, it seems often to be a detached portion of a manor which
is in part dependent on, and yet in part independent of, the
main body. Probably at the berewick the lord has some demesne
land and some farm buildings, a barn or the like, and the villeins
of the berewick are but seldom called upon to leave its limits;
but the lord has no hall there, he does not consume its produce
upon the spot, and yet for some important purposes the berewick
is a part of the manor. The berewick might well be some way

---

[1] D. B. i. 101 b; iv. 107.   [2] D. B. i. 41.   [3] D. B. i. 230.
[4] D. B. i. 338–9.   [5] D. B. i. 220, Tingdene.
[6] D. B. ii. 15 b, 17 b.   [7] D. B. ii. 385 b.
        [8] The form *bereuita* is exceedingly common, but must, we think, be due to a
mistake; *c* has been read as *t*.

off from the hall; a manor in Hampshire had three berewicks
on the mainland and two in the Isle of Wight[1].

Then again in the north and east the manor is often the centre of an extensive but very discrete territory known as its soke. One says that certain lands are 'soke' or are 'the soke,' or are 'in the soke' of such a manor, or that 'their soke belongs' to such a manor. One contrasts the soke of the manor with the 'inland' and with the berewicks[2]. The soke in this context seems to be the territory in which the lord's rights are, or have been, of a justiciary rather than of a proprietary kind[3]. The manor of the eastern counties is a discrete, a dissipated thing. Far from lying within a ring fence, it often consists of a small nucleus of demesne land and villein tenements in one village, together with many detached parcels in many other villages, which are held by 'free men' and sokemen. In such a case we may use the term *manerium* now in a wider, now in a narrower sense. In valuing the manor, we hardly know whether to include or exclude these free men. We say that the manor 'with the free men' is worth so much[4], or that the manor 'without the free men' is worth so much[5], that the manor is worth £10 and that the free men pay 40 shillings[6], that Thurmot had soke over the manor and over three of the free men while the Abbot of Ely had soke over the other three[7].

(margin note: Manor and soke.*)*

[1] D. B. i. 38 b, Edlinges. Some of the 'wicks' seem to have been dairy farms. D. B. i. 58 b: 'et wika de 10 pensis caseorum.' On the Glastonbury estates we find persons called *wikarii*, each of whom has a *wika*. Glastonbury Rentalia, 39: 'Thomas de Wika tenet 5 acras et 50 oves matrices et 12 vaccas... Philippus de Wika tenet unum ferlingum et 50 oves matrices et 12 vaccas.' Ibid. 44: 'A. B. tenet unum ferlingum et 50 oves matrices et 12 vaccas pro 1 sol. pro wika.' Ibid. 48: 'Ricardus de Wika tenet 5 acras et 50 oves matrices et 12 vaccas. Alanus de Wika eodem modo.' Ibid. p. 51.

[2] D. B. i. 350: 'In Osgotebi et Tauelebi 2 bo[vatae] inland et 1 bo[vata] soca huius manerii.' D. B. i. 338 b: 'Hiboldeston est bereuuita non soca et in Grangeham sunt 2 car[ucatae] inland et in Springetorp dim. car[ucata] est inland. Reliqua omnis est soca.'

[3] When therefore, as is often the case, we find that the occupants of 'the soke' are not sokemen but villeins, this seems to point to a recent depression of the peasantry.

[4] D. B. ii. 330 b: 'In illo manerio...sunt 35 liberi homines....Tunc valuerunt liberi homines 4 libras. Manerium cum liberis hominibus valet modo 24 libras.'

[5] D. B. ii. 358 b: 'Hoc manerium exceptis liberis tunc valuit 30 solidos.'

[6] D. B. ii. 289 b.   [7] D. B. ii. 285 b.

From one extreme we may pass to the other extreme. If there were huge manors, there were also tiny manors. Let us begin in the south-west of England. Quite common is the manor which is said to have land for but one team; common also is the manor which is said to have land for but half a team. This means, as we believe, that the first of these manors has but some 120 acres of arable, while the second has but 60 acres or thereabouts. 'Domesday measures' are, it is well known, the matter of many disputes; therefore we will not wholly rely upon them, but will look at some of these 'half-team' manors and observe how much they are worth, how many tenants and how much stock they have upon them.

(i) A Somersetshire manor[1]. Half the land is in demesne; half is held by 7 bordiers. The only plough beasts are 4 oxen on the demesne; there are 3 beasts that do not plough, 20 sheep, 7 acres of underwood, 20 acres of pasture. It is worth 12*s.*, formerly it was worth 10*s.*

(ii) A Somersetshire manor[2]. A quarter of the land is in demesne; the rest is held by 2 villeins and 3 bordiers. The men have one team; apparently the demesne has no plough-oxen. No other animals are mentioned. There are 140 acres of wood, 41 acres of moor, 40 acres of pasture. It is worth 12*s.* 6*d.* and has been worth 20*s.*

(iii) A Somersetshire manor[3]. All the land, save 10 acres, is in demesne; 2 bordiers hold the 10 acres. There is a team on the demesne; there are 2 beasts that do not plough, 7 pigs, 16 sheep, 4 acres of meadow, 7 of pasture. Value, 6*s.*

(iv) A Somersetshire manor[4]. The whole of the arable is in demesne; the only tenant is a bordier. There are 4 plough-oxen and 11 goats and 7 acres of underwood. Value, 6*s.*

(v) A Devonshire manor[5]. To all seeming all is in demesne and there are no tenants. There are 4 plough-beasts, 15 sheep, 5 goats, 4 acres of meadow. Value, 3*s.*

(vi) A Devonshire manor[6]. Value, 3s. All seems to be in demesne; we see no tenants and no stock.

We have been at no great pains to select examples, and yet smaller manors may be found, manors which provide arable land for but two oxen. Thus

[1] D. B. iv. 397; i. 93 b, Ichetoca.
[2] D. B. iv. 411; i. 94 b, Tocheswilla.
[3] D. B. iv. 398; i. 93 b, Pilloc.
[4] D. B. iv. 341; i. 96, Sordemanneford.
[5] D. B. iv. 355; i. 116 b, Labera.
[6] D. B. iv. 367; i. 112 b, Oplomia.

(vii)   A Somersetshire manor[1] occupied by one villein. We read nothing of any stock. Value, 15*d*.

(viii)   A Somersetshire manor[2] with 3 bordiers on it. Value, 4*s*.

(ix)   A Somersetshire manor[3] with one bordier on it. Value, 30*d*.

The lowest value of a manor in this part of the world is, so far as we have observed, one shilling; that manor to all appearance was nothing but a piece of pasture land[4]. Yet each of these holdings is a *mansio*, and the Bishop of Winchester's holding at Taunton is a *mansio*.

From one side of England we will journey to the other side; from Devon and Somerset to Essex and Suffolk. We soon observe that in describing the holdings of the 'free men' and sokemen of this eastern district as they were in King Edward's day, our record constantly introduces the term *manerium*. A series of entries telling us how 'a free man held *x* hides or carucates or acres' will ever and anon be broken by an entry that tells us how 'a free man held *x* hides or carucates or acres for a manor'[5]. We soon give up counting the cases in which the manor is rated at 60 acres. We begin counting the cases in which it is rated at 30 acres and find them numerous; we see manors rated at 24 acres, at 20, at 15, at 12 acres. But this, it may be said, tells us little, for these manors may be extravagantly underrated[6]. Let us then look at a few of them. *Small manors in the east.*

(i)   In Espalle Siric held 30 acres for a manor; there were always 3 bordiers and one team and 4 acres of meadow; wood for 60 pigs and 13 beasts. It was then worth 10*s*.[7]

(ii)   In Torentuna Turchetel a free man held 30 acres for a manor; there were always 2 bordiers and one team and a half. It is worth 10*s*.[8]

(iii)   In Bonghea Godric a free man held 30 acres for a manor; there were 1 bordier and 1 team and 2 acres of meadow. It was then worth 8*s*.[9]

[1] D. B. iv. 338; i. 95 b, Aisseforda.
[2] D. B. iv. 395; i. 93, Terra Colgrini.
[3] D. B. iv. 394; i. 93, Rima.
[4] D. B. iv. 338; i. 95 b, Aisseforda.
[5] As the term *manerium* is often represented by the mere letter *M* or *m*, we will refer to some cases in which it is written in full. D. B. ii. 295 b: '40 acras pro uno manerio'; Ibid. 311 b: 'In eadem villa est 1 liber homo de 40 acris et tenet pro manerio.'
[6] The question whether the acreage stated in the Suffolk survey is real or rateable can not be briefly debated. We hope to return to it.
[7] D. B. ii. 322 b, 323.   [8] D. B. ii. 323.   [9] D. B. ii. 288.

(iv) Three free men and their mother held 30 acres for a manor. There was half a team. Value, 5s.[1]

(v) In Rincham a free man held 30 acres for a manor. There were half a team and one acre of meadow. Value, 5s.[2]

(vi) In Wenham Ælfgar a free man held 24 acres for a manor. Value, 4s.[3]

(vii) In Torp a free man held 20 acres for a manor. One team; wood for 5 pigs. Value, 40d.[4]

(viii) In Tudenham Ælfric the deacon, a free man, held 12 acres for a manor. One team, 3 bordiers, 2 acres of meadow, 1 rouncey, 2 beasts that do not plough, 11 pigs, 40 sheep. Value, 3s.[5]

We are not speaking of curiosities; the sixty acre manor was very common in Essex, the thirty acre manor was no rarity in Suffolk.

The manor as a peasant's holding

Now it is plain enough that the 'lord' of such a manor,—or rather the holder of such a manor, for there was little lordship in the case,—was often enough a peasant, a tiller of the soil. He was under soke and under commendation; commended it may be to one lord, rendering soke to another. Sometimes he is called a sokeman[6]. But he has a manor. Sometimes he has a full team, sometimes but half a team. Sometimes he has a couple of bordiers seated on his land, who help him in his husbandry. Sometimes there is no trace of tenants, and his holding is by no means too large to permit of his cultivating it by his own labour and that of his sons. No doubt in the west country even before the Conquest these petty *mansiones* or *maneria* were being accumulated in the hands of the wealthy. The thegn who was the *antecessor* of the Norman baron, sometimes held a group, a geographically discontinuous group, of petty manors as well as some more substantial and better consolidated estates. But still each little holding is reckoned a manor, while in the east of England there is nothing to show that the nameless free men who held the manors which are said to consist of 60, 40, 30 acres had usually more than one manor apiece. When therefore we are told that

[1] D. B. ii. 309.   [2] D. B. ii. 297 b.   [3] D. B. ii. 377.
[4] D. B. ii. 333.   [5] D. B. ii. 423.
[6] D. B. ii. 316: 'In Aldeburc tenuit Uluricus sochemannus Edrici T. R. E. 80 acras pro manerio.' Ibid. 353: 'Nordberiam tenuit Eduinus presbyter sochemannus Abbatis 30 acras pro manerio.'

already before the Conquest England was full of manors, we must reply: Yes, but of what manors[1]?

Now were the differences between various manors a mere difference in size and in value, a student of law might pass them by. Our notion of ownership is the same whether it be applied to the largest and most precious, or to the smallest and most worthless of things. But in this case we have not to deal with mere differences in size or value. The examples that we have given will have proved that few, if any, propositions of legal import will hold good of all *maneria*. We must expressly reject some suggestions that the later history of our law may make to us. 'A manor has a court of its own':—this is plainly untrue. To say nothing of extreme cases, of the smallest of the manors that we have noticed, we can not easily believe that a manor with less than ten tenants has a court of its own, yet the number of such manors is exceedingly large. 'A manor has freehold tenants':—this of course we must deny, unless we hold that the *villani* are freeholders. 'A manor has villein or customary tenants':—even this proposition, though true of many cases, we can not accept. Not only may we find a manor the only tenants upon which are *liberi homines*[2], but we are compelled to protest that a manor need not have any tenants at all. 'A manor must contain demesne land':—this again we can not believe. In one case we read that the whole manor is being farmed by the villeins so that there is nothing in demesne[3], while in other cases we are told that there is nothing in demesne and see

Definition of a manor.

---

[1] We have taken our examples of small manors from the east and the southwest because Little Domesday and the Exeter Domesday give details which are not to be had elsewhere. But instances may be found in many other parts of England. Thus in Sussex, i. 24, two free men held as two manors land rated at a hide and sufficient for one team ; it is now tilled by four villeins. In the Isle of Wight, D. B. i. 39 b, five free men held as five manors land sufficient for two teams ; it is now tilled by four villeins. In Gloucestershire, D. B. i. 170, is a manor worth ten shillings with two serfs upon it ; also a manor rated at one virgate. In Derbyshire, D. B. i. 274 b, land sufficient for four teams and rated as four carucates had formed eight manors. In Nottinghamshire, D. B. i. 285 b, land sufficient for a team and a half and valued at ten shillings had formed five manors for five thegns, each of whom had his hall.

[2] D. B. ii. 380 : 'In Thistledona tenet 1 liber homo Ulmarus commendatus S. Eldrede 60 acras pro manerio et 5 liberi homines sub se.'

[3] D. B. i. 127 b : 'Wellesdone tenent canonici S. Pauli....Hoc manerium tenent villani ad firmam canonicorum. In dominio nil habetur.'

no trace of any recent change[1]. Thus, one after another, all the familiar propositions seem to fail us, and yet we have seen good reason to believe that *manerium* has some exact meaning. It remains that we should hazard an explanation.

The manor and the geld.
A manor is a house against which geld is charged. To the opinion that in some way or another the definition of a manor is intimately connected with the great tax we shall be brought by phrases such as the following : 'Richard holds Fivehide of the Earl which Brihtmær held in King Edward's time for forty acres and for a manor[2].'—'Two free men who were brothers, Bondi and Ælfric held it for two hides and for two manors[3].' When we say that a man holds land 'as' or 'for' (*pro*) forty acres, we mean that his holding, be its real size what it may, is rated to the geld at forty acres. If we add the words 'and as (or for) one manor,' surely we are still speaking of the geld. For one moment the thought may cross our minds that, besides a tax on land, there has been an additional tax on 'halls,' on houses of a certain size or value ; but this we soon dismiss as most unlikely. To raise but one out of many objections : had there been such a house-tax, it would have left plain traces of itself in those 'Geld Inquests' of the south-western counties that have come down to us. Rather we regard the matter thus :— The geld is a land-tax, a tax of so much per hide or carucate. In all likelihood it has been assessed according to a method which we might call the method of subpartitioned provincial quotas. The assumption has been made that a shire or other large district contains a certain number of hides ; this number has then been apportioned among the hundreds of that shire, and the number allotted to each hundred has been apportioned among the vills of that hundred. The common result is that some neat number of hides, five, ten or the like is attributed

---

[1] D. B. i. 235 b: Billesdone, 'In dominio nil fuit nec est.' Ibid. 166 b, Glouc.: 'Isdem Willelmus [de Ow] tenet Alvredestone. Bondi tenuit T. R. E. Ibi 3 hidae geldantes. Nil ibi est in dominio, sed 5 villani et 3 bordarii habent 3 carucas.'...'Isdem Willelmus tenet Odelavestone. Brictri filius Algari tenuit. Ibi nil in dominio nisi 5 villani cum 5 carucis.' D. B. iv. 396: 'Rogerius habet 1 mansionem quae vocatur P....et reddit gildum pro dimidia virgata ; hanc potest arare 1 carruca. Hanc tenet Anschetillus de Rogerio. Ibi habet Anschetillus 4 bordarios qui tenent totam illam terram et habent ibi 1 carrucam et 1 agrum prati, et reddit 10 solidos.'

[2] D. B. ii. 31.   [3] D. B. ii. 59 b.

to the vill[1]. This again has been divided between the holdings
in that vill. Ultimately it is settled that for fiscal purposes
a given holding contains, or must be deemed to contain, this
or that number of hides, virgates, or acres. Thus far the
system makes no use of the *manerium*. But it now has to
discover some house against which a demand may be made
for every particular penny of geld. Despite the 'realism' of
the system, it has to face the fact that, after all, taxes must be
paid by men and not by land. Men live in houses. It seeks
the tax-payer in his house. Now, were all the occupiers of land
absolute owners of the land that they occupied, even were it
true that every acre had some one person as its absolute owner,
the task would be simple. A schedule of five columns, such
we are familiar with, would set forth ' Owner's Name,' ' Place
of Residence,' ' Description of Geldable Property,' ' Hidage,'
' Amount due.' But the occupier is not always the owner;
what is more, there is no absolute ownership. Two, three, four
persons will be interested in the land; the occupier will have
a lord and that lord a lord; the occupier may be a serf, a villein,
a sokeman; there is commendation to be considered and soke
and all the infinite varieties of the power to ' withdraw' the
land from the lord. Rude and hard and arbitrary lines must
be drawn. Of course the state will endeavour to collect the
geld in big sums. It will endeavour to make the great folk
answer for the geld which lies on any land that is in any way
subject to their power; thus the cost of collecting petty sums
will be saved and the tax will be charged on men who are
solvent. The central power may even hold out certain advantages to the lord who will become responsible for the geld
of his tenants or justiciables or commended men. The hints
that we get in divers counties that the lord's 'inland' has borne
no geld seem to point in this direction, though the arrangements about this matter seem to have varied from shire to
shire[2]. On the pipe rolls of a later day we see that the geld
charged against the magnates is often ' pardoned.' For one
reason the king can not easily tax the rich; for another he

---

[1] I leave this sentence as it stood before Mr Round had published in his
Feudal England the results of his brilliant researches. Of the 'five hide unit'
I already knew a good deal; of the ' six carucate unit' I knew nothing.

[2] Round, Domesday Studies, i. 109.

122 *Domesday Book.*

can not easily tax the poor; so he gets at the poor through the rich. The small folk will gladly accept any scheme that will keep the tax-collector from their doors, even though they purchase their relief by onerous promises of rents and services. The great men, again, may find advantage in such bargains; they want periodical rents and services, and in order to obtain them will accept a certain responsibility for occasional taxes. This process had gone very far on the eve of the Conquest. Moreover the great men had enjoyed a large liberty of paying their geld where they pleased, of making special compositions with the king, of turning some wide and discrete territory into a single geld-paying unit, of forming such 'manors' as Taunton or Berkeley or Leominster.

Classification of men for the geld.

In King Edward's day, the occupiers of the soil might, so it seems to us, be divided by the financier into three main classes. In the first class we place the man who has a manor. He has, that is, a house at which he is charged with geld. He may be a great man or a small, an earl or a peasant; he may be charged at that house with the geld of a hundred hides or with the geld of fifteen acres. In the second class we place the villeins, bordiers, cottiers. The geld apportioned to the land that they occupy is demanded from their lord at his manor, or one of his manors. How he recoups himself for having to make this payment, that is his concern; but he is responsible for it to the king, not as guarantor but as principal debtor. But then, at least in the east and north, there are many men who fall into neither of these classes. They are not villeins, they are sokemen or 'free men'; but their own tenements are not manors; they belong to or 'lie in' some manor of their lord. These men, we think, can be personally charged with the geld; but they pay their geld at their lord's hall and he is in some measure bound to exact the payment.

Proofs of connexion between the manor and the geld.

Any thing that could be called a strict proof of this theory we can not offer; but it has been suggested by many facts and phrases which we can not otherwise explain. In the first place, our record seems to assume that every holding either is a manor or forms part of a manor[1]. Then we are told how

---

[1] D. B. i. 35: 'In Driteham tenet Ricardus [filius Gisleberti] 1 hidam et dimidiam. Ælmar tenuit de Rege E. pro uno manerio....In eadem Driteham est 1 hida et dimidia quam tenuit Aluric de Rege E. pro uno manerio, et postea

lands 'geld' at or in some manor or at the *caput manerii.*
Thus lands which lie many miles away from Tewkesbury, but
which belong to the manor of Tewkesbury, 'geld in Tewkesbury[1].' Sometimes the same information is conveyed to us
by a phrase that deserves notice. A piece of land is said to
'defend itself' in or at some manor, or, which is the same
thing, to have its *wara* or render its *wara*, that is to say,
its defence, its answer to the demand for geld, there[2]. 'In
Middleton two sokemen had 16 acres of land and they rendered
their *wara* in the said Middleton, but they could give and sell
their land to whom they pleased[3].' When we are told that
certain lands are *in warnode Drogonis* or *in warnode Archiepiscopi*, it is meant that the lands belong to Drogo or the
Archbishop for the purpose of 'defence' against the geld[4].
It is not sufficient that land should be taxed, it must be taxed
'in' some place, which may be remote from that in which,
as a matter of physical fact, it lies[5]. One clear case of a free
tenant paying his geld to his lord is put before us :—'Leofwin
had half a hide and could withdraw with his land and he
paid geld to his lord and his lord paid nothing[6].' Besides
this we have cases in which the lord enjoys the special privilege

dedit illam terram uxori suae et filiae ad aecclesiam de Certesy, sicuti homines
de hundredo testantur. Ricardus [filius Gisleberti] calumniatur. Non iacet
ulli manerio, nec pro manerio tenet, set liberata fuit ei et modo 3 hidae geldant
pro una hida et dimidia.' To say of the second of these two plots that it
neither is a manor nor yet belongs to a manor, is to say that it is shirking the
geld. D. B. i. 48: 'Walerannus tenet Dene....Ista tera non adiacet ulli suo
manerio.' Here *suo*=*Waleranni*. Waleran seems to be holding land without
good title.

[1] D. B. i. 163 b, Clifort. D. B. i. 58 b : 'In Winteham tenet Hubertus de
Abbate 5 hidas, de terra villanorum fuerunt 4, et geldaverunt cum hidis
manerii.'

[2] The word *wara* means defence ; it comes from a root which has given us,
wary, warrant, warn, guarantee, weir, etc. See Vinogradoff, Villainage, 243.

[3] D. B. i. 212.

[4] D. B. i. 340, 366, 368. Is not the last part of the word A.-S. *notu*,
(business, office)?

[5] D. B. i. 132 b : 'Hoc manerium tenuit Heraldus Comes et iacuit et iacet in
Hiz [Hitchin, Herts] sed wara hujus manerii iacuit in Bedefordscire T. R. E. in
hundredo de Maneheue.' D. B. i. 190, 'Haec terra est bereuuicha in Neuport
[Essex] set wara ejus iacet in Grantebrige.' When in the survey of Oxfordshire,
i. 160, it is said, 'Ibi 1 hida de *warland* in dominio,' the taxed land is contrasted
with the inland, which in this county has gone untaxed.

[6] D. B. i. 28.

of collecting the geld from his tenants and keeping it for his own use[1]. A remarkable Kentish entry tells us that at Peckham the archbishop had an estate which had been rated at six sullungs, and then that 'of the land of this manor a certain man of the archbishop held a half-sullung which in King Edward's day gelded with these six sullungs, although being free land it did not belong to the manor save for the purpose of the scot[2].' Here we have land so free that the one connexion between it and the manor to which it is attributed consists in the payment of geld—it gelds along with the other lands of the manor. In the great lawsuit between the churches of Worcester and Evesham about the lands at Hamton, the former contended that these lands should pay their geld along with the other estates of the bishop[3].

Land gelds in a manor.

Let us observe the first question that the commissioners are to ask of the jurors. What is the name of the *mansio*? Every piece of geldable land is connected with some *mansio*, at which it gelds. Let us observe how the commissioners and the jurors proceed in a district where the *villae* and the *mansiones* or *maneria* are but rarely coincident. The jurors of the Armingford hundred of Cambridgeshire are speaking of their country vill by vill. They come to the vill of Abington[4]. Abington, they say, was rated at five hides. Of these five hides the king has a half-hide; this lies in Litlington. Earl Roger has one virgate; this lies in his manor of Shingay. Picot the sheriff has a half-virgate; this lies and has always lain in Morden. In what sense important to the commissioners or their master can a bundle of strips scattered about in the fields of Abington be said to lie in Litlington, in Shingay, or in Morden? We answer that it gelds there.

Geld and hall.

Hence the importance of the hall. It is the place where geld is demanded and paid. A manor without a hall is a

---

[1] See the cases of the monks of Bury and the canons of S. Petroc, above, p. 55.

[2] D. B. i. 4 b: 'De terra huius manerii ten[uit] unus homo archiepiscopi dimid. solin et cum his 6 solins geldabat T. R. E. quamvis non pertineret manerio nisi de scoto quia libera terra erat.' The *scotum* in this context seems to be or to include the geld. Compare D. B. i. 61 b: 'Haec terra iacet et appreciata est in Gratentun quod est in Oxenefordscire et tamen dat scotum in Berchescire.' D. B. ii. 11: 'In Colecestra habet episcopus 14 domos et 4 acras non reddentes consuetudinem praeter scotum nisi episcopo.'

[3] See above, p. 85.   [4] Hamilton, Inquisitio, 60.

thing to be carefully noted, otherwise some geld may be lost[1]. A man's land has descended to his three sons: if 'there is only one hall,' but one demand for geld need be made; if 'each has his hall,' there must be three separate demands. When we are told that two brothers held land and that each had his house (*domus*) though they dwelt in one court (*curia*), a nice problem is being put before us:—Two halls, or one hall—Two manors or one manor[2]?

The petty *maneria* of Suffolk, what can they be but The petty manors. holdings which geld by themselves? The holders of them are not great men, they have no tenants or just two or three bordiers; sometimes they can not 'withdraw' their lands from their lords. But still they pay their own taxes at their own houses.

In supposing that forces have been at work which tend The lord and his man's taxes. to make the lord responsible for the taxes of his men, we are not without a warrant in the ancient dooms. 'If a king's thegn or a lord of land (*landrica*) neglects to pay the Rome penny, let him forfeit ten half-marks, half to Christ, half to the king. If a "townsman" withholds the penny, let the lord of the land pay the penny and take an ox from the man, and if the lord neglects to do this, then let Christ and the king receive the full *bót* of 12 ores[3].' The right of doing justice is also the duty of doing justice. It is natural that the lord with soke should become a tax-gatherer, and he will gladly guarantee the taxes if thereby he can prevent the king's officers from entering his precinct and meddling with his justiciables. At no time has the state found it easy to collect taxes from the poor; over and over again it has been glad to avail itself of the landlord's intermediation[4].

Our theory that while the lord is directly and primarily Distinction between villeins and sokemen. responsible for the geld of his villeins, he is but subsidiarily responsible for the geld of those of his sokemen or 'free men'

---

[1] Above, p. 110.　　　　[2] D. B. i. 35 b.

[3] Northumbrian Priests' Law, 58, 59, (Schmid, p. 369.)

[4] An Act of 1869 (32–3 Vic. c. 41) allowed the owners of certain small houses to agree to pay the rates which under the ordinary law would become due from the occupiers, and authorized the vestries to allow such owners a commission of 25 per cent. See also the instructive recital in 59 Geo. III. c. 12, sec. 19:—The small occupiers are evading the poors' rate, and the owners exact higher rents than they would otherwise get, on the ground that the occupiers can not be effectually assessed.

who are deemed to belong to his manor, is founded in part
on what we take to have been the wording of King William's
writ[1], in part on the form taken by the returns made thereto.
The writ draws a marked line between the villein and the
sokeman. The king wishes to know how much land each
sokeman, each *liber homo*, holds; he does not care that any
distinction should be drawn between the lord's demesne lands
and the lands of the villeins. And, on the whole, his commands
are obeyed. A typical entry in the survey of East Anglia
will first describe in one mass the land held by the lord and
his villeins, will tell us how many carucates this land is rated
at, how many teams there are on the demesne, and how many
the men have, then it will enumerate sheep and pigs and
goats, and then, as it were in an appendix, it will add that
so many sokemen belong to this manor and that between them
they hold so many carucates or acres[2]. In Suffolk even the
names of these humble tenants are sometimes recorded[3]. And
then, we have seen[4] that there is some doubt as to whether
or no these men are or are not to be reckoned as part of the
manor for all purposes. We have to say that the manor ' with
the free men,' or ' without the free men ' is worth so much.

The lord's
subsidiary
liability.
After all, we are only supposing that the fashion in which
the danegeld was put in charge resembled in some of its
main outlines the fashion in which a very similar tax was
put in charge under Richard I. In 1194 the land-tax that
was levied for the payment of the king's ransom seems to
have been assessed according to the hidage stated in Domesday
Book[5]. Then in 1198 a new assessment was made. We are
told that the king ordained that every baron should with
the sheriff's aid distrain his men to pay the tax cast upon
them, and that if, owing to the baron's default, distresses were

---

[1] See above, p. 24.

[2] E.g. D. B. ii. 389 b, 'Clarum tenuit Aluricus pro manerio 24 car. terrae
T. R. E. Tunc 40 villani....Tunc 12 carucae in dominio....Tunc 36 carucae
hominum....Huic manerio semper adiacent 5 sochemani cum omni consuetudine
1 car. terrae et dim. Semper 1 caruca et dimidia.'

[3] E.g. D. B. ii. 339: 'In eadem villa 14 liberi homines commendati, Godricus
faber et Edricus et Ulnotus et Osulfus et Uluricus et Stanmarus et Leuietus et
Wihtricus et Blachemanus et Mansuna et Leuinus et Ulmarus et Ulfah et alter
Ulfah et Leofstanus de 40 acris et habent 2 carucas et valent 10 solidos.'

[4] Above, p. 115.

[5] Rolls of the King's Court, Ric. I. (Pipe Roll. Soc.), p. xxiv. But apparently
there had been considerable rearrangements in some of the counties.

not made, then the amount due from the baron's men should be seized from the baron's own demesne and he should be left to recoup himself as best he could[1]. Now it is a liability of this sort that we are venturing to carry back into the Confessor's day. The lord is responsible to the state as principal, and indeed as sole, debtor for so much of the geld as is due from his demesne land and from the land of his *villani,* while as regards any lands of 'free men' or sokemen which are attached to his manor, his liability is not primary nor absolute; he is bound to take measures to make these men pay their taxes; if he fails in this duty, then their taxes will become due from his demesne[2].

When we read that in Nottinghamshire the relief of the thegn who had six manors or less was three marks, while his who had more than six manors was eight pounds[3], this may seem to hint that some inferior limit was set to the size of the manor. If so, it was drawn at a very low point in the scale of tenements. Possibly some general rule had compelled all men who held less than a bovate or half-virgate to 'add' themselves to the manor of some lord. But the Nottinghamshire rule is rude and arbitrary. He who has seven houses against which geld is charged is a big man. On the other hand, it is probable that the Norman lords brought with them some notion, and not a very modest notion, of what a reasonably sufficient *manerium* should be. The king has in some cases rewarded them by a promise of ten or twenty manors without specifying very carefully what those manors are to be like. He has promised Count Eustace a hundred manors[4]. Thus we would explain a not uncommon class of entries:—'fourteen free men commended to Wulfsige were delivered to Rainald

Manors distributed to the Frenchmen.

---

[1] Hoveden, iv. 46. The important words are these: 'Statutum etiam fuit quod quilibet baro cum vicecomite faceret districtiones super homines suos; et si per defectum baronum districtiones factae non fuissent, caperetur de dominico baronum quod super homines suos restaret reddendum, et ipsi barones ad homines suos inde caperent.' The baron's *homines* we take to be freeholders; he would be absolutely liable for the tax cast upon his villeinage. As to the tax of 1198 see Eng. Hist. Rev. iii. 501, 701; iv. 105, 108.

[2] In Dial. de Scac. ii. 14, the author tells us that until recently if a baron who owed money to the crown was insolvent, the goods of his knights could be seized. The idea of subsidiary liability is not too subtle for the time.

[3] Above, p. 108.

[4] D. B. ii. 9: 'set Comes Eustachius 1 ex illis [hidis] tenet que non est de suis c. [100] mansionibus.'

to make up (*ad perficiendum*) this manor of Carlington[1].'—
in Berningham a free man held 20 acres of land and this
was delivered to Walter Giffard to make up Letheringsett[2].'—
'Peter claims the land which belonged to seventeen free men
as having been delivered to him to make up this manor[3].'—
'This land was delivered to Peter to make up some, but his
men do not know what, manor[4].' The small 'free men' of
the east have been 'added to' manors to which they did not
belong in King Edward's day. A few of the free men of
Suffolk still 'remain in the king's hand' ready to be delivered
out to complete the manors of their conquerors[5]. Here too
we may perhaps find the explanation of the entry which says
that Hugh de Port held Wallop 'for half a manor[6].' The
king has promised him a dozen or score of manors; and this
estate at Wallop worth but fifteen shillings a year, really no
gentleman would take it for a manor.

Summary.   Such then is the best explanation that we can offer of
the *manerium* of Domesday Book. About details we may
be wrong, but that this term has a technical meaning which
is connected with the levy of the danegeld we can not doubt.
It loses that meaning in course of time because the danegeld
gives way before newer forms of taxation. It never again
acquires a technical meaning until the late days when retrospective lawyers find the essence of a manor in its court[7].

---

[1] D. B. ii. 233 b.   [2] D. B. ii. 242 b.   [3] D. B. ii. 258.
[4] D. B. ii. 258.   [5] D. B. ii. 447.   [6] D. B. i. 45 b.
[7] Two objections to our theory may be met by a note. (1) Some manors are
free of geld, and therefore to make our definition correct we ought to say that a
manor is a tenement which either pays its geld at a single place or which would
do so were it not freed from the tax by some special privilege. A *manerium* does
not cease to be a *manerium* by being freed from geld. (2) In later days we may
well find a manor holden of another manor, so that a plot of land may be
within two manors. If this usage of the term can be traced back into Domesday
Book as a common phenomenon, then our doctrine is in great jeopardy. But
we have noticed no passage which clearly and unambiguously says that a tract
of land was *at one and the same time* both a *manerium* and also a part of
another *manerium*. To this we must add that of the distribution of *maneria*
T. R. E. we only obtain casual and very imperfect tidings. If T. R. W. a free
man has been 'added to' a *manerium*, the commissioners have no deep interest in
the inquiry whether T. R. E. his tenement was itself an independent *manerium*.
A great simplification has been effected and the number of *maneria* has been
largely reduced.

§ 7. *Manor and Vill.*

After what has now been said, it is needless to repeat
that in Domesday Book the *manerium* and the *villa* are
utterly different things[1]. In a given case the two may coincide,
and throughout a great tract of England such cases were
common and we may even say that they were normal. But
in the east this was not so. We may easily find a village
which taken as a whole has been utterly free from seignorial
domination. Orwell in Cambridgeshire will be a good example[2].

Manorial and non-manorial vills.

In King Edward's day this vill of Orwell was rated at
4 hides: probably it was somewhat underrated for at the
date of the survey it was deemed capable of finding land for
nearly 6 teams. The following table will show who held the
four hides before the Conquest:—

The vill of Orwell.

	H.	V.	A.
Two sokemen, men of Edith the Fair		$\frac{2}{3}$	
A sokeman, man of Abp Stigand		$1\frac{1}{3}$	
A sokeman, man of Robert Wimarc's son		$1\frac{1}{3}$	
A sokeman, man of the King		$\frac{2}{3}$	
A sokeman, man of Earl Ælfgar		$1\frac{1}{3}$	
A sokeman, man of Earl Waltheof		3	
A sokeman, man of the King		$\frac{1}{3}$	
Sigar a man of Æsgar the Staller		$1\frac{1}{3}$	
Turbert a man of Edith the Fair		$3\frac{1}{4}$	5
Achil a man of Earl Harold		1	
A sokeman of the King		1	
S^t. Mary of Chatteris		$\frac{1}{3}$	
S^t. Mary of Chatteris		$\frac{1}{4}$	
	4	0	0[3]

It will be seen that eight of the most exalted persons in
the land, the king, the archbishop, three earls, two royal
marshals or stallers, and that mysterious lady known as Edith
the Fair, to say nothing of the church of Chatteris, had a
certain interest in this little Cambridgeshire village. But
then how slight an interest it was! Every one of the tenants

---

[1] D. B. ii. 174: 'Hec villa fuit in duobus maneriis T. R. E.' Ibid. i. 164:
'De his 2 villis fecit Comes W. unum manerium.'

[2] Inquisitio, 77–9.

[3] This result comes out correctly if $1\,\text{H} = 4\,\text{V} = 120\,\text{A}$. For the state of this
vill T. R. W. see Round, Feudal England, 40.

was free to 'withdraw himself,' ' to give or sell his land.' Now
we can not say that all of them were peasants. Achil the
man of Harold seems to have had other lands in the neighbouring villages of Harlton and Barrington[1]. It is probable
that Turbert, Edith's man, had another virgate at Kingston[2]:
he was one of the jurors of the hundred in which Orwell lay[3].
Sigar the man of Æsgar was another juror, and held land
at Thriplow, Foxton, Haslingfield and Shepreth; he seems
to have been his lord's steward[4]. But we may be fairly certain
that the unnamed sokemen tilled their own soil, though perhaps
they had help from a few cottagers. And they can not have
been constantly employed in cultivating the demesne lands.
of their lords. They must go some distance to find any such
demesne lands. The Wetherley hundred, in which Orwell
lies, is full of the sokemen of these great folk : Waltheof, for
example, has 3 men in Comberton, 4 in Barton, 3 in Grantchester, 1 in Wratworth : but he has no demesne land, and if
he had it, he could not get it tilled by these scattered tenants.
The Fair Edith has half a hide in Haslingfield and we are
told that this belongs to the manor of Swavesey. Now at
Swavesey Edith has a considerable manor[5], but it can not have
got much in the way of labour out of a tenant who lived at
Haslingfield, for the two villages are a long ten miles apart.
As to the king's sokemen, their only recorded services are
the *avera* and the *inward*. The former seems to be a carrying
service done at the sheriff's bidding and to be only exigible
when the king comes into the shire, while *inward* seems to
be the duty of forming a body guard for the king while he
is in the shire :—if in any year the king did not come, a small
sum of money was taken instead[6].

[1] His plot at Orwell is said to belong to Harlton. Then at Harlton we find
an Achil with sokemen under him, and though in D. B. he is described as a
king's thegn, this is not incompatible with his being the man of Harold for
some of his lands. At Barrington Achillus Danaus homo Haroldi has a holding
of 40 acres.

[2] Inquisitio, 86.   [3] Ibid. 68.   [4] Ibid. 43, 44, 45, 73, 76.

[5] D. B. i. 195.

[6] D. B. i. 139: 'De consuetudine 1 averam inveniebat cum Rex in scyra
veniebat, si non 5 den. reddebat.' D. B. i. 190, '[Sochemanni in Fuleberne]
reddunt per annum 8 libras arsas et pensatas et unoquoque anno 12 equos et
12 inguardos si Rex in vicecomitatu veniret, si non veniret 12 sol. et 8 den.;
T. R. E. non reddebant vicecomiti nisi averas et inguardos vel 12 sol. et 8 den.
et superplus invasit Picot [vicecomes] super Regem.'

Lest it should be thought that in picking out the village of Orwell we have studiously sought a rare case, we will here set out in a tabular form what we can learn of the state of the hundred in which Orwell lies. The Wetherley hundred contained twelve vills: it was a land of true villages which until very lately had wide open fields[1]. In the Confessor's day the lands in it were allotted thus:—

A Cambridgeshire hundred.

CAMBRIDGESHIRE. WETHERLEY HUNDRED[2].

I. COMBERTON. A vill of 6 hides.

		H.	V.	A.		C.	B.
1.	Seven sokemen of the King	1	1	0 ⎫			
	A sokeman, man of Earl Waltheof ⎱		3	0 ⎬		4	0
	A sokeman, man of Abp Stigand ⎰			⎭			
2.	A man of Earl Waltheof		1	15		1	0
3.	A sokeman, man of the King		1	0 ⎫			
	A sokeman, man of Abp Stigand		1	15 ⎬		2	0
	A sokeman, man of Earl Waltheof		1	15 ⎭			
4.	The King	2	2	0		5	0
		5	3	15[3]		12	0

II. BARTON. A vill of 7 hides.

		H.	V.	A.		C.	B.
1.	Two sokemen, men of Earl Waltheof	1	1	15 ⎫			
	A sokeman, man of Earl Waltheof		3	15[4] ⎬		5	0
	A sokeman, man of Earl Waltheof		1	0 ⎭			
2.	Juhael the King's hunter	1	0	0		1	0
3.	A sokeman, man of Edith the Fair		2	0 ⎫			
4.	Twenty-three sokemen of the King	3	0	0 ⎭		6	0
		7	0	0		12	0

[1] Wratworth has completely disappeared from the modern map; its territory seems to be included in that of the present Orwell. See Rot. Hund. ii. 559 and Lysons, Magna Britannia, ii. 243. A small hamlet called Malton seems to represent it. Whitwell also is no longer the name of a village, while the modern Coton is not mentioned in D. B. There is now a Whitwell Farm near the village of Coton, but in the parish of Barton. The modern Coton does not seem to be the ancient Whitwell, for on Subsidy Rolls we may find Whitwell annexed to Barton and Coton to Grantchester.

[2] The figures in our first column represent the division of the vill among the Norman lords. H. V. A. stand for Hides, Virgates, Acres. By C. and B. we signify the Carucae and Boves for which ' there was land.'

[3] There is some small error in this case.

[4] A small conjectural emendation.

III. GRANTCHESTER. A vill of 7 hides[1].

	H.	V.	A.	C.	B.
1. Five sokemen, men of the King		3	0	1	0
2. Two sokemen, men of the King	2	1	0 }	6	0
A sokeman, man of Æsgar the Staller		2	0 }		
3. A sokeman, man of Earl Ælfgar		3	0 }	4	0
Three sokemen, men of Earl Waltheof	2	0	0 }		
4. Godman a man of Edith the Fair		1	15	1	0
5. Juhael the King's hunter		1	0		4
6. Wulfric, the King's man			15		3
	7	0	0	12	7

IV. HASLINGFIELD. A vill of 20 hides.

	H.	V.	A.	C.	B.
1. The King	7	1	0	8	0
2. Five sokemen, men of the King	3	0	0 }	4	0
A sokeman, man of Æsgar the Staller	1	3	0 }		
3. Ealdred a man of Edith the Fair	1	0	15	1	4
4. Edith the Fair, belonging to Swavesey		2	0		4
5. Sigar a man of Æsgar the Staller	5	0	0	6	0
6. Two sokemen of the King	1	1	3	2	0
7. Merewin, a man of Edith the Fair			12	0	0
	20	0	0	22	0

V. HARLTON. A vill of 5 hides.

	H.	V.	A.	C.	B.
1. Achil, a King's thegn and under him five sokemen of whom four were his men while the fifth was the man of Ernulf	4	0	0	6	0
2. Godman a man of Æsgar the Staller	1	0	0	1	0
	5	0	0	7	0

VI. BARRINGTON. A vill of 10 hides.

	H.	V.	A.	C.	B.
1. Eadric Púr a King's thegn		3	0 }		
Fifteen sokemen, men of the King	4	1	15 }		
Four sokemen, men of Earl Ælfgar	2	0	15 }	11	0
Three sokemen, men of Æsgar the Staller	1	0	0 }		
Eadric Púr, holding of the Church of Chatteris			15 }		
2. The Church of Chatteris	2	0	0	4	0
3. Ethsi, holding of Robert Wimarc's son			20		3
4. Achil the Dane, a man of Earl Harold			40		6
5. A sokeman, man of the King			15		2
	11	0	0[2]	17	3

[1] The Inq. Com. Cant. says 6 hides.
[2] An error of one hide in the particulars. The two records do not fully agree.

		H.	V.	A.	C.	B.
VII.	**SHEPRETH.** A vill of 5 hides.					
1.	Four sokemen, men of the King	2	0	15	2	2
	A sokeman, man of Earl Ælfgar					
2.	The Church of Chatteris	1	1	15	1	4
3.	Sigar a man of Æsgar the Staller	1	0	0	1	0
4.	Heming a man of the King		1	15		4
5.	The Church of Ely			15		2
		5	0	0	5	4
VIII.	**ORWELL.** A vill of 4 hides.					
1.	Two sokemen, men of Edith the Fair			20		
	A sokeman, man of Abp Stigand		1	10		
	A sokeman, man of Robert Wimarc's son		1	10	1	4
	A sokeman, man of the King			20		
	A sokeman, man of Earl Ælfgar		1	10		
2.	A sokeman, man of Earl Waltheof		3	0	1	0
	A sokeman, man of the King			10		
3.	Sigar, a man of Æsgar the Staller		1	10		4
4.	Turbert, a man of Edith the Fair		3	12½	1	4
5.	Achil, a man of Earl Harold		1	0		2
6.	A sokeman, man of the King		1	0		3
7.	The Church of Chatteris			10		1
8.	The Church of Chatteris			7½		½
		4	0	0	5	2½
IX.	**WRATWORTH.** A vill of 4 hides.					
1.	A sokeman, man of Edith the Fair		3	10		
	A sokeman, man of Abp Stigand		3	0		
	A sokeman, man of Earl Ælfgar		1	10	3	0
	A sokeman, man of Robert Wimarc's son			10		
	A sokeman, man of the King			20		
2.	A sokeman, man of Earl Waltheof		2	20	1	0
	A sokeman, man of Robert Wimarc's son			10		
3.	A sokeman, man of Edith the Fair		1	10		4
4.	A sokeman, man of the King		1	0		3
5.	Two sokemen, men of the King		2	0		4
		4	0	0	5	3
X.	**WHITWELL.** A vill of 4 hides.					
1.	A sokeman, man of Earl Ælfgar		1	20		
	A sokeman, man of Robert Wimarc's son		1	0	1	4
	A sokeman, man of the King		2	0		
2.	A sokeman, man of Abp Stigand			15		
	A sokeman, man of Edith the Fair			10		4
	[A sokeman]			15		
3.	Six sokemen, men of the King	1	1	0		
	A sokeman, man of Robert Wimarc's son		2	0	2	0
	A sokeman, man of Earl Ælfgar		1	0		
4.	Godwin a man of Edith the Fair		2	0	1	0
		4	0	0	5	0

XI. WIMPOLE. A vill of 4 hides.

		H.	V.	A.	C.	B.
1.	Edith the Fair	2	2	15	3	0
2.	Earl Gyrth	1	1	15	2	0
		4	0	0	5	0

XII. ARRINGTON. A vill of 4 hides.

		H.	V.	A.	C.	B.
1.	Ælfric, a King's thegn	1	1	10 ⎫		
	A sokeman, man of Earl Waltheof	1	0	0 ⎪		
	A sokeman, man of the Abbot of Ely	1	0	0 ⎬	8	0
	A sokeman, man of Robert Wimarc's son			20 ⎭		
2.	A man of Edith the Fair		2	0		4
		4	0	0[1]	8	4

The Wetherley sokemen. Now if by a 'manor' we mean what our historical economists usually mean when they use that term, we must protest that before the Norman Conquest there were very few manors in the Wetherley hundred. In no one case was the whole of a village coincident with a manor, with a lord's estate. The king had considerable manors in Comberton and Haslingfield. Sigar had a manor at Haslingfield; the church of Chatteris had a manor at Barrington besides some land at Shepreth; Wimpole was divided between Edith and Earl Gyrth; Harlton between Achil and Godman. But in Barton, Grantchester, Shepreth, Orwell, Wratworth, Whitwell and Arrington we see nothing manorial, unless we hold ourselves free to use that term of a little tenement which to all appearance might easily be cultivated by the labour of one household, at all events with occasional help supplied by a few cottagers. Indeed it is difficult to say what profit some of the great people whose names we have mentioned were deriving from those of their men who dwelt in the Wetherley hundred. We take the Mercian earl for example[2]. One of the sokemen of Grantchester, four of the sokemen of Barrington, one of the sokemen of Shepreth, one of the sokemen of Orwell, one of the sokemen of Wratworth, two of the sokemen of Whitwell were Ælfgar's men. That Ælfgar got a little money or a little provender out of them is probable, that they did some carrying service for him is possible and perhaps they aided him at harvest time on some manor

---

[1] A small emendation justified by Inq. Eliensis (Hamilton, p. 110).

[2] Ælfgar died before King Edward; Freeman, Norman Conquest, ed. 3, iii. 469, places his death in or about 1062.

of his in another part of the county; but that they were not
the tillers of his land seems clear[1].

What is more, our analysis of this Wetherley hundred enables
us to drive home the remark that very often a sokeman was
not the sokeman of his lord or, in other words, that he was not
under seignorial justice[2]. Ælfgar had ten sokemen scattered
about in six villages. Did he hold a court for them? We
think not. Did they go to the court of some distant manor?
We think not. The court they attended was the Wetherley
hundred-moot. One of the sokemen in Arrington was in a somewhat exceptional position—exceptional, that is, in this hundred.
Not only was he the man of the Abbot of Ely, but his soke
belonged to the Abbot; and if he sold his tenement, and this
he could do without the Abbot's consent, the soke over his land
would 'remain' to the Abbot[3]. He was not only his lord's
man but his lord's justiciable and probably attended some
court outside the hundred. But for the more part these men
of Wetherley were not the justiciables of their lords. It was
a very free hundred when the Normans came there: much too
free for the nation's welfare we may think, for these sokemen
could go with their land to what lord they pleased. Also be it
noted in passing that the churches have little in Wetherley.

In 1086 there had been a change. The sokemen had
disappeared. The Norman lords had made demesne land where
their English *antecessores* possessed none. Count Roger had
instituted a seignorial court at Orwell. He had borrowed
three sokemen 'to hold his pleas' from Picot the sheriff and
had refused to give them up again[4]. Apparently they had
sunk to the level of *villani*. Two centuries afterwards we

The sokeman and seignorial justice.

Changes in the Wetherley hundred.

---

[1] The history of the earldoms during Edward's reign is exceedingly obscure.
See Freeman's elaborate note: Ibid., 555. In particular Cambridgeshire seems
to have lain now in one and now in another earldom. Thus it comes about
that Cambridgeshire sokemen are commended some to Ælfgar, some to Waltheof,
some to Harold, some to Gyrth. Ælfgar, for example, had at one time been
earl in East Anglia. Men who had commended themselves to an earl would,
unless they 'withdrew themselves,' still be his men though he had ceased to be
earl of their county.

[2] See above, p. 105. Observe how frequently our record speaks of 'sochemanni *homines* Algari' and the like. These sokemen are Ælfgar's men; but
are not properly his sokemen.

[3] Inq. Com. Cant. 110. This is from the Inquisitio Eliensis. Compare
p. 83.

[4] Inq. Com. Cant. 77–8.

see the hundred of Wetherley once more. There is villeinage
enough in it. The villein at Orwell, for example, holds only
10 acres but works for his lord on 152 days in the year, besides
boon-days[1]. And yet we should go far astray if we imposed
upon these Cambridgeshire villages that neat manorial system
which we see at its neatest and strongest in the abbatial cartularies. The villages do not become manors. The manors
are small. The manors are intermixed in the open fields.
There are often freeholders in the village who are not the
tenants of any lord who has a manor there. A villein will
hold two tenements of two lords. The villein of one lord will
be the freeholder of another. The 'manorial system' has been
forced upon the villages, but it fits them badly[2].

Manorial-
ism in Cam-
bridge-
shire.

In the thirteenth century the common field of a Cambridgeshire village was often a very maze of proprietary rights, and
yet the village was an agrarian whole. Let us take, for
example, Duxford as it stood in the reign of Edward I.[3] We
see 39 villein tenements each of which has fourteen acres in
the fields. These tenements are divided between five different
manors. Four of our typical 'townsmen' hold of Henry de
Lacy, who holds of Simon de Furneaux, who holds of the Count
of Britanny, who holds of the king. Two hold of Ralph of
Duxford, who holds of Basilia wife of Baldwyn of St George,
who holds of William Mortimer, who holds of Simon de
Furneaux, who holds of the Count of Britanny, who holds
of the king. Eight hold of the Templars, who hold of Roger
de Colville, who holds of the Earl of Albemarle, who holds
of the king. Nine hold of William le Goyz, who holds of
Henry of Boxworth, who holds of Richard de Freville, who
holds of the king. Sixteen hold of John d'Abernon, who
holds of the Earl Marshal, who holds of the king. Three of
the greatest 'honours' in England are represented. Three
monasteries and two parochial churches have strips in the
fields. And yet there are normal tenements cut according
to one pattern, tenements of fourteen acres the holders of

[1] Rot. Hund. ii. 558.

[2] One instance may suffice. In Sawston (Rot. Hund. ii. 575–80) are three
manors, *A*, *B*, *C*; *A* has a sub-manor. One Thomas Dovenel holds in villeinage
of the lord of *A*; in villeinage of the lord of *B*; in freehold of the lord of *B*;
in freehold of a tenant of the lord of *B*; in freehold of a tenant of a tenant of
the lord of *B*.

[3] Rot. Hund. ii. 580.

which, though their other services may differ, pay for the more part an equal rent[1]. The village seems to say that it must be one, though the lords would make it many. And then we look back to the Confessor's day and we see that a good part of Duxford was held by sokemen[2].

Perhaps we shall be guilty of needless repetition; but what is written in Domesday Book about *maneria* is admirably designed for the deception of modern readers whose heads are full of 'the manorial system.' Therefore let us look at two Hertfordshire villages. In one of them there is a *manerium* which Ralph Basset holds of Robert of Ouilly[3]. It has been rated at 4, but is now rated at 2 hides. There is land for 4 teams. In demesne are 2 teams; and $3\frac{1}{2}$ *villani* with 2 sokemen of 1 hide and 5 *bordarii* have 2 teams. There are 1 cottager and 1 serf and a mill of 10 shillings and meadow for 3 teams. It is now worth £3; in King Edward's day it was worth £5. Now here, we say, is a pretty little manor of the common kind. Let us then explore its past history. 'Five sokemen held this manor.' Yes, we say, before the Conquest this manor was held in physically undivided shares by five lords. Their shares were small and they were humble people; but still they had a manor. But let us read further. 'Two of them were the men of Brihtric and held $1\frac{1}{2}$ hides; other two were the men of Osulf the son of Frane and held $1\frac{1}{2}$ hides; and the fifth was the man of Eadmer Atule and held a hide.' We will at once finish the story and see how Robert of Ouilly came by this manor. 'No one of these five sokemen belonged to his *antecessor* Wigot; every one of them might sell his land. One of them bought (i.e. redeemed) his land for nine ounces of gold from King William, so the men of the hundred say, and afterwards turned for protection to Wigot.' So Robert's title to this manor is none of the best. But are we sure that before the Conquest there was anything that we should call a manor? These five sokemen who have unequal shares, who have three different lords, who hold in all but 4 team-lands, whose land is worth but £5, do not look like a set of co-parceners to whom a 'manor' has descended. When Robert of Ouilly has got his manor there are upon it 2 sokemen,

The soke-men and the manors.

---

[1] On four out of the five manors the rent is 2*s*. 3*d*.; on the fifth 3*s*. 0*d*.

[2] Inq. Com. Cant. 41.   [3] D. B. i. 137 b.

3 villeins, 5 *bordarii*, a cottager and a serf. It was not a splendid manor for five lords.

We turn over a few pages. Hardouin of Eschalers has a manor rated at 5½ hides[1]. It contains land for 8 teams. In demesne are 2 hides less 20 acres, and 3 teams; 11 *villani* with the priest and 5 *bordarii* have 5 teams. There are 4 cottagers and 6 serfs. It is worth £9; in the Confessor's day it was worth £10. Who held this manor in the past? Nine sokemen held it. Rather a large party of joint lords, we say; but still, families will grow. Howbeit, we must finish the sentence :—' Of these, one, Sired by name, was the man of Earl Harold and held 1 hide and 3 virgates for a manor; another, Alfred, a man of Earl Ælfgar, held 1½ hides for a manor; and the other seven were sokemen of King Edward and held 2 hides and 1 virgate and they supplied the sheriff with 9 pence a year or 2¼ *averae* (carrying services).' No, we have not been reading of the joint holders of a ' manor'; we have been reading of peasant proprietors. Two of them were substantial folk; each of the two held a *manerium* at which geld was paid ; the other seven gelded at one of the king's *maneria* under the view of his bailiffs. *Maneria* there have been everywhere; but ' manors' we see in the making. Hardouin has made one under our eyes.

We hear the objection that, be it never so humble, a manor is a manor. But is that truism quite true ? If all that we want for the constitution of a manor is a proprietor of some land who has a right to exact from some other man, or two or three other men, the whole or some part of the labour that is necessary for the tillage of his soil, we may indeed see manors everywhere and at all times. Even if we introduce a more characteristically medieval element and demand that the tillers shall be neither menial servants nor labourers hired for money, but men who make their living by cultivating for their own behoof small plots which the proprietor allows them to occupy, still we shall have the utmost difficulty if we would go behind manorialism. But suppose for a moment that we have a village the land of which is being held by nine sokemen, each of whom has a hide or half-hide scattered about in the open fields, and each of whom controls the labour of a couple of serfs, shall we not be misleading the public and ourselves if we speak of nine

[1] D. B. i. 141 b.

manors or even of nine 'embryo manors'? At any rate it is clear enough that if these estates of the sokemen are 'embryo manors,' then these embryos were deposited in the common fields. In that case the common fields, the hides and yard-lands of the village are not the creatures of manorialism.

We have seen free villages; we have seen a free hundred. We might have found yet freer hundreds had we gone to Suffolk. We have chosen Cambridgeshire because Cambridge-shire can not be called a Danish county, except in a sense in which, notwithstanding the wasted condition of Yorkshire, about one half of the English nation lived in Danish counties. When men divide up England between the three laws, they place Cambridgeshire under the Danelaw; but to that law they subject about one half of the inhabitants of England. There may have been many men of Scandinavian race in Cam-bridgeshire; but we find hundreds not wapentakes, hides not carucates, while among the names of villages there are few indeed which betray a Scandinavian origin. The Wetherley hundred was not many miles away from the classic fields of Hitchin[1]. *The Danes and free-dom.*

But in truth we must be careful how we use our Dane. Yorkshire was a Danish county in a sense in which Cambridge-shire was not Danish; it was a land of trithings and wapentakes, a land without hides, where many a village testified by its name to a Scandinavian settlement. And yet to all appearance it was in the Confessor's day a land where the manors stood thick[2]. Then we have that wonderful contrast between Yorkshire and Lincolnshire which Ellis summed up in these figures:— *The Danish counties.*

	Sochemanni	Villani	Bordarii
Lincolnshire	11,503	7,723	4,024
Yorkshire	447	5,079	1,819

Perhaps this contrast would have been less violent if Yorkshire had not been devastated: but violent it is and

[1] Inq. Com. Cant., pp. 108–110. As names of the Abbot of Ely's sokemen in Meldreth and neighbouring villages we have Grimmus, Alsi Cild, Wenesi, Alsi, Leofwinus, Ædricus, Godwinus, Almarus, Aluricus frater Goduuini, Ædriz, Alsi Berd, Alricus Godingessune, Wenestan, Alwin Blondus, Alfuuinus, Alure-dus, Alricus Brunesune, Alware, Hunuð, Hunwinus, Brizstanus. This does not point to a preponderance of Norse or Danish blood.

[2] Owing to the wasted condition of Yorkshire, the information that we obtain of the T. R. E. is meagre and perfunctory. But what seems character-istic of this county is a holding of two or three ploughlands which we might fairly call an embryo manor.

must be. It will provoke the remark that the 'faults' (if any faults there be) in a truly economic stratification of mankind are not likely to occur just at the boundaries of the shires, whereas so long as each county has a court from which there is no appeal to any central tribunal, we may expect to find that lines which have their origin in fiscal practice will be sharp lines and will coincide with the metes and bounds of jurisdictional districts.

The contrast between villeins and sokemen. Nor should it escape remark that the names by which a grand distinction is expressed are in their origin very loose terms and etymologically ill-fitted to the purpose that they are serving. In English the *villanus* is the *túnesman* or, as we should say, the villager. And yet to all seeming the sokeman is essentially a villager. What is more the land where the sokemen and 'free men' lived was a land of true villages, of big villages, of limitless 'open fields,' whereas the hamleted west was servile. Then again *sokeman* is a very odd term. If it signified that the man to whom it is applied was always the justiciable of the lord to whom he was commended, we could understand it. Even if this man were always the justiciable of a court that had passed into private hands, we could still understand it. But apparently there are plenty of sokemen whose soke 'is' or 'lies' in those hundred courts that have no lord but the king. The best guess that we can make as to the manner in which they have acquired their name is that in an age which is being persuaded that some 'service' must be done by every one who holds land, suit of court appears as the only service that is done by all these men. They may owe other services; but they all owe suit of court. If so we may see their legal successors in those freeholders of the twelfth century who are 'acquitting' their lords and their villages by doing suit at the national courts[1]. But when a new force comes into play (and the tribute to the pirate was a new and a powerful force) new lines of demarcation must be drawn, new classes of men must be formed and words

---

[1] See the early extents in Cart. Rams. iii. Thus (242) at Hemingford: 'R. V. tenet tres virgatas et dimidiam et sequitur hundredum et comitatum.... R. H. tenet duas virgatas et sequitur hundredum et comitatum.' Elsworth (249): 'R. filius T. duas virgatas. Pro altera sequitur comitatum et hundredum; pro altera solvit quinque solidos.' Brancaster (261): 'Cnutus avus Petri tenebat terram suam libere in tempore Regis Henrici et sequebatur comitatum et hundredum, et fuit quietus ab omni servitio.' See also Vinogradoff, Villainage, 441 ff.

will be borrowed for the purpose with little care for etymological niceties. One large and widely-spread class may find a name for itself in a district where the ordinary 'townsmen' or villagers are no longer treated as taxpayers responsible to the state, while some practice peculiar to a small part of the country may confer the name of 'sokemen' on those tillers of the soil who are rated to the geld. We are not arguing that this distinction, even when it first emerged, implied nothing that concerned the economic position of the villein and the sokeman. The most dependent peasants would naturally be the people who could not be directly charged with the geld, and the peasants who could not pay the geld would naturally become dependent on those who would pay it for them; still we are not entitled to assume that the fiscal scheme accurately mirrored the economic facts, or that the varying practice of different moots and different collectors may not have stamped as the villeins of one shire those who would have been the sokemen of another[1].

Be this as it may, any theory of English history must face the free, the lordless, village and must account for it as for one of the normal phenomena which existed in the year of grace 1066. How common it was we shall never know until the material contained in Domesday Book has been geographically rearranged by counties, hundreds and vills. But whether common or no, it was normal, just as normal as the village which was completely subject to seignorial power. We have before us villages which, taken as wholes, have no lords. What is more, it seems obvious enough that, unless there has been some great catastrophe in the past, some insurrection of the peasants or the like, the village of Orwell—and other villages might be named by the dozen—has never had a lord. Such lordships as exist in it are plainly not the relics of a dominion which has been split up among divers persons by the action of gifts and inheritances. The sokemen

Free villages.

---

[1] Some thirty years ago the whole political world of England was agitated by controversy about 'the compound householder.' Was he to have a vote? The historian of the nineteenth century will not treat the compound householders as forming one homogeneous class of men whose general status could be marked off from that of other classes. Nor, it is to be hoped, will etymological guesses lead him to believe that the compound householder held a compound house. He will say that a landlord 'compounded for' the rates of the aforesaid householder. *Mutatis mutandis* may not the villein have been the compound householder of the eleventh century?

of Orwell have worshipped every rising sun. One has commended himself to the ill-fated Harold, another to the ill-fated Waltheof, a third has chosen the Mercian Ælfgar, a fourth has placed himself under the aspiring Archbishop; yet all are free to 'withdraw.' We have here a very free village indeed, for its members enjoy a freedom of which no freeholder of the thirteenth century would even dream, and in a certain sense we have here a free village community. How much communalism is there? Of this most difficult question only a few words will now be said, for our guesses about remote ages we will yet a while reserve.

Village communities.

In the first place, we can not doubt that the 'open field system' of agriculture prevails as well in the free villages as in those that are under the control of a lord. The sokeman's hide or virgate is no ring-fenced 'close' but is composed of many scattered strips. Again, we can hardly doubt that the practice of 'co-aration' prevailed. The sokeman had seldom beasts enough to make up a team. It is well known that the whole scheme of land-measurements which runs through Domesday Book is based upon the theory that land is ploughed by teams of eight oxen. It is perhaps possible that smaller teams were sometimes employed; but when we read that a certain man 'always ploughed with three oxen[1],' or 'used to plough with two oxen but now ploughs with half a team[2],' or 'used to plough with a team but now ploughs with two oxen[3],' we are reading, not of small teams, but of the number of oxen that the man in question contributed towards the team of eight that was made up by him and his neighbours. When of a piece of land in Bedfordshire it is said that 'one ox ploughs there,' this means that the land in question supplies but one ox in a team of eight[4]; and here and not in any monstrous birth do we find the explanation of 'terra est dimidio bovi et ibi est semibos[5]':— there is a sixteenth part of a teamland and its tenant along with some other man provides an ox. There may have been light ploughs as well as heavy ploughs, but the heavy plough must have been extremely common, since the term 'plough team' (*caruca*) seems invariably to mean a team of eight.

The villagers as co-owners.

Then one notable case meets our eye in which the owner-

[1] D. B. ii. 204: '3 liberi homines...semper arant cum 3 bobus.'
[2] D. B. ii. 184 b.   [3] D. B. ii. 192 b.   [4] D. B. i. 211.
[5] D. B. i. 218 b. Compare the 'dimidius porcus' of ii. 287.

ship of land, of arable land, seems to be attributed to a village community. In Goldington, a village in Bedfordshire, Walter now holds a hide; there is land for one team and meadow for half a team. 'The men of the vill held this land in common and could sell it[1].' Apparently the men of the vill were Ælfwin Sac a man of the Bishop of Lincoln who held half a team-land and 'could do what he liked with it,' nine sokemen who held three team-lands between them, three other sokemen who held three team-lands, and Ælfmær a man of Asgil who held three team-lands[2]. How it came about that these men, besides holding land in severalty, held a tract in common, we are left to guess. Nor can we say whether such a case was usual or unusual. Very often in Little Domesday we meet an entry which tells how x free men held y acres and had z teams; for example, how 15 free men held 40 acres and had 2 teams[3]. In general we may well suppose that each of them held his strips in severalty, but we dare not say that such a phrase never points to co-ownership.

Then as to such part of the land as is not arable:—Even in the free village a few enclosed meadows will probably be found; but the pasture ground lies open for 'the cattle of the vill.' At the date of the survey, though several Norman lords have estates in one vill, the common formula used in connexion with each estate is, not 'there is pasture for the cattle of this manor, or of this land,' but 'there is pasture for the cattle of the vill.' Occasionally we read of 'common pasture' in a context which shows that the pasture is common not to several manorial lords but to the villeins of one lord[4]. In the hundred of Coleness in Suffolk there is a pasture which is common to all the men of the hundred[5]. But, as might be expected, we hear little of the mode in which pasture rights were allotted or regulated. Such rights were probably treated as appurtenances of the arable land:—'The canons of Waltham claim as much

The waste land of the vill.

---

[1] D. B. i. 213 b: 'Hanc terram tenuerunt homines villae communiter et vendere potuerunt.'

[2] D. B. i. 210, 212 b, 213 b.

[3] D. B. i. 214: 'In Meldone Johannes de Roches occupavit iniuste 25 acras super homines qui villam tenent.' This is a vague phrase.

[4] e.g. D. B. i. 112 b: 'Colsuen homo Episcopi Constantiensis aufert ab hoc manerio communem pasturam quae ibi adiacebat T. R. E. et etiam T. R. W. quinque annis.'

[5] D. B. ii. 339 b.

wood as belongs to one hide[1].'   If the rights of user are known, no one cares about the bare ownership of pasture land or wood land :—it is all one whether we say that Earl Edwin is entitled to one third of a certain wood or to every third oak that grows therein[2].

Co-owner-
ship of
mills.

Sometimes the ownership of a mill is divided into so many shares that we are tempted to think that this mill has been erected at the cost of the vill.   In Suffolk a free man holds a little *manerium* which is composed of 24 acres of land, 1½ acres of meadow and 'a fourth part of the mill in every third year[3]':—he takes his turn with his neighbours in the enjoyment of the revenue of the mill.   We may even be led to suspect that the parish churches have sometimes been treated as belonging to the men of the vill who have subscribed to erect or to endow them.   In Suffolk a twelfth part of a church belongs to a petty *manerium* which contains 30 acres and is cultivated by two bordiers with a single team[4].   When a parish church gets its virgate by 'the charity of the neighbours[5],' when nine free men give it twenty acres for the good of their souls[6], we may see in this some trace of communal action.

The system
of virgates
in a free
village.

Incidentally we may notice that the system of virgate holdings seems quite compatible with an absence of seignorial control.   In the free village, for example in Orwell, we shall often find that one man has twice, thrice or four times as much as another man :—the same is the case in the manorialized villages of Middlesex, where a villein may have as much as a hide or as little as a half-virgate ; but all the holdings will bear, at least in theory, some simple relation to each other.   Thus in Orwell the virgates are divided into thirds and quarters, and in several instances a man has four thirds of a virgate.   In Essex and East Anglia, though we may find many irregular and many very small holdings, tenements of 60, 45, 40, 30, 20, 15 acres are far commoner than they would be were it not that a unit of 120 acres will very easily break into such pieces.   Domesday Book takes no notice of family law and its 'vendere potuit' merely excludes the interference of the lord and does not imply that a man is at liberty to disappoint his expectant heirs.

[1] D. B. i. 140 b.
[2] D. B. i. 75 : 'tercia vero pars vel tercia quercus erat Comitis Eduini.'
[3] D. B. ii. 404 b : ' et in tercio anno quarta pars mol[endini].'
[4] D. B. ii. 291 b.   [5] D. B. ii. 24 b.   [6] D. B. ii. 438.

Very possibly there has been among the small folk but little giving or selling of land.

Nor is a law which gives the dead man's land to all his sons as co-heirs a sufficient force to destroy the system of hides and virgates when once it is established by some original allotment. In the higher ranks of society we see large groups of thegns holding land in common, holding as the Normans say 'in parage.' We can hardly doubt that they are co-heirs holding an inheritance that has not been physically partitioned[1]. Sometimes it is said of a single man that he holds in parage[2]. This gives us a valuable hint. Holding in parage implies that one of the 'pares,' one of the parceners,—as a general rule he would be the eldest of them—is answerable to king and lord for the services due from the land, while his fellows are bound only to him; they must help him to discharge duties for which he is primarily responsible[3]. This seems the import of such passages as the following—'Five thegns held two bovates; one of them was the *senior* (the elder, and we may almost say the lord) of the others[4]'—'Eight thegns held this manor; one of them Alli, a man of King Edward, was the *senior* of the others[5]'—'Godric and his brothers held three carucates; two of them served the third[6]'—'Chetel and Turver were brothers and after the death of their father they divided the land, but so that Chetel in doing the king's service should have help from Turver his brother[7]'—'Siwate, Alnod, Fenchel and Aschil divided the land of their father equally, and they held in such wise that if there were need for attendance in the king's host and Siwate could go, his brothers were to aid him [with money and provisions]; and on the next occasion another brother was to go and Siwate like the rest was to help him; and so on down

The vir-gates and inherit-ance.

---

[1] D. B. i. 83 : 'sex taini in paragio,' 'quatuor taini in paragio.' Ibid. 83 b : 'novem taini in paragio.' Ibid. 168 b : 'quinque fratres tenuerunt pro 5 maneriis et poterant ire quo volebant et pares erant.'

[2] D. B. i. 96 b: 'dim. hida quam tenebat T. R. E. unus tainus in paragio.' Ibid. 40 : 'Brictric tenuit de episcopo in paragio.'

[3] But it was possible for several men to be holding in parage and yet for each of them to have a separate *manerium*. This seems to imply that their holdings were physically separate and that each holding was separately liable for geld, though as regards other matters, e.g. military service, the division was ignored.

[4] D. B. i. 291.   [5] D. B. i. 145 b.   [6] D. B. i. 341.
[7] D. B. i. 354.

the list; but Siwate was the king's man[1].' No doubt similar
arrangements were made by co-heirs of lowlier station[2]. The
integrity of the tenement is maintained though several men
have an interest in it. In relation to the lord and the state
one of them represents his fellows. When the shares become
very small, some of the claimants might be bought out by the
others[3].

The farm.   But, to return to the village, we must once more notice
that the Canons of St Paul's have let their manor of Willesden
to the villeins[4]. This leads us to speculate as to the incidence
and collection of those great provender rents of which we read
when royal manors are described. In King Edward's day a
royal manor is often charged with the whole or some aliquot
share of a 'one night's farm,' that is one day's victual for the
king's household. Definite amounts of bread, cheese, malt,
meat, beer, honey, wool have to be supplied; thus, for example,
Cheltenham must furnish three thousand loaves for the king's
dogs and King's Barton must do the like[5]. Then too Edward
the sheriff receives as the profits of the shrievalty of Wiltshire, 130 pigs, 32 bacons, certain quantities of wheat, malt,
oats, and honey, 400 chicken, 1600 eggs, 100 cheeses, 100 lambs,
52 fleeces[6]. Between the king and the men of the manor, no
doubt there stands a farmer, either the sheriff or some other
person, who is bound to supply the due quantity of provender;
but to say that this is so does not solve the problem that is
before us. We have still to ask how this due quantity is
obtained from the men of the village. It is a quantity which
can be expressed by round figures; it is 3000 dog-cakes, or
the like. We do not arrive at these pretty results by adding
up the rents due from individuals. Again, just in the counties
which are the homes of freedom we hear much of sums of

---

[1] D. B. i. 375 b: 'Siuuate et Alnod et Fenchel et Aschil equaliter et pariliter
diviserunt inter se terram patris sui T. R. E. et ita tenuerunt ut si opus fuit
expeditione Regis et Siuuate potuit ire, alii fratres iuverunt eum. Post istum,
ivit alter et Siuuate cum reliquis iuvit eum; et sic de omnibus. Siuuate tamen
fuit homo Regis.'

[2] D. B. i. 206: 'sex sochemanni id est Aluuoldus et 5 fratres eius habuerunt
4 hid. et dim. ad geldum.'

[3] D. B. i. 233: 'Hanc terram tenuerunt 2 fratres pro 2 maneriis, et postea
emit alter ab altero partem suam et fecit unum manerium de duobus T. R. E.'

[4] D. B. i. 127 b: 'Hoc manerium tenent villani ad firmam canonicorum.'

[5] D. B. i. 162 b.

[6] D. B. i. 69.

money that are paid to a lord by way of free will offering[1]. In
Norfolk and Suffolk the villagers will give a yearly *gersuma*,
in Lincoln they will pay a yearly *tailla*, and this will be a neat
round sum; very often it is 20 shillings, or 40 or 10.

In this particular we seem to see an increase of something
that may be called communalism, as we go backwards. Of
course in the cartularies of a later age we may discover round
sums of money which, under the names of 'tallage' or 'aid'
are imposed upon the vill as a whole; but in general we may
accept the rule that tributes to be paid by the vill as a whole,
in money or in kind, are not of recent origin. They are more
prominent in the oldest than in other documents. As examples,
we may notice the 'cornage' of the Boldon Book—one vill
renders 20 shillings, another 30 shillings for cornage[2]; also the
contributions of sheep, poultry, bread and cloth which the vills
of Peterborough Abbey bring to the monks on the festival of
their patron saint—one vill supplying ten rams and twenty
ells of cloth, another four rams, five ells of cloth, ten chicken
and three hundred loaves[3]. But then we have to notice that
a village which has to pay a provender rent or even a *tailla*
or *gersuma* is not altogether a free village. Its communal
action is called out by seignorial pressure.

And as we go backwards the township seems to lose such
definiteness as is given to it by the police law of the thirteenth
century[4]. This was to be expected, for such law implies a
powerful, centralized state, which sends its justices round the
country to amerce the townships and compel these local
communities to do their duties. Once and once only does
the township appear in the Anglo-Saxon dooms. This is
in a law of Edgar. If a man who is on a journey buys
cattle, then on his return home he must turn them onto the
common pasture, 'with the witness of the township.' If he
fails to do so, then after five nights the townsmen are to give
information to the elder of the hundred, and in that case
they and their cattle-herd will be free of blame, and the
man who brought the cattle into the town will forfeit them,

Round sums raised from the villages.

The township and police law.

---

[1] D. B. ii. 118 b Yarmouth: 'De gersuma has 4 libras dant burgenses gratis
et amicitia.'

[2] Thus D. B. iv. 568: 'Due ville reddunt 30 sol. de cornagio.' Ib. 570:
'Queryngdonshire reddit 76 sol. de cornagio.'

[3] Black Book of Peterborough, *passim.*   [4] Hist. Engl. Law, i. 550.

half to the lord and half to the hundred. If, on the other hand, the townsmen fail in the duty of giving information, their herd will pay for it with his skin[1]. The township has very little organization of which the state can make use. It does not seem even to have an 'elder' or head-man, and, from the threat of a flogging, we may gather that its common herdsman will be a slave. Purchases of cattle can not be made 'with the witness of the township'; the purchaser ought to seek out two or three of those twelve standing witnesses who are appointed for every hundred[2]. So again, in the twelfth century we see the finder of a stray beast bringing it into the vill; he conducts it to the church-door and tells his story to the priest, the reeve and as many of the best men of the vill as can be got together. Then the reeve sends to the four neighbouring vills, calls in from each the priest, the reeve and three or four men and recounts the tale in their presence. Then on the following day he goes to the head-man of the hundred and puts the whole matter before him and delivers up the beast to him, unless indeed the place where it was found straying was within the domain of some lord who had sake and soke[3]. Here again, the organization of the township appears to be of a most rudimentary kind. It has no court, unless its lord has sake and soke; it has no power to detain an estray for safe custody. In this very simple case it requires the help of other vills and must transmit the cause to the hundred court. And so again, though there may be some reason for thinking that at one time the murder fine—the fine payable if the slayer of a foreigner was not arrested—was primarily exigible from the vill in which the corpse was found, the hundred being but subsidiarily liable, still this rule seems to have been soon abandoned and the burden of the fine, a fine far too heavy for a single vill, was cast upon the hundred[4]. For all this, however, the law knew and made use of the township. The Domesday commissioners required the testimony of the priest, the reeve and six *villani* of every vill. So soon as the law about suit to the hundred court becomes at all plain, the suit is due rather from vills than from men, and the burden is discharged by the lord of the vill or

[1] Edgar IV. 8. 9.   [2] Ibid. 6.
[3] Leg. Edw. Conf. 24.
[4] Leg. Edw. Conf. 15.   Compare Leg. Henr. 91;   Leg. Will. Conq. I. 22;
Leg. Will. Conq. III. 3.

his steward, or, if neither of them can attend, then by the priest, the reeve and four of the vill's best men[1].

How could these requirements be met by a vill which had no lord? It would be a fair remark that the existence of such vills is not contemplated by the Norman rulers. The men who will represent the vill before the Domesday commissioners will in their eyes be *villani*. This assumption is becoming true enough. We have seen Orwell full of sokemen; in 1086 there is never a sokeman in it; there is no one in it who is above the rank of a villein. Count Roger and Walter Giffard, Count Alan and Geoffrey de Mandeville can make such arrangements about the suit of Orwell, the reeveship of Orwell, as they think fit. Everywhere the Frenchmen are consolidating their manors, creating demesne land where their English *antecessores* had none, devising scientific frontiers, doing what in them lies to make every vill a manor. Thus is evolved that state of things which comes before us in the thirteenth century. The work of the foreigners was done so completely that we can see but very little of the institutions that they swept away.

On the whole, however, we shall do well not to endow the free township of the Confessor's day with much organization. We may be certain that, at least as a general rule, it had no court; we may doubt very gravely whether it always had any elder, head-man, or reeve. Often it was a small and yet a heterogeneous, and a politically distracted body. Some of its members might be attached to the house of Godwin, some had sworn to live and die for the house of Leofric. Just because it is free it has few, if any, communal payments to make. Only if it comes under a single lord will it have to render a provender rent, a *tailla* or *gersuma*. As a sphere for communal action there remains only the regulation of the arable lands, the woods and waste. We can not say for certain that these give scope for much regulation. The arable strips are held in severalty; if by chance some of them are held in common, this in all probability is a case rather of co-ownership than of communal ownership. The pasture rights may well be regarded as appurtenances of the arable strips. The practice of 'co-aration' need not be enforced by law; the man who will not help his neighbours must be content to see his own land unploughed. The course of agriculture is fixed and will not be often or easily

The free village and Norman government.

Organization of the free village.

---

[1] Leg. Henr. 7 § 7.

altered. The 'realism' which roots every right and duty in
a definite patch of soil, the rapid conversion of new arrangements into immemorial customs, the practice of taking turn
and turn about, the practice of casting lots, these will do much
towards settling questions such as our modern imaginations
would solve by means of a village council. No doubt, from
time to time a new departure is made; new land is reclaimed
from the waste, perhaps the pasture rights are stinted or re-
distributed, a mill is built or a church is endowed;—but all
this requires no periodic assemblies, no organization that we
dare call either permanent or legal. Once in five years or so
there may be something to be done, and done it will be by
a resolution of the villagers which is or calls itself an unanimous
resolution. If the Cambridgeshire townships had been landowning corporations, each of them would have passed as a single
unit into the hands of some Norman baron. But this did not
happen. On the contrary, the Norman barons had to content
themselves with intermixed strips; the strips of Ælfgar's men
went to Count Roger, the strips of Edith's men went to Count
Alan. We are far from denying the existence of a communal
sentiment, of a notion that somehow or another the men of
the vill taken as a whole owned the lands of the vill, but this
sentiment, this notion, if strong was vague. There were no
institutions in which it could realize itself, there was no form
of speech or thought in which it could find an apt expression.
It evaded the grasp of law. At the touch of jurisprudence the
township became a mere group of individuals, each with his
separate rights[1].

§ 8. *The Feudal Superstructure.*

The higher
ranks of
men.

It remains that we should speak very briefly of the higher
ranks of men and the tenure by which they held their land.
Little accurate information can be extorted from our record.
The upper storeys of the old English edifice have been de-
molished and a new superstructure has been reared in their
stead. It is not the office of Domesday Book to tell us much
even of the new nobility, of the services which the counts

---

[1] It is possible that the entry (i. 204) which tells how the sokemen of
Broughton enjoyed the smaller *wites* points to a free village court; but we have
put another interpretation upon this; see above, p. 99.

and barons are to render to the king in return for their handsome endowments:—as to the old nobility, that has perished. Still there are some questions that we ought to ask.

The general theory that all land tenure, except indeed the tenure by which the king holds land in demesne, is dependent tenure, seems to be implied, not only by many particular entries, but also by the whole scheme of the book. Every holder of land, except the king, holds it of (*de*) some lord, and therefore every acre of land that is not royal demesne can be arranged under the name of some tenant in chief. Even a church will hold its land, if not of the king, then of some other lord[1]. The terms of the tenure are but very rarely described, for Domesday Book is no feodary. Just now and again a tenure *in elemosina* is noticed and in some of these cases this term seems already to bear the technical sense that it will have in later days; the tenant owes a spiritual, but no secular service[2]. A few instances of what later lawyers would call a 'tenure by divine service,' as distinct from a tenure in frank-almoin, may be found[3]. A few words here and there betray the existence of tenure by knight's service and of castle guard[4]. In the *servientes Regis* who have been enfeoffed in divers counties we may see the predecessors of the tenants by serjeanty[5]. We shall remark, however, the absence of those abstract terms which are to become the names of the various tenures. We read of *servientes, sochemanni, villani, burgenses*, but not of *seriantia[6], socagium, villenagium, burgagium*. As we pursue our retrogressive course through the middle ages, we do not find that the law of personal condition becomes more and more distinct from the law of land tenure; on the contrary, the two become less and less separable.

Dependent tenure.

---

[1] D. B. i. 91: 'Ecclesia Romana beati Petri Apostoli tenet de Rege Peritone.' Ib. 157: 'Ecclesia Sancti Dyonisii Parisii tenet de Rege Teigtone. Rex Edwardus ei dedit.' Ib. 20 b: 'Abbas de Grestain tenet de Comite 2 hidas in Bedingham.'

[2] Hist. Eng. Law, i. 220.

[3] D. B. i. 218 b: 'Rex vero Willelmus sibi postea in elemosina concessit, unde pro anima Regis et Regine omni ebdomada 2 feria missam persolvit.' D. B. ii. 133: 'et cantat unaquaque ebdomada tres missas.'

[4] D. B. i. 3: 'reddit unum militem in servitio Archiepiscopi.' Ib. 10 b: 'servitium unius militis.' Ib. 32: 'servitium unius militis.' Ib. 151 b: 'inveniebat 2 loricatos in custodiam de Windesores.'

[5] Hist. Eng. Law, i. 268.

[6] But D. B. i. 218 b gives us 'tenet in ministerio Regis.'

Feudum.   It has sometimes been said that a feudal tenure was the only kind of land tenure that the Norman conquerors could conceive. In a certain sense this may be true, but we should have preferred to say that probably they could not easily conceive a kind of tenure that was not dependent:—every one who holds land (except he be the king) holds it of someone else. The adjective 'feudal' was not in their vocabulary, and their use of the word *feudum*—occasionally we meet the older *feum*¹—is exceedingly obscure. Very rarely does it denote a tenure or a mass of rights; usually, though it may connote rights of a certain order, it denotes a stretch of land; thus we may read of the fee of the Bishop of Bayeux, thereby being meant the territory which the bishop holds. Occasionally, however, we hear of a man holding land *in feudo*. One instance may be enough to show that such a phrase did not imply military tenure:—'William the Chamberlain held this manor *in feudo* of the Queen [Matilda] at a rent of £3 a year and after her death he held it in the same fashion of the king².' All sense of militariness, and all sense of precariousness, that the word has ever had in its continental history, seems to be disappearing. Already the process has begun which will make it applicable to every person who has heritable rights in land. William the Chamberlain is, we take it, already a fee farmer, that is, a rent-paying tenant with heritable rights³. As to the word *beneficium*, which *feum* or *feudum* has been supplanting, we shall hardly find it with its old meaning. It seems to be holding its own only within the sphere of ecclesiastical rights, where the 'benefice' will survive until our own day⁴.

¹ D. B. i. 4 b: 'De terra huius manerii tenet Godefridus in feuo dimid. solin.' Ib. 36 b: 'Humfridus Camerarius tenet de feuo Reginae Cumbe.' Ib. 336 b: 'Ipsam [domum] clamat Normannus Crassus de feuo Regis.'

² D. B. i. 129 b: 'Postea Willelmus Camerarius tenuit de Regina in feudo pro 3 lib. per annum de firma, et post mortem Reginae eodem modo tenuit de Rege.'

³ But, as in general a farmer would have no heritable rights, holding in fee may be contrasted with holding in farm. D. B. i. 230 b: 'Has terras habet Goduinus de Rege ad firmam, Dislea vero tenet de Rege in feudo.' So again it may be contrasted with the husband's rights in his wife's marriage portion. D. B. i. 214 b: 'De ista terra tenet Pirotus 3 hidas de maritagio suae feminae et unam hidam et terciam partem unius hidae tenet in feudum de Nigello.'

⁴ D. B. i. 158: Robert de Ouilly holds forty-two houses in Oxford, some meadow-land and a mill 'cum beneficio S. Petri,' i.e. together with the benefice of S. Peter's church. Elsewhere, i. 273, we read that King William gave a

A yet more interesting and equally foreign word is not *Alodium.* unfrequently used, namely, *alodium.* The Norman commissioners deemed that a large number of English tenants in Kent, Sussex, Surrey and Hampshire and some in Berkshire had been *alodiarii* or *aloarii* and had held *in alodium* or *sicut alodium.* The appearance of this term in one district and in one only is far from proving that there had been anything peculiar in the law of that district. It may well be a mere chance that the *liberi homines* of other counties are not called *alodiaries.* Still in Hampshire, where alodiaries abounded, it was not every free man holding land who had an *alod*[1]. Perhaps we shall be right in thinking that the term pointed to heritability :—the free man who holds land but has no *alod* has only an estate for life. Certainly it does not mean that the tenant has no lord. The alodiary may hold his alod 'of' his lord[2]; he may owe service to his lord[3]; he may pay a relief[4]; he may have no power 'to withdraw himself with his land' from his lord[5]. The Norman lawyers had no speculative objection to the existence of alodiaries ; it in no way contradicted such doctrine of tenure as they had formed. In 1086 there were still alodiaries in Berkshire[6], and in royal charters of a much later day there is talk of the alodiaries of Kent as of an existing class[7]. It is just possible that William's commissioners saw some difference between holding *in feudo* and holding *in alodio.*

---

manor to the monks of Burton ' pro beneficio suo ' ; but the meaning of this is by no means clear.

[1] D. B. i. 44 b : ' Duo liberi homines tenuerunt de Alwino sed non fuit alod.' The same phrase occurs on f. 46.

[2] D. B. i. 22 : ' Aluuard et Algar tenuerunt de Rege pro 2 maneriis in alodia....Ælueua tenuit de Rege Edwardo sicut alodium.' Ib. 26 : ' Godwinus Comes tenuit et de eo 7 aloarii.'

[3] D. B. i. 60 b : ' Duo alodiarii tenuerunt T. R. E....unus servivit Reginae, alter Bundino.'

[4] D. B. i. 1 : ' Quando moritur alodiarius, Rex inde habet relevationem terrae.'

[5] D. B. i. 52 b : ' Has hidas tenuerunt 7 alodiarii de Episcopo nec poterant recedere alio vel ab illo.'

[6] D. B. i. 63 b : ' Ibi sunt 5 alodiarii.'

[7] See charter of John for St Augustin's, Canterbury, Rot. Cart. p. 105 : ' omnes allodiarios quos eis habemus datos.' This phrase seems to descend through a series of charters from two charters of the Conqueror in which the ' swa fele þegna swa ic heom togeleton habbe ' of the one appears in the other as ' omnes allodiarios.' If so, we get from the Conqueror's own chancery the equation þegn = alodiarius. Hist. Mon. S. August. 349–50.

If ever they contrasted the two words, they may have hinted that while the *feudum* has been given by the lord to the man, the *alodium* has been brought by the man to the lord; but we can not be very certain that they ever opposed these terms to each other[1]. Such sparse evidence as we can obtain from Normandy strengthens our belief that the wide, the almost insuperable, gulf that modern theorists have found or have set between 'alodial ownership' and 'feudal tenure' was not perceptible in the eleventh century[2]. It can be no part of our task to trace the history of these terms *alodium* and *feudum* behind the date at which they are brought into England, but hereafter we shall see that here in England a process had been at work which, had these terms been in use, would have brought the alod very near to the feud, the feud very near to the alod.

Application of the formula of dependent tenure.

It is probable that this process had gone somewhat further in Normandy than in England. It is probable that the Normans knew that in imposing upon all English lands 'the formula of dependent tenure' they were simplifying matters. They seem to think, and they may be pretty right in thinking, that every English land-holder had held his land under (*sub*) some lord; but apparently they do not think that every English land-holder had held his land of (*de*) some lord. Not unfrequently they show that this is so. Thus one Sigar holds a piece of Cambridgeshire *of* Geoffrey de Mandeville; he used to hold it *under* Æsgar the Staller[3]. We catch a slight shade of difference between the two prepositions; *sub* lays stress on the lord's power, which may well be of a personal or justiciary, rather than of a proprietary kind, while *de* imports a theory about the origin of the tenure; it makes the tenant's rights look like derivative rights:—it is supposed that he gets his land from

[1] D. B. i. 23: in two successive entries we have ' Offa tenuit de Episcopo in feudo......Almar tenuit de Goduino Comite in alodium.' So again, i. 59: 'Blacheman tenuit de Heraldo Comite in alodio...Blacheman tenuit in feudo T. R. E.' The suggestion has been made that *alodium* represents *book-land*; see Pollock, Land Laws, ed. 3. p. 27; Eng. Hist. Rev. xi. 227; but we gravely doubt whether the humbler *alodiarii* had books. The author of the Quadripartitus renders *bócland* by *terra hereditaria, terra testimentalis, terra libera,* and even by *feudum* (Edg. ii. 2); *alodium* occurs in the Instituta Cnuti. After this we can hardly say for certain that D. B. does not use *alodium* and *feodum* as equivalents, both representing a heritable estate, as absolute an ownership of land as is conceivable.

[2] Hist. Eng. Law, i. 46.   [3] D. B. i. 197.

his lord. And at least in the eastern counties—so it may well have seemed to the Normans—matters sadly needed simplification. Even elsewhere and when a large estate is at stake they can not always get an answer to the question ' Of whom was this land holden¹?' Still they thought that some of the greatest men in the realm had held their lands, or some of their lands, of the king or of someone else. The formulas which are used throughout the description of Hampshire and some other counties seem to assume that every holder of a manor, at all events if a layman, had held it *of* the king, if he did not hold it *of* another lord. Tenure *in feudo* again they regarded as no innovation². They saw the work of subinfeudation:—Brihtmær held land of Azor and Azor of Harold; we may well suppose that Harold held it of the king and that some villeins held part of it of Brihtmær, and thus we see already a feudal ladder with no less than five rungs³. They saw that the thegns owed ' service ' to their lords⁴. They saw the heriot; they sometimes called it a relief⁵. We can not be sure that this change of names imported any change in the law; when a burgess of Hereford died the king took a heriot, but if he could not get the heriot he took the dead man's land⁶. They saw that in certain cases an heir had to ' seek ' his ancestor's lord if he wished to enjoy his ancestor's land⁷. They saw that many a free man could not give or sell his land without his lord's consent. They saw that great and powerful men could not give or sell their land without the king's consent⁸.

¹ D. B. i. 238 b: ' Reliquas autem 7 hidas et dimidiam tenuit [*sic*] Britnodus et Aluui T. R. E., sed comitatus nescit de quo tenuerint.'

² D. B. i. 23: ' Offa tenuit de episcopo in feudo.' Ib. i. 59 b: ' Blacheman tenuit in feudo T. R. E.'

³ D. B. i. 28 b: ' Bricmar tenuit de Azor et Azor de Heraldo...Terra est 2 carucis. In dominio est una et 2 villani et 2 bordarii cum dimidia caruca.'

⁴ D. B. i. 75 b: ' De eadem terra ten[ent] 3 taini 3 hidas et reddunt 3 libras excepto servicio.' Ib. 86 b: ' Huic manerio est addita dimidia hida. Tres taini tenebant T. R. E. et serviebant preposito manerii per consuetudinem absque omni firma donante.'

⁵ D. B. i. 1: 'Quando moritur alodiarius, Rex inde habet relevationem terrae.'

⁶ D. B. i. 179: ' Burgensis cum caballo serviens, cum moriebatur, habebat Rex equum et arma eius. De eo qui equum non habebat, si moreretur, habebat Rex aut 10 solidos aut terram eius cum domibus.'

⁷ D. B. i. 50 b: ' Alric tenet dimidiam hidam. Hanc tenuit pater eius de Rege E. Sed hic Regem non requisivit post mortem Godric sui avunculi qui eam custodiebat.'

⁸ D. B. i. 238 b: ' Huic aecclesiae dedit Aluuinus vicecomes Cliptone

Military
tenure.   They saw something very like military tenure. No matter
with which we have to deal is darker than the constitution of
the English army on the eve of its defeat. We may indeed
safely believe that no English king had ever relinquished the
right to call upon all the free men of his realm to resist an
invader. On the other hand, it seems quite clear that, as a
matter of fact, 'the host' was no longer 'the nation in arms.'
The common folk of a shire could hardly be got to fight outside
their shire, and ill-armed troops of peasants were now of little
avail. The only army upon which the king could habitually
rely was a small force. The city of Oxford sent but twenty
men or twenty pounds[1]: Leicester sent twelve men[2]: Warwick
sent ten[3]. In Berkshire the law was that, if the king called out
the host, one soldier (*miles*) should go for every five hides and
should receive from each hide four shillings as his stipend for
two months' service. If the man who was summoned made
default, he forfeited all his land to the king; but there were
cases in which he might send one of his men as a substitute,
and for a default committed by his substitute he suffered no
forfeiture, but only a fine of fifty shillings[4]. It is probable that
a similar 'five hide rule' obtained throughout a large part of
England. The borough of Wilton was bound to send twenty
shillings or one man 'as for an honour of five hides[5].' When
an army or a fleet was called out, Exeter 'served to the amount
of five hides[6].' All this points to a small force of well armed

concessu Regis Edwardi et filiorum suorum pro anima sua.' Ib. 59: 'De hoc
manerio scira attestatur, quod Edricus qui eum tenebat deliberavit illum filio
suo qui erat in Abendone monachus ut ad firmam illud teneret et sibi donec
viveret necessaria vitae donaret; post mortem vero eius manerium haberet.
Et ideo nesciunt homines de scira quod abbatiae pertineat, neque enim inde
viderunt brevem Regis vel sigillum. Abbas vero testatur quod in T. R. E. misit
ille manerium ad aecclesiam unde erat et inde habet brevem et sigillum R. E.'
    [1] D. B. i. 154: 'Quando Rex ibat in expeditione, burgenses 20 ibant cum eo
pro omnibus aliis, vel 20 libras dabant Regi ut omnes essent liberi.'
    [2] D. B. i. 230: 'Quando Rex ibat in exercitu per terram, de ipso burgo
12 burgenses ibant cum eo.'
    [3] D. B. i. 238: 'Consuetudo Waruuic fuit, ut eunte rege per terram in
expeditionem, decem burgenses de Waruuic pro omnibus aliis irent.'
    [4] D. B. i. 57 b.
    [5] D. B. i. 64 b: 'Quando Rex ibat in expeditione vel terra vel mari, habebat
de hoc burgo aut 20 solidos ad pascendos suos buzecarlos, aut unum hominem
ducebat secum pro honore 5 hidarum.'
    [6] D. B. i. 100: 'Quando expeditio ibat per terram aut per mare serviebat
haec civitas quantum 5 hidae terrae.'

soldiers. For example, 'the five hide rule' would be satisfied if Worcestershire sent a contingent of 240 men. But not only was the army small; it was a territorial army; it grew out of the soil.

At first sight this 'five hide rule' may seem to have in it little that is akin to a feudal system of knights' fees. We may suppose that it will work thus:—The host is summoned; the number of hides in each hundred is known. To despatch a company of soldiers proportioned to the number of the hides, for example twenty warriors if the hundred contains just one hundred hides, is the business of the hundred court and the question 'Who must go?' will be answered by election, rotation or lot. But it is not probable that the territorializing process will stop here, and this for several reasons. An army that can not be mobilized without the action of the hundred moots is not a handy force. While the hundredors are deliberating the Danes or Welshmen will be burning and slaying. Also a king will not easily be content with the responsibility of a fluctuating and indeterminate body of hundredors; he will insist, if he can, that there must be some one person answerable to him for each unit of military power. A serviceable system will not have been established until the country is divided into 'five-hide-units,' until every man's holding is such an unit, or is composed of several such units, or is an aliquot share of such an unit. Then again the holdings with which the rule will have to deal are not homogeneous; they are not all of one and the same order. It is not as though to each plot of land there corresponded some one person who was the only person interested in it; the occupiers of the soil have lords and again those lords have lords. The king will insist, if he can, that the lords who stand high in this scale must answer to him for the service that is due from all the lands over which they exercise a dominion, and then he will leave them free to settle, as between themselves and their dependants, the ultimate incidence of the burden:—thus room will be made for the play of free contract. At all events when, as is not unusual, some lord is the lord of a whole hundred and of its court, the king will regard him as personally liable for the production of the whole contingent that is due from that hundred. In this way a system will be evolved which for many practical purposes will be indistinguishable from the system of knights' fees, and all this without any

The army and the land.

help from the definitely feudal idea that military service is the return which the tenant makes to the lord for the gift of land that the lord has made to the tenant.

Feudalism and army service.

That this process had already done much of its work when the old English army received its last summons, we can not doubt, though it is very possible that this work had been done sporadically. We see that the land was being plotted out into five-hide-units. In one passage the Norman clerks call such a unit an honour, an ‘honour of five hides[1].’ There is an old theory based upon legal texts that such an honour qualifies its lord or owner to be a thegn. If a ceorl prospers so that he has five hides ‘to the king’s útware,’ that is, an estate rated as five hides for military purposes, he is worthy of a thegn’s wergild[2]. Then the Anglo-Saxon charters show us how the kings have been endowing their thegns with tracts of territory which are deemed to contain just five or some multiple of five hides[3]. The thegn with five hides will have tenants below him; but none of them need serve in the host if their lord goes, as he ought to go, in person. Then each of these territorial units continues to owe the same quantum of military service, though the number of persons interested in it be increased or diminished, and thus the ultimate incidence of the duty becomes the subject-matter of private arrangements. That is the point of a story from Lincolnshire which we have already recounted:—A man’s land descends to his four sons; they divide it equally and agree to take turns in doing the military service that is due from it; but only the eldest of them is to be the king’s man[4]. Then we see that the great nobles lead or send to the war all the *milites* that are due from the lands over which they have a seignory. There are already wide lands which owe military service—we can not put it otherwise—to the bishop of Winchester as lord of Taunton:— they owe ‘attendance in the host along with the men of the bishop[5].’ The churches of Worcester and Evesham fell out about certain lands at Hamton; one of the disputed questions

---

[1] Above, p. 156, note 5.

[2] Schmid, App. vii. c. 2. § 9–12; App. v; Pseudoleges Canuti (i.e. Instituta Cnuti) 60, 61 (Schmid, p. 431).

[3] Of this we shall speak in another Essay.

[4] D. B. i. 375 b; above, p. 145.

[5] D. B. i. 87 b: ‘Istae consuetudines pertinent ad Tantone......profectio in exercitum cum hominibus episcopi......Hae duae terrae non debent exercitum.’

was whether or no Hamton ought to do its military service
'in the bishop's hundred of Oswaldslaw' or elsewhere[1]. This
question we take to be one of great importance to the bishop.
Lord of the triple hundred of Oswaldslaw, lord of three
hundred hides, he is bound to put sixty warriors into the field
and he is anxious that men who ought to be helping him to
make up this tale shall not be serving in another contingent.

But from Worcestershire we obtain a still more precious
piece of information. The custom of that county is this:—
When the king summons the host and his summons is disregarded by one who is a lord with jurisdiction, 'by one who is
so free a man that he has sake and soke and can go with his
land where he pleases,' then all his lands are in the king's
mercy. But if the defaulter be the man of another lord and
the lord sends a substitute in his stead, then he, the defaulter,
must pay forty shillings to his lord,—to his lord, not to the
king, for the king has had the service that was due; but if the
lord does not send a substitute, then the forty shillings which
the defaulter pays to the lord, the lord must pay to the king[2].
A feudalist of the straiter sort might well find fault with this
rule. He might object that the lord ought to forfeit his land,
not only if he himself fails to attend the host, but also if he
fails to bring with him his due tale of *milites.* Feudalism was
not perfected in a day. Still here we have the root of the
matter—the lord is bound to bring into the field a certain
number of *milites,* perhaps one man from every five hides, and
if he can not bring those who are bound to follow him, he must
bring others or pay a fine. His man, on the other hand, is
bound to him and is not bound to the king. That man by
shirking his duty will commit no offence against the king.
The king is ceasing to care about the ultimate incidence of
the military burden, because he relies upon the responsibility
of the magnates. How this system worked in the eastern
counties where the power of the magnates was feebler, we can

Default of service.

---

[1] See above, p. 85, note 3.

[2] D. B. i. 172: 'Quando Rex in hostem pergit, si quis edictum eius vocatus
remanserit, si ita liber homo est ut habeat socam suam et sacam et cum terra
sua possit ire quo voluerit, de omni terra sua est in misericordia Regis.
Cuiuscumque vero alterius domini homo si de hoste remanserit et dominus eius
pro eo alium hominem duxerit, 40 sol. domino suo qui vocatus fuit emendabit.
Quod si ex toto nullus pro eo abierit, ipse quidem domino suo 40 sol. dabit,
dominus autem eius totidem solidis Regi emendabit.'

not tell. It is not improbable that one of the forces that is attaching the small free proprietors to the manors of their lords is this ' five hide rule'; they are being compelled to bring their acres into five-hide-units, to club together under the superintendence of a lord who will answer for them to the king, while as to the villeins, so seldom have they fought that they are ceasing to be 'fyrd-worthy[1].' But in the west we have already what in substance are knights' fees. The Bishop of Worcester held 300 hides over which he had sake and soke and all customs; he was bound to put 60 *milites* into the field; if he failed in this duty he had to pay 40 shillings for each deficient *miles*. At the beginning of Henry II.'s reign he was charged with 60 knights' fees[2].

The new military service.

We are not doubting that the Conqueror defined the amount of military service that was to be due to him from each of his tenants in chief, nor are we suggesting that he paid respect to the rule about the five hides, but it seems questionable whether he introduced any very new principle. A new theoretic element may come to the front, a contractual element:—the tenant in chief must bring up his knights because that is the service that was stipulated for when he received his land. But we cannot say that even this theory was unfamiliar to the English. The rulers of the churches had been giving or 'loaning' lands to thegns. In so doing they had not been dissipating the wealth of the saints without receiving some 'valuable consideration' for the gift or the loan (*lǽn*); they looked to their thegns for the military service that their land owed to the king. To this point we must return in our next essay ; but quite apart from definitely feudal bargains between the king and his magnates, between the magnates and their dependants, a definition of the duty of military service which connects it with the ownership of land (and to such a definition men will come so soon as the well-armed few can defeat the ill-armed many) will naturally produce a state of things which will be patient of, even if it will not engender, a purely feudal explanation. If one of the men to whom the Bishop of Worcester looks for military service makes a default, the fine that is due from him will go to the bishop, not to the king. Why so ? One explanation will be that the bishop has over him a sake and soke of the very highest order,

---

[1] See above, p. 77, note 1.   [2] See Round, *Feudal England*, 249.

which comprehends even that *fyrd-wíte*, that fine for the neglect of military duty, which is one of the usually reserved pleas of the crown[1]. Another explanation will be that this man has broken a contract that he made with the bishop and therefore owes amends to the bishop:—to the bishop, not to the king, who was no party to the contract. Sometimes the one explanation will be the truer, sometimes the other. Sometimes both will be true enough. As a matter of fact, we believe that these men of the Bishop of Worcester or their predecessors in title have solemnly promised to do whatever service the king demands from the bishop[2]. Still we can hardly doubt which of the two explanations is the older, and, if we attribute to the Norman invaders, as perhaps we may, a definite apprehension of the theory that knight's service is the outcome of feudal compacts, this still leaves open the inquiry whether the past history of military service in Frankland had not been very like the past history of military service in England. Already in the days of Charles the Great the duty of fighting the Emperor's battles was being bound up with the tenure of land by the operation of a rule very similar to that of which we have been speaking. The owner of three (at a later time of four) manses was to serve; men who held but a manse apiece were to group themselves together to supply soldiers. Then at a later time the feudal theory of free contract was brought in to explain an already existing state of things[3].

Closely connected with this matter is another thorny topic, namely, the status of the thegn and the relation of the thegn to his lord. In the Confessor's day many *maneria* had been held by thegns; some of them were still holding their lands when the survey was made and were still called thegns. The king's

The thegns.

---

[1] D. B. i. 208: 'Testantur homines de comitatu quod Rex Edwardus dedit Suineshefet Siuuardo Comiti soccam et sacam, et sic habuit Haroldus comes, praeter quod geldabant in hundredo et in hostem cum eis ibant.' It is here noted that though Harold had sake and soke over Swineshead, it paid its geld and did its military duty in the hundred. Our record would hardly mention such a point unless very often the exaction of geld and military service was one of the rights and duties of the lord who had sake and soke.

[2] In the next chapter we shall speak of the bishop's land-loans.

[3] See the capitularies of 807 and 808 (ed. Boretius, pp. 134, 137). Also, Fustel de Coulanges, Les transformations de la royauté, 515 ff. It may well be doubted whether the five-hide rule had not been borrowed by English kings from their Frankish neighbours. Stubbs, Const. Hist. i. 208 ff.

thegns were numerous, but the queen also had thegns, the earls had thegns, the churches had thegns and we find thegns ascribed to men who were neither earls nor prelates but themselves were thegns[1]. Many of the king's thegns were able to give or sell the lands that they held, 'to go to whatever lord they pleased[2].' On the other hand, many of the thegns of the churches held lands which they could not 'withdraw' from the churches[3]; in other words 'the thegn-lands' of the church could not be separated from the church[4]. The Conqueror respected the bond that tied them to the church. The Abbot of Ely complained to him that the foreigners had been abstracting the lands of S[t]. Etheldreda. His answer was that her demesne manors must at once be given back to her, while as for the men who have occupied her thegnlands, they must either make their peace with the abbot or surrender their holdings[5]. Thus the abbot seems to have had the benefit of that forfeiture which his thegns incurred by espousing the cause of Harold. We see therefore that the relation between thegn, lord and land varied from case to case. The land might have proceeded from the lord and be held of the lord by the thegn as a perpetually inheritable estate, or as an estate granted to him for life, or granted to him and two successive heirs[6]; on the other hand, the lord's hold over the land might be slight and the bond between thegn and lord might be a mere commendation which the thegn could at any time dissolve. Again, the relation between thegn and lord is no longer conceived as a menial, 'serviential' or ministerial relation. The *Taini Regis* are

---

[1] D. B. i. 152 b: 'duo teigni homines Alrici filii Goding.' Ib. 'Hoc manerium tenuit Azor filius Toti teignus Regis Edwardi et alter teignus homo eius tenuit unam hidam et vendere potuit.'

[2] D. B. i. 84 b: at the end of a list of royal thegns 'Omnes qui has terras T. R. E. tenebant, poterant ire ad quem dominum volebant.'

[3] D. B. i. 41: 'Tres taini tenuerunt de episcopo et non potuerunt ire quolibet.'

[4] D. B. i. 91: 'Hae terrae erant tainland in Glastingberie T. R. E. nec poterant ab aecclesia separari.'

[5] Hamilton, Inquisitio, pp. xviii. xix.

[6] D. B. i. 66 b: 'De hac eadem terra 3 hidas vendiderat abbas cuidam taino T. R. E. ad aetatem trium hominum, et ipse abbas habebat inde servitium, et postea debet redire ad dominium.' Ib. i. 83 b: 'Ipsa femina tenet 2 hidas in Tatentone quae erant de dominio abbatiae de Cernel; T. R. E. duo teini tenebant prestito.'

often contrasted with the *Servientes Regis*[1]. The one trait
of thegnship which comes out clearly on the face of our
record is that the thegn is a man of war[2]. But even this trait
is obscured by language which seems to show that there has
been a great redistribution of military service. Though there
is no Latin word that will translate *thegn* except *miles*, though
these two terms are never contrasted with each other, and
though there are thegns still existing, still of these two terms
one belongs to the old, the other to the new order of things[3].
Thus thegnship is already becoming antiquated and we are left
to guess from older dooms and later Leges what was its essence
in the days of King Edward.

The task is difficult for we can see that this institution has
undergone many changes in the course of a long history and
yet can not tell how much has remained unchanged. We begin
by thinking of thegnship as a relation between two men. The
thegn is somebody's thegn. The household of the great man,
but more especially the king's household, is the cradle of
thegnship. The king's thegns are his free servants—servants
but also companions. In peace they have duties to perform
about his court and about his person; they are his body-guard
in war. Then the king—and other great lords follow his
example—begins to give lands to his thegns, and thus the
nature of the thegnship is modified. The thegn no longer lives
in his lord's court; he is a warrior endowed with land. Then
the thegnship becomes more than a relationship, it becomes a
status. The thegn is a 'twelve hundred man'; his wergild
and his oath countervail those of six ceorls. This status
seems to be hereditary; the thegn's sons are 'dearer born'
than are the sons of the ceorl[4]. But we can not tell how far

Nature of thegnship.

[1] D. B. i. 64 b: 'Herman et alii servientes Regis...Odo et alii taini Regis ..
Herueus et alii ministri Regis.' Ib. 75: 'Guddmund et alii taini...Willelmus
Belet et alii servientes Regis.'

[2] D. B. i. 56 b (Berkshire custom): 'Tainus vel miles Regis dominicus
moriens, pro relevamento dimittebat Regi omnia arma sua et equum unum cum
sella, alium sine sella.'

[3] D. B. i. 83: 'Bricsi tenuit miles Regis E.' Such entries are rare.
D. B. i. 66: 'De eadem terra huius manerii ten[ent] duo Angli....Unus ex eis
est miles iussu Regis et nepos fuit Hermanni episcopi.' Here the king compels
an Englishman to become a *miles*. D. B. i. 180 b: 'Quinque taini...habebant
sub se 4 milites.' The warrior was not necessarily of thegnly rank.

[4] See the passages collected by Schmid, Gesetze, p. 667.

this principle is carried. We can not easily reconcile this hereditary transmission of thegn-right with the original principle that thegnship is a relation between two men. We may have thegns who are nobody's thegns, or else we may have persons entitled to the thegnly wergild who yet are not thegns. What is more, since the law which regulates the inheritance of land does not favour the first-born, we may have poor thegns and landless thegns. Yet another principle comes into play. A duty of finding well armed warriors for the host is being territorialized; every five hides should find a soldier. The thegn from of old has to attend the host with adequate equipment; the men who under the new system have to attend the host with horse and heavy armour are usually thegns. Then the man who has five hides, and who therefore ought to put a warrior into the field, is a thegn or is entitled to be a thegn. The ceorl obtains the thegnly wergild if he has an estate rated for military purposes at five hides. Another version of this tradition requires of the ceorl who 'thrives to thegn-right' five hides of his own land, a church, a kitchen, a house in the *burh*, a special office in the king's hall. To be 'worthy of thegn-right' may be one thing, to be a thegn, another. To be a thegn one must be some one's thegn. The prosperous ceorl will be no thegn until he has put himself under some lord. But the bond between him and his lord may be dissoluble at will and may hardly affect his land. It is, we repeat, very difficult to discover how these various principles were working together, checking and controlling each other in the first half of the eleventh century. Several inconsistent elements seem to be blended. There is the element of hereditary caste :—the thegn transmits thegnly blood to his offspring. There is the element of personal relationship :—he is the thegn of some lord and owes fealty to that lord. There is the military element :—he is a warrior who has horse and heavy armour and is bound to fight the nation's battles. Connected with this last there is the proprietary element :—each five hides must send a warrior to the host; the man with five hides is entitled to become, perhaps he may be compelled to become a thegn, a warrior[1].

[1] In their treatment of the thegnship of the last days before the Conquest, Maurer lays stress upon the proprietary element, Schmid upon the hereditary. See Little, Gesiths and Thegns, E. H. R. iv. 723.

On the whole, we gather from Domesday Book that the military element is subduing the others. The thegn is the man who for one reason or another is a warrior. For one reason or another, we say; for the class of thegns is by no means homogeneous. On the one hand, we see the thegns of the churches, who have been endowed by the prelates in order that they may do the military service due from the ecclesiastical lands. Many of the prelates have thegns, and for the creation of thegnlands by the churches it would not be easy to find any explanation save that which we have already found in the territorialization of military service. The thegn might pay some annual 'recognition' to the church, he might send his labourers to help his lord for a day or two at harvest time; but we may be sure that he was not rack-rented and that, if military service be left out of account, the church was a loser by endowing him. Here the land proceeds from the lord to the thegn; the thegn can not give or sell it; the holder of that land can have no lord but the church; if he forfeits the land, he forfeits it to the church. But, on the other hand, we see numerous king's thegns who are able 'to go to what lord they please.' We may see in them landed proprietors who by the play of 'the five hide rule' have become bound to serve as warriors. We may be fairly certain that they have not been endowed by the king, otherwise they would not enjoy the liberty, that marvellous liberty, of leaving him, of putting themselves under the protection and the banner of some earl or some prelate. Not that every thegn will (if we may borrow phrases from a later age) possess a full 'thegn's fee' or owe the service of a whole warrior. Large groups of thegns we may see who obviously are brothers or cousins enjoying in undivided shares the inheritance of some dead ancestor. They may take it in turns to go to the war; the king may hold the eldest of them responsible for all the service; but each of them will be called a thegn, will be entitled to a thegnly wergild and swear a thegnly oath. Still, on the whole, the thegn of Domesday Book is a warrior, and he holds—though perhaps along with his coparceners—land that is bound to supply a warrior.

In the main all thegns seem to have the same legal status, though they may not be all of equal rank. All of them seem to have the wergild of twelve hundred shillings. A law of Cnut, after describing the heriot of the earl, distinguishes two classes of thegns; there is 'the king's thegn who is nighest to him' and whose heriot includes four horses and 50 mancuses of gold, and 'the middle thegn' or 'less thegn' from whom he gets but one horse and one set of arms or £2.[1] This law should we think be read in connexion with the rule that is recorded by Domesday Book as prevailing in the shires of Derby and Nottingham:—the thegn who had fewer than seven manors paid a relief of 3 marks to the sheriff, while he who had seven and upwards paid £8 to the king[2]. A rude line is drawn between the richer. and the poorer thegns of the king. The former deal immediately with the king and pay their reliefs directly to him; the latter are under the sheriff and their reliefs are comprised in his farm. Thus the wealthy thegns, like the *barones maiores* of later days, are 'nigher to' the king than are the 'less-thegns' or those *barones minores* who in a certain sense are their successors.

The great lords. The kings, the earls and the churches have of course many demesne manors. Of the ecclesiastical estates we shall speak in our next essay, for they can be best examined in the light that is cast upon them by the Anglo-Saxon charters. Here we will merely observe that some of the churches have not only large, but well compacted territories. The abbey of St. Etheldreda, for example, besides having outlying manors, holds the two hundreds which make up the isle of Ely; her property in Cambridgeshire is valued at £318[3]. The earls also are rich in demesne manors and so is the king.

The king as landlord. King William is much richer than King Edward was. The Conqueror has been chary in appointing earls and consequently he has in his hand, not only the royal manors, but also a great many comital manors, to say nothing of some other estates which, for one reason or another, he has kept to himself. Edward had been rich, but when compared with his earls he had not been extravagantly rich. In Somersetshire, for example, there were twelve royal manors which may have brought in a revenue of £500 or thereabouts, while there were fifteen comital manors which were worth nearly £300[4]. The royal demesne had been a scattered territory; the king had something in most shires, but was far richer in some than in others.

---

[1] Cnut, ii. 71.   [2] D. B. i. 280 b.
[3] Hamilton, Inquisitio, 121.   [4] Eyton, Somerset, i. 84.

It was not so much in the number of his manors as in their size and value that he excelled the richest of his subjects. Somehow or another he had acquired many of those vills which were to be the smaller boroughs and the market towns of later days. We may well suppose that from of old the vills that a king would wish to get and to keep would be the flourishing vills, but again we can not doubt that many a vill has prospered because it was the king's.

Among the manors which William holds in the south-west a distinction is drawn by the Exeter Domesday. The manors which the Confessor held are 'The King's Demesne which belongs to the kingdom,' while those which were held by the house of Godwin are the 'Comital Manors[1].' So in East Anglia certain manors are distinguished as pertaining or having pertained to the kingdom or kingship, the *regnum* or *regio*[2]. This does not seem to have implied that they were inalienably annexed to the crown, for King Edward had given some of them away. Neither when it speaks of the time of William, nor when it speaks of the time of Edward, does our record draw any clear line between those manors which the king holds as king and those which he holds in his private capacity, though it may just hint that certain ancient estates ought not to be alienated. The degree in which the various manors of the crown stood outside the national system of finance, justice and police we can not accurately ascertain. Some, but by no means all, pay no geld. Of some it is said that they have never paid geld. Perhaps in these ingeldable manors we may see those which constituted the royal demesne of the West Saxon kings at some remote date. Of the king's vill of Gomshall in Surrey it is written : 'the villeins of this vill were free from all the affairs of the sheriff[3],' as though it were no general truth that with a royal manor the sheriff had nothing to do.

The ancient demesne.

---

[1] D. B. iv. 75: 'Dominicatus Regis ad Regnum pertinens in Devenescira.' Ib. 99 : 'Mansiones de Comitatu.' Eyton, Somerset, i. 78.

[2] D. B. ii. 119: 'Hoc manerium fuit de regno, sed Rex Edwardus dedit Radulfo Comiti.' Ib. 144: 'Suafham pertinuit ad regionem et Rex E. dedit R. Comiti.' Ib. 281 b: 'Terra Regis de Regione quam Rogerus Bigotus servat.' Ib. 408 b: 'Tornei manerium Regis de regione.' Mr Round, Feudal England, p. 140, treats *regio* as a mere blunder; but it may well stand for *kingship*.

[3] D. B. i. 30 b: 'Huius villae villani ab omni re vicecom[itis] sunt quieti.'

The comi-
tal manors.
        As with the estates of the king, so with the estates of
the earls, we find it impossible to distinguish between private
property and official property. Certain manors are regarded
as the 'manors of the shire' (*mansiones de comitatu*[1]); certain
vills are 'comital vills[2],' they belong to 'the consulate[3].' Hereditary right tempered by outlawry was fast becoming the
title by which the earldoms were holden. The position of the
house of Leofric in Mercia was far from being as strong as the
position of the house of Rolf in Normandy, and yet we may
be sure that King Harold would not have been able to treat
the sons of Ælfgar as removable officers. But one of the best
marked features of Domesday Book, a feature displayed on
page after page, the enormous wealth of the house of Godwin,
seems only explicable by the supposition that the earlships
and the older ealdormanships had carried with them a title
to the enjoyment of wide lands. That enormous wealth had
been acquired within a marvellously short time. Godwin was
a new man: nothing certain is known of his ancestry. His
daughter's marriage with the king will account for something;
Harold's marriage with the daughter of Ælfgar will account
for something, for instance, for manors which Harold held in
the middle of Ælfgar's country[4]; and a great deal of simple
rapacity is laid to the charge of Harold by jurors whose testimony is not to be lightly rejected[5]; but the greater part of the
land ascribed to Godwin, his widow and his sons, seems to
consist of *comitales villae*.

Private
rights and
govern-
mental
revenues.
        The wealth of the earls is a matter of great importance. If
we subtract the estates of the king, the estates of the earls, and
the estates of the churches—and, as we shall see hereafter, the
churches had obtained the bulk of their wealth directly from

[1] D. B. iv. 99.
[2] Pseudoleges Canuti (=Liebermann's Instituta Cnuti), 55 (Schmid, p. 430):
'Comitis rectitudines secundum Anglos istae sunt communes cum rege: tertius
denarius in villis ubi mercatum convenerit, et in castigatione latronum, et
comitales villae, quae ad comitatum eius pertinent.'
[3] D. B. ii. 118 b: 'Terre Regis in Tetford...est una leugata terre in longa et
dim. in lato de qua Rex habet duas partes: de his autem duabus partibus tercia
pars in consulatu iacet.' But this seems to mean that only this part of the land
is in the county of Norfolk. Ibid. i. 246: in Stafford the king has twenty-two
houses 'de honore comitum.'   [4] D. B. i. 246.
[5] Ellis, Introduction, i. 313. When twenty years after Harold's death a
question about the title to land is at issue, there seems no reason why the jurors
should tell lies about Harold.

the kings,—if we subtract again the lands which the king, the earls, the churches have granted to their thegns, the England of 1065 will not appear to us a land of very great landowners, and we may obtain a valuable hint as to one of the origins of feudalism. A vast amount of land is or has recently been held by office-holders, by the holders of the kingship, the earlships, or the ealdormanships. We seem to see their proprietary rights arising in the sphere of public law, growing out of governmental rights, which however themselves are conceived as being in some sort proprietary. Many a passage in Domesday Book will suggest to us that a right to take tribute and a right to take the profits of justice have helped to give the king and the earls their manors and their seignories. Even in his own demesne manors the king is apt to appear rather as a tribute taker than as a landowner. Manors of very unequal size and value have had to supply him with equal quantities of victuals; each has to give 'a night's farm' once a year. Then from the counties at large he has taken a tribute; from Oxfordshire, for example, £10 for a hawk, 20 shillings for a sumpter horse, £23 for dogs and 6 sesters of honey[1]; from Worcestershire £10 or a Norway hawk, 20 shillings for a sumpter horse[2]; from Warwickshire £23 for 'the dog's custom,' 20 shillings for a sumpter horse, £10 for a hawk and 24 sesters of honey[3]. The farm of the county that the sheriff pays is made up out of obscure old items of this sort. Many men who are not the king's tenants must assist him in his hunting, must help in the erection of his deer-hays[4]. Then there are the *avera* and the *inwards* that are exacted by the king or his sheriff from sokemen who are not the king's men. The sheriff also is entitled to provender rents; out of 'the revenues which belong to the shrievalty' of Wiltshire, Edward of Salisbury gets pigs, wheat, barley, oats, honey, poultry, eggs, cheeses, lambs and fleeces; and besides this he seems to have 'reveland' which belongs to him as sheriff[5]. Then we see curious payments in money and renders

---

[1] D. B. i. 154 b.   [2] D. B. i. 172.   [3] D. B. i. 238.

[4] D. B. i. 56 b: Berkshire custom, 'Qui monitus ad stabilitionem venationis non ibat 50 sol. Regi emendabat.' See also the Hereford custom, Ib. 179; also Rectitudines (Schmid, App. III.) c. 1.

[5] D. B. i. 69. But the meaning of *reveland* is obscure. The most important passages about it are in D. B. i. 57 b (Eseldeborne), 181 (Getune). D. B. i. 83: 'Hanc tenet Aiulf de Rege quamdiu erit vicecomes.'

in kind made to some royal or some comital manor by the holders of other manors. In Devonshire, Charlton which belongs to the Bishop of Coutances, Honiton which belongs to the Count of Mortain, Smaurige which belongs to Ralph de Pomerai, Membury which belongs to William Chevre, Roverige which belongs to S^t. Mary of Rouen, each of these manors used to pay twenty pence a year to the royal manor of Axminster[1]. In Somersetshire there are manors which have owed *consuetudines*, masses of iron and sheep and lambs to the royal manors of South Perrott and Cury, or the comital manors of Crewkerne and Dulverton[2]. Then again, we find that pasture rights are connected with justiciary rights:—Godwin had a manor in Hampshire to which belonged the third penny of six hundreds, and in all the woods of those six hundreds he had free pasture and pannage[3]; the third penny of three hundreds in Devonshire and the third animal of the moorland pastures were annexed to the manor of Molland[4]. Many things seem to indicate that the distinction between private rights and governmental powers has been but faintly perceived in the past.

The English state.   If now we look at that English state which is the outcome of a purely English history, we see that it has already taken a pyramidal or conical shape. It is a society of lords and men. At its base are the cultivators of the soil, at its apex is the king. This cone is as yet but low. Even at the end of William's reign the peasant seldom had more than two lords between him and the king, but already in the Confessor's reign he might well have three[5]. Also the cone is obtuse: the angle at its apex will grow acuter under Norman rulers. We can indeed obtain no accurate statistics, but the number of landholders who were King Edward's men must have been much larger than the tale of the Norman tenants in chief. In the geographical distribution of the large estates under William there is but little more regularity than there was under his predecessor. In Cheshire and in Shropshire the Conqueror

[1] D. B. i. 100.
[2] D. B. i. 86, 86 b, 92, 97; so in Devonshire, 117 b: 'Hoc manerium debet per consuetudinem in Tavetone manerium Regis aut 1 bovem aut 30 denarios.'
[3] D. B. i. 38 b.
[4] D. B. i. 101: 'Ipsi manerio pertinet tercius denarius de hundredis Nortmoltone et Badentone et Brantone et tercium animal pasturae morarum.'
[5] Above, p. 155.

formed two great fiefs for Hugh of Avranches and Roger of Montgomery, well compacted fiefs, the like of which England had not yet seen. But the units which William found in existence and which he distributed among his followers were for the more part discrete units, and seldom did the Norman baron acquire as his honour any wide stretch of continuous territory. Still a great change took place in the substance of the cone, or if that substance is made up of lords and men and acres, then in the nature of, or rather the relation between, the forces which held the atoms together. Every change makes for symmetry, simplicity, consolidation. Some of these changes will seem to us predestined. To speculate as to what would have happened had Harold repelled the invader would be vain, and certainly we have no reason for believing that in that case the formula of dependent tenure would ever have got hold of every acre of English land and every right in English land. The law of 'land loans' (*Lehnrecht*) would hardly have become our only land law, had not a conqueror enjoyed an unbounded power, or a power bounded only by some reverence for the churches, of deciding by what men and on what terms every rood of England should be holden. Had it not been for this, we should surely have had some *franc alleu* to oppose to the *fief,* some *Eigen* to oppose to the *Lehn*. But if England was not to be for ever a prey to rebellions and civil wars, the power of the lords over their men must have been—not indeed increased, but—territorialized ; the liberty of 'going with one's land to whatever lord one chose' must have been curtailed. As yet the central force embodied in the kingship was too feeble to deal directly with every one of its subjects, to govern them and protect them. The intermediation of the lords was necessary ; the state could not but be pyramidal ; and, while this was so, the freedom that men had of forsaking one lord for another, of forsaking even the king for the ambitious earl, was a freedom that was akin to anarchy. Such a liberty must have its wings clipt ; free contract must be taught to know its place ; the lord's hold over the man's land must become permanent. This change, if it makes at first for a more definite feudalism, or (to use words more strictly) if it substitutes feudalism for vassalism, makes also for the stability of the state, for the increase of the state's power over the individual, and in the end for the disappearance of feudalism. The freeholder of the thirteenth century is much more like the subject of a modern state than was the free man of the Confessor's day who could place himself and his land under the power and warranty of whatever lord he chose. Lordship in becoming landlordship begins to lose its most dangerous element; it is ceasing to be a religion, it is becoming a 'real' right, a matter for private law. Again, we may guess, if we please, that but for the Norman Conquest the mass of the English peasantry would never have fallen so low as fall it did. The 'sokemen' would hardly have been turned into 'villeins,' the 'villeins' would hardly have become 'serfs.' And yet the villeins of the Confessor's time were in a perilous position. Already they were occupying lands which for two most important purposes were reckoned the lands of their lords, lands for which their lords gelded, lands for which their lords fought. Even in an English England the time might have come when the state, refusing to look behind their lords, would have left the protection of their rights to a *Hofrecht*, to 'the custom of the manor.'

Last words. It is, we repeat it, vain to speculate about such matters, for we know too little of the relative strength of the various forces that were at work, and an accident, a war, a famine, may at any moment decide the fate, even the legal fate, of a great class. And above all there is the unanswerable question whether Harold or any near successor of his would or could have done what William did so soon as the survey was accomplished, when he proved that, after all, the pyramid was no pyramid and that every particle of it was in immediate contact with him, and 'there came to him all the land-sitting men who were worth aught from over all England, whosesoever men they were, and they bowed themselves to him, and became this man's men[1].'

§ 9. *The Boroughs.*

Borough and village. Dark as the history of our villages may be, the history of the boroughs is darker yet; or rather, perhaps, the darkness seems blacker because we are compelled to suppose that it conceals from our view changes more rapid and intricate than

[1] Chron. ann. 1085.

those that have happened in the open country. The few paragraphs that follow will be devoted mainly to the development of one suggestion which has come to us from foreign books, but which may throw a little light where every feeble ray is useful. At completeness we must not aim, and in our first words we ought to protest that no general theory will tell the story of every or any particular town[1].

In the thirteenth century a legal, though a wavering, line is drawn between the borough and the mere vill or rural township[2]. It is a wavering line, for stress can be laid now upon one and now upon another attribute of the ancient and indubitable boroughs, and this selected attribute can then be employed as a test for the claims of other towns. When in Edward I.'s day the sheriffs are being told to bid every borough send two burgesses to the king's parliaments, there are somewhat more than 150 places to which such summonses will at times be addressed, though before the end of the middle ages the number of 'parliamentary boroughs' will have shrunk to 100 or thereabouts[3]. Many towns seem to hover on the border line and in some cases the sheriff has been able to decide whether or no a town shall be represented in the councils of the realm. Yet if we go back to the early years of the tenth century, we shall still find this contrast between the borough and the mere township existing as a contrast whence legal consequences flow. Where lies the contrast? What is it that makes a borough to be a borough? That is the problem that we desire to solve. It is a legal problem. We are not to ask why some places are thickly populated or why trade has flowed in this or that channel. We are to ask why certain vills are severed from other vills and are called boroughs.

We may reasonably wish, however, since mental pictures must be painted, to know at the outset whereabouts the line

The borough in cent. xiii.

The number of the boroughs.

---

[1] A sketch of the principal argument of this section was published in Eng. Hist. Rev., xi. 13, as a review of Keutgen's Untersuchungen über den Ursprung der deutschen Stadtverfassung. The origin of the French and German towns has become the theme of a large and very interesting literature. A good introduction to this will be found in an article by M. Pirenne, L'origine des constitutions urbaines, Revue historique, liii. 52, lvii. 293, and an article by Mr Ashley, Quarterly Journal of Economics, vol. x. July, 1896. The continuous survival of Roman municipal institutions even in Gaul seems to be denied by almost all modern students.

[2] Hist. Eng. Law, i. 625.   [3] Stubbs, Const. Hist. iii. 448.

will be drawn, and whether when we are speaking of the Conqueror's reign and earlier times we shall have a large or a small number of boroughs on our hands. Will it be a hundred and fifty, or a hundred, or will it be only fifty? At once we will say that some fifty boroughs stand out prominently and will demand our best attention, though a second and far less important class was already being formed.

The aid-paying boroughs of cent. xii.

In the middle of the twelfth century the Exchequer was treating certain places in an exceptional fashion. It was subjecting them to a special tax in the form of an *auxilium* or *donum*. This fact we may take as the starting point for our researches. Now if we read the unique Pipe Roll of Henry I.'s reign and the earliest Pipe Rolls of Henry II.'s we observe that an 'aid' or a 'gift' is from time to time collected from the 'cities and boroughs,' and if we put down the names of the towns which are charged with this impost, we obtain a remarkable result[1]. Speaking broadly we may say that the only towns which pay are 'county towns.' For a large part of England this is strictly true. We will follow the order of Domesday Book, beginning however with its second zone. If London is in Middlesex[2], it is Middlesex's one borough. In Hertfordshire is Hertford. In Buckinghamshire is Buckingham, but no aid can be expected from it. In Oxfordshire is Oxford. In Gloucestershire is Gloucester, but Winchcombe also asserts its burghal rank. In Worcestershire is Worcester, while Droitwich appears occasionally with a small gift. Hereford is the one borough of Herefordshire. Turning to the third zone, we pass rapidly through Cambridgeshire, Huntingdonshire, Bedfordshire and Northamptonshire; each has its borough. This will be true of Leicestershire also; but Leicester is by this time so completely in the hands of its earl that the king gets nothing from it. Nor, it would seem, does he get anything from Warwick. Half in Warwickshire, half in Staffordshire lies Tamworth; Stafford also pays. At times Bridgenorth appears beside Shrewsbury. Nothing is received from Chester, for it is the head of a palatinate. Derby, Nottingham and York are the only representatives of their shires. Lincolnshire

---

[1] We must exclude cases in which the king takes an aid from his whole demesne, e.g. for his daughter's marriage, for in such a case many royal manors which have no right to be called boroughs must make a gift.

[2] Round, Geoffrey de Mandeville, 347, has excellent remarks on this point.

has Stamford on its border as well as Lincoln in its centre. Norfolk has Thetford as well as Norwich; but Suffolk has only Ipswich and Essex only Colchester.

In the southern zone matters are not so simple. Kent contains Canterbury and Rochester; Surrey contains Guildford and Southwark; Sussex only Chichester. Hampshire has Winchester; Southampton is receiving special treatment. Wallingford represents Berkshire. When we get to Wiltshire and Dorset we are in the classical land of small boroughs. There are various little towns whose fate is in the balance; Marlborough and Calne seem for the moment to be the most prominent. In Somersetshire, whatever may have been true in the past, Ilchester is standing out as the one borough that pays an aid. Exeter has now no second in Devonshire. If there is a borough in Cornwall, it makes no gift to the king. *Aid-paying boroughs in the south.*

We may obtain some notion of the relative rank of these towns if we set forth the amounts with which they are charged in 1130 and in 1156, though the materials for this comparison are unfortunately incomplete. *List of aids.*

	Pipe Roll 31 Hen. I	Pipe Roll 2 Hen. II		Pipe Roll 31 Hen. I	Pipe Roll 2 Hen. II
	£	£		£	£
London	120	120	Wiltshire boroughs	17	
Winchester	80		Calne		1
Lincoln	60	60	Dorset boroughs	15	
York	40	40	Huntingdon	8	8
Norwich	30	33⅓	Ipswich	7	3⅓
Exeter		20	Guildford	5	5
Canterbury	20	13⅓	Southwark	5	5
Colchester	20[1]	12⅔[1]	Hertford	5	
Oxford	20	20	Stamford	5	
Gloucester	15	15	Bedford	5	6⅔
Wallingford	15		Shrewsbury		5
Worcester		15	Droitwich		5
Cambridge	12	12	Stafford	3⅓	3⅓
Hereford		10	Winchcombe	3	5
Thetford	10		Tamworth	2¾	1¼[2]
Northampton	10		Ilchester		2½
Rochester		10	Chichester[3]		
Nottingham } Derby }	15	15			

[1] Nearly.
[2] This may come only from the Staffordshire part of Tamworth.
[3] Chichester pays in later years; but very little.

Now we are not putting this forward as a list of those English towns that were the most prosperous in the middle of the twelfth century. We have made no mention of flourishing seaports, of Dover, Hastings, Bristol, Yarmouth. Nor is this a list of all the places that are casually called *burgi* on rolls of Henry II.'s reign. That name is given to Scarborough, Knaresborough, Tickhill, Cirencester and various other towns. New tests of 'burgality' (if we may make that word) are emerging and old tests are becoming obsolete. We see too that some towns are dropping out of the list of aid-paying boroughs. In 1130 Wallingford has thrice failed to pay its aid of £15 and the whole debt of £45 must be forgiven to the burgesses *pro paupertate eorum*[1]. So Wallingford drops out of this list. Probably Buckingham has dropped out at an earlier time for a similar reason. But still this list, especially in the form that it takes in Henry I.'s time, is of great importance to those who are going to study the boroughs of Domesday Book. It looks like a traditional list. It deals out nice round sums. It is endeavouring to keep Wallingford on a par with Gloucester and above Northampton. It is retaining Winchcombe.

If we make the experiment, we shall discover that this catalogue really is a good prologue to Domesday Book. We will once more visit the counties which form the second zone. The account that our record gives of Hertfordshire has a preface. That preface deals with the borough of Hertford and precedes even the list of the Hertfordshire tenants in chief. Buckingham in Buckinghamshire and Oxford in Oxfordshire are similarly treated. In Gloucestershire the city of Gloucester and the borough of Winchcombe are described before the body of the county is touched. In Worcestershire, Herefordshire, Cambridgeshire, Huntingdonshire, Bedfordshire, Northamptonshire, Leicestershire, Warwickshire, Staffordshire[2], Shropshire, Cheshire, Derbyshire, Nottinghamshire[3] and Yorkshire the same procedure is adopted: the account of the shire's city or borough precedes the account of the shire. In Lincolnshire the description of the county is introduced by the description

[1] Pipe Roll, 31 Hen. I. p. 139.

[2] Was the blank space in D. B. i. 246 left for the borough of Tamworth? This borough is incidentally mentioned in D. B. i. 238, 246, 246 b.

[3] But the account of the two sister boroughs here falls between the accounts of the two sister counties.

of Lincoln and Stamford; also of Torksey, which had been a place of military importance and seems to have been closely united with the city of Lincoln by some governmental bond[1]. Convenient arrangement is not the strong point of 'Little Domesday'; but what is said therein of Colchester is said at the very end of the survey of Essex, while Norwich, Yarmouth and Thetford stand at the end of the royal estates in Norfolk, and Ipswich stands at the end of the royal estates in Suffolk.

If now we enter the southern zone and keep in our minds the scheme that we have seen prevailing in the greater part of England, we shall observe that the account of Kent has a prologue touching Dover, Canterbury and Rochester. In Berkshire an excellent account of Wallingford precedes the rubric *Terra Regis.* Four places in Dorset are singled out for prefatory treatment, namely, Dorchester, Bridport, Wareham and Shaftesbury. In Devon Exeter stands, if we may so speak, above the line, and stands alone, though Barnstaple, Lidford and Totness are reckoned as boroughs. Of the other counties there is more to be said. If we compare the first page of the survey of Somerset with the first pages that are devoted to its two neighbours, Dorset and Devon, we shall probably come to the conclusion that the compilers of the book scrupled to put any Somerset vill on a par with Exeter, Dorchester, Bridport, Wareham and Shaftesbury. In each of the three cases the page is mapped out in precisely the same fashion. The second column is headed by *Terra Regis.* A long way down in the first column begins the list of tenants in chief. The upper part of the first column contains in one case the account of Exeter, in another the account of the four Dorset boroughs, but in the third case, that of Somerset, it is left blank. In Wiltshire Malmesbury and Marlborough stand above the line; but, if we look to the foot of the page, we shall suspect that the compilers can not easily force their general scheme upon this part of the country. In Surrey no place stands above the line. Guildford is the first place mentioned on the *Terra Regis*; Southwark seems to be inadequately treated on a later page. The case of Sussex is like that of Somerset; the list of the tenants in chief is preceded by a blank space. In Hampshire a whole column

Southern boroughs in Domesday.

---

[1] D. B. i. 337. It is even called a *suburbium* of Lincoln, though it lies full 10 miles from the city.

is left blank.　On a later page the borough of Southampton has a column to itself; in the next column stands the *Terra Regis* of the Isle of Wight.　And now let us turn back to the Middlesex that we have as yet ignored.　Nearly two columns, to say nothing of some precedent pages, are void[1].

The boroughs and the plan of Domesday Book.

Now we must not be led away into speculations which would be vain.　We must not, for example, inquire whether the information that had been obtained touching London and Winchester was too bulky to fill a room that had been left for it.　We must not inquire whether something was to be said of Chichester or Hastings, of Ilchester or of Bristol that has not been said.　But apparently we may attribute to King William's officials a certain general idea.　It is an idea which suits the greater part of England very well, though they find difficulties in their way when they endeavour to impose it on some of the counties that lie south of the Thames.　The broad fact stands clear that throughout the larger part of England the commissioners found a town in each county, and in general one town only, which required special treatment.　They do not locate it on the *Terra Regis*; they do not locate it on any man's land.　It stands outside the general system of land tenure.

The borough on no man's land.

For a while, then, let us confine our attention to these county towns, and we shall soon see why it is that they are rarely brought under any rubric which would describe them as pieces of the king's soil or pieces of some one else's soil.　The trait to which we allude we shall call (for want of a better term) the tenurial heterogeneity of the burgesses.　In those boroughs that are fully described we seldom, if ever, find that all the burgesses have the same landlord.　Of course there is a sense in which, according to the view of the Domesday surveyors and of all later lawyers, every inch of borough land is held of one landlord, namely, the king; but in that sense every inch of England has the same landlord.　The fact that we would bring into relief is this, that normally the burgesses of the borough do not hold their burgages immediately of one and the same lord; they are not 'peers of a tenure'; the group that they constitute is not a tenurial group.　Far rather we shall

---

[1] The one glimpse that I have had of the manuscript suggested to me (1) that the accounts of some of the boroughs were postscripts, and (2) that space was left for accounts of London and Winchester.　The anatomy of the book deserves examination by an expert.

find that, though there will be some burgesses holding immediately of the king, there will be others whose titles can be traced
to the king only through the medium of other lords. And the
mesne lord will often be a very great man, some prelate or
baron with a widespread honour. Within the borough he will,
to use the language of Domesday Book, 'have' or 'hold' a
small group of burgesses, and sometimes they will be reckoned
as annexed to or as 'lying in' some manor distant from the
town. It seems generally expected that the barons of the
county should have a few burgages apiece in the county town.
This arrangement does not look new. Seemingly the great
men of an earlier day, the *antecessores* of the Frenchmen, have
owned town-houses: not so much houses for their own use, as
houses or 'haws' (*hagae*) in which they could keep a few
'burgesses.'

Some examples of this remarkable arrangement should be Hetero-
given. First we will look at Oxford. The king has many geneous
houses; the Archbishop of Canterbury has 7; the Bishop of the
Winchester 9; the Bishop of Bayeux 18; the Bishop of boroughs.
Lincoln 30; the Bishop of Coutances 2; the Bishop of Hereford
3; the Abbot of St Edmund's 1; the Abbot of Abingdon 14;
the Abbot of Eynsham 13. And so with the worldly great:—
the Count of Mortain has 10; Count Hugh has 7; the Count
of Evreux 1; Robert of Ouilly 12; Roger of Ivry 15; Walter
Giffard 17:—but we need not repeat the whole long list[1].

It is so at Wallingford; King Edward had 8 virgates on
which were 276 houses, and they paid him £11 rent; Bishop
Walkelin of Winchester has 27, which pay 25 shillings; the
Abbot of Abingdon has two acres, on which are 7 houses paying
4 shillings; Milo Crispin has 20 houses, which pay 12 shillings
and 10 pence; and so forth[2]. Further, it is said that the
Bishop's 27 houses are valued in Brightwell; and, turning to
the account of Brightwell, there, sure enough, we find mention
of the 25 shillings which these houses pay[3]. Milo's 20 houses
are said to 'lie in' Newnham; he has also in Wallingford 6
houses which are in Hazeley, 1 which is in Stoke, 1 which is in
Chalgrove, one acre with 6 houses which is in Sutton, one acre
with 11 houses which is in Bray; 'all this land' we are told
'belongs to Oxfordshire, but nevertheless it is in Wallingford.'

---

[1] D. B. i. 154.   [2] D. B. i. 56.   [3] D. B. i. 58.

Yes, Milo's manor of Chalgrove lies five, his manor of Hazeley lies seven miles from Wallingford; nevertheless, houses which are physically in Wallingford are constructively in Chalgrove and Hazeley. That we are not dealing with a Norman novelty is in this case extremely plain. Wallingford is a border town. We read first of the Berkshire landowners who have burgesses within it. There follows a list of the Oxfordshire 'thegns' who hold houses in Wallingford. Archbishop Lanfranc and Count Hugh appear in this context as 'thegns' of Oxfordshire.

Examples of heterogeneity.

When we have obtained this clue, we soon begin to see that what is true of Oxford and Wallingford is true even of those towns of which no substantive description is given us. Thus there are 'haws' or town-houses in Winchester which are attached to manors in all corners of Hampshire, at Wallop, Clatford, Basingstoke, Eversley, Candover, Strathfield, Minstead and elsewhere. Some of the manors to which the burghers of London were attached are not, even in our own day, within our monstrous town ; there are some at Banstead and Bletchingley in Surrey, at Waltham and Thurrock in Essex. But in every quarter we see this curious scheme. At Warwick the king has in his demesne 113 houses, and his barons have 112[1]. Of the barons' houses it is written : 'These houses belong to the lands which the barons hold outside the borough and are valued there.' Or turn we to a small town:—at Buckingham the barons have 26 burgesses; no one of them has more than 5.[2] The page that tells us this presents to us an admirable contrast between Buckingham and its future rival. Aylesbury is just an ordinary royal manor and stands under the rubric *Terra Regis.* Buckingham is a very petty townlet; but it is a borough, and Count Hugh and the Bishop of Coutances, Robert of Ouilly, Roger of Ivry, Arnulf of Hesdin and other mighty men have burgesses there. As a climax we may mention the case of Winchcombe. The burgages in this little town were held by many great people. About the year 1100 the king had 60; the Abbot of Winchcombe 40; the Abbot of Evesham 2; the Bishop of Hereford 2; Robert of Bellême 3; Robert Fitzhamon 5, and divers other persons of note had some 29 houses among them[3]. However poor, however small Winchcombe

---

[1] D. B. i. 238. [2] D. B. i. 143.

[3] Ellis, Introduction, ii. 446; Winchcombe Land-boc, ed. Royce, p. xiv; Stevenson, Rental of Gloucester, p. ix.

may have been, it radically differed from the common manor and the common village.

We have seen above how in the Conqueror's day the Abbey of Westminster had a manor at Staines[1] and how that manor included 48 burgesses who paid 40s. a year. Were those burgesses really in Staines, and was Staines a borough? No, they were in the city of London. The Confessor had told his Middlesex thegns how he willed that St Peter and the brethren at Westminster should have the manor (*cotlif*) of Staines with the land called Staninghaw (*mid ðam lande Stæningehaga*) within London and all other things that had belonged to Staines[2]. Is not the guess permissible that Staining Lane in the City of London[3], wherein stood the church of St Mary, Staining, was so called, not 'because stainers lived in it,' but because it once contained the haws of the men of Staines? We must be careful before we find boroughs in Domesday Book, for its language is deceptive. Perhaps we may believe that really and physically there were forty-six burgesses in the vill of St Albans[4]; but, after what we have read of Staines, can we be quite sure that these burgesses were not in London? The burgesses who *de iure* 'are in' one place are often *de facto* in quite another place.

We may for a moment pass over two centuries and turn to the detailed account of Cambridge given to us by the Hundred Rolls, the most elaborate description that we have of any medieval borough. Now in one sense the 'vill' or borough of Cambridge belongs to the king, and, under him, to the burgesses, for they hold it of him *in capite* at a fee-farm rent. But this does not mean that each burgess holds his tenement of the corporation or *communitas* of burgesses, which in its turn holds every yard of land of the king in chief. It does not even mean that each burgess holds immediately of the king, the *communitas* intervening as farmer of the king's rents[5]. No, the titles of the various burgesses go up to the king by many various routes. Some of them pay rents to the officers of the borough who are the king's farmers; but many of them do not. The Chancellor and Masters of the University, for example, hold three messuages in the vill of Cambridge; 'but'

Burgesses attached to manors.

Tenure of the borough and tenure of land within the borough.

[1] D. B. i. 128, 128 b; and above, p. 111. [2] K. 855 (iv. 211).
[3] Stow, Survey, ed. Strype, Bk. iii. p. 121. [4] D. B. i. 135 b.
[5] Hist. Eng. Law, i. 636.

say the sworn burgesses 'what they pay for the same, we do not know and can not discover[1].' How could it be otherwise? Domesday Book shows us that the Count of Britanny had ten burgesses in Cambridge[2]. Count Alan's houses will never be held in chief of the crown by any burgess: they will form part of the honour of Richmond to the end of time. We may take another example which will show the permanence of proprietary arrangements in the boroughs. From an account of Gloucester which comes to us from the year 1100 or thereabouts we learn that there were 300 houses in the king's demesne and 313 belonging to other lords. From the year 1455 we have another account which tells of 310 tenements paying landgavel to the king's farmers and 346 which pay them nothing[3].

The king and other landlords. Perhaps no further examples are needed. But this tenurial heterogeneity seems to be an attribute of all or nearly all the very ancient boroughs, the county towns. In some cases the king was the landlord of far the greater number of the burgesses. In other cases the bishop became in course of time the lord of some large quarter of a town in which his cathedral stood. At Canterbury and Rochester, at Winchester and Worcester, this process had been at work from remote days; the bishops had been acquiring land and 'haws' within the walls[4]. But we can see that in Henry I.'s day there were still four earls who were keeping up their interest in their burgesses at Winchester[5]. In the later middle ages we may, if we will, call these places royal boroughs and the king's 'demesne boroughs,' for the burgesses derive their 'liberties' directly from the king. But we must keep these ancient boroughs well apart from any royal manors which the king has newly raised to burghal rank. In the latter he will be the immediate landlord of every burgess; in the former a good deal of rent will be paid, not to him, nor to the community as his farmers, but to those who are filling the shoes of the thegns of the shire.

---

[1] Rot. Hund. ii. 361.   [2] D. B. i. 189.

[3] Rental of Gloucester, ed. W. H. Stevenson: Gloucester, 1890, p. x.

[4] There are many examples in Kemble's Codex.

[5] Pipe Roll, 31 Hen. I. p. 41: 'Vicecomes reddit compotum de £80 de auxilio civitatis....Et in perdonis....Comiti de Mellent 25 sol....Comiti de Lerecestria 35 sol....Comiti de Warenna 16 sol....Comiti Gloecestriae 116 sol. et 8 den.' See also the Liber Wintoniae, D. B. iv. 531 ff.

This said, we will turn back our thoughts to the oldest days. The oldest burh. The word that deserves our best attention is *burh*, the future *borough*, for little good would come of an attempt to found a theory upon the Latin words, such as *civitas, oppidum* and *urbs* which occur in some of those magniloquent land-books[1]. Now it seems fairly clear that for some long time after the Germanic invasions the word *burh* meant merely a fastness, a stronghold, and suggested no thick population nor any population at all. This we might learn from the map of England. The hill-top that has been fortified is a *burh*. Very often it has given its name to a neighbouring village[2]. But, to say nothing of hamlets, we have full two hundred and fifty parishes whose names end in *burgh, borough* or *bury*, and in many cases we see no sign in them of an ancient camp or of an exceptionally dense population. It seems a mere chance that they are not *tons* or *hams, worths* or *thorpes*. Then again, in Essex and neighbouring shires it is common to find that in the village called *X* there is a squire's mansion or a cluster of houses called *X-bury*. Further, we can see plainly from our oldest laws that the palisade or entrenchment around a great man's house is a *burh*. Thus Alfred: The king's *burh-bryce* (the sum to be paid for breaking his *burh*) is 120 shillings, an

---

[1] In the A.-S. land-books the word *civitas* is commonly applied to Worcester, Winchester, Canterbury, and other such places, which are both bishops' sees and the head places of large districts. But (K. v. p. 180) Gloucester is a *civitas*, and for some time after the Conquest it is rather the county town than the cathedral town that bears this title. Did any one ever speak of Selsey or Sherborne as a *civitas*? In 803 (K. v. p. 65) the bishops of Canterbury, Lichfield, Leicester, Sidnacester, Worcester, Winchester, Dunwich, London and Rochester style themselves bishops of *civitates*, while those of Hereford, Sherborne, Elmham and Selsey do not use this word. But an inference from this would be rash.

[2] An interesting example is this. In 779 Offa conveys to a thegn land at Sulmonnesburg. The boundaries mentioned in the charter are those of the present parish of Bourton-on-the-Water. 'Sulmonnesburg...is the ancient camp close to Bourton which gave its name to the Domesday Hundred of Salmanesberie, and at a gap in the rampart of which a Court Leet was held till recently.' See C. S. Taylor, Pre-Domesday Hide of Gloucestershire, Trans. Bristol and Gloucestershire Archæol. Soc. vol. xviii. pt. 2. As regards the names of hills and of villages named from hills there may occasionally be some difficulty in marking off those which go back to *beorh* (*berry, berrow, barrow*) from those which go back to *burh* (*burgh, borough, bury*). Mr Stevenson tells me that in the West of England the termination *-borough* sometimes represents *-beorh*.

archbishop's 90 shillings, another bishop's 60 shillings, a twelve-hundred man's 30 shillings, a six-hundred-man's 15 shillings, a ceorl's edor-bryce (the sum to be paid for breaking his hedge) 5 shillings[1]. The ceorl, whose *wer* is 200 shillings, will not have a *burh*, he will only have a hedge round his house; but the man whose *wer* is 600 shillings will probably have some stockade, some rude rampart; he will have a *burh*.

The king's burh.

We observe the heavy *bót* of 120 shillings which protects the king's *burh*. May we not see here the very first stage in the legal history of our boroughs? We pass over some centuries and we read in a statement of the Londoners' customs that a man who is guilty of unlawful violence must pay the king's *burh-bryce* of five pounds[2]. And then the Domesday surveyors tell us how at Canterbury every crime committed in those streets which run right through the city is a crime against the king, and so it is if committed upon the high-roads outside the city for the space of one league, three perches and three feet[3]. This curious accuracy over perches and feet sends us to another ancient document:—'Thus far shall the king's peace (*grið*) extend from his *burhgeat* where he is sitting towards all four quarters, namely, three miles, three furlongs, three acre-breadths, nine feet, nine hand-breadths, nine barley-corns[4].' And then we remember how Fleta tells us that the verge of the king's palace is twelve leagues in circumference, and how within that ambit the palace court, the king's most private court, has jurisdiction[5].

The special peace of the burh.

Has not legal fiction been at work since an early time?

[1] Alfred, 40; Ine, 45.

[2] Aethelr. iv. 4. The Quadripartitus is our only authority for these *Instituta*; but Dr Liebermann (Quadrip. p. 138) holds that the translator had in front of him a document written before the Conquest. Schmid would read *borh-bryce*; see p. 541; but this emendation seems needless. Has not the sum been Normanized? The king's *burh-bryce* used to be 120 (i.e. in English 'a hundred') shillings, and a hundred *Norman* shillings make £5. So according to the Berkshire custom (D. B. i. 56 b) he who by night breaks a *civitas* pays 100 shillings to the king and not (it is noted) to the sheriff.

[3] D. B. i. 2: 'Concordatum est de rectis callibus quae habent per civitatem introitum et exitum, quicunque in illis forisfecerit, regi emendabit.' See the important document contained in a St Augustin's Cartulary and printed in Larking, Domesday of Kent, Appendix, 35: 'Et omnes vie civitatis que habent duas portas, hoc est introitum et exitum, ille sunt de consuetudine Regis.'

[4] Schmid, App. XII; Leg. Henr. c. 16.

[5] Fleta, p. 66; see also 13 Ric. II. stat. 1. cap. 3.

Has not the sanctity of the king's house extended itself over a group of houses? The term *burh* seems to spread outwards from the defensible house of the king and with it the sphere of his *burh-bryce* is amplified. Within the borough there reigns a special peace. This has a double meaning:—not only do acts which would be illegal anywhere become more illegal when they are done within the borough, but acts which would be legal elsewhere, are illegal there. King Edmund legislating against the blood-feud makes his *burh* as sacred as a church; it is a sanctuary where the feud may not be prosecuted[1]. If in construing such a passage we doubt how to translate *burh*, whether by *house* or by *borough*, we are admitting that the language of the law does not distinguish between the two. The Englishman's house is his castle, or, to use an older term, his *burh*; the king's borough is the king's house, for his house-peace prevails in its streets[2].

Our oldest laws seem to know no *burh* other than the strong house of a great (but he need not be a very great) man. Early in the tenth century, however, the word had already acquired a new meaning. In Æthelstan's day it seems to be supposed by the legislator that a moot will usually be held in a *burh*. If a man neglects three summonses to a moot, the oldest men of the *burh* are to ride to his place and seize his goods[3]. Already a *burh* will have many men in it. Some of them will be elder-men, aldermen. A moot will be held in it. Very possibly this will be the shire-moot, for, since there is riding to be done, we see that the person who ought to have come to the moot may live at a distance[4]. A little later the *burh* certainly has a moot of its own. Edgar bids his subjects seek the *burh-gemót* as well as the *scyr-gemót* and the *hundred-gemót*. The borough-moot is to be held thrice a year[5]. At least from this time forward, the borough has a court. An important line is thus drawn between the borough and the mere *tún*. The borough has a court; the village has none, or, if the villages are getting

The town and the burh.

---

[1] Edmund, ii. 2.

[2] See also Schmid, App. IV. (Be griðe and be munde), § 15: 'If any man fights or steals in the king's *burh* or the neighbourhood (the 'verge'), he forfeits his life, if the king will not concede that he be redeemed by a *wergild*.'

[3] Æthelstan, ii. 20.

[4] K. 1334 (vi. p. 195): a contract made at Exeter before Earl Godwin and all the shire.

[5] Edgar, iii. 5; Cnut, ii. 18.

courts, this is due to the action of lords who have sake and soke and is not commanded by national law. National law commands that there shall be a moot thrice a year in every *burh*.

The building of boroughs. The extension of the term *burh* from a fortified house to a fortified group of houses must be explained by those who are skilled in the history of military affairs. It is for them to tell us, for example, how much use the Angles and Saxons in the oldest days made of the entrenched hill-tops, and whether the walls of the Roman towns were continuously repaired[1]. Howbeit, a time seems to have come, at latest in the struggle between the Danish invaders and the West-Saxon kings, when the establishment and maintenance of what we might call fortified towns was seen to be a matter of importance. There was to be a cluster of inhabited dwellings which as a whole was to be made defensible by ditch and mound, by palisade or wall. Edward the Elder and the Lady of the Mercians were active in this work. Within the course of a few years burgs were 'wrought' or 'timbered' at Worcester, Chester, Hertford, Witham in Essex, Bridgnorth, Tamworth, Stafford, Warwick, Eddisbury, Warbury, Runcorn, Buckingham, Towcester, Maldon, Huntingdon[2]. Whatever may be meant by the duty of repairing burgs when it is mentioned in charters coming from a somewhat earlier time, it must for the future be that of upholding those walls and mounds that the king and the lady are rearing. The land was to be burdened with the maintenance of strongholds. The land, we say. That is the style of the land-books. Land, even though given to a church, is not to be free (unless by exceptional favour) of army-service, bridge-work and borough-bettering or borough-fastening. Wall-work[3] is coupled with bridge-work; to the duty of maintaining the county bridges is joined the duty of constructing and repairing the boroughs. Shall we say the 'county boroughs'?

The shire and its borough. Let us ask ourselves how the burden that is known as *burh-bót*, the duty that the Latin charters call *constructio, munitio, restauratio, defensio, arcis* (for *arx* is the common

---

[1] Mention is made of the walls of Rochester and Canterbury in various charters from the middle of cent. viii onwards: K. vol. i. pp. 138, 183, 274; vol. ii. pp. 1, 26, 36, 57, 86; vol. v. p. 68.

[2] Green, Conquest of England, 189–207.

[3] For instance, K. iii. pp. 5, 50.

term) will really be borne. Is it not highly probable, almost certain, that each particular tract of land will be ascript to some particular *arx* or *castellum*[1], and that if, for instance, there is but one *burh* in a shire, all the lands in that shire must help to better that *burh*. Apportionment will very likely go further. The man with five hides will know how much of the mound or the wall he must maintain, how much ' wall-work' he must do. We see how the old bridge-work becomes a burden on the estates of the county landowners. From century to century the Cambridgeshire landowners contribute according to their hidage to repair the most important bridge of their county, a bridge which lies in the middle of the borough of Cambridge. Newer arrangements, the rise of castles and of borough communities, have relieved them from the duty of ' borough-fastening;' but the bridge-work is apportioned on their lands.

The exceedingly neat and artificial scheme of political geography that we find in the midlands, in the country of the true 'shires,' forcibly suggests deliberate delimitation for military purposes. Each shire is to have its borough in its middle. Each shire takes its name from its borough. We must leave it for others to say in every particular case whether and in what sense the shire is older than the borough or the borough than the shire: whether an old Roman chester was taken as a centre or whether the struggles between Germanic tribes had fixed a circumference. But a policy, a plan, there has been, and the outcome of it is that the shire maintains the borough[2].

There has come down to us in a sadly degenerate form a document which we shall hereafter call ' The Burghal Hidage[3].' It sets forth, so we believe, certain arrangements made early in the tenth century for the defence of Wessex against Danish

Military geography.

[1] K. 1154 (v. 302): 'adiacent etiam agri quamplurimi circa castellum quod Welingaford vocitatur.'—K. 152 (i. 183): 'castelli quod nominatur Hrofescester.' —K. 276 (ii. 57): 'castelli Hrobi.'

[2] A beautiful example is given by Staffordshire and Warwickshire. Each has its borough in its centre, while Tamworth on the border is partly in the one shire, partly in the other. See Pipe Roll, 31 Hen. I. 75, 76, 107, 108. As to these Mercian shires, see Stubbs, Const. Hist., i. 123 ; Green, Conquest of England, 237: ' Hertfordshire, Buckinghamshire and Bedfordshire are other instances of purely military creation, districts assigned to the fortresses which Eadward raised at these points.'

[3] See our index under *Burghal Hidage*. Mr W. H. Stevenson's valuable aid in the identification of these burgs is gratefully acknowledged.

inroads. It names divers strongholds, and assigns to each a large number of hides. A few of the places that it mentions we have not yet found on the map. Beginning in the east of Sussex and following the order of the list, we seem to see Hastings, Lewes, Burpham (near Arundel), Chichester, Porchester, Southampton, Winchester, Wilton, Tisbury (or perhaps Chisenbury), Shaftesbury, Twyneham, Wareham, Bredy, Exeter, Halwell near Totness, Lidford, Barnstaple, Watchet, Axbridge; then Langport and Lyng (which defend the isle of Athelney), Bath, Malmesbury, Cricklade, Oxford, Wallingford, Buckingham, Eastling near Guildford, and Southwark. Corrupt and enigmatical though this catalogue may be, it is of the highest importance. It shows how in the great age of burg-building the strongholds had wide provinces which in some manner or another were appurtenant to them, and it may also give us some precious hints about places in Wessex which once were national burgs but which forfeited their burghal character in the tenth century. Guildford seems to have risen at the expense of Eastling and Totness at the expense of Halwell, while Tisbury, Bredy and Watchet (if we are right in fancying that they are mentioned) soon lost caste. Lyng is not a place which we should have named among the oldest of England's burgs, and yet we have all read how Alfred wrought a 'work' at Athelney. In Wessex burgs rise and fall somewhat rapidly. North of the Thames the system is more stable. Also it is more artificial, for north of the Thames civil and military geography coincide.

The shire's wall-work Let us now look once more at the Oxford of Domesday Book. The king has twenty 'mural houses[1]' which belonged to Earl Ælfgar; they pay 13s. 2d. He has a house of 6d. which is constructively at Shipton; one of 4d. at Bloxham; one of 30d. at Risborough and two of 4d. at Twyford in Buckinghamshire. 'They are called mural houses because, if there be need and the king gives order, they shall repair the wall.' There follows a list of the noble houseowners, an archbishop, six bishops, three earls and so forth. 'All the above hold these houses free because of the reparation of the wall. All the houses that are called "mural" were in King Edward's time free of everything except army service and wall-work.' Then of Chester we read this[2]:—'To repair the wall and the bridge, the reeve

---

[1] D. B. i. 154. [2] D. B. i. 262 b.

called out one man from every hide in the county, and the lord whose man did not come paid 40s. to the king and earl.' The duty of maintaining the bulwark of the county's borough is incumbent on the magnates of the county. They discharge it by keeping haws in the borough and burgesses in those haws[1].

We may doubt whether the duty of the county to its borough has gone no farther than mere 'wall-work.' A tale from the older Saxony may come in well at this point. When the German king Henry the Fowler was building burgs in Saxony and was playing the part that had lately been played in England by Edward and Æthelflæd, he chose, we are told, the ninth man from among the *agrarii milites*; these chosen men were to live in the burgs; they were to build dwellings there for their fellows (*confamiliares*) who were to remain in the country tilling the soil and carrying a third of the produce to the burgs, and in these burgs all *concilia* and *conventus* and *convivia* were to be held[2]. Modern historians have found in this story some difficulties which need not be noticed here. Only the core of it interests us. Certain men are clubbed together into groups of nine for the purpose of maintaining the burg as a garrisoned and victualled stronghold in which all will find room in case a hostile inroad be made.

Turning to England we shall not forget how in the year 894 Alfred divided his forces into two halves; half were to take the field, half to remain at home, besides the men who were to hold the burgs[3]; but at all events we shall hardly go astray if we suggest that the thegns of the shire have been bound to keep houses and retainers in the borough of their shire and that this duty has been apportioned among the great estates[4]. We find that the baron of Domesday Book has a

Henry the Fowler and the German burgs.

The shire thegns and their town houses.

---

[1] It will be understood that we are not contending for an exact correspondence between civil and military geography. Oxford and Wallingford are border towns. Berkshire men help to maintain Oxford, and Oxfordshire men help to maintain Wallingford.

[2] Widukind, i. 35. For comments see Waitz, Heinrich V. 95; Richter, Annalen, iii. 8; Giesebrecht, Kaiserzeit (ed. 5), i. 222, 811; Keutgen, Ursprung der deutschen Stadtverfassung, p. 44. Giesebrecht holds that Edward's measures may well have been Henry's model.

[3] A.-S. Chron. ann. 894.

[4] A charter of 899 (K. v. p. 141) professes to tell how King Alfred, Abp Plegmund and Æthelred ealdorman of the Mercians held a moot 'de instauratione urbis Londoniae.' One result of this moot was that two plots of land inside the walls, with hythes outside the walls, were given by the king,

few burgesses in the borough and that these few burgesses 'belong' in some sense or another to his various rural manors. Why should he keep a few burgesses in the borough and in what sense can these men belong some to this manor and some to that? To all appearance this arrangement is not modern. King Edmund conveyed to his thegn Æthelweard an estate of seven hides at Tistead in Hampshire and therewith the haws within the burg of Winchester that belonged to those seven hides[1]. When the Bishop of Worcester loaned out lands to his thegns, the lands carried with them haws in the 'port' of Worcester[2]. We have all read of the ceorl who 'throve to thegn-right.' He had five hides of his own land, a church and a kitchen, a bell-tower and a *burh-geat-setl,* which, to our thinking, is just a house in the 'gate,' the street of the *burh*[3]. He did not acquire a town-house in order that he might enjoy the pleasures of the town. He acquired it because, if he was to be one of the great men of the county, he was bound to keep in the county's *burh* retainers who would do the wall-work and hoard provisions sent in to meet the evil day when all men would wish to be behind the walls of a *burh*.

The knights in the borough.

We have it in our modern heads that the medieval borough is a sanctuary of peace, an oasis of 'industrialism' in the wilderness of 'militancy.' Now a sanctuary of peace the borough is from the very first. An exceptional and exalted peace reigns over it. If you break that peace you incur the king's *burh-bryce.* But we may strongly suspect that the first burg-men, the first *burgenses,* were not an exceptionally peaceful folk. Those *burhwaras* of London who thrashed Swegen[4] and chose kings were no sleek traders; nor must we speak contemptuously of 'trained bands of apprentices' or of 'the civic militia.' In all probability these burg-men were of all men

the one to the church of Canterbury, the other to the church of Worcester. How will the *instauratio* of London be secured by such grants?

[1] K. 1144 (v. 280). Other cases: K. 663 (Chichester), 673 (Winchester), 705 (Warwick), 724 (Warwick), 746 (Oxford), 1235 (Winchester).

[2] K. 765–6, 805.

[3] Schmid, App. V. This might mean a seat (of justice) in the gate of his own *burh.* But this document will hardly be older than, if so old as, cent. x., by which time we should suppose that *burh* more often pointed to a borough than to a strong house. We may guess that in the latter sense it was supplanted by the *hall* of which we read a great deal in Domesday. See above, p. 109. However, it does not seem certain that O. E. *geat* can mean *street.*

[4] A.-S. Chron. ann. 994.

in the realm the most professionally warlike. Were we to say that in the boroughs the knightly element was strong we might mislead, for the word *knight* has had chivalrous adventures. However, we may believe that the *burgensis* of the tenth century very often was a *cniht*, a great man's *cniht*, and that if not exactly a professional soldier (professional militancy was but beginning) he was kept in the borough for a military purpose and was perhaps being fed by the manor to which he belonged. These knights formed gilds for religious and convivial purposes. At Cambridge there was a gild of thegns, who were united in blood-brotherhood. We can not be certain that all these thegns habitually lived in Cambridge. Perhaps we should rather say that already a Cambridgeshire club had its head-quarters in Cambridge and there held its 'morning-speeches' and its drinking bouts. These thegns had 'knights' who seem to have been in some sort inferior members of the gild and to have been bound by its rules[1]. Then we hear of 'knight-gilds' at London and Canterbury and Winchester[2]. Such gilds would be models for the merchant-gilds of after-days, and indeed when not long after the Conquest we catch at Canterbury our first glimpse of a merchant-gild, its members are calling themselves knights: knights of the chapman-gild[3]. Among the knights who dwelt in the burg such voluntary societies were the more needful, because these men had not grown up together as members of a community. They came from different districts and had different lords. In this heterogeneity we may also see one reason why a very stringent peace, the king's own house-peace, should be maintained, and why the borough should have a moot of its own. When compared with a village there is something artificial about the borough.

This artificiality exercised an influence over the later fate of *Burh-bót and castle-guard.* the boroughs. The ground had been cleared for the growth of a new kind of community, one whose members were not bound together by feudal, proprietary, agricultural ties. But the strand that we have been endeavouring to trace is broken at

[1] Thorpe, Diplomatarium, 610. When the Confessor sends a writ to London he addresses it to the bishop, portreeve and burh-thegns. See K. iv. pp. 856, 857, 861, 872.

[2] Gross, Gild Merchant, i. 183, 189.

[3] Gross, op. cit. ii. 37.

the Conquest. The castle arises. It is garrisoned by knights who are more heavily armed and more professionally militant than were their predecessors. The castle is now what wants defending; the knights who defend it form no part of the burghal community, and perhaps 'the castle fee' is in law no part of the borough. And yet let us see how in the twelfth century the king's castle at Norwich was manned. It was manned by the knights of the Abbot of St Edmund's. One troop served there for three months and then was relieved by another, and those who were thus set free went home to the manors with which the abbot had enfeoffed them and which they held by the service of castle-guard[1]. Much in this arrangement is new; the castle itself is new; but it is no new thing, we take it, that the *burh* should be garrisoned by the knights of abbots or earls. And who built the castles, who built the Tower of London? Let us read what the chronicler says of the year 1097:—Also many shires which belonged to London for work[2] were sorely harassed by the wall that they wrought around the tower, and by the bridge, which had been nearly washed away, and by the work of the king's hall that was wrought at Westminster. There were shires or districts which from of old owed this work or work of this kind to London-bury[3].

Borough and market.

Long before the Conquest, however, a force had begun to play which was to give to the boroughs their most permanent characteristic. They were to be centres of trade. We must not exclude the hypothesis that some places were fortified and converted into burgs because they were already the focuses of such commerce as there was. But the general logic of the process we take to have been this:—The king's *burh* enjoys a special peace: Even the men who are going to or coming from it are under royal protection: Therefore within its walls men can meet together to buy and sell in safety: Also laws which are directed against theft command that men shall not buy and sell elsewhere: Thus a market is established: Traders begin to

---

[1] Hist. Eng. Law, i. 257.

[2] A.-S. Chron. ann. 1097: 'Eac manege sciran þe mid weorce to Lundenne belumpon...' Thorpe thought good to substitute *scipan* for *sciran*.

[3] D. B. i. 298. Outside York were some lands which gelded with the city; 'et in tribus operibus Regis cum civibus erant.' This refers to the *trinoda necessitas*.

build booths round the market-place and to live in the borough.
A theory has indeed been brilliantly urged which would find
the legal germ of the borough rather in a market-peace than in
the peace of a burg[1]. But this doctrine has difficulties to meet.
A market-peace is essentially temporary, while the borough's
peace is eternal. A market court, if it arises, will have a
jurisdiction only over bargains made and offences committed
on market-days, whereas the borough court has a general
competence and hears pleas relating to the property in houses
and lands. Here in England during the Angevin time the
'franchise,' or royally granted right, of holding a market is quite
distinct from the legal essence of the borough. Lawful markets
are held in many places that are not boroughs; indeed in the
end by calling a place 'a mere market-town' we should imply
that it was no borough. Already in Domesday Book this seems
to be the case. Markets are being held and market-tolls are
being taken in many vills which are not of burghal rank[2].
Perhaps also we may see the borough-peace and the market-
peace lying side by side. In the Wallingford of the Confessor's
day there were many persons who had sake and soke within
their houses. If any one spilt blood and escaped into one of
those houses before he was attached, the owner received the
blood-wite. But it was not so on Saturdays, for then the money
went to the king 'because of the market[3].' Thus the king's
borough-peace seems to be intensified on market-days; on
those days it will even penetrate the houses of the immunists.
So at Dover some unwonted peace or 'truce' prevailed in the
town from S[t]. Michael's Day to S[t]. Andrew's: that is to say,
during the herring season[4].

The establishment of a market is not one of those indefinite Establish-
phenomena which the historian of law must make over to the markets
historian of economic processes. It is a definite and a legal act.
The market is established by law. It is established by law
which prohibits men from buying and selling elsewhere than in
a duly constituted market. To prevent an easy disposal of

---

[1] Sohm, Die Entstehung des deutschen Städtewesens: Leipzig, 1890.
[2] Ellis, Introduction, i. 248–253.
[3] D. B. i. 56 b.
[4] D. B. i. 1. Black Book of the Admiralty, ii. 158: 'the herring season,
that is from S[t]. Michael's Day to S[t]. Clement's (Nov. 23).' S[t]. Andrew's Day
is Dec. 1.

stolen goods is the aim of this prohibition. Our legislators are always thinking of the cattle-lifter. At times they seem to go the full length of decreeing that only in a ' port' may anything be bought or sold, unless it be of trifling value; but other dooms would also sanction a purchase concluded before the hundred court. He who buys elsewhere runs a risk of being treated as a thief if he happens to buy stolen goods[1]. Official witnesses are to be appointed for this purpose in every hundred and in every *burh*: twelve in every hundred and small *burh*, thirty-three in a large *burh*[2]. Here once more we see the *burh* co-ordinated with the hundred. A by-motive favours this establishment of markets. Those who traffic in the safety of the king's *burh* may fairly be asked to pay some toll to the king. They enjoy his peace; perhaps also the use of royal weights and measures, known and trustworthy, is another part of the valuable consideration that they receive. First and last throughout the history of the boroughs toll is a matter of importance[3]. It gives the king a revenue from the borough, a revenue that he can let to farm. Also, though we do not think that the borough court was in its origin a mere market court, the disputes of the market-place will provide the borough court with plentiful litigation, and in this quarter also the king will find a new source of income. Among the old land-books that which speaks most expressly of the profits of jurisdiction as the subject-matter of a gift is a charter which concerns the town of Worcester. Æthelred and Æthelflæd, the ealdorman and lady of the Mercians, have, at the request of the bishop, built a *burh* at Worcester, and they declare that of all the rights that appertain to their lordship both in market (*on ceapstowe*) and in street, within the *burh* and without, they have given half to God and S[t]. Peter, with the witness of King Alfred and all the wise of Mercia. The lord of the church is to have half of all, be it land-fee, or fiht-wite, stealing, wohceapung (fines for buying or selling contrary to the rules of the market) or borough-wall-scotting[4]. Quite apart from

---

[1] Edward, i. 1; Æthelstan, ii. 12, 13; iv. 2; vi. 10; Edmund, iii. 5; Edgar, iv. 7–11; Leg. Will. i. 45; Leg. Will. iii. 10. See Schmid, Glossar. s. v. *Marktrecht*.

[2] Edgar, iv. 3–6. We should expect rather 36 than 33, and *xxxvi* might easily become *xxxiii*.

[3] K. 280 (ii. 63), 316 (ii. 118).

[4] Kemble, Cod. Dip. 1075 (v. 142); Kemble, Saxons, ii. 328; Thorpe, 136:

the rent of houses, there is a revenue to be gained from the borough.

Another rule has helped to define the borough, and this rule also has its root among the regalia. No one, says King Æthelstan, is to coin money except in a port; in Canterbury there may be seven moneyers, four of the king, two of the bishop, one of the abbot; in Rochester three, two of the king, one of the bishop; in London-borough eight; in Winchester six; in Lewes two; in Hastings one; in Chichester one; in Hampton two; in Wareham two; in Exeter two; in Shaftesbury two, and in each of the other boroughs one[1]. Already, then, a *burh* is an entity known to the law: every *burh* is to have its moneyer.

We have thus to consider the *burh* (1) as a stronghold, a place of refuge, a military centre: (2) as a place which has a moot that is a unit in the general, national system of moots: (3) as a place in which a market is held. When in the laws this third feature is to be made prominent, the *burh* is spoken of as a *port*, and perhaps from the first there might be a *port* which was not a *burh*[2]. The word *port* was applied to inland towns. To this usage of it the *portmoot* or *portmanmoot* that in after days we may find in boroughs far from the coast bears abiding testimony. On the other hand, except on the seaside, this word has not become a part of many English place names[3]. If, as seems probable, it is the Latin *portus*, we apparently learn from the use made of it that at one time the havens (and some of those havens may not have been in England) were the only known spots where there was much buying and selling. But be it remembered that a market-place, a *ceap-stow*, does not

Moneyers in the burh.

Burh and port.

'ge landfeoh, ge fihtwite, ge stale, ge wohceapung, ge burhwealles sceatinge.' In D. B. i. 173 it is said that the Bishop of Worcester had received the third penny of the borough. Apparently in the Confessor's day he received £6, the third of a sum of £18. As to the early history of markets, see the paper contributed by Mr C. I. Elton to the Report of the Royal Commission on Market Rights, 1889.

[1] Æthelstan, ii. 14.

[2] The general equivalence of *port* and *burh* we may perhaps infer from Æthelstan, ii. 14: No one is to coin money outside a *port*, and there is to be a moneyer in every *burh*.

[3] Stockport, Langport, Amport, Newport-Pagnell, Milborne Port, Littleport are instances. But a very small river might be sufficient to make a place a haven.

imply a resident population of buyers and sellers; it does not imply the existence of retailers[1].

Military and commercial elements in the borough.

We can not analyse the borough population; we can not weigh the commercial element implied by *port* or the military element implied by *burh*; but to all seeming the former had been rapidly getting the upper hand during the century which preceded the making of Domesday Book. If we are on the right track, there was a time when the thegns of the shire must have regarded their borough haws rather as a burden than as a source of revenue. They kept those haws because they were bound to keep them. On the other hand, the barons of the Conqueror's day are deriving some income from these houses. Often it is very small. Count Hugh, for example, has just one burgess at Buckingham who pays him twenty-six pence a year[2]. All too soon, it may be, had the boroughs put off their militancy. Had they retained it, England might never have been conquered. Houses which should have been occupied by 'knights,' were occupied by chapmen.

The borough and agriculture.

But this is not the whole difficulty. Even if we could closely watch the change which substitutes a merchant or shopkeeper for a 'knight' as the typical burg-man or burgess, we should still have to investigate an agrarian problem. Very likely we ought to think that even on the eve of the Conquest the group of men which dwells within the walls is often a group which by tilling the soil produces a great part of its own food,

[1] Seemingly if this O.-E. *port* is not Lat. *portus*, it is Lat. *porta*, and there is some fascination about the suggestion that the *burh-geat*, or in modern German the *Burg-gasse*, in which the market is held, was described in Latin as *porta burgi*. In A.D. 762 (K. i. p. 133) we have a house 'quae iam ad Quenegatum urbis Dorouernis in foro posita est.' In A.D. 845 (K. ii. p. 26) we find a 'publica strata' in Canterbury 'ubi appellatur Weoweraget,' that is, the gate of the men of Wye. But what we have to account for is the adoption of *port* as an English word, and if our ancestors might have used *geat*, they need not have borrowed. In A.D. 857 (K. ii. p. 63) the king bestows on the church of Worcester certain liberties at a spot in the town of London, 'hoc est, quod habeat intus liberaliter modium et pondera et mensura sicut in porto mos est ad fruendum.' To have public weights and measures is characteristic of a *portus* (=haven). The word may have spread outwards from London. Dr Stubbs (Const. Hist. i. 439) gives a weighty vote for *porta*; but the continental usage deserves attention. Pirenne, Revue historique, lvii. 75 : 'Toutes les villes anciennes [en Flandre] s'y forment au bord des eaux et portent le nom caractéristique de *portus*, c'est-à-dire de débarcadères. C'est de ce mot *portus* que vient le mot flamand *poorter*, qui désigne le bourgeois.' See D. B. i. 181 b : 'in Hereford Port.'

[2] D. B. i. 143.

though some men may be living by handicraft or trade and some may still be supported by those manors to which they 'belong.' In one case the institutions that are characteristic of *burh* and *port* may have been superimposed upon those of an ancient village which had common fields. In another an almost uninhabited spot may have been chosen as the site for a stronghold. In the former and, as we should fancy, the commoner case a large choice is open to the constructive historian, for he may suppose that the selected village was full of serfs or full of free proprietors, that the soil was royal demesne or had various landlords. In one instance he may think that he sees the coalescence of several little communities that were once distinct; in another the gradual occupation of a space marked out by Roman walls. The one strong hint that is given to us by Domesday Book and later documents is that our generalities should be few and that, were this possible, each borough should be separately studied.

As a rule, quite half of the burgesses in any of those county towns that are fully described in the survey are the king's own burgesses, and in some cases his share is very large. This suggests that the land on which the borough stands has been royal land and that the king provided the shire thegns with sites for their haws. For their haws they have sometimes been paying him small rents. On the other hand, at Leicester, though the king has some 40 houses, the great majority belong to Hugh of Grantmesnil. He has about 80 houses which pertain to 17 different manors and which may in the past have been held by many different thegns; but he also holds 110 houses which are not allotted to manors and which have probably come to him as the representative of the earls and ealdormen of an older time[1]. This looks as if in this case the soil had been not royal but 'comital' land at the time when the place was fortified and when the landowners of the shire, including perhaps the king, were obliged to build houses within the wall. But though we fully admit that each of our boroughs has lived its own life, our evidence seems to point to the conclusion that in those truly ancient boroughs of which we have been speaking, though there might be many inhabitants who held and who cultivated arable land lying without the walls, there were from a remote time other burgesses who were

Burgesses as cultivators.

[1] D. B. i. 230.

not landowners and were not agriculturists and yet were men of importance in the borough. If we look, for example, at the elaborate account of Colchester we shall first read the names of the king's burgesses. 'Of these 276 burgesses of the king, the majority have one house and a plot of land of from one to twenty-five acres; some possess more than one house and some have none; they had in all 355 houses and held 1296 acres of land[1]'. But these were not the only burgesses. Various magnates had houses which were annexed to their rural manors. Count Eustace (to name a few) had 12, Geoffrey de Mandeville 2, the Abbot of Westminster 4, the Abbess of Barking 3, and seemingly to these houses no strips in the arable fields were attached[2]. Thus, though many of the burgesses may till the soil, the borough community is not an agrarian community. We can not treat it as a village community that has prospered and slowly changed its habits. A new principle has been introduced, an element of heterogeneity. The men who meet each other in court and market, the men who will hereafter farm the court and market, are not the shareholders in an agricultural concern.

Burgage tenure.

That tenurial heterogeneity of which we have been speaking had another important effect. When in later days a rural manor is being raised to the rank of a *liber burgus*, the introduction of 'burgage tenure' seems to be regarded as the very essence of the enfranchisement[3]. Probably this feature had appeared in many boroughs at an early date. The lord with lands in Oxfordshire may have been bound to keep a few houses and retainers in Oxford. If, however, the commercial element in the town began to get the better of the military element, if Oxford became a centre of trade, then a house in Oxford could be let for a money rent. In Domesday Book the barons are drawing rents from their borough houses. If any return is to be made by the occupier to the owner it will take the form of a money rent; it can hardly take another form. Thus tenure at a money rent would become the typical tenure of a burgage tenement. It will be a securely heritable tenure, because the landlord is an absentee and has too few tenants in

---

[1] Cutts, Colchester, 65; Round in The Antiquary, vol. vi. (1882) p. 5.
[2] D. B. ii. 106–7. See Round, op. cit., p. 252.
[3] Hist. Eng. Law, i. 629.

the town to require the care of a resident reeve. But there
may have been many dwellers in some of the boroughs who
were bound to help in the cultivation of a stretch of royal or
episcopal demesne that lay close to the walls. In the west
some of the king's burgesses seem to have been holding under
onerous terms. At Shrewsbury, which lies near the border of
Wales where every girl's marriage gave rise to an *amobyr*, a
maid had to pay ten, a widow twenty shillings when she took a
husband, and a relief of ten shillings was due when a burgess
died[1]. At Hereford the reeve's consent was necessary when a
burgage was to be sold, and he took a third of the price. When
a burgess died the king got his horse and arms (these Hereford
burgesses were fighting men); if he had no horse, then ten
shillings 'or his land with the houses.' Any one who was too
poor to do his service might abandon his tenement to the reeve
without having to pay for it. Such an entry as this seems to tell
us that the services were no trivial return for the tenement[2].

On the other hand, we may see at Stamford what seem to
be the remains of a very free group of settlers, presumably
Danes. The town contains among other houses 77 houses of
sokemen 'who hold their lands in demesne and seek lords
wherever they please, and over whom the king has nothing
but wite and heriot and toll.' These may be the same persons
who hold 272 acres of land and pay no rent for it[3]. At
Norwich, again, we seem to hear of a time when the burgesses
were free to commend themselves to whomever they would, and
were therefore living in houses which were all their own, and
for which they paid no rent[4]. It is very possible that, so far as
landlordly rights are concerned, there was as much difference
between the eastern and the western towns as there was
between the eastern and the western villages. Still if we
look at borough after borough, tenure at a money rent is the
tenure of the burgage houses that we expect to find, and such
a tenure, even if in its origin it has been precarious, is likely to

Eastern and western boroughs.

[1] D. B. i. 252.

[2] D. B. i. 179. So at Chester (i. 262 b) it is considered possible that the
heir will not be able to pay the relief of ten shillings and will forfeit the
tenement.

[3] D. B. i. 336.

[4] D. B. ii. 116. See also the case of Thetford (D. B. ii. 119), where there
had been numerous burgesses who could choose their lords.

become heritable and secure. As to the shire thegns, they have in some cases paid to the king small rents for their haws; but in others, for example at Oxford, tenure by wall-work has been their tenure, and when in other towns we find them paying rent to the king we may perhaps see commuted wall-work.

Common property of the burgesses.

Traces are few in Domesday Book of any property that can be regarded as the property of a nascent municipal corporation, and even of any that can be called the joint or common property of the burgesses. In general each burgess holds his house in the town of the king or of some other lord by a several title, and, if he has land in the neighbouring fields, this also he holds by a several title. 'In the borough of Nottingham there were in King Edward's day 183 burgesses and 19 *villani*. To this borough belong 6 carucates of land for the king's geld and one meadow and certain small woods...This land was divided between 38 burgesses and [the king] received 75s. 7d. from the rent of the land and the works of the burgesses.' 'In the borough of Derby there were in King Edward's day 243 resident burgesses....To this borough belong 12 carucates of land for the geld, but they might be ploughed by 8 teams.' This land was divided among 41 burgesses who had 12 teams[1].' In these cases we see plainly enough that such arable land as is in any way connected with the borough has been held by but a few out of the total number of the burgesses. Therefore we must deal cautiously with entries that are less explicit. When, for example, in the description of Stamford we read

The community as land-holders.

"Lagemanni et burgenses habent cclxxii. acras sine omni consuetudine[2]," we must not at once decide that there is any ownership by the burgesses as a corporation, or any joint ownership, or even that all the burgesses have strips in these fields, though apparently the burgesses who have strips pay no rent for them. This is the fact and the only fact that the commissioners desire to record. They do not care whether every burgess has a piece, or whether (as was certainly the case elsewhere) only some of them held land outside the walls. When of Norwich we read 'et in burgo tenent burgenses xliii. capellas[3],' we do not suppose that all the Norwich burghers have chapels, still less that they hold the forty-three chapels

---

[1] D. B. i. 280.　　　　　[2] D. B. i. 336 b.

[3] D. B. ii. 117.

as co-owners, still less that these chapels belong to a corporation. We remember that the Latin language has neither a definite nor an indefinite article. Therefore when of 80 acres at Canterbury, which are now held by Ralph de Colombiers, we read 'quas tenebant burgenses in alodia de rege,' we need not suppose that these acres had belonged to *the* (i.e. to all the) burgesses of Canterbury[1]. So of Exeter it is written: 'Burgenses Exoniae urbis habent extra civitatem terram xii. caruc[arum] quae nullam consuetudinem reddunt nisi ad ipsam civitatem.' This, though another interpretation is possible, may only mean that there are outside the city twelve plough-lands which are held by burgesses whose rents go to make up that sum of £18 which is paid to the king, or rather in part to the sheriff and in part to the queen dowager, as the ferm of the city[2]. Concerning Colchester there is an entry which perhaps ascribes to the community of burgesses the ownership or the tenancy of fourscore acres of land and of a strip eight perches in width surrounding the town wall; but this entry is exceedingly obscure[3]. Another dark case occurs at Canterbury. We are told that the burgesses or certain burgesses used to hold land of the king 'in their gild[4].' Along with this we must read another passage which states how in the same city the Archbishop has twelve burgesses and thirty-two houses which 'the clerks of the vill hold in their gild.' Apparently in this last case we have a clerical club

---

[1] D. B. i. 2. In 923 (K. v. p. 186) we hear of land outside Canterbury called *Burhuuare bocaceras*, apparently acres booked to [certain] burgesses.

[2] D. B. i. 100.

[3] D. B. ii. 107: 'In commune burgensum iiii. xx. acrae terrae; et circa murum viii. percae; de quo toto per annum habent burgenses lx. sol. ad servicium regis si opus fuerit, sin autem, in commune dividunt.' As to this most difficult passage, see Round, Antiquary, vol. vi. (1882) p. 97. Perhaps the most natural interpretation of it is that the community or commune of the burgesses holds this land and receives by way of rent from tenants, to whom it is let, the sum of 60 shillings a year, which, if this be necessary, goes to make up what the borough has to pay to the king, or otherwise is divisible among the burgesses. But, as Mr Round rightly remarks, 60 shillings for this land would be a large rent.

[4] D. B. i. 2: 'Ipsi quoque burgenses habebant de rege 33 acras terrae in gildam suam.' Another version says, '33 agros terre quos burgenses semper habuerunt in gilda eorum de donis omnium regum.' The document here cited is preserved in a cartulary of St Augustin, and is printed in Larking, Domesday of Kent, App. 35. It is closely connected with the Domesday Survey and is of the highest interest.

or fraternity holding land, and the burgher's gild may be of much the same nature, a voluntary association. Not very long after the date of Domesday, for Anselm was still alive, an exchange of lands was made between the convent (*hired, familia*) of Christ Church and the 'cnihts' of the chapman gild of Canterbury. The transaction takes place between the 'hired' on the one hand, the 'heap' (for such is the word employed) on the other. The witnesses to this transaction are Archbishop Anselm and the 'hired' on the one hand, Calveal the portreeve and 'the eldest men of the heap' on the other[1]. But to see a municipal corporation in the burghers' gild of Domesday Book would be very rash. We do not know that all the burghers belonged to it or that it had any governmental functions[2].

Rights of common.

We may of course find that a group of burgesses has 'rights of common;' but rights of common, though they are rights which are to be enjoyed in common, are apt to be common rights in no other sense, for each commoner has a several title to send his beasts onto the pasture. Thus 'all the burgesses of Oxford have pasture in common outside the wall which brings in [to the king] 6s. 8d[3].' The soil is the king's; the burgesses pay for the right of grazing it. The roundness of the sum that they pay seems indeed to hint at some arrangement between the king and the burgesses taken in mass; but probably each burgess, and the lord of each burgess, regards a right of pasture as appurtenant to a burgage tenement. The case is striking, for we have seen how heterogeneous a group these Oxford burgesses were[4]. No less than nine prelates, to say nothing of earls and barons, had burgesses in the city. We must greatly doubt whether there is any power in any assembly of the burgesses to take from the Bishop of Winchester or the Count of Mortain the customary rights of pasture that have been enjoyed by the tenants of his tenements.

Absence of communalism in the boroughs.

We might perhaps have guessed that the boroughs would

---

[1] Gross, Gild Merchant, ii. 37.

[2] We do not even know for certain that when our record says that the burgesses and the clerks held land 'in gildam suam,' more was meant than that the land was part of their geldable property. See Gross, Gild Merchant, i. 189. In the Exon Domesday the geld is *gildum*.

[3] D. B. i. 154.   [4] See above, p. 179.

be the places of all others in which such communalism as there
was in the ancient village community would maintain and
develop itself, until in course of time the borough corporation,
the ideal borough, would stand out as the owner of lands
which lay within and without the wall. But, if we have not
been going astray, we may see why this did not happen, at
least in what we may call the old national boroughs. The
burgensic group was not homogeneous enough. We may suppose that some members of it had inherited arable strips and
pasture rights from the original settlers; but others were
'knights' who had been placed in the haws of the shire-thegns,
or were merchants and craftsmen who had been attracted by
the market, and for them there would be no room in an old
agrarian scheme. Indeed it is not improbable that, even as
regards rights of pasture, there was more difference between
burgess and burgess than there was between villager and
villager. In modern times it is not unknown that some of
the burgesses will have pasture rights, while others will have
none, and in those who are thus favoured we may fancy that
we see the successors in title of the king's tenants who turned
out their beasts on the king's land[1].

We have seen that in the boroughs a group of men is
formed whose principle of cohesion is not to be found in
land tenure. The definition of a burgess may involve the
possession of a house within or hard by the walls; but the
burgesses do not coalesce as being the tenants or the men
of one lord; and yet coalesce they will. They are united in
and by the moot and the market-place, united under the king
in whose peace they traffic; and then they are soon united
over against the king, who exacts toll from them and has
favours to grant them. They aspire to farm their own tolls,
to manage their own market and their own court. The king's

*The
borough
community
and its
lord.*

---

[1] In modern York the freemen inhabiting the different wards had rights of
pasture varying from ward to ward: Appendix to Report of Municipal
Corporations' Commissioners, 1835, p. 1745. York is one of the towns in
which we may perhaps suppose that there has been a gradual union of several
communities which were at one time agrarianly distinct. See D. B. i. 298.
Dr Stubbs seems to regard this as a common case and speaks of 'the townships
which made up the *burh*' (Const. Hist. i. 101). We can not think that the
evidence usually points in this direction, and have grave doubts as to the
existence within the walls of various communities that were called townships.
Within borough walls we must not leap from parish to township.

rights are pecuniary rights ; he is entitled to collect numerous
small sums. Instead of these he may be willing to take a
fixed sum every year, or, in other words, to let his rights to
farm.

The farm
of the
borough.

This step seems to have been very generally taken before
the Conquest. Already the boroughs were farmed. Now the
sums which the king would draw from a borough would be
of several different kinds. In the first place, there would be
the profits of the market and of the borough court. In the
second place, there would be the gafol, the 'haw-gavel' and
'land-gavel' arising from tenements belonging to the king
and occupied by burgesses. In the third place, there might
be the danegeld ; but the danegeld was a tax, an occasional
tax, and for the moment we may leave it out of our consideration. Now the profits of the market and court seem to
have been farmed. The sums that they bring in to the king
are round sums. The farmer seems to have been the sheriff or
in some cases the king's portreeve. We can find no case in
which it is absolutely clear to our minds that the borough itself,
the *communitas burgi*, is reckoned to be the king's farmer.
Again, the king's gafol, that is his burgage rents, may be farmed :
they are computed at a round sum. Thus at Huntingdon
ten pounds are paid by way of land-gafol, and we may be fairly
certain that the sum of the rents of the individual burgesses
who held their tenements immediately of the king (there were
other burgesses who belonged to the Abbot of Ramsey) did
not exactly make up this neat sum[1]. In this case, however,
the sum due to the king from his farmer, probably the sheriff,
in respect of the land-gafol is expressly distinguished from
the sum that he has to pay for the farm of the borough (*firma
burgi*):—at least in its narrowest sense, the *burgus* which is
farmed is not a mass of lands and houses, it is a market and
a court[2]. But, though we find no case in which the community
of the borough is unambiguously treated as the king's farmer,
there are cases in which it seems to come before us as the
sheriff's farmer. 'The burgesses' of Northampton pay to the
sheriff £30. 10s. per annum :—'this belongs to his farm[3].' The
sheriff of Northamptonshire is liable to the king for a round

---

[1] D. B. i. 203. As to the whole of this matter see Mr Round's paper on
Domesday Finance in Domesday Studies, vol. i.

[2] Hist. Eng. Law, i. 635.   [3] D. B. i. 219.

sum as the farm of the shire, but 'the burgesses' of Northampton are liable to the sheriff for a round sum. This may
mean that for this round sum they are jointly and severally
liable, while, on the other hand, they collect the tolls and fines,
perhaps also the king's burgage rents, and have an opportunity
of making profit by the transaction.

We must not be in haste to expel the sheriff from the The sheriff
boroughs of the shire, or to bring the burgesses into immediate borough's
contact with the king's treasury. We must remember that farm.
at the beginning of Henry II.'s reign there is scarcely an
exception to the rule that the boroughs of the shire are in
the eyes of auditors at the Exchequer simply parts of that
county which the sheriff farms. So far as the farm is concerned, the royal treasury knows nothing of any boroughs[1].
The sheriff of Gloucestershire, for example, accounts for a
round sum which is the farm of his county ; neither he nor
any one else accounts to the king for any farm of the borough
of Gloucester. If, as is most probable, the borough is being
farmed, it is being farmed by some person or persons to whom,
not the king, but the sheriff has let it for a longer or shorter
period at a fixed rent. Here, again, we see the likeness between
a borough and a hundred. The king lets the shire to farm ;
the shire includes hundreds and boroughs; the sheriff 'lets
the hundreds to farm; the sheriff lets the boroughs to farm.'
A few years later a new arrangement is made. The king
begins to let the borough of Gloucester to farm. A sum of
£50 (blanch) is now deducted from the rent that the sheriff
has been paying for his shire, and, on the other hand, Osmund
the reeve accounts for £55, which is the rent of the borough.
We must not antedate a change which is taking place very
gradually in the middle of the twelfth century. Nor must we
at once reject the inference that, as the bailiffs to whom the
sheriff lets the hundreds are chosen by him, so also the bailiffs
or portreeves to whom he lets the boroughs are or have been
chosen by him. It seems very possible that one of the first

---

[1] The case of London is anomalous; but not so anomalous as it is often
supposed to be. On this point see Round, Geoffrey de Mandeville, 347 ff. On
the Pipe Roll of 2 Hen. II. (pp. 24, 28) the citizens of Lincoln are accounting
for a farm of £180, while the sheriff in consequence of this arrangement is
credited with £140 (blanch) when he accounts for the farm of the shire. This
is as yet a rare phenomenon.

steps towards independence that a borough takes is that its burgesses induce the sheriff to accept their nominee as his farmer of the town if they in mass will make themselves jointly and severally liable for the rent. These movements take place in the dark and we can not date them; but to antedate them would be easy.

The community and the geld. We also see that the 'geld' that the borough has to pay is a round sum that remains constant from year to year. Cambridge, for example, is assessed at a hundred hides, Bedford at half a hundred[1]. Now we have good reason to believe that, in the open country also, a round sum of geld or (and this is the same thing) a round number of hides had been thrown upon the hundreds, that the sum thrown upon a hundred was then partitioned among the vills, and that the sum thrown upon a vill was partitioned among the persons who held land in the vill. In the open country, however, when once the partition had been made, the number of hides that was cast upon the land of any one proprietor seems to have been fixed for good and all[2]. If we suppose, for example, that a vill had been assessed at ten hides and that five of those units had been assigned to a certain Edward, then Edward or his successors in title would always have to pay for five hides, and would have to pay for no more although the other proprietors in the vill obtained an exemption from the tax or were insolvent. In short, the tax though originally distributed by a partitionary method was not repartitionable. On the other hand, in the boroughs a more communal arrangement seems to have prevailed. In some sense or another, the whole borough, no matter what its fortunes might be, remained answerable for the twenty, fifty or a hundred hides that had been imposed upon it. Such a difference would naturally arise. In the open country the taxational hidation was supposed to represent and did represent, albeit rudely, a state of facts that had once existed. The man who was charged with a hide ought in truth to have had one of those agrarian units that were commonly known as hides. But when a borough was charged with hides, a method of taxation that was adapted to and suggested by rural arrangements was being inappropriately applied to what had become

[1] As to the round sums cast on the boroughs, see Round in Domesday Studies, i. 117 ff.; also Round, Feudal England, 156.

[2] This may not have been the case in East Anglia.

or would soon become an urban district. Thus the gross sum
that is cast upon the borough does not split itself once and for
all into many small sums each of which takes root in a
particular tenement. The whole sum is exigible from the
whole borough every time a geld is imposed. It is repartitionable.

For all this, however, we must be careful not to see more
communalism or more local self-government than really exists.
At first sight we may think that we detect a communal or a
joint liability of all the burgesses for the whole sum that is
due from the borough in any one year. 'The English born'
burgesses of Shrewsbury send up a piteous wail[1]. They still
have to pay the whole geld as they paid it in the Confessor's
day, although the earl has taken for his castle the sites of
fifty-one houses, and other fifty houses are waste, and forty-
three French burgesses hold houses which used to pay geld,
and the earl has given to the abbey, which he has founded,
thirty-nine burgesses who used to pay geld along with the
others. But, when we examine the matter more closely, we
may doubt whether there is here any joint and several (to say
nothing of any corporate) liability. Very various are the modes
in which a land-tax or house-tax may be assessed and levied.
Suppose a tax of £100 imposed upon a certain district in which
there are a hundred houses. Suppose it also to be law that,
though some of these houses come to the hands of elemosynary
corporations (which we will imagine to enjoy an immunity from
taxation) still the whole £100 must be raised annually from the
householders of the district. For all this, we have not as yet
decided that any householder will ever be liable, even in the
first instance, for more than his own particular share of the
£100. A readjustment of taxation there must be. It may
take one of many forms. There may be a revaluation of the
district, and the £100 may be newly apportioned by some
meeting of householders or some government officer. But,
again, the readjustment may be automatic. Formerly there
were 100 houses to pay £100. Now there are 90 houses to
pay £100. That each of the 90 must pay ten-ninths of a pound
is a conclusion that the rule of three draws for us. In the
middle ages an automatic readjustment was all the easier
because of the common assumption that the value of lands

[1] D. B. i. 252.

and houses was known to every one and that one virgate in a manor was as good as another, one 'haw' in a borough as good as another[1]. We do not say that the complaint of the burgesses at Shrewsbury points to no more than an automatic readjustment of taxation which all along has been a taxation of individuals; still the warning is needful that the exaction at regular or irregular intervals of a fixed amount from a district, or from the householders or inhabitants of a district, an amount which remains constant though certain portions of the district obtain immunity from the impost, does not of necessity point to any kind of liability that is not the liability of one single individual for specific sums which he and he only has to pay; nor does it of necessity point to any self-governing or self-assessing assembly of inhabitants[2].

No corporation implied by the farming of the borough.

Returning, however, to the case of Northampton, it certainly seems to tell us of a composition, not indeed between the burgesses and the king, but between the burgesses and the sheriff. 'The burgesses of Northampton pay to the sheriff £30. 10s.' We may believe that 'the burgesses' who pay this sum have a chance of making a profit. If so, 'the burgesses' are already beginning to farm 'the borough.' From this, nevertheless, we must not leap to corporate liability or corporate property. Very likely the sheriff regards every burgess of Northampton as liable to him for the whole £30. 10s.; very certainly, as we think, he does not look for payment merely to property which belongs, not to any individual burgess nor to any sum of individual burgesses, but to 'the borough' of Northampton. Nor if the burgesses make profit out of tolls and fines, does it follow that they have a permanent common

[1] D. B. i. 298. Of York we read: 'In the geld of the city are 84 carucates of land, each of which gelds as much as one house in the city.' This seems to point to an automatic adjustment. To find out how much geld any house pays, divide the total sum that is thrown upon York by the number of houses + 84.

[2] Mr Round (Domesday Studies, i. 129) who has done more than anyone else for the elucidation of the finance of Domesday, has spoken of 'the great Anglo-Saxon principle of *collective liability.*' This may be a useful term, provided that we distinguish (a) liability of a corporation for the whole tax whenever it is levied; (b) joint and several liability of all the burgesses for the whole tax whenever it is levied; (c) liability of each burgess for a share of the whole tax, the amount that he must pay in any year being affected by an increase or decrease in the number of contributories.

purse; they may divide the surplus every year[1], or we may suspect them of drinking the profits as soon as they are made.

Entries which describe the limits that are set to the duty of military or of naval service may seem more eloquent. Thus of Dover we are told that the burgesses used to supply twenty ships for fifteen days in the year with twenty-one men in each ship, and that they did this because the king had released to them his sake and soke[2]. Here we seem to read of a definite transaction between the king of the one part and the borough of the other part, and one which implies a good deal of governmental organization in the borough. We would say nothing to lessen the just force of such a passage, which does not stand alone[3]; but still there need be but little more organization in the borough of Dover than there is in Berkshire. It was the custom of that county that, when the king summoned his host, only one soldier went from every five hides, while each hide provided him with four shillings for his equipment and wages[4]. We may guess that in a county such a scheme very rapidly 'realized' itself and took root in the soil, that in a borough there was less 'realism,' that there were more frequent readjustments of the burden; but the difference is a difference of degree.

Of anything that could be called the constitution of the boroughs, next to nothing can we learn. We may take it that in most cases the king's farmer was the sheriff of the shire; in some few cases, as for example at Hereford, the reeve of the borough may have been directly accountable to the king[5]. We know no proof that in any case the reeve was an elected officer. Probably in each borough a court was held which was a court for the borough; probably it was, at least as a general rule, co-ordinate with a hundred court, and indeed at starting the borough seems to be regarded as a vill which is also a hundred[6].

Borough and county organization.

Government of the boroughs.

---

[1] See the entry touching Colchester, above, p. 201, note 3.

[2] D. B. i. 1.

[3] D. B. i. 238. The custom of Warwick was that when the king made an expedition by land ten burgesses of Warwick should go for all the rest. He who did not go when summoned [summoned by whom?] paid 100 shillings to the king; [so his offence was against the king not against the town.] And if the king went against his enemies by sea, they sent him four boat-swains or four pounds in money.

[4] D. B. i. 56 b.   [5] D. B. i. 179.

[6] At Chester (D. B. i. 262 b) the twelve civic *iudices* paid a fine if they were

The action of this court, however, like the action of other hundred courts, must as time went on have been hampered by the growth of seignorial justice. The sake and soke which a lord might have over his men and over his lands were certainly not excluded by the borough walls. He had sometimes been expressly told that he might enjoy these rights 'within borough and without borough.' It is difficult for us to realize the exact meaning that 'sake and soke' would bear when ascribed to a prelate or thegn who had but two or three houses within the town. Perhaps in such cases the town houses were for jurisdictional purposes deemed to be situate within some rural manor of their lord. But in a borough a lord might have a compact group of tenants quite large enough to form a petty court. In such a case the borough court would have the seignorial courts as rivals, and many a dispute would there be. At Lincoln one Tochi had a hall which undoubtedly was free 'from all custom'; but he had also thirty houses over which the king had toll and forfeiture. So the burgesses swore; but a certain priest was ready to prove by ordeal that they swore falsely[1]. In these cases the lord's territory would appear in later times as a little 'liberty' lying within the borough walls. The middle ages were far spent before such liberties had become mere petty nuisances[2]. In the old cathedral towns, such as Canterbury and Winchester, the bishop's jurisdictional powers and immunities were serious affairs, for the bishop's tenants were numerous[3]. Nevertheless, in the great and ancient boroughs, the boroughs which stand out as types and models, there was from a very remote time a court, a borough-moot or portman-moot, which was not seignorial, a court which was a unit in a national system of courts.

The borough court. Of the form that the borough court took we can say little. Perhaps at first it would be an assembly of all the free burg-men or port-men. As its business increased in the large boroughs, as it began to sit once a week instead of thrice a year, a set

absent without excuse from the 'hundret.' This seems to mean that their court was called a hundred moot. It is very possible that, at least in the earliest time, the moot that was held in the borough had jurisdiction over a territory considerably larger than the walled space, and in this case the urban would hardly differ from the rural hundred. A somewhat new kind of 'hundred' might be formed without the introduction of any new idea.

[1] D. B. i. 336.   [2] Hist. Eng. Law, i. 631.
[3] Green, Town Life, vol. i. ch. xi.

of persons bound to serve as doomsmen may have been formed,
a set of aldermen or lawmen whose offices might or might
not be hereditary, might or might not 'run with' the possession of certain specific tenements. A 'husting' might be
formed, that is, a house-thing as distinct from a 'thing' or
court held in the open air. Law required that there should
be standing witnesses in a borough, before whom bargains
and sales should take place. Such a demand might hasten
the formation of a small body of doomsmen. In Cambridge
there were lawmen of .thegnly rank[1]; in Lincoln there were
twelve lawmen[2]; in Stamford there had been twelve, though
at the date of Domesday Book there were but nine[3]; we read
of four *iudices* in York[4], and of twelve *iudices* in Chester[5].
So late as 1275 the twelve lawmen of Stamford lived on in
the persons of their heirs or successors. There are, said a
jury, twelve men in Stamford who are called lawmen because
their ancestors were in old time the judges of the laws (*iudices
legum*) in the said town; they hold of the king in chief; by
what service we do not know; but you can find out from
Domesday Book[6]. Over the bodies of these, presumably Danish,
lawmen there has been much disputation. We know that
taken individually the lawmen of Lincoln were holders of
heritable franchises, of sake and soke. We know that among
the twelve *iudices* of Chester were men of the king, men of
the earl, men of the bishop; they had to attend the 'hundred,'
that is, we take it, the borough court. We know no more;
but it seems likely that we have to deal with persons who
collectively form a group of doomsmen, while individually each
of them is a great man, of thegnly rank, with sake and soke
over his men and his lands; his office passes to his heir[7]. On
the whole, however, we must doubt whether the generality of
English boroughs had arrived at even this somewhat rudimentary stage of organization. In 1200 the men of Ipswich,
having received a charter from King John, decided that there

---

[1] D. B. i. 189.   [2] D. B. i. 336 b.   [3] D. B. i. 336 b.
[4] D. B. i. 298.   [5] D. B. i. 262 b.   [6] R. H. i. 354-6.

[7] Besides the well known English books, see a paper by Konrad Maurer,
Sitzungsberichte der Akademie der Wissenschaften zu München, Philosoph.-
philolog. Classe, 1887, vol. ii. p. 363. In the Leges Edw. Conf. 38 § 2, the
'lagemanni et meliores homines de burgo' seem to serve as inquest men, rather
than doomsmen; while the *lahmen* of the document concerning the Dunsetan
(Schmid, App. i.) seem to be doomsmen.

should be in their borough twelve chief portmen, 'as there were in the other free boroughs in England,' who should have full power to govern and maintain the town and to render the judgments of its court[1]. Now Ipswich has a right to be placed in the class of ancient boroughs, of county towns, and yet to all appearance it had no definite class of chief men or doomsmen until the year 1200. Still we ought not to infer from this that the town moot had been in practice a democratic institution. There may be a great deal of oligarchy, and oligarchy of an oppressive kind, though the ruling class has never been defined by law. Domesday Book allows us to see in various towns a large number of poor folk who can not pay taxes or can only pay a poll tax. We must be chary of conceding to this crowd any share in the dooms of the court[2].

Definition of the borough. But what concerns the government of the boroughs has for the time been sufficiently said by others. In our few last words we will return to our first theme, the difference between the borough and the mere township.

Mediatized boroughs. We have seen that in Domesday Book a prominent position is conceded to certain towns. They are not brought under any rubric which would place them upon the king's or any other person's land. It must now be confessed that there are some other towns that are not thus treated and that none the less are called boroughs. If, however, we remember that burgesses often are in law where they are not in fact, the list that we shall make of these boroughs will not be long. Still such boroughs exist and a few words should be said about them. They seem to fall into two classes, for they are described as being on the king's land or on the land of some noble or prelate. Of the latter class we will speak first. It does not contain many members and in some cases we can be certain that in the Confessor's day the borough in question had no other lord than the king. Totness is a case in point. It now falls under the title *Terra Judhel de Tottenais*; but we are told that King Edward held it in demesne[3]. In Sussex we

---

[1] Gross, Gild Merchant, ii. 114 ff.; Hist. Eng. Law, i. 642.

[2] D. B. ii. 290, Ipswich: 'Modo vero sunt 110 burgenses qui consuetudinem reddunt et 100 pauperes burgenses qui non possunt reddere ad geltum Regis nisi unum denarium de suis capitibus.' D. B. ii. 116, Norwich: 'Modo sunt in burgo 665 burgenses anglici et consuetudines reddunt, et 480 bordarii qui propter pauperiem nullam reddunt consuetudinem.'

[3] D. B. i. 108 b.

see that Steyning, Pevensey and Lewes are called *burgi*[1],
Steyning is placed on the land of the Abbot of Fécamp,
Pevensey on that of the Count of Mortain and Lewes on that
of William of Warenne; but at Lewes there have been many
haws appurtenant to the rural manors of the shire thegns[2].
In Kent the borough of Hythe seems to be completely under
the archbishop[3]. He has burgesses at Romney over whom he
has justiciary rights, but they serve the king[4]. The 'little
borough called Fordwich' belonged to the Abbot of S[t] Augustin. But of this we know the history. The Confessor gave
him the royal two-thirds, while the bishop of Bayeux as the
successor of Earl Godwin gave him the comital one-third[5].
Further north, Louth in Lincolnshire and Newark in Nottinghamshire seem to be accounted boroughs; they both belong
to the bishop of Lincoln; but in the case of Newark (which
was probably an old *burh*) we may doubt whether his title is
very ancient[6]. We are told that at Tatteshall, the Pontefract
of later days[7], there are sixty 'minute burgesses,' that is, we
take it, burgesses in a small way. Ilbert de Lacy is now their
lord; but here again we may suspect a recent act of mediatiza-
tion[8]. Grantham in Lincolnshire is placed on the Terra Regis;
it had belonged to Queen Edith; there were, however, seventy-
seven tofts in it which belonged to 'the sokemen of the thegns,'
that is, to the sokemen of the thegns of the shire[9]. Then in
Suffolk we see that Ipswich is described at the end of the section
which deals with the royal estates; a similar place is found for
Norwich, Yarmouth and Thetford in the survey of Norfolk[10].
But for Dunwich we must look elsewhere. There were burgesses at Dunwich; but to all seeming the royal rights over

[1] Whether the *novum burgum* mentioned in D. B. i. 17 is Winchelsea or
Rye or a new town at Hastings seems to be disputable. See Round, Feudal
England, 568.

[2] D. B. i. 26 b, 27.   [3] D. B. i. 4 b.

[4] D. B. i. 4 b. See also, 10 b.   [5] D. B. i. 12.

[6] D. B. i. 345, 283 b. It has been said that Leofric gave Newark to the see.

[7] Dodsworth's Yorkshire Notes, ed. R. Holmes (reprinted from Yorkshire
Archaeological Journal), p. 126.

[8] D. B. i. 316 b. The estate is ingeldable and therefore looks like an
ancient possession of the king.

[9] D. B. 337 b: ' Toftes sochemanorum teignorum.' Some commentators
have seen here ' sokemen thegns '; but the other interpretation seems far more
probable.

[10] Had these towns been described in Great Domesday, they would probably
have been definitely placed outside the *Terra Regis*.

the town had passed into the hands of Eadric of Laxfield[1]. The successor of the same Eadric has burgesses among his tenants at Eye[2]. There are burgesses at Clare, though Clare belongs altogether to the progenitor of the lordly race which will take its name from this little town[3]. But at least in this last case, the burgesses may be new-comers, or rather perhaps we may see that an old idea is giving way to a newer idea of a borough, and that if men engaged in trade or handicraft settle round a market-place and pay money-rents to a lord they will be called burgesses, though the town is no national fortress. At Berkhampstead 52 burgesses are collected in a *burbium,* but they may be as new as the two *arpents* of vineyard[4]. We must not say dogmatically that never in the days before the Conquest had a village become a borough while it had for its one and only landlord some person other than the king, some bishop, or some thegn. This may have happened at Taunton. In 1086 there were burgesses at Taunton and it enjoyed ' burh-riht,' and yet from a very remote time it had belonged to the bishops of Winchester. But the cases in which we may suppose that a village in private hands became a *burgus* and that this change took place before the Norman invasion seem to be extremely few. In these few the cause of the change may have been that the king by way of special favour imposed his *burhgriᵭ* upon the town and thereby augmented the revenue of its lord[5].

[1] D. B. ii. 311, 312, 385.   [2] D. B. ii. 319 b.

[3] D. B. ii. 389 b: ' semper unum mercatum modo 43 burgenses.' For Sudbury, see D. B. ii. 286 b; for Beccles, 369 b.

[4] D. B. i. 136 b: ' In burbio huius villae 52 burgenses.' The word *burbium* looks as if some one had argued that as *suburbium* means an annex to a town, therefore *burbium* must mean a town. But the influence of *burh, burg, bourg* may be suspected. A few pages back (132) the *burgum* of Hertford seems to be spoken of as ' hoc suburbium.' It is of course to be remembered that *burgus* or *burgum* was a word with which the Normans were familiar: it was becoming the French *bourg.* It is difficult to unravel any distinctively French thread in the institutional history of our boroughs during the Norman age; but the little knot of traders clustered outside a lord's castle at Clare or Berkhampstead, at Tutbury, Wigmore or Rhuddlan may have for its type rather a French *bourg* than an English *burh.* Indeed at Rhuddlan (i. 269) the burgesses have received the law of Breteuil.

[5] For Taunton, see D. B. i. 87 b: ' Istae consuetudines pertinent ad Tantone: burgeristh, latrones, pacis infractio, hainfare, denarii de hundred, denarii S. Petri, ciricieti.' Compare the document which stands as K. 897 (iv. 233): ' Ðæt is ærest...seo men redden into Tantune cirhsceattas and

As to the boroughs that are regarded as standing on the king's land, these also seem to be few and for the more part they are small. There are burgesses at Maldon[1]; but Maldon is not placed by the side of Colchester[2]; it is described among the royal estates. There are burgesses at Bristol[3]; but Bristol is not placed beside Gloucester and Winchcombe. Perhaps we should have heard more of it, if it had not, like Tamworth, stood on the border of two counties. In the south-west the king's officials seem to be grappling with difficulties as best they may. In Dorset they place Dorchester, Bridport, Wareham and Shaftesbury above the rubric *Terra Regis*[4], and we can not find that they reckon any other place as a borough. In Devonshire we see Exeter above the line; Lidford and Barnstaple, however, are called boroughs though they are assigned to the king's land, and (as already said) Totness is a borough, though it is mediatized and is described among the estates of its Breton lord[5]. No borough in Somerset is placed above the line, though we learn that the king has 107 burgesses in Ilchester who pay him 20 shillings[6], and that he and others have burgesses at Bath[7]. Perhaps the space that stands vacant before the list of the tenants in chief should have been filled with some words about these two towns. Axbridge, Langport and Milborne seem to be boroughs; Axbridge and Langport occur in that list of ancient fortresses which we have called The Burghal Hidage[8]. Wells was an episcopal, Somerton a royal manor; we have no reason for calling either of them a borough. In Hampshire another of the ancient fortresses, Twyneham (the modern Christ Church) is still called *burgus*, but seems to be finding its level among the royal manors[9]. In Wiltshire Malmesbury and Marlborough are placed above the line. We learn that the king receives £50 from the *burgus* of Wilton[10], and we also learn incidentally that various lords have burgesses in that town; for example, the bishop of Salisbury has burgesses in Wilton who belong to his manor of Salisbury[11]. Old Salisbury ('old Sarum' as we foolishly call it) seems to be a mere manor

burhgerihtu.' See also K. 1084 (v. 157): 'ut episcopi homines [apud Tantun] tam nobiles quam ignobiles...hoc idem ius in omni haberent dignitate quo regis homines perfruuntur, regalibus fiscis commorantes.'

[1] D. B. ii. 5 b. [2] D. B. ii. 104. [3] D. B. i. 163.
[4] D. B. i. 75. [5] D. B. i. 100, 108 b.
[6] D. B. i. 86 b. [7] D. B. i. 87. [8] See above, p. 188.
[9] D. B. 38 b, 44. [10] D. B. 64 b. [11] D. B. 66.

belonging to the bishop; but the king receives its third penny. He receives also the third penny of Cricklade, which we have named before now as one of the old Wessex strongholds, and several of the county magnates had burgesses there. On the other hand Calne, Bedwind and Warminster are reckoned to be manors on the king's land. Burgesses belong to them; but whether those burgesses are really resident in them may not be quite certain[1]. Devizes we can not find. That puzzles should occur in this quarter is what our general theory might lead us to expect. In the old home of the West-Saxon kings there may well have been towns which had long ago secured the name and the peace of royal burgs, though they manifested none of that tenurial heterogeneity which is the common mark of a borough. A town, a village, which not only belonged to the king but contained a palace or house in which he often dwelt, would enjoy his special peace, and might maintain its burghal dignity long after there was little, if any, real difference between it and other manors or villages of which the king was the immediate landlord. Already in 1086 there may have been 'rotten boroughs,' boroughs that were rotten before they were ripe[2].

Attributes of the borough.

A borough belongs to the genus *villa* (*tún*). In age after age our task is to discover its *differentia*, and the task is hard because, as age succeeds age, changes in law and changes in fact are making the old distinctions obsolete while others are becoming important. Let us observe, then, that already when Domesday Book was in the making those ancient

---

[1] The burgesses belonging to Ramsbury are really at Cricklade: D. B. i. 66.

[2] It seems very possible that already before the Conquest some boroughs had fallen out of the list. In cent. x. we read, for example, of a *burh* at Towcester and of a *burh* at Witham in Essex. We must not indeed contend that a shire-supported town with tenurial heterogeneity came into existence wherever Edward the Elder or the Lady of the Mercians 'wrought a *burh*.' But still during a time of peace the walls of a petty *burh* would be neglected, and, if the great majority of the inhabitants were the king's tenants, there would be little to distinguish this place from a royal village of the common kind. See for Towcester, D. B. i. 219 b; for Witham, D. B. ii. 1 b. In later days we may see an old borough, such as Buckingham, falling very low and sending no burgesses to parliament. It will be understood that we have not pledged ourselves to any list of the places that were boroughs in 1066. There are difficult cases such as that of St Albans; see above, p. 181. But, we are persuaded that few places were deemed *burgi*, except the shire towns.

attributes of which we have been speaking were disappearing or were fated soon to disappear. We have thought of the typical borough as a fortified town maintained by a district for military purposes. But already the shire thegns have been letting their haws at a rent and probably have been letting them to craftsmen and traders. Also the time has come for knight-service and castles and castle-guard. We have thought of the typical borough as the sphere of a special peace. But the day is at hand when a revolution in the criminal law will destroy the old system of *wer* and *wíte* and *bót*, and the king's peace will reign always and everywhere[1]. We have thought of the typical borough as a town which has a court. But the day is at hand when almost every village will have its court, its manorial court. New contrasts, however, are emerging as the old contrasts fade away. Against a background of villeinage and week-work, the borough begins to stand out as the scene of burgage tenure. The service by which the burgess holds his tenement is a money rent. This may lead to a large increase in the number of boroughs. If a lord enfranchises a manor, abolishes villein customs, takes money rents, allows his tenants to farm the court and perhaps also to farm a market that he has acquired from the king, he will be said to create a *liber burgus*[2]. Merchant gilds, elected bailiffs, elected mayors and common seals will appear and will complicate the question. There will follow a time of uncertainty and confusion when the sheriffs will decide as suits them best which of the smaller towns are boroughs and which are not.

If the theory that we have been suggesting is true, all or very nearly all our ancient boroughs (and we will draw the line of ancientry at the Conquest) are in their inception royal

Classification of boroughs.

---

[1] A last relic of the old borough peace may be found in Britton's definition of burglary (i. 42): 'Burglars are those who feloniously in time of peace break churches, or the houses of others, or the walls or gates of our cities or boroughs (*de nos citez ou de nos burgs*).'

[2] By a charter of enfranchisement a lord might introduce burgage tenure and abolish 'servile customs'; but it must be, to say the least, doubtful whether he could, without the king's licence, confer upon a village the public status of a borough and e.g. authorize it to behave like a hundred before the justices in eyre. This is one of the reasons why sheriffs can draw the line where they please, and why some towns which have been enfranchised never obtain a secure place in the list of parliamentary boroughs.

boroughs. The group of burgesses when taken as a whole had no superior other than the king. His was the peace that prevailed in the streets; the profits of the court and of the market were his, though they were farmed by a reeve. Rarely, however, was he the landlord of all the burgesses. In general not a few of them lived in houses that belonged to the thegns of the shire. We must be careful therefore before we speak of these towns as ' boroughs on the royal demesne.' For the more part, the compilers of Domesday Book have refused to place them on the *Terra Regis*. In course of time some of them will be currently spoken of as boroughs on or of the royal demesne. The rights of those who represent the thegns of the shire will have become mere rights to rent, and, their origin being forgotten, they will even be treated as mere rent-charges[1]. The great majority of the burgesses will in many instances be the king's immediate tenants and he will be the only lord of that incorporeal thing, ' the borough,' the only man who can grant it a charter or let it to farm. But we must distinguish between these towns and those which at the Conquest were manors on the king's land. These latter, if he enfranchises them, will be boroughs on the royal demesne in an exacter sense. So, again, we must distinguish between those ancient boroughs which the king has mediatized and those manors of mesne lords which are raised to the rank of boroughs. We have seen that from the ancient borough the king received a revenue of tolls and fines. Therefore he had something to give away. He could mediatize the borough. Domesday Book shows us that this had already been done in a few instances[2]. At a later time some even of the county towns passed out of the king's hands into the hands of earls. This happened at Leicester and at Warwick. The earl succeeded to the king's rights, and the burgesses had to go to the earl for their liberties and their charters. But such cases are very distinct from those in which a mesne lord grants

---

[1] Hist. Eng. Law, i. 630. When it is being said that if land in the borough escheats, it always escheats to the king, the mesne tenures are already being forgotten within the borough, just as in modern times we have forgotten them in the open country. The burgher's power of devising his land made escheat a rare event, and so destroyed the evidence of mesne tenure.

[2] See above, p. 212. Also the king might give away an undivided share of the borough. Apparently the church of Worcester had received the third penny of the city ever since the day when the *burh* was wrought by the ealdorman and lady of the Mercians. See above, p. 194.

an enfranchising charter to the men of a place which has hitherto been one of his manors, and by speaking of boroughs which are 'on the land of mesne lords' we must not confuse two classes of towns which have long had different histories. In the ancient boroughs there is from the first an element that we must call both artificial and national. The borough does not grow up spontaneously; it is made; it is 'wrought'; it is 'timbered.' It has a national purpose; it is maintained 'at the cost of the nation' by the duty that the shire owes to it. This trait may soon have disappeared, may soon have been forgotten, but a great work had been done. In these nationally supported and heterogeneously peopled towns a new kind of community might wax and thrive.

ESSAY II.

ENGLAND BEFORE THE CONQUEST.

Object of this Essay. No one can spend patient hours in examining the complex web disclosed by Domesday Book without making some theories, at least some guesses, about the political, social and economic threads of which that web has been woven. But if we here venture to fashion and state a few such theories or such guesses, it is with no hope that they will be a complete explanation of old English history. For, in the first place, we are to speak mainly of the things of the law, of legal ideas and legal forms, and once for all we may protest that we have no wish to overestimate their importance. The elaborate and long continued development to which we point when we speak of 'feudalism,' can not be fully explained by any discussion of legal ideas and legal forms. On the other hand, it can not be fully explained without such discussion, for almost all that we can know about it is to be found in legal documents. In the second place, we are to make a selection. Certain phases of our oldest legal history, notably those which are called 'constitutional,' have been so fully treated by classical books, that at the present moment there is no good reason why we should traverse the ground that has been covered. Therefore if, for example, we say little or nothing of the ancient Germanic *comitatus* or of the relationship between lord and man in so far as it is a merely personal relationship, this will not be because we have overlooked these matters; it will be because there is nothing to be gained by our repeating what has been well and sufficiently said by Dr Konrad Maurer, Dr Reinhold Schmid, Dr Stubbs and others. And if, again, we lay great stress on what may be called the ecclesiastical phase of the feudalizing process, this will not be because we think it the only phase, it will be because we think that too little attention has been paid by English writers to the influence which the churches exercised upon temporal affairs by means of their endowments. The day for an artistically proportioned picture of the growth of feudalism has not yet come; the day for a quantitative analysis of the elements of feudalism may never come; for the present we must be content if we can bring out a few new truths or set a few old truths in a new light. The vast and intricate subject may be approached from many different quarters. If we can make some little progress along our chosen path, we shall be all the more willing to admit that progress along other paths is possible.

It can not but be, however, that this part of our work should be controversial, though it need not be polemical. We are told that 'in spite of all the labour that has been spent on the early history of England, scholars are still at variance upon the most fundamental of questions: the question whether that history began with a population of independent freemen or with a population of dependent serfs[1]'. Some exception may be taken to this statement. No one denies that for the purposes of English history slavery is a primitive institution, nor that in the seventh and eighth centuries there were many slaves in England. On the other hand, no one will assert that we can ascertain, even approximately, the ratio that the number of slaves bore to the number of free men. Moreover such terms as 'dependent' and 'independent' are not words that we can profitably quarrel over, since they are inexact and ambiguous. For all this, however, it may well be said that there are two main theories before the world. The one would trace the English manor back to the Roman villa, would think of the soil of England as being tilled from the first mainly by men who, when they were not mere slaves, were *coloni* ascript to the land. The other would postulate the existence of a large number of free men who with their own labour tilled their own soil, of men who might fairly be called free 'peasant proprietors' since they were far from rich and had few slaves or servants, and yet who were no mere peasants since they habitually bore arms in the national host. What may be considered for the moment as a variant on this latter doctrine would place the ownership of the soil, or of

Marginal note: Fundamental controversies as to Anglo-Saxon history.

---

[1] Ashley, Introduction to Fustel de Coulanges, Origin of Property in Land, p. vii.

large tracts of the soil, not in these free peasants taken as individuals, but in free village communities.

The Romanesque theory unacceptable.Now we will say at once that the first of these theories we can not accept if it be put forward in a general form, if it be applied to the whole or anything like the whole of England. Certainly we are not in a position to deny that in some cases, a Roman villa having come into the hands of a Saxon chieftain, he treated the slaves and *coloni* that he found upon it in much the same way as that in which they had been theretofore treated, though even in such a case the change was in all probability momentous, since large commerce and all that large commerce implies had perished. But against the hypothesis that this was the general case the English language and the names of our English villages are the unanswered protest. It seems incredible that the bulk of the population should have been of Celtic blood and yet that the Celtic language should not merely have disappeared, but have stamped few traces of itself upon the speech of the conquerors[1]. This we regard as an objection which goes to the root of the whole matter and which throws upon those who would make the English nation in the main a nation of Celtic bondmen, the burden of strictly proving their thesis. The German invaders must have been numerous. The Britons were no cowards. They contested the soil inch by inch. The struggle was long and arduous. What then, we must ask, became of the mass of the victors? Surely it is impossible that they at once settled down as the 'dependent serfs' of their chieftains. Again, though it is very likely that where we find a land of scattered steads and of isolated hamlets, there the Germanic conquerors have spared or have been unable to subdue the Britons or have adapted their own arrangements to the exterior framework that was provided by Celtic or Roman agriculture, still, until Meitzen[2] has been refuted, we are compelled to say that our true villages, the nucleated villages with large 'open fields,' are not Celtic, are not Roman, but are very purely and typically German. But this is not all. Hereafter we shall urge some other objections. The

[1] The gradual disappearance in recent times of the Irish language is no parallel case, for this is a triumph of the printing press. Mr Stevenson tells me that the number of unquestioned cases of a word borrowed from Celtic in very ancient times is now reduced to less than ten.

[2] Meitzen, Siedelung und Agrarwesen der Germanen, especially ii. 120 ff.

doctrine in question will give no rational explanation of the
state of things that is revealed to us by the Domesday Survey
of the northern and eastern counties and it will give no
rational explanation of seignorial justice.   This being so, we
seem bound to suppose that at one time there was a large
class of peasant proprietors, that is, of free men who tilled the
soil that they owned, and to discuss the process which substitutes for peasant proprietorship the manorial organization.

Though we can not deal at any length with a matter which
lies outside the realm of legal history, we ought at once to
explain that we need not regard this change as a retrogression.
There are indeed historians who have not yet abandoned the
habit of speaking of feudalism as though it were a disease of
the body politic.   Now the word 'feudalism' is and always will
be an inexact term, and, no doubt, at various times and places
there emerge phenomena which may with great propriety be
called feudal and which come of evil and make for evil.   But if
we use the term, and often we do, in a very wide sense, if we
describe several centuries as feudal, then feudalism will appear
to us as a natural and even a necessary stage in our history :
that is to say, if we would have the England of the sixteenth
century arise out of the England of the eighth without passing
through a period of feudalism, we must suppose many immense
and fundamental changes in the nature of man and his
surroundings.   If we use the term in this wide sense, then
(the barbarian conquests being given us as an unalterable fact)
feudalism means civilization, the separation of employments,
the division of labour, the possibility of national defence, the
possibility of art, science, literature and learned leisure ; the
cathedral, the scriptorium, the library, are as truly the work of
feudalism as is the baronial castle.   When therefore we speak,
as we shall have to speak, of forces which make for the
subjection of the peasantry to seignorial justice and which
substitute the manor with its villeins for the free village, we
shall—so at least it seems to us—be speaking not of abnormal
forces, not of retrogression, not of disease, but in the main of
normal and healthy growth.   Far from us indeed is the cheerful
optimism which refuses to see that the process of civilization is
often a cruel process ; but the England of the eleventh century
is nearer to the England of the nineteenth than is the England
of the seventh—nearer by just four hundred years.

Feudalism as a normal stage.

This leads to a remark which concerns us more deeply. As regards the legal ideas in which feudalism is expressed a general question may be raised. If we approach them from the standpoint of modern law, if we approach them from the standpoint of the classical Roman law, they are confused ideas. In particular no clear line is drawn between public and private law. Ownership is *dominium*; but governmental power, jurisdictional power, these also are *dominium*. Office is property; taxes are rents; governmental relationships arise *ex contractu*. Then within the province of private law the ideas are few; these few have hard work to do; their outlines are blurred. One *dominium* rises above another *dominium*, one seisin over another seisin. Efforts after precision made in comparatively recent times by romanizing lawyers serve only to show how vague was the subject-matter with which they had to deal. They would give the lord a *dominium directum*, the vassal a *dominium utile*; but then, when there has been further subinfeudation, this vassal will have a *dominium utile* as regards the lord paramount, but a *dominium directum* as regards the sub-vassal. So again, as we shall see hereafter, the gift of land shades off into the 'loan' of land, the 'loan' into the gift. The question then occurs whether we are right in applying to this state of things such a word as 'confusion,' a word which implies that things that once were distinct have wrongfully or unfortunately been mixed up with each other, a word which implies error or retrogression.

Now, no doubt, from one point of view, namely that of universal history, we do see confusion and retrogression. Ideal possessions which have been won for mankind by the thought of Roman lawyers are lost for a long while and must be recovered painfully. Lines that have been traced with precision are smudged out, and then they must be traced once more. If we regard western Europe as a whole, this retrogression appears as a slow change. How slow—that is a much controverted question. There are, for example, historians who would have us think of the Gaul of Merovingian times as being in the main governed by Roman ideas and institutions, which have indeed been sadly debased, but still are the old ideas and institutions. There are other historians who can discover in this same Gaul little that is not genuinely German and barbarous. But at any rate, it must be admitted that somehow or another a retrogression takes place, that the best legal ideas of the ninth and tenth centuries are not so good, so modern, as those of the third and fourth. If, however, we take a narrower view and fix our eyes upon the barbarian hordes which invade a Roman province, shall we say that their legal thought gradually goes to the bad, and loses distinctions which it has once apprehended? To turn to our own case—Shall we say that Englishmen of the eighth century mark the line that divides public from private law, while Englishmen of the eleventh century can not perceive it?

No one perhaps to such a question would boldly say: Yes. And yet, when it comes to a treatment of particulars, an affirmative answer seems to be implied in much that has been written even by modern historians. They begin at the beginning and attribute precise ideas and well-defined law to the German conquerors of Britain. If they began with the eleventh century and thence turned to the earlier time, they might come to another opinion, to the opinion that in the beginning all was very vague, and that such clearness and precision as legal thought has attained in the days of the Norman Conquest has been very gradually attained and is chiefly due to the influence which the old heathen world working through the Roman church has exercised upon the new. The process that is started when barbarism is brought into contact with civilization is not simple. The hitherto naked savage may at once assume some part of the raiment, perhaps the hat, of the white man. When after a while he puts these things aside and learns to make for himself clothes suitable to the climate in which he lives and the pursuits in which he is engaged, we see in this an advance, not a relapse; and yet he has abandoned some things that belong to the white man. Even so when our kings of the eighth century set their hands to documents written in Latin and bristling with the technical terms of Roman law, to documents which at first sight seem to express clear enough ideas of ownership and alienation, we must not at once assume that they have grasped these ideas. In course of time men will evolve formulas which will aptly fit their thought, for example, the 'feudal' charter of feoffment with its *tenendum de me* and its *reddendo mihi*. Externally it will not be so Roman or (we may say it) so modern a document as was the land-book of the eighth century, and yet in truth there has

The contact of barbarism and civilization.

M.   15

been progress not retrogress. Words that Roman lawyers would have understood give way before words which would have been nonsense to them, *feoffamentum, liberatio seisinae* and the like. This is as it should be. Men are learning to say what they really mean.

And now let us remember that our materials for the legal history of the long age which lies behind Domesday Book are scanty. A long age it is, even if we measure it only from the date of Augustin's mission. The Conqueror stands midway between Æthelbert and Elizabeth. To illustrate five hundred years of legal history we have only the dooms and the land-books. The dooms are so much taken up with the work of keeping the peace and punishing theft that they tell us little of the structure of society or of the feudalizing process, while as to what they imply it is but too easy for different men to form different opinions. Some twelve hundred land-books or charters, genuine and spurious, are our best, almost our only, evidence, and it must needs be that they will give us but a partial and one-sided view of intricate and many-sided facts[1].

§ 1. *Book-land and the Land-book.*

Now these charters or land-books are, with hardly any exceptions, ecclesiastical title-deeds. Most of them are deeds whereby lands were conveyed to the churches; some are deeds whereby lands were conveyed to men who conveyed them to the churches. Partial, one-sided and in details untrustworthy though the testimony that they bear may be, there is still one general question that they ought to answer and we ought to ask. Domesday Book shows us many of the churches as the lords of wide and continuous tracts of land. Now about this

---

[1] We shall use, and cite by the letter *K.*, Kemble's Codex Diplomaticus Aevi Saxonici. We shall refer by the letters *H. & S.* to the third volume of the Councils and Ecclesiastical Documents edited by Haddan and Stubbs, by the letter *T.* to Thorpe's Diplomatarium, by the letter *B.* to Birch's Cartularium, by the letter *E.* to Earle's Land Charters. Reference will also be made to the two collections of facsimiles, namely, the four volumes which come from the British Museum and the two which come from the Ordnance Survey. We are yet a long way off a satisfactory edition of the land-books. A model has been lately set by Prof. Napier and Mr Stevenson in their edition of the Crawford Collection of Early Charters, Oxford, 1895.

important element in the feudal structure the land-books ought
to tell us something. They ought to tell us how the churches
acquired their territories; they ought to tell us what class of
men made gifts of land to the churches; they ought to tell us
whether those gifts were of big tracts or of small pieces. For
example, let us remember how Domesday Book shows us that
four minsters, Worcester, Evesham, Pershore and Westminster,
were lords of seven-twelfths of Worcestershire, that the church
of Worcester was lord of one quarter of that shire and lord of
the triple hundred of Oswaldslaw. How did that church
become the owner of a quarter of a county, to say nothing of
lands in other shires? We ought to be able to answer this
question in general terms, for among the charters that have
come down to us there is no series which is longer, there is
hardly a long series which is of better repute, than the line of
the land-books which belonged to the church of Worcester.
They come to us for the more part in the form of a cartulary
compiled not long after the Conquest by the monk Heming at
the instance of Bishop Wulfstan[1].

Now the answer that they give to our question is this:— How the
churches
With but few exceptions, the donors of these lands were kings acquired
or under-kings, kings or under-kings of the Mercians, kings of their lands.
the English, and the gifts were large gifts. Very often the
charter comprised a tract of land which in Domesday Book
appears as a whole vill or as several contiguous vills. Seldom
indeed is the subject-matter of the gift described as being a
villa or a *vicus*:—the king merely says that he gives so many
manses or the land of so many *manentes* at a certain place.
Still, if we compare these charters with Domesday Book, we
shall become convinced that very often the land given was of
wide extent. For example, Domesday Book tells us that the
church of Worcester holds Sedgebarrow (Seggesbarue) where
it has four hides for geld, but eight plough teams. How was
this acquired? The monks answer that three centuries ago,
in 777, Aldred the under-king of the Hwiccas gave them

---

[1] Heming's Cartulary was published by Hearne. It has been said that
some of the documents in this collection which Kemble accepted as genuine
commit the fault of supposing that the old episcopal minster was dedicated to
St. Mary, whereas it was dedicated to St. Peter. See Robertson, Historical
Essays, 195. However, where Heming's work can be tested it generally gains
credit.

viculum qui nuncupatur aet Segcesbaruue iiii. mansiones, that land having been giving to him by Offa king of the Mercians in order that the soul of the *subregulus* might have something done for it[1]. In the Conqueror's reign the Archbishop of Canterbury held a great estate in Middlesex of which Harrow was the centre, and which contained no less than 100 hides. Already in 832 the archbishop or his church had 104 hides at Harrow[2]. Here we will state our belief, its grounds will appear in another essay, that the ' manses ' that the kings throw about by fives and tens and twenties, are no small holdings, but hides each of which contains, or is for fiscal purposes deemed to contain, some 120 acres of arable land together with stretches, often wide stretches, of wood, meadow and waste, the extent of which varies from case to case. From the seventh century onwards the kings are giving large territories to the churches. One instance is beyond suspicion, for Bede attests it. In 686 or thereabouts Æthelwealh king of the South Saxons gave to Bishop Wilfrid the land of eighty-seven families in the promontory of Selsey, and among its inhabitants were two hundred and fifty male and female slaves[3]. This gift comprised a spacious tract of country; it comprised what then were, or what afterwards became, the sites of many villages[4]. But to whichever of our oldest churches we turn, the story that it proclaims in its title-deeds is always the same:—We obtained our lands by means of royal grants; we obtained them not in little pieces, here a few acres and there a few, but in great pieces. Canterbury and Winchester echo the tale that is told by Worcester. Another example may be given. It is one that has been carefully examined of late. In 739 King Æthelheard of Wessex gave to Forthhere bishop of Sherborne twenty *cassati* at the place called ' Cridie.' Thereby he disposed of what now are ' the parishes of Crediton, Newton St. Cyres, Upton Pyne, Brampford Speke, Hittesleigh, Drewsteignton, Colebrooke, Morchard Bishop, Sandford, Kennerleigh and the modern parish of Sherwood, part of Cheriton Bishop, and possibly the

---

[1] D. B. i. 173 b ; K. 131 (i. 158); B. i. 311.

[2] D. B. i. 127; K. 230 (i. 297) ; B. i. 558.

[3] Hist. Eccl. iv. 13 (ed. Plummer, i. 232).

[4] See the spurious charter of Cædwalla, K. 992 (v. 32) which purports to show where the 87 manses lay. According to it, the gift comprised some places which lay well outside the promontory of Selsey. But more of this hereafter.

whole of Clannaborough.' He disposed of the whole and more
than the whole of the modern 'hundred' of Crediton[1]. Then,
to choose one last instance, it is said that already in 679 Osric
of the Hwiccas gave to an abbess *centum manentes qui adiacent
civitati quae vocatur Hât Bathu*[2]. It is not unlikely that this
means that a king newly converted to Christianity disposed by
one deed of many square leagues of land, namely, of the hundred
of Bath[3]. The kingdom of the Hwiccas was not boundless. If
Osric executed a few more charters of this kind he would soon
have 'booked' it all.

Let us then examine with some care the charters that come
to us from the earliest period, a period which shall begin with
the year 600 and end with the year 750. From this time we
have some forty charters sufficiently genuine for our present
purpose. With hardly an exception the grantor is a king or
an under-king, while the grantee is a dead saint, a church, a
bishop, an abbot, or a body of monks. If the grantee is a
layman, the gift is made to him in order that he may found a
minster. If this purpose is not expressed, it is to be understood. Thus in 674 or thereabouts Wulfhere king of the
Mercians gives five manses to his kinsman Berhtferth as a
perpetual inheritance. Berhtferth is to have full power to give
them to whom he pleases, and we are not told that he proposes
to devote them to pious uses. Nevertheless, the king makes
the gift 'for the love of Almighty God and of his faithful
servant S[t]. Peter[4].' In other cases the lay donee is to hold
the land 'by church right' or 'by minster right[5].' Indeed
there seems to be no single deed of this period which does not
purport upon its face to be in some sort an ecclesiastical act, an
act done for the good of the church[6].

The earliest books.

---

[1] Napier and Stevenson, Crawford Charters, p. 43. Some of the best work
that has been done towards connecting Domesday Book with the A.-S. land-books
will be found in a paper on the Pre-Domesday Hide of Gloucestershire : Transactions of Bristol and Gloucestershire Arch. Soc. vol. xviii., by Mr C. S. Taylor.

[2] K. 12 (i. 16); B. i. 69; H. & S. 129 ; Plummer, Bede, ii. 247. The charter
itself is open to grave suspicion.

[3] C. S. Taylor, The Pre-Domesday Hide of Gloucestershire.

[4] E. p. 4; B. M. Facsim. iv. 1.

[5] K. 83 (i. 100): 'in possessionem aecclesiasticae rationis et regulae...in ius
monasticae rationis.' K. 90 (i. 108): 'in possessionem iuris ecclesiastici.'
K. 101 (i. 122): 'ut sit aecclesiastici iuris potestate subdita in perpetuum.'

[6] K. 54 (i. 60) is a gift to an abbess, for compare K. 36 (i. 41). We here

Exotic character of the book.   These charters are documents of ecclesiastical origin; they are also documents of foreign origin. The bishops and abbots have brought or have imported models from abroad. The 'books' that they induce the kings to sign are full of technical phrases which already have an ancient history. By way of illustration we will notice one point at which there is an instructive resemblance and an instructive contrast. On the Continent a grantor of lands ends his conveyance with a 'penal stipulation.' If an heir of his controverts the deed, he is to pay a certain sum, and none the less the conveyance is to remain in full force. In England we can not thus stipulate for a pecuniary penalty; the land-book is still so purely an ecclesiastical affair that the punishment of its violator must be left to the church and to God. So instead of stipulating that he shall pay money, we stipulate that he shall be excommunicated and, if impenitent, damned, but we do not forget to add that none the less the conveyance shall remain as valid and effectual as ever. 'If anyone,' says Eadric of Kent, 'shall attempt to go against this gift, let him be separated from all Christianity and the body and blood of Jesus Christ, *manentem hanc donationis chartulam*[1] *in sua nihilominus firmitate.*' Such words may look somewhat out of place in their new surroundings; but they are part of a venerable formula[2].

The book purports to confer ownership.   But what is the model to which in the last resort these documents go back? A conveyance by a Roman landowner. He has in the land full and absolute *dominium* and is going to transfer this to another. Let us observe that the recorded motive which prompts a king to set his cross, or rather Christ's cross, to a land-book is a purely personal motive. He wishes to save his soul, he desires pardon for his crimes[3]. Of the welfare of his realm he says nothing; but his soul must be saved. Sometimes he will give land to an under-king or to an

leave out of account the early lease for lives granted by Bp. Wilfrid, K. 91 (i. 109), an important document, but one which must be mentioned in another context.

[1] An accusative absolute.

[2] Eadric's deed is K. 27 (i. 30). See also Hlothar's charter K. 16 (i. 20) and Suaebraed's, K. 52 (i. 59); B. M. Facs. i. plates 1, 3. With these should be compared the forms in Rozière, Formules, i. 208–255. On pp. 235, 253 will be found instances, one from the very ancient Angevin collection, another from Marculf, in which the breaker of the charter is threatened, not only with a money penalty, but also with excommunication and damnation.

[3] K. Nos. 12, 16, 32, 36, 48, 52, 56, 67, etc.

ealdorman, for they also have souls and may desire salvation[1]. He is acting as a private landowner might act. Then he uses terms and phrases which belong to the realm of pure private law. He asserts in the most energetic of all the words that the law of the lower empire could provide that he is a landowner and that he is going to transfer landownership. The land in question is *tellus mea*[2] or it is *terra iuris mei*[3]. Then it is the very land itself that he gives, the land of so many manses, 'with all the appurtenances, fields, pastures, woods, marshes.' It is no mere right over the land that he gives, but the very soil itself. Next let us observe the terms in which the act of conveyance is stated:—*perpetualiter trado et de meo iure in tuo transscribo terram…ut tam tu quam posteri tui teneatis, possideatis et quaecunque volueris de eadem terra facere liberam habeatis potestatem*[4]. The Latin language of the time had no terms more potent or precise than these. Or again: *aliquantulam agri partem…Waldhario episcopo in dominio donare decrevimus*[5]. Or again: *aeternaliter et perseverabiliter possideat abendi vel dandi cuicumque eligere voluerit*[6]. But it is needless to multiply examples.

No doubt then, if we bring to the interpretation of these instruments the ideas of an earlier or of a later time, the ideas of ancient Rome or of modern Europe, we see the king as a landowner conferring on the churches landownership pure and simple. The fact on which our constitutional historians have laid stress, namely, that sometimes (for we must not overstate the case) the king says that the bishops and his great men are consenting to his deed, important though it may be in other contexts, is of little moment here. The king is put before us as the owner of the land conveyed; it is, he says, *terra mea*, *terra iuris mei*. The rule, if rule it be, that he must not give away his land without the consent of bishops and nobles in no way denies his ownership. However, we are at the moment more concerned with the fact, or seeming fact, that what he gives to the churches is ownership and nothing less. *Does the book really confer ownership?*

But if we loyally accept this seeming fact and think it over, to what conclusions shall we not be brought, when we remember *The book really conveys a superiority.*

---

[1] K. 131 (i. 158). [2] K. 1. [3] K. Nos. 27, 35, 77, 79, 999, 1006, 1007.
[4] K. 35 (i. 39); E. 13; B. M. Facs. i. 2.
[5] K. 52 (i. 59); E. 16; B. M. Facs. i. 3.
[6] E. 4; B. M. Facs. iv. 1.

how wide were the lands which the churches acquired from the
kings, when we think once more how by virtue of royal gifts
the church of Worcester acquired a quarter of a county? When
these lands were given to the church were they waste lands?
It is plain that this was not the common case. Already there
were manses, there were arable fields, there were meadows,
there were tillers of the soil. One of two conclusions seems to
follow. Either the king really did own these large districts,
and the tillers of the soil were merely his slaves or *coloni*,
who were conveyed along with the soil, or else the clear and
emphatic language of the charters sadly needs explanation.
Now if we hold by the letter of the charters, if we say that
the king really does confer landownership upon the churches,
there will be small room left for any landowners in England
save the kings, the churches and perhaps a few great nobles.
This is a theory which for many reasons we can not adopt; no
one can adopt it who is not prepared to believe that Britain
was conquered by a handful of chieftains without followers.
The only alternative course seems that of saying that many
of the land-books even of the earliest period, despite their
language, convey not the ownership of land, but (the term
must be allowed us) a 'superiority' over land and over free
men.

A modern
analogy.
Let us for a moment remember that the wording of a
modern English conveyance might easily delude a layman or
a foreigner. An impecunious earl, we will say, sells his ancient
family estate. We look at the deed whereby this sale is
perfected. The Earl of *A.* grants unto *B. C.* and his heirs all
the land delineated on a certain map and described in a certain
schedule. That in substance is all that the deed tells us. We
look at the map; we see a tract of many thousand acres, which,
besides a grand mansion, has farm-houses, cottages, perhaps,
entire villages upon it. The schedule tells us the names of
the fields and of the farm-houses. Like enough no word will
hint that any one lives in the houses and cottages, or that any
one, save the seller, has any right of any kind in any part of
this wide territory. But what is the truth? Perhaps a
hundred different men, farmers and cottagers, have rights of
different kinds in various portions of the tract. Some have
leases, some have 'agreements for leases,' some hold for terms
of years, some hold from year to year, some hold at will. The

rights of these tenants stand, as it were, between the purchaser and the land that he has bought. He has bought the benefit, and the burden also, of a large mass of contracts. But of these things his conveyance says nothing[1]. And so again, in the brief charters of the thirteenth century a feoffor will say no more than that he has given *manerium meum de Westona*, as though the manor of Weston were some simple physical object like a black horse, and yet under analysis this *manerium* turns out to be a complex tangle of rights in which many men, free and villein, are concerned.

But it will be said that all this is the result of 'feudalism.' It implies just that dismemberment of the *dominium* which is one of feudalism's main characteristics. Undoubtedly in the twelfth century the free tenant in fee simple who holds land 'in demesne' can have, must have, a lord above him, who also holds and is seised of that land and who will speak of the land as his. But we are now in the age before feudalism, in the seventh and eighth centuries. Are we to believe that the free owner of Kemble's 'ethel, hid, or alod' might have above him, perhaps always had above him, not merely a lord (for a personal relation of patronage between lord and man is not to the point), but a landlord: one who would speak of that 'ethel, hid or alod' as *terra iuris mei*: one who to save his soul would give that land to a church and tell the bishop or abbot to do whatever he pleased with it? If we believe this, shall we not be believing that so far as English history can be carried there is no age before 'feudalism'? Convey-ance of su-periority in early times.

We will glance for a moment at two transactions which took place near the end of the seventh century. Bede tells how Æthelwealh king of the South Saxons was persuaded to become a Christian by Wulfhere king of the Mercians. The Mercian received the South Saxon as his godson and by way of christening-gift gave him two provinces, namely the Isle of Wight and the territory of the Meanwari in Wessex, perhaps the hundreds of Meon in Hampshire[2]. Then the same Bede Illustra-tions.

---

[1] Davidson, Precedents in Conveyancing, i. 88 (ed. 1874): 'In conveying estates, it is not usual to refer to the leases affecting the same, unless the leases are for a long term of years, or beneficial, or otherwise not of the ordinary type.'

[2] Hist. Eccl. iv. c. 13 (ed. Plummer, i. 230). In the O. E. version the words are: 'Ond se cyning... him to godsuna onfeng and to tacne ðære sibbe him twa

tells us that the same Æthelwealh gave to Bishop Wilfrid a land of eighty-seven families, to wit, the promontory of Selsey: he gave it with its fields and its men, among whom were two hundred and fifty male and female slaves[1]. A modern reader will perhaps see here two very different transactions. In the one case he sees 'the cession of a province' by one king to another, and possibly he thinks how Queen Victoria ceded Heligoland to her imperial grandson:—the act is an act of public law, a transfer of sovereignty. In the other case he sees a private act, the gift of an estate for pious uses. But Bede and his translator saw little, if any, difference between the two gifts: in each case Bede says 'donavit'; the translator in the one case says 'forgeaf,' in the other 'geaf and sealde.' Now it will hardly be supposed that the Isle of Wight had no inhabitants who were not the slaves or the *coloni* of the king, and, that being so, we are not bound to suppose that there were no free landowners in the promontory of Selsey. May it not be that what Æthelwealh had to give and gave to Wilfrid was what in our eyes would be far rather political power than private property?

What had the king to give?

But over the free land of free landowners what rights had the king which he could cede to another king or to a prelate, saying withal that the subject of his gift was land? He had, as we think, rights of two kinds that were thus alienable; we may call them fiscal rights and justiciary rights, though such terms must be somewhat too precise when applied to the vague thought of the seventh and eighth centuries. Of justiciary rights we shall speak below. As to the rights that we call fiscal, we find that the king is entitled to something that he calls *tributum, vectigal,* to something that he calls *pastus, victus,* the king's *feorm* ; also there is military service to be done, and the king, when making a gift, may have a word to say about this.

The king's alienable rights.

Now it must at once be confessed that the charters of this early period seldom suggest any such confusion between political power and ownership as that which we postulate. Still from time to time hints are given to us that should not be ignored. Thus a Kentish king shortly after the middle of the

mægþe forgeaf, ðæt is Wiht ealond and Meanwara mægþe on West Seaxna ðeode.'

[1] Hist. Eccl. iv. c. 13 (ed. Plummer, i. 232).

eighth century gave to the church of Rochester twenty plough-
lands, not only 'with the fields, woods, meadows, pastures,
marshes and waters thereto pertaining,' but also 'with the
tributum which was paid thence to the king[1].' Such a phrase
would hardly be appropriate if the king were giving land of
which he was the absolute owner, land cultivated for him by
his slaves.

A little more light is thrown on the matter by the first
rude specimens of a clause that is to become common in after
times, the clause of immunity. Already in the seventh century
Wulfhere of Mercia, having made a gift of five manses, adds:
'Let this land remain free to all who have it, from all earthly
hardships, known or unknown, except fastness and bridge and
the common host[2].' So in 732 a king of Kent says: 'And no
royal due shall be found in it henceforth, saving such as is
common to all church lands in this Kent[3].' Æthelbald of
Mercia says: 'By my royal power I decree that it be free for
ever from all tribute of secular payments, labours and burdens,
so that the said land may render service to none but Almighty
God and the church[4].' Yet more instructive, if we may rely
upon it, is the foundation charter of Evesham Abbey. Æthelweard has given twelve manses: he then says, 'I decree that
for the future this land be free from all public tribute, purveyance, royal works, military service (*ab omni publico vectigali,
a victu, ab expeditione, ab opere regio*) so that all things in
that place which are valuable and useful may serve the church
of S[t]. Mary, that is to say, the brethren serving [God] there;
save this, that if in the island belonging to the said land there
shall chance to be an unusual supply of mast, the king may

Military service as a burden on land.

---

[1] K. 114 (i. 139); E. 49: 'et cum omni tributo quod regibus inde dabatur.'
So by a deed of A.D. 762, K. 109 (i. 133), B. i. 272, a thegn states that king
Æthelbert gave him a *villa* 'cum tributo illius possidendam' and then proceeds
to give this *villa* to a church 'cum tributo illius.'

[2] E. 4; B. M. Facs. iv. 1: 'et semper liber permaneat omnibus habentibus
ab omnibus duris secularibus, notis et ignotis, praeter arcem et pontem ac
vulgare militiam.'

[3] K. 77 (i. 92); E. 24; B. M. Facs. i. 6: 'Et ius regium in ea deinceps
nullum repperiatur omnino, excepto dumtaxat tale quale generale est in univer-
sis ecclesiasticis terris quae in hac Cantia esse noscuntur.'

[4] K. 90 (i. 108); E. 40: 'Et ut ab omni tributo vectigalium operum onerumque saecularium sit libera in perpetuum, pro mercede aeternae retributionis,
regali potestate decernens statuo; tantum ut deo omnipotenti ex eodem agello
aecclesiasticae servitutis famulatum impendat.'

have pasture for fattening one herd of pigs, but beyond this no pasture shall be set out for any prince or potentate[1].' Now in the first place, these charters speak as though military service is due from land :—I (says the king) declare this land to be free from the 'fyrd,' from the *expeditio*—or—I declare that it is free from all earthly burdens, except military service and the duty of repairing bridge and burh. We are not saying that there is already military tenure, but we do say that already the 'fyrd' is conceived as a burden on land, in so much that the phrase 'This land is—or is not—to be free of military service' has a meaning. But after all, land never fights: men fight. Of what men then is the king speaking when he says that the land is, or is not, free from the *expeditio?* Not of the donees themselves, for they are bishops and monks and serve in no army but God's. Not of the slaves who are on the land, for they are not 'fyrd-worthy.' He is speaking of free men who live on the land; he is declaring that when he has, if so modern a term be suffered, 'attorned' them to the church, they will still have to serve in warfare, or he is de-claring that they will be free even from this duty to the state in order that the land may be the more absolutely at the service of God and His stewards.

The king's *feorm.* Then military service, along with the duty of repairing bridges and fastnesses, belongs to a genus of dues, of which unfortunately we get but a vague description. There are *vectigalia publica, opera regia, onera saecularia,* there is *tributum,* there is *victus.* How much of the information that we get about these matters from later days we may carry back with us to the earliest period it is difficult to say. Apparently the king, the under-king, even the ealdorman, has a certain right of living at the expense of his subjects, of making a progress through the villages and quartering himself, his courtiers, his huntsmen, his dogs and horses upon the folk of the townships, of exacting a 'one night's farm' from this village, a 'two nights' farm' from that. The men who have to bear these exactions may well be free men and free land-

---

[1] K. 56 (i. 64); H. & S. iii. 278; B. i. 171. The charter is of fairly good repute, but nothing that comes from Evesham is beyond suspicion. It is almost impossible to translate these early books without making their language too definite. How, for instance shall we render 'nulli, neque principi, neque praefecto, neque tiranno alicui pascui constituantur'?

owners; still over them the king has certain rights and rights that .he can give away. According to our interpretation of the charters, it is often enough such rights as these that the king is giving when he says that he is giving *terram iuris mei.* He declares, it will be observed, that the land is to be free from *vectigalia* and *opera* to which it has heretofore been subject. But does he mean by this to benefit the occupiers of the soil? No, he has no care whatever to relieve them. Bent on saving his soul, his care is that the land shall be wholly devoted to the service of God. As we understand the matter, whatever *vectigalia* and *opera* the king has hitherto exacted from these men the church will now exact. The king has conveyed what he had to convey, a superiority over free landowners.

It is permissible to doubt whether modern historians have Nature of the *feorm.* fully realized the extent of the rights which the king had over the land of free landowners. In the middle of Ine's laws, which follow each other in no rational order, we suddenly come upon an isolated text, which says this: 'For 10 hides "to foster" 10 vessels of honey, 300 loaves, 12 ambers of Welsh ale, 30 of clear [ale], 2 old [i.e. full grown] oxen or 10 wethers, 10 geese, 20 hens, 10 cheeses, an amber full of butter, 5 salmon, 20 poundsweight of fodder and a hundred eels[1].' The context throws no light upon the sentence; but in truth no sentence in Ine's laws has a context. What is its meaning? We can not but think that this *foster* is the king's *victus*[2]. Once a year from every ten hides he is entitled to this *feorm.* Perhaps it is a 'one night's *feorm*'; for it may be enough to support a king of the seventh century and a modest retinue during twenty-four hours. Still it will be no trifling burden upon the land, even if we suppose the hide to have 120 arable acres or thereabouts. Suppose that the king transfers his right over a single hide to some bishop or abbot, the donee will be entitled to receive from that hide a rent which can not be called insignificant. We dare not argue that this law is a general law for the whole of Wessex. It may refer only to some newly settled and allotted districts. There are other

---

[1] Ine, 70, § 1.

[2] Thorpe, Gloss. s. v. *Foster*, thinks that this law has to do with the fostering of a child. Schmid is inclined to hold that it speaks of a rent payable to a landlord.

hints in these laws of Ine of some large land-settlement, an
allotment of land among great men who have become bound
to bring under cultivation a district theretofore waste[1]. But
it is difficult to dissociate the *foster* of these laws from the
victus of the charters, and, quite apart from this disputable
passage, we have plenty of proof that the king's *victus* was an
incumbrance which pressed heavily upon the lands of free
landowners[2]. If in England the duty of feeding the king as
he journeys through the country developed into a regular
tax or rent this would not stand alone. That duty plays a
considerable part in the Scandinavian law-books, and in the
Denmark of the thirteenth century we may find arrangements
which are very like that set forth in Ine's law. Every hundred
(*herad*), taken as a whole, has to contribute something towards
the king's support. Often it is a round sum of money; but
often it will consist of provisions necessary to maintain the
king's household during a night or two or three nights (*servicium
unius noctis, servicium duarum noctium*). Then the 'service of
two nights' is accurately defined. It consists of, among other
things, 26 salted pigs, 14 live pigs, 16 salted oxen, 16 salted
sheep, 360 fowls, 180 geese, 360 cheeses, corn, malt, fodder,
butter, herrings, stock-fish, pepper and salt. This revenue
stands apart from the revenue derived from the crown lands;
it is regarded as a tax rather than a rent; but it is to this

---

[1] Ine, 64–6: 'He who has 20 hides must show 12 hides of cultivated land if
he wishes to go away. He who has 10 hides shall show 6 hides of cultivated
land. He who has 3 hides let him show one and a half.' The persons
with whom these laws deal are certainly not *ascripti glebae*; they are very great
men. Then we must read c. 63: 'If a gesithcundman go away, then may he
have his reeve with him and his smith and his child's fosterer'; and then c. 68:
'If a gesithcundman be driven off, let him be driven from the dwelling (botle),
not from the set land (naes þaere setene).' The king's gesiths have been taking
up large grants of waste land and putting under-tenants on the soil. These
great folk must not fling up their holdings until they have brought the land into
cultivation. If they do abandon their land, they may take away with them only
three of their dependants. If they are evicted by some adverse claimant this is
not to harm their under-tenants; they are to be driven from the *botl*, that is
from the chief house, but not from the land that they have set out to husbandmen. These last are to enjoy a secure title. We must leave to linguists the
question whether we have rightly understood the difficult *seten*; but these
chapters, together with c. 67, which deals with the relations between these
lords and their husbandmen, seem to point to some great scheme for colonizing
a newly-conquered district.
[2] Kemble, Saxons, i. 294–8; ii. 58.

extent rooted in the soil, that the amount due from each hundred (*herad*) is fixed[1]. There is a great deal to make us think that at a quite early time in England such arrangements as this had been made. If we look at the charters we find that the king is always giving away manses in fives and tens, fifteens and twenties. This symmetry, this prevalence of a decimal system, we take to be artificial; already the manse, or hide, is a fiscal unit, a fraction of a district which has to supply the king with food or with money in lieu of food[2].

Whatever be the origin of the king's *feorm*—and if we find it in the voluntary gifts which yet barbarous Germans make to their kings, we may none the less have to admit that it has been touched by the influence of the Roman *tributum*— it becomes either a rent or a tax. We may call it the one, or we may call it the other, for so long as the recipient of it is the king, the law of the seventh and eighth centuries will hardly be able to tell which it is[3]. The king begins to give it away: in the hands of his donees, in the hands of the churches, it becomes a rent. This is not all, however, that the king has to give, or that the king does give, when he says that he is giving land. That he may be giving away the profits of justice, that he may be giving jurisdiction itself, we shall argue hereafter. But probably he has even in early days yet other things to give, and at any rate in course of time he discovers that such is the case. He can give the right to take toll, he can give market rights[4]. It is by no means impossible that he has forest rights, some general claim to place uncultivated land under his ban, if he would hunt therein, and some general claim to the nobler kinds of fish[5]. Then again, in the eleventh

Tribute and rent.

---

[1] Karl Lehmann, Abhandlungen zur Germanischen Rechtsgeschichte, 1888; Liber Census Daniae, ed. O. Nielsen, 1879.

[2] Cnut's law (II. 62) about this matter seems to imply that in consequence of the immunities lavishly bestowed by his predecessors, the old 'king's *feorm*' was only leviable from lands which were deemed to be the king's lands, but that Cnut's reeves had been demanding that this *feorm* should be supplemented by other lands. The king of his grace forbids them to do this. The old *feorm* has been changed into a rent of crown lands; a vague claim to 'purveyance' is abolished, but will appear again after the Conquest.

[3] In the A.-S. Chron. ann. 991, 1007, 1011, the Danegeld appears as a *gafol*; but this is the common word for a rent paid by a tenant to his landlord.

[4] Kemble, Saxons ii. 73–6.

[5] Already in 749 Æthelbald of Mercia in a general privilege for the churches (H. & S. iii. 386) says, 'Sed nec hoc praetermittendum est, cum necessarium

century we find men owing services to the king which he still
receives rather as king than as landlord, and the sporadic
distribution of these services seems to show that they are not
of modern origin. Such are, for example, the 'inwards' and
the 'averages' which are done by the free men of Cambridgeshire[1]. We are told in a general way that the thegn owes fyrd-
fare, burh-bót and brycg-bót, but that from many lands—the
lands comprised within no privilege, no franchise—'a greater
land-right arises at the king's ban'; for there is the king's
deer-hedge to be made, there are warships to be provided, there
are sea-ward and head-ward[2]. Every increase in the needs
of the state, in the power of the state, gives the king new
rights in the land, consolidates his seignory over the land. If
a fleet be formed to resist the Danes, the king has something
to dispose of, a new immunity for sale. If a geld be levied
to buy off the Danes, the king can sell a freedom from this
tax, or he can tell the monks of S[t]. Edmundsbury that they
may levy the tax from their men and keep it for their own
use[3]. This, we argue, is not a new abuse, a phenomenon which
first appears in the evil feudal time when men began to confuse
imperium with *dominium*, kingship with landlordship, office
with property, tax with rent. On the contrary, we must begin
with confusion. In some of the very earliest land-books that
have come down to us what the king really gives, when he
says that he is giving land, is far rather his kingly superiority
over land and landowners than anything that we dare call
ownership[4].

Mixture of
ownership
and superi-
ority.

Not that this is always the case. Very possible is it that
from the first the king had villages which were peopled mainly
by his theows and læts, and intertribal warfare may have
increased their number. But the charters, for all their apparent precision, will not enable us to distinguish between these
cases and others in which the villages are full of free land-

constat aecclesiis Dei, quia Æthelbaldus Rex, pro expiatione delictorum suorum
et retributione mercedis aeternae, famulis Dei propriam libertatem in fructibus
silvarum agrorumque, sive in caeteris utilitatibus fluminum vel raptura piscium,
habere donavit.'

[1] See above, p. 55.   [2] Rectitudines c. 1 (Schmid, App. III.).
[3] See above, p. 169.
[4] Schröder, Die Franken und ihr Recht, Zeitsch. d. Savigny Stiftung,
iii. 62–82, has argued that, from the first times of the Frankish settlement
onwards, the king has a *Bodenregal*, an *Obereigenthum* over all land.

owners and their slaves. The charters are not engendered by the English facts; they are foreign, ecclesiastical, Roman. By such documents, to our thinking, the king gives what he has to give. In one case it may be a full ownership of a village or of some scattered steads; in another it may be a superiority, which when analyzed will turn out to be a right of exacting supplies of provender from the men of the village; in a third, and perhaps a common case, the same village will contain the *mansi serviles* of the king's slaves and the *mansi ingenuiles* of free landowners. He no more thinks of distinguishing by the words of his charter his governmental power over free men and their land from his ownership of his slaves and the land that they are tilling, than his successor of the eleventh or twelfth century will think of making similar distinctions when he bestows a 'manor' or an 'honour.'

We have been suggesting and shall continue to suggest The king's superiority. that at a very early time, a time beyond which our land-books will not carry us, the king is beginning to discover that the whole land which he rules is in a certain and a profitable sense his land. He can give it away; he can barter it in exchange for spiritual benefits, and this he can do without wronging the free landholders who are in possession of that land, for what he really gives is the dues (it is too early to say the 'service') that they have owed to him and will henceforth owe to his donee. Let us remember that his successors will undoubtedly be able to do this. In a certain sense, Henry II., for example, will have all England to give away. If we were to put an extreme case, we might have to reckon with possible rebellions; but every single hide of England Henry can give without wronging any one. Suppose that C has been holding a tract as the king's tenant in chief by service worth £5 a year, Henry can make a grant of that land to B, and by this grant C will not be wronged. Henceforth C will hold of B, and B of the king. Suppose that, on the occasion of this grant, services worth £2 a year are reserved, then the king has it in his power to grant the land yet once more: to grant it, let us say, to the Abbot of A, who is to hold in frankalmoin; C will not be wronged, B will not be wronged. What the king has done with one hide he can do with every hide in England; piece by piece he can give all England away. We have been suggesting and shall continue to suggest that at a very early time, even in the first days of English Christianity, the king is beginning to discover that he has some such power as that which his successors will exercise. This barbarous chieftain learns that his political sway over the folk involves a proprietary and alienable element of which he can make profit. It involves a right to *feorm* and a right to *wites*. The beef and the cheese and the Welsh ale that he might have levied from a district he invests, if we may so speak, in what he is being taught to regard as the safest and most profitable of all securities. He obtains not only remission of his sins, but also the friendship and aid of bishops and clergy. And so large stretches of land are 'booked' to the churches. It is to be feared that if the England of the sixth century had been visited by modern Englishmen, the Saxon chieftains would have been awakened to a consciousness of their 'booking' powers by offers of gin and rifles.

Book-land and church right.

In its original form and when put to its original purpose the land-book is no mere deed of gift; it is a dedication. Under the sanction of a solemn anathema, a tract of land is devoted to the service of God. A very full power of disposing of it is given to the bishop or the abbot, who is God's servant. As yet the law has none of those subtle ideas which in after ages will enable it to treat him as 'a corporation sole' or as 'a trustee,' nor can the folk-law meddle much with the affairs of God. The bishop or abbot must be able to leave the land to whom he pleases, to institute an heir. Thus 'book-land' stands, as it were, outside the realm of the folk-law. In all probability the folk-law of this early period knows no such thing as testamentary power. Testamentary power can only be created by the words of a book, by an anathema. But laymen are not slow to see that they can make use of this new institution for purposes of their own, which are not always very pious purposes. By a pretext that he is going to construct a minster, a man will obtain a book garnished with the crosses of bishops. One day calling himself an abbot and the next day calling himself a king's thegn, a layman among ecclesiastics, an ecclesiastic among laymen, he will shirk all duties that are owed to state and church. Already Bede complains of this in a wise and famous letter. He advocates a resumption of these inconsiderate and misplaced gifts, and reproves the

prelates for subscribing the books[1]. His letter may have done
good; but laymen still obtained books which authorized them
to hold land 'by church right.' Thus Offa of Mercia gave to
an under-king lands at Sedgebarrow 'in such wise that he
might have them during his life, and in exercise of full power
might leave them to be possessed by church right[2].' There-
upon the *subregulus*, as a modern English lawyer might say,
executed this power of appointment in favour of the church of
Worcester. The same Offa gave land to his thegn Dudda so
that by church right he might enjoy it during his life and
leave it on his death to whom he would[3].

We must wait for a later age before we shall find the
kings freely booking lands to their thegns without any allusion
to ecclesiastical purposes. Indeed it may be said that the
Anglo-Saxon land-book never ceases to be an ecclesiastical
instrument. True that in the tenth century the kings are
booking lands to their thegns with great liberality; true also
that there is no longer any pretence that the land so booked
will go to endow a church; but let us observe these books
and let us not ignore the recitals that they contain. Why
does the king make these grants? He says that it is because
he hopes for an eternal reward in the everlasting mansions.
This has perhaps become an empty phrase: but it has a
history. Also it is needed in order to make the deed a logical
whole. Let us observe the sequence of the clauses:—' Whereas
the fashion of this world passeth away but the joys of heaven
are eternal; therefore I give land to my thegn so that he may
enjoy it during his life and leave it on his death to whomsoever
he pleases, and if any one shall come against this charter may
he perish for ever; I have confirmed this gift with the sign
of Christ's holy cross[4].' Some piety in the harangue (*arenga*)
is necessary in order to lead up to the anathema and the cross;

Book-land and testament.

---

[1] Epistola ad Ecgbertum (ed. Plummer, i. 405).

[2] K. 131 (i. 158).

[3] K. 137 (i. 164); B. M. Facs. i. 10. A few words are illegible, but the land
is given 'in ius ecclesiasticae liberalitatis in perpetuum possid[endam].'

[4] Æthelwulf makes a grant to a thegn, K. 269 (ii. 48), 'pro expiatione
piaculorum meorum et absolutione criminum meorum.' In course of time the
piety of the recitals becomes more and more perfunctory. It becomes a philo-
sophic reflection on the transitoriness of earthly affairs and finally evaporates,
leaving behind some commonplace about the superiority of written over unwritten
testimony.

it justifies the intervention of the bishops, who also will make crosses and thereby will be denouncing the church's ban against any one who violates the charter. And who, we may ask, is likely to violate the charter? The donee's kinsfolk may be tempted to do this if the donee makes use of that testamentary power which has been granted to him (as, for instance, by leaving the land to a church) more especially because it may be very doubtful whether in impeaching such a testament they will not have the folk-law on their side. Such in brief outline is—so we think—the history of book-land. It is land (or rather in many cases a superiority) held by royal privilege[1] under the sanction of the anathema.

§ 2. *Book-land and Folk-land.*

What is folk-land?

With 'book-land' is contrasted 'folk-land.' Therefore of folk-land a few words must be said. What is folk-land? A few years ago the answer that historians gave to this question was this: It is the land of the folk, the land belonging to the folk. Dr Vinogradoff has argued that this is not the right answer[2]. His argument has convinced us; but, as it is still new, we will take leave to repeat it with some few additions of our own.

Folk-land in the texts.

The term 'folk-land' occurs but thrice in our texts. It occurs in one law and in two charters. The one law comes from Edward the Elder[3] and all that it tells us is that folk-land is the great contrast to book-land. Folk-land and book-land seem to cover the whole field of land tenure. Possibly this law tells us also that while a dispute about folk-land will, a dispute about book-land will not, come before the shiremoot:— but we hardly obtain even this information[4]. Then we have the two charters. Of these the earlier is a deed of Æthelbert of Kent dated in 858[5]. The king with the consent of his great men and of the prelates gives to his thegn Wulflaf five plough-lands at Washingwell (*aliquam partem terrae iuris mei*) in exchange for land at Marsham. He declares that the land

---

[1] Bede (ed. Plummer, i. 415): 'ipsas quoque litteras privilegiorum suorum.'
[2] Vinogradoff, Folkland, Eng. Hist. Rev. viii. 1.
[3] Edw. i. 2.   [4] Schmid, p. 575.
[5] K. 281 (ii. 64); B. M. Facs. ii. 33.

at Washingwell is to be free from all burdens save the three usually excepted, the land at Marsham having enjoyed a similar immunity. The boundaries of Washingwell are then stated. On the west it is bounded by the king's folk-land (*cyninges folcland*) which Wighelm and Wulflaf have. So much for the deed itself. On its back there is an endorsement to the following effect : ' This is the land-book for Washingwell that Æthelbert the king granted to Wulflaf his thegn in exchange for an equal amount of other land at Marsham ; the king granted and booked to Wulflaf five sullungs of land at Washingwell for the five sullungs at Marsham and the king made that land at Marsham his folk-land (" did it him to folk-land ") when they had exchanged the lands, save the marshes and the salterns at Faversham and the woods that belong to the salterns.' Now this deed teaches us that there was land which was known as ' the king's folk-land,' and that it was in the occupation of two men called Wighelm and Wulflaf, the latter of whom may well have been the Wulflaf who made an exchange with the king. The endorsement tells us that when the king received the land at Marsham he made it his folk-land, ' he did it him to folk-land.'

The other charter is of greater value. It is the will of the Ealdorman Alfred and comes from some year late in the ninth century[1]. He desires in the first place to state who are the persons to whom he gives his inheritance and his book-land. He then gives somewhat more than 100 hides, including 6 at Lingfield and 10 at Horsley, to his wife for her life, 'with remainder,' as we should say, to their daughter. More than once he calls this daughter ' our common bairn,' thus drawing attention to the fact that she is not merely his daughter, but also his wife's daughter. This is of importance, for in a later clause we hear of a son. 'I give to my son Æthelwald three hides of book-land: two hides on Hwætedune [Waddon], and one at Gatatune [Gatton] and therewith 100 swine, and, if the king will grant him the folk-land with the book-land, then let him have and enjoy it: but if this may not be, then let her [my wife] grant to him whichever she will, either the land at Horsley or the land at Lingfield.' Such are the materials which must provide us with our knowledge of folk-land.

The will of Alfred the Ealdorman.

---

[1] K. 317 (ii. 120); T. 480; B. ii. 195.

We must examine Alfred's will somewhat carefully. The
testator has a wife, a son, a daughter. He leaves the bulk
of his book-land to his wife for life with remainder to his
daughter. For his son he makes a small provision (only three
hides) out of his book-land, but he expresses a wish that the
king will let that son have the folk-land, and, if this wish be
not fulfilled, then that son is to have either ten or else six
hides out of the book-land previously given to the wife and
daughter. We see that, even if he gets these few hides, the
son will obtain but a small part of a handsome fortune. 'If
the king will grant him the folk-land'—this may suggest that
a man's folk-land will not descend to his heir. But another,
and, as it seems to us, a far more probable explanation is open.
The son is 'my son,' the daughter is 'our common bairn.'
May not the son be illegitimate, or may not his legitimacy
be doubtful, for legitimacy is somewhat a matter of degree?
The ealdorman may have contracted a dubious or a morganatic
marriage. We can see that he does not feel called upon to
do very much for this son of his. He expresses a hope that
the king as supreme judge will hold the son to be legitimate,
or sufficiently legitimate to inherit the folk-land, which he
does not endeavour to bequeath.

The king like other persons can have both folk-land, and
book-land. We have just heard of 'the king's folk-land': we
turn to the important deed whereby King Æthelwulf booked
land to himself[1]. Alms, it says, are the most perdurable of
possessions; one ought to minister to the necessities of others
and so make to oneself friends of the mammon of unrighteousness; therefore I King Æthelwulf with the consent and leave
of my bishops and great men have booked to myself twenty
manses so that I may enjoy them and leave them after my
death to whomsoever I please in perpetuity: the land is to
be free from all tribute and the like, save military service
and the repair of bridges. Then the description of the land
thus booked is preceded by the statement: 'These are the
lands which his wise men (*senatores*) conceded to Æthelwulf.'
Now the full meaning of this famous instrument we can not
yet discuss. To put it briefly, our explanation will be that
over his book-land the king will have powers which he will

---

[1] K. 260 (ii. 28); B. ii. 33; B. M. Facs. ii. 30.

not have over his folk-land; in particular he will have that testamentary power which will enable him to become friendly with the mammon of unrighteousness and secure those eternal mansions that he desires. But we have introduced this charter here because, though it says no word of folk-land, it forms an important part of the case of those who contend that folk-land is land belonging to the people[1].

Another weighty argument is derived from the fact that there are but very few charters of the kings which do not in some formula or another profess that many illustrious persons have consented to or have witnessed the making of the deed. We have no desire to detract from the significance of this fact, still we ought to examine our documents with care. Such words as a charter has about 'consent' may occur in two different contexts. They may occur in close connexion with the words of gift, 'the operative words,' as our conveyancers say, or they may occur in the eschatocol, the clause which deals with the execution and attestation of the instrument. If we come across two deeds, one of which tells us how 'I king Æthelwulf with the consent and leave of my bishops and great men give land to a church or a thegn,' while the other says nothing of consent until it tells us how 'This charter was written on such a day *his testibus consentientibus*,' we must not at once treat them as saying the same thing in two different ways.

For this purpose we may divide our charters into three periods. The first begins with the few genuine charters of the seventh century and ends in the reign of Egbert, the second endures until the reign of Edward the Elder, the third until the Norman Conquest. It will be well understood that we draw no hard line; each period has its penumbra; but the years 800 and 900 or 925 may serve to mark very rudely the two limits of the middle period. Now a clause in the body of the deed stating that the gift is made by the consent of the witan is characteristic of this middle period. Any one who wishes to forge a royal land-book of the ninth century should insert this clause; any one who wishes to forge a deed

The consent of the witan.

Consent and witness in the land-books.

---

[1] In K. 1019 (v. 58) there is talk of Offa having booked land to himself, and in K. 1245 (vi. 58) Edgar seems to perform a similar feat without mentioning the consent of the witan, though they attest the deed. See Stubbs, Const. Hist. i. 145.

of the tenth or of the eighth century should think twice before he makes use of it. To be more exact, it becomes a common form under Cenwulf of Mercia and Egbert of Wessex ; it grows very rare under Æthelstan[1]. In the meanwhile it serves as a common form, and it appears in deeds wherein the king says in forcible terms that he is disposing of his land and his inheritance[2]. During the last of our three periods all that is ascribed to the great men whose crosses follow the king's cross is little, if anything, more than the function of witnesses. A deed of Æthelstan's day will end with some such formula as the following : ' this book was written at such a place and time, and its authority was confirmed by the witnesses whose names are written below.' But very often there is no such concluding formula : we have simply the list of witnesses and their crosses, and of each of them it is said that he consented and subscribed. Later in the tenth century the formula which introduces the names of the witnesses will hardly admit that they in any sense confirmed the transaction; it will say merely, ' This book was written on such a day *his testibus consentientibus quorum nomina inferius caraxantur.*' On this will follow the names and crosses; and of each bishop—but not as a general rule of any other witness—it will be said that he has done something for the stability of the deed. To convey this information, the scribe rings the changes on a score of Latin words—*subscripsi, consensi, consolidavi, corroboravi, confirmavi, conscripsi, consignavi, adquievi, praepinxi, praepunxi, praenotavi,* and so forth, thereby showing that he has no very clear notion as to what it really is that the bishop does. But this degradation of what seems to be a formula of assent into a formula of attestation has been noticed by others[3], and it is more to our purpose to examine the charters of the earliest period, for then, if at any time, the folk-land should have appeared in its true character as the land of the people.

Attestation of the earliest books.   Now during our earliest period instruments which contain in conjunction with their operative words any allusion to the

---

[1] From Alfred and Edward the Elder we have hardly enough genuine charters to serve as materials for an induction, but Edward's reign seems the turning point.

[2] A.D. 838, K. 1044 (v. 90): Egbert gives 'aliquantulam terrae partem meae propriae hereditatis...cum consilio et testimonio optimatum meorum.' A.D. 863, K. 1059 (v. 116): Æthelred ' cum consensu ac licentia episcoporum ac principum meorum ' gives ' aliquam partem agri quae ad me rite pertinebat.'

[3] Stubbs, Const. Hist. i. 212.

consent of the great men of the realm are exceedingly rare[1]. A commoner case is that in which the eschatocol says something about consent. We will collect a few examples.

I have confirmed this with the sign of the holy cross with the counsel of Laurence the bishop and of all my *principes* and have requested them to do the like[2].

I have impressed the sign of the holy cross and requested fit and proper witnesses to subscribe[3].

I have confirmed this gift with my own hand and have caused fit and proper witnesses, my companions (*comites*), to confirm and subscribe[4].

This formula, undoubtedly of foreign origin, was common in Kent[5]. From Wessex and the middle of the eighth century, we twice obtain a fuller form.

These things were done in such a year; and that my munificent gift may be the more firmly established (*firmius roboretur*) we have associated with ourselves the fit and proper witnesses and ‘adstipulators’ whose names and descriptions are set forth below to subscribe and confirm this privilege of the aforesaid estate (*praedictae possessionis privilegium*[6]).

More frequently however the document has nothing that can be called a clause of attestation. It simply gives us the names and the crosses of the witnesses. Occasionally over against each name, or each of the most important names, is set some word or phrase describing this witness's act. He has subscribed, or he has consented, or he has consented and subscribed, or perhaps he has confirmed[7].

---

[1] We know of but four specimens earlier than 750. The first is a deed whereby Wulfhere of Mercia makes a grant ‘cum consensu et licentia amicorum et optimatum meorum’: E. 4; B. M. Facs. iv. 1. The second is a deed whereby Hlothar of Kent makes a grant with the consent of Abp Theodore, his (Hlothar's) brother's son Eadric and all the princes; K. 16 (i. 20); B. M. Facs. i. 1. The third, known to us only through a copy, is one by which Æthelbald of Mercia makes a grant ‘cum consensu vel episcoporum vel optimatum meorum’; K. 83 (i. 100). By a fourth deed, K. 27 (i. 30), Eadric grants land ‘cum consensu meorum patriciorum’; but this also we only get from a copy.

[2] K. 1 (i. 1); A.D. 604. Æthelbert for Rochester.

[3] K. 43 (i. 50); B. i. 140: A.D. 697, Wihtræd.—K. 47 (i. 54); E. 17; B. M. Facs. i. 4: Wihtræd.—K. 77 (i. 92); E. 24; B. M. Facs. i. 6: A.D. 732, Æthelbert.—K. 132 (i. 160); E. 54; B. M. Facs. ii. 4: A.D. 778, Egbert.

[4] K. 85 (i. 102); E. 32: Eadbert for Rochester. Of this deed we have but a transcript. The formula of attestation is very curious and may have been distorted either by the original scribe or the copyist.

[5] K. 157 (i. 189), Offa of Mercia uses this eschatocol, but in a Kentish gift.

[6] K. 1006-7 (v. 47-8); B. i. 256-7.   [7] K. 79 (i. 95).

Now we ought not to draw inferences from these phrases
without knowing that in the Latin of this period such words
as *confirmare, corroborare, adstipulari* are the proper words
whereby to describe the act of those who become witnesses to
the execution of a deed[1]. Our kings are making use, though
it is a lax use, of foreign formulas; what is more, they are
adopting the formulas of private deeds. They have no chancellor, as the Frankish kings have, and they do not, as the
Frankish kings do, dispense with that *rogatio testium* which
is one of the usual forms of private law[2]. On the continent of
Europe all this talk about confirmation, corroboration and
consent would by no means imply that the witnesses were
more than witnesses. The line which divides attestation from
participation is really somewhat fine, and though well enough
apprehended by modern lawyers, would not easily be explained
to a barbarian ealdorman. A witness does consent to the
execution of the instrument which he attests, though he may
be utterly ignorant of its import, and, if the law demands that
such an instrument shall be attested, then it may well be said
of the witness that by attesting it he makes it firm, he
confirms it. Until he attested it, it was not a valid instrument[3].
Now we are not saying that the magnates, more especially the
bishops, who attested these ancient charters thought of themselves as mere witnesses. Had that been so, a clause expressing
the consent of the whole body of great men would hardly have
crept into the charters; and it does creep in gradually during
the last half of the eighth century[4]. A similar development

[1] Brunner, Rechtsgeschichte der Röm. u. German. Urkunde, pp. 220–8;
Giry, Manuel de diplomatique, 614. Bede in his famous letter (ed. Plummer,
i. 417) uses the technical *astipulari* to describe the action of the prelates who
set their crosses to the king's charters. It occurs also in a charter of 791,
K. 1015 (v. 53–4). See also K. 691 (iii. 289), 'constipulatores.'

[2] Brunner, op. cit. 158. Dr Brunner thinks that the precedents for A.-S.
charters came direct from Rome rather than from any other quarter (p. 187);
but he fully admits that these charters when compared with foreign instruments
show a certain formlessness.

[3] Under our own law we may conceive a case in which a man would be
compelled to die unwillingly intestate because one of the two people present at
his death-bed capriciously refused to witness a will.

[4] The transition is marked by the following charters.—K. 104, 105, 108, 113,
in these we have the mere rogation of fit and proper witnesses.—K. 114 (a
Kentish deed which Kemble ascribes to 759–765), in this the clause of attestation
speaks of the counsel and consent of the *optimates* and *principes*.—K. 118,
Uhtred of the Hwiccas makes a grant with the consent and licence of Offa king

has been noticed in the charters of the German kings. A clause expressing the consent of the great folk rarely occurs in the Merovingian or the early Carolingian charters, unless they belong to certain exceptional classes. It is said to become common under the weak rule of Lewis the Child; then for a while it becomes rare again, and then once more common under Henry III and Henry IV, though consent and witness are hardly to be distinguished[1].

Perhaps from the first in England the cross of at least one bishop was much to be desired or was almost indispensable, for the anathema which the charter pronounces will be a solemn sentence of excommunication when it comes from a bishop, while it will be at best a pious wish if it comes from the king; and it is well to have the cross of every bishop, so that the breaker of the charter may find himself excommunicated in every diocese. This is not all; we may well believe that from the first the king was more or less bound to consult with his great men before he alienated his land. The notion that land could be alienated at all may not have been very ancient, and the king when giving land away may have been expected to pay some regard to the welfare of his realm[2]. The discovery that he had an alienable superiority over free land and free landowners would sharpen this rule. Some of these early donations are to our minds more like cessions of political power than gifts of land; they make over to bishops and abbots rights which the king has exercised rather as king than as landowner. A wholesome practice grows up which is embodied in the clause that states the consent of the witan,

Function of the witan.

---

of the Mercians and of his (Offa's) bishops and *principes.*—K. 120, the witnesses are described as *condonantes.*—K. 121, 122, (A.D. 774) the clause of attestation says 'cum sacerdotibus et senioribus populi more testium subscribendo.'—K. 131, 'testium ergo et consentientium episcoporum ac principum meorum signa et nomina pro firmitatis stabilimento hic infra notabo.'—A clause of this kind becomes common with Offa, see K. 134, 137, 138, 148, 151, but occasionally there are relapses and the signatories merely appear as 'fit and proper' or 'religious' witnesses. But it is not until after 800 that, save as a rare exception, the consent of the magnates is brought into connexion with the operative words.

[1] Bresslau, Urkundenlehre, i. 697.

[2] Bede's letter to Egbert (ed. Plummer, i. 405) and his account of Benedict Biscop (ib. 364) show that it was expected of the king that he should provide land for young warriors of noble race; but no word implies that the land out of which the provision was to be made was 'folk-land,' nor is it clear that the young warrior was to have a book.

and, even when this clause has disappeared, still it is in the presence and with the witness of his councillors that the king makes his grants. This is no purely English phenomenon. When a Norman duke hands his charter to be roborated and confirmed by his *fideles*, we do not infer that he is disposing of land that is not his[1]. But it is very remarkable that in the earliest English charters the consent of an overlord is treated as a far more serious thing than the consent of the nobles[2].

The king and the people's land.

Of some value though this 'constitutional check' may have been, we can not regard it as a relic of a time when there was land which in any accurate sense of the term was owned by the people. The recorded action of the witan in relation to the king's grants does not become more prominent, it becomes less prominent, as we go backwards and reach the heptarchic days. But that is not all. Is it not marvellous that there should be land owned by the people and yet that we should have to discover this momentous fact from a few casual phrases occurring in three documents of the ninth and tenth centuries? Are we to suppose that whenever the king is giving away land, this land is the land of the people? Why do not the charters say so? Repeatedly the king speaks of the land that he gives as ' my land' (*terram iuris mei*), and this too in charters which state that the witan give their consent to the grant. Never by any chance does a scribe slip into any such phrase as *terram gentis meae, terram gentis Merciorum* or the like. And how came it about that from the very earliest time the king could devote the people's land to the salvation of his own peculiar soul? But, it will be said, no doubt the king had private estates besides having a power over ' the unallotted lands of the nation,' and those private estates he could give away as he pleased.

---

[1] See William's charter for Fécamp, Neustria Pia, p. 224.

[2] A.D. 692–3, K. 35 (i. 39); B. M. Facs. i. 2: a grant by ' Hodilredus parens Sebbi...cum ipsius consensu'; ' ego Sebbi rex Eastsaxonorum pro confirmatione subscripsi.'—A.D. 704, K. 52 (i. 59); B. M. Facs. i. 3: 'Ego Sueabræd rex Eastsaxonorum et ego Pæogthath cum licentia Ædelredi regis.'—A.D. 706, K. 56 (i. 64), 'Ego Æthiluueard subregulus...consentiente Coenredo rege Merciorum.'—A.D. 721–46, K. 91 (i. 109), Æthelbald of Mercia attests a lease made by the bishop of Worcester.—A.D. 759, K. 105 (i. 128); B. M. Facs. ii. 2: three brothers, each of whom is a *regulus*, make a gift 'cum licentia et permissione Regis Offan Merciorum.'—A.D. 767, 770, K. 117–8 (i. 144–5): two gifts by Uhtred, *regulus* of the Hwiccas, 'cum consensu et licentia Offani Regis Merciorum.'—A.D. 791? K. 1016 (v. 54): 'Ego Aldwlfus dux Suð-Saxonum...cum consensu et licentia Offae regis Merciorum.'

But then, how are we to distinguish between those charters whereby he disposed of his own and those whereby he disposed of national lands? The formula which expresses the consent of the wise will certainly not serve our turn. It leads, as we have seen, to a distinction between different ages, not to a classification of the various charters of one and the same king.

Some historians have supposed that at the outset there was a clear distinction between the king's private estates and those national lands which were becoming the domains of the crown. Now a vague distinction between what belonged to the king as king and what belonged to him—if we may use so modern a phrase—in his private capacity, we may admit, while at the same time we gravely doubt whether the language or the thought of the eighth or ninth century had any forms in which this distinction could be precisely expressed. Even within the ecclesiastical sphere, where traditions of Roman law may have lingered and where dead saints presented themselves as persons capable of acquiring land, it was by no means easy to distinguish the bishop's property from his church's property. We may find a deed whereby some king for the love of God or the salvation of his soul gives land to a certain bishop, and states in strong, clear words that the donee is to have the most absolute power of giving and selling and even, for this sometimes occurs, of bequeathing the land[1]. We shall probably believe that the king intends that this land shall go to increase the territory of the church, and yet we dare not make the bishop either 'a trustee' or 'a corporation sole.'

As to the king, it would be on his death that the necessity of drawing some distinction between his two capacities would first present itself. Perhaps a brother of his would be elected to the kingdom and his children would be passed by. Clearly this brother should have those lands which have supplied the king with the main part of his revenue, and yet it would be hard that the dead man's children should be portionless. However, we may strongly suspect that in the earliest time cases of this nature were settled as they arose without the establishment of any general rule, and that even on the eve of the Norman Conquest no definite classification of the king's estates had been framed. We dare not expect the rule to be more definite than

King's land and crown land.

Fate of the king's land on his death.

[1] K. 113 (i. 137).

that which settled the title to the kingship, and how exceedingly indefinite the latter was the historians of our constitution have explained. Hereditary and elective elements were mixed up in the title; we can define neither the one nor the other. That 'superiority' over all the land of his kingdom of which we have spoken above, though it might be alienated piecemeal among the living, would pass from the dead king to his elected successor. On the other hand, some kings were careful to have certain lands booked to themselves and to obtain from their nobles 'an express power of testamentary appointment.' But very possibly there was a wide fringe of disputable matter. King Alfred's will, with all that he says about what had been done by himself, his father and his brothers, seems to tell us that a prudent king would obtain the consent of his councillors to any disposition that he made of land that was in any sort his. Also it seems to bear witness to a strong feeling that the reigning king should enjoy at any rate the bulk of the lands that his predecessor had enjoyed[1].

The new king and the old king's heir.

In one of his charters Æthelred the Unready is made to tell a long and curious story[2]:—' My father, king Edgar, gave certain lands to the minster at Abingdon. On his death the wise men elected as king my brother Edward, and put me in possession of the lands which belonged to the king's sons. Among these were the lands given to Abingdon; they were forcibly taken from the monks. Whether this was lawful or unlawful those wise men know best. Then my brother Edward died and I became possessed, not only of the lands which belonged to the king's sons, but also of the royal lands. I do not wish to incur my father's curse, and therefore I intend to substitute for his gift a compensation out of my own proper inheritance. The land that I am now going to dispose of I acquired by gift from certain persons whose names I state.'—We seem to see here

---

[1] K. 314 (ii. 112); 1067 (v. 127); Liber de Hyda, 57. On the death of Æthelbald, two of his sons, Æthelred and Alfred, seem to have made over the lands which had been devised to them by their father to Æthelbert, the reigning king, so that he might enjoy them during his life. Then again, on Æthelbert's death, Alfred would not insist upon a partition but allowed his share to remain in the possession of Æthelred, the reigning king. See also Eadred's will, Liber de Hyda, 153 ; he seems to have a good deal of land of which he can dispose freely.

[2] K. 1312 (vi. 172).

three kinds of land, the *regales terrae* which pass from king to king, the lands 'entailed,' if we may use that term, on the king's family (*regii pueri*), and lands which come to a king by way of gift or the like and constitute his *propria hereditas*. But the wise men seem to have violated three solemn books which they themselves or their predecessors had attested, and we can but say with king Æthelred '*quam rem si iuste aut iniuste fecerint ipsi sciant*[1].' There can be but little law about such matters so long as the title to the kingship is indefinable[2].

This distinction between the lands which would pass from king to king and the lands which would pass from the king to his heirs or to his devisees may have been complicated with another distinction. Domesday Book tells us that some, but by no means all, of the lands held by the Confessor were and had always been free of geld, and this freedom from taxation may imply other immunities. It is possible that, as in later times, certain 'ancient demesnes of the crown' already stood outside the national system of taxation, justice and police, that the ealdorman of the shire and the shire-moot had no jurisdiction over them, and that they were administered by reeves yet more personally dependent on the king than was the shire-reeve. It is possible, however, that the two distinctions cut each other, for when the king booked land to himself he, at all events on some occasions, inserted in the charter a clause of immunity, the very object of which was to put the land outside the general, national system. To this distinction the famous exchange which Æthelbert effected with his thegn Wulflaf may point. It says that when, instead of Washingwell, the king accepted Marsham, 'he did it him to folk-land.' The land at Marsham was no longer to enjoy that immunity which it had enjoyed while it was in the hands of the thegn, it was to come under the sway of the sheriff and of the national courts. However, it is much easier for us to dream dreams about such a transaction than to discover the truth. *Ancient demesne and its immunity.*

If the folk-land was the land of the people and if the king when he booked land to a church or a thegn was usually booking *Rights of individuals in national land.*

---

[1] The violated books are in Chron. Abingd. i. 314, 317, 334.

[2] Were it possible for us to say that the kingship was elective, this would be but a beginning of difficulties. For example, we should raise a question which in all probability has no answer, were we to ask whether a majority could bind a minority.

folk-land and converting it into book-land, how are we to think of the land that still is folk-land? Is it land that has not yet been brought into cultivation; is it land in which no proprietary interests, save that of the folk, exist? Now we are far from saying that the king never grants land that is waste and void of inhabitants; but it is plain enough that this is not the common case. The charter deals in the first instance with manses, *villae*, *vici*, houses, túns, with cultivated fields and meadows. Waste land (it may be) is given in large quantities, but merely as appurtenant to the profitable core of the gift. We see too that individual men have rights in the folk-land; Alfred the ealdorman has folk-land and hopes that on his death it will pass to his son; King Æthelbert has folk-land and it is occupied by Wighelm and Wulflaf; King Edward the Elder supposes that the title to folk-land may be in dispute between two persons and that this dispute will come before the sheriff. What then the folk owns, if it owns anything at all, is not (if we may introduce such feudal terms) 'land in demesne' but 'land in service,' in other words, a superiority or seignory over land. We must add that it is a superiority over free men and over men who have titles that can be the subject of law-suits in the county court. And now we must ask, What profit does the nation get out of this superiority? Shall we say that the *tributum*, the *vectigal* paid to the king is to be regarded as rent paid to the nation, that the *opera regia*, the *victus*, the *pastus*, are services rendered by the tenant to the people, or shall we say that the folk's right over this land is proved by its serving as the fund whereon the king can draw when he desires to save his soul? Then, if on the other hand we make the tillers of the folk-land mere tenants at will, there will be little room left for any landowners, for any 'peasant proprietors.' To meet this difficulty it has been supposed that, at all events at a remote time, there was much land that was neither folk-land nor book-land. The allotments which the original settlers received were neither folk-land nor book-land.

The *alod*.   In order to describe those allotments the words *alod* and *ethel* have been used, and other terms, such as 'family land' and 'heir land,' have been invented. But in the laws and the charters we do not meet with these phrases. The law of Edward the Elder seems to set before us book-land and folk-land as exhausting the kinds of land. 'He who deforces any one of his right, be it in book-land, be it in 'folk-land' must pay a penalty. It is difficult to believe that this law says nothing of one very common kind of land, still more difficult to believe that already in the first half of the ninth century the amount of the so-called *alod*, *ethel*, or 'heir-land,' had become so small that it might be neglected. So far as we can see, book-land from first to last was only held by the churches and by very great men. The books that we have, more especially the later books, are with hardly any exceptions furnished with clauses of immunity, clauses which put the land outside the national system of police, and, as we think, of justice also. It is not to be imagined for one moment that the numerous *liberi homines* who even in the Conqueror's reign held land in Essex and East Anglia had books. To say that book-land had consumed the ancient *alod* or *ethel*, is in truth to say that all land was privileged.

We turn once more to Edward's law. Land, it would seem, *Book-land* is either book-land or folk-land. Book-land is land held by *and privi-* *lege.* book, by a royal and ecclesiastical *privilegium*. Folk-land is land held without book, by unwritten title, by the folk-law. 'Folk-land' is the term which modern historians have rejected in favour of the outlandish *alod*. The holder of folk-land is a free landowner, though at an early date the king discovers that over him and his land there exists an alienable superiority. Partly by alienations of this superiority, partly perhaps by gifts of land of which the king is himself the owner, book-land is created.

Edward's law speaks as though it were dealing with two *Kinds of* different kinds of land. But really it is dealing with two *land and* *kinds of* different kinds of title. We, and even our statutes, habitually *right.* speak of freehold land, copyhold land, leasehold land, yet we know that the same piece of land may be at one and the same time freehold, copyhold and leasehold. All land is freehold land; every rood has its freeholder. Bracton habitually spoke of land held by frankalmoin, land held by knight's service, land held in socage, but he knew well enough that a single acre might be held at one and the same time by many different tenures. Just so, we take it, the same land might be both book-land and folk-land, the book-land of the minster, the folk-land of the free men who were holding—not indeed 'of'—but still 'under' the minster. They or their ancestors had held under the king, but the king had booked their land (which also in a certain sense was his land) to a church. The mental effort, the abstraction,

that would be required of us were we to speak of various
'estates, rights and titles,' we try to avoid by speaking as
though the distinction that was to be indicated were a distinction between various material things, and as though a freehold
or copyhold quality were, like fertility or sterility, an attribute
of the soil.   Even so abstract a term as 'estate' is soon debased
by the vulgar mouth: estates are ploughed; men 'shoot over'
their estates.   'Book-land' is a briefer term than 'land held by
book-right'; 'folk-land' is a briefer term than 'land held by
folk-right.'   The same piece of land may be held by book-right
and by folk-right; it may be book-land and folk-land too.

And now we must turn to consider another element in the
king's alienable superiority.   We must speak of jurisdiction.

§ 3.   *Sake and Soke.*

Import-
ance of
seignorial
justice. Of all the phenomena of feudalism none seems more essential
than seignorial justice.   In times gone by English lawyers and
historians have been apt to treat it lightly and to concentrate
their attention on military tenure.   For them 'the introduction
of the military tenures' has been 'the establishment of the
feudal system.'   But when compared with seignorial justice,
military tenure is a superficial matter, one out of many effects
rather than a deep-seated cause.   Seignorial justice is a
deep-seated cause of many effects, a principle which when once
introduced is capable of transfiguring a nation.   Of the origin
and antiquity of this principle, however, some even of our most
illustrious historians have spoken with great hesitation and
therefore we shall spend some time in examining the texts which
reveal what can be known about it, admitting once for all that
they leave much room for differences of opinion.

Theory of
the modern
origin of
seignorial
justice. Since the doctrine to which we have come would trace
seignorial justice back to a remote time, we shall do well to
state at the outset an extreme version of the opposite doctrine,
a version which has been elaborately set forth in a learned and
spirited essay[1].—On the eve of the battle of Hastings a seignorial court was still a new thing in England.   It was a Norman

[1] Adams, The Anglo-Saxon Courts of Law (Essays in Anglo-Saxon Law,
p. 1).   Hallam, Middle Ages (ed. 1837), vol. ii. p. 416, says that of the right of
territorial jurisdiction 'we meet frequent instances in the laws and records of

precursor of the Norman Conquest. England owes it to Edward the Confessor, who was 'half-Norman by birth and wholly Norman by education and sympathies.' It came to us with 'a new theory of constitutional law.' From the reign of no older king can any evidence be produced of the existence—at any rate of the legalized existence—of private courts. True, there are charters that give to the holders of great estates the profits of jurisdiction; but a grant of the profits of jurisdiction is one thing, jurisdiction itself is another. True, that one man might have *soke* over another, but this does not mean that he had jurisdiction; at the most it means that he was entitled to the profits of justice, to wites, to fines and amercements. 'No instance can be found before the Norman times in which *sócn* means jurisdiction. *Sócn* had a technical meaning of its own which is always rigorously observed. The idea of jurisdiction, on the other hand, was expressed by an equally technical word, the meaning of which is also rigorously observed. This is *sacu*, a word which has strangely vanished from our legal vocabulary, but is still preserved, even in its technical sense, by the German *sache*[1].'

Now it will not be disputed that in Domesday Book and the Leges Henrici this distinction is obliterated. *Soke* means jurisdiction and '*sake* and *soke*' is but a pleonastic phrase, which means no more than *soke*[2]. Nor is it disputable that on the vigil of the Conquest a great deal of jurisdiction was wielded by the lords. Not a few of the 'hundreds' were in private hands, and, apart from hundredal jurisdiction, a lord might have and often had sake and soke over his own lands. It is not denied that Edward the Confessor had freely granted to churches and other lords large rights of justice,—not merely rights to the profits of jurisdiction, but jurisdiction itself. The question is whether what he did was new. *Sake and soke in the Norman age.*

For one moment longer we may dwell on the indisputable *The Confessor's writs.*

the Anglo-Saxons, though not in those of early date.' The one charter older than Edward the Confessor that he cites is one of the Croyland forgeries. Kemble's opinion seems to have fluctuated; Saxons, i. 177 note, ii. 397, Cod. Dipl. i. xliv–xlvii. K. Maurer, Krit. Ueberschau, ii. 57, thinks that the existence of the private court is proved for Cnut's reign, but not for any earlier time. Dr Stubbs, Const. Hist. i. 119, seems to doubt whether it can be traced far beyond the days of Cnut. Zinkeisen, Die Anfänge der Lehngerichtsbarkeit in England (1893, a Berlin doctoral dissertation), criticizes Mr Adams's theory.

[1] Essays, pp. 43–4. [2] See above, p. 84.

17—2

fact that he dealt out jurisdictional rights with a lavish hand. This we gather, not so much from his Latin land-books, as from English writs in which he announces to the bishop, earl, sheriff and great men of a county that he has given land in that county to some church 'with sake and soke and toll and team'; sometimes he adds 'with infangennethef, grithbrice, foresteal, hamsocn, flymena-fyrmth,' and so forth. Sometimes the donees are to have these rights in all their own lands. Sometimes he gives them the hundredal jurisdiction over lands that are not their own. Thus to S^t. Benet of Ramsey he gives soken over all the men in a hundred and a half—over all the men who are 'moot-worthy, fyrd-worthy, and fold-worthy,' whosesoever men they may be: that is to say (as we understand it) he gives a jurisdiction over all the free men of the district, the men who attend the moots, who attend the host and who are not compelled by any *soca faldae* to send their sheep to a seignorial fold, and this although those men be bound to S^t. Benet neither by tenure nor by personal commendation[1]. Again, he concedes that the donee's tenants shall be quit of shires and hundreds[2]. Again, he gives the favoured church taxational power: whenever the king takes a geld, be it army-geld, or ship-geld, the monks may impose a similar tax upon the township and keep the proceeds to their own use[3]. In short, it seems not too much to say that any delegation and appropriation of justice of which our Norman kings were guilty had an ample warrant in the practice of S^t. Edward.

Cnut's practice.

Now the theory which would make him an innovator in this matter receives a rude shock from a writ of Cnut[4]. The king announces that the Archbishop of Canterbury is to be worthy throughout his lands of his sake and soke and grithbrice, hamsocn, foresteal, infangennethef and flymena-fyrmth. Until

---

[1] K. 853 (iv. 208); E. 343.

[2] The clearest instance is in the Waltham charter, K. 813 (iv. 154), but some details of this are not beyond suspicion. See also the writs for Westminster, K. 828 (iv. 191), 857 (iv. 213); Ordn. Facs. vol. ii. pl. 9.

[3] Charter for S^t. Edmund's, K. 1346 (vi. 205). See the account of Bury S^t. Edmunds in D. B. ii. 372: 'et quando in hundreto solvitur ad geltum 1 lib. tunc inde exeunt 60 den. ad victum monachorum.'

[4] First printed from a copy in the MacDurnan Gospels by J. O. Westwood in Palaeographia Sacra, with a facsimile, plate 11. Accepted by Kemble and printed by him in Archaeological Journal, xiv. 61; Earle, 232; Freeman, Norman Conquest, ii. 52.

the genuineness of this writ, which does not stand quite alone[1], be disproved, the charge that has been brought against Edward fails. He was but following in the steps of the great Dane, though it may be that he rushed forward where his predecessor had trod cautiously.

Having seen what Cnut could do upon occasion, we turn to Cnut's law. the famous passage in his dooms which declares what 'rights the king has over all men[2].' In Wessex and Mercia (in the Danelaw the list is somewhat different) he has hamsocn, foresteal, flymena-fyrmth and fyrd-wite 'unless he will honour a man yet further and grant him this worship.' Now if we had not before us his writ for the archbishop, we might perhaps argue that this law merely decreed that the profits of certain pleas were not to be covered by the 'farms' paid to the king by the sheriffs and other national officers. But in the writ we see that Cnut allows to the archbishop just the excepted rights, just that 'worship' which men are not to have as a general rule. Nor surely can we say that what is conceded is, not jurisdiction itself, but merely the profits of jurisdiction. The archbishop is to have *sake* as well as *soke*, and those who have contended for the strictest interpretation of royal grants have not contended that the former of these words can mean anything but 'causes,' 'pleas,' 'jurisdiction.' Therefore when it is interpreted by the aid of this writ, Cnut's law seems to imply that private jurisdiction is a common thing. The king is already compelled to protest that there are certain pleas of the crown that are not covered by vague and general words.

Now express grants of *sake* and *soke* first become apparent The book to us in documents of a certain class, a class that we do not writ. get before the last years of the tenth century. It is necessary therefore that we should make a short digression into the region of 'diplomatics.' The instruments of the Confessor's reign, and we may add of the Norman reigns, which we loosely call royal charters or royal land-books divide themselves somewhat easily into two main classes, which we will call respectively (1) charters and (2) writs. These names are not very happy, still they are

---

[1] See the writ for S^t. Paul's, K. 1319 (vi. 183). Mr Adams (p. 44) stigmatizes this as an evident forgery; but the reasons for this severe judgment are not apparent. See also K. 1321 (vi. 190), and the Latin writ of Harthacnut K. 1330 (vi. 192), which may have a genuine basis.

[2] Cnut, ii. 12 (Schmid, p. 276).

the best that occur to us. If we have regard to the form of the
instrument, the distinction is evident. The charter is with rare
exceptions in Latin. It begins with an invocation of the Triune
God or perhaps with a sacred monogram. On the other hand,
there is no address to mortal men; there is no salutation. There
follow a pious *arenga* setting forth how good a thing it is to
make gifts, how desirable it is, since men are very wicked, that
transactions should be put into writing. Then the king states
that he gives, or has given, or will give—the use of the future
tense is not uncommon—certain land to a certain person. Then
comes a clause which we shall hereafter call 'the clause of
immunity':—the land is to be free from certain burdens. Then
comes the anathema or damnatory clause, threatening all
breakers of the charter with excommunication here and torment
hereafter. Then in the charters of the time before the Conquest
the boundaries of the land are described in English. Then
comes the sign of the cross touched by the king's hand and
the crosses of the witan or nobles who 'attest' or 'attest and
consent to' the grant. In the writ all is otherwise. In the
Confessor's day it is usually, in the Norman reigns it is sometimes, an English document. It begins, not with an invocation,
but with a salutation;—the king greets his subjects or some
class of his subjects: King Edward greets 'Herman bishop and
Harold earl and all my thegns in Dorset,' or 'Leofwin bishop
and Edwin earl and all my thegns in Staffordshire':—and then
he tells them something. He tells them that he has granted
lands or liberties to a certain person. There follows a command
or a threat—'I command and firmly enjoin that none shall
disturb the grantee,' 'I will not suffer that any man wrong the
grantee.' The boundaries are not described. There is seldom
any curse. The king makes no cross. If any witnesses are
mentioned, they are few and they do not make crosses.

Differences
between
book and
writ. Now these formal differences correspond more or less
exactly to a substantial difference. As every modern lawyer
knows, a written document may stand in one of two relations
to a legal transaction. On the one hand it may itself be the
transaction: that is to say, the act of signing, or of signing and
delivering, the document may be the act by which certain
rights are created or transferred. On the other hand, the
instrument may be but evidence of the transaction. Perhaps
the law may say that of such a transaction it will receive no

evidence save a document written and signed; perhaps it may
say that the testimony of documents is not to be contradicted
by word of mouth; but still the document is only evidence,
though it may be incontrovertible evidence, of the transaction;
the transaction may have been complete before the document
was signed[1]. This material distinction is likely to express
itself in points of form; for instance, such a phrase as 'I
hereby give' is natural in the one case; such a phrase as
'Know all men by this writing that I have given' is appropriate
in the other. Instruments of both kinds were well enough
known in the Frankish kingdom; their history has been traced
back into the history of Roman conveyancing[2]. It would be
out of place were we here to discuss the question whether the
Anglo-Saxon land-book was a dispositive or merely an evidential
document; suffice it to say that with rare exceptions the instruments that are of earlier date than the Confessor's reign are in
form charters and not writs. On the other hand, the documents
of the Angevin kings which treat of gifts of lands and liberties,
though we call them charters, are in form (if we adopt the
classification here made) not charters but writs. In form they
are evidential rather than dispositive; they are addressed to
certain persons—all the king's lieges or a class of the lieges—
bidding them take notice that the king has done something,
has given lands, and then adding some command or some
threat. This command or threat makes them more than
evidential documents; the *Sciatis me dedisse* is followed by a
Quare volo et firmiter praecipio; it is not for no purpose that
the king informs his officers or his subjects of his having made
a gift; still in form they are letters, open letters, 'letters
patent,' and the points of difference between the Angevin
charter and the Angevin 'letters patent' (strictly and properly
so called) are few, technical and unimportant when compared
with the points of difference which mark off these two classes
of documents from the ancient land-book[3]. In short before

---

[1] Thus if a statute requires written and signed evidence of an agreement, a
letter in which the writer says, 'True, I made such and such an agreement, but
I am not going to keep it,' may be evidence enough; see *Bailey* v. *Sweeting*,
9 C. B. N. S. 843.

[2] Brunner, Carta und Notitia (Commentationes in honorem T. Mommsen);
Brunner, Zur Rechtsgeschichte der Röm. u. Germ. Urkunde.

[3] Both the Angevin charter and the Angevin letters patent are in what we
call 'writ-form.' The main formal difference is that the charter professes to be

the end of the twelfth century, the writ-form or letter-form with its salutation, its 'Know ye,' its air of conveying information coupled with commands, has entirely supplanted the true charter-form with its dispositive words and its air of not merely witnessing, but actually being, a gift of land.

Anglo-Saxon writs.

But to represent this as a contrast between English instruments and Norman or French instruments would be a mistake. In the first place, we have a few documents in writ-form that are older than the days of the Norman-hearted Edward. As already said, we have a writ from Cnut and it has all those features of Edward's writs which have been considered distinctively foreign. We have another writ from the same king. The king addresses Archbishop Lyfing, Abbot Ælfmær, Æthelric the shireman 'and all my thegns twelvehinde and twihinde.' He tells them that he has confirmed the archbishop's liberties and threatens with the pains of hell any one who infringes them[1]. We have a writ from Æthelred the Unready, and a remarkable writ it is. He addresses Ælfric the ealdorman, Wulfmær and Æthelweard and all the thegns in Hampshire and tells them how he has confirmed the liberties of bishop Ælfheah and how large tracts of land are to be reckoned as but one hide—an early example of 'beneficial hidation[2].' Secondly, the solemn charter with its invocation, its pious harangue, its dispositive words, its religious sanction, its numerous crosses, its crowd of attesting and consenting witnesses, was in use in Normandy before and after the conquest of England. Thirdly, the Norman kings of England used it upon occasion. Much they did by writ. The vast tracts of land that they had at their disposal would naturally favour the conciser form; but some of the religious houses thought it well to obtain genuine land-books of the old English, and (we must add) of the old Frankish type. The king's seal was not good enough for them; they would have the king's cross and the crosses of his wife, sons, prelates and barons. The ultimately complete victory of what we have called the writ-form over what we have called the charter-form may perhaps be rightly described as a result of the Conquest,

witnessed by a number of the king's councillors, while *Teste Meipso* does for letters patent. This distinction is coming to the front about the year 1200.

[1] K. 731 (iv. 9); T. 308.

[2] K. 642 (iii. 203); compare D. B. i. 41.

an outcome, that is, of the strong monarchy founded by William of Normandy and consolidated by Henry of Anjou, but it can not be rightly described as the victory of a French form over an English form; and a very similar change was taking place in the chancery of the French kings[1].

We may say then that the appearance of words clearly and indisputably conceding jurisdictional rights is contemporaneous with the appearance of a new class of diplomata, namely royal writs as contrasted with royal charters or land-books. We may add that it is contemporaneous with the appearance of royal diplomata couched in the vernacular language. This

Sake and soke appear when writs appear.

---

[1] The Conqueror's charter for Exeter reproduced in Ordnance Facsimiles, vol. ii. is a fine specimen of the solemn charters referred to above. A considerable number of specimens, genuine and spurious (for our present purpose a forgery is almost as valuable as a true charter), will be found in the Monasticon, e.g. i. 174, Rufus for Rochester; i. 266, Rufus for Bath; ii. 109–111, 126, Henry I. for Abingdon; i. 163, Henry I. for Rochester; ii. 65–6, Henry I. for Evesham; ii. 267, Henry I. for Bath; ii. 539, Henry I. for Exeter; iii. 448, Henry I. for Malvern; vi. (1) 247, Henry I. for Merton; iii. 406, Stephen for Eye. Nor was this solemn form employed only by kings:—See Monast. ii. 385-6, Earl Hugh for Chester; iii. 404, Robert Malet for Eye; v. 121, Hugh de la Val for Pontefract; v. 167, William of Mortain for Montacute; v. 190, Simon of Senlis for S[t]. Andrew Northampton; v. 247, Stephen of Boulogne for Furness; v. 316, Richard Earl of Exeter for Quarr; v. 628, Ranulf of Chester for Pulton. As to Normandy, see the charters in the Neustria Pia and the Gallia Christiana. A charter of Henry II. for Fontenay recites a charter by which the ancestors of Jordan Tesson founded the abbey with the consent of Duke William, also a charter of Duke William, 'quae cartae crucibus sunt signatae secundum antiquam consuetudinem'; Neustria Pia, p. 80; Gallia Christiana, xi. Ap. col. 82. It is probable that during the Norman reigns the king's cross was considered more valuable even than the king's seal; Monast. iv. p. 18, Henry I. says, 'hanc donationem confirmo ego Henricus rex et astipulatione sanctae crucis et appositione sigilli mei'; Ibid. ii. 385-6, Earl Hugh confirms a gift 'non solum sigillo meo sed etiam sigillo Dei omnipotentis, id est, signo sanctae crucis.' It is not implied in our text that every specimen of each of the two forms of instrument that we have mentioned will always display all the characteristics that have been noticed. There is no reason, for example, why in a solemn charter the king should not speak in the past tense of the act of gift, and as a matter of fact he does so in some of the Anglo-Saxon books, while, on the other hand, an instrument which begins with a salutation may well have the words of gift in the present tense (this is by no means uncommon in Anglo-Norman documents); nor of course is it necessary that an instrument in writ-form should be authenticated by a seal instead of a cross. Again, a solemn charter with crosses and pious recitals may begin with a salutation. We merely point out that the diplomata of Edward the Confessor and his Norman successors tend to conform to two distinct types. As to this matter see the remarks of Hickes, Dissertatio Epistolaris, p. 77; Hardy, Introduction to Charter Rolls, xiv., xxxvi.

may well lead us to two speculations. In the first place, is it not very possible that many ancient writs have been lost? The writ was a far less solemn instrument than the land-book, and it is by no means certain that the writs of the Confessor were intended to serve as title-deeds or to come to the custody of those for whose benefit they were issued. King Edward greets the bishop of London, Earl Harold, the sheriff and all the thegns of Middlesex and tells them how he has given land to S^t. Peter and the monks of Westminster, and how he wills that they enjoy their sake and soke. The original document is presented to the bishop, the earl, or the sheriff (to all of them perhaps as they sit in their shire moot) and we can not be certain that after this the monks ought to have that document in their possession, that it ought not to be kept by the sheriff, or perhaps returned to the king with an indorsement expressive of obedience. Many hundred writs must King William have issued in favour of his barons—this is plain from Domesday Book—and what would we not give for a dozen of them? Secondly, it is well worth notice that 'sake and soke' begin to appear so soon as royal diplomata written in English become common, and when we observe the formulas which enshrine these words we find some difficulty in believing that such formulas are new or foreign. Let us listen to one.

> saca and socne
> toll and team
> griðbrice and hamsocne
> and foresteal
> and alle oðre gerihte
> inne tid and ut of tide
> binnan burh and butan burh
> on stræte and of stræte.

Surely this alliteration and this rude rhythm tell us that the clause has long been fashioning itself in the minds and mouths of the people and is no piece of a new-fangled ' chancery-style[1].' And one other remark about language will occur to us. In many respects the law Latin of the middle ages went on becoming a better and better language until, in the thirteenth century, it became a very good, useful and accurate form of

---

[1] The curious formula, Schmid, App. XI., already has ' ne sace ne socne.' This seems to suppose that it is a common thing for a man to have sake and soke over his land.

speech. But it gained this excellence by frankly renouncing all attempts after classicality, all thought of the golden or the silver age, and by freely borrowing from English whatever words it wanted and making them Latin by a suffix. The Latin of the Anglo-Saxon land-books is for all practical purposes a far worse language, just because it strives to be far better. It wanted to be good Latin, and even at times good Greek. The scribe of the ninth or tenth century would have been shocked by such words as *tainus, dreinus, smalemannus, sochemannus* which enabled his successors to say precisely what they wanted. He gives us *provincia* instead of *scira, satrapes* instead of *aldermanni*, and we read of *tributum* and *census* when we would much rather have read of *geldum* and *gablum*. It was out of the question that he should be guilty of such barbarisms as *saca et soca*. If he is to speak to us of these things, he will do so in some phrase which he thinks would not have disgraced a Roman orator—in a phrase, that is, which will not really fit his thought.

The traditions, the legends, current in later times, can not be altogether neglected. The prelates of the thirteenth century often asserted that some of their franchises, and in particular their hundred courts, had been given to their predecessors in an extremely remote age. Thus the bishop of Salisbury claimed the hundred of Ramsbury in Wiltshire by grant of King Offa of Mercia[1]; the Abbot of Ramsey claimed the hundred of Clackclose in Norfolk by grant of King Edgar[2]. On such claims we can lay but very little stress, for if the church had held its 'liberties' from before the Conquest, the exact date at which it had acquired them was of little importance and their origin would easily become the sport of guess-work and myth. But occasionally we can say that there must in all probability be some truth in the tale. Such is the case with the famous hundred of Oswaldslaw in Worcestershire. When the Domesday survey was made this hundred belonged to the church of Worcester. Worcestershire was deemed to comprise twelve hundreds and Oswaldslaw counted for three of them[3]. Oswaldslaw contained 300 hides, and to all seeming the whole shire contained 1200 hides or thereabouts. Even in the thirteenth century a certain tripleness seems to be

Traditional evidence of sake and soke.

[1] R. H. ii. 231.   [2] R. H. ii. 458.   [3] D. B. i. 172 b.

displayed by this hundred; the bishop holds his hundred court in three different places, namely, outside the city of Worcester, at Dryhurst and at Wimborntree[1]. Now the story current in S[t]. Mary's convent was that this triple hundred of Oswaldslaw received its name from Oswald, the saintly bishop who ruled the church of Worcester from 960 to 992. A charter was produced, perhaps the most celebrated of all land-books, that *Altitonantis Dei largiflua clementia*, which, after many centuries, was to prove the King of England's dominion over the narrow seas[2]. According to this charter Edgar, Oswald's patron, threw together three old hundreds, Cuthbertslaw, Wolfhereslaw, and Wimborntree to form a domain for the bishop and his monks[3]. Could we accept the would-be charter as genuine, could we even accept it as a true copy of a genuine book (and this we can hardly do)[4], there would be an end of all controversy as to the existence of seignorial justice in the year 964, for undoubtedly it contains words which confer jurisdiction[5]. Upon these we will not rely: the fact remains that in Domesday Book there appears this hundred of Oswaldslaw, that it is treated as a triple hundred, as three hundreds, that the bishop has jurisdiction over it, that the sheriff has no rights within it, that it looks like a very artificial aggregate of land, for pieces of it lie intermixed with other hundreds and

[1] R. H. ii. 283.

[2] Hale, Worcester Register, pp. xxx, 21 b; K. Appendix, 514 (vi. 237); Hickes, Dissertatio Epistolaris, i. 86; at the end of his dissertation Hickes gives a facsimile of the instrument.

[3] A record of 825 (H. & S. iii. 596–601) mentions a place 'in provincia Huicciorum' called Oslafeshlau; the editors of the Councils say 'Oslafeshlau is probably the original name of the hundred which now, either from some act of S[t]. Oswald or by an easy corruption, is called Oswaldslaw.' One of Oswald's books (K. iii. 160) mentions 'Oswald's hlaw' among the boundaries of Wulfringtune, i.e. Wolverton, a few miles east of Worcester. It is very likely that the true name of the hundred is Oswald's hlaw, i.e. Oswald's hill, not Oswald's law, though the mistake was made at an early time. But the story told by the charter as to the fusion of three old hundreds is corroborated by Domesday, and in the thirteenth century one of the three courts was still held at Wimborntree.

[4] But Dr Stubbs, Const. Hist. i. 118, relies on part of this charter and it is not like ordinary forger's work. If, as is highly probable, there has been some 'improvement' of the charter, such improvement seems to have favoured, not the church of Worcester as against the king, but the monks as against the bishop.

[5] 'cum tolle et teame, saca et socne, et infangenetheof, et proprii iuris debitum transgressionis, et poenam delicti quae Anglice dicitur ofersæwnesse, et gyltwyte.'

pieces of it lie surrounded by Gloucestershire. In 1086 the church of Worcester had to all appearance just those rights which the *Altitonantis* professed to grant to her; already they were associated with the name of Oswald; already they were regarded as ancient privileges. 'Saint Mary of Worcester has a hundred called Oswaldslaw, in which lie 300 hides, from which the bishop of the said church, by a constitution of ancient times, has the profits of all sokes and all the customs which belong thereto for his own board and for the king's service and his own, so that no sheriff can make any claim for any plea or for any other cause:—this the whole county witnesses[1].' Surely the whole county would not have spoken thus of some newfangled device of the half-Norman Edward. Such a case as this, so great a matter as the utter exclusion of the sheriff from one quarter of the shire, we shall hardly attempt to explain by hypothetical usurpations. These liberties were granted by some king or other. If they were granted by the Confessor, why was not a charter of the Confessor produced? Why instead was a charter of Edgar produced, perhaps re-written and revised, perhaps concocted? The easiest answer to this question seems to be that, whatever may be the truth about this detail or that, the *Altitonantis* tells a story that in the main is true. The diplomatist's scepticism should in this and other instances be held in check by the reflexion that kings and sheriffs did not permit themselves to be cheated wholesale out of valuable rights, when the true state of the facts must have been patent to hundreds of men, patent to all the men of Oswaldslaw and to 'the whole county' of Worcester[2].

We may now turn to the genuine books of an earlier time and patiently examine their words. It is well known that

Criticism of the earlier books.

---

[1] D. B. i. 172 b: 'Ecclesia S. Mariae de Wirecestre habet unum hundret quod vocatur Oswaldeslau in quo iacent ccc. hidae. De quibus episcopus ipsius ecclesiae a constitutione antiquorum temporum habet omnes redditiones soch-arum et omnes consuetudines inibi pertinentes ad dominicum victum et regis servitium et suum, ita ut nullus vicecomes ullam ibi habere possit querelam, nec in aliquo placito, nec in alia qualibet causa. Hoc testatur totus comitatus.'

[2] Another example is Edgar's charter for Ely, A.D. 970 K. 563 (iii. 56), which bestows the soke over the two hundreds which lie within the Isle, five hundreds in Essex, and all other lands of the monastery. Kemble was inclined to accept the A.-S. version of the charter. It purports to be obtained by bishop Æthelwold and, if genuine, is closely connected with the Oswaldslaw charter; both testify to unusual privileges obtained by the founders of the new monasticism.

an Anglo-Saxon land-book proceeding from the king very commonly, though not always, contains a clause of immunity. Sometimes a grant of immunity is the essence of the book; the land in question already belongs to a church, and the bishop or abbot now succeeds in getting it set free from burdens to which it has hitherto been subject. What is now granted to him is 'freedom,' 'liberty,' 'freóls'; the book is a *freóls-bóc*[1]; it may be that he is willing to pay money, to give land, to promise prayers in return for this franchise, this *libertas*[2]. Thus, for example, King Ceolwulf of Mercia grants a *libertas* to the Bishop of Worcester, freeing all his land from the burden of feeding the king's horses, and in consideration of this grant the bishop gives to the king five hides of land for four lives and agrees that prayers shall be said for him every Sunday[3].

The clause of immunity.   Now in an ordinary case the clause of immunity will first contain some general words declaring the land to be free of burdens in general, and then some exceptive words declaring that it is not to be free from certain specified burdens[4]. Both parts of the clause demand our attention. The burdens from which the land is to be free are described by a large phrase. Usually both a substantive and an adjective are employed for the purpose; they are to be freed *ab omni terrenae servitutis iugo—saecularibus negotiis—mundiali obstaculo—mundialibus causis—saecularibus curis—mundialibus coangustiis—cunctis laboribus vitae mortalium.* The adjectives are remarkable, for they seem to suggest a contrast. The land is freed from all earthly, worldly, secular, temporal services. Does this not mean that it is devoted to services that are heavenly, sacred, spiritual[5]? True, that in course of time we may find this

---

[1] E.g. K. 1298 (vi. 149), 'Dis is seo freolsboc to ðan mynstre æt Byrtune.'

[2] E.g. K. 277 (ii. 58), 278 (ii. 60).

[3] A.D. 875; K. 306 (ii. 101); B. ii. 159.

[4] Unsuspected charters of the seventh and eighth centuries are so few, that we hardly dare venture on any generalities about their wording. But already in a charter attributed to 674, E. p. 4, Brit. Mus. Facs. iv. 1, something very like the 'common form' of later days appears; it appears also in a charter of A.D. 691–2, K. 32 (i. 35), E. p. 12, of which we have but a fragmentary copy, and before the end of the eighth century it appears with some frequency; see e.g. Offa's charter of 774, K. 123 (i. 150): 'sit autem terra illa libera ab omni saecularis rei negotio, praeter pontis, arcisve restaurationem et contra hostes communem expeditionem.'

[5] Occasionally the contrast is expressly drawn, e.g. by Æthelbald, K. 90 (i. 108): 'ut ab omni tributo vectigalium operum onerumque *saecularium* sit

same formula used when the king is giving land, not to a church, but to one of his thegns; but still in its origin the land-book is ecclesiastical; 'book-right' is the right of the church, *ius ecclesiasticum*[1], and we may well believe that the phraseology of the books, which in substance remains unaltered from century to century, was primarily adapted to pious gifts. It is by no means improbable that in the middle of the eighth century Æthelbald of Mercia by a general decree conceded to all the churches of his kingdom just that freedom from all burdens, save the *trinoda necessitas*, that was usually granted by the clause of immunity contained in the land-books, and we can hardly say with certainty that half a century before this time Wihtræd had not granted to all the churches of Kent a yet larger measure of liberty, a liberty which absolved them even from the *trinoda necessitas*[2]. Turning from the adjectives to the substantives that are used, we find them to be wide and indefinite words; the lands are to be free from all worldly services, burdens, troubles, annoyances, affairs, business, causes, matters and things. Sometimes a more definite word is added such as *tributum, vectigal, census,* and clearly one main object of the clause is to declare that the land is to pay nothing to the king or his officers; it is to be free of rent and taxes,

---

libera...tantum ut Deo omnipotenti ex eodem agello *aecclesiasticae* servitutis famulatum inpendat.'

[1] See above, p. 229.

[2] Privilege of Wihtræd, A.D. 696–716, Haddan and Stubbs, iii. 238: 'Adhuc addimus maiorem libertatem. Inprimis Christi ecclesiae cum omnibus agris ad eam pertinentibus, similiter Hrofensi ecclesiae cum suis, caeterisque praedictis omnibus ecclesiis Dei nostri, subiciantur pro salute animae meae, meorumque praedecessorum, et pro spe caelestis regni ex hac die, et deinceps concedimus et donamus ab omnibus difficultatibus saecularium servitutis, a pastu Regis, principum, comitum, nec non ab operibus, maioribus minoribusve gravitatibus: et ab omni debitu vel pulsione regum tensuris liberos eos esse perpetua libertate statuimus.' See also the act by which Æthelbald confirmed this privilege in 742, H. & S. iii. 340, B. i. 233–6. According to one version of this act, the *trinoda necessitas* is, according to another it is not, excepted. The learned editors of the Councils speak of 'the suspicions common to every record that notices the Privilege of Wihtræd.' We are treading on treacherous ground. See also the less suspicious Act of Æthelbald, A.D. 749, H. & S. iii. 386: 'Concedo ut monasteria et aecclesiae a publicis vectigalibus et ab omnibus operibus oneribusque, auctore Deo, servientes absoluti maneant, nisi sola quae communiter fruenda sunt, omnique populo, edicto regis, facienda iubentur, id est, instructionibus pontium, vel necessariis defensionibus arcium contra hostes, non sunt renuenda.'

scotfree and gafolfree[1]. Occasionally particular mention is made of a duty of entertaining the king, his court, his officers, his huntsmen, dogs and horses, also of a duty of entertaining his messengers and forwarding them on their way[2]. Thus, for example, Taunton, which belonged to the bishop of Winchester, had been bound to provide one night's entertainment for the king and nine nights' entertainment for his falconers and to support eight dogs and a dog-ward, to carry with horses and carts to Curry and to Williton whatever the king might need, and to conduct wayfarers to the neighbouring royal vills. To obtain immunity from these burdens the bishop had to give the king sixty hides of land[3].

Discussion of the words of immunity.

No doubt it is a sound canon of criticism that, when in a grant precise are followed by vague words, the former should be taken to explain, and, it may be, to restrain the latter. If, for example, land be freed 'from taxes and all other secular burdens,' we may well urge that the 'other secular burdens' which the writer has in his mind are burdens akin to taxes. And of course it is fair to say that in our days a grant of private justice would be an extremely different thing from a grant of freedom from fiscal dues. But what, we must ask, does this freedom from fiscal dues really mean when it is granted by an Anglo-Saxon land-book? When the monks or canons obtain a charter freeing this territory from all *tributum* and *census*, from all *pastiones* and so forth, is it intended that the occupiers of the soil shall have the benefit of this grant? Not so. The religious have been stipulating for themselves and not for their men. The land has been freed from service to the king in order that it may serve the church[4]; the church will take what the king has hitherto taken or it will take an equivalent. In a writ of Edward the Confessor this appears very plainly. Whenever men pay a geld to the king, be it an

[1] A.D. 1066, Edward the Confessor for Westminster, K. 828 (iv. 191): 'scotfre and gavelfre.'

[2] Kemble, Codex, vol. i. Introduction liii–lvi., collects some of the best instances. Offa for a valuable consideration frees certain lands belonging to the church of Worcester from *pastiones*; 'nec non et trium annorum ad se pertinentes pastiones, id est sex convivia, libenter concedendo largitus est': K. 143 (i. 173), B. i. 335.

[3] A.D. 904, K. 1084 (v. 157).

[4] A.D. 826, Egbert for Winchester, K. 1037 (v. 81): 'Volo etiam ut haec terra libera semper sit...nullique serviat nisi soli episcopo Wentano.'

army-geld or a ship-geld, the men of S^t. Edmund are to pay a like geld to the abbot and the monks[1]. Probably this principle has been at work all along. The king has had no mind to free the *manentes, casati, tributarii* of the church from any *tributum* or *vectigal.* What has hitherto been paid to him, or some equivalent for it, will now go to the treasury of the church. Thus, even within the purely fiscal region, we see that the object of the immunity is to give the church a grip on those who dwell upon the land. But we must read the clause to its end.

As is well known, it usually proceeds to except certain burdens, to declare that the land is not to be free from them. These burdens, three in number, are on a few occasions spoken of as the *trinoda necessitas.* That term has become common in our own day and is useful. The land is not to be free from the duty of army-service, the duty of repairing strongholds, the duty of repairing bridges. An express exception of this *trinoda necessitas* out of the general words of immunity is extremely common. Moreover there are charters which speak as though no lands could ever be free from the triple charge[2], and a critic should look with some suspicion upon any would-be land-book which expressly purports to break this broad rule. But besides some books which do expressly purport to free land from the *trinoda necessitas*[3], we have a considerable number of others which grant immunity in wide terms and make no exception of army-service, bridge-bote or burh-bote[4], and we are hardly entitled to reject them all merely because they do not conform to the general principle[5]. More to our

The trinoda necessitas.

---

[1] K. 1346 (vi. 205). Compare Fustel de Coulanges, L'Immunité Mérovingienne, Revue historique, xxiii. 21.

[2] E.g. K. 1117 (v. 231): 'tribus semotis causis a quibus nullus nostrorum poterit expers fore'; K. v. pp. 259, 283, 334.

[3] To this class belong the foundation charter of Evesham mentioned above, p. 235, and Offa's charter for S^t. Albans, K. 161 (i. 195), which Haddan and Stubbs, iii. 469, are unwilling to decisively reject. Cenwulf's charter for Abingdon, K. 214 (i. 269), H. & S. iii. 556, sets a limit to the amount of military service that is to be demanded. Æthelstan's charter for Crediton, recently printed by Napier and Stevenson, Crawford Charters, p. 5, frees land from the *trinoda necessitas.*

[4] E.g. K. i. p. 274; ii. pp. 14, 15, 24, 26, 83 ; v. pp. 53, 62, 81.'

[5] Observe how Bede describes a gift made by Oswy in the middle of the seventh century; Hist. Eccl. iii. 24 (ed. Plummer, i. 178): 'donatis insuper duodecim possessiunculis terrarum in quibus *ablato studio militiae terrestris*, ad exercendam militiam caelestem etc.'

M.   18

purpose is it to notice that, though a grant of jurisdictional powers would be an extremely different thing from a grant of immunity from army-service, the duty of attending the national or communal courts is extremely like the duty of attending the host, and it would not be extravagant to argue that when the king says 'I free this land from all secular burdens except those of fyrd-fare, burh-bote and bridge-bote,' he says by implication 'I free this land from suit to shires and hundreds.'

The *ángild.*　　But yet more important is it to notice that charters of the ninth century frequently except out of the words of immunity not three burdens, but four. In addition to the *trinoda necessitas,* some fourth matter is mentioned. Its nature is never very fully described, but it is hinted at by the terms *ángild, singulare pretium, pretium pro pretio.* In connexion with these charters we must read others which exempt the land from 'penal causes,' or *wíte-rǽden* and others which expressly grant to the donee the 'wites' or certain 'wites' issuing from the land; also we shall have to notice that there are dooms which decree that certain 'wites' are to be paid to the land-lord or *land-ríca.* Now *ángild (singulare pretium)* is a technical term in common use[1]. When a crime has been committed—theft is the typical crime which the legislators have ever before their eyes—the *ángild* is the money compensation that the person who has been wronged is entitled to receive, as contrasted with any wite or fine that is payable to the king. We find, then, a charter saying that certain land—not certain persons, but certain land—is to be free from all secular burdens save the *ángild,* and in some cases it will be added that the land is to pay nothing, not one farthing, by way of wite, or that nothing is 'to go out to wite[2].' Of the various interpretations that might possibly be put upon such words one may be at once rejected. It is not the intention of the king who makes or of the church which receives the grant that crimes committed on this land shall go unpunished. No lord would wish his territory to be a place where men might murder and steal with impunity. We may be certain then that if a crime be committed, there is to be a wite; but it is

---

[1] The passages in the dooms which mention it are collected in Schmid, Glossar, s. v. *ángild.* They are discussed by Maurer, Krit. Ueberschau, ii. 32.

[2] The clauses of immunity which mention the *ángild* will be collected in a note at the end of this section.

not to go outside the land; the lord himself is to have it. But how is the lord to enforce his right to the wite,—must he sue· for it in the national or communal courts, or has he a court of his own?

This question is difficult. The ancient charters, however nearly they may go to telling us that the donee will do justice within his territory, never go quite that length. There is, however, a book granted by Cenwulf of Mercia in 816 to the church of Worcester which adds to the clause of immunity these words—'and if a wicked man be three times captured in open crime, let him be delivered up at the king's tún (*vicum regalem*)[1].' This seems to tell us that only the worst offenders will be delivered up to the royal or national officers and to imply that the bishop may do justice upon all others. Then there are two books in favour of the church of Abingdon, the one granted by Cenwulf in 821, the other by Egbert in 835, which, though their language is very obscure, seem to tell us that if one of the 'men of God' (by which phrase are meant the 'vassals' of the church of Abingdon) be accused of any crime, the overseer of the church may swear away the charge by his own oath, and that, if he dare not swear, he may pay the *ángild* to the plaintiff and, this done, will have justice over the offender[2]. Another ancient book suggests that the lord of an immunity, when he had to pay the *ángild* for one of his men, could not be forced to cross the boundary of his land. On that boundary some mixed tribunal would meet consisting partly of his men and partly of outsiders[3]. Then, again, there are the books which either give the lord the *furis comprehensio* or else exempt his land from the *furis comprehensio*. Now when a

The right to wites and the right to a court.

---

[1] K. 210 (i. 265); B. i. 497; H. & S. iii. 585. The clause in question is not found in every copy of the charter. If some monk is to be accused of tampering with the book, there seems just as much reason for charging him with having omitted a clause which limited, as for charging him with inserting a clause which recognized, the jurisdiction of the church.

[2] These clauses will be discussed in a note at the end of this section.

[3] A.D. 841, K. 250 (ii. 14): 'Liberabo ab omnibus saecularibus servitutibus... regis et principis vel iuniorum eorum, nisi in confinio reddant rationem contra alium.' Compare K. 117 (i. 144): 'nisi specialiter pretium pro pretio ad terminum.' Also Leg. Henr. 57 § 1: 'Si inter compares vicinos utrinque sint querelae, conveniant ad divisas.' Ibid. 57 § 8: 'aliquando in divisis vel in erthmiotis.' Ibid. 9 § 4: 'Et omnis causa terminetur, vel hundreto, vel comitatu, vel hallimoto soccam habentium, vel dominorum curiis, vel divisis parium.' See above, p. 97.

writ of Cnut or Edward the Confessor tells us that a lord is to
have *infangennethef* we do not doubt that he is to have the
right which bore that name in later days, the right to hold a
court for and to hang thieves who are caught in seisin of the
stolen goods, and to the *furis comprehensio* of the older books
we can hardly give another meaning.   And the apparent
equivalence of the two phrases 'You shall hold this land with
thief-catching' and 'You shall hold this land free of thief-
catching' illustrates our argument that to exempt land from
public or national justice is to create private or seignorial
justice[1].   We may see this in later days; a lord who holds
land 'free and quit of frankpledge' assumes the right to hold a
view of frankpledge, and we can not say that he is wrong in so
doing[2].

The Taun-
ton book.   Lastly, in a book of fairly good repute we may read of the
grand liberties with which in 904 King Edward endowed the
Bishop of Winchester's large estate at Taunton—that estate
which in subsequent centuries was to become the classical
example of colossal manors.   'I have,' says the king, 'granted
to Christ that the men of the bishop, noble as well as non-noble,
living on the said land shall be worthy of the same right that is
enjoyed by those who dwell on the demesnes of the crown, and
that jurisdiction in all secular causes shall be exercised to the
use of the bishops in the same manner as that in which
jurisdiction is exercised in matters pertaining to the king[3].'
This is the more important because it suggests, what like
enough is true, that the king himself is one of the first of all
'immunists'; his own estates, the ancient demesne of the

---

[1] A.D. 828, K. 223 (i. 287): 'cum furis comprehensione intus et foris';
A.D. 842, K. 253 (ii. 16) 'ut...furis comprehensione...terra secura et immunis...
permaneat'; A.D. 850, K. 1049 (v. 95) a similar form; A.D. 858, K. 281
(ii. 64), a similar form; A.D. 869, K. 300 (ii. 95), a similar form; A.D. 880,
K. 312 (ii. 109): 'cum furis comprehensione.' See Kemble's remarks, C. D.
vol. i. p. xlvi.

[2] Hist. Eng. Law, i. 565.

[3] K. 1084 (v. 157); B. ii. 272: 'Christo concessi ut episcopi homines tam
nobiles quam ignobiles in praefato rure degentes hoc idem ius in omni haberent
dignitate quo regis homines perfruuntur regalibus fiscis commorantes, et omnia
saecularium rerum iudicia ad usus praesulum exerceantur eodem modo quo
regalium negotiorum discutiuntur iudicia.' Similar words occur in a confirmation by Edgar, K. 598 (iii. 136), which Kemble rejects. This contains an
English paraphrase of the Latin text.

crown, already stand outside the national system of finance, justice and police[1].

But so careful must we be in drawing inferences from singular instances, so wary of forgeries, that in the end we can not dispense with arguments which rest rather upon probabilities than upon recorded facts. It is conceded that the 'immunist' (it is convenient to borrow a term that French writers have coined) is entitled to many of the fines and forfeitures that arise from offences committed within his territory. Is it, we must ask, probable that any ealdorman or sheriff will be at pains to exact and collect these fines and forfeitures for the immunist's benefit? Now it is true that in later days a few lords enjoyed a comparatively rare franchise known as *amerciamenta hominum*. When their men were amerced in the king's court the amercements were paid into the exchequer, and then the lord would petition to have them paid out to him[2]. But this was an uncommon and an exalted franchise. As a general rule, the person in whose name a court is held, be he king or lord, gets the profits of the court. No one in the middle ages does justice for nothing, and in the ninth century the days when national officers would be paid by salary were far distant. When the king declares that nothing is to 'go out' of the immunist's lands 'by way of wite,' then to our thinking he declares that, save in exceptional cases, he and his officers will neither meddle nor make with offences that are committed within that territory. Again, though we may reject this charter and that, there can be little doubt that before the end of the tenth century, the territory held by a church sometimes coincided with a jurisdictional district, with a hundred or group of hundreds. When this was so, and the church enjoyed a full immunity, it was almost of necessity the lord of the court as well as the lord of the land. Why should the sheriff hold that court, why should he appoint a bailiff for that hundred, if never thereout could he get one penny for his own or the king's use?

We must once more remember that even in the days of full grown feudalism the right to hold a court was after all rather a fiscal than a jurisdictional right. We call it jurisdictional,

The immunist and the wite.

Justice and jurisdiction.

---

[1] Compare K. 821 (iv. 171): 'swa freols on eallan thingan eall swa thaes cinges agen innland.'

[2] Hist. Eng. Law, i. 570.

but still, at least normally, the lord was, neither in his own person, nor yet in the person of his steward, the judge of the court[1]. His right was not in strictness a right *ius dicendi*, for the suitors made the judgments. When analysed it was a right to preside over a court and to take its profits. Very easy therefore is the transition from a right to 'wites' to such 'jurisdiction' as the feudal lord enjoys. When once it is established that all the fines of a hundred court are to go to a bishop, that no sheriff or bailiff will get anything by going to hold that court, then the court already is 'in the bishop's hands.'

The Frank-ish immu-nity.

This, however, can not be treated as a merely English question. Parallel to the English *fréols-bóc* runs the Frankish *carta immunitatis*, and, if the former has given rise to the question whether it conceded jurisdictional rights, the latter has given rise, not merely to the same question, but to much learned controversy. Now it is highly probable that the English 'immunity' is not independent of the Merovingian 'immunity'; still the terms of the former do not seem to have been copied from those of the latter, and it is a significant fact that two different formulas should be equally open to the blame of not deciding just that most important question which according to our ideas they ought to decide. The Frankish formula is addressed by the king to his subordinates and declares that no public officer (*nullus iudex publicus*) is to enter the land of the immunist for the purpose of hearing causes, levying *freda* (which answer to our 'wites'), making distresses or exacting pledges; but, like our English formula, it says no word of any court to be held or any jurisdiction to be exercised by the immunist. It would be impertinent to give here any lengthy account of the various opinions about this matter that have been held by foreign scholars, still more impertinent to pronounce any judgment upon them, but even those writers who seem most inclined to minimize the scope of the immunity are forced to admit that, as a mere matter of fact, the immunist by virtue of his immunity is enabled to hold a court for his territory. That seignorial courts were growing up even in the Merovingian time, that such courts there were even in the sixth century, there seems little or no doubt, even though it be denied that they were the creatures of these

[1] Hist. Eng. Law, i. 580.

clauses of immunity. On the whole, to whichever side of the channel we look, we seem compelled, alike by the words of the charters and by the controversies which they have occasioned, to believe that in the eyes of the kings and the immunists seignorial jurisdiction, that right to hold a court which seems to us so strange a right, was not a matter of the first importance, not worth conceding, not worth denying. Who is to have the profits of justice?—that is a momentous question. But if it be decided that they are to go to the bishop, then the king will have no further care for them:—the bishop may and must get them for himself. As to the 'justiciables,' it may well be that they are very indifferent about the matter, not impossible that the burden of suit will be alleviated if the lord establishes a court of his own, or if an old court passes into his hands[1].

One other question should be raised, even if we can find for it no certain answer. Is not seignorial jurisdiction very closely connected at its root with ecclesiastical jurisdiction? Of course in more recent times the two are thoroughly distinct from each other. The bishop, besides being a spiritual judge, will be a feudal lord with many manorial courts and many chartered franchises; but any court that he holds as a lord will have

Seignorial and ecclesiastical jurisdiction.

---

[1] Few questions in Frankish history have been more warmly contested than this, whether the immunist had a jurisdiction within his territory. On the one hand, it has been contended that there is no evidence older than 840 that he exercised jurisdiction even as between the inhabitants of that territory. On the other hand, it has been said that already in 614 he has civil jurisdiction in disputes between these inhabitants, besides a criminal jurisdiction over them, which however does not extend to the graver crimes. A few references will suffice to put the reader in the current of this discussion; Löning, Geschichte des Deutschen Kirchenrechts, ii. 731; Brunner, D. R. G. ii. 298; Schröder, D. R. G. 174; Beauchet, Histoire de l'organisation judiciaire en France, 74; Beaudoin, Étude sur les origines du régime féodal (Annales de l'enseignement supérieur de Grenoble, vol. i. p. 43); Fustel de Coulanges, L'Immunité Mérovingienne (Revue Historique, xxii. 249, xxiii. 1). One of the most disputed points is the character of the court held by an abbot, which is put before us by the very ancient Formulae Andecavenses, a collection attributed to the sixth or, at the latest, to the early years of the seventh century. It has been asserted and denied that this abbot of Angers is exercising the powers given to him by an immunity; some have said that he, or rather his steward, is merely acting as an arbitrator; Brunner, Forschungen, 665, explains him as one of the *mediocres iudices* of decaying Roman law. On the whole, the balance of learning is inclining to the opinion that, even in the Merovingian time, there were great churches and other lords with courts which wielded power over free men, and that the 'immunities,' even if they were not intended to create such courts, at all events made them possible, or, as Fustel says, consecrated them.

nothing to do with the court that he holds as a bishop. The constitution and procedure of the one will differ at every point from the constitution and procedure of the other. The one belongs to the temporal order and is subject to the king's court, the other belongs to the spiritual order and is in no sense below the royal tribunal. Thus it is when feudal law and canon law have reached their full stature. But even from the twelfth century we may get a hint that the distinction has not always been so sharply marked. We may read how in Henry I.'s day the Bishop of Bath ' with his friends and barons' heard a cause in which Modbert claimed lands that were held by the monks of Bath. The proceedings took place under a royal writ and ought, we should say, to have been in all respects temporal proceedings; but in framing the judgment two bishops, three archdeacons and several 'clerks and chaplains' took the leading part, while the lay tenants of the bishop stood by as witnesses[1]. In this context we must remember that in the twelfth century the clergy were contending that land given to a church in frankalmoin is outside the sphere of secular justice[2], and, while this contention was being urged, it was easily possible that a bishop should hold an amphibious court:—Over the claim that Modbert is making the bishop has jurisdiction, either because the monks are holding the land of him as his tenants, or because that land has been given to God and the saints by an ancient book which denounced the anathema against all who should violate it. Going back yet further, we see, at all events in France, that the claim of the clergy to hold their lands and seignories exempt from all temporal jurisdiction has been intimately connected with the claim of the clergy that they themselves need not answer before a lay tribunal. A learned man has said that the exemption of the clergy from the temporal courts was 'the first step towards the feudalization of justice[3].' If our English documents do not make this plain, if the relations between church and state were more harmonious in England than elsewhere (and because more harmonious therefore more indefinite and to the modern student more perplexing), still we can see that the main idea of the English *fréols-bóc* is the liberation of a tract of ground from all secular

---

[1] Madox, Hist. Exch. i. 109 ; Bigelow, Placita Anglo-Normannica, 114.
[2] Hist. Eng. Law, i. 224–30.
[3] Nissl, Der Gerichtsstand des Clerus im Fränkischen Reich, 247.

troubles, all temporal burdens, all earthly service. The land is dedicated to God and the saints, or, if it is not dedicated in the strictest sense, it is given for God's sake and the welfare of the donor's soul; it is within the ban of the church. And so the men who sit upon the land of the church of Abingdon, laymen though they be, are *homines Dei*, the men of God[1]. As such, should they not be subject to the jurisdiction of the church?

At this point we may profitably remember that the juris- Criminal justice of theChurch.
diction which in later days appears as the 'criminal jurisdiction' of ecclesiastical tribunals (the jurisdiction which, for example, those tribunals exercise when they chastise a man for incest, fornication or perjury) was but slowly disengaged from the general mass of penal jurisdiction that was wielded by moots in which the bishop occupied a prominent seat. Moreover, the bishop's justice did not escape that fiscal taint which pervaded the whole system of criminal law. As in some cases the king is entitled to a *wite*, so in others the *wite* falls to the bishop. For instance, we see traces of a rude *concordat*, which, when incest or adultery is committed, subjects the woman to the bishop, the man to the king[2]; and then from Domesday Book we learn that in the borough of Lewes the upshot of this partition is that the king will get 8*s.* 4*d.* from the man while the adulteress pays a like sum to the archbishop of Canterbury[3]. And so ecclesiastical jurisdiction becomes a source of income, a matter to be fought for and bargained for. The monks of Battle will claim that within the *banlieu* of their abbey all the 'forfeitures of Christianity' belong to them and not to the bishop of Chichester[4]. What is more, they will connect their claim to purely temporal justice with their possession of ordeal pits, and here we may see another link between the hundred-moots and the churches[5]. The churches have made money out

---

[1] K. 214 (i. 269); 236 (i. 312).
[2] Edw. & Guth. 4; Leg. Henr. 11, § 5. [3] D. B. i. 26.
[4] Chron. de Bello, 26–7: 'Et si forisfacturae Christianitatis quolibet modo infra leugam contigerint, coram abbate definiendae referantur. Habeatque ecclesia S. Martini emendationem forisfacturae; poenitentiam vero reatus sui rei ab episcopo percipiant.'
[5] Battle Custumals (Camden Soc.), 126: 'Septem hundreda non habent fossas nisi apud Wy, et ideo habemus ij. denarios: Archiepiscopus tamen et Prior de novo trahunt homines suos ad fossas: Abbas de S. Augustino non habet.'

of the ordeal.   Long after the English prelates had been
forbidden to hold spiritual pleas in the hundred courts,
Alexander III. was compelled to speak sharply to the archbishop of Canterbury touching the conduct of archdeacons who
exacted thirty pence from every man or woman who went to the
fire or the water for purgation[1].

Antiquity
of sei-
gnorial
courts.

No doubt the theory to which we have been led implies
that in the eighth or even in the seventh century, there were
in England 'immunists' who had jurisdiction within their
territories, and further it implies that a royal grant of land in
the ninth and tenth centuries generally included, and this as
a matter of 'common form,' a grant of jurisdiction.   We cannot
see either in the history of England or in the history of the
Frankish Empire any reason why we should shrink from these
conclusions.   Further, it must be admitted that if the clause of
immunity conveys, or permits the growth of, seignorial jurisdiction, this jurisdiction is of an exalted kind, for no causes are
excepted out of it, unless it be by the words about the *ángild*,
and even those words drop out from the charters in course of
time.   Those words about the *ángild* imply, to our thinking,
that the immunist will have jurisdiction over any dispute which
arises between two men of the enfranchised territory, and also
that if an action against one of these men be brought by a
'foreigner' in a court outside the precinct, the immunist can
obtain 'cognizance' of the action by appearing in that court
and paying the *ángild*.   When the words about the *ángild*
disappear, this means that the immunist is obtaining a yet
further measure of 'liberty':—whenever one of his men is sued
he can 'crave his court' and need not, as a condition for
obtaining it, offer to pay what is due to the plaintiff.   The
highest criminal jurisdiction was probably excepted from the
grant.   Being a grant of wites, it will not extend to the
'bootless' the 'unemendable' crimes.   But Cnut's attempt to
save for himself certain pleas of the crown looks to us like the
effort of a strong king to recover what his predecessors have
been losing[2].   And then Cnut himself and the Confessor,—the
latter with reckless liberality—expressly grant to the churches

[1] c. 3, X. 5, 37: 'Accepimus...quod archidiaconi Conventrensis episcopatus...
in examinatione ignis et aquae triginta denarios a viro et muliere quaerere
praesumunt.'
[2] Cnut II. 12–15.

just those very reserved pleas of the crown. The result is that
the well endowed immunist of S^t. Edward's day has jurisdiction
as high as that which any palatine earl of after ages enjoyed.
No crime, except possibly some direct attack upon the king's
person, property or retainers, was too high for him. It is the
reconstruction of criminal justice in Henry II.'s time, the new
learning of felonies, the introduction of the novel and royal
procedure of indictment, that reduce the immunist's powers
and leave him with nothing better than an unintelligible list
of obsolete words[1]. In this matter of seignorial justice England
had little to learn from Normandy. On the contrary, the
Norman counts and barons were eager to secure the uncouth
phrases which gave to the English immunist his justice, ' haute,
moyenne et basse justice.'

Our next question must be whether in the days before the
Conquest a franchise or immunity was the only root of private
jurisdiction: in other words, whether any jurisdiction was
implied in the mere relation between lord and man or between
lord and tenant. This also is a question which will hardly be
finally answered if regard be had only to the English documents.
For France it is the question whether the *senior*, as such, has
jurisdiction over his *vassus*, or again, whether he has jurisdiction
over his *vassus* if, as is usually the case in the Carlovingian age,
the *vassus* holds a *beneficium* given to him by his *senior*. The
English dooms which deal with what we may call the justiciary
relationship between lord and man closely resemble in many
respects the Frankish capitularies which touch the same
subject; both sets of documents seem to evade the simple
question that we put to them. But as regards the continent it
may here be enough to say that, though there have been many
debates, the current of learning seems to have set decidedly in
favour of the doctrine that neither in Merovingian nor yet in
Carlovingian times had the *senior*, unless he was an immunist,
a jurisdiction over his men. Such a jurisdiction has not been
developed when the midnight hides everything from our view.
When the morning comes, feudal justice stands revealed,
though nowhere perhaps is it governed by that simple principle
that ultimately prevailed in England, namely, that any and
every lord, no matter his personal rank or the rank of his
tenement, has civil justice over his tenants.

*Justice,
vassalage
and tenure.*

[1] Hist. Eng. Law, i. 564.

The lord's
duty when
his man is
accused.

The possibility of debate about this matter is afforded by texts of an earlier age, which at times seem to speak of the lord as 'doing justice' when a charge is brought against any of his men[1]. Our English run parallel with the Frankish texts. The state in its organization of justice and police does not treat the contract between man and lord, between *senior* and *vassus*, as a matter of indifference, still less as a danger to society. We must not think of feudalism or vassalism as of something which from the very first is anti-national and anarchic. In its earliest stages it is fostered by the state, by the king, by national law. The state demands that the lordless man of whom no right can be had shall have a lord[2]. It makes the lord responsible for the appearance of his men in court to answer accusations[3]. It is not unlikely that the whole system of frankpledge grows out of this requirement. In some instances the state may go further; it may treat the lord, not merely as bound to produce his man, but as responsible for his man's evil deeds. But, at all events, any one who has a charge to make against a lord's man must in the first instance demand justice of the lord. If without making such a demand, making it repeatedly, he brings the charge before the king, he must pay the same fine that the lord would have paid had he been guilty of a default of justice[4]. 'Of a default of justice' we say and are compelled to say. It is phrases such as this that have occasioned controversy. To an ear attuned to the language of feudalism they seem to imply a seignorial court in which the lord 'does justice' or 'holds full right' to the demandant. But to all appearance they have gradually changed their meaning. Originally a lord 'does right' to the demandant by producing in a public court the man against whom the claim is urged; or he does it by satisfying the claim, and in that case he seems entitled to exact from his man, not merely a sum which will compensate the outlay, but also the 'wite' or fine which in another case would have gone to the king or some national officer. He has thus 'done justice' and may have the usual profit that comes of doing justice. Probably we ought to distinguish between a

---

[1] Beaudoin, op. cit. p. 94 ff.   [2] Æthelstan, ii. 2.
[3] Konrad Maurer, Krit. Ueberschau, ii. 30 ff.
[4] Æthelstan, ii. 3. Observe how in the Latin version 'se hlaford the rihtes wyrne' becomes 'dominus qui rectum difforciabit.'

laxer and a stricter measure of responsibility, between the
lord's responsibility for his men in general and his responsibility
for such of his men as form his *familia*, in the language of
later days his *mainpast*; but our texts do not lay much stress
upon this distinction, and, as a matter of remote history, the
relation between lord and man may grow out of the relation
between the head of a household and the members of it[1].

At any rate, in numberless cases the law begins to interpose
a third person, namely, the wrong-doer's lord, between the
wrong-doer and the wronged : it is to this lord that the
claimant should in the first instance address himself. The lord
who does his duty by the king and the nation is he who keeps
a tight hold on his men, who chooses them carefully, who
dismisses them if they are bad subjects, who ' does justice ' and
' holds full right ' if any of them be accused. Then, on the
other hand, he has the right and duty of ' warranting ' his men.
If, as will often happen, the bond between a lord and his man
is complicated with the bond between landlord and tenant,
then, as in later days, if the tenant's title be impeached, he will
vouch his lord to warranty and the lord will defend the action.
But, besides this, within limits that are not well defined, the
lord is the man's *defensor* or *tutor*[2]. It is expected of him by
morality, if not by law, that he will take upon himself the
responsibility for his man's acts if they be not open crimes.
He must stand by his men and see them through all trouble[3].

Duty of the lord.

For a while the state approves all this. The dangerous
person is, not the lord, whose wide lands are some security for
his good behaviour, but the lordless man of whom no right can
be had. Somehow or another theft must be suppressed. This
is the determination of our strongest kings, of our wisest
' witan.' That they are raising up over against the state
another power, the power of seignorial justice, they do not see.
And, after all, these ' witan ' both laymen and clerks are
themselves great lords, and the king is the lordliest of them all.
Thus the foundation for a feudal jurisdiction is laid. Still
between the lord's duty of producing his men and his right to
hold a court of and for his men there is to our eyes a great

The state requires the lord to ' do right.'

---

[1] K. Maurer, Krit. Ueberschau, ii. 32, 40, 41. Ine, 22, is of great importance
on account of its antiquity.

[2] D. B. ii. 18 b: ' inde vocat dominum suum ad tutorem.' See above, p. 71.

[3] Leg. Henr. 57, § 8; 82, §§ 4, 5, 6.

gulf. We have seen above that this gulf had not been bridged even in the Confessor's, even in the Conqueror's day[1]. Nor to our thinking would it have been bridged but for the creation of 'immunities' upon a grand scale. The first origin of the immunity we have sought in the efforts of the clergy to obtain lands which should be utterly exempt from 'all earthly burdens,' 'all worldly business.' But this effort unites with the stream of tendency that we have now been watching. The state will be grateful to the church if it will 'hold all the men of God to right' and do judgment between them and upon them.

The *land-ríca* as immunist. There is also a long series of dooms going back as far as Æthelstan's reign which give certain fines and forfeitures to one who is described as the *land-hláford* or the *land-ríca*. Remarkable they are, for they seem to assume that wherever a crime is committed there will be forthcoming some-one who will answer to the title 'the land-lord' or 'the territorial magnate.' In some sense or another they presuppose that there is *Nulle terre sans seigneur*. But who is this 'landlord'? According to our thinking, he is the lord of the hundred or else the lord who has a charter of immunity comprehending the land in question, and, if there be no person answering to this description, then he is the king. In the first place, in certain dooms relating to London we are told that, when a thief is caught and slain, his property is to be divided into two parts, of which his wife takes one, while the other is divided between the king and 'the association' (perhaps we may say 'the gild') which was engaged in the pursuit and capture; 'but if it be book-land or bishop's-land, the landlord takes half with the association in common[2].' This seems to mean that there will be a lord to share in the proceeds of the forfeiture if, but only if, the scene of the capture be land that is within an immunity. It is assumed, not without warrant in the land-books, that the man who has book-land always, or almost always, enjoys an immunity, while as to the bishop's-land, whether the bishop be holding it in demesne or have granted it out to his thegns, that no doubt will be protected by an ample charter. So again, in another law 'the lord' receives the thief's *wer* 'if he [the lord] is worthy of his wite[3]': that is to say, the lord

---

[1] See above, p. 89.
[2] Æthelstan, vi. (Iudicia Civitatis Lundoniae), 1.
[3] Æthelred, i. 1, § 7.

receives it if he is in enjoyment of an immunity which confers upon him a right to 'wites.' Then again, in several cases we find that the land-lord or *land-ríca* shares the proceeds of a fine with the hundred or wapentake[1]. This, as we think, points to the fact that the hundreds and wapentakes are passing into private hands. These laws are severe laws against criminals. They urge all men to the pursuit of the flying thief and they hold out a reward to those who are active in this duty. The men of the hundred are to have half the thief's property, while the lord (who in many cases will be the lord of the hundred) is to have the other half. He is to have no more, even though his charter may seem to give him more. So again, in certain cases an accused person must find security that he will stand a trial, and the gage is to be given 'half to the *land-ríca*, half to the wapentake[2].' This *land-ríca* is the lord of the wapentake. In another instance the gage must be given half to the *land-ríca* and half to the king's port-reeve[3]. Then there are cases in which the 'land-lord' is to take possession of cattle that have been irregularly acquired and are presumably stolen, and is to preserve them until their true owner shall make his appearance[4]. These provisions, which seem the foundation of the 'franchise of waif and stray,' suggest that the 'land-lord' is the president of the court into which the owner must go when he wishes to prove his title; were this not so, the king's reeve would be the person who would have the custody of the unclaimed beasts. Certainly our explanation of these passages assumes that a hundred is often in private hands and it assumes that, when this is not the case, then the king is regarded as the lord of the hundred. But in so doing it merely assumes that the state of things revealed by Domesday Book is about a century old. When in that record we read that the soke of four and a half hundreds in Oxfordshire 'belongs to' the royal manor of Bensington, that the soke of two hundreds 'belongs to' the royal manor of Headington, that the soke of other two hundreds 'belongs to' the royal manor of Bampton, we see that the king is the lord, the proprietor, of those hundreds which have no other lord[5].

---

[1] Edgar, I. 2, 3; III. 7; IV. 2, § 8; Æthelred, I. 1; III. 3, 4, 7.
[2] Æthelred, III. 3, 4.   [3] Æthelred, III. 7.
[4] Edgar, IV. 2, § 11; Æthelred, I. 3.
[5] D. B. i. 154. See above, p. 92.

From the laws now before us we infer that this is no very new arrangement. But of course it is possible that those laws have divers cases in view. It may be that within the hundred there is an immunity, a privileged township or manor, and that a thief is caught there. Who is to have the profits which arise from the crime and condemnation? The answer is: Half shall go to the hundred, half to the *land-ríca*, that is to say, half goes to the doomsmen, or perhaps to the lord, of the hundred court, half to the immunist. The lord under the general words of his charter might perchance claim the whole; but, in order that all the hundredors may have an interest in the pursuit of thieves, it is otherwise decreed. But where is justice to be done, in the hundred court or in the court of the immunist? That is a question of secondary importance to which our laws do not address themselves. Very probably justice will be done in the hundred court, or again it is not impossible that a mixed tribunal consisting partly of the men of 'the franchise,' partly of the men of 'the geldable' will meet upon the boundary of the immunist's land[1]. Our main point must be that the land-lord or *land-ríca* of these laws is an immunist, or is the king, who, where there is no immunity, occupies the position of an immunist.

The immunist's rights over free men. We see too that the immunist's rights extend over free men and over free landowners. If a man is guilty of heathenry he must, if he be a king's thegn, pay ten half-marks, half to Christ and half to the king, but if he be another 'landowning man' then he pays six half-marks, half to Christ and half to the *land-ríca*[2]. The landowner normally has a land-lord above him. We see also that the lord is made liable for the payment of dues which are ultimately exigible from those who are dwelling within his territory. 'If a king's thegn or other *land-ríca* makes default in paying Peter's pence, he must pay ten half-marks, half to Christ and half to the king; if a "towns-man" makes a similar default, the *land-ríca* must pay the penny and take an ox from the defaulter, and if the *land-ríca* neglects to do this, then Christ and the king shall receive the full *bót* of twelve ores[3].' Such is the manner in

---

[1] See above, p. 275.

[2] Northumbrian Priests' Law, Schmid, App. II. 48–9.

[3] Ibid. 57, 58. See also the texts which give the lord a share with the bishop in the penalty for neglect to pay tithe, viz. Edgar, II. 3; Æthelred, VIII. 8; Cnut, I. 8.

which the lord's power is consolidated. He begins to stand between his free men and the state, between his free men and the church.

Another consequence of the argument in which we have been engaged is that, at least a century before the Conquest, the great immunists were granting immunities to their dependants. From this consequence we shall not flinch. Bishop Oswald, for example, was an immunist on a splendid scale, and when he loaned land to a knight and said that the land was to be 'free from all secular service' save the *trinoda necessitas*, he loaned not merely land, but immunity and jurisdiction. On one occasion, adopting a formula that has lately come before us, he said that nothing was to go out of the land by way of *wite* [1]. By this we understand that he gave to his thegn any wites which might thereafter be incurred by the inhabitants of the manses which were comprised in the loan, and further that he gave him the right to hold a court. Domesday Book requires us to believe that such transactions had not been uncommon [2].

Will our attempt to explain the land-books create too many holders of sake and soke? We do not think so, for we do not think that the number of land-books should be indefinitely multiplied by our imaginations. If we look in Domesday Book at the counties which lie south of the Thames, we shall indeed see that the total amount of land of which the churches are tenants in chief is very large. But the number of these landowning churches is small. When we have named seven episcopal and a dozen abbatial minsters we have disposed of by far the greater bulk of the church lands in this district, and these minsters are as a general rule just those which have transmitted to us in cartularies and chronicles the story of their acquisitions. To churches that were destroyed by the Danes we may allot some charters; but we should have no warrant for the supposition that royal diplomata have perished by the hundred and left no trace behind. In the shires of York, Lincoln, Nottingham, Derby we might allow sake and soke to every English prelate who appears as a tenant in chief and yet not raise to twelve [3] the number of the ecclesiastical

Delegation of justiciary rights.

Number of immunists.

---

[1] K. 498 (ii. 386).   [2] See above, p. 100.

[3] The Archbishop of York, the bishops of Durham, Chester, Lincoln and (for one manor) Salisbury, the abbots of York, Peterborough, Ramsey, Croyland, Burton and (for one manor) Westminster.

immunists who had lands in this wide region. As to the lay holders of sake and soke, they were not very many though they held broad lands; also they belonged for the more part to an exalted class[1]. However, here as elsewhere we must admit that every attempted explanation discloses new problems.

NOTE.

The Ángild Clause.

As we have said above, (p. 274), there are certain charters in which the clause of immunity makes mention of the *ángild* (*pretium pro pretio, singulare pretium*). We will here collect the obscure texts in which this difficult term occurs.

First, however, we will call attention to a passage in Domesday's account of Worcestershire (D. B. i. 175 b), which throws some light on the matter. Westminster Abbey holds 200 hides and Pershore Abbey holds 100 hides. 'The county says that the church of Pershore is entitled to church-scot from all the 300 hides [its own 100 and Westminster's 200], to wit, from every hide on which a free man dwells one load of corn on Sᵗ. Martin's day, (if he has more hides than one, they are free), and if that day be infringed [i.e. if payment be not made thereon], he who has kept back the corn must pay elevenfold, but first must pay what is due [i.e. he altogether pays twelve loads—"God's property and the church's twelve-fold" (Æthelb. 1.)]; and the Abbot of Pershore will have a wite (*forisfactura*) from his own 100 hides, such as he ought to have from his own land ; but from the other 200 hides he will have the multifold payment of the corn that is due (*habet summam et persolutionem*) and the Abbot of Westminster has the wite (*forisfacturam*).' For *solvere et persolvere*, see Laws of William (Select Charters) c. 5; for *solta et persolta*, see Dial. de Scac. ii. 10.

If then, a Westminster tenant fails to pay church-scot to Pershore, he must make *bót* (very ample *bót*) to Pershore, but his *wite* will go to his own lord ; nothing is to 'go out to *wite*' from the Westminster land. We will now turn to the land-books. We take them to be saying in effect that in such a case as that put by Domesday the grantee of the immunity is to have his man's wite, though the restitutory *bót* will go to another.

(i) A.D. 767. Uhtred of the Hwiccas. K. 117 (i. 144); B. i. 286: 'interdicimus ut si aliquis in hac praenominatam terram aliquid foras furaverit alicui solvere aliquid nisi specialiter pretium pro pretio ad terminum ad poenam nihil foras.' We should place a stop after *terminum.* Then the last clause means 'nothing shall go out to wite.' The mention of the *terminus* suggests a payment at the boundary of the immunist's land.

---

[1] D. B. i. 280 b ; i. 337.

(ii) [Questionable]. A.D. 799. Cenwulf. K. 176 (i. 213); B. i. 411: 'de partibus vero et de causis singulare solvere pretium et nihil aliud de hac terra.'

(iii) A.D. 799–802. Pilheard. K. 116 (i. 142); B. i. 284: 'ut ab omnium fiscalium redituum operum onerumque seu etiam popularium conciliorum vindictis nisi tantum pretium pro pretio liberae sint in perpetuum.'

(iv) A.D. 814. Cenwulf of Mercia for the church of Worcester. K. 206 (i. 259); B. i. 489: 'exceptis his, expeditione et pontis constructione, et singulare pretium foras, nihilque ad poenam resolvat.'

(v) Cenwulf of Mercia for the church of Worcester. K. 215 (i. 271); B. i. 507: 'exceptis his, arcis et pontis constructione et expeditione et singulare pretium foras adversum aliud; ad poenam vero neque quadrantem minutam foras resolvat.'

(vi) A.D. 822. Ceolwulf of Mercia for Archbishop Wilfred. K. 216 (i. 272); B. i. 508: 'liberata permaneat in aefum nisi is quattuor causis quae nunc nominabo, expeditione contra paganos ostes, et pontes constructione sui [=seu] arcis munitione vel destructione in eodem gente, et singulare pretium foras reddat, secundum ritam gentes illius, et tamen nullam penam foras alicui persolvat.'

(vii) A.D. 831. Wiglaf of Mercia for the archbishop. K. 227 (i. 294); B. i. 556: 'nisi his tantum causis, expeditione et arcis munitione pontisque constructione et singulare pretium contra alium.'

(viii) A.D. 835. Egbert of Wessex for Abingdon. K. 236 (i. 312); B. i. 577: 'de illa autem tribulatione que witereden nominatur sit libera, nisi tamen singuli pretium solverit ut talia accipiant. Fures quoque quos appellant weregeldðeofas si foras rapiantur, pretium eius dimidium illi aecclesiae, et dimidium regi detur, et si intus rapitur totum reddatur ad aecclesiam.'

(ix) A.D. 849. Berhtwulf of Mercia for his thegn Egbert. K. 262 (ii. 34); B. ii. 40: 'Liberabo ab omnibus saecularibus servitutibus…nisi in confinio rationem reddant contra alium.'

(x) A.D. 855. Burhred of Mercia for the church of Worcester. K. 277 (ii. 58); B. ii. 88: 'nisi tantum quattuor causis, pontis et arcis, et expeditione contra hostes, et singulare pretium contra alium, et ad poenam nihil foras resolvat.

(xi) A.D. 883. Æthelred of Mercia for Berkeley. K. 313 (ii. 110); B. ii. 172: 'and þæt ic þæt mynster fram æghwelcum gafolum gefreoge þe to þiode hlafarde belimpeð, littles oððe micles, cuðes ge uncuðes, butan angilde wið oþrum and fæsten gewerce and fyrd socne and brycg geweorce……æghwelces þinges to freon ge wið cyning, ge wið ealdorman, ge wið gerefan æghwelces þeodomes, lytles and micles, butan fyrd socne and fæsten geworce and brycg geworce and angylde wið oðrum and noht ut to wite.'

(xii) A.D. 888. Æthelred of Mercia for a thegn. K. 1068 (v. 133); B. ii. 194: 'liberam hanc terram describimus ab omnibus causis nisi singulare pretium contra aliud ponat et modum ecclesiae.' Is the *modus* [or *modius*] of the church the church-scot?

In a few other cases the immunity mentions penal causes, 'witeræden,' and no express exception is made of the *ángild.* Thus :—

(xiii) A.D. 842. Æthelwulf for a thegn. K. 253 (ii. 16); B. ii. 13: 'ut regalium tributum et principali dominacione et vi coacta operacione et poenalium condicionum furis comprehensione...secura...permaneat.'

(xiv) [Questionable]. A.D. 844. Æthelwulf for Malmesbury ; one of the documents reciting the famous 'donation.' K. 1048 (v. 93); B. ii. 26; H. & S. iii. 630: 'ut sit tutus et munitus ab omnibus saecularibus servitutis, fiscis regalibus, tributis maioribus et minoribus, quod nos dicimus witereden.'

(xv) A.D. 877. Bp. Tunbert. K. 1063 (v. 121); B. ii. 163: 'a taxationibus quod dicimus wite redenne.'

The most detailed and at the same time the most hopelessly obscure information that we get is such as can be obtained from two Abingdon charters.

A.D. 821. Cenwulf. K. 214 (i. 269); B. i. 505; H. & S. iii. 556 : 'Si pro aliquo delicto accusatur homo Dei aecclesiae ille custos solus cum suo iuramento si audeat illum castiget. Sin autem ut recipiat aliam iusticiam huius vicissitudinis conditionem praefatum delictum cum simplo praetio componat.'

A.D. 835. Egbert. K. 236 (i. 312); B. i. 577; H. & S. iii. 613. The same clause, but with *alienam* instead of *aliam.* Also the following:— 'De illa autem tribulatione que witereden nominatur sit libera nisi tamen singuli [*corr.* singulare ?] pretium solverit ut talia accipiant [accipiat ?].'

This is very dark. Our best guess as to its meaning is this:—If a man of God, that is, a tenant of the church, is accused of crime, the *custos* of the church (this may mean the abbot, but more probably points to his reeve) may by his single oath purge the accused. But if he dare not do this, then he (the abbot or reeve) may pay the *bót* that is claimed, and by performing this condition he may obtain a transfer (*vicissitudo*) of the cause and do what other justice remains to be done, i.e. he may exact the *wite.* So in the second charter the abbot may pay the *bót*, the *singulare pretium*, and so obtain a right to exact the wite :—he makes the payment *ut talia* [i.e. *witereden*] *accipiat.* In guessing that *vicissitudo* points to a transfer of a suit, we have in mind the manner in which the Leges Henrici, 9 § 4, speak of the 'transition' of causes from court to court. The case that is being dealt with by these charters we take to be one in which an outsider in a 'foreign' court sues one of the abbot's tenants. The abbot can swear away the charge, or if he dares not do this, can obtain cognizance of the cause (in the language of a later day *potest petere curiam suam*) and therewith the right to the *wite*, but must in this case pay the restitutory *bót*, or rather, perhaps, find security that this shall be paid to the plaintiff in case he is successful. The clause may also imply that a multiple *bót* can not be exacted from the immunist's men, e.g. such a *bót* as we saw the Abbot of Pershore exacting from the Westminster men ; but this is a minor question.

§ 4. *Book-land and Loan-land.*

We can not say that from the first the gift of book-land The book and the gift.
establishes between the donee and the royal donor any such
permanent relation as that which in later times is called tenure.
What the king gives he apparently gives for good and all. In
particular, a gift of land to a church is 'an out and out gift';
nay more, it is a dedication. Still, even within the sphere of
piety and alms, we sometimes find the notion that in consequence of the gift the donee should do something for the
donor. Cnut frees the lands of the church of Exeter from all
burdens except military service, bridge-repair and 'assiduous
prayers[1],' and thus the title by which the churches hold their
lands is already being brought under the rubric *Do ut des*.
Turning to the books granted to laymen, we see that, at all
events from the middle of the tenth century onwards, they
usually state a *causa*, or as we might say 'a consideration,' for
the gift. Generally the gift is 'an out and out gift.' Words
are used which expressly tell us that the donee is to enjoy the
land during his life and may on his death give it to whomsoever he chooses. Nothing is said about his paying rent or
about his rendering in the future any service to the king in
return for the land. The 'consideration' that is stated in the
instrument is, if we may still use such modern terms, 'a past
consideration.' The land comes rather as a reward than as a
retaining fee. Sometimes indeed the thegn pays money to the
king and is in some sort a buyer of the land, though the king
will take credit for generosity and will talk of giving rather
than of selling[2]. More often the land comes as a reward to
him for obedience and fidelity or fealty. Already the word
fidelitas is in common use ; we have only to render it by *fealty*
and the transaction between the king and his thegn will be apt
to look like an infeudation, especially when the thegn is
described by the foreign term *vassallus*[3]. Even the general

---

[1] K. 729 (iv. 3).

[2] It is noticeable that the verb *syllan* usually means 'to give.' Words such
as *vendere* are avoided.

[3] A.D. 941, K. 390 (ii. 234) condemned by Kemble : 'amabili vassallo meo.'—
A.D. 952, K. 431 (ii. 302): 'cuidam vassallo.'—A.D. 956? K. 462 (ii. 338): 'meo
fideli vassallo.'—A.D. 967, K. 534 (iii. 11): 'meo fideli vassallo.'—A.D. 821,

rule that the king is rewarding a past, rather than stipulating for a future fealty, is not unbroken. Thus as early as 801 we find Cenwulf of Mercia and Cuthræd of Kent giving land to a thegn as a perpetual inheritance ' but so that he shall remain a faithful servant and unshaken friend to us and our magnates[1].' So again, in 946 King Edmund gives land to a faithful *minister* ' in order that while I live he may serve me faithful in mind and obedient in deed and that after my death he may with the same fealty obey whomsoever of my friends I may choose[2].' The king, it will be seen, reserves the right to dispose by will of his thegn's fealty. A continuing relation is established between the king and his successors in title on the one hand, the holder of the book-land and his successors in title on the other.

Book-land and service. However, as already said, the gift supposes that the personal relationship of lord and thegn already exists between the donor and the donee before the gift is made. This relationship was established by a formal ceremony; the thegn swore an oath of fealty, and it is likely that he bent his knee and bowed his head before his lord[3]. The Normans saw their homage in the English commendation[4]. The fidelity expected of the thegn is not regarded as a debt incurred by the receipt of land. And if the king does not usually stipulate for fidelity, still less does he stipulate for any definite service, in particular for any definite amount of military service. The land is not to be free of military service :—this is all that is said. However, to say this is to say that military service is already a burden on land. Already it is conceivable—very possibly it is true—that some of the lands of the churches have been freed even from this burden[5]. What is more, if we may believe the Abingdon charters, the ninth century is not far advanced before the king is occasionally making bargains as to the amount of military

K. 214 (i. 269): ' expeditionem cum 12 vassallis et cum tantis scutis exerceant.' After the Norman Conquest the word is very rare in our legal texts.

[1] K. 179 (i. 216): ' eo videlicet iure si ipse nobis et optimatibus nostris fidelis manserit minister et inconvulsus amicus.'

[2] K. 408 (ii. 263): ' eatenus ut vita comite tam fidus mente quam subditus operibus mihi placabile obsequium praebeat, et meum post obitum cuicunque meorum amicorum voluero eadem fidelitate immobilis obediensque fiat.'

[3] The terms of the oath are given in Schmid, App. X.

[4] See above, p. 69.

[5] See above, p. 69.

service that the lands of the churches shall render. Abingdon
need send to the host but twelve vassals and twelve shields[1].
Likewise we see that on the eve of the Conquest, though other
men who neglected the call to arms might escape with a fine of
forty shillings, it was the rule, at least in Worcestershire, that
the free man who had sake and soke and could 'go with his
land whither he would' forfeited that land if he was guilty of a
similar default[2]. With this we must connect those laws of
Cnut which say that the man who flees in battle, as well as
the man who is outlawed, forfeits his book-land to the king, no
matter who may be his lord[3].

Such rules when regarded from one point of view may well
be called feudal. Book-land having been derived from, is
specially liable to return to the king. It will return to him
if the holder of it be guilty of shirking his military duty or of
other disgraceful crime. To this we may add that if these rules
betray the fact that the holder of this king-given land may
none the less have commended himself and his land to some
other lord against whose claims the king has to legislate,
thereby they disclose a feudalism of the worst, of the centri-
fugal kind. The ancient controversy as to whether 'the
military tenures' were 'known to the Anglo-Saxons' is apt to
become a battle over words. The old power of calling out all
able-bodied men for defensive warfare was never abandoned; but
it was not abandoned by the Norman and Angevin kings. The
holder of land was not spoken of as holding it by military
service; but it would seem that in the eleventh century the king,
save in some pressing necessity, could only ask for one man's
service from every five hides, and the holder of book-land
forfeited that land if he disobeyed a lawful summons[4]. Whether
a man who will lose land for such a cause shall be said to hold
it by military service is little better than a question about the
meaning of words. At best it is a question about legal logic.
We are asked to make our choice (and yet may doubt whether
our ancestors had made their choice) between the ideas of
misdemeanour and punishment on the one hand and the idea
of reentry for breach of condition on the other.

The same vagueness enshrouds the infancy of the escheat

Military service.

Escheat of book-land.

---

[1] K. 214 (i. 269); H. & S. iii. 556.
[2] D. B. i. 172; see above, p. 159.   [3] Cnut, ii. 13, 77.
[4] See above, p. 156.

propter defectum tenentis. Already in 825 a king tells how he gave land to one of his *praefecti* who died intestate and without an heir, 'and so that land by the decree of my magnates was restored to me who had before possessed it[1].' Here we seem to see the notion that when a gift has spent itself, when there is no longer any one who can bring himself within the words of donation, the given land should return to the giver. In another quarter we may see that when the king makes a gift he does not utterly abandon all interest in the land that is given. Cenwulf of Mercia in a charter for Christ Church at Canterbury tells us that King Egbert gave land to a certain thegn of his who on leaving the country gave it to the minster; but that Offa annulled this gift and gave away the land to other thegns, saying that it was unlawful for a thegn to give away without his lord's witness (*testimonio*) the land given to him by his lord[2]. Cenwulf restored the land to the church; but he took money for it, and he does not say that Offa had acted illegally. There is much to show that the 'restraint on alienation' is one of the oldest of the 'incidents of tenure.' Our materials do not enable us to formulate a general principle, but certain it is that the holders of book-land, whether they be laymen or ecclesiastics, very generally obtain the consent of the king when they propose to alienate their land either *inter vivos* or by testament. We may not argue from this to any definite condition annexed to the gift, or to any standing relationship between the donor and the donee like the 'tenure' of later times. After all, it is a very natural thought that a reward bestowed by the king should not be sold or given away. The crosses and stars with which modern potentates decorate their *fideles,* we do not expect to see these in the market[3]. The land that the king has booked

---

[1] K. 1035 (v. 76). The charter is not beyond suspicion, but Kemble has received, and the editors of the Councils (H. & S. iii. 607) have refused to condemn it.

[2] K. 1020 (v. 60); B. i. 409; H. & S. iii. 528.

[3] See Brunner, Die Landschenkungen der Merowinger und der Agilolfinger, Forschungen, p. 6: 'He who receives an order acquires in the insignia of the order which are delivered to him an ownership of an extremely attenuated kind. He can not give them away or sell them or let them out or give them in dowry. When he dies they go back to the giver.' We are not aware of any English decision on such matters as these. In a charter for Winchester (B. ii. 238) Edward the Elder is represented as saying that the land that he gives to the church is never to be alienated. If, however, the monks must sell or

to his thegn is an 'honour' and the giver will expect to be
consulted before it passes into hands that may be unworthy of
it. It may be just because the gift of book-land is made by
the king and corroborated by all the powers of church and state,
that the book is conceived as exercising a continuous sway over
the land comprised in it. The book, it has well been said, is
the *lex possessionis* of that land[1]. It can make the land descend
this way or that way, and the land will come back to the king
if ever the power of the book be spent. What is more, from
the first we seem to see a germ of our famous English rule that
if a gift be made without 'words of inheritance' the gift will
endure only during the life of the donee:—will endure, we say,
for a gift is no mere act done once for all but a force that
endures for a longer or a shorter period. Certain it is that
most of the charters are careful to say that the gift is not thus
to come to an end but is to go on operating despite the donee's
death[2].

And even when, as is generally the case, the book made in
favour of a lay-man says that the donee is to have the power
of leaving the land to whomsoever he may please, or to such
heirs as he may choose, we still must doubt whether his
testamentary power is utterly unrestrained, whether he will not
have to consult the royal donor when he is making his will.
The phenomena which we have here to consider are very
obscure, because we never can be quite certain why it is that a
testator is seeking the king's aid. We have to remember that
the testament is an exotic, ecclesiastical institution which is
likely to come into collision with the ancient folk-law. From
an early time the church was striving in favour of the utmost
measure of testamentary freedom, for formless wills, for nuncu-

Alienation of book-land.

---

exchange it, then they may return it 'to that royal family by whom it was
given to them.'

[1] Brunner, Zur Rechtsgeschichte d. röm. u. germ. Urkunde, p. 190; Hist.
Eng. Law, ii. 12.

[2] See Brunner, Landschenkungen, Forschungen, p. 1. In this paper
Dr Brunner appealed to our English law, in order that he might settle the
famous controversy between Waitz and Roth as to the character of the gifts
of land made by the Merovingians. On p. 5 he denies that our rule about
'words of inheritance' should be called feudal. Its starting point is the
principle that the quality [an English lawyer would add—and the quantity
also] of the 'estate' (*Besitzrecht*) can be determined by the donor's words, by a
lex donationis imposed by the donor on the land.

pative wills[1]. The very largeness of its claims made impossible any definite compromise between church-right and folk-right. So far as we can see, no precise law is evolved as to when and how and over what a man may exercise a power of testation. The church will support testaments of the most formless kind; on the other hand, the heirs of the dead man will endeavour, despite the anathema, to break his will, and sometimes they will succeed[2]. Consequently the testator will endeavour to obtain the crosses of the bishops and the consent of the king. He has already a book which tells him that he may leave the land to a chosen heir; but if he be prudent he will not trust to this by itself. Kings change their minds.

The heriot and the testament.

Then the law about heriots complicates the matter. The heriot has its origin in the duty of the dying thegn or of his heirs to return to his lord the arms which that lord has given or lent to him. We have to use some such vague phrase as 'given or lent'; we dare not speak more precisely[3]. A time comes when the king provides his thegn, no longer with arms, but with land; still the heriot is rendered[4]. In the tenth century this render is closely connected with the exercise of testamentary power. The thegn offers a heriot with a prayer that 'his will may stand.' He presents swords and money to the king in order that he may be worthy of his testament[5]. When we find such phrases as this, we can not always be certain that the land of which the testator is going to dispose is land over which a book purports to give him testamentary

---

[1] Brunner, Geschichte der Urkunde, p. 200.

[2] Heming's Cartulary, i. 259. 'Post mortem autem eius, filius eius... testamentum patris sui irritum faciens....' Ibid. p. 263: 'Brihtwinus...eandem terram Deo et Sanctae Mariae obtulit, eundemque nepotem suum monachum fecit. Filius eius etiam, Brihtmarus nomine, pater ipsius iam dicti Edwini monachi, cum heres patris extitisset,...ipsam...villam monasterio dedit.' Hist. Eng. Law, ii. 250.

[3] Brunner, Forschungen, p. 22; Hist. Eng. Law, i. 292.

[4] Crawford Charters (ed. Napier and Stevenson), pp. 23, 126. Early in cent. xi. a bishop in his testament declares how he gives 'to each retainer his steed which he had lent him.'

[5] See the wills collected by Thorpe; p. 501: gift to the queen for her mediation that the will may stand. Ibid. p. 505: 'And bishop Theodred and ealdorman Eadric informed me, when I gave my lord the sword that king Edmund gave me...that I might be worthy of my testament (*mine quides wirde*). And I never...have done any wrong to my lord that it may not so be.' Ibid. p. 519: 'And I pray my dear lord for the love of God that my testament may stand.' See also pp. 528, 539, 543, 552, 576.

power; he may be hoping that the king's aid will be sufficient to enable him to bequeath the unbooked land that he holds[1]. In other cases he may be endeavouring to dispose of lands that have merely been 'loaned' to him for his life by the king. But this will hardly serve to explain all the cases, and we so frequently find the holder of book-land applying for the king's consent when he is going to make an alienation of it *inter vivos* that we need not marvel at finding a similar application made when he is about to execute a testament[2].

This having been said, we shall not be surprised to find that in ancient times the difference between a gift of land and a loan of land was not nearly so well marked as it would be by modern law. The loan may be regarded as a temporary gift, the gift as a very permanent, if not perpetual, loan. We know how this matter looks in the law of Bracton's age. By feoffment one gives land to a man for his life, or one gives it to him and the heirs of his body, or to him and his heirs: but in any case, the land may come back to the giver. The difference between the three feoffments is a difference in degree rather than in kind; one will operate for a longer, another for a shorter time; but, however absolute the gift may be, the giver never parts with all his interest in the land[3]. Or we may put it in another way:—in our English law usufruct is a temporary *dominium* and *dominium* is a usufruct that may be perpetual. Or, once more, adopting the language of modern statutes, we may say that the tenant for life is no usufructuary but 'a limited owner.' We are accustomed to bring this doctrine into connexion with rules about dependent tenure:—the donor, we say, retains an interest in the land because he is the tenant's lord. But, on looking at the ancient land-books, we may find

The gift and the loan.

---

[1] Thus ealdorman Alfred disposes (but with the consent of the king and all his witan) of his 'heritage' as well as of his book-land; Thorpe, 480. Lodge, Essays on A.-S. Law, p. 108, supposes a certain power of regulating the descent of 'family land' within the family.

[2] K. 414 (ii. 273): 'Ego Wulfricus annuente et sentiente et praesente domino meo rege...concessi...terram iuris mei...quam praefatus rex Eadredus mihi dedit in perpetuam hereditatem cum libro eiusdem terrae.'—K. 1130 (v. 254): 'Ego Eadulfus dux per concessionem domini mei regis...concedo...has terras de propria possessione mea quas idem...rex dedit in perpetuam hereditatem.'—K. 1226 (vi. 25): 'Ego Ælfwordus minister Regis Eadgari concedo... annuente domino meo rege...villam unam de patrimonio meo.'

[3] Except in the cases, comparatively rare before the statute *Quia Emptores*, in which the feoffee is to hold of the feoffor's lord.

reason to suspect that the confusion of loans with gifts and gifts with loans (if we may speak of confusion where in truth the things confounded have never as yet been clearly distinguished) is one of the original germs of the rule that all land is held of the king. After all, the king—and he is by far the greatest giver in the country and his gifts are models for all gifts—never can really part with all the rights that he has in the land that he gives, for he still will be king of it and therefore in a sense it will always be part of his land. To maintain a sharp distinction between the rights that he has as king and the rights that he has as landlord, jurisprudence is not as yet prepared.—But we must look at the land-loan more closely.

The *pre-carium.* Foreign historians have shown how after the barbarian invasions one single form of legal thought, or (if we may borrow a term from them), one single legal 'institute' which had been saved out of the ruins of Roman jurisprudence, was made to do the hard duty of expressing the most miscellaneous facts, was made to meet a vast multitude of cases in which, while one man is the owner of land, another man is occupying and enjoying it by the owner's permission. This institute was the *precarium.* Originally but a tenancy at will, it was elaborated into different shapes which, when their elaboration had been completed, had little in common. For some reason or another one begs (*rogare*) of a landowner leave to occupy a piece of land; for some reason or another the prayer is granted, the grantor making a display of generosity and speaking of his act as a 'benefit' (*beneficium*), an act of good-nature and liberality. An elastic form is thus established. The petitioner may, or may not, promise to pay a rent to his benefactor; the benefactor may, or may not, engage that the relationship shall continue for a fixed term of years, or for the life of the petitioner or for several lives. Usually this relationship between petitioner and benefactor is complicated with the bond of patronage: the former has commended himself to the latter, has come within his power, his protection, his trust (*trustis*), has become his *fidelis*, his *homo*. At a later time the inferior is a *vassus*, the superior is his *senior*, for the word *vassus*, which has meant a menial servant, spreads upwards. Then the *precarium*, as it were, divides itself into various channels. One of its streams encompasses the large province of humble tenancies, wherein the peasants obtain land from the churches and other owners on more or less arduous conditions, or reserve a right to occupy so long as they live the lands that they have given to the saints. Another stream sweeps onward into the domain of grand history and public law. The noble obtains a spacious territory, perhaps a county, from the king by way of 'benefaction'; the *precarium* becomes the *beneficium*, the *beneficium* becomes the *feudum*[1]. The king can not prevent the *beneficia*, the *feuda*, from becoming hereditary.

The analogous English institution was the *læn* or, as we now say, loan. If in translating a German book we render *Lehn* by *fief*, *feud*, or *fee*, we should still remember that a *Lehn* is a loan. And no doubt the history of our ancient land-loans was influenced by the history of the *precarium*. We come upon the technical terms of continental law when King Æthelbald forbids any one to beg for a benefit or benefice out of the lands that have been given to the church of Winchester[2]. There was need for such prohibitions. Edward the Elder prayed the bishop of this very church to lend him some land for his life; the bishop consented, but expressed a fervent hope that there would be no more of such requests, which in truth were very like commands. It would seem that some of the English kings occasionally did what had been done on a large scale in France by Charles Martel or his sons, namely, they compelled the churches to grant benefices to lay noblemen[3]. When bishop Oswald of Worcester declared how he had been lending lands to his thegns, he used a foreign, technical term: '*beneficium* quod illis *praestitum* est[4].' But it is clear that the English conception of a land-loan was very lax; it would blend

---

[1] Fustel de Coulanges, Les origines du système féodal; Brunner, D. R. G. i. 209–12.

[2] K. 1058 (v. 115); B. ii. 89: 'et nullus iam licentiam ulterius habeat Christi neque sancti Petri...neque ausus sit ulterius illam terram praedictam *rogandi in beneficium*.'

[3] K. 1089 (v. 166); B. ii. 281. See also K. 262 (ii. 33); B. ii. 40; Birhtwulf of Mercia takes a lease for five lives from the church of Worcester and assigns it to a thegn. The consideration for this lease is a promise that for the future he will not make gifts out of the goods of the church.

[4] K. 1287 (vi. 124). The verb *praestare* was the regular term for describing the action of one who was constituting a *precarium* or *beneficium*. In K. 1071 (v. 138) Bp Werferth of Worcester obtains a lease for three lives having petitioned for it; 'terram...humili prece deprecatus fui.'

with the conception of a gift. To describe transactions of one and the same kind, if such verbs as *commodare* and *lǽnan* and *lǽtan* were used[1], such words as *conferre, concedere, tribuere, largiri* and *donare* were also used[2]. A loan is a temporary gift, and the nature of the transaction remains the same whether the man to whom the loan is made does, or does not, come under the obligation of paying rent or performing services.

Loans of church lands to the great.
Unfortunately our materials only permit us to study one branch of the loan; the aristocratic branch we may call it. No doubt the lords, especially the churches, are from an early time letting or 'loaning' lands to cultivators. Specimens of such agricultural leases we do not see and cannot expect to see, for they would hardly be put into writing. But at an early time we do see the churches loaning lands, and wide lands, to great men. This is a matter of much importance. One other course in the feudal edifice is thus constructed. We have seen the churches interposed between the king and the cultivators of the soil; the churches have become landlords with free land-holders under them. And now it is discovered that the churches have a superiority which they can lend to others. We see already a four-storeyed structure. There are the cultivator, the church's thegn, the church, the king. Very great men think it no shame to beg boons from the church. Already before 750 the bishop of Worcester has granted five manses to 'Comes Leppa' for lives[3]; before the century is out the abbot of Medeshamstead has granted ten manses to the 'princeps' Cuthbert for lives[4]. In 855 the bishop of Worcester gives eleven manses to the ealdorman of the Mercians and his wife for their lives[5]; in 904 a successor of his makes a similar gift[6]. But we have seen that the king himself was not above taking a loan from the church. Indeed powerful men insist on having loans, and the churches, in order to protect themselves against importunities, obtain from the king this among their other immunities, namely, that no lay man is to beg boons from them, or that no lease is to be for longer than the lessee's

---

[1] For *commodare* see K. v. pp. 166, 169, 171; for *lǽnan*, ibid. 162; for *lǽtan*, ibid. 164.

[2] See Bp Oswald's leases.

[3] K. 91 (i. 109).　　　　　　　　　[4] K. 165 (i. 201).

[5] K. 279 (ii. 61).　　　　　　　　　[6] K. 339 (ii. 149).

life[1]. In such cases we may also see the working of a second motive : the church is to be protected against the prodigality of its own rulers. The leases made by the prelates seem usually to have been for three lives. This compass is so often reached, so seldom exceeded[2] that we may well believe that the English church had accepted as a rule of sound policy, if not as a rule of law, the novel of Justinian which set the limit of three lives to leases of church lands[3].

Occasionally the lease is made in consideration of a sum of money paid down ; occasionally the recipient of the land comes under an express obligation to pay rent. An early example shows us the abbot of Medeshamstead letting ten manses to the 'princeps' Cuthbert for lives in consideration of a gross sum of a thousand shillings and an annual *pastus* or 'farm' of one night[4]. The bishop of Worcester early in the ninth century concedes land to a woman for her life on condition that she shall cleanse and renovate the furniture of the church[5]. On the other hand, when land is 'loaned' to a king or a great nobleman, this may be in consideration of his patronage and protection ; the church stipulates for his *amicitia*[6]. We may say that he becomes the *advocatus* of the church, and the patronage exercised by kings and nobles over the churches is of importance, though perhaps it was not quite so serious a matter in England as it was elsewhere.

The consideration for the loan.

But from our present point of view by far the most interesting form that the loan takes is the loan to the thegn or the *cniht*. Happily it falls out that we have an excellent opportunity of studying this institution. We recall the fact

S[t]. Oswald's loans.

[1] See the charter of Cenwulf for Winchcombe, H. & S. iii. 572 and the editors' note at 575. See also K. 610 (iii. 157), 1058 (v. 115), 1090 (v. 169).

[2] K. 262 (ii. 33) is a lease for five lives by the church of Worcester ; but the lessee is a king.

[3] Nov. 7, 3. See Brunner, Zur Rechtsgeschichte der röm. u. germ. Urkunde, 187. Theodore of Tarsus would perhaps have known this rule. It does not belong to the general western tradition of Roman law, but is distinctly Justinianic.

[4] K. 165 (i. 201). The 'limitation' is not very plain ; but we seem to have here a lease for two lives.

[5] K. 182 (i. 220).

[6] K. 262 (ii. 33) ; B. ii. 40 : lease by church of Worcester to the king for five lives : 'et illi dabant terram illam ea tamen conditione ut ipse rex firmius amicus sit episcopo praefato et familia in omnibus bonis eorum.' K. 279 (ii. 61) : lease by the same church to a *dux* and his wife with stipulation for *amicitia*.

that by the gifts of kings and underkings the church of Worcester had become entitled to vast tracts of land in Worcestershire and the adjoining counties. Now between the years 962 and 992 Bishop Oswald granted at the very least some seventy loans comprising in all 180 manses or there-abouts[1]. In almost all cases the loan was for three lives. In a few cases the recipient was a kinsman of the bishop, in a few he was an ecclesiastic; far more generally he is described as 'minister meus,' 'fidelis meus,' 'cliens meus,' 'miles meus,' 'my knight,' 'my thegn,' 'my true man.' When the 'cause' or consideration for the transaction is expressed it is 'ob eius fidele obsequium' or 'pro eius humili subiectione atque famulatu': a recompense is made for fealty and service. Any thing that could be called a stipulation for future service is very rare. A definite rent is seldom reserved[2]. Sometimes the bishop declares that the land is to be free from all earthly burdens, save service in the host and the repair of bridges and strongholds. To those excepted imposts he sometimes adds church-scot, or the church's rent, without specifying the amount. Sometimes he seems to go further and to say that the land is to be free from everything save the church's rent (*ecclesiasticus census*)[3]. In so doing he gives a hint that the recipients of the lands will have something to pay to, or something to do for the church. Were it not for this, we might well think that these loans were made solely in con-sideration of past services, of obedience already rendered, and that at most the recipient undertook the vague obligation of being faithful and obsequious in the future.

Sᵗ. Os-wald's let-ter to Edgar.

But happily for us Sᵗ. Oswald was a careful man of business

---

[1] These are preserved in Heming's Cartulary; see K. 494–673.

[2] In K. 498 (ii. 386) the *aecclesiasticus census* is two *modii* of clean grain; in K. 511 (ii. 400) the lessee must mow once and reap once 'with all his craft'; in K. 508 (ii. 398) he must sow two acres with his own seed and reap it; in K. 661 (iii. 233) is a similar stipulation.

[3] In many cases the clause of immunity has become very obscure owing to a copyist's blunder. It is made to run thus: 'Sit autem terra ista libera omni regi nisi aecclesiastici censi.' Some mistake between *rei* and *regi* may be suspected. What we want is what we get in some other cases, e.g. K. 651, 652, viz. 'libera ab omni saecularis rei negotio.' The following forms are somewhat exceptional; K. 530 and 612, 'butan ferdfare and walgeworc and brycgeworc *and circanlade*'; K. 623, 666, 'excepta sanctae dei basilicae suppeditatione et ministratione'; K. 625, 'exceptis sanctae dei aecclesiae necessitatibus et utilitatibus.'

and put on record in the most solemn manner the terms on
which he made his land-loans. The document in which he did
this is for our purposes the most important of all the documents
that have come down to us from the age before the Conquest[1].
It takes the form of a letter written to King Edgar. We will
give a brief and bald abstract of it[2]:—' I am (says the bishop)
deeply grateful to you my lord, for all your liberality and will
remain faithful to you for ever. In particular am I grateful to
you for receiving my complaint and that of God's holy Church
and granting redress by the counsel of your wise men[3]. Therefore I have resolved to put on record the manner in which I
have been granting to my faithful men for the space of three
lives the lands committed to my charge, so that by the leave
and witness of you, my lord and king, I may declare this
matter to the bishops my successors, and that they may know
what to exact from these men according to the covenant that
they have made with me and according to their solemn promise.
I have written this document in order that none of them may
hereafter endeavour to abjure the service of the church. This
then is the covenant made with the leave of my lord the king
and attested, roborated and confirmed by him and all his wise
men. I have granted the land to be held under me (*sub me*)
on these terms, to wit, that every one of these men shall fulfil
the whole law of riding as riding men should[4], and that they
shall pay in full all those dues which of right belong to the
church, that is to say *cricscoott, toll,* and *tace* or *swinscead,*
and all other dues of the church (unless the bishop will excuse
them from any thing), and shall swear that so long as they

---

[1] Kemble gives it in Cod. Dipl. 1287 (vi. 124) and in an appendix to vol. i.
of his history. Also he speaks of it in Cod. Dipl. i. xxxv., and there says that
it is 'a laboured justification' by Bp Oswald of his proceedings. To my mind
it is nothing of the kind. Oswald is proud of what he has done and wishes
that a memorial of his acts may be carefully preserved for the benefit of the
church. Of course, if regarded from our modern point of view, the form of the
document is curious. The bishop seems engaged in an attempt to bind his lessees
by his own unilateral account of the terms to which they have agreed. But his
object is to have of the contract a record which has been laid before the king
and the witan and which, if we are to use modern terms, will have all the force
of an act of parliament, to say nothing of the anathema.

[2] In places its language becomes turbid and well-nigh untranslatable.

[3] It may be that the bishop has just obtained from the king a grant or
confirmation of the hundredal jurisdiction over what is to be Oswaldslaw.

[4] K. vi. 125: 'hoc est ut omnis equitandi lex ab eis impleatur quae ad
equites pertinet.'

possess the said land they will be humbly subject to the commands of the bishop. What is more, they shall hold themselves ready to supply all the needs of the bishop; they shall lend their horses; they shall ride themselves, and be ready to build bridges and do all that is necessary in burning lime for the work of the church[1]; they shall erect a hedge for the bishop's hunt and shall lend their own hunting spears whenever the bishop may need them. And further, to meet many other wants of the bishop, whether for the fulfilment of the service due to him or of that due to the king, they shall with all humility and subjection be obedient to his domination and to his will[2], in consideration of the benefice that has been loaned to them, and according to the quantity of the land that each of them possesses. And when the term for which the lands are granted has run out, it shall be in the bishop's power either to retain those lands for himself or to loan them out to any one for a further term, but so that the said services due to the church shall be fully rendered. And in case any shall make wilful default in rendering the aforesaid dues of the church, he shall make amends according to the bishop's *wite*[3] or else shall lose the gift and land that he enjoyed. And if any one attempt to defraud the church of land or service, be he deprived of God's blessing unless he shall make full restitution. He who keeps this, let him be blessed; he who violates this,

---

[1] K. vi. 125 : 'et ad totum piramiticum opus aecclesiae calcis atque ad pontis aedificium ultro inveniantur parati.' The translation here given is but guesswork; we suppose that *piramiticus* means ' of or belonging to fire (πῦρ).'

[2] Ibid.: 'insuper ad multas alias indigentiae causas quibus opus est domino antistiti frunisci, sive ad suum servitium sive ad regale explendum, semper illius archiductoris dominatui et voluntati qui episcopatui praesidet......subditi fiant.' Is *archiductor* but a fine name for the bishop? We think not. In the Confessor's day Eadric the Steersman was 'ductor exercitus episcopi ad servitium regis' (Heming, i. 81), and it would seem from this that the tenants were to be subject to a captain set over them by the bishop. But in the famous, if spurious, charter for Oswaldslaw (see above, p. 268) Edgar says that on a naval expedition the bishop's men are not to serve under the ordinary officers 'sed cum suo archiductore, videlicet episcopo, qui eos defendere et protegere debet ab omni perturbatione et inquietudine.' This would settle the question, could we be certain that the words ' videlicet episcopo ' were not the gloss of a forger who was improving an ancient instrument. For our present purpose, however, it is no very important question whether the *archiductor*, the commander in chief of these tenants, is the bishop himself or an officer of his.

[3] Ibid. : 'praevaricationis delictum secundum quod praesulis ius est emendet.'

let him be cursed: Amen. Once more, my lord, I express my gratitude to you. There are three copies of this document; one at Worcester, one deposited with the Archbishop of Canterbury and one with the Bishop of Winchester.'

Now we may well say that here is feudal tenure. In the first place, we notice a few verbal points. The recipient of the *læn* has received a *beneficium* from the bishop, and if he will not hold the land *de episcopo*, none the less he will hold it *sub episcopo*. Then he is the bishop's *fidelis*, his *fidus homo*, his 'hold and true man,' his thegn, his knight, his soldier, his *minister*, his *miles*, his *eques*. Then he takes an oath to the bishop, and seemingly this oath states in the most energetic terms his utter subjection to the bishop's commands. What is more, he swears to be faithful and obedient because he has received a *beneficium* from the bishop, and the amount of his service is measured by the quantity of land that he has received. Then again, we see that he holds his land by service; if he fails in his service, at all events if he denies his liability to serve, he is in peril of losing the land, though perhaps he may escape by paying a pecuniary fine. As to the services to be rendered, if we compare them with those of which Glanvill and Bracton speak, they will seem both miscellaneous and indefinite; perhaps we ought to say that they are all the more feudal on that account. The tenant is to pay the church-scot, the *ecclesiasticus census* of other documents. This, as we learn from Domesday Book, is one load (*summa*) of the best corn from every hide of land, and unless it be paid on S^t. Martin's day, it must be paid twelve-fold along with a fine[1]. He must pay toll to the bishop when he buys and sells; he must pay *tace*, apparently the pannage of a later time, for his pigs. He must go on the bishop's errands, provide him with hunting-spears, erect his 'deer-hedge' when he goes to the chase. There remains a margin of unspecified services; for he must do what he is told to do according to the will of the bishop. But, above all, he is a horseman, a riding man and must fulfil 'the law of riding.' For a moment we are tempted to say 'the law of chivalry.' This indeed would be an anachronism; but still he is bound to ride at the bishop's command. Will he ride only on peaceful errands? We doubt it. He is

Feudalism in Oswaldslaw.

---

[1] D. B. 174. Compare the entry on f. 175 b relating to the church-scot of Pershore.

bound to do all the service that is due to the king, all the forinsec service[1] we may say. A certain quantity of military service is due from the bishop's lands; his thegns must do it. As already said, the obligation of serving in warfare is not yet so precisely connected with the tenure of certain parcels of land as it will be in the days of Henry II., but already the notion prevails that the land owes soldiers to the king, and probably the bishop has so arranged matters that his territory will be fully 'acquitted' if his *equites*, his *milites* take the field. Under what banner will they fight? Hardly under the sheriff's banner. Oswald is founding Oswaldslaw and within Oswaldslaw the sheriff will have no power. More probably they will follow the banner of S‍ᵗ. Mary of Worcester. This we know, that in the Confessor's reign one Eadric was steersman of the bishop's ship and commander of the bishop's troops[2]. This also we know, that in the suit between the churches of Worcester and of Evesham that came before the Domesday commissioners, one of the rights claimed by the bishop against the abbot was that the men of two villages, Hamton and Bengeworth, were bound to pay geld and to fight along with the bishop's men[3]. And then, suppose that Danes or Welshmen or Englishmen make a raid on the bishop's land, is it certain that he will communicate with the ealdorman or the king before he calls upon his knights to defend and to avenge him? Still we must not bring into undue relief the military side of the tenure.

Oswald's riding men.
These men may be bound to fight at the bishop's call, but fighting is not their main business; they are not professional warriors. They are the predecessors not of the military tenants of the twelfth century, but of the *radchenistres*, and *radmanni* of Domesday Book, the *rodknights* of Bracton's text, the thegns and drengs of the northern counties who puzzle the lawyers of the Angevin time. Point by point we can compare the tenure of these *ministri* and *equites* of the tenth with that of the thegns and drengs of the twelfth and thirteenth centuries and at point after point we find similarity, almost identity. They pay

---

[1] Hist. Eng. Law, i. 217. See also D. B. i. 165 b, Hinetune.

[2] Heming, i. 81: 'Edricus qui fuit, tempore regis Edwardi, stermannus navis episcopi et ductor exercitus eiusdem episcopi ad servitium regis.' D. B. i. 173 b: 'Edricus stirman' held five hides of the bishop.

[3] Heming, i. 77: 'Et [episcopus] deracionavit socam et sacam de Hamtona ad suum hundred de Oswaldes lawe, quod ibi debent placitare et geldum et expeditionem...persolvere.'

rent; they have horses and their horses are at the service of
their lord ; they must ride his errands, carry his stores, assist
him in the chase; they must fight if need be, but the exact
nature of this obligation is indefinite[1]. Dependent tenure is
here and, we may say, feudal tenure, and even tenure by knight's
service, for though the English *cniht* of the tenth century differs
much from the knight of the twelfth, still it is a change in
military tactics rather than a change in legal ideas that is
required to convert the one into the other. As events fell out
there was a breach of continuity; the English thegns and
drengs and knights either had to make way for Norman *milites*,
or, as sometimes happened, they were subjected to Norman
milites and constituted a class for which no place could readily
be found in the new jurisprudence of tenures. But had Harold
won the day at Hastings and at the same time learnt a lesson
from the imminence of defeat, some peaceful process would
probably have done the same work that was done by forfeitures
and violent displacements. The day for heavy cavalry and
professional militancy was fast approaching when Oswald subjected his tenants to the *lex equitandi*.

Yet another of those feudal phenomena that come before us   Heritable
in the twelfth century may easily be engendered by these loans; loans.
we mean the precarious inheritance, the right to 'relieve' from
the lord the land that a dead man held of him[2]. In speaking
of Oswald's loans as 'leases for three lives' we have used a loose
phrase which might lead a modern reader astray. Oswald does
not let land to a man for the lives of three persons named in
the lease and therefore existing at the time when the lease is
made; rather he lets the land to a man and declares that it
shall descend to two successive heirs of his. The exact extent
of the power that the lessee has of instituting an heir, in other
words of devising the land by testament, instead of allowing it
to be inherited *ab intestato*, we need not discuss; suffice it that
the lessee's rights may twice pass from ancestor to heir, or from
testator to devisee[3]. Now such a lease may cover the better

---

[1] Maitland, Northumbrian Tenures, Eng. Hist. Rev. v. 625.

[2] Hist. Eng. Law, i. 288.

[3] In this respect Oswald's leases seem to have closely resembled a form of
lease, known as *manusfirma*, which became common in the France of the
eleventh century: Lamprecht, Beiträge zur Geschichte des französischen
Wirthschaftslebens, pp. 59, 60.

part of a century. A time will come when the land ought to return to the church that gave it; but for some eighty years it will have 'been in one family' and twice over it will have been inherited. Is it very probable that the bishop will be able to oust the third heir? Will he wish to do so, if three generations of thegns or knights have faithfully served the church? May we not be fairly certain that this third heir will get the land on the old terms, if he will 'recognize' the church's right to turn him out? As a matter of fact we see that Oswald's successors have great difficulty in recovering the land that he has let[1]. In the middle ages he who allows land to descend twice has often enough allowed it to become heritable for good and all. Despite solemn charters and awful anathemas he will have to be content with a relief[2].

Wardship and mar-
riage.　　But at least, it will be said, there was no 'right of wardship and marriage.' We can see the beginning of it. In 983 Oswald let five manses to his kinsman Gardulf. Gardulf is to enjoy the land during his life; after his death his widow is to have it, if she remains a widow or if she marries one of the bishop's subjects[3]. So the bishop is already taking an interest in the marriages of his tenants; he will have no woman holding his land who is married to one who is not his man. And then Domesday Book tells us how in the Confessor's day one of Oswald's successors had disposed of an heiress and her land to one of his knights[4].

Seignorial
jurisdic-
tion.　　Still, it will be urged, the feudalism here displayed is imperfect in one important respect. These tenants of the church of Worcester hold their land under contracts cognizable

[1] Heming, i. 259: 'Ac primo videndum quae terrae trium heredum temporibus accommodatae sint, post quorum decessum iuri monasterii redderentur, quaeve postea iuxta hanc conventionem redditae, quaeve iniuste sunt retentae, sive ipsorum, qui eas exigere deberent, negligentia, sive denegatae sint iniquorum hominum potentia.' See also the story told by Heming on p. 264.

[2] Lamprecht, op. cit. p. 61, says that it was quite uncommon for the French landlord to get back his land if once he let it for three lives. One of the Worcester leases, but one stigmatized by Kemble (ii. 152), is a lease for three lives 'nisi haeredes illius tempus prolixius a pontifice sedis illius adipisci poterint.'

[3] K. 637 (iii. 194): 'si in viduitate manere decreverit, vel magis nubere voluerit, ei tamen viro qui episcopali dignitati supradictae aecclesiae sit subiectus.'

[4] D. B. i. 173: 'Hanc terram tenuit Sirof de episcopo T. R. E., quo mortuo dedit episcopus filiam eius cum hac terra cuidam suo militi, qui et matrem pasceret et episcopo inde serviret.'

by the national courts; they do not hold by any special feudal law, they are not subject to any feudal tribunal. Now if when we hear of 'feudalism,' we are to think of that orderly, centralized body of land-law which in Henry III.'s day has subjected the whole realm to its simple but mighty formulas, the feudalism of Oswald's land-loans is imperfect enough. But then we must remind ourselves that never in this country does feudal law (the *Lehnrecht* of Germany) become a system to be contrasted with the ordinary land law (*Landrecht*)[1], and also we must observe that already in Oswald's day the thegns of the church of Worcester were in all probability as completely subject to a private and seignorial justice as ever were any freeholding Englishman. What court protected their tenure, what court would decide a dispute between them and the bishop? Doubtless—it will be answered—the hundred court. But in all probability that court, the court of the great triple hundred of Oswaldslaw was already in the hand of the bishop who gave it its name[2]. The suits of these tenants would come into a court where the bishop would preside by himself or his deputy, and where the doomsmen would be the tenants and justiciables of the bishop—not indeed because tenure begets jurisdiction (to such a generalization as this men have not yet come)—but still, the justice that these tenants will get will be seignorial justice.

Now how far we should be safe in drawing from Oswald's loans and Oswaldslaw any general inferences about the whole of England is a difficult question. It is clear that the bishop was at great pains to regulate the temporal affairs of his church. He obtained for his leases the sanction of every authority human and divine, the consent of the convent, the ealdorman, the king, the witan; he deposited the covenant with the king, with the archbishop of Canterbury, with the bishop of Winchester. Also we must remember that he had lived in a Frankish monastery, and that, at least in things monastic, he was a radical reformer. Nor should it be concealed that in Domesday Book the entries concerning the estates of the church of Worcester stand out in bold relief from the monotonous background. Not only is the account of the hundred of Oswaldslaw prefaced by a statement which in forcible words lays stress on its complete subjection to the bishop, but in numerous cases the tenure of

Oswaldslaw and England at large.

---

[1] Hist. Eng. Law, i. 214.
[2] See above, p. 267.

the nobler and freer tenants within that hundred is described as being more or less precarious :—they do whatever services the bishop may require ; they serve 'at the will of the bishop'; no one of them may have any lord but the bishop ; they are but tenants for a time and when that time is expired their land will revert to the church[1].

Inferences from Oswald's loans. However, we should hesitate long before we said that Oswald's land-loans were merely foreign innovations. His predecessors had granted leases for lives ; other churches were granting leases for lives, and the important document that he sent to the king proves to us that we can not trust our Anglo-Saxon lease or land-book to contain the whole of the terms of that tenure which it created. Suppose that this unique document had perished, how utterly mistaken an opinion should we have formed of the terms upon which the thegns and knights of the church of Worcester held their lands ! We should have heard hardly a word of money payments, no word of the oath of subjection, of the *lex equitandi*, of the indefinite obligation of obeying whatever commands the bishop might give. It may well be that the thegns and knights of other churches held on terms very similar to those that the bishop of Worcester imposed. Even if we think that Oswald was an innovator, we must remember that the adviser of Edgar, the friend of Dunstan, the reformer of the monasteries, the man who for thirty years was Bishop of Worcester and for twenty years Archbishop of York, was able to make innovations on a grand scale. What such a man does others will do. The yet safer truth that what Oswald did could be done, should not be meaningless for us. In the second half of the tenth century there were men willing to take land on such terms as Oswald has described.

Economic position of Oswald's tenants. These men were not peasants. The land that Oswald gave them they were not going to cultivate merely by their own labour and the labour of their sons and their slaves, though we

---

[1] D. B. i. 172 b: 'Hae praedictae ccc. hidae fuerunt de ipso dominio aecclesiae, et si quid de ipsis cuicunque homini quolibet modo attributum vel praestitum fuisset ad serviendum inde episcopo, ille qui eam terram praestitam sibi tenebat nullam omnino consuetudinem sibimet inde retinere poterat nisi per episcopum, neque terram retinere nisi usque ad impletum tempus quod ipsi inter se constituerant, et nusquam cum ea terra se vertere poterat......Kenewardus tenuit et deserviebat sicut episcopus volebat......Ricardus tenuit ad servitium quod episcopus voluit......Godricus tenuit serviens inde episcopo ut poterat deprecari......Godricus tenuit ad voluntatem episcopi.'

are far from saying that they scorned to handle the plough. We have in Domesday Book a description of their holdings, and it is clear that in the Confessor's day, when some of Oswald's leases must yet have been in operation, the lessees had what we should describe as small manors with villeins and cottagers upon them. Thus, for example, Eadric the Steersman, who led the bishop's host, had an estate of five hides which in 1086 had three *villani* and four *bordarii*, to say nothing of a priest, upon it[1]. Like enough, what the bishop has been 'loaning' to his thegns has been by no means always 'land in demesne,' it has been 'land in service': in other words, a superiority, a seignory. Thus, as we say, another course of the feudal edifice is constructed. Above the cultivator stands the thegn or the *cniht*, who himself is a tenant under the bishop and who owes to the bishop services that are neither very light nor very definite. We can not but raise the question whether the cultivators, if we suppose them to be in origin free landowners, can support the weight of this superstructure without being depressed towards serfage. But we are not yet in a position to deal thoroughly with this question[2].

We must now return for a moment to the relation that exists between the loan and the book. *Lénland* is contrasted with *bócland*; but historians have had the greatest difficulty in discovering the principle that lies beneath this distinction[3]. Certainly we can not say that, while book-land is created and governed by a charter, there will be no written instrument, no book, creating and governing the *lén*. We have books which in unambiguous terms tell us that they bear witness to loans. Nor can we say that the holder of book-land will always have a perpetual right to the land, 'an estate in fee simple,' an estate to him and his heirs. In many cases a royal charter will create a smaller estate than this; it will limit the descent of the land

Loan-land and book-land.

---

[1] D. B. 173 b.

[2] Oswald's tenants closely resemble the *ministeriales* of foreign bishops ; see Waitz, Verfassungsgeschichte, v. 283–350. Oswald's *lex equitandi* may be compared with what is said (ibid. p. 293) of a bishop of Constance: 'quibus omnibus hoc ius constituit, ut cum abbate equitarent eique domi forisque ministrarent, equos suos tam abbati quam fratribus suis quocumque necesse esset praestarent, monasterium pro posse suo defensarent.'

[3] Kemble, Saxons, i. 310 ff. ; K. Maurer, Krit. Ueb. i. 104; Essays in Anglo-Saxon Law, No. ii. (Lodge) ; Brunner, Geschichte d. röm. u. germ. Urkunde, 182.

to the heirs male of the donee. Moreover the written leases for three lives of which we have been speaking are ' books.' Thus in 977 Oswald grants three manses to his thegn Eadric for three lives, and the charter ends with a statement which tells us in English that Oswald the archbishop is booking to Eadric his thegn three hides of land which Eadric formerly held as *lǽnland*[1]. A similar deed of 985 contains a similar statement; five hides which Eadric held as *lǽnland* are now being booked to him, but booked only for three lives[2]. In yet another of Oswald's charters we are told that the donee is to hold the land by way of book-land as amply as he before held it by way of *lǽnland*[3]. After this it is needless to say that book-land may be burdened with rents and services. But indeed it would seem that Oswald's thegns and knights held both book-land and *lǽnland*. It was book-land because it had been booked to them, and yet very certainly it had only been loaned to them[4].

Book-land in the dooms. Let us then turn to the laws and read what they say about book-land. Two rules stand out clearly. Æthelred the Unready declares that every *wíte* incurred by a holder of book-land is to be paid to the king[5]. Cnut declares that the book-land of the outlaw, whosesoever man he may be, and of the man who flies in battle is to go to the king[6]. These laws seem to put before us the holder of book-land as standing by reason of his land in some specially close relationship to the king. If we may use the language of a later day, the holder of book-land is a tenant in chief of the king, and this even though he may have commended himself to someone else. On the other hand, if the holder of *lǽnland* commits a grave crime, his land reverts, or escheats or is forfeited to the man who made the *lǽn*[7]. And yet, though this be so and though Oswald's thegns will in some sense or another be holding book-land, we may be quite certain that should one of them be outlawed the bishop will claim the

---

[1] K. 617 (iii. 164).   [2] K. 651 (iii. 216).

[3] K. 679 (iii. 258).

[4] K. 1287 (vi. 125): 'propter beneficium quod eis praestitum est.' D. B. i. 173 b. It may cross the reader's mind that the leases of which Oswald speaks in his letter to Edgar are not the transactions recorded in the charters that have come down to us, but other and unwritten leases. But Domesday Book and the stories told by Heming make against this explanation.

[5] Æthelr. i. 1, § 14.   [6] Cnut, ii. 13, 77.

[7] K. 328 (ii. 133): A certain Helmstan is guilty of theft 'and mon gerehte ðæt yrfe cinge forðon he wes cinges mon and Ordlaf feng to his londe forðan hit wæs his læn ðæt he on sæt.'

land. Indeed he is careful about this as about other matters. Often he inserts in his charter a clause saying that, whatever the grantee may do, the land shall return unforfeited to the church.

Any solution of these difficulties must be of a somewhat speculative kind. We fashion for ourselves a history of the book and of the land-loan which runs as follows:—The written charter first makes its appearance as a foreign and ecclesiastical novelty. For a very long time it is used mainly, if not solely, as a means of endowing the churches with lands and superiorities. It is an instrument of a very solemn character armed with the anathema and sanctioned by the crosses of those who can bind and loose. Usually it confers rights which none but kings can bestow, and which even kings ought hardly to bestow save with the advice of their councillors. A mass of rights held under such a charter is book-land, or, if we please, the land over which such rights are exercisable, is book-land for the grantee. In course of time similar privileges are granted by the kings to their thegns, though the book does not thereby altogether lose its religious traits. It is long before private persons begin to use writing for the conveyance or creation of rights in land. The total number of the books executed by persons who are neither kings, nor underkings, nor prelates of the church, was, we take it, never very large; certainly the number of such books that have come down to us is very small.

Nothing could be more utterly unproved than the opinion that in Anglo-Saxon times written instruments were commonly used for the transfer of rights in land. Let us glance for a moment at the documents that purport to have come to us from the tenth century. Genuine and spurious we have near six hundred. But we exclude first the grants made by the kings, secondly Oswald's leases and a few similar documents executed by other prelates, thirdly a few testamentary or quasi-testamentary dispositions made by the great and wealthy. Hardly ten documents remain. Let us observe their nature. The ealdorman and lady of the Mercians make a grant to a church in royal fashion[1]; but in every other case in which we have a document which we can conceive as either transferring rights in land or as being formal evidence of such a transfer, the consent of the king or of the king and witan to the

Relation of loan-land to book-land.

Royal and other books.

[1] K. 330 (ii. 136).

transaction is stated, and with hardly an exception the king
executes the document[1]. Even the holder of book-land who
wished to alienate it, for example, the thegn who wished to
pass on his book-land to a church, did not in general execute
a written conveyance. One of three courses was followed.
The donor handed over his own book, the book granted by the
king, and apparently this was enough; or the parties to
the transaction went before the king, delivered up the old
and obtained a new book; or the donor executed some brief
instrument—sometimes a mere note endorsed on the original
book—stating how he had transferred his right[2]. But in any
case, according to the common usage of words, a usage which
has a long history behind it, it is only the man who is holding
under a royal privilege who has 'book-land.' It is to this
established usage that the laws refer when they declare that
the king and no lower lord is to have the *wíte* from the holder
of book-land, and that when book-land is forfeited it is forfeited
to the king. For all this, however, if you adhere to the letter,
book-land can only mean land held by book. Now from a
remote time men have been 'loaning' land, and prelates when
they have made a loan have sometimes executed a written
instrument, a book. A prelate can pronounce the anathema
and the recipient of the *lǽn* may well wish to be protected, not
merely by writing, but by Christ's rood. When therefore
Bishop Oswald grants a written lease to one of his thegns
who heretofore has been in enjoyment of the land but has had
no charter to show for it, we may well say that in the future
this thegn will have book-land, though at the same time he
has but loan-land. We have no scruple about charging our
ancestors with having a confused terminology. The confusion
is due to a natural development; 'books' were formerly used
only for one purpose, they are beginning to be used for many
purposes, and consequently 'book-land' may mean one thing in

[1] K. 414 (ii. 273): conveyance by Wulfric with the king's consent.—K. 491
(ii. 379): conveyance by Wulfstan with consent of king and witan, who execute
the deed.—K. 690-1 (iii. 286-8): conveyances by Æscwig executed by king and
witan.—K. 1124, 1130 (v. 246-54): conveyances confirmed by king and
bishops.—K. 1201 (v. 378): exchange with king's consent.—K. 1226 (vi. 25):
conveyance by a thegn reciting king's consent. A few documents we must leave
unclassified; K. 499, 591, 693; we do not know how they were executed or
what was their evidential value.

[2] Brunner, Geschichte d. röm. u. germ. Urkunde, p. 175.

one context, another in another. We may say that every one
who holds under a written document holds book-land, or we
may still confine the name 'book' to that class of books which
was at one time the only class. The king's charters, the king's
privileges, have been the only books; they are still books in a
preeminent sense. Just so in later days men will speak of
'tenure in capite' when what they really mean is 'tenure in
capite of the crown by military service[1].'

But there is a deeper cause of perplexity. Once more we *The gift
and the
loan.*
must repeat that the gift shades off into the loan, the loan into
the gift. The loan is a gift for a time. It is by words of
donation ('I give,' 'I grant') that Oswald's *beneficia* are
praestita to his knights and thegns. Conversely, the king's
most absolute gift leaves something owing and continuously
owing to him; it may be prayers, it may be fealty and obedience.
And having considered by how rarely good fortune it is that
we know the terms of Oswald's land-loans, how thoroughly
we might have mistaken their nature but for the preservation
of a single document, we shall be very cautious in denying that
between many of the holders of book-land and the king there
was in the latter half of the tenth century a relationship for
which we have no other name than feudal tenure. If Oswald's
charters create such a tenure, what shall we say of the numerous
charters whereby Edred, Edwy, Edgar and Æthelred grant land
to their thegns in consideration of fealty and obedience? Must
not these thegns fulfil the whole *lex equitandi*; will they not
lose their lands if they fail in this service? True that the
rights conferred upon them are not restrained within the
compass of three lives but are heritable *ad infinitum*. But
does this affect the character of their tenure? Can we—we
can not in more recent times—draw any inference from 'the
quantum of the estate' to 'the quality of the tenure'? On the
whole, we are inclined to believe that the practice of loaning
lands affected the practice of giving lands, there being no sharp
and formal distinction between the gift and the loan, and that
when Edward the Confessor died no great injustice would
have been done by a statement that those who held their lands
by royal books held their lands 'of' the king. This at least we
know, that the formula of dependent tenure ('*A* holds land of
B') was current in the English speech of the Confessor's day

[1] Hist. Eng. Law, i. 212.

and that some of the king's thegns held their land 'of' the king[1]. We may guess that those old terms 'book-land' and 'loan-land' would soon have disappeared even from an unconquered England, for it was becoming plain that the book bears witness to a loan. A new word was wanted; that word was *feudum*.

§ 5. *The Growth of Seignorial Power.*

Subjection of freemen.   We now return to our original theme, the subjection to seignorial power of free land-holders and their land, for we now have at our command the legal machinery, which, when set in motion by economic and social forces, is capable of effecting that subjection. Let us suppose a village full of free land-holders. The king makes over to a church all the rights that he has in that village, reserving only the *trinoda necessitas* and perhaps some pleas of the crown. The church now has a superiority over the village, over the ceorls; it has a right to receive all that, but for the king's charter, would have gone to him.

The royal grantee and his land.   In the first place, it has a right to the *feorm*, the *pastus* or *victus* that the king has hitherto exacted. We should be wrong in thinking that in the ninth century (whatever may have been the case in earlier times) this exaction was a small matter. In 883 Æthelred ealdorman of the Mercians with the consent of King Alfred freed the lands of Berkeley minster from such parts of the king's *gafol* or *feorm* as had until then been unredeemed. In return for this he received twelve hides of land and thirty mancuses of gold, and then in consideration of another sixty mancuses of gold he proceeded to grant a lease of these twelve hides for three lives[2]. The king had been deriving a revenue from this land 'in clear ale, in beer, in honey, in cattle,

---

[1] K. 843 (iv. 201): 'swa full and swa forð swa Đurstan min huskarll hit furmest of me heold.'—K. 846 (iv. 205): 'swa full and swa forð swa Sweyn mi may hit formest of me held.'—K. 826 (iv. 190): 'swa Ælfwin sy nunne it heold of ðan minstre.'—K. 827 (iv. 190): 'swa Sihtric eorll of ðan minstre þeowlic it heold.' If K. 1237 (vi. 44) be genuine (and Kemble has not condemned it) then already in the middle of the tenth century 'Goda princeps tenuit terram de rege,' nor only so, 'tenuit honorem de rege'; but this document is unacceptable. At best it may be a late Latin translation of an English original.

[2] K. 313 (ii. 110); T. 129; B. ii. 172.

in swine and in sheep.' In Domesday Book a 'one night's farm' is no trifle; it is all that the king gets from large stretches of his demesne[1]. Having become entitled to this royal right, the church would proceed to make some new settlement with the villagers. Perhaps it would stipulate for a one night's farm for the monks, that is to say, for a provender-rent capable of supporting the convent for a day. In the middle of the ninth century a day's farm of the monks of Canterbury comprised forty sesters of ale, sixty loaves, a wether, two cheeses and four fowls, besides other things[2]. When once a village is charged in favour of a lord with a provender-rent of this kind, the lord's grip upon the land may easily be tightened. A settlement in terms of bread and beer is not likely to be stable. Some change in circumstances will make it inconvenient to all parties and the stronger bargainer will make the best of the new bargain. The church will be a strong bargainer for it has an inexhaustible treasure-house upon which to draw. We, however, concerned with legal ideas, have merely to notice that the law will give free play to social, economic and religious forces which are likely to work in the lord's favour.

But a village charged with a 'provender-rent' may seem far enough removed from the typical manor of the twelfth and thirteenth centuries. In the one we see the villagers cultivating each for his own behoof and supplying the lord at stated seasons with a certain quantity of victuals; in the other the villagers spend a great portion of their time in tilling the lord's demesne land. In the latter case the lord himself appears as an agriculturist: in the former he is no agriculturist, but merely a receiver of rent. The gulf may seem wide; but it is not impassable. One part, the last part, of a process which surmounts it is visible. In the eleventh and twelfth centuries the lords, though they have much land in demesne, still reckon the whole or part of what they are to receive from each manor in terms of 'farms'; the king gets a one night's farm from this manor, the convent of Ramsey gets a fortnight's farm from that manor[3]. But we can conceive how the change begins. The monks are not going to travel, as a king may have travelled, from village

Provender rents and the manorial economy.

---

[1] In many cases the one night's farm is reckoned at £100 or thereabouts; Round, Feudal England, 112.
[2] K. 477 (ii. 354); T. 509.
[3] Vinogradoff, Villainage, 301.

to village feasting at the expense of the folk. They are going to live in their monastery; they want a regular supply of victuals brought to them. They must have an overseer in the village, one who will look to it that the bread and beer are sent off punctually and are good. In the village over which they already have a superiority they acquire a manse of their very own, a *mansus indominicatus* as their foreign brethren would call it. When once they are thus established in the village, piety and other-worldliness will do much towards increasing their demesne and strengthening their position[1].

The church and the peasants. We have argued above that in the first instance it was not by means of the petty gifts of private persons that the churches amassed their wide territories. The starting point is the alienation of a royal superiority. Still there can be little doubt that the small folk were just as careful of their souls as were their rulers. They make gifts to the church. Moreover, the gift is likely to create a dependent tenure. They want to give, and yet they want to keep, for their land is their livelihood. They surrender the land to the church: but then they take it back again as a life-long loan. Thus the church has no great difficulty about getting demesne. But further, it gets dependent tenants and a dependent tenure is established. Like enough on the death of the donor his heirs will be suffered to hold what their ancestor held. Very possibly the church will be glad to make a compromise, for it may be doubtful whether these *donationes post obitum*[2], or these gifts with reservation of an usufruct, can be defended against one, who, not having the fear of God before his eyes, will make a determined attack upon them. Gradually the church becomes more and more interested in the husbandry of the village. It receives gifts; it makes loans; it substitutes labour services to be done on its demesne lands for the old *feorm* of provender. It is rash to draw inferences from the fragmentary and obscure laws of Ine; but one of them certainly suggests that, at least in some district of Wessex, this process was going on rapidly at the end of the seventh century, so rapidly and so oppressively that the king had to step in to protect the smaller folk. The man who has

[1] Even T. R. W. and in a thoroughly manorial county such as Hampshire we may find a village in which the lord has no demesne. See e.g. D. B. i. 41 b, Alwarestoch.

[2] Hist. Eng. Law, ii. 315.

taken a yard of land at a rent is being compelled not only to pay but also to labour. This, says the king, he need not do unless he is provided with a house[1].

Now we are far from saying that the manorial system of rural economy is thus invented. From the time of the Teutonic conquest of England onwards there may have been servile villages, Roman villas with slaves and *coloni* cultivating the owner's demesne, which had passed bodily to a new master. We have no evidence that is capable of disproving or of proving this. What we think more probable is that in those tracts where true villages (nucleated villages, as we have before now called them[2]) were not formed, the conquerors fitted themselves into an agrarian scheme drawn for them by the Britons, and that in the small scattered hamlets which existed in these tracts there was all along a great deal of slavery[3]. But, at any rate, the church was a cosmopolitan institution. Many a prelate of the ninth and tenth centuries, Bishop Oswald for one, must have known well enough how the foreign monasteries managed their lands, and, whatever controversies may rage round questions of remoter history, there can be no doubt that by this time the rural economy of the church estates in France was in substance that which we know as manorial. Foreign precedents in this as in other matters may have done a great work in England[4]. All that we are here concerned to show is that there were forces at work which were capable of transmuting a village full of free landholders into a manor full of villeins.

Besides the rights transferred to it by the king, the church would have other rights at its command which it could employ for the subjection—we use the word in no bad sense—of the peasantry. By the law of God it might claim first-fruits and tenths. The payment known as *ciric-sceat*, church-scot, is a very obscure matter[5]. Certainly in laws of the tenth century it seems to be put before us as a general tax or rate, due from all lands, and not merely from those lands over which a church has the lordship. On the other hand, both in earlier and in later docu-

Growth of the manorial system.

Church-scot and tithe.

---

[1] Ine, 67. See Schmid's note.
[2] See above, p. 15.
[3] See Meitzen, Siedelung und Agrarwesen der Germanen, ii. 97 ff.
[4] Stubbs, Const. Hist. i. 223.
[5] The subject is treated at length by Kemble, Saxons, ii. 490 and App. D, and Schmid, p. 545.

ments it seems to have a much less general character. In some
of the earlier it looks like a due, we may even say a rent
(*ecclesiasticus census*) paid to a church out of its own lands,
while in the later documents, for example in Domesday Book,
it appears sporadically and looks like a heavy burden on some
lands, a light burden on others. The evidence suggests that
the church had attempted and on the whole had failed, despite
the help of kings and laws, to make this impost general. That
in some districts it was a serious incumbrance we may be sure.
On those estates of the church of Worcester to which we have
often referred, every hide was bound to pay upon S^t. Martin's
day one horse-load (*summa*) of the best corn that grew upon it.
He who did not pay upon the appointed day incurred the
outrageous penalty of paying twelve-fold, and in addition to this
a fine was inflicted[1]. If the bishop often insisted on the letter
of this severe rule, he must have reduced many a free ceorl to
beggary. It is by no means certain that the duty of paying tithe
has not a somewhat similar history. Though in this case the
impost became a general burden incumbent on all lands, it may
have been a duty of perfect obligation for the subjects of the
churches, while as yet for the mass of other landowners it was
but a religious duty or even a counsel of perfection. At any
rate, this subtraction of a tenth of the gross produce of the
earth is no light thing : it is quite capable of debasing many
men from landownership to dependent tenancy.

Jurisdic-
tional
rights of
the lord.

Another potent instrument for the subjection of the free
landowners would be the jurisdictional rights which passed
from the king to the churches and the thegns. At first this
transfer would appear as a small matter. The president of a
court of free men is changed :—that is all. Where the king's
reeve sat, the bishop or the bishop's reeve now sits ; fines which
went to the royal hoard now go to the minster ; but a moot of
free men still administers folk-right to the justiciables of the
church. However, in course of time the change will have
important effects. In the first place, it helps to bind up suit
of court with the tenure of land. The suitor goes to the bishop's
court because he holds land of which the bishop is the lord. If,
as will often be the case, he wishes to escape from the burden-
some duty, he will pay an annual sum in lieu thereof, and here
is a new rent. Then again all the affairs of the territory are

[1] D. B. i. 174. Compare Ine, 4 ; Æthelr. viii. 11 ; Cnut, i. 10.

now periodically brought under the bishop's eye; he knows, or his reeves know, all about every one's business and they have countless opportunities of granting favours and therefore of driving bargains. Moreover it is by no means unlikely that the lord will now have something to say about the transfer of land, for it is by no means unlikely that conveyances will be made in court, and that the rod or *festuca* which serves as a symbol of possession will be handed by the seller to the reeve and by the reeve to the purchaser. We need not regard the conveyance in court as a relic of a time when a village community would have had a word to say if any of its members proposed to assign his share to an outsider. There are many reasons for conveying land in court. We get witnesses there, and no mere mortal witnesses but the testimony of a court which does not die. Then, again, there may be the claims of expectant heirs to be precluded and perhaps they can be precluded by a decree of the court. The seller's kinsfolk can be ordered to assert their rights within some limited time or else to hold their peace for ever after, so that the purchaser will hold the land under the court's ban[1]. And thus the rod passes through the hands of the president. But 'nothing for nothing' is a good medieval rule. The lord will take a small fine for this *land-cóp*, this sale of land, and soon it may seem that the purchaser acquires his title to the land rather from the lord than from the vendor[2].

Yet another turn is given to the screw, if we may so speak, when the state and the church begin to hold the lord answerable for taxes which in the last resort should be paid by the tenant[3]. This, when we call to mind the huge weight of the danegeld, will appear as a matter of the utmost importance. Before the end of the tenth century—this is the picture that we draw for ourselves—large masses of free peasants were in sore straits and were in many ways subject to their lords. Many of them were really holding their tenements by a more or less precarious tenure. They had taken 'loans' from their lord and become bound to pay rents and work continuously on his inland. Others of them may have had ancient ancestral

[margin note: The lord and his man's taxes.]

---

[1] Hist. Eng. Law, ii. 95.

[2] Æthelred, iii. 3; Schmid, App. II. 67 and Schmid, Glossar. s. v. *land-ceáp*.

[3] See above, pp. 55, 122, 125.

titles which could have been traced back to free settlers and free conquerors; but for centuries past a lord had wielded rights over their land. The king's *feorm* had become the lord's *gafol*, and this, supplemented by church-scot and by tithes, may have been turned into *gafol* and week-work. The time came for a new and heavy tax. •This was a crushing burden, and even had the geld been collected from the small folk it would have had the effect of converting many of them from landowners into landborrowers[1]. But a worse fate befell them. They were so poor that the state could no longer deal with them; it dealt with their lord; he paid for their land. It follows that in the eye of the state their land is his land. Less and less will the national courts and the folk-law recognize their titles; the lord 'defends' this land against all the claims of the state; therefore the state regards it as his. Hence what seems the primary distinction drawn by Domesday Book—that between the soke-man and the *villanus*. The *villanus* is not rated to the land-tax. Some men are not rated to the geld because they have but precarious titles; other men have precarious titles because they are not rated to the geld. A wide and a legally definable class is formed of men who hold land and who yet are fast losing the warranty of national law. When once the country is full of lords with sake and soke, a very small change, a very small exhibition of indifference on the part of the state, will deprive the peasants of this warranty and condemn them to hold, not by the law of the land, but by the custom of their lord's court.

Depression of the free ceorl.

To this depth of degradation the great mass of the English peasants in the southern and western counties—the *villani, bordarii, cotarii* of Domesday Book—may perhaps have come before the Norman Conquest. There may have been no courts which would recognize their titles to their land, except the courts of their lords. We are by no means certain that even this was so; but they must fall deeper yet before they will be the 'serf-villeins' of the thirteenth century.

---

[1] See above, p. 6. In a charter of Æthelred, K. 689 (iii. 284), Abp. Sigeric, the reputed inventor of the danegeld, is represented as pledging a village of thirty manses in order that he may pay the money demanded by the pirates. He thus raises 90 pounds of purest silver and 200 mancuses of purest gold. If the mancus was the eighth of a pound (Schmid, p. 595) we have 90 pounds of silver and 25 of gold, or in all perhaps £390. The whole danegeld of Kent under Henry II. was less than £106. For other transactions of a similar kind, see Crawford Charters, 76.

However, the conditions which would facilitate such a farther The slaves.
fall had long been prepared, for slavery had been losing some of
its harshest features. Of this process we have said something
elsewhere[1]. What the church did for the slave may have been
wisely and was humanely done; but what it did for the slave
was done to the detriment of the poorer classes of free men.
By insisting that the slave has a soul to be saved, that he can
be sinned against and can sin, that his marriage is a sacrament,
we obliterate the line between person and thing. On the other
hand, in the submission of one person to the will of another, a
submission which within wide limits is utter and abject, the
church saw no harm. Villeinage and monasticism are not
quite independent phenomena; even a lawyer could see the
analogy between the two[2]. And a touch of mysticism dignifies
slavery:—the bishop of Rome is the serf of the serfs of God;
an earl held land of Westminster Abbey 'like a *theow*[3].' One
of the surest facts that we know of the England of Cnut's time
is that the great folk were confounding their free men with
their theowmen and that the king forbad them to do this. We
see that one of the main lines which has separated the rightless
slave from the free ceorl is disappearing, for the lord, as suits
his interest best, will treat the same man now as free and now
as bond[4].

We might here speak of the numerous causes for which in a Growth of
lawful fashion a free man might be reduced into slavery, and manors from
were we to do so, should have to notice the criminal law with below.
its extremely heavy tariff of *wer* and *wite* and *bót*. But of this
enough for the time has been said elsewhere[5], and there are
many sides of English history at which we can not even glance.
However, lest we should be charged with a grave omission, we
must explain that the processes which have hitherto come
under our notice are far from being in our eyes the only
processes that tended towards the creation of manors. We
have been thinking of the manors as descending from above
(if we may so speak) rather than as growing up from below.
The alienation of royal rights over villages and villagers has
been our starting point, and it is to this quarter that we are

---

[1] See above, p. 27.   [2] Hist. Eng. Law, i. p. 416.

[3] K. 1327 (iv. 190): 'swa full and swa forð swa Sihtric eorll of ðan ministre
þeowlic it heold.'

[4] Cnut, ii. 20.   [5] Hist. Eng. Law, ii. p. 458.

inclined to look for the main source of seignorial power. But, no doubt, within those villages which had no lords—and plenty of such villages there were in 1065—forces were at work which made in the direction of manorialism. They are obscure, for they play among small men whose doings are not recorded. But we have every reason to suppose that in the first half of the eleventh century a fortunate ceorl had many opportunities of amassing land and of thriving at the expense of his thriftless or unlucky neighbours. Probably the ordinary villager was seldom far removed from insolvency : that is to say, one raid of free-booters, one murrain, two or three bad seasons, would rob him of his precious oxen and make him beggar or borrower. The great class of *bordarii* who in the east of England are subjected to the sokemen has probably been recruited in this fashion[1]. And so we may see in Cambridgeshire that a man will some-times have half a hide in one village, a virgate in another, two-thirds of a virgate in a third. He is 'thriving to thegn-right.' Then, again, some prelate or some earl will perhaps obtain the commendation of all the villagers, and his hold over the village will be tightened by a grant of sake and soke, though, if we may draw inferences from Cambridgeshire, this seems to have happened rarely, for the sokemen of a village have often shown a marvellous disagreement among themselves in their selection of lords, and seem to have chosen light-heartedly between the house of Godwin and the house of Leofric as if they were but voting for the yellows or the blues. We fully admit that these forces were doing an important work; but they were doing it slowly and it was not nearly achieved when the Normans came. Nor was it neat work. It tended to produce not the true and compact manerio-villar arrangement, but those loose, dissipated manors which we see sprawling awkwardly over the common fields of the Cambridge-shire townships[2].

Theories which connect the English manor with the Roman villa.

We have been endeavouring to show that the legal, social and economic structure revealed to us by Domesday Book can be accounted for, even though we believe that in the seventh century there was in England a large mass of free landowning ceorls and that many villages were peopled at that time and at

[1] Chron. Petrob. 166 : 'Sunt etiam in eadem scira 15 undersetes qui nullum servicium faciunt nisi husbondis in quorum terra sedent.'
[2] See above, p. 136.

later times chiefly by free landowning ceorls and their slaves. We have now to examine the evidence that is supposed to point to a contrary conclusion and to connect the English manor of the eleventh century with the Roman villa of the fifth. Two questions should be distinguished from each other—(1) Have we any proof that during those six centuries, especially during the first three of them, the type of rural economy which we know as 'manorial' was prevalent in England? (2) Have we any proof that the tillers of the soil were for the more part slaves or unfree men? We will move backwards from Domesday Book.

In the first place reliance has been placed on the document known as *Rectitudines Singularum Personarum*[1]. Of the origin of this we know nothing; we can not say for certain that it is many years older than the Norman Conquest. Apparently it is the statement of one who is concerned in the management of great estates and is desirous of imparting his knowledge to others. It first sets forth the right of the thegn. He is worthy of the right given to him by his book. He must do three things in respect of his land, namely, fyrdfare, burh-bote and bridge-work. From many lands however 'a more ample landright arises at the king's ban': that is to say, the thegn is subject to other burdens, such as making a deer-hedge at the king's *hám*, providing warships[2] and sea-ward and head-ward and fyrd-ward, and almsfee and church-scot and many other things. Then we hear of the right of the *geneat*. It varies from place to place. In some places he must pay rent (*land-gafol*) and grass-swine yearly, and ride and carry and lead loads, work and support his lord[3], and reap and mow and hew the deer-hedge and keep it up, build and hedge the *burh* and make new roads for the *tún*, pay church-scot and almsfee, keep head-ward and horse-ward, go errands far and near wherever he is directed. Next we hear of the cottier's services. He works one day a week and three days in harvest-time. He ought not to pay rent. He ought to have five acres more or less. He pays hearth-penny on Holy

The Recti-tudines.

---

[1] Schmid, App. III. p. 370; Seebohm, English Village Community, p. 129. See also Liebermann's article in Anglia, ix. 251, where the *Gerefa*, which seems to be a second part of this document, is printed.

[2] We here adopt Schmid's conjecture: 'and scorp to friðscipe [*corr.* fyrdscipe].'

[3] Ibid.: 'and hlaford feormian,' and supply a feorm (firma) for his lord.

Thursday as every free man should. He 'defends' or 'acquits' his lord's inland when there is a summons for seaward or for the king's deer-hedge or the like, as befits him, and pays church-scot at Martinmas. Then we have a long statement as to the services of the *gebúr*. In some places they are heavy, in others light. On some land he must work two days a week and three days at harvest by way of week-work. Besides this there is rent to be paid in money and kind. There is ploughing to be done and there are boon-works. He has to feed dogs and find bread for the swine-herd. His beasts must lie[1] in his lord's fold from Martinmas to Easter. On the land where this custom prevails the *gebúr* receives by way of outfit two oxen and one cow and six sheep and seven sown acres upon his yard-land. After the first year he is to do his services in full and he is to receive his working tools and the furniture for his house. We then hear of the special duties and rights of the bee-keeper, the swine-herd, the follower, the sower, ox-herd, shepherd, beadle, woodward, hayward and so forth.

Discussion of the Rectitudines.

Now, according to our reading of this document, there stand below the thegn, but above the serfs (of whom but few words are said[2]) three classes of men—there is the *geneat*, there is the *gebúr* and there is the *cotsetla*. The boor and the cottier are free men; the cottier pays his hearth-penny, that is his Romescot, his Peter's-penny, on Holy Thursday as every free man does; but both boor and cottier do week-work. On the other hand the *geneat* does no week-work. He pays a rent, he pays a grass-swine (that is to say he gives a pig or pigs in return for his pasture rights), he rides, he carries, he goes errands, he discharges the forinsec service due from the manor, and he is under a general obligation to do whatever his lord commands. He bears a name which has originally been an honourable name; he is his lord's 'fellow[3].' His services strikingly resemble those which S[t]. Oswald exacted from his *ministri*, his *equites*, his *milites*[4]. Almost every word that is said of the *geneat* is true of those very substantial persons who took land-loans from the

---

[1] The text says that he must lie at his lord's fold; but probably it refers to the *soca faldae*. See above, p. 76.

[2] Of the serfs we hear (c. 8, 9) what they are to receive, but not what they ought to do; their services are unlimited.

[3] Schmid, p. 596: Maurer, K. U. ii. 405.

[4] See above, p. 305, also Maurer, K. U. ii. 406.

church of Worcester. The *geneat* (who becomes a *villanus* in
the Latin version of our document that was made by a Norman
clerk of Henry I.'s reign) is a riding-man, radman, radcniht,
with a horse, a very different being from the *villanus* of the
thirteenth century[1]. On the other hand, in the *gebúr* of this
document we may see the *burus*, who is also the *colibertus* of
Domesday Book[2], and he certainly is in a very dependent
position, for his lord provides him with cattle, with instruments
of husbandry, even with the scanty furniture of his house. We
dare not indeed argue from this text that the *villanus* of
Domesday Book does not owe week-work, for the writer who
rendered *geneat* by *villanus* was quite unable to understand
many parts of the document that he was translating[3]; but when
we place the *Rectitudines* by the side of the survey we can
hardly avoid the belief that the extremely dependent *gebúr* of
the former is represented, not by the *villanus*, but by the *burus*
or *colibertus* of the latter. However, over and over again the
author of the *Rectitudines* has protested that customs vary.
He will lay down no general rule; he does but know what
goes on in certain places[4].

In 956 King Eadwig gave to Bath Abbey thirty manses at The Tiden-
ham case.

---

[1] He is to 'work' for his lord; but then see how Oswald speaks of his
knights and radmen : 'semper illius...dominatui et voluntati...cum omni
humilitate et subiectione subditi fiant secundum ipsius voluntatem.' Cf. D. B. i.
172 b : 'deserviebat sicut episcopus volebat'...'tenuit ad servitium quod
episcopus voluit.' The translator who turned him into a *villanus* was
capable of turning the king's *geneat* of Ine's law into a *colonus*, a *colonus* with a
wergild of 1200 shillings ! See Schmid, p. 29.

[2] See above, p. 36.

[3] See e.g. cap. i., where it is pretty clear that he can not translate *scorp*. So
in the Latin version of Edgar II. c. 1 he renders *geneatland* by *terra
villanorum*. But about such a matter as this the testimony of the Quadripartitus is of no value. See Liebermann, Gerefa, Anglia, ix. 258.

[4] Mr Seebohm, p. 130, commits what seems to me the mistake of saying
that the cottiers and boors are 'various classes of geneats.' To my thinking a
great contrast is drawn between the *geneat* and the *gebúr* both in this document
and in the account of Tidenham. So in Edgar II. c. 1 the contrast is between
land which the great man has in hand and land which he has let to his
'fellows,' his *equites* and *ministri*. See Konrad Maurer, K. U. ii. 405–6.
Such words as *gebúr* and *burus* are obviously very loose words and it is likely
that many a man who answered to the description of the *gebúr* given by the Rectitudines appears in Domesday Book, which in general cares only about fiscal
distinctions, as a *villanus* or *bordarius*. But we have clear proof that the
surveyors saw a class of *buri* (=*coliberti*) who were distinct from the ordinary
villani. See above, p. 36.

Tidenham in Gloucestershire[1]. A cartulary compiled in the twelfth century contains a copy of his gift, and remote from this it contains a statement of the services due from the men of Tidenham. It is possible, but unlikely, that this statement represents the state of affairs that existed at the moment when the minster received the gift; to all appearance it belongs to a later date[2]. It begins by stating that at Tidenham there are 30 hides, 9 of inland and 21 'gesettes landes,' that is 9 hides of demesne and 21 hides of land set to tenants. Then after an account of the fisheries, which were of importance, it tells us of the services due from the *geneat* and from the *gebúr*. The *geneat* shall work as well on the land as off the land, whichever he is bid, and ride and carry and lead loads and drive droves 'and do many other things.' The *gebúr* must do week-work, of which some particulars are stated, and he also must pay rent in money and in kind. Here again a well marked line is drawn between the *geneat* and the *gebúr*. Here again the *geneat*, like the *cniht* or *minister* of Oswaldslaw, is under a very general obligation of obedience to his lord; but he is a riding man and there is nothing whatever to show that he is habitually employed in agricultural labour upon his lord's demesne. As to the *gebúr*, he has to work hard enough day by day, and week by week, though of his legal status we are told no word.

The Stoke case.

In a Winchester cartulary, 'a cartulary of the lowest possible character,' there stands what purports to be a copy of the charter whereby in the year 900 Edward the Elder gave to the church of Winchester 10 *manentes* of land 'æt Stoce be Hysseburnan' together with all the men who were thereon at the time of Alfred's death and all the men who were 'æt Hisseburna' at the same period. Edward, we are told, acquired the land 'æt Stoce' in exchange for land 'æt Ceolseldene' and 'æt Sweoresholte [Sparsholt].' At the end of the would-be charter stand the names of its witnesses. Then follows in English (but hardly the English of the year 900) a statement of the services

---

[1] K. 452 (ii. 327). See also Two Chartularies of Bath Abbey (Somerset Record Society), pp. 5, 18, 19.

[2] K. iii. 449; E. 375: Seebohm, 148. Both documents come from MS. C.C.C. Camb. cxi. The conveyance is on f. 57, the statement of services on f. 73. The statement of services immediately precedes the lease of Tidenham to Stigand, K. 822 (iv. 171). Thus we have really better reason for referring that statement to the very eve of the Norman Conquest than to 956. See also Kemble, Saxons, i. 321, and Maurer, K. U. ii. 406.

which the ceorls shall do 'to Hysseburnan.' Then follow the boundaries. Then the eschatocol of the charter and the list of witnesses is repeated[1]. On the face of the copy are three suspicious traits: (1) the modernized language, (2) the repeated eschatocol, (3) the description of the services, for the like is found in no other charter. This is not all. Two other documents in the same cartulary bear on the same transaction. By the first Edward gave to the church of Winchester 50 *manentes* 'æt Hysseburnan' which he had obtained by an exchange for land 'æt Merchamme[2].' By the second he gave to the church of Winchester 50 *manentes* 'ad Hursbourne' and other 10 'ad Stoke[3].' The more carefully these three documents are examined, the more difficult will the critic find it to acquit the Winchester monks of falsifying their 'books' and improving Edward's gift. Therefore this famous statement about the ceorls' services is not the least suspicious part of a highly suspicious document. It is to this effect:—'From each *hiwisc* (family or hide), at the autumnal equinox, forty pence and six church *mittan* of ale and three sesters of loaf-wheat. In their own time they shall plough three acres and sow them with their own seed, and in their own time bring it [the produce of the sown land] to barn. They shall pay three pounds of gafol barley and mow half an acre of gafol-mead in their own time and bring it to the rick; four fothers of split gafol-wood for a shingle-rick in their own time and sixteen yards of gafol-fencing in their own time. And at Easter two ewes with two lambs, but two young sheep may be counted for an old one; and they shall wash and shear sheep in their own time. And every week they shall do what work they are bid, except three weeks, one at Midwinter, one at Easter and the third at the Gang Days.' Here no doubt, as in the account of Tidenham, as in the *Rectitudines*, we see what may fairly be called the manorial economy. The lord has a village; he has demesne land (*inland*) which is cultivated for him by the labour of his tenants; these tenants pay *gafol* in money or in kind; some of them (the *geneat* of Tidenham, the *geneat* of the *Rectitudines*) assist him when called upon to do so; others

---

[1] K. 1077 (v. 146; iv. 306); T. 143; Kemble, Saxons, i. 319; Seebohm, 160. But the form of the instrument as given in the Codex Wintoniensis is best seen in B. ii. 240. We have quoted above the estimate of this Codex formed by Mr Haddan and Dr Stubbs (Councils, iii. 638).

[2] B. ii. 238.   [3] B. ii. 239.

work steadily from day to day; in many particulars the extent of the work due from them is ascertained; whether they are free men, whether they are bound to the soil, whether the national courts will protect them in their tenure, whether they are slaves, we are not told.

Inferences
from these
cases.
That such an arrangement was common in the eleventh century we know; a solitary instance of it comes to us professedly from the first year of the tenth, and certainly from a cartulary that is full of lies. To draw general inferences from a few such instances would be rash. What should we believe of 'the English village of the eleventh century' if the one village of which we had any knowledge was Orwell in Cambridgeshire[1]? What should we believe of 'the English village of the thirteenth century' if our only example was a village on the ancient demesne? The traces of a manorial economy that have been discovered in yet remoter times are few, slight and dubious. A passage in the laws of Ine[2] seems to prove that there were men who had let out small quantities of land, 'a yard or more,' to cultivators at rents and who were wrongfully endeavouring to get from their lessees work as well as *gafol*. The same law may prove the highly probable proposition that some men had taken 'loans' of manses and were paying for them, not only by *gafol*, but by work done on the lord's land. That already in Ine's day there were many free men who were needy and had lords above them, that already the state was beginning to consecrate the relation between lord and man as a security for the peace and a protection against crime is undoubted[3]. But this does not bring us very near to the Roman *villa*. Nor shall we see a *villa* wherever the dooms or the land-books make mention of a *hám* or a *tún*, for the meanest ceorl may have a *tún* and will probably have a home of his own[4].

The *villa*
and the
vicus.
It is said that the England of Bede's day was full of *villae* and that Bede calls the same place now *villa* and now *vicus*[5].

---

[1] See above, p. 129.   [2] Ine, 67.

[3] Ine, 39. The man who leaves his lord (not his lord's land, but his lord) without license, or steals himself away into another shire, is to pay 60 shillings (no trivial sum) to his lord.

[4] Surely the law, Hloth. and Ead. c. 15, which begins 'If a man receive a guest three nights in his own home (an his agenum hame)' is not directed only against the lords of manors. See Meitzen, Siedelung und Agrarwesen, ii. 123.

[5] Ashley, Translation of Fustel de Coulanges, Origin of Property, p. xvi.

But before we enter on any argument about the use of such words, we ought first to remember that neither Bede nor the scribes of the land-books were trained philologists. London is a *villa*[1], but it is also a *civitas, urbs, oppidum, vicus,* a *wíc,* a *tún,* a *burh,* and a *port.* When we see such words as these used promiscuously we must lay but little stress upon the occurrence of a particular term in a particular case. Suppose for a moment that in England there were many villages full of free landholders : what should they be called in Latin ? They should, it is replied, be called *vici* and they should not be called *villae,* for a *villa* is an estate. But it is part of the case of those who have used this argument that at the time of the barbarian invasions the Roman world was full of *villae,* so full that every or almost every *vicus* was situated on and formed part of a *villa*[2]. We are therefore exacting a good deal from Bede, from a man who learnt his Latin in school, if we require him to be ever mindful of this nice distinction. We are saying to him : ' True it is that a knot of neighbouring houses with the appurtenant lands is habitually called a *villa* ; but then this word introduces the notion of ownership ; the *villa* is an unit in a system of property law, and, if your village is not also an estate, a *praedium,* then you should call it *vicus* and not *villa.*' To this we must add that, while the word *villa* did not until after the Norman Conquest force its way into English speech, the word *vicus* became an English word at a very early period[3]. It became our word *wick* and it became part of a very large number of place-names[4]. The Domesday surveyors found *herdwicks* and *berewicks* in many parts of the country[5].

[1] K. 220 (i. 280) : ' ad regalem villam Lundoniae perveniens.'

[2] Fustel de Coulanges, L'Alleu, ch. vi. There is much to be said on the other side ; see Flach, Les origines de l'ancienne France, ii. pp. 47–62. As to the *villa* of the Lex Salica, see Blumenstok, Entstehung des deutschen Immobiliareigenthums, i. 219 ff.

[3] The suggestion that *villa* appears in some of our place-names as the termination *-well* runs counter, so Mr Stevenson tells me, to rules of phonology.

[4] See Bosworth's Dictionary ; Kemble, Cod. Dipl. iii. p. xli. In the translation of S^t. Mark viii. 23, 26 both *wíc* and *tun* are used as equivalents for *vicus* :—' eduxit eum extra vicum…et si in vicum introieris' = ' and lædde hine butan þa wic……and ðeah þu on tun ga.' Even in France the word *vicus* becomes part of numerous place-names : see Flach, op. cit. i. p. 53.

[5] There is something curious about the use made of *wick.* It is often used to distinguish a hamlet or small cluster of houses separate from the main village. Thus in the parish of X we shall find X-*wick.* The *berewicks* and

Moreover we can see that in the Latin documents *villa* is used in the loosest manner. London is a *villa*; but a single house, a single ' haw,' in the city of Canterbury or the city of Rochester is a *villa*[1].

Notices of manors in the charters.

If we carefully attend to the wording of the land-books, we shall find the manorial economy far more visible in the later than in the earlier of them. The Confessor gives to Westminster 'ða cotlife Perscore and Dorhurste' with all their lands and all their berewicks[2]. He gives the cotlif Eversley and all things of right belonging thereto, with church and mill, with wood and field, with meadow and heath, with water and with moor[3]. From 998 we have a gift of a 'heafod-botl,' a capital mansion, we may say, and its appurtenances[4]. In earlier times we may sometimes find that the subject matter of the royal gift is spoken of as forming a single unit; it is a *villa*, or it is a *vicus*. But rarely is the thing that is given called a *villa* except when the thing that is given is just a single hide[5]. If a charter freely disposes of several *villae*, meaning thereby villages, we shall probably find some other reasons for assigning that charter, whatever date it may bear, to the eleventh, the twelfth or a yet later century[6]. Sometimes in old books the king will say that he is giving a *vicus*, a *vicus* of five or eight or ten *tributarii*[7]. Much more frequently he will not speak thus; he will not speak as though the subject matter of his gift had a physical unity and individuality. 'I give,' he will say, 'so

herdwicks of D. B. (see above, p. 114) seem to be small clusters. On the other hand London is a *wic*; Hloth. and Ead. 16.

[1] K. 1041 (v. 88): 'in Dorobernia etiam civitate unam villam donabo ad quam pertinet quinque iugera terrae et duo prata.' K. 276 (ii. 57): 'dabo unam villam, quod nos Saxonice an haga dicimus.' K. 259 (ii. 26): 'villam unam ab orientale parte muri Doroverniae civitatis.'

[2] K. 829 (iv. 191).

[3] K. 845 (iv. 204). In a passage which has been interpolated into one copy of the A.-S. Chronicle (Thorpe, p. 220) we read 'And se biscop......bohte þa feala cotlif æt se king.'

[4] Crawford Charters, pp. 22, 125; K. 1293 (vi. 138).

[5] Thus K. 109 (i. 133): 'villam unam...quae iam ad Quenegatum urbis Dorovernensis in foro posita est.' It is not denied that in some quite early charters a king gives a *villa* or *villula*, e.g. K. 209 (i. 264): 'Heallingan cum villulis suis'; see also K. 140 (i. 169), in which *villula* and *viculus* are used as synonyms.

[6] A good example is that abominable forgery K. 984 (v. 2), Wulfhere's charter for Peterborough.

[7] For example, K. 117-8-20 (i. 144-7).

many *manentes, tributarii,* or *casati* in the place known as *X,*'
or 'I give a certain part of my land, to wit, that of so many
manentes, tributarii, or *casati* at the spot which men call *Y.*'
Such language does not suggest that the manses thus given are
subservient to one dominant and dominical manse or manor; it
is very unlike the language of the twelfth century[1]. Such
words as *fundus* and *praedium* are conspicuously absent, and
ager usually means but a small piece of land, an acre. Foreign
precedents would have suggested that when an estate was to be
conveyed it should be conveyed *cum servis et ancillis,* or *cum
mancipiis et accolabus*; such clauses are rare in our English
land-books[2].

But, it will be said, at all events the king is giving persons, The *mansa*
and the
manens.
men, as well as land; he is giving *manentes, casati, tributarii.*
What is more these are foreign words and they describe the
'semi-servile' occupants of the soil. Now it is true that
sometimes he gives *manentes, casati, tributarii,* though more
often he gives either so many manses (*mansas*), or 'the land of
so many *manentes, casati, tributarii,*' while in Kent he gives
plough-lands or sullungs. But we think it plain that in
England these Latin words were used simply to describe the
extent, or rather the rateable extent, of land, without much
reference to the number or the quality of its occupants.
The *terra unius manentis,* even the *unus casatus* when that
is the subject of a conveyance, is like Bede's *terra unius
familiae,* the unit known to Englishmen as the *hiwisc,* or *hide*[3].
Hence it is that reference is so often made to repute and
estimation. 'I give,' says Egbert, 'a certain portion of land to

---

[1] One of the earliest instances of what looks like manorial organization will
be found in K. 201 (i. 253); B. i. 485. In 814 Cenwulf gives to the Abp. of
Canterbury a plough-land: 'et hoc aratrum cum omnibus utensilibus bonis ad
mansionem in grafon æa [Graveney] æternaliter concessum est.'

[2] A.D. 880, K. 311 (ii. 107): 'Insuper etiam huic donationi in augmentum
sex homines, qui prius pertinebant ad villam regiam in Beonsinctune, cum
omni prole stirpeque eorum ad eandem conscripsimus aecclesiam.' A.D. 889,
K. 315 (ii. 117): 'cum hominibus ad illam pertinentibus.' A.D. 962, K. 1239
(vi. 49): 'vineam......cum vinitoribus.' In late documents penned in English it
is common to convey land 'with meat and with man.' Instances are collected
in Crawford Charters, 127.

[3] Therefore we sometimes meet with the form *cassata,* while *manens* is
treated as a feminine word; K. i. 301; B. i. 573: 'has x. manentes......
dividendas dimisit.' So Asser (ed. Camden, p. 4) says that Æthelwulf ordered
that one poor man should be fed and clothed 'per omnem hereditariam terram
suam semper in x. manentibus.'

the amount, as I estimate, of five *casati*,' or (it may be) ' of twenty *manentes*[1].' Nothing can be easier than to count whether there be four, five, or six ' semi-servile ' households on a given piece of land. Far easier would it be to do this than to do what is habitually done, namely, to set forth the boundaries of the land with laborious precision. But there is already an element of estimation, of appreciation, in these units. Already they are units in a system of taxation. Hence also it is that so very frequently what the king gives is just exactly five, or some multiple of five, of these units[2]. Rating is a rough process; five and ten are pleasant numbers.

The hide.　　But against the argument which would see in every conveyance of ' five *manentes* ' or of ' the land of five *casati* ' a conveyance of five semi-servile households with their land we have another objection to urge. Here we will state it briefly; a fuller statement would take us far away from our present theme. If the land-books of the churches are to lead up to Domesday Book, the unit conveyed as *terra unius manentis* (*casati, tributarii*) is a hide with some 120 acres of arable land, the land appropriate to a plough-team of eight oxen. Had the semi-servile *manens* as a general rule 120 arable acres, a plough-team of eight oxen? We do not believe it, and those who have most strongly insisted on the servility or ' semi-servility ' of the tillers of the soil, do not believe it. They would give the *gebúr* but a quarter of a hide and but two beasts of the plough. That being so, it should be common ground that the *terra unius manentis* (*casati, tributarii*) can not be construed as ' the land occupied by one semi-servile tenant.' An explanation of the fact that land is conveyed by reference to units so large as the hide of 120 acres and that these units are spoken of as though each household would normally have one of them must be sought elsewhere; we can not here pause to find it. But in any

---

[1] K. 1033 (v. 73): 'aliquam portionem terrae......in modum videlicet ut autumo v. cassatorum.' K. 1308 (v. 83): 'aliquam portionem terrae......in modum videlicet ut autumo xx. manentium.' K. 565 (iii. 64): 'quoddam ruris clima sub aestimatione decem cassatorum.' K. 573 (iii. 87): 'ruris quandam particulam, denis ab accolis aestimatam mansiunculis.' K. 602 (iii. 146): ' quoddam rus x. videlicet mansarum quantitate taxatum.'

[2] Let us open the Cod. Dipl. at the beginning of Edmund's reign (ii. 218). The number of manses given in twenty-five consecutive charters is as follows : 10, 20, 10, 10, 9, 10, 15, 7, 8, 20, 10, 3, 5, 20, 30, 3, 6, 5, 3, 7, 20, 20, 5, 8, 5.

case these foreign terms should give us little trouble. When
he hears such words as *manens, casatus, tributarius*, the man
who has lived in Gaul may hear some undertone of servility or
'semi-servility.' We do not discuss this matter; it may be so.
But look at the words themselves, what do they primarily
mean? A *manens* is one who dwells upon land, a *casatus* is
one to whom a *casa* has been allotted, a *tributarius* pays
tributum; the free English landowner pays a *tributum* to the
king[1]. We must make the best we can of a foreign, an
inappropriate tongue, and the best that we make is often
very bad, especially when we have a taste for fine writing.
And so England is full of villas which are Roman and satraps
who, no doubt, are Persian.

And whence, we must ask, comes that system of intermixed
'strip-holding' that we find in our English fields? Who laid
out those fields? The obvious answer is that they were laid
out by men who would sacrifice economy and efficiency at the
shrine of equality. Each manse is to have the same number of
strips; the strips of one manse must be neither better nor
worse than those of its neighbour and therefore must be
scattered abroad over the whole territory of the village. That
this system was not invented by men who owned large continuous tracts is plain. No such owner would for one moment
dream of cutting up his land in this ridiculous fashion, and of
reserving for his own manse, not a ring-fenced demesne, but
strips lying here and there, 'hide-meal and acre-meal' among
the strips of his serfs. That is not the theory. No one
supposes that a Roman landowner whose hands were free
allowed the soil of his villa to be parcelled out in accordance
with this wasteful, cumbrous, barbarous plan. So his hands
must not be free; the soil of which he becomes the owner must
already be plotted out in strips, and these strips must be so
tightly bound up into manses, that he scruples to overturn an
existing arrangement, and contents himself with appropriating
a few of the manses for his own use and compelling the
occupants of the others to labour for him and pay him rents.
In this there is nothing impossible; but we have only deferred,
not solved the problem. Who laid out our English fields and

The strip-holding and the villa.

---

[1] It seems almost necessary to protest that to-day our landowners are not
semi-servile occupants of the soil, though they pay land taxes, house taxes,
income taxes and rates innumerable.

tied the strips into manses ? That this work was done by the Britons before they were brought under the Roman yoke does not seem very probable. Celtic rural economy, whenever it has had a chance of unfettered development, has made for results far other than those that are recorded by the larger half of the map of England. If throughout England the Romans found so tough a system of intermixed manses that, despite all its absurdities, they could not but spare it, then the Britons who dwelt in the land that was to be English were many centuries in advance of the Britons who dwelt in the land that was to be Welsh. To eke out this hypothesis another must be introduced. The Teutonic invaders of Britain must be brought from some manorialized province. So, after all, the model of the English field may have been 'made in Germany.' Somehow or another it was made in South Germany by semi-servile people, whose semi-servility was such a half-and-half affair that they could not be prevented from sacrificing every interest of their lords at the shrine of equality[1].

The lords and the strips. We are far from saying that wherever there is strip-holding, there liberty and equality have once reigned[2]. It is very possible that where a barbarian chieftain obtained a ring-fenced allotment of conquered soil, he sometimes divided it into scattered strips which he parcelled out among his unfree dependants. But if he did this, he did it because his only idea of agriculture was derived from a village formed by men who were free and equal. The maintenance of a system of intermixed strip-holding may be due to seignorial power, and a great deal of the rigidity of the agrarian arrangements that we see in the England of the thirteenth century may be due to the same cause. Seignorial power was not, at least in origin, absolute ownership. It had to make the best it could of an existing system. For the lord's purposes that system was at its best when it was rigid and no tenement was partible. But assuredly this plan was not originally invented by great proprietors who were seeking to get the most they could out of their land, their slaves and their capital.

---

[1] I can not but think that Fustel de Coulanges knew his business thoroughly well, and that if the German is to be taught his proper and insignificant place, the less that is said of intermixed 'strip-holding' the better, though to ignore it utterly was, even in France, a bold course.

[2] Meitzen, op. cit. i. 431–41.

That we have not been denying the existence of slavery will be plain. Indeed we may strongly suspect that the men who parcelled out our fields were for the more part slave-owners, though slave-owners in a very small way. To say nothing of Welshmen, there was quite enough inter-tribal warfare to supply the ceorl with a captive. But it was not for the sake of slaves or serfs or 'semi-servile' folk that the system of intermixed strips was introduced. *The ceorl and the slave*

Lastly, the theory which would derive the English manor from the Roman *villa* must face the grave problem presented to it by the account which Domesday Book, when speaking of the Confessor's day, gives of the eastern and northern counties, of a large quarter of all England, and of just that part of England which was populous. We see swarms of men who are free men but who are subject, they and their land, to various modes and degrees of seignorial power. The modes are many, the degrees are gentle. Personal, tenurial, justiciary threads are woven into a web that bewilders us. Here we see the work of commendation, there the work of the land-loan, and there again what comes of grants of sake and soke. We see the formation of manors taking place under our eyes, and as yet the process is by no means perfect. In village after village there is nothing that our economic historians would consent to call a manor. Now, no doubt, the difference between the east and the west is, at least in part, due to Danish invasions and Danish settlements. But how shall we picture to ourselves the action of the Danes? Is it to be supposed that they found the Anglo-Roman manor-villa a prevalent and prosperous institution, that they destroyed it and put something else in its place, put in its place the village of free peasants who could 'go with their land' to what lord they pleased? If so, then we have to face the question why these heathen Danes acted in a manner so different from that in which their predecessors, the heathen Angles and Saxons, had acted. Surely one part of the explanation is that the inswarming barbarians checked the manorializing process that was steadily at work in Wessex and Mercia. We do not say that this is the whole explanation. We have seen how free were many of the Cambridgeshire villages and have little reason to believe that they had been settled by Danes[1]. The west country is the country to which we shall naturally look for *The condition of the Danelaw.*

[1] See above, p. 139.

the most abundant traces of the *Wealh theow*.   There it is that
we find numerous *servi*, and there that we find rather *trevs* than
villages.   But also we have hardly a single land-book of early
date which deals with any part of the territory that became the
Danelaw.   Many a book the Danes may have burnt when they
sacked the monasteries.   They sacked the monasteries, burnt
the books and freed the land.   But still we may doubt whether
the practice of booking lands to the churches had gone far in
East Anglia and the adjacent shires when they were once more
overwhelmed by barbarism.   No doubt in course of time the
churches of the east became rich : Ely and St Edmunds, Peterborough and Ramsey, Croyland and Thorney.   But, even when
supplemented by legend and forgery, their titles to wide territories can seldom be compared for antiquity to the titles that
might have been pleaded by the churches of Kent and Wessex and
the Severn Valley.   Richly endowed churches mean a subjected
peasantry.   And thus we may say of the Danes that if in a
certain sense they freed the districts which they conquered, they
in the same sense enslaved the rest of England.   Year by year
Wessex and Mercia had to strain every nerve in order to repel
the pagans, to fit out fleets, build burgs and keep armies always
in the field.   The peasant must in the end bear the cost of this
exhausting struggle.   Meanwhile in the north and the east the
process that makes manors has been interrupted ; it must be
begun once more.   It was accomplished by men some of whom
had Scandinavian blood in their veins, but who were not
heathens, not barbarians : it was accomplished by Normans
steeped in Frankish feudalism.

§ 6.   *The Village Community.*

The village community. We have argued for an England in which there were many
free villages.   It remains for us to say a word of the doctrines
which would fill England with free landowning village communities.   Here we enter a misty region where arguments
suggested by what are thought to be 'survivals' and inferences
drawn from other climes or other ages take the place of documents.   We are among guesses and little has as yet been proved.

The popular theory. A popular theory teaches us that land belonged to communities before it belonged to individuals.   This theory has the

great merit of being vague and elastic; but, as it seems to think itself precise, and probably owes some of its popularity to its pretence of precision, we feel it our duty to point out to it its real merit, its vague elasticity.

It apparently attributes the ownership of land to communities. It contrasts communities with individuals. In so doing it seems to hint, and yet to be afraid of saying, that land was owned by corporations before it was owned by men. The hesitation we can understand. No one who has paid any attention to the history of law is likely to maintain with a grave face that the ownership of land was attributed to fictitious persons before it was attributed to men. But if we abandon ownership by corporations and place in its stead co-ownership, then we seem to be making an unfortunate use of words if we say that land belonged to communities before it belonged to individuals. Co-ownership is ownership by individuals. When at the present day an English landowner dies and his land descends to his ten daughters, it is owned by individuals, by ten individuals. If each of these ten ladies died intestate leaving ten daughters, the land would still be owned by individuals, by a hundred individuals. *[margin: Co-owner-ship and ownership by corporations.]*

The distinction that modern law draws between the land-owning corporation and the group of co-owners is as sharp as any distinction can be. It will be daily brought home to any one who takes an active share in the management of the affairs of a corporation, for example, a small college which has a master, six fellows and eight scholars. A conveyance of land to the college and a conveyance of land to these fifteen men would have utterly different effects. A corporation may be deep in debt while none of its members owes a farthing. Now we may suspect, and not without warrant, that in a remote past these two very different notions, namely that of land owned by a corporation and that of land owned by a group of co-owners, were intimately blent in some much vaguer notion that was neither exactly the one nor exactly the other. We may suspect that could we examine the conduct of certain men who lived long ago we should be sorely puzzled to say whether they were behaving as the co-owners of a tract of land'or as the members of a corporation which was its owner. But to fashion for ourselves any clear and stable notion of a *tertium quid* that is neither corporate ownership nor co-ownership, but partly the *[margin: 'Communities' as owners.]*

one and partly the other, seems impossible[1]. Therefore if, in accordance with the popular theory, we attribute the ownership of lands to 'communities,' we ought to add that we do not attribute it to corporations and that we are fully aware that co-ownership can not be sharply contrasted with ownership by individuals.

Possession and ownership.

Also since we are apt to fall into the trick of talking about possession when we mean ownership or proprietary right, we need not perhaps ask pardon for the remark that land owned by a group of three joint tenants may be possessed in many different ways. The three may be jointly possessing the whole; each may be severally possessing a physically divided third; the whole may be possessed by one of them or by some fourth person; the possession may be rightful or wrongful.

But there is a graver question that must be raised. When we say that land belonged to communities before it belonged to individuals, are we really speaking of ownership or of something else?

Ownership and governmental power.

At the present day no two legal ideas seem more distinct from each other than that of governmental power and that of proprietary right. The 'sovereign' of Great Britain (be the sovereignty where it may) is not the owner of Great Britain, and if we still say that all land is 'held of' the king, we know that the abolition of this antique dogma, this *caput mortuum*, might be easily accomplished without any perceptible revolution in the practical rules of English law. A landowner in the United States does not 'hold of' the State or the people or the government of the State. The 'eminent domain' of the State is neither ownership nor any mode of ownership. Further, we conceive that the sovereign person or sovereign body can, without claiming any ownership in the soil, place many restrictions on the use that an owner may make of his land. A law may prohibit owners from building on certain lands: those lands are still their lands. Again, the supposed law may be not a negative but a positive rule; it may require that the owners of certain lands shall build upon them, or shall till them, or shall keep them as pasture[2]: still neither state nor sovereign

---

[1] This seems to me the net outcome of the long and interesting controversy which has divided the Germanists as to the nature of the German *Genossenschaft*.

[2] This is no extravagant hypothesis. See e.g. Stat. 7 Hen. VIII. c. 1 Thacte advoidyng pullyng downe of townes.

will be owner of those lands or have any proprietary interest in
them. Our law may subject certain lands to a land-tax to be
paid to the state in money, or to a tithe to be paid to the
church in kind, but the state will not and the church will not be
part-owner of those lands. Our state may habitually expropriate
owners, may take their lands from them because they are felons
or because their lands are wanted for the construction of railways. We may conceive it expropriating owners who have
done no wrong and yet are to have no compensation ; but until
the expropriation takes place the state does not own the land.
As with land, so with chattels. The owner of a cart may find
that it is impressed for the purpose of military transport[1] and
yet the cart is his and not the state's.

Similar powers may be exercised by persons or bodies that
are not sovereign, for example, by the governor of a province,
by a county council or a municipal corporation. Suppose that
the owners of land situate within a certain borough are pro-
hibited by a by-law from placing on their soil any buildings
the plans of which have not been approved by the town council.
Carry this supposition further :—suppose that the town council
is a 'folk-moot' which every inhabitant of the borough may
attend. Still, according to our thinking, there would here be
no communal ownership and no division of ownership between
individuals and a corporation. If we thought it well to say
that in such a case the community would have some kind of
'eminent domain' over the land of individuals, we should have
to add that this kind of eminent domain was not a proprietary
right, but merely governmental power, a power of making general
rules and issuing particular commands. Nor would the case
be altered if the expressed object of such rules and commands
was the interest, it may even be the pecuniary interest, of the
men of the town. The erection of buildings may be controlled
in order that the town may be wholesome and sightly, or we
may conceive that landowners in the suburbs are compelled
to keep their land as market-gardens or as dairy-farms in
order that vegetables or milk may be cheap :—for all this the
town council or community of townsfolk would have no property
in the land.

But though this be so, we can not doubt that could we
trace back these ideas to their origin, we should come to a

Ownership and the powers of subordinate governors.

Evolution of sovereignty and ownership.

[1] See Army Act, 1881, 44 and 45 Vic. c. 58, sec. 115.

time when they were hardly distinct from each other. The language of our medieval law tells us that this is so. The one word *dominium* has to cover both proprietary rights and many kinds of political power; it stands for ownership, lordship, sovereignty, suzerainty. The power that Edward I. wields over all England, the power that he claims over all Scotland, all Gascony, the right that he has in his palace of Westminster, the right that he has in his war-horse, all these are but modes of *dominium*. Then we imagine a barbarous horde invading a country, putting its inhabitants to the sword and defending it against all comers. Doubtless in some sort the land is its land. But in what sort? In the sort in which Queen Victoria or the British nation has lands in every quarter of the globe, the sort in which all France belongs to the French Republic, or the sort in which Blackacre is the land of John Styles? Have the barbarians themselves answered this question? Have they asked it[1]?

Communal ownership as a stage. Now if we are going to confuse sovereignty with ownership, *imperium* with *dominium*, political power with proprietary right, why then let our socialists and collectivists cease their striving and sing *Te Deum*. Already their ideal must be attained. Every inch of the soil of France, to name one instance, 'belongs' to the French Republic. But, if we would not be guilty of this confusion, then we must be very careful before we assent to the proposition that in the normal course of history (if indeed in such a context history can be said to have a normal course) the ownership of land by communities appears before the ownership of land by individuals. Even if we put aside all such criticisms as would be legal quibbles in the eyes of impatient theorists, and refuse to say whether the 'community' is a mass of men, an ideal person or *tertium quid*, we still are likely to find that the anthropologists will be against us. We are now told by one of the acutest of explorers that, if we leave out of account as no true case of ownership the sort of

---

[1] Flach, Les origines de l'ancienne France, ii. 45, referring to the classical passages in Cæsar and Tacitus, says: 'Ce serait un abus de mots de dire que la tribu ou que le clan sont propriétaires. La tribu (*civitas*) a la souveraineté du territoire, les clans de leurs subdivisions ont l'usage des parts qui leur sont assignées. La conception même de la propriété est exclue par la nature des terres : étendue de friches toujours renaissantes et en surabondance toujours : *superest ager.*' See also Dargun, Ursprung des Eigenthums, Zeitschrift für vergleichende Rechtswissenschaft, v. 55.

inchoate sovereignty which an independent tribe of hunters may exercise over a piece of the world's surface, 'ownership of land by individuals' is to be found at a much lower grade in the scale of civilization than that at which 'communal ownership' makes its first appearance[1]. Communal ownership, it is said, is not seen until that stage is reached at which the power of the chieftain is already a considerable force and the work of centralization is progressing. With these inductions we do not meddle; but if the anthropologist will concede to the historian that he need not start from communalism as from a necessary and primitive *datum*, a large room will be open for our guesses when we speculate about the doings of a race of barbarians who have come into contact with Roman ideas. Even had our anthropologists at their command materials that would justify them in prescribing a normal programme for the human race and in decreeing that every independent portion of mankind must, if it is to move at all, move through one fated series of stages which may be designated as Stage *A*, Stage *B*, Stage *C* and so forth, we still should have to face the fact that the rapidly progressive groups have been just those which have not been independent, which have not worked out their own salvation, but have appropriated alien ideas and have thus been enabled, for anything that we can tell, to leap from Stage *A* to Stage *X* without passing through any intermediate stages. Our Anglo-Saxon ancestors did not arrive at the alphabet, or at the Nicene Creed, by traversing a long series of 'stages'; they leapt to the one and to the other.

But in truth we are learning that the attempt to construct a normal programme for all portions of mankind is idle and unscientific. For one thing, the number of such portions that we can with any plausibility treat as independent is very small. For another, such is the complexity of human affairs and such their interdependence, that we can not hope for scientific laws which will formulate a sequence of stages in any one province of man's activity. We can not, for instance, find a law which deals only with political and neglects proprietary arrangements, or a law which deals only with property and neglects religion. So soon as we penetrate below the surface, each of the cases whence we would induce our law begins to look extremely

A normal sequence of stages.

---

[1] Dargun, Ursprung des Eigenthums, Zeitschrift für vergleichende Rechtswissenschaft, v. 1 (1884). See also Hildebrand, Recht und Sitte, Jena, 1896.

unique, and we shall hesitate long before we fill up the blanks
that occur in the history of one nation by institutions and
processes that have been observed in some other quarter. If
we are in haste to drive the men of every race past all the
known 'stages,' if we force our reluctant forefathers through
agnatic *gentes* and house-communities and the rest of it, our
normal programme for the human race is like to become a
grotesque assortment of odds and ends.

Was land owned by village communities? It is an interesting question whether in the history of our
own people we ought to suppose any definite 'stage' inter-
mediate between the introduction of steady agriculture and
the ownership of land by individuals. To say the least, we
have no proof that among the Germans the land was continuously tilled before it was owned by individuals or by those
small groups that constituted the households. This seems
to be so whether we have regard to the country in which the
Germans had once lived as nomads or to those Celtic and
Roman lands which they subdued. To Gaul and to Britain
they seem to have brought with them the idea that the
cultivable land should be allotted in severalty. In some cases
they fitted themselves into the agrarian framework that they
found; in other cases they formed villages closely resembling
those that they had left behind them in their older home. But
to all appearance, even in that older home, so soon as the village
was formed and had ploughed lands around it, the strips into
which those fields were divided were owned in severalty by the
householders of the village. Great pains had been taken to
make the division equitable; each householder was to have
strips equal in number and in value, and to secure equivalence
each was to have a strip in every part of the arable territory.
But our evidence, though it may point to some co-operation in
agriculture, does not point to a communistic division of the
fruits[1]. Nor does it point to a time when a village council or a
majority of villagers conceived that it had power to re-allot the

---

[1] In the A.-S. laws about tithes there is really no hint of communalism.
When a landowner has ploughed his tenth acre, he is to assign that acre, or
rather the crop that it will bear next year, to the church. That is all; and
though it may be a rude plan, it is compatible with the most absolute
individualism. Mr Seebohm, Village Community, 114, however, seems to think
otherwise. As to the Welsh laws, we beg an enormous question if we introduce
them into this context. A distribution of acres when the ploughing is done is
just what we do not see in England.

arable strips at regular or irregular intervals[1]. On the contrary, the individual's hold upon his strips developed very rapidly into an inheritable and partible ownership. No doubt this ownership grew more intense as time went on. It is a common remark that during yet recent ages the ownership of land that is known to our law has been growing more intense. This is true and patent enough; the landowner has gained powers of alienation that his predecessors did not enjoy. Possibly the only ownership of land that was known to the Lex Salica was inalienable and could be inherited only by sons of the dead owner. Then again, in old days a trespass that did no harm would have been no trespass. 'Nominal damages' are no primitive institution, and for a long time a man may have had no action if strange cattle browsed over land on which no crop of corn was ripening[2]. But this growing intensity of ownership may be seen also in the case of movable goods. Indeed there is a sense in which English law may be said to have known a full ownership of land long ages before it knew a full ownership of chattels[3]. What, however, we are concerned to observe is that the German village community does not seem to have resisted this development of ownership or set up for itself any antagonistic proprietary claim. It sought no more as regards the arable fields than a certain power of regulating their culture, and in old times the *Flurzwang*, the customary rotation of crop and fallow, must have appeared less as the outcome of human ordinance than as an unalterable arrangement established by the nature of things in general and of acre strips in particular[4].

[1] As to the famous words of Tacitus 'Agri pro numero cultorum ab uniuersis in uices [*al.* inuicem] occupantur' and the proposal to read *uniuersis vicis*, one of the best suggestions yet made (Meitzen, Siedelung, iii. 586) is that Tacitus wrote merely *ab uniuersis occupantur*, that a copyist repeated the word *uniuersis*, and that other copyists tried to make sense of nonsense.

[2] As to the state of things represented by the Lex Salica see Blumenstok, Entstehung des deutschen Immobiliareigenthums, Innsbruck, 1894, pp. 196 ff.

[3] Hist. Eng. Law, ii. 155. It may be convenient now-a-days to say that *ownership* implies a power of alienation. See Pollock, Jurisprudence, 166. But to insist on this usage in such discussions as that in which we are engaged would lead to needless circumlocution. The question that is before us is whether as a complaint to which a court of law will give audience 'This acre is mine' is more modern than 'This acre is ours.'

[4] As to the whole of this matter see Meitzen, op. cit., especially iii. 574–589. As regards arable land in this country the only 'survivals' which point to anything that should be called communal ownership are singularly inconclusive.

Meadows, pasture and wood. Thus, so far back as we can see, the German village had a solid core of individualism. There were, however, lands which in a certain sense belonged to it and which were not allotted for good and all among its various members. For one thing, the meadows were often subjected to a more communal scheme. In the later middle ages we may see them annually redistributed by rotation or by lot among the owners of the arable. The meadows, which must be sharply distinguished from the pasture, were few, and, as we may see from Domesday and other records, they were exceedingly valuable. Probably their great but varying value stood in the way of any permanent partition that would have seemed equitable. Still they were allotted annually and the right to an allotment 'ran with' the house and the arable strips. But again, there were woods and pastures. If we must at once find an owner for this *Almende*, we may be inclined to place the ownership in a village community, though not without remembering that if this community may develop into a land-owning corporation, it may develop into a group of co-owners. But in all likelihood the question as to the whereabouts of ownership might go unanswered and unasked for a long time. Rights of user exercisable over these woods and pastures were attached to the ownership of the houses and the arable strips, and such 'rights of common' may take that acutely individualistic form which they seem to have taken in the England of the thirteenth century. The freeholder of 'ancient arable,' whose tenement represents one of the original shares, has a right to turn out beasts on the waste, on the whole waste and every inch of it, and of this right nor lord, nor community can deprive him[1]. Perhaps we may attribute to our law about this matter an unusual and, in a certain sense, an abnormal individualism. In the much governed England of the Angevin time, the strong

They relate to small patches of arable land held by burgesses : that is to say, they relate to places in which a strong communal sentiment was developed during the later middle ages, and they do not relate to communities that ought to be called agricultural. The 'burgess plot' is not large enough to have been any man's livelihood when cultivated in medieval fashion, and it may well be modern. It is demonstrable that in one case a very 'archaic' arrangement was deliberately adopted in the nineteenth century by burgesses who preferred 'allotment grounds' to pasture rights. Maitland, Survival of Archaic Communities, Law Quarterly Review, ix. 36.

[1] Hist. Eng. Law, i. 610–12.

central power encouraged every freeholder to look to it for relief against all kinds of pressure seignorial or communal. Elsewhere a village moot may assume and retain some control over these pasture rights. But still the untilled land, the waste, the *Almende*, exists mainly, if not solely, for the benefit of a small group of tenements that are owned and possessed in severalty. As to the ownership of the land that is subject to the rights of pasture, it is a nude, a very nude *dominium*, and for a long while no one gives it a thought.

In a favourable environment the German village community may and will become a landowning corporation. But many dangers lie before it: internal as well as external dangers. We must not think of it as a closely knit body of men. The agrarian is almost the only tie that keeps it together. Originally the men who settle down in a village are likely to be kinsmen. Some phrases in the continental folk-laws, and some perhaps of our English place-names, point in this direction. But (explain this how we will) the German system of kinship, which binds men together by the sacred tie of blood-feud, traces blood both through father and through mother, and therefore will not suffer a 'blood-feud-kin' to have either a local habitation or a name[1]. Very soon, especially if daughters or the sons of daughters are allowed (and very ancient Frankish laws allow them) to inherit the dead man's land, a man who lives in one village will often be closer of kin to men who live in other villages than to his neighbours. The village community was not a *gens*. The bond of blood was sacred, but it did not tie the Germans into mutually exclusive clans. Nor did it hold them in large 'house-communities,' for the partible inheritance seems as a general rule to have been soon partitioned[2]. Nor again may we ascribe to the German house-father much power over his full-grown sons[3].

Moreover, the village community was not a body that could declare the law of the tribe or nation. It had no court, no jurisdiction. If moots were held in it, these would be

The bond between neighbours.

Feebleness of the village community.

---

[1] Hist. Eng. Law, ii. 238. A hypothetical practice of endogamy will hardly give us the requisite explanation, for on the whole the church seems to have encountered little difficulty in imposing its extravagantly exogamous canons. To persuade the converts not to marry their *affines* was a much harder task.

[2] Heusler, Institutionen, 229.

[3] As to the ownership of land by 'families,' see Hist. Eng. Law, ii. 242.

comparable rather to meetings of shareholders than to sessions
of a tribunal. In short, the village landowners formed a group
of men whose economic affairs were inextricably intermixed, but
this was almost the only principle that made them an unit,
unless and until the state began to use the township as its
organ for the maintenance of the peace and the collection of
taxes. That is the reason why we read little of the township
in our Anglo-Saxon dooms[1]. Only as the state's pressure
increases, does the vill become one of the public institutions of
the kingdom. We may even exaggerate the amount of agricultural co-operation that was to be found within it. Beyond
the age in which the typical peasant is a virgater contributing
two oxen to a team of eight, our English evidence seems to
point to a time when the normal 'townsman' held a hide and
had slaves and oxen enough for its cultivation. Nor in all
probability was the village community a large body. We may
doubt whether in the oldest days it usually comprised more
than some ten shareholders[2].

Absence of organization. Whatever might come in course of time, we must not
suppose that the village had much that could be called a
constitution. In particular, we must be careful not to carry
too far back the notion that votes will be counted and that
the voice of a majority will be treated as the voice of all.
When that marvellous title *De migrantibus* raises a corner of
the curtain and gives us our only glance into a village of newly
settled Salian Franks, the one indisputable trait that we see
among much that is disputable is that the new-comer must
leave the village if one villager objects to his presence. His
presence, we may suppose, might be objectionable because
it might add to the number of those who enjoyed wood, waste
and water in common; but any one villager can insist on his
departure. Out of this state of things 'communal ownership'
may grow; but all the communalism that we see at present
is very like individualism[3]. Above all, we must not picture
these village lands as 'impressed with a trust' in favour of

---

[1] See above, p. 147.   [2] Of this in the next essay.

[3] A valuable and interesting discussion of the proprietary system of the Lex
Salica will be found in Blumenstok, Entstehung des deutschen Immobiliareigenthums, Innsbruck, 1894. This will serve as a good introduction to the
large literature which surrounds the *De migrantibus*. The least probable of all
interpretations seems that given by Fustel de Coulanges.

unborn generations or as devoted to 'public purposes.' If in course of time small folk, cottiers, 'under-settles' and the like, are found in the village, they will have to struggle for rights in the waste, and the rights, if any, that they get will be meagre when compared with those of the owners of 'whole lands' and 'half lands.' An oligarchy of peasant proprietors may rule the waste and the village.

Thus even in favourable circumstances there were many difficulties to be overcome if the communalism, such as it was, of the village community was to be maintained and developed. But where the village was founded upon conquered soil the circumstances were not favourable. If the Germans invaded Gaul or Britain, the very fields themselves seemed to rebel against communalism and to demand a ring-fenced severalty. Throughout large tracts in Gaul the barbarians were content to adapt themselves to the shell that was provided for them. A certain aliquot share of every estate might be taken from its former owner and be allotted to a Burgundian or a Goth according to a uniform plan[1]. Throughout other large tracts villages of the Germanic type were founded; a large part of northern Gaul was studded with such villages, and it may be well for us to remember that some of our Norman subjugators came to us from a land of villages, if others came from a land of isolated homesteads[2]. There can be little doubt that in Britain numerous villages were formed which reproduced in all essentials the villages which Saxons and Angles had left behind them on the mainland, and as little doubt that very often, in the west and south-west of Britain, German kings and eorls took to themselves integral estates, the boundaries and agrarian arrangement whereof had been drawn by Romans, or rather by Celts[3]. *The German village on conquered soil.*

Then the invasions and the long wars called for a rapid development of kingship. Very quickly the Frankish kingship became despotism. In England also the kings became powerful and the hereditary nobles disappeared. There was taxation. The country was plotted out according to some rude scheme to provide the king with meat and cheese and ale[4]. Then came bishops and priests with the suggestion that he should *Development of kingly power.*

---

[1] See Meitzen, op. cit. i. 526–35.
[2] Meitzen, i. 517 and the Maps 66 *a*, 66 *b* in the Atlas.
[3] Meitzen, ii. 97–122.　　　　　[4] See above, p. 237.

devote his revenues to the service of God and with forms of conveyance which made him speak as if the whole land were his to give away. Here, so we have argued, was the beginning of a process which placed many a village under a lord. The words of this lord's 'book' told him that he was owner, or at least lord, of this village 'with its woods and its pastures.' The men of the village might or might not maintain all their accustomed rights, but at any rate no expansion of those rights beyond the ancient usage was possible. The potentialities of the waste (if we may so speak) had been handed over to a lord; the future was his.

Free villages in England. We must not, however, repeat what has been lengthily said above touching the growth of the manorial system, though we are painfully aware that we have neglected many phases of the complicated process. Here let us remember that this process was not complete in the year 1066, and let us look once more at the free villages in the east; for example, at Orwell[1]. Who owned the land that served as a pasture for the *pecunia villae*? Shall we place the ownership in the thirteen holders of the arable strips into which the four hides were divided, or in a corporation whereof they were the members, or in their various lords, those eight exalted persons to whom they were commended, or shall we say that here is *res nullius*? The supposition that the lords are owners of the waste we may briefly dismiss. The landholders are free to 'withdraw themselves' and seek other lords. That the land is *res nullius* we may also positively deny, if thereby be meant that it lies open to occupation. Let a man of the next village turn out his beasts there and he will find out fast enough that he has done a wrong. But who will sue him? Will all the villagers join as co-plaintiffs or will the village corporation appear by its attorney? Far more in accordance with all that we see in later days is it to suppose that any one of the men of Orwell who has a right to turn out beasts can resent the invasion[2]. This brings to

---

[1] See above, p. 129.

[2] Throughout the historical time, so far as we know, the right of every commoner has been well protected against strangers. He might drive off the stranger's beasts, impound them, and, at all events if he had been incommoded, might sue for damages. See *Marys's case*, 9 Coke's Reports, 111 b; *Wells* v. *Watling*, 2 W. Blackstone's Reports, 1233. He needed no help from his neighbours.

our notice the core of individualism that lies in the centre of the village. The houses and the arable strips are owned in severalty, and annexed to these houses and arable strips are pasture rights which are the rights of individuals and which, it may be believed, seem to exhaust the utility of the waste. What remains to dispute about? A nude, a very nude *dominium*, which is often imperceptible.

Not always imperceptible. From time to time these Orwell people in town meeting assembled may have taken some grave resolution as to the treatment of the waste. They may now and then have decided to add to the amount of arable and diminish the amount of pasture. But occasional measures of this sort, for which a theoretical, if not a real, unanimity is secured, will not generate a regulative organ, still less a proprietary corporation. In decade after decade a township-moot at Orwell would have little to do. The moot of the Wetherley hundred is the court that deems dooms for the men of Orwell. If the lands of Orwell had been steadily regarded as the lands of a corporation they would have passed in one lump to some one Norman lord. But such corporate feeling as there was was weak. The men of Orwell had been seeking lords, each man for himself, in the most opposite quarters. Many of the virgates that are physically in one village have, as we have seen[1], been made 'to lie in' other villages; for the free man can carry his land where he pleases. When this is so, he is already beginning to feel that the tie which keeps him in a village community is a restraint that has, perhaps unfortunately, been imposed upon him and his property by ancient history.

The fate of these lordless communities and of their waste was still trembling in the balance when King Harold fell. To guess what would have happened had he held his own is not easy. It is possible that what was done by foreigners would have been done, though less rapidly, by lords of English race, and that by consolidating soke and commendation into a firm landlordship and then making among themselves treaties of partition, they would have acquired the ownership of the pasture land subject to the rights of common. It is perhaps more probable that in some cases the old indeterminate state of things might have been maintained until the idea of a fictitious personality had spread from the chapter-house to the

The village meeting.

What might have become of the free village.

[1] See above, pp. 13, 124.

M.

23

borough and from the borough to the village. Then the ownership of the soil might have been attributed to a corporation of
which the freeholders in the village were the members. One
famous case which came to light in the seventeenth century may
warn us that throughout the middle ages there were here and
there groups of freeholders, and even of customary tenants, who
were managing agrarian affairs in a manner which feudalism
could not explain and our English law would not warrant, for
they were behaving as though they were members of a landowning corporation[1]. Often in the east of England the manors
must have been so intermixed that village meetings, not however of a democratic kind, may have dealt with business which
lay outside the competence of any seignorial court. We know
little and, it is to be feared, must be content to know little of
such meetings. They were not sessions of a tribunal; they
kept no rolls; the law knew them not. But we dare not say
that if all seignorial pressure had been removed, the village
lands would have been preserved as communal lands for modern
villagers. Where there was no seignorial pressure, no joint and
several liability for dues, the tie was lax between the owners
of the strips in the village fields; and if there was a corporate
element in their union, there was also a strong element of
co-ownership. Had they been left to themselves, we can not
say with any confidence that they would not sooner or later
have partitioned the waste. Was it not their land, and might
they not do what they liked with their own?

Mark com-
munities.
One other question may be touched. It was the fashion
in England some years ago that those who spoke of village
communities should say something of 'the Germanic mark.'
What they said seemed often to imply that the German village
community was a mark community. This was a mistake. It
seems indeed that there were parts of Germany in which the
word 'mark' was loosely used[2]; but the true *Markgenossenschaft*
was utterly different from the *Dorfgenossenschaft*, and the lands
with which it dealt were just those lands that belonged to no
village[3]. In the country which saw the Germans becoming an
agricultural race, the lands belonging to the villages were but
oases in a wild territory. In later days some large piece of this

---

[1] I refer to the much discussed case of Aston and Cote. See Law Quarterly
Review, ix. 214.

[2] Meitzen, op. cit. i. 573.   [3] Ibid. i. 122–60.

territory is found to be under the control of a 'mark-community,' whose members are dwelling here and there in many different villages and exercise rights over the land (for the more part it is forest land[1]) that belongs to no village but constitutes the mark. Traces of what might have become 'the mark system' may perhaps be found in England; but not where they have been usually sought.

We read of a tract in Suffolk which is common pasture for the whole hundred of Coleness[2]. Instances in which a piece of land is common pasture for many vills were by no means uncommon in the thirteenth century. They grow rarer as time goes on. Our law provided but a precarious and uncomfortable niche for them under the rubric *common pur cause de vicinage*[3]. These are the traces of what in different surroundings might have become, and perhaps were near to becoming, mark communities. In the thirteenth century the state seems to have been already enforcing the theory that every inch of land ought to lie within the territory of some vill[4]. This was a police measure. The responsibility of one set of villagers was not to cease until the boundary was reached where the responsibility of another set began. But even in recent times there have been larger moors in the north of England which 'belonged' (we will use a vague word) to two or more townships in common. At any rate, we must not take back this theory that the vills exhaust the land into the days of the Germanic settlement[5]. In some districts the vills must have been separated from each other by wide woods, and in all likelihood large portions of these woods were not proper to any one village, but were regarded as belonging, in some sense or another, to a group of villages. However, land of this kind was just the land which was most exposed to an assertion of

Intercommoning between vills.

[1] Therefore its assembly is a *Holtding*, and a *Holzgraf* presides there: Meitzen, op. cit. i. 125.

[2] D. B. ii. 339 b: 'In hundret de Coleness est quedam pastura communis omnibus hominibus de hundret.' At Rhuddlan (D. B. i. 269) Earl Hugh has given to Robert half the castle, half the burg, and 'half of the forests which do not pertain to any vill of the said manor.' This, however, is in Wales.

[3] Hist. Eng. Law, i. 608.

[4] Ibid. i. 547.

[5] Blomefield, Hist. Norfolk, iv. 691 gives an account of an extremely fertile tract of pasture known as Tilney Smeeth upon which the cattle of seven 'towns' intercommoned.

royal ownership, and we imagine that a mark community had from the first little chance of organizing itself in England[1]. But we have already made too many guesses.

Last words.

We must not be in a hurry to get to the beginning of the long history of law. Very slowly we are making our way towards it. The history of law must be a history of ideas. It must represent, not merely what men have done and said, but what men have thought in bygone ages. The task of reconstructing ancient ideas is hazardous, and can only be accomplished little by little. If we are in a hurry to get to the beginning we shall miss the path. Against many kinds of anachronism we now guard ourselves. We are careful of costume, of armour and architecture, of words and forms of speech. But it is far easier to be careful of these things than to prevent the intrusion of untimely ideas. In particular there lies a besetting danger for us in the barbarian's use of a language which is too good for his thought. Mistakes then are easy, and when committed they will be fatal and fundamental mistakes. If, for example, we introduce the *persona ficta* too soon, we shall be doing worse than if we armed Hengest and Horsa with machine guns or pictured the Venerable Bede correcting proofs for the press; we shall have built upon a crumbling foundation. The most efficient method of protecting ourselves against such errors is that of reading our history backwards as well as forwards, of making sure of our middle ages before we talk about the 'archaic,' of accustoming our eyes to the twilight before we go out into the night.

---

[1] If we are right in supposing that very generally a royal land-book disposes of a whole village, then if it proceeds to give rights in the *communis silva*, it is probably speaking of a wood that is not regarded as annexed to that village but of one which is common to various villages. The intercommoning of vills in a forest is illustrated by the famous Epping case, *Commissioners of Sewers* v. *Glasse*, Law Reports, 19 Equity, 134. But for the king's rights in forest land, a ' mark community ' might have grown up in Epping. On the other hand, but for the king's rights, the land might long ago have been partitioned among the mark-men.

ESSAY III.

THE HIDE.

WHAT was the hide? However unwilling we may be to What was the hide? face this dreary old question, we can not escape it. At first sight it may seem avoidable by those who are interested in the general drift of national life, but have no desire to solve petty problems or face unnecessary difficulties. The history of weights and measures, some may say, is probably very curious and no doubt is worth study; but we, who shall be amply satisfied if we understand the grand movements and the broad traits, must leave this little province, as we must leave much else, to antiquarian specialists. Unfortunately, however, that question about the hide is 'pre-judicial' to all the great questions of early English history.

If our choice lay between 30 and 40 acres, or again be- Importance of the question. tween a long and a short hundred, then indeed we might refuse to take part in the conflict. But between the advocates of big hides of 120 acres or thereabouts and the advocates of little hides of 30 acres or thereabouts there should be no peace. In the construction of early English history we shall adopt one style of architecture if we are supplied with small hides, while if our materials consist of big hides an entirely different 'plan and elevation' must be chosen. Let us take one example. We find the kings giving away manses or hides by fives and tens. What are they really doing? Are they or are they not giving away whole villages? Obviously this question is pre-judicial to many another. Our whole conception of the Anglo-Saxon kingship will be profoundly affected by our attribution or our denial to the king of an alienable superiority over villages that are full of free landowners. This question, therefore, we should have upon our hands even if we thought that we could rear the fabric of political and constitutional history without first laying an economic foundation. But the day for such castles in the air is passing.

Howbeit, we must not talk in this pompous way of castles or foundations. We are not going to lay foundations, nor even to choose a site. We hope to test a few materials and perhaps to show how a site may some day be acquired.

Hide and manse in Bede. From the Norman Conquest so far back as we can go, a certain possessory unit or a certain typical tenement is being thrust upon our notice by the laws, the charters, the historians[1]. We may begin with Bede. When he is going to speak of the area or the capacity of a tract of land, be it large or be it small, he refers to a certain unit or type, namely, the land of one family (*terra unius familiae*). The abbess Hild acquires the land of one family and erects a religious house upon it[2]; king Oswy gives away twelve tracts of land, each of which consists of 'the *possessiones* of ten families'[3]; the kingdom of the South Saxons contains the land of 7,000 families[4]. We see that already Bede is thinking rather of the size or capacity of a tract of soil than of the number of households that happen to be dwelling there. 'The measure (*mensura*) of the Isle of Wight is, according to the English mode of reckoning, 1200 families[5].' 'The isle of Thanet is no small island: that is to say, according to the customary English computation, it is of 600 families[6].' Some apology is due from a scholar who writes in Latin and who writes thus; so Bede tells us that he is using the English mode of reckoning; he is literally translating some English term.

Hide and manse in the land-books. When his own book is rendered into English that term will reappear. Usually it reappears in the form *híd*, but occasionally we have *hiwisc* or *hiwscipe*. There seems no room for

---

[1] The word *tenement* will be often employed hereafter. Has it become needful to protest that a *tenement* need not be a house? If my body is my soul's 'frail tenement,' that is not because my body holds my soul (a reprobate error), but because (for this is better philosophy and sound law) my soul holds my body. But, to descend from these heights, it will be a thousand pities if a vulgar blunder compels us to abandon the excellent *tenement* in favour of the feeble *holding* or the over-worked *estate*.

[2] Hist. Eccl. lib. 4, c. 21 (23), ed. Plummer, i. 253.

[3] Ibid. lib. 3, c. 24, ed. cit. i. 178.

[4] Ibid. lib. 4, c. 13, ed. cit. i. 230.

[5] Ibid. lib. 4, c. 14 (16), ed. cit. i. 237.

[6] Ibid. lib. 1, c. 25, ed. cit. i. 45.

doubt that *hiwisc* and the more abstract *hiwscipe* mean a
household, and very little room for doubt that *híd* springs
from a root that is common to it and them and has the same
primary meaning[1]. Elsewhere we may find an equivalence
between the hide and the *hiwisc* :—'If a Welsh man thrives
so that he has a *hiwisc* of land and can render the king's
gafol, then his wergild is 120 shillings; but if he attains only
to a *half-hide* then his wergild is 80 shillings[2].' In the charters
also we may now and then find that the land to be conveyed
is a *hiwisc*[3], or is the land of one *familia*[4]. However, the
common English term is *hide*, while the scribes of the land-
books, who as yet are above inventing a Latin *hida*, ring the
changes on half-a-dozen phrases[5]. We begin with *terra unius
manentis, terra unius casati, terra unius tributarii*, which keep
clearly before our eyes the fact or the theory that the normal
householder, the normal taxpayer, will possess one of these
units. At a little later time the more convenient *mansa*
(sometimes *mansio*[6] or *mansiuncula*) becomes popular, and we
may see also that men are beginning to speak of manents,
casates, tributaries 'of land,' much as they would speak of
acres or perches of land[7]. So far as we can see, all these
terms are being used as though they were absolutely equivalent. If a clerk has to describe several different tenements,
he will write of *manentes* in one clause and *casati* in the
next, merely because a repetition of the same term would be

[1] If, as Mr Seebohm suggests (Village Community, p. 398), this word meant
the skin of an ox, some one would assuredly have Latined it by *corium*, and not
by *terra unius familiae* (*manentis* etc.)

[2] Schmid, App. VII. (Wergilds), 2, § 7. By comparing this with Ine 32 we
get an even more explicit equation: 'Gif Wylisc mon hæbbe hide londes'='Gif
Wilisc mon geþeo þæt he hæbbe hiwisc landes.'

[3] K. 271 (ii. 52), a forgery: 'æt Cemele tien hyda, æt Domeccesige þriddehalf
hiwisce.'—K. 1077 (v. 146): 'æt hilcan hiwisce feowerti penega.'—K. iii. 431:
'ðæs anes hiwisces boc...ðas oðres hiwisces.'—K. 1050 (v. 98). See also Crawford Charters, 127, for *hiwscipe*.

[4] K. 1006 (v. 47): 'de terra iuris mei aliquantulam portionem, iuxta mensuram
scilicet decem familiarum.' See also K. 1007.

[5] The would-be Latin *hida* occurs already in K. 230 (i. 297), but is rare
before the Conquest. On the other hand, as an English word *híd* is in constant
use.

[6] K. 131 (i. 159); K. 140 (i. 169).

[7] Thus, to give one early example, K. 1008 (v. 49): 'duodecim tributarios
terrae quae appellantur Ferrinig.' So in K. 124 (i. 151) we have the neuter form
manentia.

inelegant[1]. In Kentish charters we read more of the *aratrum*
and the *sullung* than of the manse and the hide; but apparently
we have here other names for what is a similar and in some
sort an equivalent unit[2]; and it is by no means unknown that
Kentish tenements will be called manses and hides[3].

The large
hide and
the manor-
ial arrange-
ment.
Now if we ask whether the type to which reference is thus
made is a tenement comprising about six-score acres of arable
land, we are asking a question of the gravest importance.
For let us look at some of the consequences which will flow
from an affirmative answer. Let it be granted that, long
before the Norman Conquest, the hide has become an unit
in an unwieldy system of taxation, which has been governed
by false assumptions and vitiated by caprice, until the fiscal
hide in a given case may widely diverge from its original or
indeed from any fixed type. None the less, this system has
for its base the theory that the typical man of Anglo-Saxon
law, the typical householder or taxpayer, has a hide, has land
enough for a team of oxen, has 120 arable acres. The language
of the charters supposes that this is so. No doubt the supposition is, as every supposition of this kind must be, untrue;
but still it must have a core of truth, and in the remotest
age this core will be at its largest. Men will not fall into
a habit of speaking of 120 arable acres or thereabouts as the
tenement of one family or of one householder, unless as a
matter of fact the tenement of one family or of one householder has in a preponderant number of cases some such
content as this. Suppose, for example, that the Anglo-Saxon
kingdoms of the sixth century had been composed chiefly of
lords, whose estates ranged from 600 acres to some much
larger quantity, and of ' semi-servile' cultivators, the average
size of whose tenements was 30 acres, such a usage of words
as that which we are considering could never have struck

---

[1] A good instance in Egbert's Dialogue, H. & S. iii. 404. For how many
hides may the clergy swear? A priest may swear 'secundum numerum 120
tributariorum'; a deacon 'iuxta numerum 60 manentium'; a monk 'secundum
numerum 30 tributariorum.' Here *tributarii* alternates with *manentes* for the
same reason that *secundum* alternates with *iuxta*. So K. 143 (i. 173): '*manentes
...casati...manentes...casati.*'

[2] See Schmid, p. 611.

[3] See, for instance, Werhard's testament (A.D. 832), K. 230 (i. 297): 'Otteford
100 hidas, Grauenea 32 hidas.' These are Kentish estates. Hereafter we shall
give some reasons for thinking that the Kentish *sullung* may have a history that
is all its own.

root. Either the small tenement of the cultivator or the big tenement of his lord must have been taken as the typical 'manse,' the typical 'land of one householder.' Let us at once press home this argument, though at present it involves a hypothesis, for in the dull disquisitions that follow we may be cheered by the thought that great questions are at stake. If in the oldest time the typical 'land of one householder' had 120 arable acres, the manorial system was not prevalent, not dominant, in England. It will be admitted on all hands that this would be much too large a tenement for a serf or a semi-servile *colonus*. On the other hand, it is much too small a tenement for any one who is going to play the part of a manorial lord, unless we use the term *manorial* in so wide a sense that it becomes useless. For how many tenants will this manorial lord, who is to be taken as the typical householder, have upon his 120 acres? If his arrangements are at all like those revealed to us by Domesday Book, he will keep at least one-third of his land in demesne, and there will remain but 80 acres for the *coloni*. Shall we give him three *coloni*, or four or five? We can hardly give him a larger number. Furthermore, it is quite clear that this 'manorial lord' will not own a village. The villages as we see them in the earliest charters and thence onward into Domesday Book contain five, ten, fifteen hides. Our manorial lord must be content to take his hide in little scraps scattered about among the scraps of some ten or twenty other 'manorial lords' whose hides are similarly dispersed in the open field of a village. All this seems to follow inevitably if once we are satisfied that the hide of the old days had 120 arable acres or thereabouts; for the hide is the land of one typical householder[1].

Now for a long time past there has been among historians Our course.

---

[1] Mr Seebohm, Village Community, p. 395, admits that the *familia* of Bede and the *casatum* of the charters is the hide, and that the hide has 120 acres. This does not prevent him from holding (p. 266) that when Bede speaks of king Oswy giving to a church twelve *possessiunculae*, each of ten families, we must see *decuriae* of slaves, 'the bundle of ten slaves or semi-servile tenants.' He seems also to think that while the hide was 'the holding of the full free landholder,' the *hiwisc* was the holding of a servile family. But the passage which he cites in a note (Wergilds, § 7) seems to disprove this, for there undoubtedly, as he remarks, *hiwisc* = hide. It is the passage quoted above on p. 359. The Welshman gets a wergild of 120 shillings (three-fifths of an English ceorl's wergild) by acquiring a *hiwisc* or (Ine 32) *hide* of land. Why the *hide* should not here mean what it admittedly means elsewhere is not apparent.

and antiquaries a good deal of agreement in favour of this large hide, but against it appeal may be made to honoured names, such as those of Kemble and Eyton[1]. Also it must be confessed that in favour of much smaller hides, or at least of much smaller hides for the earliest days, some weighty arguments may be advanced. In order that they may be understood, and perchance refuted, we must pursue a long and devious course and must raise by the way many questions, touching which we have no right to an opinion: questions about agriculture, questions about land measurement, perhaps even physiological questions. Also it is our misfortune that, as we stumble through the night, we must needs stumble against some of our fellow adventurers.

§ 1. *Measures and Fields.*

Permanence and change in agrarian history.
At the present moment there is no need for arguments which insist upon the immutable character of ancient agrarian arrangements. If we take up a map of a common field drawn in the eighteenth century, the lines that we see upon it are in the main very old. The scheme seems fashioned for the purpose of resisting change and compelling the men of one age to till the land as their fathers tilled it. Nothing but an unanimous agreement among those who are not likely to agree can break up that prison-house of cells in which agriculture has been cramped and confined. Rather, it may be, the student who is perusing the 'estate map' and who is fascinated by the possession of a new tool for picking historical locks, should warn himself that, though there has been permanence, there has also been change, and that in a far-off time changes of a certain sort came quickly. True that in the current of agricultural progress there is a rapid acceleration as it flows towards

---

[1] Though Eyton has (for some reason that we can not find in his published works) allowed but 48 'gheld acres' to the 'gheld hide,' he can hardly be reckoned as an advocate of the Small Hide. His doctrine, if we have caught it, is that the hide has never been a measure of size. This raises the question— How comes it then that the fractions into which a hide breaks are indubitably called (gheld) 'acres'? Why not ounces, pints, pence?

our own day. We may easily go back to an age when the introduction of a new process or new implement was rare. On the other hand, if we fix our attention on the map of any one village and contemplate its strips and balks and virgates, the hazard involved in an assumption of their antiquity will increase swiftly when we have left behind us the advent of Duke William and are urging our inferential career towards Hengest or, it may be, towards Cæsar.

Let us look, for example, at the changes that take place in some Essex villages during the twenty years that precede the Domesday Inquest. The following table shows them: Rapidity of change in old times.

	Villani	Bordarii	Servi	Lord's teams	Men's teams
Teidana[1], T. R. E.	5	3	4	2	4
T. R. W.	1	17	0	3	3
Waldena[2], T. R. E.	66	17	16	8	22
T. R. W.	46	40	20	10	22
Hame[3], T. R. E.	32	16	3	5	8
T. R. W.	48	79	3	4	12
Benefelda[4], T. R. E.	10	2	7	3	7
T. R. W.	9	11	4	3	4
Wimbeis[5], T. R. E.	26	18	6	3	21
T. R. W.	26	55	0	3	15

These are but specimens of the obscure little revolutions that are being accomplished in the Essex villages. In general there has been a marked increase in the number of *bordarii*, at the expense of the villeins on the one part and the serfs on the other[6], and this, whatever else it may represent, must tell us of a redistribution of tenements, perhaps of a process that substitutes the half-virgate for the virgate as the average holding of an Essex peasant. The jar of conquest has made such revolutions easy[7].

But, it will be said, though the 'bundles' of strips be cut in half, the main features of the field remain constant. Let us, however, look at Yorkshire, where for fifteen years an immense tract of land has been lying 'waste.' Have we any Devastation of villages.

---

[1] D. B. ii. 47 b.   [2] Ibid. 61.   [3] Ibid. 64.
[4] Ibid. 65.   [5] Ibid. 69 b.   [6] See above, p. 35.
[7] For this reason I do not feel sure that Mr F. Baring (Eng. Hist. Rev. xi. 98) has conclusively proved his case when he accuses D. B. of omitting to notice the free tenants on the estates of the Abbey of Burton.

reason to believe that when agriculture slowly steals back into this desert there will be a mere restoration of the defaced map ? Surely not. If for a few years an ' open field ' lies waste, there will be no mere restoration. For one thing, many of the old outlines will have utterly vanished. Even if the acres were already divided by the so-called ' balks ' (and we can not be sure that they always were[1]), the balk was but a narrow strip of unploughed sward and would hardly be perceptible when the whole field was once more a sheet of grass and weeds. For another thing, new settlers would probably begin by ploughing only a small portion of the old field. It is likely enough that their measuring rod would not be even approximately equal to the rod employed in a previous century, and they would have ample opportunity for the introduction of novelties, for the substitution of three fields for two and for all that such a change implies. Now William's deliberate devastation of the north is but one final and grandiose exploit of an ancient kind of warfare. After his day agrarian history becomes more stable because invasions cease and the character of civil warfare changes. The strife between York and Lancaster, between King and Parliament, passes like a thunderstorm over the fields; it damages the crops; but that is all, and Bosworth ' Field ' and Naseby ' Field ' will next year be tilled in the same old way. A raid of the Danes, a feud between Angle and Saxon, was a different affair. The peasants fought. Men, women and children were sold as slaves. Also there was deliberate devastation. ' They make a wilderness and call it peace.' What else should they call it, when a foodless wilderness is the most scientific of all frontiers ? Readers of the English Chronicle will doubt whether there is any village in England that has not been once, or more than once, a deserted village. And if we must reckon with war, there is famine also to be reckoned with. When in a few brief words the English Chronicler tells us that in 1043 there was mickle hunger in the land so that the sestar of corn sold for sixty pence and

---

[1] The antiquity and universality of the balk must not be taken for granted ; see Meitzen, op. cit. i. 86 ; iii. 319. However, in recent times balks did occur within the shots (this Meitzen seems to doubt) as may be seen to-day at Upton St. Leonards, Co. Gloucester. Mr Seebohm, op. cit. 4, 382, claims the word *balk* for the Welsh ; but see New Eng. Dict. and Skeat, Etymol. Dict. In this, as in many another case, the Welsh claim to an English word has broken down.

even more[1], he is, like enough, telling us of a disaster which depopulated many a village and forced many a villager to bow his head for meat in those evil days[2]. Agrarian history becomes more catastrophic as we trace it backwards.

And, putting on one side the ravages of war and famine, we must call to mind the numerous hints that our map gives us of village colonization[3]. Men did not make two contiguous villages at one time and call them both Hamton. Names are given to places in order that they may be distinguished from neighbouring places. So when we see two different villages, called Hamton and Other Hamton, lying next each other, we may be fairly certain that they are not of equal antiquity, and it is not unlikely that the one is the offshoot and daughter of the other[4]. There are about one hundred and fifty Newtons and Newtowns in England. Every instance of colonization, every new settlement in the woods, gave scope for the introduction of novelties, such scope as was not to be found in after days when men stood thicker on the soil and all the best land was already tilled[5].

Village colonies.

Therefore we must not trust a method of husbandry or a scheme of land-measures much further than we can see it. Nothing, for example, could be rasher than the assumption that the 'three-course system' of tillage was common in the England of the seventh century[6]. We have a little evidence that it was practised in the eleventh[7], perhaps some evidence,

Antiquity of the three-field system.

[1] A.-S. Chron. ad ann. 1043. Henry of Huntingdon, p. 192, took the sestar of this passage to be a horse-load. Even if we accept his version, the price would be high when compared with the prices recorded on the Pipe Rolls of Henry II.; for which see Hall, Court Life, 219, 220. But, though the point can not be argued here, we may strongly suspect that the chronicler meant something that is almost infinitely worse, and that his sestar was at the very least as small as our bushel. We know of no English document which suggests a *sextarius* that would be comparable with a horse-load.

[2] Geatfled's will, K. 925 (iv. 263).　　　[3] See above, p. 14.

[4] Observe the clumsy nomenclature illustrated by K. 816 (iv. 164), a deed forged for the Confessor :—'Middletun et oðer Middletun...Horningdun et oðer Horningdun...Fifehyda et oðer Fifehyda.'

[5] See in this context the interesting letter of Bp. Denewulf to Edward the Elder, K. 1089 (v. 166). An estate of 72 hides, a very large estate, came to the bishop almost waste. He prides himself on having now tilled 90 acres!

[6] A good programme of this system is given by Cunningham, Growth of English Industry, i. 71.

[7] Rectitudines, 4, § 3 ; Seebohm, Village Community, 141. Mr Seebohm's inference is ingenious and plausible. See also Andrews, Old English Manor, 248.

that it was not unknown in the ninth[1]. But 'the two-course system' can be traced as far[2], and seems to have been as common, if not commoner, in the thirteenth century[3]. If on a modern map we see a village with 'trinity fields,' we must not at once decide that those who laid them out sowed two in every year, for it is well within the bounds of possibility that two were left idle[4]. An agriculture of this kind was not unknown in the Yorkshire of the fourteenth century[5], and indeed we read that in the eighteenth 'one crop and two fallows' was the traditional course in the open field of a Suffolk village[6].

Differences between the different shires. We have time enough on our hands. Between Domesday Book and the withdrawal of the legions lies as long an interval as that which separates the Conqueror from Mr Arthur Young. Also we have space enough on our hands. Any theory that would paint all England as plotted out for proprietary and agricultural purposes in accordance with a single pattern would be of all theories the least probable. We need not contrast Kent with Westmoreland, or Cornwall with Norfolk, for our

[1] K. 259 (ii. 26), A.D. 845: Gift of 19 acres near the city of Canterbury, 6 acres in one place, 6 in another, 7 in a third.

[2] K. 241 (ii. 1), A.D. 839: Gift of 24 acres, 10 in one place, 14 in another.— K. 339 (ii. 149), A.D. 904: Gift of 60 acres of arable to the south and 60 to the north of a certain stream.—K. 586 (iii. 118): 'and 30 æcra on ðæm twæm feldan dallandes.'

[3] See e.g. Glastonbury Rentalia (Somerset Record Soc.) pp. 14, 15, 55, 67, 89, 119, 128–9, 137–8, 155, 166, 192, 195, 208, 219. A system which leaves half the land idle in every year is of course quite compatible with the growth of both winter and spring corn. When, as is not uncommon, the villeins have to do between Michaelmas and Christmas twice as much ploughing as they will do between Christmas and Lady Day, this seems to point to a scheme which leaves one field idle and divides the other between winter and spring corn in the proportion of 2 : 1. Even in the fourteenth century a three-field system seems to have been regarded in some places as 'high farming.' Larking, Domesday of Kent, App. p. 23: Extent of Addington, A.D. 1361: 'Et sunt ibidem 60 acrae terrae arabilis, de quibus duae partes possunt seminari per annum, *si bene coluntur*.' For evidence of the three-field system, see Nasse, Agricultural Community, Engl. transl. 53.

[4] Meitzen, op. cit. ii. 592.

[5] Turton, Forest of Pickering (North Riding Record Society), 148 ff. Twenty years ago A. E. enclosed an acre; sown eight times with spring corn; value of a sown acre 1*s.*, of an unsown, 4*d.* Twenty-two years ago E. C. enclosed a rood; sown seven times with oats, value 6*d.* a year; value, when unsown, 1*d.* a year. In the same book are many instances of a husbandry which alternates oats with hay.

[6] Scrutton, Commons and Common Fields, 118, citing a Report to the Board of Agriculture.

maps seem to tell us that Somerset differed from Wiltshire and Dorset. The settlement of a heathen folk loosely banded together under a war-lord was one thing; the conquest of a new province by a Christian king who was advised by foreign bishops and had already been taught that he had land to 'book,' would be another thing. If, as seems possible, we read in Ine's laws of a 'plantation' of some parts of Somerset effected by means of large allotments made to the king's gesiths, who undertake to put tillers on the soil[1], we must not at once infer that this is an old procedure, for it may be very new, and may have for its outcome an agrarian arrangement strikingly unlike that which existed in the heart of the older Wessex.

Moreover there are upon the face of our map many cases which seem to tell us that in the oldest days the smallest district that bore a name was often large, and therefore that the territory which subserved a single group of homesteads was often spacious. One example we will take from Norfolk. We find a block of land that now-a-days consists of eleven parishes, namely, Wiggenhall S^t. Mary the Virgin, Wiggenhall S^t. German, Wiggenhall S^t. Peter, Wiggenhall S^t. Mary Magdalen, Tilney cum Islington, Tilney All Saints, Tilney S^t. Lawrence, Terrington S^t. Clement, Terrington S^t. John, Walpole S^t. Peter, Walpole S^t. Andrew[2]. In such a case we can hardly suppose that all these villages belong to the same age, even if we are not entitled to infer that the later villages were not founded until the day for parish churches had arrived. This being so, it is highly probable that some villages were formed at all stages of the feudalizing process, and therefore that a historical account of 'the' English township, or even of 'the' English nucleated village, would of necessity be untrue. And, while this East Anglian specimen is still before us, we may notice another interesting trait. In the Marshland Fen there is a considerable tract of ground which consists of 'detached portions' of these and other villages. Each has been given a block there, a fairly rectangular block. At one point the partition is minute. A space of less than 36 acres has been cut up so that no less than six villages shall have a piece, a

New and old villages.

---

[1] Ine, 63–68, 70. See above, p. 238.

[2] A very fine instance is found on the north coast of Norfolk:—Burnham Deepdale, B. Norton, B. Westgate, B. Sutton, B. Thorpe, B. Overy. As to this see Stevenson, E. H. R. xi. 304.

rectangular piece of it[1]. It seems very possible that this fen
has at some time been common ground for all these villages,
and, as already said, it is in this quarter that we may perhaps
find traces of something that resembled the ' marks' of Germany[2]. The science of village morphology is still very young,
and we must not be led away into any discussion of its elements ;
but there is the more reason why we should take to heart those
warnings that it already gives us, because what we can read of
hides is to be found for the more part in documents proceeding
from a central power, which, for governmental and fiscal purposes,
endeavours to preserve fictitious continuity and uniformity in
the midst of change and variety. However, we must draw
nearer to our task.

History of
measures.

As regards land measurement, we may be fairly certain that
in the days before the Norman Conquest there was little real,
though much nominal uniformity. The only measures for the
size of things with which nature has equipped the natural man
are his limbs. For the things that he handles he uses his
thumb, span, cubit, ell ; for the ground upon which he walks,
his foot and his pace. For large spaces and long distances he
must have recourse to ' time-labour-units,' to the day's journey
and the morning's ploughing. Then gradually, under the
fostering care of government, steady equations are established
between these units :—twelve thumbs, for instance, are to
make a foot. Thus the measures for land are brought into
connexion with the more delicate measures used for cloth and
similar stuff. Then an attempt to obtain some standard less
variable than the limb may forge a link between thumbs and
grains of corn. Another device is the measuring rod. One
rod will represent the arm of an average man ; a longer rod
may serve to mediate between the foot which is short and
the acre or day's ploughing which is large. In laying out a
field in such wise that it shall consist of equal pieces, each
of which can be ploughed in a forenoon, we naturally use a
rod. We say, for example, that to plough a strip that is 4 rods
wide and 40 long is a fair day's work. For some while there is

[1] Index Map of Ordnance Survey of Norfolk. Six-inch Map of Norfolk, LVI.
Another instance occurs near Yarmouth along the banks of the Waveney. Even
if the allotment was the result of modern schemes of drainage, it still might be
a satisfaction of very ancient claims.

[2] See above, p. 355.

no reason why the rods employed in two neighbouring villages should be strictly or even approximately equal[1]. Taxation is the great force that makes for standard land measures. Then a king declares how many thumbs there ought to be in the cloth-ell or cloth-yard. At a later time he actually makes cloth-ells or cloth-yards and distributes them, keeping an ultimate standard in his own palace. Thenceforward all other units tend to become mere fractions or multiples of this royal stick. The foot is a third, the thumb or inch a thirty-sixth part thereof. Five and a half cloth-measuring yards make a royal land-measuring rod. Plot out a space which is four rods by forty, you will have an acre.

The whole story, if ever it be told at length, will be intricate; but we believe that a general persuasion that land-measurements ought to be fixed by law and by reference to some one carefully preserved standard is much more modern than most people think. Real accuracy and the establishment of a measure that is to be common to the whole realm first emerge in connexion with the measurement of cloth and such like. There is a delightful passage in the old Scotch laws which tells us that the ell ought to contain 37 inches meted by the thumbs of three men, 'þat is to say, a mekill man and a man of messurabill statur and of a lytill man[2].' We have somewhere read that in Germany, if a perch of fifteen feet was to be manufactured, the first fifteen people who chanced to come out of church contributed each a foot towards the construction of the standard. At an early time, however, men were trying to find some class of small things which were of a fairly invariable length and hit upon barley-corns. This seems to have happened in England before the Norman Conquest[3]. Instead of taking the 'thoume' of 'a man of messurabill statur' for your inch, you are to take three barley-corns, 'iii bear cornys gud and chosyn but tayllis (i.e. without the tails)'[4]. But the twelfth century was drawing to an end before

Slow growth of uniformity.

---

[1] Fines (ed. Hunter) i. 242: 'sex acras terrae mensuratas per legalem perticam eiusdem villae [de Haveresham].'

[2] Acts of Parliament of Scotland, i. 309.

[3] Schmid, Gesetze, App. XII.: 'three feet and three hand breadths and three barley corns.'

[4] Acts of Parliament of Scotland, i. 309. Compare Statutes of the Realm, i. 206: 'Tria grana ordei sicca et rotunda faciunt pollicem.' This so-called Statute of Admeasurement has not been traced to any authoritative source.

any decisive step was taken to secure uniformity even in the measurement of cloth. In Richard I.'s day guardians of weights and measures are to be appointed in every county, city and borough; they are to keep iron *ulnae*[1]. At this time or a little later these *ulnae*, ells or cloth-yards were being delivered out by a royal officer to all who might require them, and that officer had the custody of the ultimate standards[2]. We may doubt whether the laws which require in general terms that there shall be one measure throughout the realm had measures of land in view[3]. A common standard is not nearly as necessary in this case as it is in the case of cloth. Even in our own day men do not buy land by the acre or the perch in the same sense as that in which they buy cloth or cotton by the yard. Very rarely will anyone name a price for a rood and leave it to the other bargainer to decide which out of many roods shall be included in the sale. Nevertheless, the distribution of iron *ulnae* was important. An equation was established between the cloth measure and the land measure: five-and-a-half *ulnae* or cloth-yards make one royal perch. After this we soon find that land is occasionally measured by the iron *ulna* of the king[4].

Superficial measure.

The scheme of computation that we know as 'superficial measure' was long in making itself part of the mental furniture of the ordinary man. Such terms as 'square rod' and 'square mile' were not current, nor such equations as that which tells us how 144 square inches make a square foot. Whatever may have been the attainments of some cloistered mathematicians, the man of business did not suppose that he could talk of size without talking of shape, and indeed a set of terms which speak of shapeless size is not very useful until men have enough of geometry and trigonometry to measure spaces that are not rectangular parallelograms. The enlightened people of the thirteenth century can say that

Probably, like many of the documents with which it is associated, it is a mere note which lawyers copied into their statute books.

[1] Hoveden, iv. 33: 'et ulna sit ferrea.'   [2] Britton, ii. 189.

[3] Magna Carta is careful of wine, beer, corn and cloth ; not of land.

[4] Gloucester Corporation Records, ed. Stevenson, p. 80. Near the year 1200 a grant is made of land in Gloucester measuring in breadth 30 feet 'iuxta ferratam virgam Regis.' Ducange, s. v. *ulna*, gives examples from the Monasticon. The iron rod was an iron ell. Were standard perches ever made and distributed? Apparently the only measure of length of which any standard was made was the *ulna* or cloth-yard.

if an acre is x perches long it is y perches wide[1]. They can compare the size of spaces if all the lines be straight and all the angles right; and for them an acre is no longer of necessity ten times as long as it is broad. But they will not tell us (and they do not think) that an acre contains z 'square perches.' This is of some importance to students of Domesday Book. Very often the size of a tract of land is indicated by the length of two lines:—The wood or the pasture is x leagues (furlongs, perches, feet) in length and y in breadth. Now, to say the least, we are hasty if we treat this as a statement which gives us size without shape. It is not all one to say that a wood is a league long and a league wide and to say that it is two leagues long and half a league wide. The jurors are not speaking of superficial content, they are speaking of length and breadth, and they are either giving us the extreme diameters of the irregularly shaped woods and pastures, or (and this seems more probable) they are making rough estimates of mean diameters. If we go back to an earlier time, the less we think of 'superficial measure' the better[2].

Let us recall the main features of our modern system, giving them the names that they bore in medieval Latin.

The modern system.

Linear Measure.

12 inches (*pollices*) = 1 foot (*pes*); 3 feet = 1 yard (*ulna*); 5·5 yards = 1 rod, pole, perch (*virga, pertica, perca*); 40 perches = 1 furlong (*quarentina*); 8 furlongs = 1 mile (*mille*); 12 furlongs = 1 *leuua, leuca, leuga* (league)[3].

Superficial Measure.

144 square inches = 1 square foot; 9 square feet = 1 square yard; 30·25 square yards = 1 square perch; 40 square perches = 1 rood; 4 roods = 1 acre[4].

---

[1] See the apocryphal Statute of Admeasurement, Stat., vol. i. p. 206.

[2] If the jurors had superficial measure in their heads and were stating this by reference to two straight lines, they would make the length of one of these lines a constant (e.g. one league or one furlong). This is not done: the space is 6 furlongs in length by 3 in breadth, 14 furlongs in length by 4 in breadth, 9 furlongs and 1 perch in length by 5 furlongs and 2 perches in breadth (instances from Norfolk) or the like. They are endeavouring to indicate shape as well as size. See the method of measurement adopted in K. 594 (iii. 129): 'and ðær ðæt land unbradest is ðer hit sceol beon eahtatyne fota brad.'

The league of 12 furlongs has dropped out of modern usage; it is very prominent in D. B., where miles, though not unknown, are rare.

[4] Our foot is ·30479 meters. Our perch is very close to 5 meters. Our acre 40·467 ares. A hide of 120 acres would be 48·56 hectares.

In the thirteenth century these outlines are already drawn ; but, as we have seen, if we are to breathe the spirit of the time, we ought to say (while admitting that acres may be variously shaped) that the normal acre is 4 perches in width and 40 perches (= 1 furlong) in length. The only other space that we need consider is the quarter of an acre, our rood. That ought to be 1 perch in width and 1 furlong (= 40 perches) in length. The breadth of the acre is still known to all Englishmen, for it is the distance between the wickets.

The ancient elements of land measure.

This system has been generated by the corelation ot cloth-measures and land-measures. If we are going back to remote times, we must expel the cloth-measures as intruders. What then is left is very simple ; it is this:—the human foot, a day's ploughing and a measuring stick which mediates between feet and acres. That stick has had many names. Our arithmetic books preserve three, 'rod, pole or perch'; it has also been known as a $g\bar{a}d$ or *goad* and a *lug* : but probably its oldest name is *yard* (*gyrd*). It is of some importance that we should perceive that our modern yard of three feet is not one of the very ancient land-measures. It is a 'cloth-yard' not a land-yard. In medieval documents the Latin name for it is *ulna*[1], and probably the oldest English name for it is *eln, elle, ell*. There seems to have been a shifting of names. The measuring rod that was used for land had so many names, such as *perch, rod, pole, goad, lug*, that it could afford, if we may so speak, to dispense with the additional name of *yard*, which therefore might stand for the much shorter rod that was used by the clothiers. However, even in our own century men have been speaking of 'yards of land' in a manner which implies that at one time a yard, when mentioned in this context, was the same thing as the perch. When they have spoken of a 'yard of land' they have meant sometimes a quarter of an acre (our rood) and sometimes a much larger space. In 1820 a 'yard of land' means, we are told, a quarter of an acre in Wiltshire, while in Buckinghamshire it stands for a tract

---

[1] Statutes of the Realm, i. 206 : 'Tres pedes faciunt ulnam.' Though this equation gets established, the *ulna* or cloth-yard seems to start by being an arm's length. See the story that Henry I. made his own arm a standard : Will. Malmesb. Gesta Regum., ii. 487. Britton, i. 189, tells us that the *aune* contains two cubits and two thumbs (inches). Our yard seems too long to be a step.

which varies from 28 to 40 acres[1]. This last application of
the term we shall consider by and by. A yard of land or
rood of land (*rood* and *rod* are all one) is a quarter of an acre,
because an acre is four rods or 'yards' or perches in width,
and, when an acre is to be divided, it is always, and for a very
good reason, divided by lines parallel to its long sides. So
though the rood or yard of land may in course of time take
other shapes and even become a shapeless size, it ought to be a
rod or 'yard' in width and forty rods or one furlong in length.

So we start with the human foot, the day's ploughing and
a rod. How much borrowing there has been in this matter
by race from race is an obscure question. For example, the
mediation of a rod between the foot and the day's work is
common to the Roman and the Germanic systems. Here the
similarity ends, and the vast differences which begin seem
to have exceedingly deep roots. We can not be content with
saying that the Roman puts two oxen in the plough and
therefore draws short furrows, whereas the German puts eight
oxen and draws long furrows. There seems to be a radical
disagreement between them as to what a plough should be
and what a plough should do[2]. To these matters we can make
but the slightest reference, nor dare we touch the problems of
Celtic history. Somehow or another the Germans come to the
rule that generally an acre or day's work should be four rods
wide and, if possible, about forty rods long[3]. *The German acre.*

It is very probable that in England this rule prevailed
at a remote time. Throughout the middle ages and on to
our own day there have been many 'acres' in England which
swerved markedly from what had become the statutory type,
and in some cases a pattern divergent from the statutory
pattern became 'customary' in a district. But apparently
these customary acres commonly agree with the royal standard
in involving the equation: 1 acre = 4 perches × 40 perches[4]. In
Domesday Book and thence onwards the common Latin for
furlong is *quarentina*, and this tells us of furrows that are forty *English acres.*

[1] Second Report of Commissioners for Weights and Measures, Parliamentary Papers, 1820, Reports, vol. vii.

[2] As to all this see Meitzen, op. cit. i. 272 fol.

[3] The ratio 10 : 1 is not the only one that is well represented in Germany. The practice of making the acre four rods wide is more universal. As we shall see below, length must take its chance.

[4] Morgan, England under the Normans, 19.

perches long. It is when we ask for the number of feet in
a perch that we begin to get various answers, and very various
they are. The statutory number, the ugly 16·5, looks like
a compromise[1] between 15 and 18, both of which numbers seem
to have been common in England and elsewhere. This is
the royal equation in the thirteenth century; it has been
found near the middle of the twelfth[2]; more at present we
Small
acres. cannot say. Short perches and small acres have been very
common in the south of England. In 1820 some information
about the customary acre was collected[3]:—In Bedfordshire it
was 'sometimes 2 roods.' In Dorsetshire 'generally 134 [in-
stead of 160] perches.' In Hampshire, 'from 107 to 120
perches, but sometimes 180.' In Herefordshire, 'two-thirds
of a statute acre,' but 'of wood, an acre and three-fifths or 256
perches.' In Worcestershire, 'sometimes 132 or 141 perches.'
In Sussex, '107, 110, 120, 130 or 212 perches'; '*short acre*,
100 or 120 perches'; '*forest acre*, 180 perches.' Then as to
rods, the 'lug or goad' of Dorsetshire had 15 ft. 1 in.; in
Hertfordshire, 20 feet; in Wiltshire, 15 or 16½ or 18. The
wide prevalence of rods of 15 feet can not be doubted, and
it seems possible that rods with as few as 12 feet have been
in use[4]. An acre raised from a 12 foot rod would, if feet
were invariable, be little more than half our modern statute
acre. Nowhere do we see any sure trace of a rod so short
as the Roman *pertica* of ten *pedes*, though the scribes of the
land-books will give the name *pertica* to the English *gyrd*[5].

Large
acres. In northern districts the 'customary' acre grows larger.
In Lincolnshire it is said to be '5 roods, particularly for copyhold land'; but small acres were known there also[6]. In
Staffordshire, 'nearly 2¼ acres.' In Cheshire, 'formerly and
still in some places 10,240 square yards' (pointing to a rod
of 24 feet). In Westmoreland, '6760 square yards' (pointing

---

[1] Pollock, E. H. R. xi. 218.

[2] Morgan, op. cit. 19, citing Monasticon, iv. 421.

[3] Second Report of the Commissioners for Weights and Measures, Parliamentary Papers, 1820, Reports, vol. vii. The information thus obtained might
have been better sifted. When it is said that a certain customary perch
contains 15 feet 1 inch, these feet and inches are statute feet and statute inches.
Probably this perch had exactly 15 'customary' feet. So, again, it is likely
that every 'customary' acre contained 160 'customary' perches.

[4] See below, p. 382.   [5] Compare Meitzen, op. cit. ii. 560.

[6] Morgan, op. cit. 22.

to a rod of 19½ feet), also the so-called 'Irish acre' of 7840 square yards (pointing to a rod of 21 feet). There is much evidence that rods of 20 and 21 feet were often used in Yorkshire and Derbyshire. Rods of 18, 19½, 21, 22½ and 24 feet were known in Lancashire. A writer of the thirteenth century speaks as if rods of 16, 18, 20, 22 and 24 feet were in common use, and mentions none shorter[1]. As just said, the Irish plantation acre was founded on a rod of 21 feet. The Scotch acre also is larger than the English; it would contain about 6150·4 instead of 4840 of our square yards; it is formed from a rod of 6 Scotch ells. On the other hand, the acres which have prevailed in Wales seem to be small; one type had 4320 of our square yards, another 3240.

There has been variety enough. Even if the limits of variation are given by rods of 12 and 24 feet, this will enable one acre to be four times as large as another. Whether before the twelfth century there was anything that we ought to call a standard rod, a royal rod for all England, must be very doubtful. In royal and other land-books references are made to furlongs, to acre-breadths, to yards or rods or perches, and to feet as to known measures of length[2], but whether a kingly gift is always measured by a kingly rod we do not know. The Carolingian emperors endeavoured to impose a rod upon their dominions; it seems to have been considerably shorter than our statute perch[3]. In this province we need not expect many Norman novelties. We see from Domesday Book that the Frenchmen introduced the ancient Gallic *arpentum*[4] as a measure for vineyards[5]; but most of the vines were of

Anglo-Saxon rods and acres.

---

[1] Anonymous Husbandry, see Walter of Henley, ed. Lamond, p. 69.

[2] K. 296 (ii. 87): 6 *virgae* in length and 3 in breadth.—K. 339 (ii. 149): 28 roda lang and 24 roda brad.—K. 507 (ii. 397): 12 gerda lang and 9 gerda brad.—K. 558 (iii. 229): 'tres perticas'='þreo gyrda.'—K. 772 (iv. 84): 12 *perticae*.—K. 787 (iv. 115): a *pertica* and a half.—K. 814 (iv. 160): dimidiam virgam et dimidiam quatrentem.—K. 1103 (v. 199): 75 gyrda.—K. 1141 (v. 275): 6 gyrda.—K. 1087 (v. 163): 3 furlongs and 3 mete-yards=an unknown quantity +12 yards+13 yards+43 yards and 6 feet+20 yards and 6 feet+7 yards and 6 feet+5 yards. This charter is commended to geometers. We see, however, that the 'yard' in question is longer than 6 feet; it is connected with our perch, not with our cloth yard. Schmid, App. XII.: 3 miles, 3 furlongs, 3 acre-breadths, 9 feet, 9 hand-breadths and 9 barley-corns.

[3] Meitzen, op. cit. ii. 554. This *virga regalis* is set down at 4·70 meters; our statute perch stands very close to 5 meters.

[4] Meitzen, op. cit. i. 278.   [5] Ellis, Introduction, i. 116.

their own planting, and the mere fact that they used this measure only for the vineyards seems to tell us that they were content with English rods and English acres[1]. In Normandy the perches seem to have ranged upwards from 16 to 25 feet[2]; so that 16·5 would not have hit the average. On the whole, our perch seems to speak of a king whose interests and estates lay in southern England and who struck a mean between 15 and 18. Whoever he was, we owe him no thanks for the 'undecimal' element that taints our system[3].

Customary acres and forest acres.

But we must be cautious in drawing inferences from loose reports about 'customary' measures. Village maps and village fields have yet to be seriously studied. We may in the meanwhile doubt whether in some districts to which the largest acres are ascribed, such acres are normal or are drawn in the oldest villages. We may suspect them of being 'forest acres.' If once a good many of these abnormal units are distributed in a district, they will by their very peculiarity attract more than their fair share of attention and will be spoken of as characteristic of that district. In Germany, as well as in England, we find forest acres which are much larger than common acres and are meted by a rod which is longer than the common rod[4]. Possibly men have found a long rod convenient when they have large spaces to measure, but we fancy that the true explanation would illustrate the influence exercised by taxation on systems of measurement. Some scheme of allotment or colonization is being framed; an equal tribute is to be reserved from the allotted acres. If, however, there is uncleared woodland to be distributed, rude equity, instead of changing the tribute on the acre, changes the acre's size and uses a long rod for land that can not at once be tilled[5].

---

[1] The use of *quarentina* for furlong may be due to the Normans.

[2] Delisle, Études sur la condition de la classe agricole en Normandie, 531–2.

[3] We find from D. B. i. 166 that there was a royal *sextarius*; but (i. 162, 238) other *sextarii* were in use.

[4] Meitzen, op. cit. ii. 564. Thus in Köln, the Morgen is 31·72 ares, the Waldmorgen 38·06 ares. In Brunswick the Feldmorgen is 25·02 ares, the Waldmorgen 33·35 ares. So in Sussex the common acres are small; the forest acre = 180 (instead of 160) perches. So in Herefordshire the common acre is put down at two-thirds of the statute acre, but an acre of wood is more than an acre and a half of statute measure.

[5] Registr. Honor. Richemund., Ap., p. 11, Agard says: 'In the Arrentation of Assarts of Forests made in Henry III.'s and Edward I.'s times, for forest ground the commissioners let the land *per perticam xx. pedum*,' though by this time the

Also fields that were plotted out by Normans were likely to have large acres, and as the perches of Normandy seem to have been longer than most of the perches that were used in France, we may perhaps infer that the Scandinavian rods were long and find in them an explanation of the big acres of northern England. But at present such inferences would be precarious.

Whether in its origin the land-measuring rod is a mere representative of a certain number of feet or is some instrument useful for other purposes seems to be dubious. One of the names that it has borne in English is *goad*; but most of our rods would be extravagantly long goads[1]. Possibly the width of four oxen yoked abreast has exercised some influence upon its length[2]. When a rod had once found acceptance, it must speedily have begun to convert that 'time-labour-unit,' the acre, into a measured space. Already in the land-books we read of acres of meadow[3]; this is no longer a contradiction in terms. Still there can be no doubt that our acre, like the *jurnale*, *Tagwerk*, *Morgen* of the Continent, has at its root the tract that can be ploughed in a day, or in a forenoon:—in the afternoon the oxen must go to the pasture[4]. Now, when

The acre and the day's work.

16·5 foot perch was the established royal measure for ordinary purposes. In a Buckinghamshire Fine levied in John's reign (Hunter, i. 242) we find acres of land which are measured ' by the lawful perch of the vill,' while acres of wood are measured 'by the perch of the king.' Ibid. 13, 178 : a perch of 20 feet was being used in the counties of Bedford and Buckingham, though Bedfordshire is notorious for small acres. The obscure processes that go on in the history of measures might be illustrated from the report cited above, p. 374, note 3 ; the length of the 'customary' perch varies inversely with the difficulty of the work to be done. In Herefordshire a perch of fencing was 21 feet, a perch of walling 16·5. And so forth.

[1] Morgan, op. cit. 27, suggests a double goad. The *gād* of modern Cambridgeshire has been a stick 9 feet long; but the surveyor put eight into the acre-breadth, reckoning two of these *gāds* to the customary pole of 18 feet. See Pell, in Domesday Studies, i. 276, 296. A rod that is 18 feet long is a clumsy thing and perhaps for practical purposes it has been cut in half. Meitzen, op. cit., i. 90 : Two hunting-spears would make a measuring rod. See also Hanssen, Abhandlungen, ii. 210.

[2] Seebohm, op. cit. 119. Welsh evidence seems to point this way.

[3] K. 529 (iii. 4) : ' 12 æceras mædwa.'—K. 549 (iii. 33).—K. 683 (iii. 263).

[4] When Walter of Henley, p. 8, is making his calculations as to the amount of land that can be ploughed in a day, he assumes that the work will be over *a noune*. The ' by three o'clock ' of his translator is too precise and too late. At whatever hour nones should have been said, the word *noon* became our name for twelve o'clock. See also Seebohm, op. cit. 124.

compared with their foreign cousins, our statute perch is a long
rod and our statute acre is a decidedly large 'day-work-unit[1].'
It seems to tell of plentiful land, sparse population and poor
husbandry. This is of some importance. There is a good deal
of evidence pointing to the conclusion that, whereas in the
oldest days men really ploughed an acre in a forenoon, the
current of agricultural progress made for a while towards the
diminution of the space that was covered by a day's labour.
In Ælfric's dialogue the ploughman complains that each day
he must till 'a full acre or more[2].' His successor, the poetic
Piers, had only a half-acre to plough[3]. In monastic cartularies
which come from southern counties, where we have no reason
to suspect exceptionally large acres, the villein seems often to
plough less than an acre[4]. Then that enlightened agriculturist,
Walter of Henley, enters upon a long argument to prove to his
readers that you really can plough seven-eighths of an acre
in a forenoon, and even a whole acre if you are but engaged
in that light kind of ploughing which does for a second
fallowing[5]. Five centuries later another enlightened agriculturist, Arthur Young, discovered that 'from North Leach,
through Gloucestershire, Monmouthshire, and Glamorganshire,
light and middling turnip-land etc.' was being ploughed at the
rate of half an acre to one acre a day by teams of 'eight oxen;
never less than six; or four and two horses.' This, he says,
was being done 'merely in compliance with the obstinacy of
the low people,' for 'the labourers will not touch a plough
without the usual number of beasts in it[6]'. Mr Young could
not tell us of 'these vile remnants of barbarity without a great

---

[1] Meitzen, op. cit., ii. 565. The rods known in Germany range upwards
from very short South German rods which descend from the Roman *pertica* to
much longer rods which lie between 4 meters and 5. Our statute perch just
exceeds 5 meters. Then the ordinary (not forest) *Morgen* rarely approaches
40 ares, while our statute acre is equivalent to 40·46 ares. However, the
Scandinavian *Tonne* is yet larger and recalls the big acres of northern England.
In France perches of 18 feet were common, and in Normandy yet longer perches
were used, but we do not know that the French *acre* or *journal* contained
160 square perches.

[2] Seebohm, op. cit. 166.

[3] Seebohm, op. cit. 19.

[4] Thus e.g. Glastonbury Rentalia, 68 : 'if he has eight oxen he shall plough
every Thursday [during certain seasons] three roods [*perticatas*].'

[5] Walter of Henley, 9.

[6] Tour through the Southern Counties, ed. 3 (1772), pp. 298–301.

degree of disgust[1]'. But we are grateful. We see that an
acre of light land was the maximum that these 'low people'
with their eight oxen would plough in a day, and we take it
that at one time the voice of reforming science had urged men
to diminish the area ploughed in a given time, to plough
deeper and to draw their furrows closer. The old tradition
was probably well content with a furrow for every foot. Walter
of Henley proposed to put six additional furrows into the acre[2].
Hereafter we shall see that some of the statistics given by
Domesday Book fall in with the suggestion that we are here
making. Also we may see on our maps that the strip which
a man has in one place is very often not an acre but a half-
acre. Now, in days when men really ploughed an acre at a
stretch, such an arrangement would have involved a waste
of time, since, when the morning's work was half done, the
plough would be removed from one 'shot' to another[3].

At length we reach the fields, and at once we learn that
there is something unreal in all our talk of acre and half-acre
strips. In passing we may observe that some of our English
meadows which show by their 'beds' that they were not always
meadows, seem to show also that the boundaries of the strips
were not drawn by straight rods, but were drawn by the plough.
The beds are not straight, but slightly sinuous, and such, it is
said, is the natural course of the old plough; it swerves to the
left, and this tendency is then corrected by those who guide it[4].
But, apart from this, land refuses to be cut into parallelograms
each of which is 40 rods long and 4 wide. In other words, the
'real acres' in an open field diverge widely from the ideal acre
that was in the minds of those who made them. *The real acres in the fields.*

Let us recall a few features of the common field, though
they will be familiar to all who have read Mr Seebohm's book[5]. *The 'shots.'*

---

[1] Tour through the Southern Counties, p. 127.

[2] Walter of Henley, 9.

[3] Young, View of Agriculture of Oxfordshire, p. 104. In Oxfordshire in the
early years of this century many ploughs with four horses 'go out for 3 roods,'
after all improvements in ploughs and in horses.

[4] Meitzen, op. cit. 88. Dr Taylor in Domesday Studies, i. 61, gives a
somewhat different explanation. The ploughman walked backwards in front of
the beasts, and, when near the end of the furrow, used his right arm to pull
them round.

[5] Among the land-books those that most clearly indicate the intermixture of
strips are K. 538 (iii. 19),—648 (iii. 210),—692 (iii. 290),—1158 (v. 310),—1169
(v. 326),—1234 (vi. 39),—1240 (vi. 51),—1276 (vi. 108),—1278 (vi. 111).

A natural limit to the length of the furrow is set by the endurance of oxen. From this it follows that even if the surface that lies open is perfectly level and practically limitless, it will none the less be broken up into what our Latin documents call *culturae*[1]. The *cultura* is a set of contiguous and parallel acre-strips; it tends to be a rude parallelogram; two of its sides will be each a furlong ('furrowlong') in length, while the length of the other sides will vary from case to case. We commonly find that every great field (*campus*) is divided into divers *culturae*, each of which has its own name. The commonest English equivalent for the word *cultura* seems to have been *furlong*, and this use of *furlong* was very natural; but, as we require that term for another purpose, we will call the *cultura* a *shot*. So large were the fields, that the annual value of an acre in one shot would sometimes be eight times greater than that of an acre in another shot[2]. To such differences our ancestors were keenly alive. Hence the dispersion of the strips which constitute a single tenement.

Delimitation of shots.

But to make 'shots' which should be rectangular and just 40 feet long was often impossible. Even if the surface of the field were flat, its boundaries were the irregular curves drawn by streams and mounds. In order to economize space, shots running at right angles to other shots were introduced, and of necessity some furlongs were longer than others. If, however, as was often the case, men were laying out their fields among the folds of the hills, their acres would be yet more irregular both in size and in shape. They would be compelled to make very small shots, and the various furrows if 'produced' (in the geometer's sense of that word) would cut each other at all imaginable angles. On the maps we may still see them struggling with these difficulties, drawing as many rectilinear shots as may be and then compelled to parcel out as best they can the irregularly shaped patches that remain. And then we

[1] As to the names of *culturæ* the Ramsey Cartulary may be profitably consulted. Such names as Horsepelfurlange, Wodefurlonge, Benefurlange, Stapelfurlange (i. 307), Mikellefurlange (321), Stanweyfurlange, Longefurlange (331) are common. We meet also with *-wong*: Redewonge (321), Langiwange, Stoniwonge, Schortewonge, Semareswonge (341-2). Also with *-leuge* (apparently O. E. *léah*, gen. dat. *léage*): Wolnothesleuge, Edriches Leuge. Often the *cultura* is known as the Five (Ten, Twenty) Acres. Sometimes in Latin this sense of *furlong* is rendered by *quarentina*: 'unam rodam in quarentina de Newedich': Fines, ed. Hunter, i. 42.

[2] Glastonbury Rentalia, 180, 195, 208.

see that even these patches have been allotted either as acres
or as half-acres.

Therefore, when we are dealing with medieval documents, The real and the ideal acre.
we have always to remember that besides ideal acres there
were real acres which were mapped out on the surface of the
earth, and that a plot will be, and rightly may be, called an
acre though its size is not that of any ideal acre.   To tell a
man that one of these acre-strips was not an acre because it
was too small would at one time have been like telling him that
his foot was no foot because it fell short of twelve inches.   This
point is made very plain by some of the beautiful estate maps
edited by Mr Mowat[1].   We have a map of 'the village of
Whitehill in the parishe of Tackley in the countye Oxon., the
moitye or one halfe whereof belongeth to the presidente and
schollers of Corpus christi colledge in the universitye of Oxon.,
the other moitye unto Edwarde Standerd yeoman the particulars whereof soe far as knowne doe plainelye appeare in
the platte and those which are unknowne, as wastes comons
and lotte meadowes are equallye divided betweene them,
drawne in November anno domini 1605, regni regis Iacobi iij°.'
We see four great fields divided first into shots and then into
strips.   Each strip on the map bears an inscription assigning
it either to the college or to Mr Standerd, and with great
regularity the strips are assigned to the college and to
Standerd alternately.   Then on each strip is set its 'estimated'
content, and on each strip of the college land is also set its
true content.   Thus looking at one particular shot in the
South Field we read:

> ij. ac. coll. 1. 1. 36
> Edw. Stand. ij. ac.
> ij. ac. coll. 1. 2. 2
> Edw. Stand. ij. ac.
> ij. ac. coll. 1. 2. 2
> Edw. Stand. ij. ac.
> ij. ac. coll. 1. 0. 39.

This means that, going along this shot, we first come to a two-
acre-strip of college land containing by admeasurement 1 A. 1 R.
36 P.; next to a two-acre strip of Standerd's land, which the
surveyor, who was making the map for the college, was not
at pains to measure; then to a two-acre strip of college land

---

[1] Sixteen Old Maps: Oxford, Clarendon Press, 1888.

containing 1 A. 2 R. 2 P. :—and so forth. Then in the margin
of the map has been set 'A note of the contentes of the landes
in Whitehille belonginge to the colledge.' It tells us how
'theire groundes in the West Fielde by estimation 80 acres doe
conteine by statute measure 48 A. 2 R. 24 P.' The other fields
we may deal with in a table

		A.		A.	R.	P.
East Field	estimation	75	measure	51	1	25
Middle Field		58		39	3	36
South Field		103		59	2	13

It will be seen at once that the discrepancy between the
two sets of figures is not to be fully explained by the supposition that at Whitehill men had measured land by measures
differing from our statutory standards[1]. The size of a 'two-
acres' (and the land in this instance had been divided chiefly
into 'two-acres') varied not only from field to field and shot to
shot, but within one and the same shot. Each two-acre strip
has an equal breadth, but the curving boundaries of the fields
make some strips longer than others[2].

Varying size of the acres. We turn to the admirable maps of Heyford in Oxfordshire
designed in 1606. Here the land is divided among many
occupiers and cut up into a vast number of strips, to each
of which is assigned its 'estimated' and its measured content.
Thus we read :—

> dim. ac. Jo. Sheres   1. 18
> dim. ac. Ric. Elkins 1. 18
> dim. ac. Jo. Merry   1. 18.

In this part of this shot a 'half-acre' contains 1 R. 18 P. Some
of the shots in this village have fairly straight and rectangular
boundaries, so that we may, for example, find that many
successive 'half-acres' contain 1 R. 18 P. But then if we pass
to the next shot we shall find 1 R. 28 P. in the 'half-acre,' while
in a third shot we shall find but 1 R. 8 P. Yet every strip of
land is a 'half-acre' or an 'acre' or a 'acre and a half' or a
'two acres' or a 'three acres.' We see further that when
'acres' occur among 'half-acres' the strips vary in breadth
but not in length.

---

[1] The rod, however, must have been very short; perhaps it had as few as
12 feet.

[2] For many reasons this must not be taken as a typical map. We refer to
it merely as showing the relation of 'estimated' (that is of 'real') acres to an
acre-measure.

On a map of Roxton made in 1768 we have the same thing written out in English words. Thus:—

Eliz. Gardner a half	0.	1.	32
Carpenter a half	0.	1.	32
Harris an acre	0.	3.	24
Carpenter a half	0.	1.	32
Jam. Gardner an acre	0.	3.	24
Makepace a half	0.	1.	34

The result of all this is that anyone who lives in a village knows how many 'acres' its fields contain. He has not to measure anything; he has only to count strips, for he is not likely to confuse 'acres' with 'half-acres' and that is the only mistake that he could make.

If a shot had a curved boundary, little or no pains seem to have been taken to equalize the strips that lay within it by making additional width serve as a compensation for deficient length. The width of the so-called acre remained approximately constant while its length varied. Thus, to take an example from the map of Heyford, we see a shot which is bounded on the one side by a straight line and on the other by a curving road. At one end of it the acre contains 2 R. 8 P.; this increases to 2 R. 30 P.; then slowly decreases until it has fallen as low as 1 R. 36 P., and then again rises to 2 R. 2 P. When they were dividing the field, men attempted to map out shots in which approximately equal areas could be constructed; but, when a shot was once delimited, then all the acres in it were made equally broad, while their length could not but vary, except in the rare case in which the shot was a true rectangle[1]. *Irregular length of acres.*

It is probable that the whole system was made yet more visible by the practice of ploughing the land into 'beds' or ridges, which has but recently fallen out of use. In our Latin documents these ridges appear as selions (*seliones*). In English they were called 'lands,' for the French *sillon* struck no root in our language. Anyone who has walked through English grass *The selions or beds.*

---

[1] Instructive evidence about this matter was given in a Chancery suit of James I.'s reign. The deponent speaking of the fen round Ely says 'it is the use and custom...to measure the fen grounds by four poles in breadth for an acre, by a pole of 18 feet...and in length for an acre of the said grounds as it happeneth, according to the length of the furlong of the same fens, which is sometimes shorter and sometimes longer.' Quoted by O. C. Pell in Domesday Studies, i. 296.

fields will know what they looked like, for they triumph over time and change[1]. Now it would seem that a fairly common usage made four selions in each acre[2]; in other words, each acre-strip was divided longitudinally into four waves, so that the distance from crest to crest or trough to trough was a perch in length. Where this usage obtained, you could tell how many acres a shot or field contained by merely observing the undulations of the surface. Even if, as was often the case, the number of selions in the acre was not four, still the number that went to an acre of a given shot would be known, and a man might argue that a strip was an acre because in crossing it he traversed three or six terrestrial waves[3].

Acres divided lengthwise. If we look at old maps, we soon see that when an acre was divided, it was always divided by a line that was parallel, not to its short ends, but to its long sides. No one would think of dividing it in any other fashion. Suppose that you bisected it by bisecting its long sides, you would force each owner of a half-acre to turn his plough as often as if he had a whole acre. Besides, you would have uneconomical furrows; the oxen would be stopped before they had traversed what was regarded as the natural distance for beasts to go. Divide your acre into two long strips, then your folk and beasts can plough in the good old way. Hence it follows that when men think of dividing an acre they speak only of its breadth. Hence it follows that the quarter of an acre is a 'rood' or 'yard[4]' or *virga* or *virgata* of land. Its width is a rod or land-yard, and its length—but there is no need to speak of its length[5].

[1] For an explanation of this mode of ploughing, see Meitzen, op. cit. 84.

[2] Meitzen gives 6 feet as a usual width for the beds in Germany. I think that in cent. xiii. our selions were usually wider than this.

[3] The Gloucester Corporation Records, ed. Stevenson (1893), should be consulted. When small pieces of land were being conveyed, the selions were often enumerated. Thus (p. 124): 'and 13 acres of arable land...whereof one acre lies upon þistelege near Durand's land...an acre and a half being three selions... half an acre being two selions...an acre of five selions...an acre being one selion and a gore...four selions and two little gores...an acre being three selions and a head-land.' In Mr Seebohm's admirable account of the open fields there seems to me to be some confusion between the selions and the acre or half-acre strips.

[4] On Mr Mowat's map of Roxton a quarter-acre strip is a *yeard*.

[5] D. B. i. 364: 'In Staintone habuit Jalf 5 bovatas terrae et 14 acras terrae et 1 virgatam ad geldum.' This virgate is a quarter-acre. The continuous use of *virgata* in this sense is attested by Glastonbury Rentalia, 27. So in Normandy: Delisle, Études sur la condition de la classe agricole, 535. So in

How then does it happen that these terms 'virgate' and The vir-
gate.
'yard of land,' though given to a quarter of an acre, are yet
more commonly given to a much larger quantity containing
30 acres or thereabouts? The explanation is simple. The
typical tenement is a hide. If you give a man a quarter of
a hide (an equitable quarter, equal in value as well as extent
to every remaining quarter) you do this by giving him a
quarter of every acre in the hide. You give him a rood, a
yard, a *virga*[1], a *virgata* in every acre, and therefore a rood,
a yard, a *virga*, a *virgata* of a typical tenement[2].

No doubt it is clumsy to have only one term for two The double
meaning of
a yard.
quantities, one of which is perhaps a hundred-and-twenty times
as great as the other; but the context will tell us which is
meant, and the difference between the two is so large that
blunders will be impossible. In course of time there will be a
differentiation and specification of terms. To our ears, for example, *rōd* (rood) will mean one thing, *rŏd* another, *yard* a
third; but even in the nineteenth century royal commissioners
will report that a 'yard of land' may mean a quarter of an
acre or 'from 28 to 40 acres[3].' When men have not apprehended 'superficial measure' (the measurement of shapeless
size), when their only units are the human foot, a rod, an
average day's work and the tenement of a typical householder,
their language will be poor, because their thought is poor.

We have now arrived at a not insignificant truth. The The yard-
land a
fraction of
a hide.
virgate or yard-land of 30 acres or thereabouts is not a primary
unit like the hide, the rod, the acre. It is derivative; it is
compound. In its origin it is a rod's breadth in every acre
of a hide. In course of time in this case, as in other cases,
size will triumph over shape. The acre need not be ten times
as long as it is broad; the virgate need not be composed, perhaps is rarely composed, of scattered quarter-acres; quartering
acres is an uneconomical process; it leads to waste of time.

France: Ducange, s. v. *virgata* from a Register of the Chamber of Accounts:
'Quadraginta perticae faciunt virgatam: quatuor virgatae faciunt acram.' Meit-
zen, op. cit. i. 95: in Kalenberg a strip that is one rod in breadth is called a
Gert (our *yard*).

[1] In the Exeter Domesday *virga* not *virgata* is the common word. In the
Exchequer book an abbreviated form is used; but *virga* appears in i. 216 b.

[2] So again, if a *iugum* is quartered, its quarter can be called a virgate. See
Denman Ross, Hist. of Landholding, 140; Round, Feudal England, 108.

[3] See above, p. 372.

M.   25

But still the term will carry on its face the traces of an ancient history and a protest against some modern theories. The virgate in its inception can not be a typical tenement; it is a fraction of a typical tenement.

The yard-
land in
laws and
charters.

What we have here been saying seems to be borne out by the Anglo-Saxon laws and charters. They barely recognize the existence of such entities as yard-lands or virgates. The charters, it must be confessed, deal with large tracts and seldom have need to notice less than a hide. When, however, they descend below the hide, they at once come down to the acre, and this although the quantity that they have to specify is 90, or 60 or 30 acres[1]. On the other hand, any reference to such an unit as the virgate or yard-land is exceedingly rare. To judge by the charters, this is a unit which was but beginning to force itself upon men's notice in the last century before the Conquest[2]. From a remote time there may have been many tenements that were like the virgates or yard-lands of later days; but the old strain of language that is preserved in the charters ignores them, has no name for them, and, when they receive a name, it signifies that they are fractions of a householder's tenement.

[1] K. 205 (i. 259): 'circiter 30 iugera.'—K. 217 (i. 274): '30 iugera.'—K. 225 (i. 290): 'hoc est 30 iugerum'...'hoc est 85 segetum.'—K. 234 (i. 308): '150 iugera.'—K. 241 (ii. 1): '24 iugeras.'—K. 259 (ii. 26): '19 iugera.'—K. 264 (ii. 36): 'unum dimidium agrum...healve aker.'—K. 276 (ii. 57): '10 iugera.'—K. 285 (ii. 70): '80 æcra.'—K. 339 (ii. 150): 'sextig æcera earðlondes...oðer sextig.'—K. 586 (iii. 118): '30 æcra on ðæm twæm feldan.'—K. 612 (iii. 159): '2 hida buton 60 æcran.'—K. 633 (iii. 188): '3 mansas ac 30 iugerum dimensionem.'—K. 695 (iii. 295): '40 agros.'—K. 759 (iv. 59): '30 akera.'—K. 782 (iv. 106): 'fiftig æcera.'—K. 1154 (v. 303): '36 ækera yrðlandes.'—K. 1161 (v. 315): 'ter duodenas segetes'='36 æcera yrðlandes.'—K. 1211 (v. 393): '25 segetes.'—K. 1218 (vi. 1): '14 hida and...40 æcera.'

[2] Probably it occurs in Ine 67; certainly in Rectitudines 4, § 3, and in the late document about Tidenham (above, p. 330).—K. 369 (ii. 205): Boundary of a *gyrd* at Ashurst which belongs to a hide at Topsham (A.D. 937).—K. 521 (ii. 418): Edgar grants 'tres virgas.'—K. 658 (iii. 229): Æthelred grants '3 mansas et 3 perticas.'—K. 1306 (vi. 163): Æthelred grants land 'trium sub aestimatione perticarum.'—K. 772 (iv. 84): Edward Conf. grants '5 perticas.'—K. 787 (iv. 115): He grants 'unam perticam et dimidiam.'—K. 814 (iv. 160): He grants 'dimidiam virgam et dimidiam quatrentem.'—Crawford Charters, 5, 9, mortgage in 1018 of a yard of land.—K. 949 (iv. 284); 979 (iv. 307): two other examples from the eve of the Conquest.—It is more likely that these 'yards' and 'perches' of land are quarter-hides than that they are quarter-acres; 'square' perches seem to be out of the question. There are of course many instances in the charters of a *pertica*, *virga*, *gyrd* used as a measure of mere length. See above, p. 375, note 2, where a few are cited.

As an unit larger than the acre men have known nothing but the hide, the manse, the land of one family, the land of one householder. This is what we find in England: also it is found in Germany and Scandinavia[1]. The state bases its structure, its taxation, its military system, upon the theory that such units exist and can be fairly treated as equal or equivalent. This theory must have facts behind it, though in course of time the state may thrust it upon lands that it will not fit, for example, upon a land of ring-fenced property where there is no approximate equality between the various tenements. In its origin a hide will not be a measure of land. A measure is an idea; a hide is a tenement. The 'foot' does not begin by being twelve inches; it begins by being a part of the human body. The 'acre' does not begin by being 4840 square yards; it begins by being a strip in the fields that is ploughed in a forenoon. But unless there were much equality between human feet, the foot would not become a measure; nor would the acre become a measure unless the method of ploughing land were fairly uniform. A great deal of similarity between the 'real' hides or 'householder's lands' we must needs suppose if the hide becomes a measure; not only must those in any one village be much alike, there must be similarity between the villages.

After a certain sort the hide does become a measure. Bede does not believe that if the families in the Isle of Wight were counted, the sum would be just 1200. The Anglo-Saxon kings are giving away half-hides or half-manses as well as manses or hides. They can speak of three hides and thirty acres[2] or of two hides less sixty acres[3]. Men are beginning to work sums in hides and acres as they work sums in pounds and pence. Indubitably such sums are worked in Domesday Book. In the thirteenth century the hide can even be treated as a pure superficial measure. An instance is given by an 'extent' of the village of Sawston in Cambridgeshire. The content of

[1] Meitzen, op. cit. 74. In Germany the *Hufe, hoba, huoba, huba, etc.* is the unit. This word is said to be connected with the modern German *Behuf,* our *behoof*; it is the *sors*, the portion that behoves a man. In Sweden the unit is the *Mantal*, a man's share. The last word about the *tenmannetale* of Yorkshire has not been said.

[2] K. 633 (iii. 188).

[3] K. 612 (iii. 159): 'landes sumne dæl, ðæt synd 2 hida, buton 60 æcran ðæt hæft se arcebisceop genumen into Cymesige to his hame him to hwætelande.'

about two hundred small parcels of land is given in terms of acres and roods. Then an addition sum is worked and a total is stated in hides, virgates and acres, the equation that is employed being $1 \text{ H.} = 4 \text{ V.} = 120 \text{ A.}$ It is a remarkable case, because the area, not only of arable land, but of meadows, pasture, crofts, gardens and messuages is added up into hides. The hide is here a pure measure, a mere multiple of acres[1]. The men who made this 'extent' could have spoken of a hide of cloth. But this seems a rare and it is a late instance. At an earlier time the hide is conceived as consisting only of arable acres with appurtenances.

The hide as a measure of arable. A word to explain this conception. In very old times when men thought of land as the subject-matter of grants and taxes they spoke only of arable land[2]. If we are to understand their sayings and doings, we must think ourselves into an economic arrangement very different from that in which we are now immersed. We must well-nigh abolish buying and selling. Every village, perhaps every hide, must be very nearly self-sufficient. Now when once population has grown so thick that nomadic practices are forsaken, the strain of supporting mankind falls almost wholly on the ploughed land. That strain is severe. Many acres feed few people. Thus the arable becomes prominent. But further, arable implies pasture. This is not a legal theory; it is a physical fact. A householder can not have arable land unless he has pasture rights. Arable land is land that is ploughed; ploughing implies oxen; oxen, pasture. Our householder can not use a steam-plough; what is more, he can not buy hay. If he keeps beasts, they must eat. If he does not keep beasts, he has no arable land. Lastly, as a general rule men do not possess pasture land in severalty; they turn out their beasts on 'the common of the vill.' Therefore, in very old schemes of taxation and the like, pasture land is neglected : not because it is unimportant, but because it is indispensably necessary. It may be taken for granted. If a man has 120 acres of arable land, he must have adequate pasture rights; there must be in

---

[1] Rot. Hund. ii. 575. After going through the whole calculation, I have satisfied myself that the sum is worked in this way.

[2] Hence in our law Latin the word *terra* means arable land. To claim *unam acram terrae* when you meant an acre of meadow (*prati*) would have been a fatal error.

Domesday's language *pastura sufficiens carucis*. And in the
common case there will be not much more than sufficient
pasture. If there were, it would soon be broken up to provide
more corn. Every village must be self-supporting, and therefore an equilibrium of arable and pasture will be established
in every village. Thus if, for fiscal and governmental purposes,
there is to be a typical tenement, it may be a tenement of
x arable acres, and nothing need be said of any other kind
of ground.

We are going to argue that the Anglo-Saxons give 120 acres, The hide of
arable acres, to the hide. Our main argument will be that the 120 acres.
equation 1 H. = 120 A. is implied in the fiscal system revealed
by Domesday Book. But, by way of making this equation
probable, we may notice that, if we had no evidence later than
the Conquest, all that we should find on the face of the Anglo-
Saxon land-books would be favourable to this equation. In
the first place, on the only occasion on which we hear of the
content of a hide, it is put at 120 acres[1]. In the second place,
when a number of acres is mentioned, it is commonly one of
those numbers, such as 150, 90, 80, 60, 30, which will often
occur if hides of 120 acres are being partitioned[2]. The force
of this last remark may seem to be diminished if we remember
how excellent a dividend is 120. It is neatly divisible by
2, 3, 4, 5, 6, 8, 10, 12. But then we must reflect that this
very quality recommended it to organizers, more especially as
there were 240 pence in the pound.

Supposing for a moment that we bring home this equation Real and
to the Anglo-Saxon financiers, there would still remain the fiscal hides.
question how far it truthfully represented agrarian facts. To
that question no precise answer can be given: the truth lies
somewhere between two extremes. We must not for one instant
believe that England was so neat a chess-board as a rude fiscal
theory paints, where every pawn stands on its square, every
'family' in the centre of 120 acre-strips of 4 by 40 perches.
The barbarian, for all his materialism, is an idealist. He is,
like the child, a master in the art of make-believe. He sees
things not as they are, but as they might conveniently be.
Every householder has a hide; every hide has 120 acres of

---

[1] K. 1222 (vi. 12); T. 508: 'And ic Æðelgar an an hide lond ðes ðe Æulf
hauede be hundtuelti acren, ateo so he wille.' Kemble, Saxons, 117.

[2] See above, p. 386, note 1.

arable; every hide is worth one pound a year; every house-holder has a team; every team is of eight oxen; every team is worth one pound. If all this be not so, then it ought to be so and must be deemed to be so. Then by a Procrustean process he packs the complex and irregular facts into his scheme. What is worse, he will not count. He will assume that a large district has a round 1200 hides, and will then ordain that those hides must be found. We see this on a small scale if we study manorial 'extents' or village maps. The virgates are not equal; the acres are far from equal; but they are deemed to be equal[1]. Nevertheless, we must stop short of the other extreme or we shall be over-estimating the power of such government and the originality of such statesmanship as existed. Theories like those of which we are speaking are born of facts and in their turn generate new facts. Our fore-fathers really lived in a simpler and a more chess-board-like England than that which we know. There must have been much equality among the hides and among the villages. When we see that a 'hundred' in Cambridgeshire has exactly 100 hides which are distributed between six vills of 10 hides apiece and eight vills of 5 hides apiece, this simple symmetry is in part the unreal outcome of a capricious method of taxation, but in part it is a real economic fact. There was an English conquest of England, and, to all seeming, the conquest of eastern England was singularly thorough. In all probability a great many villages were formed approximately at one time and on one plan. Conveniently simple figures could be drawn, for the slate was clean[2].

Causes of divergence of fiscal from real hides.

However, at an early time the hide becomes an unit in a system of assessment. The language of the land-books tells

[1] There can be little need of examples. Glastonbury Rentalia, 152: 'S. tenet unam virgatam terrae et dimidiam, quae computantur pro una virgata.' Ibid. p. 160: 'H. tenet unam virgatam et 5 acras, quae omnia computantur pro una virgata.' Worcester Register, 62: A virgate consists of 13 acres in one field and 12½ in the other; the next virgate of 16 acres in one field and 12 in the other. In other cases the numbers are 16 and 14; 14⅔ and 11; 13 and 12½; 14 and 11; 14¾ and 11¼. Yet every virgate is a virgate.

[2] At the date of Domesday we are a long way from the first danegeld and a very long way from any settlement of Cambridgeshire; still if we analyze a symmetrical hundred, such as Armingford, we shall find that the average ten-hide vill is just about twice as rich as the average five-hide vill in men, in teams and in annual *valet*, though there will be some wide aberrations from this norm.

us that this is so[1]. Already in Ine's day we hear of the amount of victual that ten hides must find for the king's support[2]. About the end of the tenth century the duty of maintaining burgs is bound up with the possession of hides[3]. Before the end of that century heavy sums are being raised as a tribute for the Danes. For this purpose, as we shall try to show hereafter, 'hides' are cast upon shires and hundreds by those who, instead of counting, make pleasantly convenient assumptions about the capacity of provinces and districts, and in all probability the assumptions made in the oldest times were the furthest from the truth. Now and again the assessments of shires and hundreds were corrected in a manner which, so far as we are concerned, only made matters worse. It becomes apparent that hides are not of one value or nearly of one value. This becomes painfully apparent when Cornwall and other far western lands are brought under contribution. So large sums of hides are struck off the poorer counties. The fiscal 'hide' becomes a lame compromise between an unit of area and an unit of value. Then privilege confounds confusion; the estates of favoured churches and nobles are 'beneficially hidated.' But this is not all. Probably the real hides, the real old settlers' tenements, which you could count if you looked at a village and its fields, are rapidly going to pieces, and the fragments thereof are entering into new combinations. In the lordless villages economic forces of an easily imaginable kind will make for this end. Not only may we suppose some increase of population, especially where Danes swarm in, and some progress in the art of agriculture, but also the bond of blood becomes weaker and the *familia* that lives in one house grows smaller. So the hides go to pieces. The birth of trade and the establishment of markets help this process. It is no longer necessary that every tenement should be self-sufficient; men can buy what they do not grow. The formation of manors may have tended in some sort to arrest this movement. A system of equal (theoretically equal) tenements was convenient to lords who were collecting 'provender rents' and extending their powers; but under seignorial pressure virgates,

---

[1] See above, p. 336, note 1.   [2] See above, p. 237.
[3] This is proved by 'The Burghal Hidage' of which we spoke above, p. 187, and shall speak again hereafter.

rather than hides, were likely to become the prominent units. We may well believe that if to make two ears of corn grow where one grew is to benefit mankind, the lords were public benefactors, and that the husbandry of the manors was more efficient than was that of the lordless townships. The clergy were in touch with their fellows on the Continent; also the church's reeve was a professional agriculturist and might even write a tract on the management of manors[1]. There was more cooperation, more communalism, less waste. A family could live and thrive upon a virgate[2].

Effects of the divergence of fiscal from real hides. But, what concerns us at the present moment is the, for us disastrous, effect of this divergence of the fiscal from the real hide. Even if finance had not complicated the problem, we should, as we have already seen, have found many difficulties if we tried to construe medieval statements of acreage. Already we should have had three different 'acres' to think of. We will imagine that a village has 590 'acre strips' in its field. In one sense, therefore, it has 590 acres. But the ideal to which these strips tend and were meant to conform is that of acres measured by a rod of 15 feet. Measured by that rod there would, we will suppose, be 550 acres. Then, however, we may use the royal rod and say that there are 454 acres or thereabouts. But the field was divided into five tenements that were known as hides, and the general theory is that a hide (householder's land) contains, or must be supposed to contain, 120 acres. Therefore there are here 600 acres. And now a partitionary method of taxation stamps this as a vill of four hides. Consequently the 'hide' of this village may have as many as 150 or as few as 90 'acres.' It ought not to be so. It would not be so if men were always distinguishing between 'acre strips' and measured acres, between 'real' hides (which, to tell truth, are no longer real, since they are falling to pieces) and 'fiscal' or 'geld' hides. But it will be so. Here and there we may see an effort to keep up distinctions between the 'carucate for gelding' and the 'carucate for ploughing,' between

---

[1] See the Gerefa published by Dr Liebermann in Anglia, ix. 251. Andrews, Old English Manor, 246.

[2] The manner in which the old hides have really fallen to pieces but are preserving a notional existence is well illustrated by Domesday of S[t]. Paul's, 41–47. In one case a hide forms nine tenements containing respectively 30, 30, 15, 15, 5, 5, 7½, 5, 7½ acres. See Vinogradoff, Villainage, 249.

the real acre and the acre 'for defence (*acra warae*)[1]'; but men
tire of these long phrases and argue backwards and forwards
between the rateable and the real. Hence some of the worst
puzzles of Domesday Book[2].

Such being the causes of perplexity, it is perhaps surprising Acreage of
the hide in
that in the thirteenth century when, we begin to obtain a large later days.
stock of manorial extents, 'the hide' should still exhibit some
uniformity. But, unless we have been misled by a partial
induction, a tendency to reckon 120 rather than any other
number of acres to the hide is plainly perceptible. The following are the equations that prevailed on the manors of Ramsey
Abbey, which were scattered in the eastern midlands[3].

Huntingdonshire

Upwood with Raveley	1 H. = 4 V. = 80 A.
Wistow	1 H. = 4 V. = 120 A.
Broughton	1 H. = 6½ V. = 208 A.
Warboys	1 H. = 4 V. = 120 A.
Holywell	1 H. = 5 V. = 90 A.
Slepe (St Ives)	1 H. = 5 V. = 80 A.
Houghton with Wyton	1 H. = 6 V. = 108 A.
Hemingford	1 H. = 6 V. = 96 A.
Dillington	1 H. = 6 V. = 201 A.
Weston	1 H. = 4 V. = 112 A.
Brington	1 H. = 4 V. = 136 A.
Bythorn	1 H. = 4 V. = 176 A.
Gidding	1 H. = 4 V. = 112 A.
Elton	1 H. = 6 V. = 144 A.
Stukeley	1 H. = 4 V. = 96 A.
Ripton with Remington	1 H. = 4 V. = 62 A.

Northamptonshire

Barnwell	1 H. = 7 V. = 252 A.
Hemington	1 H. = 7 V. = 252 A.

Bedfordshire

Cranfield	1 H. = 4 V. = 192 A.
Barton	1 H. = 4 V. = 96 A.
Shitlingdon	1 H. = 4 V. = 48 A.

[1] Vinogradoff, Villainage, 242; Maitland, History of an English Manor,
Eng. Hist. Rev. ix. 418.

[2] See Pell, in Domesday Studies, i. 357. Almost at one and the same
moment, but in two different 'extents,' the same tenements are being described
as containing 15 and as containing 18 acres. Domesday of St. Paul's, 69: 'In
this manor the hide contains 120 acres; the old inquest said that it used not to
contain more than 80; but afterwards the lands were sought out and measured
(*exquisitae sunt terrae et mensuratae*).'

[3] Cart. Rams. iii. 208. See also the table given by Seebohm, op. cit. 37.

Hertfordshire
　　Therfield　　　　　　　　　1 H. = 4　v. = 256 A.

Suffolk
　　Lawshall　　　　　　　　　1 H. = 3　v. = 156 A.

Norfolk
　　Brancaster　　　　　　　　1 H. = 4　v. = 160 A.
　　Ringstead　　　　　　　　　1 H. = 4　v. = 120 A.

Cambridgeshire
　　Elsworth　　　　　　　　　1 H. = 4　v. = 120 A.
　　Knapwell　　　　　　　　　1 H. = 4　v. = 160 A.
　　Graveley Freehold　　　　　1 H. = 7　v. = unknown
　　　　　　　Villeinage　　　　1 H. = $6\frac{3}{4}$v. = 135 A.
　　Over　　　　　　　　　　　1 H. = 4　v. = 120 A.
　　Girton　　　　　　　　　　1 H. = 4　v. = 120 A.
　　Burwell　　　　　　　　　　1 H. = 4　v. = 120 A.

Here in thirty-one instances what we take to be the normal
equation appears but seven times, but no other equation occurs
more than twice. Moreover, so far as we have observed, the
variations in the acreage that will be ascribed to a hide are not
provincial, they are villar variations: that is to say, though we
may see that the average hide of one county would have more
acres than those that are contained in the average hide of another,
we can not affirm that the hide of a certain county or hundred
contains *a* acres, while that of another has *b* acres, and, on the
other hand, we often see a startling difference between two
contiguous villages. Lastly, where the computation of 120
acres to a hide is forsaken, we see little agreement in favour
of any other equation. In particular, though now and again
the hide of a village will perchance have 240 acres, we can
find no trace of any 'double hide' in which ingenuity might
see a link between the Roman and English systems of measurement and taxation[1]. The only other general proposition which
our evidence suggests is that a land which habitually displays

[1] A 'double hide' of 240 acres plays a part in Mr Seebohm's speculations.
His instances of it hardly bear examination. On p. 37 he produces from Rot.
Hund. ii. 629 the equation 1 H. = 6 v. of 40 A. apiece. This apparently refers
to the Ramsey manor of Brington; but Cart. Rams. ii. 43 gives 1 H. = 4 v. of
40 A., while Cart. Rams. iii. 209 gives 1 H. = 4 v. of 34 A. Then Mr Seebohm,
p. 51, cites from 'the documents of Battle Abbey given by Dugdale' the equation
1 H. = 8 v.; but this seems to refer to the statement now printed in the Battle
Cartulary (Camd. Soc.) p. xiii., where 1 H. = 4 v. As to the supposed *solanda*
of two hides, see Round, Feudal England, 103.

unusually large virgates will often be a land in which a given area of arable soil has borne an unusually light weight of taxation, and this, as we shall hereafter see, will often, though not always, be a land where a given area of arable soil has been deemed to bear an unusually small value. But this connexion between many-acred hides and light taxation is not very strongly marked in our cartularies[1].

In the land-books which deal with Kent the *aratrum* or *sulung*[2] is commoner than the hide or manse, and Domesday Book shows us that in Kent the *solin* (*sulung*) is the fiscal unit that plays the part that is elsewhere played by the hide. That same part is played in Suffolk, Norfolk, Yorkshire, Lincolnshire, and the counties of Derby, Nottingham and Leicester by the *carucata*, which has for its eighth part the *bovata*. These terms seem to be French: that is to say, they apparently formed no part of the official Latin that had been current in England[3]. We may infer, however, that they translated some English, or rather perhaps some Scandinavian terms, for only in Danish counties do we find them used to describe the geldable units. It is exceedingly doubtful whether we ought to treat this method of reckoning as older than the Danish invasions. Bede, himself a Northumbrian, uses the 'family-land' as his unit, no matter what be the part of England of which he is speaking, and his translator uses the *híd* or *hiwisc* in the same indiscriminate fashion. Unfortunately the 'carucated' shires are those which yield us hardly any land-books, and we do not know what the English jurors said when the Norman clerks wrote *carucata* and *bovata*: perhaps *plough-gate* and *ox-gate*, or *plough-gang* and *ox-gang*, or, again, a *plough of land*, for these were the vernacular words of a later age. On the whole,

The carucate and bovate.

---

[1] The virgates on the Gloucestershire manors of Gloucester Abbey contain the following numbers of acres: 36, 40, 36, 38, 48, 48, 48, 48, 50, 48, 40, 64, 64, 64, 48, 50, 60, 48, 48, 64, 18 (?), 44, 80, 48, 48, 72. See Gloucester Cartulary, vol. iii. Of the taxation and wealth of the various counties we shall speak hereafter.

[2] Napier and Stevenson, Crawford Charters, p. 47: The O. E. *sulh* (plough) is 'cognate with Lat. *sulcus*.'

[3] Both terms were in use in Normandy and some other parts of France: Delisle, Études, 538; also Ducange. In a would-be English charter of the days before the Conquest these words would be ground for suspicion. In K. 283 and 455 Kemble has printed (in documents which he stigmatizes) *caractorum*. But apparently (see B. ii. 104, iii. 94) what stands in the cartulary is *carattorum*, and this seems a mistake for the common *casatorum*. To mistake O. E. *s* for *r* is easy.

the little evidence that we have seems to point to the greater antiquity in England of a reckoning which takes the 'house-land' rather than the 'plough-land' as its unit[1].

The ox-gang. As to the bovate or ox-gang, it seems to be an unit only in the same sense as that in which the virgate or yard-land is an unit; the one is the eighth, the other is the fourth of an unit. That, in days when eight oxen are yoked to a plough, the eighth of a plough-gang should be called an ox-gang will not surprise us, though, as a matter of fact, an ox never 'goes' or ploughs in solitude[2]. In our Latin documents a third part of a knight's fee will be, not *tertia pars feodi unius militis*, but far more commonly, *feodum tertiae partis unius militis*. We do not infer from this that fractions of knights, or fractions of knight's fees are older than integral knights and integral fees. The bovate seems to have been much less widely known than the carucate, for apparently it had no place in the computation that was generally used in East Anglia, where men reckoned by carucates, half-carucates and acres and where the virgate was not absolutely unknown[3].

The fiscal carucate. In the financial system, as we have said, the carucate plays for some counties the part that is played for others by the hide. Fiscally they seem to be equivalent: that is to say, when every hide of Wessex is to pay two shillings, every carucate of Lincolnshire will pay that sum. We think also and shall try to show that the Exchequer reckons 120 acres to the carucate, or, in other words, that if a tenement taxed as a carucate were divided into six equal shares, each share would at the Exchequer be called 20 acres. The same forces, however, which have made the fiscal hide diverge widely from the 'real' hide have played upon the plough-gangs of the Danelaw. In the Boldon Book we read of many bovates with 15 acres apiece, though the figures 20, $13\frac{1}{2}$, $12\frac{1}{2}$, 12 and 8 are also represented, and, when we come to the extents of the thirteenth century, we seem to see in the north but a feeble

---

[1] See Stevenson, E. H. R. v. 143.

[2] In D. B. the *iugum* appears as a portion of a *solin*; probably as a quarter of the *solin*. D. B. i. 13: 'pro uno solin se defendit. Tria iuga sunt infra divisionem Hugonis et quartum iugum est extra.' The *iugum* has already appeared in a few Kentish land-books. In K. 199 (i. 249), B. i. 476, we find *an ioclet* which seems to be half a manse (*mansiuncula*). In K. 407 (iii. 262), B. ii. 572, we find 'an iuclæte et insuper 10 segetes (*acres*).'

[3] D. B. ii. 389 : 'In Cratingas 24 liberi homines 1 carr. terrae et 1 virg.'

tendency to any uniformity among the equations that connect carucates with acres. The numbers of the acres in a bovate given by a series of Yorkshire inquests is 7, 7, 8, 15, 12, 6, 12, 15, 15, 6, 5, 9, 10, 10, 12, 24, 4, 16, 12, 18, 8, 6, 10, 24, 32[1]. With a bovate of 4 acres, our carucate would have no more than 32. But then, in the north we may find very long rods and very large acres[2], and, where Danes have settled, we have the best reason to expect those complications which would arise from the superimposition of a new set of measures upon a territory that had been arranged to suit another set[3].

Having been led into speaking of plough-gangs, we may end these discursive remarks by a gentle protest against the use that is sometimes made of the statements that are found in the book called Fleta. It is a second-rate legal treatise of Edward I.'s day. It seems to have fallen dead from its author's pen and it hardly deserved a better fate. For the more part it is a poor abstract of Bracton's work. When it ceases to pillage Bracton, it pillages other authors, and what it says of ploughing appears to be derived at second hand from Walter of Henley[4]. Now Walter of Henley's successful and popular treatise on Husbandry is a good and important book; but we must be careful before we treat it as an exponent of the traditional mode of agriculture, for evidently Walter was an enlightened reformer. We might even call him the Arthur Young of his time. Now, it is sometimes said that according to Fleta 'the carucate' would have 160 acres in 'a two course manor' and 180 in 'a three course manor.' A reference to Walter of Henley will show him endeavouring to convince the men of his time that such amounts as these really can be ploughed, if they work hard. 'Some men will tell you that a plough can not till eight score or nine score acres by the year, but I will show you that it can.' His calculation is worth repeating. It is as follows:

Acreage tilled by a plough.

[1] Yorkshire Inquisitions (Yorks. Archæol. Soc.) passim. On p. 77 in an account of Catterick we read of 'a capital messuage worth 5s.; 32 bovates of arable land in demesne (each bovate of 6 acres at 8s.) £12. 16s.; 31½ bovates held by bondmen (each bovate of 10 acres at 13s. 4d.) £21;...2 bovates which contain 24 acres and 32 acres called Inland worth 74s. 8d.'

[2] See above, p. 375.

[3] A bovate of 13 acres seems to have prevailed in Scotland: Acts of Parliament of Scotland, i. 387.

[4] The immediate source is the Seneschaucie. See Walter of Henley, ed. Lamond, p. 84. Fleta, p. 159.

The year has 52 weeks. Deduct 8 for holy-days and other hindrances. There remain 44 weeks or 264 days, Sundays excluded.

Two course. Plough 40 acres for winter seed, 40 for spring seed and 80 for fallow (total 160) at $\frac{7}{8}$ths of an acre per day $= 182\frac{6}{7}$ days

Also plough by way of second fallowing 80 acres at an acre per day $= 80$ days

Total $\overline{262\frac{6}{7}}$ days[1].

Walter of Henley's scheme. It is a strenuous and sanguine, if not an impossible, programme. When harvest time and the holy weeks are omitted, the plough is to 'go' every week-day throughout the year, despite frost and tempest. Obviously it is a programme that can only enter the head of an enthusiastic lord who has supernumerary oxen, and will know how to fill the place of a ploughman who is ill. We have little warrant for believing that what Walter hopes to do is being commonly done in his day, less for importing his projects into an earlier age. In order that he may keep his beasts up to their arduous toil, he proposes to feed them with oats during half the year[2]. If we inferred that the Saxon invaders of England treated their oxen thus, we might be guilty of an anachronism differing only in degree from that which would furnish them with steam-ploughs. But, to come to much later days, the Domesday of S^t. Paul's enables us to say with some certainty that the ordinary team of eight beasts accomplished no such feats as those of which Walter speaks. For example, at Thorpe in Essex the canons have about 180 acres of arable land in demesne. These, it is estimated, can be tilled by one team of ten heads together with the ploughing service that is due from the tenants, and these tenants have to plough at least 80 acres, to wit, 40 in winter and 40 in Lent[3]. We must observe that to till even 120 acres according to Walter's two-course plan would mean that a plough must 'go' 180 acres in every year, and that, even if it does its acre every day, more than half the week-days in the year must be devoted to ploughing. We may, however, seriously doubt whether a scheme which

[1] Walter of Henley, pp. 6, 8, 44–5. With a three-course system the figures will be somewhat different. Plough 60 acres for winter seed, 60 for spring seed, 60 for fallow (total 180) at the rate of $\frac{7}{8}$th of an acre per day:—Total, 205$\frac{5}{7}$ days. In second fallowing plough 60 acres at an acre per day:—Grand total, 265$\frac{5}{7}$ days. Whichever system is adopted, the plough 'goes' 240 acres.

[2] Walter of Henley, p. 13,

[3] Domesday of S^t. Paul's, 38.

would plough the land thrice between every two crops had been generally prevalent[1]. Nay, we may even doubt whether the practice of fallowing had been universal[2]. Not unfrequently in our cartularies the villein is required to plough between Michaelmas and Christmas and again between Christmas and Lady Day, while nothing is said of his ploughing in the summer[3]. We are only beginning to learn a little about medieval agriculture.

However, we have now said all that we had to say by way of preface to what we fear will be a dreary and inconclusive discussion of some of those abundant figures that Domesday Book supplies. A few we have endeavoured to collect in the tables which will meet the reader's eye when he turns this page, and which will be explained on later pages.

§ 2. *Domesday Statistics.*

As a general rule the account given by Domesday Book of any manor contains three different statements about it which seem to have some bearing upon the subject of our present inquiry. (*A*) It will tell us that the manor is rated to the geld at a certain number of units, which units will in Kent be solins or sulungs and yokes (*iuga*), in Yorkshire, Lincolnshire, Derbyshire, Nottinghamshire, Leicestershire, Norfolk and Suffolk carucates and bovates (but bovates are, to say the least, rare in East Anglia), and in the rest of England hides and virgates; but acres also will from time to time appear in the statement. (*B*) It will tell us that the manor contains land for a certain number of teams, or for a certain number of oxen. (*C*) It will tell us that there are on the manor a certain number of teams, some whereof belong to the lord and some to the men.

[margin note: Domesday's three statements.]

---

[1] Meitzen, op. cit. i. 277; Andrews, op. cit. 260.

[2] Gerefa, 9 (Anglia, ix. 261): 'Me mæig in Maio and Junio and Julio on sumera fealgian.' Andrews, op. cit. 257.

[3] Thus e.g. Domesday of S[t]. Paul's, 59, Tillingham. Is it possible to fallow, when, as in this case, there is no pasture for the oxen except such as is afforded by the idle field? 'Non est ibi pastura nisi cum quiescit dominicum per wainagium....(69) Non est ibi certa pastura nisi quando terrae dominici quiescunt alternatim incultae.'

TABLE I.

	Modern Acreage	Recorded Population (Ellis)	Danegeld circ. ann. 1150			Hides, Carucates, Sulungs
	I	II	III			IV
			£	s.	d.	
Kent	975,820	12,205	105	16	10	1,224
Sussex	932,733	10,410	217	0	6	3,474
Surrey	461,230	4,383	179	16	0	1,830
Hampshire	1,037,764	10,373	184	15	4	2,588
Berkshire	461,742	6,324	205	11	4	2,473
Wiltshire	880,248	10,150	389	13	0	4,050
Dorset	632,272	7,807	248	5	0	2,277
		[7,512 E]				[2,321 E]
Somerset	1,042,488	13,764	277	10	4	2,936
		[13,307 E]				[2,951 E]
Devon	1,667,097	17,434	103	19	8	1,119
Cornwall	868,208	5,438	22	15	0	155
Middlesex	180,480 (?)	2,302	85	12	0	868
Hertford	406,932	4,927	110	1	4	1,050
Buckingham	475,694	5,420	204	14	7	2,074
Oxford	485,322	6,775	249	16	5	2,412
Gloucester	796,731	8,366	194	1	6	2,388
Worcester	480,342	4,625	101	6	0	1,189
Hereford	537,363	5,368	93	15	6	1,324
Cambridge	549,565	5,204	114	15	0	1,233
Huntingdon	233,928	2,914	71	5	0	747
Bedford	298,494	3,875	110	12	0	1,193
Northampton	639,541	8,441	119	10	9	1,356
Leicester	528,986	6,772	100	0	0	2,500 (?)
Warwick	578,595	6,574	128	12	6	1,338
Stafford	749,713	3,178	45	1	0	505
						[499 E]
Shropshire	859,516	5,080	117	18	6	1,245
Chester	[655,036]	2,349	0	0	0	512
Derby	657,550	3,041 }	112	1	11	{ 679
Nottingham	539,752	5,686 }				{ 567
Rutland	[97,273]	862	11	12	0	37
York	[3,888,351]	8,055	165	9	5	10,095
Lincoln	1,694,907	25,305	266	0	0	4,188
Essex	985,545	16,060	236	8	0	2,650
Norfolk	1,315,092	27,087	330	2	2	[2,422]
Suffolk	947,742	20,491	235	0	8	

STATISTICS.

Hides Gelding T. R. W.	Teamlands	Teams	Valet (Pearson)			
V	VI	VII	VIII			
			£	s.	d.	
		3,102	5,140	9	10	Kent
2,241		3,091	3,255	7	4	Sussex
706	1,172	1,142	1,524	4	9	Surrey
1,572	2,847	2,614				Hampshire
1,338	2,087	1,796	2,383	16	1	Berkshire
	3,457	2,997				Wiltshire
	2,303	1,762	2,656	9	8	Dorset
	[2,332 E]		[3,359	12	9 E]	
	4,858	3,804				Somerset
	[4,812 E]		[4,161	4	7 E]	
	7,972	5,542	3,220	14	3	Devon
399	2,377	1,187	662	1	4	Cornwall
	664	545	754	7	8	Middlesex
	1,716	1,406	1,541	13	11	Hertford
	2,244	1,952	1,813	7	9	Buckingham
	2,639	2,467	3,242	2	11	Oxford
		3,768	2,827	6	8	Gloucester
		1,889	991	0	6	Worcester
		2,479				Hereford
	1,676	1,443				Cambridge
	1,120	967	864	15	4	Huntingdon
	1,557	1,367	1,096	12	2	Bedford
	2,931	2,422	1,843	0	7	Northampton
		1,817	736	3	0	Leicester
	2,276	2,003	1,359	13	8	Warwick
	1,398	951	[516	16	3 E]	Stafford
		1,755				Shropshire
						Chester
	762	862	461	4	0	Derby
	1,255	1,991				Nottingham
						Rutland
						York
	5,043	4,712				Lincoln
		3,920	4,784	10	8	Essex
		4,853	4,154	11	7	Norfolk
						Suffolk

M.

TABLE II.

	Acreage div. by population	Acreage div. by teamlands	Acreage div. by teams	Population div. by teamlands
	IX	X	XI	XII
Kent	79		314	
Sussex	89		301	
Surrey	105	393	403	3·7
Hampshire	100	364	397	3·6
Berkshire	73	221	257	3·0
Wiltshire	86	254	293	2·9
Dorset	80	274	358	3·3
Somerset	75	214	274	2·8
Devon	95	209	300	2·1
Cornwall	159	365	731	2·2
Middlesex	78	271	331	3·4
Hertford	82	237	289	2·8
Buckingham	87	211	243	2·4
Oxford	71	183	196	2·5
Gloucester	95		211	
Worcester	103		254	
Hereford	100		216	
Cambridge	105	327	380	3·1
Huntingdon	80	208	241	2·6
Bedford	77	191	218	2·4
Northampton	75	218	264	2·8
Leicester	78		291	
Warwick	88	254	288	2·8
Stafford	235	536	788	2.2
Shropshire	169		489	
Chester	[278]			
Derby	216	862	762	3·9
Nottingham	94	430	271	4·4
Rutland	[112]			
York	[482]			
Lincoln	66	336	359	5·0
Essex	61		251	
Norfolk	48		270	
Suffolk	46			

AVERAGES.

Population div. by teams	Teamlands div. by teams	Total valet div. by teamlands [or by teams]			Experimental valet of teamland [or of land tilled by team]			
XIII	XIV	XV			XVI			
		£	s.	d.	£	s.	d.	
3·9		[1	13	1]	1	14	11	Kent
3·3		[1	1	0]	0	18	3	Sussex
3·8	1·02	1	6	0	1	0	8	Surrey
3·9	1·08				1	2	6	Hampshire
3·5	1·16	1	2	4	1	2	10	Berkshire
3·3	1·15				1	4	4	Wiltshire
4·4	1·30	1	3	0	1	6	8	Dorset
3·6	1·27				0	15	9	Somerset
3·1	1·43	0	8	0	0	5	3	Devon
4·5	2·00	0	5	6	0	3	8	Cornwall
4·2	1·21	1	2	8	1	1	1	Middlesex
3·5	1·22	0	17	11	0	13	11	Hertford
2·7	1·14	0	16	1	0	13	6	Buckingham
2·7	1·06	1	4	6	1	0	8	Oxford
2·2		[0	15	0]	[0	16	1]	Gloucester
2·4		[0	10	5]	[0	10	7]	Worcester
2·1					[0	9	11]	Hereford
3·6	1·16				1	2	9	Cambridge
3·0	1·15	0	15	5	0	12	2	Huntingdon
2·8	1·13	0	14	1	0	15	4	Bedford
3·4	1·21				0	9	9	Northampton
3·7					0	9	8	Leicester
3·2	1·13	0	11	11	0	10	10	Warwick
3·3	1·47	0	7	4	0	8	8	Stafford
2·8					[0	7	2]	Shropshire
								Chester
3·5	0·88	0	12	1	0	11	7	Derby
2·8	0·63				0	13	6	Nottingham
								Rutland
								York
5·3	1·07				0	17	6	Lincoln
4·0		[1	4	4]				Essex
5·5		[0	17	1]				Norfolk
								Suffolk

We may begin our investigation with a formula common in Derbyshire.

> In M [place name] habuit K [man's name] *a* car[ucatas] terrae ad geldum. Terra *b* car[ucarum *or* carucis]. Ibi nunc in dominio *d* car[ucae] et...villani et...bordarii habent *e* car[ucas].

The Lincolnshire formula is perhaps yet plainer. Instead of saying 'Terra *b* car[ucarum],' it says, 'Terra ad *b* car[ucas].' Still more instructive is a formula used in Yorkshire.

> In M habuit K *a* car[ucatas] terrae ad geldum ubi possunt esse *b* car[ucae]. Nunc habet ibi K *d* car[ucas] et...villanos et...bordarios cum *e* car[ucis].

As a variant on the phrase 'ubi possunt esse *b* car[ucae],' we have, 'quas potest arare 1 car[uca],' or 'has possunt arare *b* car[ucae][1].'

The teams on the demesne (*d*) and the teams of the tenants (*e*) are enumerated separately. The total number of the teams (*d* + *e*) we will call *c*.

Now occasionally we may find an entry concerning which the following equation will hold good: $a = b = c$: in other words, the same number will stand for the carucates at which the manor is taxed, the 'teamlands' that there are in it (or to put it another way the number of teams that 'can be there,' or the number of teams that 'can plough it'[2]) and also for the teams that are actually to be found there. Thus:—

> Terra Roberti de Todeni......In Ulestanestorp habuit Leuricus 4 car[ucatas] terrae ad geldum. Terra totidem car[ucis]. Ibi habet Robertus in dominio 1 car[ucam] et 6 villanos et 3 bordarios et 8 sochemannos habentes 3 car[ucas][3].

Here $a = b = c$. But entries so neat as this are not very common. In the first place, the number (*c*) of teams often exceeds or falls short of the number (*b*) of 'teamlands,' or, which is the same thing, the number of teams that there 'can be.' An excess of 'teamlands' over teams is common. In some parts of Yorkshire and elsewhere instead of reading

---

[1] D. B. i. 307 b, 308.

[2] It will be convenient for us to adopt this term a 'teamland' as an equivalent for the *Terra ad unam carucam* of our record, so that '*b* teamlands' shall translate *Terra ad b carucas*. The reader is asked to accept this note as an 'interpretation clause.'

[3] D. B. i. 353.

that there are so many teams, we read 'modo vasta est':—
there are no oxen there at all. But the reverse of this case
is not very uncommon. Thus we may be told that there are
3 carucates for geld, that 'there can be there 2 teams' and that
there are 4 teams[1]; we may find a manor that contains land
for but 3 teams equipped with as many as 7[2]. As to the
relation between *a* and *b*, this is not fixed. On one and the
same page we may find that *a* is equal to, greater and less
than *b*. Thus in Lincolnshire[3]:

> In Colebi habuit Siuuard 7 car. terrae ad geldum. Terra ad
> totidem car.
> In Cherchebi habuit Comes Morcar 5 car. terrae ad geldum.
> Terra ad 4 car.
> In Bodebi habuit Comes Morcar 8 car. terrae ad geldum. Terra
> ad 9 car.

Leaving now for a while the carucated part of England Southern
formulas.
and postponing our visit to Kent, we find similar formulas.
They tell us (*A*) that the manor contains a certain number of
units of assessment, (*B*) that there is land for a certain number
of teams, (*C*) that there are so many teams upon it. But
we have a new set of units of assessment; instead of carucates
and bovates, we have hides and virgates. The Huntingdonshire formula is particularly clear. It runs thus:

> In M habet K *a* hidas ad geldum. Terra *b* car[ucarum *or*
> carucis]. Ibi nunc in dominio *d* car[ucae] et...villani et...bordarii
> habentes *e* car[ucas].

The number of hides that is put before us is the number of
hides 'for geld.' So in Cheshire and Shropshire the number of
hides that is put before us is the number of 'hidae geld[antes].'
From this we easily pass to the formula that prevails in Wiltshire, Dorset, Somerset and Devon:

> K tenet M. T[empore] R[egis] E[dwardi] geldabat pro *a* hidis.
> Terra est *b* car[ucarum]. In dominio sunt *d* car[ucae] et...villani
> et...bordarii cum *e* car[ucis].

A formula common in Sussex, Surrey and several other counties
instead of telling us that this manor has *a* hides for geld, or
has *a* gelding hides, or gelds for *a* hides, tells us—what seems
exactly the same thing—that it 'defends itself' for *a* hides.

---

[1] D. B. i. 308, Trectone.   [2] D. B. i. 275 b, Burnulfestune.
[3] D. B. i 337 b.

Then we pass to counties such as Middlesex, Hertford, Buckingham and Oxford where the entry does not commonly use any words which explicitly refer to geld:—we are told that K holds M for so many hides (pro *a* hidis). Lastly, we may pass to counties, such as Warwickshire and Staffordshire where, at first sight, the entries may seem to us ambiguous. They run thus—'K holds M. There are there *a* hides. There is land for *b* teams.' Here for a moment it may seem to us that we have two different statements about the actual extent or capacity of the manor:—there are *a* hides there, but land for *b* teams. But comparing the formulas in use here with those in use in other counties, we can hardly doubt that they all come to one and the same thing:—a statement about *b*, the capacity of the manor, is preceded by a statement about its taxation, which statement may take the short form, 'There are *a* hides there,' instead of one of the longer forms, 'It gelds, or defends itself, for *a* hides,' or 'He holds *a* gelding hides, or *a* hides for geld.'

Kentish
formulas.

In Kent again, we have the three statements, though here the units of assessment are sulungs and yokes:—the land 'defends itself' for *a* sulungs; there is land there for *b* teams; there are *d* teams in demesne and the men have *e* teams.

Relation
between
the three
state-
ments.

In the hidated south, as in the carucated north, the relation between the three amounts is not invariable. We may find that $a = b = c$. It is common to find that *c* is less than *b*, but occasionally it is greater; on one and the same page we may find that *c* is equal to, is greater, is less than *b*. Then *a* is often equal to *b*, often it is less than *b*, but sometimes it is greater. We have therefore three statements about the manor, between which there is no necessary connexion of any very simple kind.

It may look pedantic, but will be convenient if, by means of the letters *A*, *B* and *C*, we try to keep distinctly before our minds 'the *A* statement' about the units of assessment, 'the *B* statement' about the 'teamlands,' or teams for which 'there is land,' and 'the *C* statement' about the existing teams. We shall find hereafter that there are certain counties in which we do not get all three statements, at least in any of their accustomed forms. In Gloucestershire, Worcestershire and Herefordshire we rarely get the *B* statement. As to Essex, Norfolk and Suffolk, we seem at first sight to obtain

A and not *B*, or *B* and not *A*, while Leicestershire will require separate treatment.

Introduction of statistics.

Now if we are ever to understand these matters, it is necessary that we should look at the whole of England. Far be it from us to say that microscopic labour spent upon one county or one hundred is wasted; often it is of the highest value; but such work is apt to engender theories which break down the moment they are carried outside the district in which they had their origin. Well would it be if the broad features of Domesday Book could be set out before us in a series of statistical tables. The task would be gigantic and could hardly be performed except by a body of men who had plenteous leisure and who would work together harmoniously. However, rather to suggest what might and some day must be done, than to parade what has been done rapidly and badly, some figures have been set forth above in two tables[1]. That they are extremely inaccurate can not be doubtful, for he who compiled them had other things to do and lacks many of the qualities which should be required of a good counter of hides. For unmethodical habits and faulty arithmetic no excuse is possible; but it will be remembered that, as matters now stand, two men not unskilled in Domesday might add up the number of hides in a county and arrive at very different results, because they would hold different opinions as to the meaning of certain formulas which are not uncommon. What is here set before the reader is intended to be no more than a distant approach towards the truth. It will serve its end if it states the sort of figures that would be obtained by careful and leisurely computers, and therefore the sort of problems that have to be solved[2].

Explanation of statistics. Acreage.

We must now explain our statistics. In Column I. we give the acreage of the modern counties[3]. A warning bracket will remind the reader that in the cases of Yorkshire, Cheshire and Rutland the modern does not coincide even approximately with the ancient boundary. To Middlesex we give a figure larger than that given by our statisticians, for they know a

[1] See pp. 400—403.

[2] We shall not complain of our tools; but Domesday Book is certainly not impeccable. As to its omissions see Eyton, Notes on Domesday (1880); also Round, Feudal England, 43.

[3] Agricultural Returns, 1895 (Board of Agriculture) p. 34. Tidal water is excluded.

county of London which has been formed at the expense of its neighbours[1]. Many minor variations should be remembered by those who would use Domesday Book for delicate purposes; for example, they must call to mind the merger in circum-ambient shires of what were once detached pieces of other counties. But of such niceties we can here take no account[2].

Popula-
tion.

In Column II. we state the 'recorded population' as com-puted by Ellis. In the cases of Dorset and Somerset we also state, and we sign with the letter *E*, the result of Eyton's labours. We must not forget that these figures give us rather the number of tenants or occupiers than the number of human beings. Our readers must multiply them by four, five or six, according to knowledge or taste, before the population of England will be attained.

Danegeld.

In Column III., for a reason that will become evident here-after, we place the amount of danegeld charged against the counties—charged against them, not actually paid by them[3]—in the middle of the twelfth century. The sources of these figures are the Pipe Rolls of 31 Henry I. and 2 and 8 Henry II. In these accounts the amount charged against a county is approximately constant. Some of the variations are probably due to a contemptuous treatment of small sums[4]; but there are cases in which a sheriff seems to have been allowed to deduct £10 or so, without any recorded explanation[5]. We choose the highest figures when there is any discord between our three rolls. The danegeld was being levied at the rate of two shillings on the hide, and therefore, if we would find the number of geldant hides, we have to multiply by ten the number of pounds that are set against the county.

Hides,
carucates,
sulungs.

Column IV. contains our estimate of *A* : in other words, of the number of hides, carucates or sulungs. As we are arguing

---

[1] The received figures are : Middlesex, 149,046, London, 75,442. From older sources we give Middlesex, 180,480: Population Abstract, 1833, vol. i. p. 376.

[2] For some good remarks on these matters see Eyton, Notes on Domesday. Lincoln, Nottingham and Northampton would require correction because of the treatment that Rutland has received. The boundary of Shropshire has under-gone changes. The inclusion of stretches of Welsh ground increases the population without adding to the hidage of some western counties.

[3] See above, p. 7.

[4] Thus Leicester is charged with £100. 0s. 0d., with £99. 19s. 11d. and with £99. 19s. 4d.

[5] In 8 Hen. II. several of the counties answer for about £10 less than had formerly been demanded from them.

for a large hide, we have thought right in doubtful cases to
lean in favour of inclusion rather than of exclusion. We count
all hides, except those ascribed to the shire's boroughs[1], even
though we are told that they have 'never' gelded. Also, when
a hide is mentioned, we count it, even though we have a strong
suspicion that the same hide is mentioned again on some other
page. Especially in Sussex, where the rapes have recently
been rearranged, this may make our figures too high[2]. Then,
again, we have frankly begged important questions by assuming
that in Domesday Book the following equations are correct.

$$1 \text{ Hide} \quad = 4 \text{ Virgates} = 120 \text{ Acres}$$
$$1 \text{ Carucate} = 8 \text{ Bovates} \; = 120 \text{ Acres}$$
$$1 \text{ Sulung} \; = 4 \text{ Yokes} \quad = 120 \text{ Acres.}$$

In the counties with which we have dealt, except Norfolk and
Essex (Suffolk we have left alone), acres are so rarely mentioned
that the error, if any, introduced by our hypothesis as to their
relation to hides and carucates will be almost infinitesimal,
and, even if we are wrong in supposing that the virgate
is the quarter of a hide and that the bovate is the eighth
of a carucate, the vitiation of our results that will be due to
this blunder will but rarely be considerable[3].

---

[1] The inclusion of the boroughs would have led to many difficulties. London,
for example, though no account is taken of it in D. B., seems to have gelded for
1200 hides. (Brit. Mus. MS. Add. 14,252, f. 126.)

[2] We omit the 'ingeldable carucates' which occur in some hidated counties.
This may introduce a little caprice. If the jurors in one of these counties
ascribe twelve carucates to a manor, we do not count them. If they had spoken
of hides which never gelded, we should have counted them; and yet we may
agree with Eyton that the two phrases would mean much the same thing. But
this source of error or caprice is not very important in our present context.
Thus we take Dorset. Eyton gives it 2321 hides and then by adding 'quasi-
hides' brings up the number to 2650. The difference between these two figures
is not large when regarded from the point that we are occupying. I have
thought that the difficulty would be better met by the warning that Wiltshire,
Dorset, Somerset and Devon contain considerable stretches of unhidated royal
demesne, than by my reckoning as hides what Eyton called 'quasi-hides.' In
the case of Dorset, Somerset and Stafford I have placed Eyton's figures below
my own and signed them with the letter *E*. I know full well that his are
much more accurate than mine. He probably gave to each county that he
examined more months than I have given weeks to the whole of England. In
comparing our results, it should be remembered that, at least in Staffordshire,
he dealt with the county boundary in a manner which, in my ignorance, I dare
not adopt.

[3] My calculations about Leicestershire are more than usually rough, owing
to the appearance of the curious 'hide' or 'hundred' or whatever it is. See on

Reduced
hidage.

Almost everywhere we may find some hides (carucates, sulungs) that do not geld and many cases in which a tract now gelds for a smaller number of hides (carucates, sulungs) than that for which it formerly paid. In four counties, however, Sussex, Surrey, Hampshire and Berkshire, we see that since William's advent there has, rightfully or wrongfully, been a large and generally distributed reduction in the tale of the gelding hides. In our Column v. we give a rough statement of the reduced number[1]. In Cornwall we read of an assessment that prevailed in the Confessor's day and of a heavier assessment. The figures which speak of this heavier assessment we place in our Column v[2].

The team-lands.

We now pass from *A* to *B*. In Column vi. we set the number of teamlands, thus answering the question *Quot carucarum [carucis] ibi est terra*. We have assumed, but this rarely has an appreciable effect on our calculations, that the land of one ox is the eighth, the land of two oxen the fourth part of the land of one team. There are certain counties where we receive no statement about the teamlands, while in certain others the statement, though it seems to be expected, is often omitted[3]. For this reason some blanks will be found in this column. In most of the other counties instances occur with more or less frequency in which nothing is said of the teamlands. In these cases we have thought it fair to assume that there were teamlands equal in number to the teams ($B = C$). The effect of this assumption will be to bring the number of teamlands (B) somewhat closer to the number of teams (C) than it would otherwise have been, but no very great harm will have thus been done to our rude statistics[4].

the one hand Stevenson, E. H. R. v. 95, and on the other Round, Feudal England, 82. Whether this unit contained 12 or 18 carucates is not of very great importance to us at the moment. But there are other difficulties in Leicestershire. In Cornwall I was compelled to make an assumption as to the peculiar *ager* or *acra* of that county; but no reasonable theory about this matter would seriously affect the number of Cornwall's hides.

[1] The usual formula is: 'Tunc se defendit pro *a* hidis, modo pro *a'*.' We place *a* in Col. iv., *a'* in Col. v.

[2] The usual formula is: 'T. R. E. geldabat pro *a* hidis; ibi tamen sunt *a'* hidae.' We place *a* in Col. iv. and *a'* in Col. v.; and we shall argue hereafter, with some hesitation, that the taxation of this county has been increased under William.

[3] The words *Terra est* are written and are followed by a blank space. Many instances in Kent and Sussex.

[4] On the other hand, when I find a statement about *B* and none about *C*, I do

Column VII. gives the number of teams. Here we assume The teams. (we shall endeavour to prove hereafter) that the *caruca* of Domesday Book always means the same, namely, eight oxen[1].

Lastly in Column VIII. we place the results attained by The values. Pearson[2] and Eyton in their endeavours to add together the various sums which the various estates in a shire are said to be worth (*valet*) or to render (*reddit*) in the Conqueror's day, and to thus obtain a total *valet* for the shire. We need hardly say that these values are 'annual values.'

The relations between our divers sets of figures are more The table of ratios. important than the figures themselves, therefore we have worked the division sums the results of which are printed in the second Table, the first seven columns whereof are filled by quotients[3]. The last column calls for more remark. The *valets* obtained for the various counties by Pearson and Eyton are somewhat precarious. They involve theories as to the relation between the values of gold and silver, as to the relation between the value of a pound reckoned by tale and a pound reckoned by weight, as to 'blanched' money and the cost of 'a night's farm.' Also a good deal is included that can hardly be called the value of land, since it comprehends, not only the value of mills and the like, but also in some cases the revenue derived from courts. In order therefore that we might compare the values given to land in the various counties, we have taken

---

not assume that $C=B$; on the contrary, I read the entry to mean that $C=0$. In other words, it is very possible that there should be teamlands without teams; but I do not think that for Domesday's purposes there can be teams (i.e. teams at work) without land that is being ploughed, though it is true that often, and in some counties habitually, C will be slightly greater than B.

[1] One of the chief difficulties in the way of accurate computation is occasioned by what we may call the complex entries. We start with some such statement as this: 'The Bishop holds Norton. It defends itself for a hides. There is land for b teams. There are d teams on the demesne and the villeins have e teams.' But then we read: 'Of this land [or of these a hides] Roger holds m hides; there are n teams on the demesne and the villeins have o teams.' Here the total number of hides is a, and not $a+m$; and I think that the total number of teamlands is b, and not b + some unstated number held by Roger; but the total number of teams is $d+e+n+o$. Entries in this form are not very uncommon, and therefore this explanation seemed to be required.

[2] Pearson, History of England, ii. 665.

[3] Col. IX. gives I. divided by II. Col. X. gives I. divided by VI. Col. XI. gives I. divided by VII. Col. XII. gives II. divided by VI. Col. XIII. gives II. divided by VII. Col. XIV. gives VI. divided by VII. Col. XV. gives VIII. divided by VI. [or if there is no VI. for this county, then by VII.].

at hazard a number of small estates in order that we might by
addition and division obtain the value of a typical teamland
with typical appurtenances. In general we have chosen ten
estates each of which has one teamland, ten estates each of
which has two teamlands and ten estates each of which has five
teamlands, and then we have divided the sum of their values
by eighty, the number of teamlands that they comprise. On
the whole, the figures that we thus obtain and place in Column
XVI. are not widely removed from those in Column XV., which
represent the quotients arising from a division of Pearson's
'county values' by the number of teamlands that are contained
in the counties[1].

An apo-
logy. In order that not too much credence and yet just credence
enough may be given to the figures that we have hastily put
together, we will set beside those that we have stated for Gloucestershire the results of a minute analysis accomplished by Mr
Charles Taylor[2]. We have set down: *Population,* 8366 (from
Ellis); *Hides,* 2388; *Teams,* 3768; *Total Valet,* £2827 6s. 8d.
(from Pearson). Mr Taylor gives: *Population,* 8239[3]; *Hides,*
2611 (or 2596); *Teams,* 3909; *Total Valet,* £3130 7s. 10d.
Now these variations are wide and may in some sort be
discreditable to those who differ from Mr Taylor[4]. But they
are not very substantial if we come to averages and ratios and
a comparison of counties. For the purposes for which we shall
use our figures, it is no great matter whether in this county
there are 2·1 or 2·2 'recorded men' to the plough-team[5]. The
broad features of Gloucestershire are that its hides fall far short
of its teams, that its recorded population is sparse, that the

---

[1] In Gloucester, Worcester, Hereford and Shropshire I was compelled to adopt
as the divisor the number of teams instead of the number of teamlands. As it
is fairly certain that these counties were 'underteamed' (*B* > *C*), the resulting
quotient (annual value of land actually tilled by a team) should be diminished
before it is compared with the figures given for other counties.

[2] C. S. Taylor, Analysis of Gloucestershire Domesday (Bristol and Gloucestershire Archaeol. Soc. 1887–9).

[3] But this is intended to include males only: the *ancillae* are left out.

[4] Mr Taylor says in his preface: 'The work has occupied a large part of my
leisure time for five years.' There is therefore some audacity in my printing my
figures beside his. It is clear that we have put different constructions upon
some of the composite entries concerning large manors. See below, p. 457.
Mr Taylor, like Eyton, computes only 48 'geld acres' to the hide; I reckon
120 acres to the hide; that, however, is in this context a trifling matter.

[5] Mr Taylor has brought out 15s. 5d. as the average *valet* of land tilled by a
team. By taking Pearson's *valet* and my teams I have brought out 15s. 0d.

average value of the land tilled by a team falls well below twenty shillings, that this shire differs markedly and in certain assignable respects from Wiltshire, where the hides exceed the teams, from Lincoln, where, despite the fen, the population is thick, from Kent, where the average value of land tilled by a team rises above thirty shillings[1].

Our figures tell of wide variations; but we may be allowed to call attention to the stability of certain ratios, a stability which is gratifying to the diffident arithmetician. In twenty-one counties we can divide 'the recorded population' by the number of teamlands. The quotient never falls as low as 2 and only twice exceeds 4[2]. For the same twenty-one counties we can divide the number of teamlands by the number of teams. Only twice will the quotient fall below 1 and only once will it touch 2. We must not, however, be led away into a general discussion of these figures. That task would require a wary and learned economist. We must keep our minds bent on what may be called the *A B C* of our subject[3].

Constancy of ratios.

Now we may start with what seems to be the most objective of our three statements, that which gives us *C*, the number of teams. We know that in *A* there is an element of estimation, of assessment; we may fear that this is true of *B* also; but an ox or a team ought to be a fact and not a theory. At the

The team.

---

[1] For Dorset and Somerset my figures can be checked by Eyton's. For Wiltshire, Devon, Cornwall, by the Geld Inquests. These give for Wiltshire (see W. H. Jones, Domesday for Wiltshire, 158 ff.) 3955 H. 3 v.; for Devon (see Devonshire Domesday, ed. Devonsh. Assoc. p. xlix.) 1029 H. 1 v. 3 F.; for Cornwall 401 H. 3 v. 1 F. I give for Wiltshire 4050 H., for Devon 1119 H., for Cornwall 399 H.

[2] Lincoln, 5·0; Nottingham, 4·4; Derby, 3·9; Surrey, 3·7; Hampshire, 3·6; Middlesex, 3·4; Dorset, 3·3; Cambridge, 3·1; Berkshire, 3·0; Wiltshire, 2·9; Hertford, Northampton, Warwick, Somerset, 2·8; Huntingdon, 2·6; Oxford, 2·5; Bedford and Buckingham, 2·4; Cornwall and Stafford, 2·2; Devon, 2·1. For Kent the figure would be near 3·9, for Sussex near 3·3, for apparently in these counties there was approximate equality between the number of teams and the number of teamlands.

[3] One word about the meaning of the *valets*. I think it very clear from thousands of examples that an estate is valued 'as a going concern.' The question that the jurors put to themselves is: 'What will this estate bring in, peopled as it is and stocked as it is?' In other words, they do not endeavour to make abstraction of the villeins, oxen, etc. and to assign to the land what would be its annual value if it were stocked or peopled according to some standard of average culture. Consequently in a few years the value of an estate may leap from one pound to three pounds or to five shillings or even to zero. Eyton, Dorset, 56, has good remarks on this matter.

outset, however, a troublesome question arises. We have assumed that whenever our record speaks of a *caruca* it means eight oxen. On the other hand, there are who maintain that whereas the *carucae* of the demesne consisted of eight, those ascribed to the villeins comprised but four oxen[1], and others have thought that the strength of Domesday's *caruca* varied from place to place with the varying practice of divers agriculturists.

Variability of the caruca. But, in the first place, it is abundantly clear that the clerk who compiled the account of Cambridgeshire from the original verdicts held himself at liberty to substitute 'half a team' for 'four oxen' and 'four oxen' for 'half a team[2].' In the second place, the theory of a variable *caruca* would in our eyes reduce to an absurdity the practice of stating the capacity of land in terms of the teams and the oxen that can plough it. We are carefully told about each estate that 'there is land for *b* teams, or for *b'* oxen, or for *b* teams and *b'* oxen.' Now if a 'team' has always the same meaning, we have here a valuable truth. If, on the other hand, a 'team' may mean eight or may mean four oxen, we are being told next to nothing. The apparently precise 'there is land for 4 teams' becomes the useless 'there is land for 32 or 16 or for some number between 32 and 16 oxen.' What could the statesmen, who were hoping to correct the assessment of the danegeld, make of so vague a statement? They propose to work sums in teams and teamlands. They spend immense pains in ascertaining that here there is 'land for half a team' or 'land for half an ox.' We are accusing them of laborious folly unless we suppose that they can at a moment's notice convert teams into oxen.

The caruca a constant. If it be allowed that in the statement (*B*) about the number of teamlands the term *caruca* has always the same meaning, we cannot stop there, but must believe that in the statement (*C*) about the number of teams this same meaning is retained. Often enough when there is equality between teamlands and teams (*C = B*), the entry takes the following form:—There is land for *b* teams and 'they' are there[3]. What are there? The

---

[1] Seebohm, Village Community, 85–6. To the contrary Round, in Domesday Studies, i. 209, and Feudal England, 35.

[2] Round, Feudal England, 35.

[3] See e.g. D. B. i. 222: 'Terra est 2 car. *Has* habent ibi 3 sochemanni et 12 bordarii.'...'Terra est 3 car. Ibi sunt *ipsae* cum 9 sochemannis et 9 bordariis.'

teams for which 'there is land': those teams which are serving
as a measure for the capacity of land. Let us try the two modes
of interpretation on the first lines that strike our eye. Here
we have two successive entries, each of which tells us that
'there is land for 6 teams[1].' If the *caruca* is a constant, we
have learnt that in one particular there is equality between
these estates. If the *caruca* is a variable, we have learnt
nothing of the kind. Let us see what we can gain by reading
further. In the one case there were 3 teams on the demesne
and the villeins had 6½; in the other there were 2 teams on the
demesne, the villeins had 2 and the sokemen 2. We want to
know whether the second of these estates is under-teamed or
over-teamed. There is land for 6 teams and there are 6 teams
on it; but 2 of these teams belong to villeins and 2 to sokemen.
If we give the villeins but 4 oxen to the team, how many shall
we give the sokemen? Shall we say 6? If so, there are
36 oxen here. Is that too many or too few or just enough for
the arable land that there is? That is an unanswerable
question, for the king's commissioners have been content with
the statement that the number of oxen appropriate to this
estate lies somewhere between 23 and 49.

Surely when we are told that 8 sokemen have '2 teams and
6 oxen' or that 9 sokemen and 5 bordiers have '3 teams and
7 oxen[2],' we are being told that the teams in question have no
less than eight oxen apiece. Surely when we are told that
there are 23 villeins and 5 bordiers with 2 teams and 5 oxen[3],
we are being told that the teams of these villeins are not teams
of four. And what are we to say of cases in which a certain
number of teams is ascribed to a number of persons who belong
to various classes, as for example when 6 villeins and 7 bordiers
and 2 sokemen are said to have 3 teams and 5 oxen[4], or where
3 villeins, 2 bordiers, a priest and a huntsman are said to have
one team and 6 oxen[5], or where 19 radknights 'with their men'
are said to have 48 teams[6]? Even if we suppose that the
officers of the exchequer have tables which tell them how many

The villeins' teams.

Ibid. i. 223 : 'Terra est 1 car. *quam* habent ibi 4 bordarii.' Ibid. i. 107 b : 'Terra
est 7 car. et *tot* ibi sunt.'
[1] D. B. i. 222, Codestoche, Lidintone.
[2] D. B. i. 289 ; 339 b, Bechelinge. [3] D. B. i. 342 b, Toresbi.
[4] D. B. i. 339, Agetorne. [5] D. B. i. 174, Lappewrte.
[6] D. B. i. 163, Berchelai.

oxen a *caruca* implies when it is attributed to a Northampton-shire sokeman or a Gloucestershire radknight, we are still setting before them insoluble problems. The radknights of Berkeley 'with their men' have 48 teams:—this may cover less than 200 or more than 300 oxen. And yet the record that is guilty of this laxity will tell us how in Bedfordshire *Terra est dimidio bovi, et ibi est semibos*[1].

The main argument that has been urged in favour of a variable *caruca* is that which, basing itself on later documents, protests that a villein ought not to have more than two oxen[2]. Now true it seems to be that if by the number of the teams belonging to the *villani* and *bordarii* of Domesday Book we divide the number of *villani* plus half the number of *bordarii* (and this would be a fair procedure), we shall obtain as our quotient a figure that will be much nearer to 2 than to 4. But it must be common ground to all who read our record that some villeins are much better supplied with oxen than are their neighbours, and that some villeins have whole teams, whatever a 'team' may mean. There is so much difference in this respect between manor and manor that we are not justified in talking of any particular number of oxen as the normal outfit of the *villanus*, and outside of Domesday Book we have far too little evidence to sanction the dogma that the average number must stand close to 2[3]. Even the villein virgater on the monastic manors of the thirteenth century is often expected to have four oxen, and his having eight is a possibility that must be contemplated[4].

The villeins' oxen.

[1] D. B. i. 218 b, Stanford. Or let us take this case (D. B. i. 148): 'Terra est 3 car. In dominio est una et 4 villani habent aliam et tercia potest fieri.' Is this third team to be a team of four or a team of eight?

[2] Seebohm, Village Community, 85.

[3] As a specimen we take 10 consecutive entries from the royal demesne in Surrey in which it is said that x villeins and y bordiers have z teams. We add half of y to x and divide the result by z. The quotients are 10·3, 4·0, 3·7, 3·5, 3·4, 2·7, 2·2, 1·9, 1·8, 1·4. If we massed the ten cases together, the quotient would be 2·8. We can easily find averages; but, even if we omit cases in which there is an exceptional dearth of oxen, the variations are so considerable that we must not speak of a type or norm.

[4] Glastonbury Rentalia, 51–2: 'S. tenet 1 virgatam terre.. et si habet 8 boves debet warectare...7 acras. Si autem pauciores habet, warectabit pro unoquoque bove octavam partem 7 acrarum.' Ibid. 61: 'R. C. tenet unam virgatam...et habebit 4 boves cum bobus domini.' Ibid. 68: 'G. tenet dimidiam hidam...et si habuerit 8 boves...' Ibid. 78: 'L. tenet 5 acras...et bis debet venire cum 1 bove et cum pluribus si habuerit...' Ibid. 98–9: 'M. tenet 1

That light as well as heavy ploughs were in use we have not Light and denied. At a little later time we see teams of six beasts and heavy ploughs. teams of ten engaged in ploughing. But the compilers of Domesday Book are not concerned with the methods of husbandry; they are registering the number of oxen. If a man has one ox which is employed as a beast of the plough, they say of him: *Arat cum uno bove*[1]. If he and another man have such an ox between them, they say: *Ibi est semibos.* If he has four oxen, they set this down as *dimidia caruca.* Instead of telling us that there are thirty-eight oxen, they speak of five teams less two oxen[2]. Twelve pence make a shilling; and, at all events at the Exchequer, eight oxen make a team.

Very lately an argument has been advanced in favour of a The team caruca, the strength of which varies from place to place. In day and many instances the Black Book of Peterborough in its de-other documents. scription of the abbatial estates will give to the demesne of a particular manor exactly the same number of teams that are ascribed to it by Domesday Book, and, while in some cases the later of these documents will tell us that there are eight oxen to the team, in others it will speak of teams of six[3]. That there is force in this argument we must admit; but many changes will take place in forty years, and we can not think that the correspondence between the two documents is sufficiently close to warrant the inference that the *caruca* of Domesday can have fewer beasts than eight. An exactly parallel argument would serve to prove that the hide of Domesday contains a variable number of fiscal 'acres.' Were it possible (but we shall see that it is not) for us to regard the teamland of Domesday as a fixed area, then we might afford to allow the strength of the team to vary; but if the teamland is no fixed area and the team has no fixed strength, then King William's inquest ends in a collection of unknown quantities.

---

virgatam...si habuerit quatuor boves...' Ibid. 129: ' S. tenet 1 virgatam...et debet invenire domino 1 carrum et 6 boves ad cariandum fenum.' Ibid. 130 : ' M. tenet dimidiam virgatam...et debet invenire 2 boves.' Ibid. 189 : Three cases in which a virgater comes to the boon days with eight oxen. Larking, Domesday of Kent, App. 33 : Customs of Hedenham : '...habebit unam virgatam terrae...item habebit quatuor boves in pasturam domini.'

[1] D. B. i. 211 : ' Terra est dim. car. et unus bos ibi arat.'
[2] D. B. i. 342 b, Toresbi.
[3] Pollock, E. H. R. xi. 813. I venture to think that Sir F. Pollock has not answered his own argument (p. 220) for a constant *caruca*.

The team-land. We turn from the team (*C*) to the teamland (*B*), and must face some perplexing questions. Reluctantly we have come to the opinion that this term 'the land of (or for) one team' does not in the first instance denote a fixed areal quantity of arable land. We have adopted this opinion reluctantly because we are differing from some of the best expositors of our record, and because it compels us to say that many of the statistical data with which that record provides us are not so useful as we hoped that they would be.

Fractional parts of the teamland. In the first place, we must notice that if this term stands for a fixed quantity, a very rude use is being made of it. We see indeed that fractional parts of a teamland can be conceived. We often meet the land of (or for) half a team; we may come upon the land of or for two oxen, one ox, half an ox. But, except in a few counties, any mention of fractions smaller than the half of a team is rare, and even halves seldom occur. Now certainly the teamland was a large unit for such treatment as this. If, for instance, we suppose that it contained 120 acres, then we must infer that in some shires the jurors who had to describe a mass of 420 acres would have called it land for 3 or else land for 4 teams, and that in most shires an odd 30 acres would have been neglected or would have done duty as half a teamland. The hides or the carucates (*A*) have often been split into small fractions where the jurors distribute integral team-lands. One example of this common phenomenon shall be given. In Grantchester lie six estates[1]:

> the first rated at 3 v. has land for 1 team,
> the second rated at 2 h. 3 v. has land for 6 teams,
> the third rated at 2 h. 3 v. has land for 4 teams,
> the fourth rated at 1½ v. has land for 1 team,
> the fifth rated at 1 v. has land for 4 oxen,
> the sixth rated at ½ v. has land for 3 oxen.

The teamland does not break up easily. As a general rule, we only hear of fractional parts of it when the jurors are compelled to deal with a tenement so small that it can not be said to possess even one teamland[2].

[1] Inq. Com. Cant. 70.

[2] Another example from a Northamptonshire column (D. B. i. 226) will show what we mean. Let H stand for hides and T for teamlands, and let the virgate be a quarter of a hide, then we have this series: 2 H (5 T), 2½ H (4 T), 4 H (8 T), 1¼ H (3 T), 1 7/12 H (4 T), ⅜ H (½ T), ¼ H (1 T), 2½ H (6 T), 1¼ H (3 T), 2 H (4 T), ⅞ H (3 T). We see that T is integral where H is fractional.

In passing we observe that this phrase, 'There is land for *x* teams' finds exact parallels in two other phrases that are not very uncommon, namely, 'There is pasture for *y* sheep' and 'There is wood for *z* pigs': also that the values given to *y* and *z* are often large and round. It may be that the jurors have in their minds equations which connect the area of a wood or pasture with its power of feeding swine or sheep, but an extremely lax use must be made of these equations when the number of sheep is fixed at a neat hundred or the number of pigs at a neat thousand, nor dare we say that the quality of the grass and trees has no influence upon the computation. *Land for oxen and wood for swine.*

Secondly, we observe that the teamland when it does break into fractional parts does not break into virgates, bovates, acres, roods, or any other units which we can regard as units in a scheme of areal measurement[1]. The eighth of a teamland is the land of (or for) an ox. If we wish to speak of the sixteenth of a teamland, we must introduce the half-ox. Now had the jurors been told to state the quantity of the arable land comprised in a tenement, they had at their command plenty of words which would have served this purpose. No sooner will they have told us that there is land for two teams, than they will add that there are five acres of meadow and a wood which is three furlongs in length by two in breadth. We infer that they have not been asked to state the area of the arable. They have been asked to say something about it, but not to state its area. *Teamland no areal unit.*

What had they been asked to say? Here we naturally turn to that well-known introduction to the Inquisitio Eliensis which professes to describe the procedure of the commissioners and which at many points corresponds with the contents of Domesday Book[2]. We read that the barons made inquiry about the number of the hides (*A*) and the number of the teams (*C*); we do not read any word about the teamlands (*B*). *Quot hidae* they must ask; *Quot carucae*[3] *in dominio et quot hominum* they must ask; *Quot carucis ibi est terra*—there is no *The commissioners and the teamlands.*

---

[1] Exceptionally we read in Kent (i. 9): 'Terra est dim. car. et ibidem sunt adhuc 30 acrae terrae.' And is not this a rule-proving exception? The jurors can not say simply 'land for half a team and thirty acres.' They say 'land for half a team and there are thirty acres in addition.'

[2] D. B. iv. 497; Inq. Com. Cant. 97.

[3] There can be little doubt that this is the right reading. See Round, *Feudal England*, 134.

such question. On the other hand, the jurors are told to give all the particulars thrice over (*hoc totum tripliciter*), once with reference to King Edward's day, once with reference to the date when the Conqueror bestowed the manor, and once with reference to the present time.

The team-lands of Great Domesday.

Now, if these be the interrogatories that the justiciars administered to the jurors, then the answering verdicts as they are recorded in Great Domesday err both by defect and by excess. On the one hand, save when they are dealing with the geld or the value of a tenement, they rarely give any figures from King Edward's day, and still seldomer do they speak about the date of the Conqueror's feoffments. Our record does not systematically report that whereas there are now four teams on this manor, there were five in the Confessor's reign and three when its new lord received it. On the other hand, we obtain the apparently unasked for information that ' there is land for five teams.'

The teams of Little Domesday.

We turn to Little Domesday and all is altered. Here the words of the writ seem to be punctually obeyed. The particulars are stated three times over, the words *tunc, post* and *modo* pointing to the three periods. Thus we learn how many teams there were when Edward was living and when the Conqueror gave the land away. On the other hand, we are not told how many teams 'could till' that land, though if the existing teams are fewer than those that were ploughing in time past, it will sometimes be remarked that the old state of things could be 'restored[1]'.

The Leicestershire formulas.

Next we visit Leicestershire. We may open our book at a page which will make us think that the account of this shire will be very similar to those reports that are typical of Great Domesday. We read that Ralph holds four carucates; that there is land for four teams; that there are two teams on the demesne while the villeins have two[2]. But then, alternating

[1] Thus, D. B. ii. 39: 'Tunc 4 carucae in dominio, post et modo 2...et 2 carucae possunt restaurari.' To use our symbols, in Essex, Norfolk and Suffolk we obtain statements about *A* and about *C*, but learn nothing about *B*, unless this is to be inferred from the increase or decrease that has taken place in *C*. We shall hereafter argue that, in spite of some appearances to the contrary, the carucates of East Anglia belong to the order *A* and not to the order *B*.

[2] Thus, D. B. i. 231: 'Rad. tenet de episcopo 4 car. terrae in Partenei. Terra est 4 car. In dominio sunt 2 et...villani habent 2 car.' Just before this

with entries which run in this accustomed form, we find others which, instead of telling us that there is land for so many teams, will tell us that there were so many upon it in the time of King Edward[1]. Perhaps, were this part of the survey explored by one having the requisite knowledge, he would teach us that the jurors of some wapentakes use the one formula while the other is peculiar to other wapentakes; but, as the record stands, the variation seems due to the compiling clerk. Be that as it may, we can hardly read through these Leicestershire entries without being driven to believe that substantially the same piece of information is being conveyed to us now in one and now in the other of two shapes that in our eyes are dissimilar. To say, 'There were four teams here in King Edward's day' is much the same as to say, 'There is land here for four teams.' Conversely, to say, 'There is land here for four teams' is much the same as to say, 'There were four teams here in King Edward's day.' For an exact equivalence we must not contend; but if the commissioners get the one piece of information they do not want the other. On no single occasion, unless we are mistaken, are both put on record[2].

When we have thought over these things, we shall perhaps fashion for ourselves some such guess as that which follows. The original scheme of the Inquest was unnecessarily cumbrous. The design of collecting the statistics of the past broke down. Let us imagine a similar attempt made in our own day. Local

Origin of the inquiry about the team-lands.

we have the other common formula: 'Rad. tenet...2 car. terrae in Toniscote. Duae car. possunt esse et ibi sunt.'

[1] Thus, D. B. i. 231 b: 'Ipsa Comitissa tenuit Dunitone. Ibi 22 car. et dimid. T. R. E. erant ibi 12 car. Modo in dominio sunt 3 et...villani...habent 12 car.'

[2] To me it looks as if the variations were due to a clerk's caprice. The Leicestershire survey fills 30 columns. Not until the top of col. 5 has the compiler, except as a rare exception, the requisite information. Then, after hesitating as to whether he shall adopt the '*x* car. possunt esse' formula, he decides in favour of 'Terra est *x* car.' This we will call Formula I. It reigns throughout cols. 5-13, though broken on three or four occasions by what we will call Formula II, namely 'T. R. E. erant ibi *x* car.' At the top of col. 14 Formula II. takes possession and keeps it into col. 16. Then I. has a short turn. Then (col. 17) II. is back again. Then follow many alternations. At the top of col. 24, however, a simplified version of II. appears; the express reference to the T. R. E. vanishes, and we have merely 'ibi fuerunt *x* car.' In the course of col. 26 this is changed to 'ibi *x* car. fuerunt.' These two versions of II. prevail throughout the last six columns, though there is one short relapse to I. (col. 28).

juries are summoned to swear communal verdicts about the number of horses and oxen that the farmers were keeping twenty years ago. Roughly, very roughly true would such verdicts be, although no foreign invasion, no influx of alien men and words and manners divides us from the fortieth year of Queen Victoria. In Essex, Norfolk and Suffolk some sort of answer about these matters was extracted from the jurors; but frequently they report that the arrangements which exist now have always existed, and by this they mean that they cannot remember any change. Now, when we fail to find in Great Domesday any similar figures, we may ascribe this to one of two causes. Either the commissioners did not collect statistics, or the compilers did not think them worthy of preservation. In some cases the one supposition may be true, in other cases the other. We may be fairly certain that in many or all counties the horses and the pigs and the 'otiose animals' that were extant in 1086 were enumerated in the verdicts[1]. Also we know that Domesday Book is no mere transcript, but is an abstract or digest, and we have cause for believing that those who made it held themselves free to vary the phrases used by the jurors, provided that no material change was thus introduced[2]. Howbeit, to come to the question that is immediately before us, our evidence seems to tell us that the commissioners and their master discovered that the original programme of the inquest was unnecessarily cumbrous. Once and again in more recent days has a similar discovery been made by royal commissioners. So some interrogatories were dropped.

Modification of the inquiry.

Then we suspect that the inquiry about the number of oxen that were ploughing in Edward's day became a more practicable, if looser, inquiry about the number of oxen capable of tilling the land. The transition would not be difficult. What King William really wants to know is the agricultural capacity of the tenement. He learns that there are now upon it so many beasts of the plough. But this number may be accidentally large or accidentally small. With an eye to future taxation, he wishes for figures expressive of the normal condition of things. But, according to the dominant idea of his

---

[1] The proof of this lies in the Inq. Com. Cant. and the Exon Domesday.

[2] This appears on a collation of D.B. with the two records mentioned in our last note. See Round, Feudal England, 26.

reign, the normal condition of things is their Edwardian condition, that in which they stood before the usurper deforced the rightful heir. And so these two formulas which we see alternating in the account of Leicestershire really do mean much the same thing: 'There is land for x teams': 'There were x teams in the time of King Edward.'

But if we suppose the justices abandoning the question 'How many teams twenty years ago?' in favour of 'How many teams can there be?' we see that, though they are easing their task and enabling themselves to obtain answers in the place of silence, they are also substituting for a matter of pure fact what may easily become a matter of opinion. They have left the actual behind and are inquiring about potentialities. They will now get answers more speedily; but who eight centuries afterwards will be able to analyze the mental processes of which these answers are the upshot? It is possible that a jury sets to work with an equation which connects oxen with area, for example, one which tells that a team can plough 120 acres. It is but too possible that this equation varies from place to place and that the commissioners do not try to prevent variations. They are not asking about area; they are asking about the number of teams requisite for the tillage of the tenement. With this and its value as data, William's ministers hope to correct the antiquated assessments. Some of the commissioners may allow the jurors to take the custom of the district as a guide, while others would like to force one equation on the whole country. Our admiration for Domesday Book will be increased, not diminished, if we remember that it is the work not of machines but of men. Some of the justices seem to have thought that the inquiry about potential teams (B) was not of the first importance, not nearly so important as the inquiries about actual teams (C) and gelding units (A). In various counties we see many entries in which *Terra est* is followed by a blank space. In Gloucester, Worcester and Hereford we find no systematic mention of teamlands, but only occasional reports which show that at certain places there might be more teams than there are. At the end of the account of the Bishop of Worcester's triple hundred of Oswaldslaw (an account so favourable to St Mary that it might have been dictated by her representative) we find the remark that in none of these manors could there be any more

Inquiry as to potential teams.

teams than now are there[1].   The bishop, who fully understands
the object of the inquest, does not mean to have his assessment
raised, and the justices are compelled to take the word of
jurors every one of whom is the vassal of S[t]. Mary.

Normal
relation
between
teams and
team-
lands.
We know so little as to the commissioners' intentions, in
particular so little as to any design on their part to force upon
the whole country some one equation connecting oxen with
area, that the task which is set before us if we would explain
the relation between the number of the teams (C) and the
number of the teamlands (B) that we find in a given county
is sometimes an intricate and perhaps insoluble problem.   If
England be taken as a whole, the two numbers will stand
very close to each other.   In some counties, for example in
Lincolnshire, if at the foot of each page we add up the particulars, we shall long remain in doubt whether B or C will be
the greater when our final sum is made.   In county after county
we shall find a large number of entries in which $B = C$, and,
though there will always be some cases in which, the tenement
being waste, C descends to zero, and others in which C is less
than B, still the deficiency will be partially redressed by
instances in which B falls short of C.   On the whole, the
relation between the two is that which we might expect.
Often there is equality; often the variation is small; but an
excess on the part of B is commoner than an excess on the
part of C, and when the waste teamlands have been brought
into the account, then in most counties B will usually exceed
C by 10 per cent. or little more.   There are, however, some
marked and perplexing exceptions to this rule[2].

As we pass through the southern counties from east to west,
the ratio borne by the teamlands to the teams steadily increases,
until ascending by leaps it reaches 1.43 : 1 (or thereabouts) in
Devon and 2 : 1 in Cornwall.   Now to all seeming we are not
in a country which has recently been devastated; it is not like
Yorkshire; we find no large number of 'waste' or unpopulated
or unvalued estates.   Here and there we may see a tenement
which has as many teams as it has teamlands; but in the

---

[1] D. B. i. 174 : 'In omnibus his maneriis non possunt esse plus carucae
quam dictum est.'

[2] When C varies from B, the statement about C will sometimes be introduced
by a *sed* or a *tamen* which tells us that things are not what they might be
expected to be.   D. B. i. 77 b : 'Terra est dimid. car. et tamen est ibi 1 car.'
D. B. i. 222 : 'Terra est dim. car. tamen 2 villani habent 1 car.'

great majority of cases the preponderance of teamlands is steadily maintained. What does this mean? One conceivable explanation we may decidedly reject. It does not mean a relatively scientific agriculture which makes the most of the ox. Nor does it mean a fertile soil[1]. Our figures seem to show that men are sparse and poor; also they are servile. We suspect their tillage to be of that backward kind which ploughs enormous tracts for a poor return. *Arva per annos mutant et superest ager.* Of the whole of the land that is sometimes ploughed, they sow less than two-thirds or a half in any one year: perhaps they sow one-third only, so that of the space which the royal commissioners reckon as three teamlands two-thirds are always idle. We must remember that in modern times the husbandry that prevailed in Cornwall was radically different from that which governed the English open fields. It was what the agrarian historians of Germany call a *Feldgrasswirtschaft*[2]. That perhaps is the best explanation which we can give of this general and normal excess of teamlands over teams. But to this we may add that systems of mensuration and assessment which fitted the greater part of England very well, may have fitted Devon, Cornwall and some other western counties very badly[3]. Those systems are the outcome of villages and spacious common fields where, without measurement, you count the 'acres' and the plough-lands or house-lands, and they refuse to register with any accuracy the arrangements of the Celtic hamlets, or rather *trevs* of the west.

[1] As a wheat-grower Devon stands in our own day at the very bottom of the English counties. Its average yield per acre in 1885–95 was 21 bushels, while Cambridge's was 32. Next above Devon stands Monmouth and then comes Cornwall.

[2] Marshall, Review of Reports to Board of Agriculture from Southern Departments, 524: 'The management of the land is uniform; here and there an exception will be found. The whole is convertible, sometimes into arable, and sometimes pasture. Arable is sown with wheat, barley, or oats, as long as it will bear any; and then grass for eight or ten years, until the land is recovered, and capable again of bearing corn.' See also p. 531: the lands go back to the waste 'in tenfold worse condition than [that wherein] they were in a state of nature.' It is just in the country which is not a country of village communities that we find this 'aration of the waste.'

[3] Some parts of Worcestershire, for example, show a marked deficiency in oxen. On the lands of Osbern Fitz Richard (14 entries) there are about 102 teams, and there 'could be' 32 more. See D. B. i. 176 b. In some parts of Cheshire also there is a great deficiency.

  It is by no means impossible that when the commissioners came to a county which was very sparsely peopled (and in Cornwall each 'recorded man' might have had near 160 acres of some sort or another all to himself) their question about the number of teamlands or about the number of teams 'that could plough there' became a question about remote possibilities, rather than about existing or probable arrangements, and that the answer to it became mere guesswork. On one occasion in Cornwall they are content with the statement that there is land for 'fifteen or thirty teams[1].' In the description of a wasted tract of Staffordshire we see six cases close together in which two different guesses as to the number of the potential teamlands are recorded[2] :—'There is land for two teams'; but 'or three' is interlined. Five times 'or two' is written above 'one.' Now this is of importance, for perhaps we may see in it the key to the treatment that wasted Yorkshire receives. How much arable land is there in this village? Well, if by 'arable land' you mean land that is ploughed, there is none. If you do not mean this, if you are speaking of a 'waste' vill where no land has been ploughed these fifteen years, then you must be content with a speculative answer[3]. If the ruined cottages were rebuilt and inhabited, if oxen and men were imported, then employment might be found for four or five teams. Called to speculate about these matters, the Yorkshire jurors very naturally catch hold of any solid fact which may serve as a base for computations. This fact they seem to find in the geld assessment. This estate is rated to the geld at two carucates; the assessment seems tolerably fair; so they say that two teams would plough the land. Or again, this estate is rated to the geld at four carucates; but its assessment is certainly too high, so let it be set down for two teamlands[4].

---

[1] D. B. i. 122 b: 'Luduham...Terra 15 car. vel 30 car.' In the Exeter book (D. B. iv. 240) two conflicting estimates are recorded : ' Luduam...In ea sunt 3 hidae terrae et reddidit gildum pro 1 hida. hanc possunt arare 15 carrucae. hanc tenet Ricardus de Comite. in ea sunt 3 hidae terrae et reddidit gildum pro 1 hida. hanc possunt arare 30 carrucae. hanc tenet Ricardus de Comite.'   [2] D. B. i. 246 b.

[3] Often a Yorkshire entry touching a waste vill gives no B. Therefore in my Tables I have omitted the number of the Yorkshire teamlands, lest hasty inferences should be drawn from it. I believe it falls between 5000 and 6000. It is much smaller than A, much greater than C.

[4] Be it remembered that these waste vills can not send deputations to meet

Even in other parts of the country the jurors may sometimes avail themselves of this device. In particular there are tracts in which they are fond of reporting that the number of teamlands is just equal to $(B = A)$ or just twice as great $(B = 2A)$ as the number of gelding carucates. We very much fear, though the ground for this fear can not be explained at this stage of our inquiry, that the figure which the jurors state when questioned about potential teams is sometimes dictated by a traditional estimate which has been playing a part in the geld assessment, and that the number of teamlands is but remotely connected with the agrarian arrangements of 1086. All our other guesses therefore must be regarded as being subject to this horrible suspicion, of which we shall have more to say hereafter[1].

This makes it difficult for us to construe the second great aberration from the general rule that the number of the teamlands in a county will slightly exceed the number of teams. In Derby and Nottingham apparent 'understocking' becomes the exception and 'overstocking' the rule. In Derby there is a good deal of 'waste' where we have to reckon teamlands but no teams, and yet on many pages the number of teams is the greater $(C > B)$. In Nottingham there seem to be on the average near 200 teams where there are but 125 teamlands. In many columns of the Lincolnshire survey, and therefore perhaps in some districts of that large and variegated county, the teams have a majority, though, if we have not blundered, they are beaten by the teamlands when the whole shire has been surveyed. It is very possible that a similar phenomenon would have been recorded in Essex and East Anglia if the inquiry in those counties had taken the form that was usual elsewhere, for the teams seem to be thick on the land. Now to interpret the steady excess of teams that we see in Derby and Nottingham is not easy. We can hardly suppose that the jurors are confessing that they habitually employ a superfluity of oxen. Perhaps, however, we may infer that in

The land of excessive teams.

the justices, and that the representatives of the wapentakes may never have seen some of those deserts of which they have to speak. 'All of these vills,' they say on one occasion (i. 301), 'belong to Preston. In sixteen of them there are a few inhabitants; but how many we do not know. The rest are waste.'

[1] See below, p. 471.

this district a given area of land will be ploughed by an
unusually large number of teams, whereas in Devon and Cornwall a given area will be ploughed, though intermittently, by
an unusually small number. In every way the contrast between
Devon and Cornwall on the one hand, Lincoln, Nottingham
and Derby on the other, is strongly marked. Of the quality of
soils something should, no doubt, be said which we are too
ignorant to say. An acre would yield more corn in Nottingham
and Derby, to say nothing of Lincoln, than in Devon and
Cornwall, though the *valets* that we find in the three Danish
shires are by no means so high as those that are displayed by
some of the southern counties. But if we ask how many
households our average teamland is supporting, then among
all the counties that we have examined Lincoln, Nottingham
and Derby stand at the very top, while Devon and Cornwall
stand with the depopulated Stafford at the very bottom of the
list[1]. Then, again, we see the contrasts between village and
trev, between Dane and Celt, between sokeman and slave.
Possibly Northampton, Derby and parts of Lincoln really are
'over-teamed': that is to say, were the land of these counties
to come to the hands of lords who held large and compact
estates, the number of plough-teams would be reduced. Where
there is freedom there will be some waste. The tenements
split into fractions, and the owner of a small piece must keep
oxen enough to draw a plough or trust to the friendliness and
reciprocal needs of his neighbours. Manorialism has this
advantage : it can make the most of the ox. Another possible
guess is that the real carucates and bovates of this district
(by which we mean the units which locally bear these names
and which are the units in the proprietary or tenurial scheme)
have few acres, fewer than would be allowed by some equation
which the royal commissioners for these counties carry in their
minds. Being assured (for example) that the bovates in a
certain village or hundred have few acres, they may be allowing
the jurors to count as three team-lands ('of imperial measure')

---

[1] Devon, 2·1; Cornwall, 2·2; Derby, 3·9; Nottingham, 4·4; Lincoln, 5·0.
The figure for Stafford is about as low as that for Cornwall; but Stafford has
been devastated. See Eyton, Staffordshire, 30. Kent and Surrey would stand
high. Kent would perhaps stand as high as Derby. But Lincoln has no peer,
unless it be Norfolk, Suffolk, or Essex. Our reason for not speaking of these
last three counties will appear by and by.

a space of arable that has been locally treated as four. So, after all, the rule that normally each teamland should have its team and that each team should till its teamland may be holding good in these counties, though the proprietary and agrarian units have differed from those that the commissioners treat as orthodox.

One last guess is lawful after what we have seen in Leicestershire. These Nottinghamshire folk may be telling how many teams there were in King Edward's time and recording a large increase in the number of oxen and therefore perhaps in the cultivated area. In this case, however, we should expect to find the *valet* greater than the *valuit*, while really we find that a fall in value is normal throughout the shire. *Attempts to explain the excess of teams.*

We must here say one parenthetical word about the account of East Anglia. In one respect it differs from the account of any other district[1]. We are told of the various landholders that they hold so many carucates or so many acres. Analogy would lead us to suppose that this is a statement touching the amount of geld with which they are charged. Though there is no statement parallel to the *Terra est b carucis* which we find in most parts of England, still there are some other counties remote from East Anglia—Gloucester, Worcester, Hereford—where no such statement is given to us. In other words, a natural first guess would be that in Norfolk and Suffolk we are informed about A and not about B. But then, it is apparent that some information about A is being given to us by a quite different formula such as we shall not meet outside East Anglia. We are told about a vill that when the hundred pays 20*s.* for the geld this vill pays so many pence— seven pence halfpenny, it may be, or eight pence three farthings. This is the formula which prescribes how much geld the landholders of the vill must pay and it says nothing of carucates or of acres. Now this might make us think that the carucates and acres which are attributed to the landholders are 'real' and not 'rateable' areas, and are to be put on a level with the teamlands (B) rather than with the hides or gelding carucates (A) of other counties. Nevertheless, on second thoughts we *Digression to East Anglia.*

---

[1] An essay by Mr W. J. Corbett which I had the advantage of seeing some time ago, and which will I hope soon be in print, will throw much new light on this matter.

may return to our first opinion. If these carucates are equivalent to the teamlands of other counties, Norfolk and Suffolk not only differ but differ very widely from the rest of England[1]. In Norfolk we make about 2,422 carucates and about 4,853 teams, and, however wide of the mark these figures may be[2], the fact that there are upon an average about two teams to every carucate is apparent on page after page of the record; often the ratio is yet higher. We have seen a phenomenon of the same kind, though less pronounced, in Nottingham; but then, if in Norfolk we proceed to divide the 'recorded population' by the number of carucates, we shall get 11 as our quotient. This is so very much higher than anything that we have seen elsewhere that we are daunted by it; for, even though we recall the possibility that a good many tenants in this free county are counted twice because they hold under two lords, still this reflection will hardly enable us to make the requisite allowance. To this it may be added that if we divide the acreage of Norfolk by its carucates and treat the carucates as teamlands, the quotient will place Norfolk among the counties in which the smallest part of the total area was under the plough. Further, it will be observed that the statement about the geldability of the vills does not enable us to bring home any particular sum to any given man. Be it granted that the sum due from a vill is fixed by the proposition that it contributes thirteen pence to every pound levied from the hundred, we have still to decide how much Ralph and how much Roger, two landholders of the vill, must contribute; and our decision will, we take it, be dictated by the statement that

[1] I have roughly added up the carucates and teams of Norfolk, a laborious task, and have seen reason to believe that the figures for Suffolk would be of the same kind.

[2] In dealing with Essex, Norfolk and Suffolk an equation connecting the hide or (as the case may be) carucate with the acre becomes of vast importance. I have throughout assumed that 120 acres make the hide or carucate. If this assumption, about which something will be said hereafter, is unjustified, my whole computation breaks down. Then in Norfolk there are (especially I think in certain particular hundreds) a good many estates for which no extent (real or rateable) is given. I have made no allowance for this. On the other hand, I believe that I have carried to an extreme in Norfolk the principle of including everything. I doubt, for example, whether some of the acres held by the parish churches have not been reckoned twice over. Also both in Essex and Norfolk I reckoned in the lands that are mentioned among the *Invasiones*, and in so doing ran the danger of counting them for a second time.

Ralph has one carucate and Roger 60 acres. We fear therefore that here again we can not penetrate through the rateable to the real[1].

About the 'land for one team' we can hardly get beyond vague guesswork, and may seriously doubt whether the inquiry as to the number of possible ploughs was interpreted in the same manner in all parts of the country. Here it may have been regarded as a reference to the good old time of King Edward, here to the local custom; there an attempt may have been made to enforce some royal 'standard measure,' and there again men were driven to speculate as to what might happen if a wilderness were once more inhabited. But unless we are mistaken, the first step towards a solution of the many problems that beset us is taken when we perceive that the jurors have not been asked to state the areal extent of the tilled or the tillable land. *The teamland no areal measure.*

Far other, as is well known, was the doctrine of one whom all students of Domesday revere. For Mr Eyton the teamland was precisely 120 of our statute acres[2]. The proof offered of this lies in a comparison of the figures given by Domesday with the superficial content of modern parishes. What seems to us to have been proved is that, if we start with the proposed equation, we shall rarely be brought into violent collision with ascertained facts, and that, when such a collision seems imminent, it can almost always be prevented by the intervention of some plausible hypothesis about shifted boundaries or neglected wastes. More than this has not been done. Always at the end of his toil the candid investigator admits that when he has added up all the figures that Domesday gives for arable, meadow, wood and pasture, the land of the county is by no means exhausted. Then the residue must be set down as 'unsurveyed' or 'unregistered' and guesses made as to its whereabouts[3]. Then further, this method involves theories *Eyton's theory.*

---

[1] Also we may remark that in many respects the survey of Essex is closely akin to the survey of East Anglia; but in Essex nothing is said about the geldability of vills and therefore, unless the Essex hides and acres belong to the order of geldable units (*A*), our record tells us nothing as to the geld of Essex: an unacceptable conclusion.

[2] Dorset, 15, 23–24.

[3] In Dorset 22,000 acres are 'designedly omitted'; in Somerset nearly 178,000; in Staffordshire nearly 246,000. Mr C. S. Taylor puts the deficiency in Gloucestershire at 200,000 or thereabouts.

about lineal and superficial measurements which are, in our eyes, precarious.

One word about this point must be said, though we can not devote much room to it. The content of various spaces, such as woods and pastures, is often indicated by a reference to linear standards, leagues, furlongs, perches, feet, and there seems to be little doubt that the main equations which govern the system are these:

$$1 \text{ league} = 12 \text{ furlongs or quarentines or acre-lengths}$$
$$= 480 \text{ perches.}$$

Now we read numerous statements which take the following form:—'It is x leagues (furlongs, perches) long and y wide,' or, to take a concrete example, 'The wood is 1 league long and 4 furlongs wide.' The question arises whether we are justified in making this mean that here is a wood whose superficial content is equal to that of a rectangular parallelogram 480 statute perches long by 160 statute perches wide. We are rash in imposing our perch of 16·5 feet on the whole England of the eleventh century, even though we are to measure arable land. We are rasher in using that perch for the measurement of woodland. But perhaps we are rasher still in supposing that the Domesday jurors have true superficial measurement in their minds[1]. We strongly suspect that they are thinking of shape as well as of size, and may be giving us the extreme diameters of the wood or some diameters that they guess to be near the mean. If a clergyman told us that his parish was 3 miles long by 2 wide, we should not accuse him of falsehood or blunder if we subsequently discovered that in shape it was approximately a right-angled triangle and contained only some 3 superficial miles. And now let us observe how rude these statements are. The Norfolk jurors are in the habit of recording the length and the breadth of the vills. Occasionally they profess to do this with extreme accuracy[2]. However, we reckon that in about 100 out of 550 cases they say that the vill is one league long by a half-league wide. This delightfully symmetrical county therefore should have quite a hundred parishes, each of which contains

---

[1] See above, p. 370.

[2] D. B. ii. 160 b : A certain vill is 1 league 10 perches long, and 1 league 4½ feet wide. Surely such a statement would never come from men who could use and were intending to use a system of superficial measurement.

close upon 720 acres. Among the 800 parishes of modern Norfolk there are not 70 whose size lies between 600 and 800 acres. We are not saying that time spent over these lineal measurements is wasted, but an argument which gets to the size of the teamland by postulating in the first place that our statute perch was commonly used for all purposes throughout England, and in the second that these lineal can be converted into superficial measurements by simple arithmetic, is not very cogent and is apt to become circular, for the teamland contains its 120 acres because that is the space left for it by parochial boundaries when we have measured off the woods and pastures, and our measurement of the woods and pastures is correct because it will leave 120 acres for every teamland.

One more word about these lineal measurements. In Norfolk and Suffolk the total area of the vills is indicated by them, and so it is in Yorkshire also. Now, unless we err, it sometimes happens that if we arithmetically deduce the total area from its recorded length and breadth, and then subtract from that area the content of any measured woods and pastures that there may be, we shall be left with too little space to give each East Anglian carucate or each Yorkshire teamland 120 acres and with far too little to allow a similar area to each East Anglian team. Try one experiment. At Shereford in Norfolk we have to force at least one carucate on which there are two teams into a space that is 3 furlongs in length by 3 in breadth[1]. That means, if our method be sound, that each team has at the utmost 45 acres to till. Try we Yorkshire. There also we shall find entries which to all appearance will not suffer us to give 120 acres to the teamland. Measured team-lands.

> In Andrebi...9 carucates for geld; there may be 6 teams...The whole half a league long and half [a league] wide[2].
> In Hotone and Bileham...a manor of 10 carucates for geld; there may be 10 teams....The whole 10 quarentines long and 8 wide[3].
> In Warlavesbi 6 carucates for geld; there may be 4 teams.... The whole half a league long and half [a league] wide[4].

---

[1] D. B. ii. 170. Or take Westbruge (ii. 206): Two carucates; two teams and a half; 'this vill is 5 furlongs in length by 3 in breadth.' If every inch of the vill is ploughed, the carucate can only have 75 acres, and each team tills but 60. I have noted many cases in which this method will not leave 120 acres for the team.   [2] D. B. i. 310.   [3] D. B. i. 307 b.
[4] D. B. i. 310. In these Yorkshire cases it is needless for us to raise the question whether the *totum* that is being measured is the manor or the vill.

It would seem then that in these cases the utmost limit
for the teamland is 60, 80, 90 acres. Then again, there are
a few precious instances in which lineal measures are used
in order to indicate the size of a piece of land the whole of
which is arable. This occurs so rarely that we may fairly
expect something exceptional. The result is bewildering. At
Thetford we hear of land that is half a league long and half
a league wide: 'the whole of this land is arable and 4 teams
can plough it[1].' Here then, but 90 acres are assigned to the
teamland. We journey to Yorkshire and first we will take
an entry which suits the Eytonian doctrine well enough.
'There are 13 carucates of land less one bovate for geld;
8 teams can plough them ... Arable land 10 quarentines long
and equally broad[2].' In this case we have 1000 acres to divide
among 8 teamlands, and this would make each teamland
125 acres:—we could hardly expect a pleasanter quotient.
But on the same page we have an entry which tells of a manor
with 60 carucates and 6 bovates for geld and 35 teamlands
where the 'arable land' is described as being '2 leagues long
and 2 [leagues] wide[3].' This gives nearly 165 acres to the teamland. There are two Lincolnshire entries which, when treated
in a similar way, give 160[4] and 225[5] acres to the teamland.
Then there is a Staffordshire entry which gives no less than
360 acres to each teamland, though it gives only 160 to each
existing team[6]. The suspicion can not but cross our minds

---

[1] D. B. ii. 118 b. [2] D. B. i. 303 b (Yorkshire, Oleslec).

[3] D. B. i. 303 b (Othelai).

[4] D. B. i. 346 b (Bastune); 4 carucates for geld; land for 4 teams; arable
land 8 quar. by 8.

[5] D. B. i. 346 b (Langetof); 6 carucates for geld; land for 6 teams; arable
land 15 quar. long and 9 wide.

[6] D. B. i. 248 b (Rolvestune); 2½ hides; land for 8 teams; 18 teams existing; arable land 2 leagues long and 1 [league] wide. Eyton (Staffordshire,
48) has a long note on this entry which makes against his doctrine that the
teamland is 120 acres. He suggests that the statement by linear measure is a
correction of the previous statement that there is land for 8 teams. Unfortunately, as we have seen, this entry does not stand alone. Morgan, op.
cit. 34, speaks of some of these entries. Those which he mentions and which
we have not noticed do not seem quite to the point. Thus (D. B. i. 263 b)
of Edesberie we read 'land for 6 ploughs...this land is a league long and equally
wide.' We are not here expressly told that all the 'land' thus measured by
lineal measure is arable. The cases of Dictune, Winetun, Grif and Bernodebi,
which he then cites, are beside the mark, for what is here measured by lineal
measure seems to be the whole area of the manor.

that as regards the amount of land that had 8 oxen for its culture there may have been as wide a difference between the various shires in the days of the Confessor as there was in the days of Arthur Young; only, whereas in the eighteenth century a little space ploughed by many oxen was a relic of barbarism, it was in the eleventh an index of prosperity, freedom, a thick population and a comparatively intense agriculture. But theories about the facts of husbandry will not dispel the whole of the fog which shrouds the Domesday teamland.

That, if all England be taken as a whole, the average teamland of Domesday Book would contain about 120 acres seems possible, and since we ourselves are committed to the belief that the old traditional hide had arable acres to this number, it may be advisable that we should examine some districts of ancient England through the medium of the hypothesis that Domesday's teamland has a long-hundred of our statute acres. In Column I. of the following table we place the result obtained if we multiply a county's teamlands (or in the case of Sussex and Gloucester the teams) by 120; and in the following columns we give the figures which show the state of the county in 1895. In order to make a rough comparison the easier, we give round figures and omit three noughts, so that, for example, 371 stands for 371,000 acres[1].

Amount of ploughed land in England.

	Arable in 1086	Arable (1895)	Permanent Pasture (1895)	Mountain and Heath Land used for grazing (1895)	Woods and Plantations (1895)	Total Acreage of Modern County
	1000 Acres	1000 Acres	1000 Acres	1000 Acres	1000 Acres	1000 Acres
Sussex	371	298	381	9	124	933
Surrey	141	133	152	12	54	461
Berkshire	251	204	163	1	36	462
Dorset	280	188	300	18	38	632
Somerset	577	207	653	48	46	1042
Devon	957	581	633	138	86	1667
Buckingham	269	165	236	2	32	476
Oxford	317	228	188	1	27	485
Gloucester	589	269	387	7	58	797
Bedford	187	155	100	1	13	298
Northampton	352	215	344	0	28	640
Lincoln	605	1017	501	2	43	1695

[1] To make safer, I take the Dorset and Somerset teamlands from Eyton, the Gloucester teams from Mr Taylor. In the modern statistics the 'arable' covers

Decrease of arable. These figures are startling enough. We are required to believe that in many counties, even in Sussex where the forest still filled a large space, there were more acres ploughed T. R. W. than are ploughed T. R. V., while in some cases the number has been reduced by one half during the intervening centuries. Were the old acres in Oxfordshire as large as our own, a good deal more than three-fifths of that county was ploughed. Much might be said of the extreme futility of ancient agriculture. Then we should have to remember the 'inclosures' of the sixteenth century; also the movement which in our own day threatens to carry us back to 'the pastoral state[1].' We should have to scrutinize those abundant marks of the plough which occur in our meadows and on our hillsides, even where we least expect them, and to distinguish those which were being made in the days of the Norman conqueror from those which tell of a much later age when 'the Corsican tyrant' threatened our shores.

The food problem. And then there is the great food problem. At this point we might desire the aid of a jury of scientific experts. We are, indeed, but ill prepared to deliver a charge or to define a clear issue, but the main question may be roughly stated thus:—South of Yorkshire and Cheshire we have some 275,000 'recorded men,' some 75,000 recorded teams and (if we allow 120 statute acres to every team) some 9,000,000 statute acres of arable land[2]. Is this supply of arable adequate or excessive for the population? Unfortunately, however, the question involves more than one unknown quantity.

What was the population? In the first place, by what figure are we to multiply the 'bare fallow' and 'grasses under rotation'; the 'permanent pasture' includes 'grass for hay,' but excludes 'mountain and heath land used for grazing'; the total acreage includes everything but 'tidal water.' To bring up the particulars to the total, we should have to add (1) a little for orchards and market gardens, and having thus obtained the sum of all the land that is within the purview of the Board of Agriculture, we should still have to add (2) the sites of towns, houses, factories, etc., (3) tenements of less than an acre whereof no statistics are obtained, (4) roads, railways, etc., (5) waste not used for pasture, rocks, sea-shore, etc., (6) non-tidal water. The area not accounted for by our figures will be smallest in an inland county which has no large towns; it will be raised by sea-shore or by manufacturing industry.

[1] Agricultural Returns, 1895, p. xiii : 'The actual loss of arable area in the interval covered by the last two decades...is 2,137,000 acres.'

[2] Mr Seebohm, Village Community, p. 103, seems to think that D. B. testifies to no more than 5 million acres of arable. But, even if we stop at the Humber, we shall have 9 million if a team tills 120.

number of ' recorded men ' before we shall obtain the total population ? Here we have to remember that nothing is said by our record about some of the largest towns and that the figures which we obtain from Norwich[1] suggest that the inhabitants of London, Winchester and the like should not be neglected, even by those who are aiming at the rudest computation. Then what we read of Bury St Edmunds[2] suggests that around every great abbey were clustered many artificers, servants and bedesmen who as a general rule were not enumerated by the jurors. We must also remember the monks, nuns and canons and the large households of barons and prelates[3]. Again, it is by no means unlikely that, despite a high rate of mortality among children, the household of the ordinary villein was upon an average larger than is the household of the modern cottager or artizan, for the blood-bond was stronger than it is now-a-days. Married brothers with their wives and children may not unfrequently have dwelt in one house and may be described in our record as a single *villanus* because they hold an undivided inheritance. On the other hand, we have seen reason to think that in the eastern villages many men may be counted more than once[4]. Shall we, for the sake of argument, multiply the recorded men by 5 ? This would give us a population of 1,375,000 souls[5].

What portion of the arable land shall we suppose to be sown in any one year ? Some grave doubts may occur to us before we put this portion higher than one half[6]. Common opinion would perhaps strike a balance between two-field and three-field husbandry. So we will suppose that out of 9 million acres 5 million are sown. *What was the field-system?*

Then comes the insoluble question about the acre's yield. Even could we state an average, this would not be very serviceable, for every district had to feed itself in every year, *What was the acre's yield?*

---

[1] D. B. ii. 116 : T. R. E. there were 1320 *burgenses.*

[2] D. B. ii. 372.

[3] It seems probable that in many cases the parish priest is reckoned among the townsmen, the *villani.*

[4] See above, p. 20.

[5] While historical economists can still dispute as to whether the population in 1346 was 5 millions, or only 2½ (Cunningham, Eng. Industry, i. 304) guesses about 1085 are premature. M. Fabre has lately estimated the population of England under Henry II. at 2,880,000. But as to this calculation, see Liebermann, Eng. Hist. Rev. xi. 746.

[6] See above, p. 366.

and the statistics of the later middle ages suggest that the difference between good and bad years was very large, while the valuations of the manors in Domesday Book seem to tell us that the difference between fertile and sterile, forward and backward counties was much wider in the eleventh century than it is in our own day. The scientific agriculturist of the thirteenth century proposed to sow an acre with two bushels of wheat and regarded ten bushels as the proper return[1]. Walter of Henley proved by figures that a three-fold return would not be remunerative, unless prices were exceptionally good, but he evidently thought of this exiguous yield as a possibility[2], and yet, as we have seen, he represents the 'high farming' of his time and in his two-course husbandry would plough the land thrice over between every two crops. In the first half of the next century we can not put the average as high as 8 bushels[3]. To eyes that look for 29 or 30, a yield of from 6 to 10 may seem pitiful; and the 'miserable husbandry' that Arthur Young saw in the west of England was producing from 15 to 20[4]. However, there are countries in which a crop of wheat which gave 10 of our bushels to one of our acres would not be very small[5]. For our present purpose, the figure that we should wish to obtain would be, not that which expressed the yield of an average year, but that which was the outcome of a bad year, for we have to keep folk alive and they can not wait for the good times. Let us then take our hypothesis from Walter of Henley. We suppose a yield of 6 bushels, 2 of which must be retained for seed. This would give us 20 million bushels as food, or, we will say, 15 bushels for every person.

Of beer.

Now, had we to deal with modern wheat and modern mills, we might argue that the bushel of wheat would weigh 60

[1] Walter of Henley, pp. 67, 71.
[2] Walter of Henley, p. 19. [3] Rogers, Hist. Agric. i. 50–1.
[4] Tour in the Southern Counties, ed. 3 (1767), p. 158. See also p. 242.
[5] Agricultural Returns, 1895, p. 239. The figures given under the year 1894 which express the average yield of a statute acre in imperial bushels are for Australasia, 8·18; India, 9·00; Russia in Europe, 10·76; United States, 12·79. Apparently in South Australia 1,577,000 acres can produce as little as 7,781,000 bushels. As I understand, Sir J. B. Lawes and Sir J. H. Gilbert reckon that for an unmanured acre in England 16 bushels would be an average return, but that if the same acre is continuously sown with wheat, the yield will decline at the rate of nearly a quarter of a bushel every year. See Journ. Agricult. Soc., 3rd Ser. vol. iv. p. 87.

pounds, that the weight of flour would be 72 per cent. of the weight of grain[1], and that every human mouth could thus be provided with a little more than 28 ounces of flour every day, or, to put it another way, with bread amounting to nine-sixteenths of a four pound loaf[2]. Some large, but indefinable, deduction should be made from this amount on the score of poor grain and wasteful processes. As the sum stands, we are at present proposing to give to each person a great deal more wheat-flour than would be obtained if the total amount consumed now-a-days in the United Kingdom were divided by the number of its inhabitants[3]. But it need hardly be said that the problem is far more complex than are our figures. In the first place, we have to withdraw from the men of 1086 a large quantity, perhaps more than a half, of the wheat-flour that we have given them in order to supply its place with other cereals[4], in particular with barley and oats, much of which, together with some of the wheat[5], will be consumed in the form of beer. And who shall fathom that ocean? *Multum biberunt de cerevisia Anglicana,* as the pope said. Their choice lay for the more part between beer and water. In the twelfth century the corn-rents paid to the bishop of Durham often comprised malt, wheat and oats in equal quantities[6]. In the next century the economy of the canons of

---

[1] This calculus was officially adopted in 1891; see a paper by Sir J. B. Lawes and Sir J. H. Gilbert in Journ. Agric. Soc., 3rd Ser., vol. iv. p. 102. I desire to express my thanks to the Secretary of the Board of Agriculture for directing my attention to this paper.

[2] I understand that the average number of loaves that can be made from 280 lbs. of flour may be put at about 90.

[3] Agricultural Returns, 1895, pp. 166, 90, 198. The old rough estimate of a quarter of wheat per head is much too high; the average is about 5·65 bushels. See the paper cited in note 1. Now-a-days we can further allot to each inhabitant of the United Kingdom an amount of cereal matter other than wheat, to wit, barley, oats, beans, peas, maize, etc. which would take for its production perhaps as much as 1·5 times the area of the land that is required for the growth of the wheat that we have allotted to him. But much of this only feeds him by feeding animals that he eats; much only feeds him very indirectly by feeding horses engaged in the production or transport of food; and some of it can not be said to feed him at all. Then, on the other hand, large quantities of potatoes, sugar and rice are being eaten.

[4] Wheat, oats, barley and peas are mentioned in D. B.; also rye (i. 257 b).

[5] Hale, Worcester Register, p. civ.

[6] Boldon Book, D. B. iv. 580–5. So in D. B. i. 69 the sheriff of Wiltshire receives equal quantities of wheat and malt and a larger quantity of oats. See also D. B. i. 179 b.

S^t. Paul's was so arranged that for every 30 quarters of wheat
that went to make bread, 7 quarters of wheat, 7 of barley and
32 of oats went to make beer[1]. The weekly allowance of every
canon included 30 gallons[2]. In one year their brewery seems to
have produced 67,814 gallons from 175 quarters of wheat, a like
quantity of barley and 708 quarters of oats[3]. With such figures
before us, it becomes a serious question whether we can devote
less than a third of the sown land to the provision of drink.
The monk, who would have growled if he got less than a gallon
a day, would, we may suppose, consume in the course of a year
20 bushels of barley or an equivalent amount of other grain: in
other words, the produce, when seed-corn is deducted, of from
two to three acres of land; and perhaps to every mouth in
England we must give half a gallon daily[4].

But if we can not make teetotallers of our ancestors (and in
very truth we can not) neither may we convert them to vege-
tarianism. What we can read of the provender-rents paid in
the days before the Conquest suggests that those who were
well-to-do, including the monks, consumed a great deal of
mutton, pork, poultry, fish, eels, cheese and honey[5]. This would
relieve the arable of part of the pressure that it would otherwise
have borne, for, though we already hear of two manors which
between them supply 6000 dog-loaves for the king's hounds[6],

*The Eng-
lishman's
diet.*

[1] Domesday of S^t. Paul's, 164*. See also Cart. Rams. iii. 231.
[2] Ibid. cxxxiv. 173.   [3] Ibid. 173.
[4] Calculations are difficult and may be misleading, not only because of the variability of medieval measures, but also because of the varying strength of beer. Mr Steele, the Chief Inspector of Excise, has been good enough to inform me that a bushel of unmalted barley weighing 42 lbs. would yield about 19·5 gallons of beer at 58°. The figures from S^t. Paul's seem to point to a strong brew, since they apparently derive but 8 gallons from the bushel of mixed grain. The ordinances of cent. xiii. (Statutes, i. 200, 202) seem to suppose that, outside the cities, the brewer, after deducting expenses and profit, could sell 8 to 12 gallons of beer for the price of a bushel of barley. If we suppose that the bushel of barley gives 18 gallons, the man who drinks his gallon a day consumes 20 bushels a year, and when the acre yields but 6 bushels of wheat, it will hardly yield more than 7 of barley. There is valuable learning in J. Bickerdyke, The Curiosities of Ale, pp. 54, 106, 154.
[5] As to both meat and drink see Ine 70, § 1; T. 460, 468, 471, 473, 474; E. 118; Æthelstan, II. 1. § 1; D. B. i. 169, rents of the shrievalty of Wiltshire. Attempts to measure the flood of beer break down before the uncertain content of the *amber, modius, sextarius,* etc. In particular I can not believe that the amber of ale contained (Schmid, p. 530; Robertson, Hist. Essays, 68) 4 of our bushels; but, do all we can to reduce it, the allowance of beer seems large.
[6] D. B. ii. 162 b : Cheltenham and King's Barton.

and also read of pigs that are fattened with corn[1], it is not very probable that any beasts, save those that laboured, got much from the arable, except the straw, and the stubble which we may suspect of having been abundantly mixed with grass and weeds. It is likely, however, that the oxen which were engaged in ploughing were fed at times with oats. Walter of Henley would keep his plough-beasts at the manger for five-and-twenty weeks in the year and would during that time give 70 bushels of oats to every eight of them[2]. At this rate our 75,000 teams would require 5,250,000 bushels of oats, and on this score we might have to deduct some 4 million bushels of wheat[3] from our 20 millions and reduce by one-fifth each person's allowance of grain. But then, it is by no means certain that we ought to transplant Walter's practices into the eleventh century; we have seen that he expected much of his oxen[4].

At first sight it may seem incredible that the average human being annually required the produce of nearly seven acres. But observe how rapidly the area will disappear. We deduct a half for the idle shift; a third of the remainder we set apart as beer-land. We have not much more than two acres remaining, and may yet have to feed oxen and horses. But suppose that we concede to every human mouth the wheat of two full acres; we can not say for certain that we are giving it a quarter of grain, even though we suppose each acre to yield more than was to be had always and everywhere in the fourteenth century[5]. *Is the arable super-abundant?*

Our doubt about the food of the oxen makes it difficult for us to state even the outlines of another important problem. Are we leaving pasture enough for the beasts? Their number was by no means small. South of the southern frontier of Cheshire and Yorkshire we must accommodate in the first place some 600,000 beasts of the plough, and in the second place and for their maintenance a sufficiency of bulls, cows and calves. *Amount of pasturage.*

---

[1] D. B. i. 205. The abbot of Peterborough is bound to find pasture for 120 pigs for the abbot of Thorney. If he can not do this, he must feed and fatten 60 pigs with corn (*de annona pascit et impinguat* 60 *porcos*).

[2] Walter of Henley, 13. Every week each ox is to have 3½ garbs of oats, and 10 garbs would yield a bushel.

[3] Now-a-days the average acre in England will produce about 29 bushels of wheat or 40 of oats. Agricultural Returns, 1895, pp. 66, 70.

[4] See above, p. 398.

[5] Rogers, op. cit. i. 51.

Now-a-days England keeps 4,723,000 head of cattle, but we have been excluding from view near a quarter of England. Then there are other animals to be provided for. Their number we can not guess, for apparently the statistics that we obtain from the south-western and eastern counties give us only the stock that is on the demesne of the manors[1]. We have seen that the peasants in East Anglia had sheep enough to make their 'fold-soke' an important social institution[2]. Also we have much evidence of large herds of pigs belonging to the villeins, though these we may send to the woods. But, attending only to the domirical stock, we will begin by looking at the manor which stands first in the Cambridgeshire Inquest. The lord has 5 teams, 8 head of not-ploughing cattle, 4 rounceys, 10 pigs and 480 sheep. Then, in the accompanying table we will give some figures from various counties which show the amount of stock that is kept where there are 200 teams or thereabouts.

	Teams (Demesne and Tenants')	Beasts not of the Plough	Horses	Goats	Pigs	Sheep
Essex	207	267	34	107	777	1657
Suffolk	200	196	30	295	676	1705
Norfolk	202	132	44	200	672	5673
Dorset	202	159	47	281	479	6160
Somerset	202	82	16	49	198	1506
Devon	205	282	16	135	173	1553
Cornwall	200	62	35	52	26	1445
Total	1418	1180	222	1119	3001	19699

Even if we look only at the flocks which belong to the holders of manors, we may have to feed a million sheep south of the Humber, and, though all England now maintains more than 15 millions, it does this by devoting a large portion of its arable to the growth of turnips and the like. No doubt, the

[1] Clearly so in some cases. See e.g. the first entry in Inq. Com. Cant. The teams of lord and villeins having been mentioned, we then read that the 'pecunia *in dominio*' consists of so many pigs, sheep, etc. Moreover, if all the cattle not of the plough were enumerated under the title *animalia*, there would not be nearly enough to renew the number of beasts of the plough. Again, when the capacity of the wood is stated in terms of the pigs that it will maintain, the number thus given will in general vastly exceed the number of pigs whose existence is recorded. Lastly, we see that at Crediton (iv. 107) where the lord has but 57 pigs, he receives every year 150 pigs from certain *porcarii*, whose herds are not counted. Throughout Sussex the lord takes one pig from every villein who has seven (i. 16 b). See also Morgan, op. cit. 56.

[2] See above, p. 76.

medieval sheep were wretched little animals; also large numbers of them were slaughtered and salted at the approach of
winter; but from the arable they got only the stubble, and
every extension of the ploughed area deteriorated the quality
besides diminishing the quantity of the pasture that was left
for their hungry mouths. As already said, our forefathers did
not live on bread and beer; bacon must have been plentiful
among them[1]. Also many fleeces were needed for their
clothing. As to meadow land (*pratum*), that is, land that was
mown, it was sparse and precious[2]; the supply of it was often
insufficient even for the lord's demesne oxen. At least in
Cambridgeshire, we find traces of a theory which taught that
every ox should have an acre of meadow; but commonly this
was an unrealized ideal[3]. In Dorset now-a-days there will be
near 95,000 acres growing grass for hay, whereas there were
not 7,000 acres of meadow in 1086[4]. Therefore we are throwing
a heavy strain on the pasture[5].

Lastly, we must not neglect, as some modern calculators do, Area of the
the sites of the villages, the straggling group of houses with villages.
their court-yards, gardens and crofts, for this deducts a sensible
piece from the conceivably tillable area. An exceedingly
minute account of Sawston in Cambridgeshire which comes
from the year 1279 shows us a territory thus divided: Messuages, Gardens, Crofts, etc., 85 acres: Arable, 1243 acres:

[1] Before we have gone through a tenth of the account of Essex, we have read
of 'wood for' near 10,000 pigs. If the woods were full and this rate were
maintained throughout the country, the swine of England would be as
numerous T. R. W. as they now are. No doubt Essex was exceptionally
wooded and many woods were understocked; still this mode of reckoning the
capacity of wood-land would only occur to men who were accustomed to see
large herds.

[2] In the thirteenth century it is common to find that the acre of meadow is
deemed to be twice or three times as valuable as the best arable acre of the
same village, and a much higher ratio is sometimes found.

[3] This appears from the parallel account of Westley given in D. B. and
Inq. Com. Cant. (p. 19) where 'pratum 2 bobus'='2 ac. prati.' Entries such
as the following are not uncommon (I. C. C. p. 13): 'Terra est 4 car.; in
dominio est una et villani habent 3 car. Pratum 1 car.' See Morgan, op. cit.
53–5.

[4] Eyton, Dorset, 146.

[5] In the above table all *vaccae*, *animalia* and *animalia ociosa* are reckoned
in the third column. I believe that the two last of these terms cover all beasts of
the bovine race that are not beasts of the plough. The horses are mostly
runcini and are kept for agricultural purposes. It may be doubted whether
destriers and palfreys are enumerated.

Meadow, 82 acres: Several Pasture, 30 acres. The neighbouring village of Whittlesford shows us: Messuages, Gardens, Crofts, etc., 35 acres: Arable, 1363 acres: Meadow, 44 acres: Several Pasture, 35 acres. In both cases we must add some unspecified quantity of Common Pasture[1]. The core of the village was not large when compared with its fields; but it can not be ignored.

Produce and value.

Recurring for a moment to our food problem, we may observe that the values that are set on the manors in Domesday Book seem to point to a very feeble yield of corn. Without looking for extreme cases, we shall often find that the value of a teamland is no more than 10 shillings. Now let us make the hypothesis most favourable to fertility and suppose that this 'value' represents a pure, net rent[2]. We will make another convenient but extravagant assumption; we will say that 24 bushels of wheat will make 365 four-pound loaves. If then a lord is to get one such loaf every day from each teamland that is valued at 10 shillings, the price of wheat will be a good deal less than 5 pence the bushel; if two daily loaves are to be had, the price of the bushel must be reduced below $2\frac{1}{2}$ pence, for the cost of grinding and baking is not negligible. Whether this last price could be assumed as normal must be very doubtful, for the little that Domesday tells us about the price of grain is told in obscure and disputable terms[3]. However, the evidence that comes to us from the twelfth[4] and thirteenth centuries[5] suggests a rough equivalence between an ox and two quarters of wheat, and in the eleventh the traditional price of the ox was 30 pence. But at any rate, the lord who has a small village with five teamlands, and who lets it to a *firmarius*, will receive a rent which, when it is stated in loaves, is by no means splendid. He will not be much of a *hláford*, or have many 'loaf-eaters' if his whole revenue is £2. 10s. or, in other words, if he is lord of but one small village in the midlands.

---

[1] Rot. Hund. ii. 570, 575. The calculation which gave these results was laborious; but I believe that they are pretty correct.

[2] On the whole, the *valet* of D. B., so far as it is precise, seems to me an answer to the question, What rent would a *firmarius* pay for this estate stocked as it is? But there are many difficulties.

[3] See the important but difficult account of the mill at Arundel: D. B. i. 23.

[4] Hall, Court Life, 221–3. The Glastonbury Inquests (Roxburgh Club) show that 36*d.* is the settled price for the ox.

[5] Rogers, Hist. Agric. i. 226, 342.

Here we must leave this question to those who are expert Varying size of acres. in the history of agriculture; but if some relief is required, it may be plausibly obtained by a reduction in the size of the ancient acre. A small piece off the village perches will mean a great piece off the 2,600 teamlands of Oxfordshire, and we seem to have the best warrant for a recourse to this device where it is most needed. The pressure upon our space appears to be at its utmost in Oxfordshire, and just for that county we have first-rate evidence of some very small acres[1]. On the other hand, in Lincolnshire and generally in the north, where we read of abnormally large acres, we seem to have room enough for them. And here may be a partial explanation of the apparent fact that the teamland of Oxfordshire does not support three, while that of Lincolnshire supports five recorded men.

In these last paragraphs we have been speaking of averages The teamland in Cambridgeshire. struck for large spaces; but if we come to some particular districts we shall have the greatest difficulty in allowing 120 acres to every teamland. This is the case in southern Cambridgeshire. In that county Domesday's list of vills is so nearly the same as the modern list of parishes that we run no great risk in comparing the ancient teamlands with the modern acreage vill by vill, if we also compare them hundred by hundred. The general result will be to make us unwilling to bestow on every teamland a long-hundred of acres. One example shall be given. The Whittlesford Hundred[2] contains five vills and we can not easily concede to it more land than is now within its boundary. In the following table we give for each vill its modern acreage, then the number of its teamlands, then the result of multiplying that number by 120.

WHITTLESFORD HUNDRED.

Sawston	1884	10	1200
Whittlesford	1969	11	1320
Duxford	3232	21[3]	2520
Hinxton	1557	16[4]	1920
Ickleton	2695	24½	2940
The Hundred	11337	82½	9900

In two cases out of five we have already come upon sheer physical impossibility. But let us suppose some rearrangement

[1] See above, p. 382.   [2] Inq. Com. Cant. 38.
[3] Or a little less.
[4] Perhaps too small. One estate was valued in Essex.

of parish boundaries and look at the whole hundred. We are giving it 9900 acres of arable and leaving 1437 for other purposes. Then we are told of 'meadow for' 37 teams and this at the rate usual in Cambridgeshire[1], means 296 acres, so that we have only 1141 left. On this we must place the sites of five villages, houses, farmyards, fourteen water-mills, cottages, gardens. Probably we want 250 acres at least to meet this demand. Not 900 acres remain for pasture. The dominical flocks and herds were not large, but the lords were receiving divers ploughshares in return for the pasture rights accorded to the tenants and in some of the vills there was not nearly enough meadow for the oxen of the villeins. It is difficult to believe that 87 per cent. of a Cambridgeshire hundred was under the plough, and that less than 8 per cent. was pasture. However, we know too little to say that even this was impossible. In the twelfth century we read of manors in which there is no pasture, except upon the arable field that is taking its turn of idleness[2]. We must remember that this idle field was not fallowed until the summer[3]; also we may suspect that much that was not corn grew on the medieval corn-land.

Saddened by our encounter with the teamlands (*B*)—and our last word about them is not yet said—we turn to the hides, carucates and sulungs (*A*). With a fair. allowance for errors we feel safe in believing that the total number mentioned by Domesday Book falls short of 70,000—and yet time was when we spoke of 60,000 knight's fees of 5 hides apiece[4]. Let us then recall once more those tales of taxation that are told by the chronicler[5]. If Cnut raised a geld of £72,000, then, even if we allow him something from those remote northern lands which William's commissioners did not enter, the rate of the impost can hardly have been less than a pound on the hide. We are not told that he raised this sum in the course of a single year; but, even if we suppose it spread over four years,

The hides of Domesday.

[1] See above, p. 443.
[2] Domesday of St. Paul's, 59, 64, 69. See above, p. 399 note 3.
[3] Hanssen, Abhandlungen, i. 163.
[4] After making an allowance of 22,000 for Suffolk (which I have not counted) and adding 500 for the land between Ribble and Mersey (which owing to some difficult problems, I have omitted), the sum would fall a little short of 68,000. The hides of London and other boroughs would raise the total. Pearson, History, i. 658, guessed 90,000 to 100,000.
[5] Above, p. 3.

it is a monstrous exaction, and we can hardly fancy that in earlier days the pirates had waited long for the £24,000 or £30,000 that were the price of their forbearance. And yet, as already said, our choice seems to lie between believing these stories and charging the annalist with reckless mendacity. Hereafter we shall argue that some ancient statements about hidage, even some made by Bede himself, deserve no credit ; but it is one thing for a Northumbrian scholar of the eighth century to make very bad guesses about the area of Sussex, and another for a chronicler of the eleventh to keep on telling us that a king levies £21,099 or £11,048 or the like, if these sums are wildly in excess of those that were demanded. As to the value of money, the economists must be heard ; but it is probable that the sea-rovers insisted on good weight[1], [and when in the twelfth century we can begin to trace the movement of prices, in particular the price of oxen, they are not falling but rising. However, we have already said our say about the enormity of the danegeld.

We are now to investigate the 'law' of A and its relation to B. We shall soon be convinced that we are not dealing with two perfectly independent variables. There will often be wide variations between the two ; A may descend to zero, while B is high, and in some counties we shall see a steady tendency which makes A decidedly higher or decidedly lower than B. And yet, if we look at England as a whole, we can not help feeling that in some sense or another A ought to be equal to B, and that, when this equation holds good, things are in a condition that we may call normal. Perhaps, as we shall see hereafter, the current notion has been that the teamland should be taxed as a hide if it lies in a district where a teamland will usually be worth about a pound a year. But for the time we will leave value out of account, and, to save words, we will appropriate three terms and use them technically. When $A = B$, there is 'equal rating'; when $A > B$, there is 'over-rating'; when $A < B$ there is 'under-rating.' We shall find, then, that in many counties there are numerous cases of equal rating. Thus in Buckinghamshire we count

cases of under-rating 136

cases of equal rating 102

cases of over-rating 115

Relation between hide and teamland.

---

[1] As to the *magnum pondus Normannorum*, see Crawford Charters, 78.

In Lincolnshire we may find an unbroken series of fourteen entries each of which gives us an instance of equal rating[1]. In both Lincolnshire and Yorkshire such cases are common, but, while in Lincolnshire over-rating is rare, in Yorkshire under-rating is very rare. Fewer are the over-rated than the under-rated counties; but there are some for which the figures can not be given, and, as immense Yorkshire is set before us as much over-rated, the balance must be nearly redressed. But further, we may see that the relation between A and B is apt to change somewhat suddenly at the border of a county. The best illustration is given by the twin shires of Leicester and Northampton, the one over-rated, the other grossly under-rated. Another good illustration is given by the south-western counties. Wiltshire is heavily over-rated; Dorset, as a whole, very equally rated; Somerset decidedly under-rated, while when we come to Devon and Cornwall we enter a land so much under-rated that, had we only the account of these two counties, the assumption that is implied in our terms 'under-rated' and 'over-rated' would never have entered our heads.

Unhidated estates.

Now for one cause of the aberration of A from B we have not far to seek; it is a cause which will make A less than B and which may reduce A to zero. It is privilege. Certain estates have been altogether exempt from geld. In particular many royal estates have been exempt. '*Nescitur quot hidae sint ibi quia non reddidit geldum*'—'*Nunquam geldavit nec scitur quot hidae sint ibi*'—'*Rex Edwardus tenuit; tunc* 20 *hidae sed nunquam geldaverunt*':—such and such like are the formulas that describe this immunity. The number of actually geldant hides is here reduced to zero, and sometimes the very term 'hides,' so usually does it imply taxation, is deemed inappropriate. But these royal estates do not stand alone. Often enough some estate of a church has been utterly freed from taxation. The bishop of Salisbury, for example, has a great estate at Sherborne which has gelded for 43 hides; but 'in this same Sherborne he has 16 carucates of land; this land was never divided into hides nor did it pay geld[2].'

Beneficial hidation.

But then again, we have the phenomenon which has aptly been called 'beneficial hidation.' Without being entirely freed from the tax, a manor has been rated at a smaller number of hides than it really contains. 'There are 5 hides' says

[1] D. B. i. 351.　　　　　　　　[2] D. B. i. 77.

a Gloucestershire entry, '3 of them geld, but by grant of the Kings Edward and William 2 of them do not geld[1].' 'There are 8 hides there' says another entry 'and the ninth hide belongs to the church of S^t. Edward; King Æthelred gave it quit [of geld][2].' 'There are 20 hides; of these 4 were quit of geld in the time of King Cnut[3].' 'The Bishop [of Winchester] holds Fernham [Fareham] in demesne; it always belonged to the bishopric; in King Edward's day it defended itself for 20 hides, and it does so still; there are by tale 30 hides, but King Edward gave them thus [i.e. granted that they should be 20 hides] by reason of the vikings, for it [Fareham] is by the sea[4].' 'Harold held it of King Edward; before Harold had it, it defended itself for 27 hides, afterwards for 16 hides because Harold so pleased. The men of the hundred never heard or saw any writ from the king which put it at that figure[5].' We have chosen these examples because they give us more information than we can often obtain; they take us back to the days of Cnut and of Æthelred; they tell us of the depredations of the vikings; they show us a magnate fixing the rateable value of his estate *ad libitum suum*. But our record is replete with other instances in which we are told that by special royal favour an estate has been lightly taxed[6]. What is more, there are many other instances in which we can hardly doubt that this same cause has been at work, though we are not expressly told of it. When in a district which as a whole is over-rated, or but moderately under-rated, we come upon a few manors which are extravagantly under-rated, then we may fairly draw the inference that there has been 'beneficial hidation.'

Certainly this will account for much, and we have reason to believe that this disturbing force had been in operation for a long time past and on a grand scale. There is an undated writ of Æthelred[7], which ordains that an immense estate of the church of Winchester having Chilcombe for its centre and containing 100 hides shall defend itself for one hide. In

Effect of privilege.

---

[1] D. B. i. 165, Alvestone.
[2] D. B. i. 165 b, Malgeresberiae.
[3] D. B. i. 252 b, Wenloch.   [4] D. B. i. 40 b.
[5] D. B. i. 32: 'postquam habuit pro 16 hidis ad libitum Heraldi.'
[6] Round, in Domesday Studies, i. 98–110.
[7] K. 642 (iii. 203).

M.   29

Domesday Book Chilcombe does defend itself for one hide though it has land for 88 teams[1]. But further, Æthelred is decreeing nothing new; his ancestors, his 'elders,' have 'set and freed' all this land as one hide 'be the same more or less.' Behind this writ stand older charters which are not of good repute. Still we can see nothing improbable in the supposition that Æthelred issued the writ ascribed to him and that what he said in it was substantially true. Before his day there may have been no impost that was known as a 'geld'; but there may have been, as we have endeavoured to show, other imposts to which land contributed at the rate of so much per hide. We suspect that 'beneficial hidation' had a long history before Domesday Book was made.

Divergence of hide from team-land. But it will not account for all the facts that are before us; indeed it will serve for few of them. Privilege can account for exceptional cases; it will not account for steady and consistent under-rating; still less will it account for steady and consistent over-rating. We must look elsewhere, and for a moment we may find some relief in the reflection that by the operation of natural and obvious causes an old rate-book will become antiquated. There will be more 'teamlands' than there are gelding hides because new land has been brought under cultivation; on the other hand, land will sometimes go out of cultivation and then there will be more gelding hides than there are teamlands. Now that there is truth here we do not doubt. As we have already said[2], the stability of agrarian affairs in these early times may easily be over-estimated. But we can not in this direction find the explanation of changes that take place suddenly at the boundaries of counties.

Partition of the geld. A master hand has lately turned our thoughts to the right quarter. There can we think be no doubt that, as Mr Round has argued, the geld was imposed according to a method which we have called the method of subpartitioned provincial quotas[3]. A sum cast upon a hundred has been divided among that hundred's vills; a sum cast upon a vill has been divided among the lands that the vill contains. It is in substance

[1] D. B. i. 41. [2] See above, p. 362.
[3] I have chosen 'subpartitioned,' because 'repartitioned' might have introduced the idea of periodical or occasional rearrangement, and this it is desirable to exclude in the present state of our knowledge.

the method which still governs our land-tax, and in this very year our attention has been pointedly called to its inequitable results. But, whereas in later centuries men distributed pounds, shillings and pence among the counties, our remoter ancestors distributed hides or carucates or acres. The effect was the same ; and it is not unlikely that they could pass with rapidity from acres to pence, because the pound had 240 pence in it and the fiscal hide had 120 acres. So the complaint urged this year that Lancashire is under-taxed and Hertfordshire over-taxed[1] would have been in their mouths the complaint that too many hides had been cast on the one county and too few on the other.

We will not repeat Mr Round's convincing arguments. Just to recall their character, we will notice the beautiful hundred of Armingford in Cambridgeshire[2]. In Edward's day it had 100 hides divided among fourteen vills, six of which had 10 hides apiece, while eight had 5 hides apiece. Before 1085 the number of hides in the hundred had been reduced from 100 to 80 ; the number of hides in each of the ' ten-hide vills' had been reduced to 8; and each ' five-hide vill ' had got rid of one of its hides. Obviously such results as these are not obtained by a method which begins by investigating the content of each landholder's tenement. The hides in the vill are imposed from above, not built up from below[3].

Distribution of hides.

We have no wish to traverse ground which must by this time be familiar to all students of Domesday. But, having in our eye certain ancient statements about the hidage of England, we will endeavour to carry the argument one step further.

The Worcestershire hidage.

In Worcestershire we have strong evidence of a neat arrangement of a whole county. In the first place, we are told that ' in this county there are twelve hundreds, whereof seven, so the shire says, are so free that the sheriff has nothing in them, and therefore, so he says, he is a great loser by his farm[4].' Then we are told that the church of Worcester has a hundred called Oswaldslaw in which lie 300 hides. Then

---

[1] See a speech by the Chancellor of the Exchequer reported in The Times for 10 July, 1896.

[2] Round, Feudal England, 50.

[3] See also Pollock, E. H. R. xi. 222.

[4] D. B. i. 172.

we remember that notorious charter (*Altitonantis*) which tells how this triple hundred of Oswaldslaw was made up of three old hundreds, called Cuthbertslaw, Wulfhereslaw and Wimborntree[1]. Then, turning to the particulars, we find that exactly 300 hides are ascribed to the various estates which S[t]. Mary of Worcester holds in this triple hundred. Those particulars are the following:—

The Worcester estate.

Chemesege	24			Norwiche	25		
Wiche	15			Overberie	6		
Fledebirie	40			Segesbarue	4		
Breodun	35	} 200		Scepwestun	2	} 25	
Rippel	25			Herferthun	3		} 100
Blochelei	38			Grimanleh	3		
Tredinctun	23			Halhegan	7		
				Cropetorn	50		

We have here preserved the order in which Domesday Book names the estates, but have added some brackets which may serve to emphasize the artificiality of the system. Then, looking back once more at our *Altitonantis*, we see Edgar adding lands to the 50 hides at Cropthorn, so that 'a perfect hundred' may be compiled, and the lands that he adds seem to be just those which in our table are bracketed with the Cropthorn estate.

The Westminster estate.

Thus we have disposed of three out of those twelve 'hundreds' of which Worcestershire is composed and also of 300 hides of land. Next we perceive that the church of Westminster is said to hold 200 hides. Reckoning up the particulars, we find, not indeed 200, but 199.

	H. V.		H. V.
Persore	2	Pidelet	5
Wiche	6	Newentune	10
Pendesham	2	Garstune	1 . 3
Berlingeham	3 . 1	Pidelet	4
Bricstelmestune	10	Peritune	6
Depeforde	10	Garstune	7
Aichintune	16	Piplintune	4 . 2
Beford	10	Piplintune	6 . 2
Longedune	30	Cumbrintune	9
Poiwic	3	Cumbrintune	10
Snodesbyrie	11	Broctune	3
Husentre	6	Stoche	15
Wich	1	Cumbrintune	2
Dormestun	5		199 . 0

[1] See above, p. 268.

Then the church of Pershore has just 100 hides; they are distributed thus :—

Persore	26
Beolege	21
Sture	20
Bradeweia	30
Lege	3
	100

It is easy to divide these manors into two groups, each of which has 50 hides. The county also tells us that the church of Pershore ought to have the church-scot from 'the whole 300 hides,' that is, as well from the 200 allotted to Westminster as from the 100 which Pershore holds[1].

Then Evesham Abbey has, we are told, 65 hides in the hundred of Fissesberge. 'In that hundred,' it is added, 'lie 20 hides of Dodingtree and 15 hides in Worcester make up the hundred.' The 65 hides which Evesham holds are allotted thus :—

Evesham	3 . 0	
Lenchewic	1 . 0	
Nortune	7 . 0	
Offenham	1 . 0	25
Liteltune	6 . 0	
Bratfortune	6 . 0	
Aldintone	1 . 0	
Wiqwene	3 . 0	
Bratfortune	6 . 0	
Badesei	6 . 2	25
Liteltune	7 . 0	
Huniburne	2 . 2	
Ambreslege	15 . 0	
	65 . 0	

We have dealt heretofore with 665 hides. Let us now reckon up all the hides in Worcestershire that we have not yet counted. The task is not perfectly straightforward, for we have to meet a few difficult questions. In order that our account may be checked by others, we will set forth its details. We will go through the survey noting all the hides which we have not already reckoned.

[1] The estate at Matma which is in the Dodingtree hundred will be accounted for below.

Worcester city	15 . 0	More	1 . 0	Glese	1 . 0
Bremesgrave	30 . 0	Betune	3 . 2	Merlie	0 . 1
¹Suchelei	5 . 0	More	0 . 1	Wich	1 . 0
Grastone	3 . 2	Edboldelege	2 . 2	Escelie	4 . 0
Cochesei	2 . 2	Eslei	6 . 0	Nordfeld	6 . 0
Willingewic	2 . 3	Eslei	1 . 0	Franchelie	1 . 0
Celdvic	3 . 0	Ridmerlege	1 . 2	Welingewiche	0 . 3
Chideminstre	20 . 0	Celdeslai	1 . 0	Escelie	1 . 0
Terdeberie	9 . 0	Estham	3 . 0	Werwelie	0 . 2
Clent	9 . 0	Ælmeleia	11 . 0	Cercehalle	2 . 0
Wich	0 . 2	Wich	10 . 0	Bellem	3 . 0
Clive	10 . 2	Sudtune	1 . 0	Hageleia	5 . 2
Fepsetanatun	6 . 0	Mamele	0 . 2	Dudelei	1 . 0
Crohlea	5 . 0	Broc	0 . 2	Suineforde	3 . 0
Hambyrie	14 . 0	Colingvic	1 . 0	Pevemore	3 . 0
Stoche	10 . 0	Mortune	4 . 0	Cradeleie	1 . 0
Huerteberie	20 . 0	Stotune	3 . 0	Belintones	5 . 0
Ulwardelei	5 . 0	Stanford	2 . 2	Witone	2 . 0
Alvievecherche	13 . 0	Scelves	1 . 0	Celvestune	1 . 0
Ardolvestone	15 . 0	Chintune	5 . 0	Cochehi	2 . 2
Boclintun	8 . 0	Beretune	2 . 0	Osmerlie	1 . 0
Cuer	2 . 0	Tamedeberie	3 . 0	Costone	3 . 0
Inteberga	15 . 2	Wich	0 . 2	Beneslei	1 . 0
Wich	1 . 0	Clistune	3 . 0	Udecote	1 . 2
Salewarpe	1 . 0	Chure	3 . 0	Russococ	5 . 0
Tametdeberie	0 . 2	Stanford	1 . 2	Stanes	6 . 0
Wich	0 . 2	Caldeslei	1 . 0	Lundredele	2 . 0
Matma	5 . 0	Cuer	1 . 0	Hatete	1 . 0
²Mortune	5 . 0	Hamme	·1 . 0	Hamtune	4 . 0
Achelenz	4 . 2	Sapie	3 . 0	Hortune	2 . 0
Buintun	1 . 0	Carletune	1 . 1	Cochesie	2 . 0
Circelenz	4 . 0	Edevent	1 . 0	Brotune	2 . 0
Actune	6 . 0	Wicelbold	11 . 0	Urso's hide	1 . 0
Lenche	4 . 0	Elmerige	8 . 0	Uptune	3 . 0
Wich	1 . 0	Croelai	5 . 0	Witune	0 . 2
Ludeleia	2 . 0	Dodeham	1 . 0	Hantune	4 . 0
Hala	10 . 0	Redmerleie	1 . 2	Tichenapletreu	3 . 0
Salewarpe	5 . 0	Hanlege	1 . 2	Cedeslai	25 . 0
Wermeslai	2 . 0	Hanlege	3 . 0	Hilhamatone	0 . 1
Linde	2 . 0	Alretune	1 . 2	Fecheham	10 . 0
Halac	1 . 0	Hadesore	2 . 0	Holewei	3 . 0
Dunclent	3 . 0	Holim	1 . 0	³Mertelai	13 . 0
Alvintune	2 . 0	Stilledune	0 . 2		539 . 0

¹ Possibly this and the four next entries should be omitted.

² We here omit the estates at Hamton and Bengeworth, about which the churches of Worcester and Evesham were disputing, for we believe that they have already been included in the Worcester estate of Cropthorn. See Round in Domesday Studies, ii. 545.

³ Perhaps add 5 hides at Suchelei ; but apparently these have been already included in the account of the King's Land.

We have here therefore 539 hides to be added to the 665 of which we rendered an account above. We thus bring out a grand total of 1204 hides. Perhaps the true total should be exactly 1200; but at any rate it stands close to that beautiful figure. And now we remember how we were told that there were 'twelve hundreds' in Worcestershire from seven of which the sheriff got nothing. Of these twelve the church of Worcester had three in its 'hundred' of Oswaldslaw, the church of Westminster two, the church of Pershore one, and the church of Evesham one. But the Evesham or Fissesberge hundred was not perfect; it required 'making up' by means of 15 hides in the city of Worcester and 20 in the hundred of Dodingtree. Thus five hundreds remain to be accounted for, and in its rubrics Domesday Book names just five, namely, Came, Clent, Cresselaw, Dodingtree and Esch. We can not allot to each of these its constituent hides, for we never can rely on Domesday Book giving all the 'hundredal rubrics' that it ought to give, and the Worcestershire hundreds were subjected to rearrangement before the day of maps had dawned[1]. An intimate knowledge of the county might achieve the reconstruction of the old hundreds. But, as it is, we seem to see enough. We seem to see pretty plainly that Worcestershire has been divided into twelve districts known as hundreds each of which has contained 100 hides. It is an anomaly to be specially noted that one of the jurisdictional hundreds, one which has been granted to the church of Evesham, has only 65 hides and can only be made up into a 'hundred' for financial purposes by adding to it 20 hides lying in another jurisdictional hundred and the 15 hides at which the city of Worcester is rated.

The moment has now come when we may tender in evidence an ancient document which professes to state the hidage of certain districts. There are three such documents which should not be confused. We propose to call them respectively (1) *The Tribal Hidage*, (2) *The Burghal Hidage*, and (3) *The County Hidage;* and this is their order of date. For the two oldest we are not yet ready. The youngest professes to give us a statement about the hidage of thirteen counties. We *The County Hidage.*

---

[1] A large hundred called Halfshire Hundred was formed. In Latin records it is *Hundredum Dimidii Comitatus.* For some light on the constitution of Dodingtree, see Round, Feudal England, 61.

have it both in Latin and in Old English. It has come down to us in divers manuscripts, which do not agree very perfectly. We will here give its upshot, placing in a last column the figures at which we have arrived when counting the hides in Domesday.

THE COUNTY HIDAGE.

	Cotton, Claudius, B. vii. f. 204 b; Kemble, Saxons, i. 493	Cotton, Vespasian, A. xviii. f. 112 b; Kemble, Saxons, i. 494	Gale, Scriptores xv. p. 748 from a Croyland MS.	MS. Jes. Coll. Ox.; Morris, Old English Miscellany, p. 145	Domesday Book (boroughs omitted)
Wiltshire	4800	4800	4800	4800	4050
Bedfordshire	1200	1000	1200	1200	1193
Cambridgeshire	2500	2500	2005	2500	1233
Huntingdonshire	850[1]	850[1]	800½	850	747
Northamptonshire	3200	4200	3200	3200	1356
Gloucestershire	2400	2000	2400	3400	2388
Worcestershire	1200	1500	1200	1200	1189
Herefordshire	1500	1500	1005	1200	1324
Warwickshire	1200	1200	1200	1200	1338
Oxfordshire	2400	2400	2400	2400	2412
Shropshire	2300	2400	2400	2400	1245
Cheshire	1300	1200	1200	1200	512
Staffordshire	500	500	....	500	505

Date of the document. Dr Liebermann has said that the text whence these figures are derived was probably compiled in English and in the eleventh century[2]. If we put faith in it, we shall be inclined to set its date at some distance before that of Domesday Book. But our first question should be whether it merits credence; whether it was written by some one who knew what he was about or whether it is wild guesswork. Now when we see that the scrupulous Eyton brought out the hides of Staffordshire at 499, or rather at 499 H $2\frac{13}{30}$ V, and that this document makes them 500, we shall begin to take it very seriously, without relying on our own 505, the result of hasty addition. We have also seen enough to say that 1200 for Worcestershire is very near the mark. As regards other counties, we set so little reliance upon our own computation, that we are not very willing to institute a comparison; but we have given Bedford-

---

[1] 'In Huntedunescyre sunt dccc hide et dimid.' This means eight and a half hundreds.

[2] Leges Anglorum, p. 7.

shire 1193 hides[1] and this document gives it 1200; we have given Oxfordshire 2412 and this document gives it 2400; we have given Gloucestershire 2388[2] and two versions of this document give it 2400. Having seen so much agreement, we must note some cases of violent discord. For Wiltshire 4800 seems decidedly too high, though we have brought the number of its hides above 4000. The figure given to Cambridgeshire is almost twice that which Domesday would justify, and the figures given to Cheshire, Shropshire and Northamptonshire are absurdly large when compared with the numbers recorded in 1086. These cases are enough to show that, though no doubt some or all of the transcribers of The County Hidage must be charged with blunders, the divergence of the copies from Domesday can not be safely laid to this account. About certain counties there is just that agreement which we might expect, when we remember how precarious our own figures are. About certain other counties there is utter disagreement. We infer therefore that the original document did not truly state the hidage as it stood in 1086; but may it not have represented an older state of things?

Let us take one case of flagrant aberration. Three copies tell us that Northamptonshire has 3200 hides; one that it has 4200. The balance of authority inclines therefore to 3200. Domesday will not give us half that number. But let us turn to the Northamptonshire Geld Roll[3], the date of which Mr Round places between the Conquest and 1075[4]. It gives the county 2663½ hides. So here we have a case in which between 1075 and 1086 a county was relieved of about half of its hides[5]. Also at 2664 we are within a moderate

The North-ampton Geld Roll.

---

[1] On a re-count I made 1185.

[2] Mr Charles Taylor gives 2595. See above, p. 412. Therefore I have once more gone through the county with his book before me. The difference between us is not altogether due to my faulty arithmetic; but arises from the different constructions that we put upon a few composite entries. In particular I can not allow the bishop of Worcester anything like the 231 hides that Mr Taylor gives him. When I find an entry in this form: 'Sancta Maria tenet H. Ibi sunt x hidae...De hac terra huius manerii Turstinus tenet y hidas in O,' I believe that x includes y, and this no matter how far the place called O may be from the place called H. My 2388 is I think a trifle too low; but I believe the number lies very close to 2400 on one side or the other.

[3] Ellis, Introduction, i. 184.   [4] Feudal England, 148.

[5] After a re-count I think that my 1356 is a little too large, and should not be surprised if the 2663½ had been exactly halved.

distance of 3200. But the Geld Roll does more than this.
It represents Northamptonshire as composed of 28 districts;
22 of these are called 'hundreds'; two are 'two-hundreds';
four are 'other-half hundreds,' or, as we might say, 'hundred-
and-a-halfs.' We work a sum:—

$$(22 + 4 + 6) \times 100 = 3200.$$

The result will increase our respect for The County Hidage.
Now, when the Geld Roll was made, some of the 'hundreds'
of Northamptonshire contained their 100 hides apiece, but
others were charged with a smaller number, which generally
was round, such as 80, 60, 40 hides; and this arrangement is
set before us as that which existed 'in the days of Edward the
king.' If therefore we put faith in The County Hidage and its
3200 hides, we must hold that it speaks to us from the earlier
part of the Confessor's reign or from some yet older time.

Value of The County Hidage. Is it too good, too neat to be true? Before we pass a
condemnatory judgment we must recall the case of Worcester-
shire, its twelve 'hundreds' and 1200 hides. Also we must
recall the case of the Armingford hundred in Cambridgeshire,
where we have seen how in William's reign an abatement
of 20 per cent. was equitably apportioned among the fourteen
villages, and the 100 hides were reduced to 80[1]. Moreover,
if in Domesday Book we pass from Northamptonshire to the
neighbouring county of Leicester, we see a startling contrast.
The former is decidedly 'under-rated'; the latter is 'over-rated.'
Leicestershire has about 2500 carucates, while Northamptonshire
has hardly more than half that number of hides. The explanation is that Northamptonshire has obtained, while Leicestershire
is going to obtain a reduction. The Pipe Rolls of the twelfth
century show us that either under Rufus or under Henry I. this
sadly over-taxed county was set down for exactly 1000 carucates.

Reductions of hidage. As to the other cases in which there is a strident discord
between Domesday and The County Hidage, the case of Chester,
where the contrast is between some 500 hides and a round
1200 will not perhaps detain us long, for we may imagine,
if we please, that the Chestershire of Cnut's day was much
larger than the territory described under that name in 1086[2].

---

[1] See above, p. 451. This is but one instance. Several other hundreds had
been similarly relieved. See Round, Feudal England, 51.

[2] My 500 (or a trifle more) for Cheshire does not include the land between
the Ribble and the Mersey. The figures given for that district are, as is well

The 2500 hides attributed to Cambridgeshire and the 2400 attributed to Shropshire may shock us, for, if they are correctly stated, they point to reductions of 50 per cent. or thereabouts. But we have seen some and are going to see some other large abatements.

On the whole, we believe that this County Hidage, though it has come to us in transcripts some or all of which are careless, is an old and trustworthy document, that it is right in attributing to the counties neat sums of hides, such as 1200 and 2400, and that it is right in representing the current of change that was flowing in the eleventh century as setting towards a rapid reduction in the number of hides. Only in one case, that of Warwickshire, have we any cause to believe that it gives fewer hides to a county than are given by Domesday; here the defect is not very large, and, besides the possibility of mistranscription, we must also remember the possibility of changed boundaries[1]. *The county quotas.*

There is one other feature of this document that we ought to notice. Let us compare the number of hides which it gives to a county with the number of 'hundreds' which that county contains according to Domesday Book. The latter number we will place in brackets[2]. *The hundred and the hundred hides.*

Bedfordshire 1200 hides [12 hundreds]: Northamptonshire 3200 [28 hundreds which, however, have been reckoned to be 32[3]]: Worcestershire 1200 [12]: Warwickshire 1200 [12]: Cheshire 1200 [12]: Staffordshire 500 [5]: Wiltshire 4800 [40]: Cambridgeshire 2500 [17]: Huntingdonshire 850 [4]: Gloucestershire 2400 [39[4]] : Herefordshire 1500 [19]: Oxfordshire 2400 [uncertain, but at least 19]: Shropshire 2400 [13].

---

known, very difficult. If we take the final statement (D. B. i. 270) about the 79 'hides' as a grand total and hold that each of these contains 6 carucates (Feudal England, 86) and that each of these carucates pays geld equivalent to that of one ordinary hide, then we have here 474 units to be added to the Cestrian 500, and yet more northerly lands may have been gelding along with Chester in Cnut's day.

[1] The various copies disagree as to whether Herefordshire shall have 1200 or 1500 hides. My figure stands about halfway between these two; but many hides were not gelding in 1086. I can not bring the Warwickshire hides down to 1200.

[2] I take the numbers of the hundreds from Dr Stubbs, Const. Hist. 106. I take them thence in order that I may not be tempted to make them rounder than they are.

[3] See above, p. 457.

[4] Mr C. S. Taylor, op. cit. 31, finds 41.

In six out of thirteen cases we seem to see a connexion of the simplest kind between the hides and the hundreds. Now in the eyes of some this trait may be discreditable to The County Hidage, for they will infer that its author was possessed by a theory and deduced the hides from the hundreds. But, after all that we have seen[1] of symmetrical districts and reductions of hidage, we ought not to take fright at this point. Other people besides the writer of this list may have been possessed by a theory which connected hides with hundreds, and they may have been people who were able to give effect to their theories by decreeing how many hides a district must be deemed to contain. Is it not even possible that we have here, albeit in faded characters, one of their decrees? But the history of the hundreds can not be discussed in a parenthesis. Some further corroboration this County Hidage will receive when hereafter we set it beside The Burghal Hidage, and we may then be able to carry Worcester's 1200 and Oxford's 2400 hides far back into the tenth century.

Comparison of Domesday hidage with Pipe Rolls.

Meanwhile, making use of our terms 'equally rated' ($A = B$), 'over-rated' ($A > B$), and 'under-rated' ($A < B$), let us briefly survey the counties as they stand in Domesday. Some help towards an estimation of their hidage is given to us by those few Pipe Rolls of the twelfth century which contain accounts of a danegeld. But we must not at once condemn as false the results of our own arithmetic merely because they do not square with the figures on these rolls. One instance will be enough to prove this. The Henries have to be content with £166 or thereabouts from Yorkshire, or, in other words, to treat it as having 1660 'carucates for geld.' We give it a little more than 10,000 and shall not admit that we have given it 8000 too many. This poor, wasted giant has been relieved and has been set below little Surrey. So again, though Leicestershire will account to Henry I. and his grandson for but £100, it most certainly had more than 1000 and more than 2000 carucates when William's commissioners visited it. On the other hand, there seem to be cases in a small group of counties in which his sons were able to recover a certain amount of geld which had been, rightfully or wrongfully, withheld or forborne during his own reign. But, taking the counties in mass, we hope that our figures are sufficiently

[1] Round, Feudal England, 44 ff.

consonant with those upon the Pipe Rolls. Absolutely consonant they ought not to be, for we have endeavoured to include the hides that are privileged from gelding, and in some shires (Hereford, for example) their number is by no means small. Also some leakage in an old tax may always be suspected, and the Pipe Rolls themselves show some unexplained variations in the amount for which a sheriff accounts, and some arithmetical errors[1].

But now we will make our tour and write brief notes as we go.

Kent is scandalously under-rated. Of this there can be no doubt, though, since in many cases blanks are left where the number of the teamlands should stand, the figures can not be fully given. There has in a few instances been a reduction in the number of geldable sulungs since the Conquest, but this does not very greatly affect the result. The under-rating seems to be generally distributed throughout the county. It had not been redressed in Henry I.'s day. Indeed on the Pipe Rolls Kent appears as paying but £105, while Sussex pays twice as much. Sussex, Surrey, Hampshire and Berkshire appear to have all been over-rated. In the Conqueror's day, however, they shuffled off large numbers of their geldant hides and were paying for considerably fewer hides than they had teamlands. Some part of this reduction was perhaps unauthorized. At any rate the sums that appear on the Pipe Rolls seem to show that in Surrey, Hampshire and Berkshire more hides were gelding under Henry I. than had been recently gelding when the survey was made; but the recovery was not sufficient to restore the state of things that existed under the Confessor. Wiltshire, so far as we can see, has always been a sorely over-rated county. It obtains no reduction under William. In the Pipe Rolls it stands at the very head of the counties. Dorset, taken as a whole, is exceedingly fairly rated. Eyton seems to have made 2321 hides and 2332 teamlands;

[Marginal note:] Under-rated and over-rated counties.

---

[1] Both statements might be illustrated from the Dorsetshire accounts. Between 2 and 8 Hen. II. the geld seems to rise from £228. 5s. to £248. 5s. but there is a blunder in the addition of the pardons in the latter roll. I believe that Mr Round has already mentioned this case somewhere. The correspondence between the Pipe Rolls and Domesday is sufficiently close to warrant our saying that the story told by Orderic of a new and severer valuation made by Rufus can have but little, if any, truth behind it. See Stubbs, Const. Hist. i. 327.

but if the royal demesne (much of which is unhidated) be left out on both sides of the account, there will be slight over-rating. Somerset is very much under-rated, even if no notice be taken of the royal demesne. Devon is grossly under-rated. Cornwall is enormously under-rated. To all appearance considerably more than 1000 teamlands have stood as 400 hides, and even this light assessment seems to be the work of the Conqueror, for in the Confessor's day the whole county seems to have paid for hardly more than 150 hides[1]. Middlesex is decidedly over-rated; but Hertford, Buckingham, Oxford, Gloucester, Worcester, Hereford, Cambridge, Huntingdon, Bedford are under-rated. The ratio borne by hides to teamlands varies from county to county. We believe that it becomes small in Gloucester and Worcester and falls much below 1 : 2 in Hereford[2]. This ratio is very small again in Warwick, Stafford, Shropshire and Cheshire. The two sister counties of Northampton and Leicester have, as already said, been very differently treated. Northampton is escaping easily, while Leicester, if we are not much mistaken, is over-rated[3]. Then however the Pipe Rolls show that before the end of Henry I.'s reign Leicester has succeeded in largely reducing its geldability. We have seen reason to believe that a similar reduction had been made in Northamptonshire shortly before the compilation of Domesday Book. Derby is under-rated; Nottingham is much under-rated. Lincoln, though under-rated, is an instance of a county in which we long doubt whether the under-rating of some will not be compensated by the over-rating of other estates. So far as we can tell, Yorkshire had been heavily over-rated; but then, the teamland of Yorkshire is very often a merely potential teamland, and we can not be certain that the jurors will give to the waste vills as many teamlands as they had before the devastation. In the end a very small sum of geld is exacted.

Hidage and value.   We have seen enough in the case of Northampton to make

[1] The common formula is: ‘T. R. E. geldabat pro *a* hidis; ibi tamen sunt *a'* hidae’ and *a'* is largely greater than *a*. I infer that *a'* represents a new and increased assessment, for the Geld Inquest seems to show Cornwall paying for 401 hides and a fraction while I make $a' = 399$.

[2] For these three counties we can not give any *B*, but must draw inferences from *C*. Clearly in Hereford *C* was often thought to be much less than *B*.

[3] As already said (above, p. 420) what we take to be Leicester's equivalent for *B* is sometimes given by an unusual formula.

us hesitate before we decide that the arrangement of hides set forth by Domesday Book is in all cases very ancient. That book shows us two different assessments of Cornwall; it shows us Sussex, Surrey, Hampshire and Berkshire relieving themselves or obtaining relief in the Conqueror's time; it shows us some Cambridgeshire hundreds disburdened of their hides. But of the great reduction in Northamptonshire we should have learnt nothing from its pages. Therefore in other cases we must be cautious, even in the scandalous case of Kent, for we can not tell that there has not been a large reduction of its sulungs in quite recent years. However, behind all the caprice and presumable jobbery, we can not help fancying that we see a certain equitable principle. We have talked of under-rating and over-rating as if we held that every teamland in the kingdom should pay a like amount. But such equality would certainly not be equity. The average teamland of Kent is worth full thirty shillings a year; the average teamland of Cornwall is barely worth five; to put an equal tax on the two would be an extreme of injustice. Now we have formed no very high estimate of the justice or the statesmanship of the English witan, and what we are going to say is wrung from us by figures which have dissipated some preconceived ideas; but they hardly allow us to doubt that the number of hides cast upon a county had been affected not only by the amount, but also by the value of its teamlands. If, starting at the east of Sussex, we journey through the southern counties, we see that over-rating prevails in Sussex, Surrey, Hampshire, Berkshire, Wiltshire, and Dorset. We see also that the *valet* of the average teamland stands rather above than below one pound. We pursue our journey. The ratio that A bears to B begins to decline rapidly and at the same time the *valets* descend by leaps and bounds. When we have reached Devon we are in a land which could not with any show of justice be taxed at the same rate per acre as that which Wiltshire might bear without complaint. Every test that we can apply shows the extreme poverty of the country that once was 'West Wales.' That poverty continues through the middle ages. We look, for example, at the contributions to the tax of 1341 and compare them with the acreage of the contributing counties. Equal sums are paid by 1020 acres in Wiltshire, 1310 in Dorset, 1740 in Somerset, 3215 in

Devon, 3550 in Cornwall[1]. We look at the subsidy of 1294[2], and, in order that Devon and Cornwall may not be put at a disadvantage by moor and sea-shore, we take as our dividend the number of acres in a county that are now-a-days under cultivation[3], and for our divisor the number of pence that the county pays. The quotients are, for Wiltshire 2·7, for Dorset 2·8, for Somerset 2·5, for Devon 6·4, for Cornwall 5·2. Retaining the same dividend, we try as a divisor the 'polls' for which a county will answer in 1377[4]. Cornwall here makes a better show; but Devonshire still displays its misery. The quotients are, for Wiltshire 16, for Dorset 14, for Somerset 15, for Devon 27, for Cornwall 17. These figures we have introduced because they support the inferences that we should draw from the *valets* and *valuits* of Domesday Book, a study of which has convinced us that the distribution of fiscal hides has not been altogether independent of the varying value of land.

Connexion between hidage and value.
But in order that we may not trust to vague impressions, let us set down in one column the number of hides (carucates or sulungs) that we have given to twenty counties and in another column the annual value of those counties in the time of King Edward as calculated by Mr Pearson[5].

	Hides, Carucates, Sulungs	Value in Pounds		Hides, Carucates, Sulungs	Value in Pounds
Kent	1224	3954	Oxford	2412	2789
Sussex	3474	3467	Gloucester	2388	2855
Surrey	1830	1417	Worcester	1189	1060
Berkshire	2473	2378	Huntingdon	747	900
Dorset	2277	2564	Bedford	1193	1475
Devon	1119	2912	Northampton	1356	1407
Cornwall	399	729	Leicester	2500	491
Middlesex	868	911	Warwick	1338	954
Hertford	1050	1894	Derby	679	631
Buckingham	2074	1785	Essex	2650	4079
				33240	38652

[1] Rogers, Hist. Agricult. i. 110.

[2] Yorkshire Lay Subsidy (Yorksh. Archæol. Soc.) p. xxxii.

[3] Total acreage under all kinds of crops, bare fallow and grass, excluding (1) nursery gardens, (2) woods and plantations, (3) mountain and heath land.

[4] Powell, East Anglia Rising, 121–3.

[5] As we are giving or trying to give the fullest number of hides whose existence is attested by D. B., and not the number gelding in 1086, we compare with it the values given by Pearson (Hist. Engl. i. 665) for the T. R. E. His values for the T. R. W. are given above, p. 401.

No one can look along these lines of figures without fancying One pound, one hide.
that some force, conscious or unconscious, has made for 'One
pound, one hide.' But we will use another test, which is in
some respects fairer, if in others it is rude. The total of the
valets or *valuits* of a county sometimes includes and sometimes
excludes the profit that the king derives from boroughs and from
county courts; also the rents of his demesne manors are sometimes stated in disputable terms. Therefore from every county
we will take eighty simple entries, some from the lands of
the churches, some from the fiefs of the barons, and in a large
county we will select our cases from many different pages. In
each case we set down the number of gelding hides (carucates,
sulungs) and the *valuit* given for the T. R. E.[1]. Our method
will not be delicate enough to detect slight differences; it will
only suffice to display any general tendency that is at work
throughout England and to stamp as exceptional any shires
which widely depart from the common rule, if common rule
there be. Using this method we find the values of the hide
(carucate, sulung) to have been as follows, our figures standing
for pounds and decimal fractions of a pound. We begin with
the lowest and end with the highest *valuit*.

Leicester 0·26, York 0·34, Surrey 0·68, Northampton 0·75, Wiltshire
0·77, Sussex 0·81, Chester 0·82, Warwick 0·84, Somerset 0·85, Buckingham 0·86, Oxford 0·87, Dorset 0·88, Berkshire 0·89, Hereford 0·91,
Gloucester 0·99, Lincoln 0·99, Derby 1·00, Huntingdon 1·02, Shropshire
1·02, Bedford 1·09, Hampshire 1·10, Worcester 1·10, Middlesex 1·15,
Essex 1·41, Devon 1·52, Hertford 1·69, Cambridge 1·73, Nottingham 1·76,
Kent 3·25, Cornwall 3·92.

Now 'One pound, one hide' seems to be the central point Equivalence of
pound and
hide.
of this series, the point of rest through which the pendulum
swings. Our experiment has been much too partial to tell
us whether a shire is slightly over-taxed or slightly under-
taxed; but, unless we have shamefully blundered, it tells us
that in some twenty out of thirty counties the aberration
from the equivalence of pound and hide will not exceed twenty-

---

[1] Suffolk and Norfolk are omitted because the relation between their
carucates and the villar geld pence is as yet uncertain. Stafford does not
provide *valuits* enough to give a stable average; but in general the *valets* and
valuits for its hides are high. I have excluded (1) royal demesne, (2) cases in
which there is any talk of 'waste,' (3) cases in which a particular manor is
obviously privileged. In Lincolnshire it is difficult to obtain good figures,
because of the way in which the sokes are valued.

five per cent. : in other words, the value of the normal hide
will not be less than 15 nor more than 25 shillings. Also we
have brought our counties into an admirable disorder. We
have snapped all bonds of race and of neighbourhood. For
example, we see the under-taxed Hampshire in the midst of
over-taxed counties ; we have divorced Nottingham from Derby
and Leicester from Northampton. The one general remark
that we can make about the geographical distribution of
taxation is that, if East Anglia is under-taxed (and this is
likely), then Kent, Essex, Suffolk, Norfolk, Cambridge and
Hertford would form a continuous block of territory that is
escaping easily.

Cases of
under-
taxation.

Kent.

The markedly exceptional cases are the most interesting.
First let us look at the worst instances of immunity. In Kent
we seem to see ' beneficial hidation ' on a gigantic scale ; but
on the whole, though the evidence is not conclusive, we do
not think that this is due to any modern privilege. We can
not doubt that for a long time past the Kentish churches
have been magnificently endowed, and yet the number of
manses and sulungs that their land-books bestow upon them
is not very large, and the number attributed to any one place
is usually small, perceptibly smaller than the number of hides
that will be comprised in a West Saxon charter. If a royal
land-book condescends to mention acres (*iugera, segetes*)[1] it
will almost certainly be a Kentish charter, and we may guess
that its acres are already fiscal acres of wide extent. To say
more would be perilous. The title-deeds of Christ Church
can not be readily harmonized with Domesday Book[2] ; perhaps
we ought to add that this is much to their credit ; but the
documents which come to us from S[t]. Augustin's and Rochester
suggest that the arrangement of sulungs which exists in the
eleventh century is ancient, or, at any rate, that the monks
knew of no older computation which dealt out these units
with a far more lavish hand[3]. In Kent the churches were

---

[1] See above, p. 386, note 1.

[2] Werhard's testament, K. 230 (i. 297), tells us of a great estate of 100 hides
at Otford, of 30 hides at Graveney and so forth. The figures are so little in
harmony with D. B. and with the other Canterbury charters that we may
suspect the 100 manses at Otford of covering many smaller estates, each of
which appears elsewhere with a name of its own.

[3] In D. B. i. 12 b S[t]. Augustin holds 30 solins at Norborne. In 618 Eadbald
of Kent, K. 6 (i. 9), gave 30 *aratra* at Nortburne ; but the deed is spurious. In

powerful and therefore may have been able to preserve a
scheme of assessment which unduly favoured a rich and prosperous shire; but we can not be certain that the hide and
the Kentish sulung have really had the same starting-point,
nor even perhaps that Kent was settled village-wise by its
Germanic invaders[1].

Devon and Cornwall ought to be 'under-rated' $(A < B)$ West Wales.
for they are very poor. What we find is that they are so much
under-rated that the hide is worth a good deal more than a
pound. Here again we are inclined to think that this under-
rating is old, perhaps as old as the subjection of West Wales.
Such land-books as we obtain from this distressful country
point in that direction, for they give but few hides and con-
descend to speak of virgates[2]. Among them is a charter pro-
fessing to come from Æthelstan which bestows 'one manse'
upon the church of S[t]. Buryan; but clearly this one manse
is a wide tract. Also this would-be charter speaks to us of
land that is measured by the arpent, and, whether or no it
was forged by French clerks after the Norman Conquest, it
may tell us that this old Celtic measure has been continuously
used in the Celtic west[3]. Be that as it may, when we are
speculating about the under-taxation of Devon and Cornwall,

D. B. 5 b, Rochester has 3 solins at Totesclive, 6 at Hallinges, 2½ at Coclestane,
3 at Mellingetes, 6 at Bronlei. In 788 Offa, K. 152 (i. 183), gave 6 *aratra* at
Trottesclib. Egbert, K. 160 (i. 193), gave 10 at Hallingas. In 880 Æthelstan,
K. 312 (ii. 109), B. ii. 168, gave 3 at Cucolanstan. Edmund, K. 409 (ii. 265),
gave 3 at Meallingas. In 998 Æthelred, K. 700 (iii. 305), gave 6 at Brunleage.
The Rochester deeds therefore may point to some reduction; but they do not
tell of any startling change.

[1] Meitzen, op. cit. ii. 101, holds that the Euti who invaded Kent fitted
themselves into an agrarian framework prepared by Celts. They came not, like
the great mass of Saxons and Angles, from a country in which villages of the
Germanic type had grown up, but from an originally Celtic land, which they
while still in the pastoral state had seized and subjugated. It is an interesting
though hazardous speculation. Certainly some cause or another keeps Kent
apart from the rest of England.

[2] Thus, K. 371 (ii. 207): Æthelstan gives to the church of Exeter 6 *perticae*
(yard-lands?). B. ii. 433: he gives one cassate to St Petroc. K. 787 (iv. 115):
the Confessor gives a *pertica* and a half in Cornwall. Crawford Charters, pp.
1–43: Æthelheard gives 20 cassates at Crediton; that is, a dozen of our
parishes. Ibid. p. 9: a single yard of land is gaged for 30 mancuses of gold.
K. 1306 (vi. 163): in 739 Æthelred gives 3 *perticae* to Athelney. K. 1324 (vi.
188): Cnut gives to Athelney *duas mansas siue* ($=et$) *unam perticam*.

[3] K. 1143 (v. 278); B. ii. 527. For the *arepennis* see Meitzen, op. cit.
i. 278, where an explanation derived from the Irish laws is given of its name.

we may remember that where the agrarian outlines were drawn by Welsh folk, the hide, though it might be imposed from above as a piece of fiscal machinery, would be an intruder among the Celtic trevs and out of harmony with its environment. The light taxation of Cambridgeshire is perhaps more wonderful, for our figures represent the hidage of the Confessor's time, and we have seen[1] how some of the hundreds in this prosperous shire (our champion wheat-grower) obtained a large abatement from the Conqueror[2]. If, in accordance with The County Hidage, we doubled the number of Cambridgeshire's hides, though it would be over-taxed, it would not be so heavily taxed as are some other counties.

Cases of over-taxation.

Extreme over-taxation is far more interesting to us at the present moment than extreme under-taxation. The latter may be the result of privilege, and in the middle ages privileges will be accorded for value received in this world or promised in another. But what are we to say of Leicester? On the face of our record it seems to have been in Edward's day the very poorest of all the counties and yet to have borne a crushing number of carucates. Under William it was beginning to prosper but still was miserably poor[3]. We have bethought ourselves of various devices for explaining this difficult case—of saying, for instance, that the Leicestershire 'carucate of land' is not a carucate for geld[4]. But this case does not stand quite alone. The Yorkshire carucates, and they are expressly called 'carucates for geld,' had been worth little. It is likely that the figure that we have given for Yorkshire is not very near the true average for that wide territory; but we examined an unusually large number of entries and avoided any which showed signs of devastation in the present or the past. Also we see that in Northamptonshire, if we take the Edwardian *valuit* and the number of hides existing in 1086, we

---

[1] See above, p. 451.

[2] The lords of Cambridgeshire may have done good service during the campaign in the Isle of Ely.

[3] Pearson's *valuit* is £491; his *valet* £736.

[4] The appearance of the curious *hida* may lead to the guess that if the geld be at two shillings, it is the Leicestershire *hida*, not the Leicestershire *carucata* which pays this sum. But (1) if the *hida* contains 18, or even 12, carucates we shall then have on our hands a case of extreme under-taxation; and (2) this will not account for the fact that an exceedingly small value is given to the land that a team ploughs.

have an over-taxed county; and yet we have reason to believe
that since 1075 it had been relieved of about half its hides.
Had this not been done, it would have stood along with
Yorkshire, and, if it once had those 3200 of which The County
Hidage speaks, it would have stood along with its sister, the
wretched Leicestershire. We might find relief in the supposition that the Leicestershire of Edward's time had been
scourged by war or pestilence; but unfortunately the jurors
often tell us how many teams were then upon the manors,
and in so doing give a marvellously small value to the land
that one team tilled. Such reports as the following are
common[1].

	Carucates	Teams T. R. E.	Teams T. R. W.	Valuit sol.	Valet sol.
Werditone	4	5	3	1	20
Castone	9	10	7	40	140
Wortone	6	6	5	40	100
Tuicros	6	6	7	3	40
Gopeshille	3	3	3	1	30
Scepa	2	3	3	2	30

What can these figures mean? They can not mean that a
tract of land was being habitually tilled by three teams and
yet was producing in the form of profit or rent no more than
the worth of one or two shillings a year. An organized attempt
to deceive King William into an abatement seems out of the
question, for he is being told of a rapid increase of prosperity.
Our best, though an unwarranted, guess is that the Leicestershire *valuit* speaks not of the Confessor's day, but of some
time of disorder that followed the Conquest, for in truth it
seems to give us but 'prairie values.' However, if we take,
not the *valuit*, but the *valet*, we still have carucates that are
worth much less than a pound, and it seems clear that the
carucate had been worth much less than a pound in the as
yet unravaged Yorkshire. On the whole, these cases, together with what we can learn of Lancashire, will dispose us
to receive with more favour than we might otherwise have
shown certain statements about the hidage of England that
have yet to be adduced. In Yorkshire, Lancashire, Leicestershire and Northamptonshire we may perhaps see the unreformed
relics of an age when the distribution of fiscal units among

[1] D. B. i. 233.

the various provinces of England was the sport of wild guess-work[1].

We have spoken of a tendency on the part of the hide to be worth a pound. Now we have no wish to represent this equitable element as all powerful or very powerful; the case of Kent is sufficient to show that it may be overruled by favouritism or privilege. There has been a 'beneficial hidation' of shires as there has been a 'beneficial hidation' of manors. Still that the kings and witan have considered the value as well as the number of teamlands seems fairly plain. Probably they have considered it in a rough, 'typical' fashion. Any one who peruses Domesday Book paying attention to the *valets* will be struck in the first place by their round-ness. If a teamland is not worth 20, it is worth 10 or 30, 5 or 40 shillings. The jurors seem to keep in their minds as types the 'one-pound-teamland,' the 'half-pound-teamland' and so forth. But then, whereas in one county 'twenty shillings' will stand for 'fair average' and in another for 'rather poor,' in a third it will indicate unusual excellence. Similarly we imagine that when fiscal hides have been distributed or re-distributed, there has been talk of typical qualities of land, of first-rate and fourth-rate land. Any tradition of Roman taxa-tion which had perdured in Britain or crossed the sea from Frankland would have taught men that this was the right method of procedure. But it is by no means certain that we can carry back this equitable principle very far[2]. Long ago the prevailing idea may have been that teamland, house-land, pound-land and fiscal hide were, or ought normally to be, all one; and then the discovery that there are wide tracts in which the worth of an average teamland is much less or somewhat

---

[1] At the end of the account of the land between Ribble and Mersey (i. 240) we are told that there were altogether 79 *hidae* which T. R. E. were worth £145. 2s. 2d. This would give a very small value for the carucate, if the *hida* of this district had six carucates; and in many cases 2s. 8d. is the value assigned to the carucate. If to a two-shilling geld the *hida* paid but two shillings, this is a bad, though not unprecedented, case of under-taxation. On the other hand, if the carucate paid two shillings, its value has been stated in some abnormal fashion. I do not think it out of the question that the *hidae* of Leicestershire and Lancashire are modern arrangements designed to give relief in some manner or another to districts which have been too heavily burdened with carucates.

[2] It may, however, have been applied to the conquered West Wales from an early time. See above, p. 467.

greater than a pound may have come in as a disturbing and differentiating force and awakened debates in the council of the nation. We may, if we like such excursions, fancy the conservatives arguing for the good old rule ' One teamland, one hide,' while a party of financial reformers has raised the cry ' One pound, one hide.' Then ' pressure was brought to bear in influential quarters,' and in favour of their own districts the witan in the moots jobbed and jerrymandered and rolled the friendly log, for all the world as if they had been mere modern politicians.

But, to be serious, it is in some conjecture such as this that we may perchance find aid when we are endeavouring to loosen one of Domesday's worst knots. We have hinted before now[1] that there are districts in which the teamland (*B*) seems to be as artificial and as remote from real agrarian life as is the hide or the gelding carucate (*A*). To any one who thinks that when we touch Domesday's teamland we have always freed ourselves from the geld system and penetrated through the rateable to the real, the following piece of the survey of Rutland may be commended. ' In Martinesleie Wapentake there is a hundred in which there are 12 carucates for geld and there can be 48 teams.' Now there is nothing curious in the fact that 48 ' real ' teamlands are rated at 12 carucates. But let us look closer. Beside one smaller estate there are in this wapentake three manors. Their arrangement is this[2] :—

Distribution of hides and of teamlands.

	Carucates for geld	Teamlands	Villeins and bordiers	Demesne teams	Men's teams
Ocheham	4	16	157	2	37
Hameldune	4	16	153	5	40
Redlinctune	4	16	196[3]	4	30
Subtenancy			24	4	5
	12	48	530	127	

Now surely the three sixteens are just as artificial as the three fours, and in what possible sense can we affirm that there is land for only 48 teams when we see that 530 tenants are actually ploughing it with 127 teams? Behind this there must be some theory or some tradition that we have not yet fathomed[4].

[1] See above, p. 427. [2] D. B. i. 293 b.
[3] And two sokemen with two teams.
[4] The artificiality or traditionality of the teamland is even more obvious in D. B. than it is in our statement. At Okeham are 4 hides; land for 16 teams. The men have 37. The king has 2 in his demesne ' et tamen aliae

Area and value as elements of geldability. We strongly suspect that in the work of distributing and reducing the geld, 'the land for one team' has been playing a part for some time past. In order to decide, for example, whether a claim for abatement was just, the statesman had to consider two elements, the number of the teamlands and their value. He would be content with round figures, indeed no others would content him or be amenable to his rude manipulation. So it is decided that some province or district has, or must be deemed to have, y teamlands. Also it is decided at this or at some other time, or perhaps from time to time, that the land in this district (regard being had to its state of cultivation) is or must be deemed to be first-class, or, as the case may be, third-class land. Then a combination of these propositions induces the conclusion that the district has x hides or carucates for geld. Then inside the district, when the process of subpartitionment begins, a similar method is pursued. There are x hides or carucates for geld to be distributed. They ought to be distributed with reference to the number and value of real teamlands. The work is rudely done in the subpartitionary fashion. A certain sub-district has $\frac{x}{a}$ hides thrown upon it; a sub-sub-district has $\frac{x}{ab}$; but this apportionment is obtained by combining a proposition about value with a partitionment of the y teamlands. The sub-sub-district has $\frac{x}{ab}$ hides, because $\frac{y}{cd}$ teamlands fall to its share and because its land is assigned to a certain class. Then, perhaps for the purpose of future rearrangements, the number of teamlands $\left(\frac{y}{cd}\right)$ is remembered as well the number of hides or gelding carucates $\left(\frac{x}{ab}\right)$. The result is that every manor in a certain district has four hides and sixteen teamlands. It is very pretty; it was never (except for technical purposes) very true, and every year makes it less true[1].

quatuor possunt esse.' So what is land for 16 teams is not only stocked but insufficiently stocked with 39. The manor of one carucate held by Leuenot seems to be another infringement of the traditional scheme, unless that carucate has been already reckoned among the four at Okeham.

[1] Many other instances suggesting the artificiality of B might be given from northern counties; e.g. in Northampton (i. 227) we have five consecutive entries in which $A = 2,\ 2,\ 2,\ 0\cdot5,\ 4$; $B = 5,\ 5,\ 5,\ 1\cdot25,\ 10$; $C = 3,\ 2,\ 5,\ 1,\ 8$. See also Round, Feudal England, 90.

That exactly this was done, we do not say and do not The equitable teamland. think; but something like it may have been done. As already remarked, we gravely doubt whether that question which the commissioners put about potential teams was understood in the same way in different counties, but we are sadly afraid that some of the answers that they obtained were references, not to existing agrarian facts, but to a fiscal history which already lay in the past and is now hopelessly obscure. A mystery of iniquity is bad, but the mysteries of archaic equity are worse. In many Anglo-Saxon arrangements we find a curious mixture of clumsiness and elaboration.

We can not quit this part of our subject without adding Artificial valets. that there are cases in which the *valuits* and *valets* look as artificial and systematic as the hides and the teamlands. On a single page we find a description of five handsome Yorkshire manors[1]. We wish to know their value in the past and the present, and what we learn is this: Brostewic valuit £56, valet £10; Chilnesse valuit £56, valet £10; Witfornes valuit £56, valet £6; Mapletone valuit £56, valet £6; Hornesse valuit £56, valet £6; and yet between these manors there are large variations in the number of the carucates and the number of the teamlands. Then we look about and see that it has been common for the first-class manor of Yorkshire, if it is the centre of an extensive soke, to be worth precisely £56[2]. We can not but fear that the value of these manors is a legal fiction, though a fiction that is founded upon fact. Their supposed worth seems fixed at a figure that will fit into some scheme, the clue to which we have not yet recovered. Everywhere we are baffled by the make-believe of ancient finance.

The obscure forces which conspired to determine the quotas The new assessments of Henry II. of the various counties might be illustrated by an episode in the reign of Henry II. The old danegeld is still being occasionally levied, and in the main the old assessment prevails. But alongside of this we see a newer tax. From time to time the king takes a gift (*donum, assisa, gersuma*) from the counties. A certain round number of marks is demanded from every shire. For this purpose a new tariff is employed, and

---

[1] D. B. i. 323 b.

[2] D. B. i. 299 Walesgrif £56; 299 b Poclinton £56; 309 Ghellinghes £56; 305 Witebi £112. It will be remembered that, as our hundred-weight (112 lbs) shows, 112 can be called a hundred.

yet it is not wholly independent of the old, for we can hardly look at it without seeing that it is so constructed as to redress in a rude fashion the antiquated scheme of the danegeld. In the first column of the following table we give, omitting fractions, the pounds that the counties contribute when a danegeld is levied, in the second and third the half-marks (6s. 8d.) that they pay by way of gift on two different occasions early in the reign of Henry of Anjou[1].

	Danegeld £	Donum of 2 Hen. II. half-marks	Donum of 4 Hen. II. half-marks
Kent	106	320	240
Sussex	217	202	160
Surrey	180	160	160
Hampshire	185		200
Berkshire	206	148	120
Wiltshire	390	200	160
Dorset	248		
Somerset	278	200	300
Devon	104	368	300
Cornwall	23		
Middlesex	86	175	80
Hertford	110	120	
Buckingham	205 }	200	240
Bedford	111 }		
Oxford	250	140	200
Gloucester	194	218	260
Worcester	101	100	120
Hereford	94	80	140
Cambridge	115	160	
Huntingdon	71	100	
Northampton	120	240	280
Leicester	100	100	160
Warwick	129	100	240
Stafford	45	80	100
Shropshire	118	80	140
Derby } Nottingham }	112	160	280
York	165	1000[2]	1000
Lincoln	266	540	600
Essex	236	400	400
Norfolk	330	400 }	400
Suffolk	235	240 }	

[1] Pipe Rolls, 2. 3. 4. 5. Hen. II. In a few cases the earlier *donum* includes a composition 'for murders and pleas.' That from Yorkshire is partly paid by York, that from Gloucestershire by Gloucester. [2] Nearly.

The variable tariff of *dona* hits most heavily just those counties which have been too favourably treated; Kent and Devon must make large 'gifts' because they pay little geld. Yorkshire, which once more is becoming prosperous, heads the new list, though it pays less geld than Surrey; and, on the other hand, Wiltshire, which makes the largest of all contributions to the ancient tax, is leniently treated. When men have acquired a vested right in an iniquitous assessment, the fertile politician neither reforms nor abolishes the old, but invents a new impost.

And now, after all these inconclusive meanderings, we will state our cheerful belief that the hide of Domesday (A) is always[1] composed of 120 acres and that the carucate for geld of Domesday (A) is always composed of 120 acres. We are speaking only of a fiscal system. Let us forget for a time that the terms that we are using can be employed to describe masses of land. Let us treat them as red and white counters. In the game played at the Exchequer the red counter called a hide is the equivalent of 120 white counters called acres. *Acreage of the fiscal hide.*

If Domesday Book is to serve its primary purpose, if it is to tell the king's officers how much geld is due, it is absolutely necessary that by some ready process they should be able to work sums in hides and acres and in carucates and acres. They must understand such statements as the following:—'it defends itself for 2 hides and 5 acres[2]': 'it gelded for 3 hides, 1 virgate and 1½ acres[3]': 'he has 5 bovates, 13 acres and 1 virgate for geld[4].' Now it is conceivable that the treasury contains a book of tables which will teach the clerks that a hide has *a* acres in Surrey and *b* acres in Devon; but this seems highly improbable. As we have already said[5], the variations between the numbers of 'real' acres that go to make 'real' hides are not provincial, they are villar variations. That the financiers at Winchester should consider villar variations is out of the question. Therefore if we can prove that in one district they employed a given equation, there is a strong presumption that they used it in other districts. And unfortunately our proof has to be of this kind, for in many counties acres are rarely mentioned and we get *Equation between hide and acres.*

[1] Except the 'hides,' if hides they be, of Leicestershire and Lancashire.
[2] D. B. i. 35 (Surrey).   [3] D. B. i. 49 b (Hants).
[4] D. B. i. 364 (Lincoln).   [5] See above, p. 394.

no sums that are worked in acres and hides. But further, if we see one equation holding good in a considerable number of cases, we shall still believe that this is the one true equation, though other cases occur in which it breaks down. We have to remember the possibility of mistranscription, the possibility of bad arithmetic, the possibility of a haughty treatment of small numbers : the actual existence of all these dangers can be amply proved. Therefore if once we have inductively obtained an equation which serves in many instances, we shall hold by it, unless the instances in which it fails point either to some one other equation or to the conclusion that the equation varies from parish to parish.

Evidence from Cambridgeshire.

Now the Cambridgeshire Inquest professes to give us the total hidage of a vill and then proceeds to allot the hides among the various tenants in chief. Sometimes when it does this it speaks of virgates and acres and thus gives us an opportunity of seeing how many acres are reckoned to the hide or to the virgate. The equation 1 H. = 4 v. is implied in many entries. But further, there are at least ten cases which assume one or both of the following equations : namely, 1 H. = 120 A. and 1 V. = 30 A. On the other hand, there are some cases in which the sum that is put before us is not rightly worked if these equations be correct; but in some of these cases the Inquisitio and Domesday Book contradict each other and in some a small quantity is neglected. The very few remaining cases point to no one rival equation, and are not too numerous to be ascribed to carelessness[1].

Evidence from the Isle of Ely.

A similar test can be applied to a part of Cambridgeshire that is not included in the Cambridgeshire Inquest but is included in the Inquisitio Eliensis. We speak of the Isle of Ely. There are entries which, having told us how many hides a manor contained, proceed to allot these among their various occupants, and, as in some of these cases a calculation by acres is mixed up with a calculation by hides, they hold out a hope that we may be able to discover how many acres were reckoned to the hide. We will begin with Ely itself. ʻ Ely defends itself for 10 hides. ...... In demesne there are 5 hides ...... and

---

[1] This part of the evidence is set out in Mr Round's Feudal England, 37–44. I have gone through all the calculations. His results are hardly different from those which I have obtained and therefore I dwell no longer on this part of the case, for it has been well stated.

there are 40 villeins with 15 acres apiece ...... and 18 cottiers
and 20 serfs[1].' Now if from the total of 10 hides we subtract
the 5 that are in demesne, this leaves 5 others, and if we divide
these 5 among the 40 villeins this gives to each villein $\frac{1}{8}$th of
a hide; but we are told that each villein has 15 acres; therefore
it follows that 120 acres make a hide. We reckon that in
eight other cases[2] the same method of computation is followed,
though in one of these a hide divided among 17 villeins
is said to give them 7 acres apiece and this shows us how a
single acre may be neglected in order to avoid a very ugly
fraction[3]. Against these cases must be set seven which give
less pleasing results[4]. In at least one of these no possible theory
will justify the arithmetic of our record as it stands[5], and
there is no accord between the remaining five.

At first sight the survey of Middlesex seems to offer ma- Evidence
terials similar to those that come to us from Cambridgeshire. from Middlesex.
Very curious and instructive they are. A Middlesex entry
will usually give us the number of hides (A), the number of
teamlands (B), the number of teams (C), and also certain particulars which state the quantity of land that there is in
demesne and the quantities held by divers classes of tenants.
The sum of these particulars we may call P. Now we begin
by hoping that P will be equal to A, and, since the particulars
often contain acres as well as hides and virgates, we hope also
to discover the equation that is involved in the sum. As an
example we will take a case in which all goes well. At Cowley
a manor defends itself for two hides; in demesne are one and
a half hides; two villeins have a half hide. Here $A = 2$ H.
and $P = 1\frac{1}{2}$ H. $+ \frac{1}{2}$ H.; so all is as it should be. But we soon
come upon cases in which, though we make no assumption
about the relation of the acre to the hide, our P refuses to
be equal to our A. Then perhaps we begin to hope that P
will be equal to B: in other words, that the sum of the quantities ascribed to lord and tenants will be equal to the number

---

[1] D. B. i. 192; iv. 107. The Inquisitio Eliensis puts the number of cottiers
at 18, while Domesday gives 28. See Hamilton's edition, p. 119.

[2] Downham, Witchford, Sutton, 'Helle,' Wilburton, Stretham, Stuntney,
Doddington.

[3] Wichford, D. B. i. 192; iv. 507; Hamilton, 119.

[4] Witcham, Whittlesey, Lindon, Wentworth, Chatteris, Wisbeach, Littleport.

[5] Wisbeach, $3\frac{1}{2}$ H. $+ 1$ v. $+ 150$ A. $+ 2\frac{1}{2}$ H. $= 10$ H.

of teamlands. But this is more fallacious than the former hope. We will put a few specimens in a table[1].

	Hides	Teamlands	Sum of particulars
Harrow (Abp. Canterbury)	100	70	$46\frac{1}{2}$ H. + 13 v. + 13 A.
Stepney (Bp. London)	32	25	$18\frac{1}{2}$ H. + $48\frac{1}{2}$ v.
Fulham (Bp. London)	40	40	$41\frac{1}{2}$ H. + 30 v.
Westminster (Abbot)	$13\frac{1}{2}$	11	10 H. + $14\frac{1}{2}$ v. + 5 A.
Sunbury (Abb. Westminster)	7	6	4 H. + $10\frac{1}{2}$ v.
Shepperton (Abb. Westminster)	8	7	$3\frac{1}{2}$ H. + 17 v. + 24 A.
Feltham (C. Mortain)	12	10	6 H. + $16\frac{1}{2}$ v.
Chelsea (Edw. of Salisbury)	2	5	1 H. + 4 v. + 5 A.

Meaning of the Middlesex entries. We seem to have here three independent statements, and, though throughout the county P shows a tendency to keep near to A, still we must not make calculations which suppose that the 'hide' of A is the 'hide' of P. Take Chelsea for example. We must not say : 2 H. = 1 H. + 4 v. + 5 A., and therefore four virgates and five acres make a hide. No, it seems possible that in these Middlesex 'particulars' we do at last touch real agrarian arrangements. At Fulham the bishop has 13 hides in demesne ; 5 villeins have 1 hide apiece ; 13 villeins have 1 virgate apiece ; 34 have a half-virgate apiece ; 22 cottiers have in all a half-hide ; Frenchmen and London burgesses have 23 hides ; so there are $41\frac{1}{2}$ hides and 30 virgates. That we take to be the real arrangement of the manor, though we are far from saying that all its hides are equal. But it gelds for only 40 hides. A virgate can not be a negative quantity. Therefore we need say no more of these Middlesex entries, only in passing let us observe that the discrepancy between P and B is often considerable, and this seems to show that the teamland of these Middlesex jurors is not in very close touch with the agrarian and proprietary allotments.

Evidence in the Geld Inquests. To yet one other quarter we have hopefully turned only to be disappointed, namely, to the so-called Geld Inquests, copies of which are placed at the beginning of the Exeter Domesday. They tell us of a geld that obviously is being levied at the rate of six shillings on the hide, and sometimes they seem to tell us expressly or implicitly the amount that an acre pays. For a moment we may think that we are obtaining

---

[1] In giving the sum of the particulars I add hides to hides, virgates to virgates, acres to acres, but I make no assumption as to the number of acres or virgates in the hide.

valuable results.   Thus at Domerham we find that 14 hides
minus 4 acres pay £4. 3s. 8d.   We conclude that each acre is
taxed at one penny and that 72 A. = 1 H.[1].   Then at Celeberge
20 H. minus 4 A. is taxed at £5. 19s. 6d.   We conclude that each
acre is taxed at three-half-pence and that 48 A. = 1 H.[2]   But
we soon come to sums which are absurd and discover that
as regards small quantities these documents are for our
present purpose quite useless.   For the Wiltshire hundreds
we have three different documents.   They do not agree in
their arithmetic.   Probably they represent the efforts of three
different computers.   Indubitably one or more of them made
blunders.   To give one example:—one of our documents begins
its account of Mere by saying that it contains 85 hides, $\frac{1}{2}$ a hide
and $\frac{1}{2}$ a virgate; the other two documents say 86 hides, $\frac{1}{2}$ a hide
and 1 virgate[3].   This is by no means the only instance of such
discrepant results.   But mere clerical or arithmetical errors
are not the only obstacle to our use of these accounts.   It
soon becomes quite evident that small amounts are dealt with
in an irregular fashion.   Thrice over we are assured that
15 H. $\frac{1}{2}$ V. paid the king £4. 11s. 0d.[4]; but they should have
paid £4. 10s. 9d., if four virgates make a hide.   Thrice over
we are assured that $64\frac{1}{2}$ H. paid £19. 6s. 10d.[5]   All suppo-
sitions as to acres and virgates apart, $64\frac{1}{2}$ H. should have paid
£19. 7s. 0d.   In Somersetshire the calculations do not speak
of acres, but they introduce us to the *fertinus* or farthing,
which is certainly meant to be the quarter of a virgate.
Numerous entries show us that 4 *fertini* = 1 virgate, and yet
when a mass of land expressed in terms of hides, virgates and
farthings is said to pay a certain sum for geld, we find that the
odd farthings are reckoned as paying, sometimes 3d., sometimes
4d., sometimes $4\frac{2}{3}$d., sometimes 5d., sometimes 6d. per farthing[6].
So again, when additions are made, odd acres are ignored.   We
are told that in a certain hundred the barons have 20 hides in
demesne, and then that this amount is made up by the following
particulars, 8 H. + 1 V. + 3 H. + 3 V. + $4\frac{1}{2}$ H. − 4 A. + $3\frac{1}{2}$ H.   It
is obvious that these particulars when added together do not
make 20 hides, though they may well make 20 hides and

[1] D. B. iv. 4, 9, 16.   [2] D. B. iv. 22.

[3] D. B. iv. 1, 6, 13.   [4] D. B. iv. 3, 8, 15 (Melchesham).

[5] D. B. iv. 3–4, 9, 15 (Chinbrige).   [6] D. B. iv. 61-2-3.

4 acres[1]. A study of these Geld Inquests has brought us reluctantly to the conclusion that, though they amply prove
that 4 v. = 1 h., they afford no proof as to the number of acres
that are reckoned to the virgate[2].

Treatment of small quantities. One word to explain that the apparent rudeness with which
small figures are treated is not due to any persuasion that
they may be safely disregarded, but is rather the natural outcome of a partitionary method of taxation. Little quantities
are lost in the process. It is known that a certain hundred
should have, for example, 80 hides and a certain vill 5 hides :
but when you come to add up the particulars you can not
bring out these round figures, perhaps because many years
ago a small error was made by some one when an estate of
$2\frac{3}{4}$ hides was being divided into 7 shares. If a mistake be
made, it can never be corrected ; the landowner who has once
or twice paid for 47 acres will refuse to pay for 48 and will
tell you that the deficient acre does not lie on his land.

Result of the evidence. The ignes fatui which dance over the survey of Middlesex
and the Geld Inquests of the south-western counties have for
a while led us from our straight path. We have seen that
in Cambridgeshire the equation 1 h. = 4 v. = 120 a. is employed
on at least twenty occasions. Now as to the rest of England
it must at once be confessed that we have no such convincing
evidence. In many counties acres of arable land are but rarely
mentioned ; parcels of land which geld for less than a hide
are generally expressed in terms of hides and virgates ; we
read, for example, not of so many acres, but of the ninth
part of a hide or of two third parts of a virgate. Thus we
are compelled for the more part to fall back upon the presumption that the treasury has but one mode of reckoning
for the whole of England.

Evidence from Essex. But we would not rest our case altogether upon probability.
In Essex we find one fairly clear case in which our equation
is used[3]. Sometimes, again, we read that a tract of land is,

---

[1] D. B. iv. 23 (Hunesberge) ; see also Langeberge on the same page.

[2] Round in Domesday Studies, i. 212 : 'I have worked through the *Inquisitio Geldi* with this special object, but found to my disappointment that the
odd acres which paid geld on this occasion did not pay at a uniform rate, some
paying twice as much as others.'

[3] D. B. ii. 19 : 'Ratendunam tenuit S. Adelred T. R. E....pro 20 hidis.
Modo pro 16 hidis et dimidia....Et 30 acras tenet Siward de S. Adelred. Modo
tenet Ranulfus Piperellus de rege, set hundret testatur de abbatia. Et 3 hidas

or gelds for, or defends itself for x hides and z acres, or for
x hides, y virgates and z acres.   Now in any entry which takes
the first of these forms we have some evidence that z acres are
less than one hide, and from any entry which takes the second of
these forms we may infer that z acres are less than one virgate.
Of course from such a statement as that 'A holds 90 or 115
or 240 acres' we draw no inference.   It is common enough in
our own day to speak of things costing thirty shillings or
eighteen pence.   But we never speak of things costing one
pound and thirty shillings, or one shilling and eighteen pence,
and we should require much proof before we thought so meanly
of our ancestors as to suppose that they habitually spoke in
this clumsy fashion.

Let us use this test.   Happily in Essex we very frequently
have a tract of land described as being x hides and z acres.

Now we read of

> a half hide and 30 acres[1],
> a hide and a half and 31 acres[2],
> a half hide and 35 acres[3],
> a half hide and 37 acres[4],
> a hide and a half and 40 acres[5],
> a hide and a half and 45 acres[6],
> a half hide and 45 acres[7],
> two hides and a half and 45 acres[8],
> a half hide and 48 acres[9],
> x hides and 80 acres[10],
> nine hides and 82 acres[11].

We have here cited twenty instances in which, as we think,
the hide exceeds 60 acres (we might have cited many others)
and twelve in which it exceeds 80 acres.   We might further
adduce instances in which our record speaks of a virgate and
10 acres, a virgate and 15 acres, and even of a virgate and
20 acres[12], and when we read of two hides less 30 acres and
two hides less 40 acres[13] we infer that a hide probably has

---

et 30 acras quas tenuit ecclesia et Leuesunus de ea T. R. E. modo tenet Eudo
de abbate.'   I think that this involves the statement :

$$16\tfrac{1}{2} \text{ H.} + 30 \text{ A.} + 3 \text{ H.} + 30 \text{ A.} = 20 \text{ H.}$$

[1] D. B. ii. 3, 11, 33, 63 b, 78 b, and in many other places.

[2] Ibid. 31.   [3] Ibid. 6 b, 42 b.   [4] Ibid. 46.

[5] Ibid. 48.   [6] Ibid. 6 b, 49, 60.   [7] Ibid. 43.

[8] Ibid. 74.   [9] Ibid. 1 b.

[10] Ibid. 11 b, 30 b, 31, 47 b.   [11] Ibid. 72.

[12] Ibid. 21 b.   [13] Ibid. 16, 15.

M.   31

not only more but considerably more than the 30, 40 or 48 acres that are allowed to it by Kemble and Eyton. Our argument is based on the belief that men do not habitually adopt extremely cumbrous forms of speech. From a single instance we should draw no inference, and therefore when we just once read of 'three hides and a half and 80 acres' we do not infer that 80 acres are less than half a hide[1].

Evidence from Essex continued. But more can be made of these returns from Essex. We will take a large number of tracts of land described in the formula 'x hides and z acres'; we will observe the various numbers for which z stands, and if we find some particular number frequently repeating itself we shall be entitled to argue that this number of acres is some very simple fraction of a hide. We will take at hazard 100 consecutive entries which contain this formula—'x hides + z acres,' where x is either an integral number or $\frac{1}{2}$. The result is that in 37 cases z is 30, in 12 it is 15, in 8 it is 40; then 35 and 20 occur 5 times; 80, 50, 45, 37, 18, 10 occur thrice, and 38 and $15\frac{1}{2}$ twice; eleven other numbers occur once apiece. There can we think be but one explanation of this. The hide contains that number of acres of which 30 is the quarter, 40 the third, 15 the eighth[2].

Further evidence. But Essex, it must be confessed, lies next to Cambridgeshire, and for the rest of England we have less evidence. Still there are entries which make against any theory which would give to the hide but 30, 40 or 48 acres. In Hertfordshire we read of 'a hide and a half and 26 acres[3].' In the same county we read of 'a half virgate and 10 acres,' and this seems to tell of a hide of at least 88 acres[4]. In Gloucestershire we read of a manor of one hide and are told that 'in this hide, when it is ploughed, there are but (*non sunt nisi*) 64 acres of land,' whence we may draw the inference that such an acreage was unusually small[5].

---

[1] D. B. ii. 79.

[2] Some other fractions into which a hide would easily break by inheritance and partition can be expressed in various ways. Thus two-thirds of a hide can be expressed as 80 A. or as 'half a hide and 20 acres.' Three-quarters of a hide appears sometimes as 'half a hide and 30 A.,' sometimes as 'a hide less 30 A.' We might add to our other arguments derived from Essex that used by Morgan (op. cit., p. 31). It seems fairly clear that the holding of Roger 'God Bless the Dames' which is called 3 v. in one place is called $\frac{1}{2}$ H. + 30 A. in another place (D. B. iv. 21 b, 96 b).

[3] D. B. i. 141 b, Wallingtone.   [4] D. B. i. 141, Stuterehele.

[5] D. B. i. 165. There is here a transition from geldable area to real area.

We pass from Mercia into Wessex. In Somersetshire we read of 'three virgates and a half and 5 acres[1],' in Dorset of 'three virgates and a half and 7 acres[2],' in Somerset of 'one and a half virgates and 8 acres[3].'

To prove that the fiscal carucate was composed of 120 (fiscal) acres is by no means easy. If, however, we have sojourned for a while in Essex and then cross the border, we can hardly doubt that in East Anglia the carucate bears to the acres the relation that is borne by those hides among which we have been living. Norfolk and Suffolk are carucated counties, but while in the other carucated counties it is usual to express the smaller quantities of land in terms of the bovate (8 bovates making one carucate) and to say nothing of acres, in East Anglia, on the other hand, it is uncommon to mention the bovate—in Suffolk we may even find the virgate[4]—and men reckon by carucates, half-carucates and acres. We allow the description of Suffolk to fall open where it pleases and observe a hundred consecutive cases in which a plot of land (as distinguished from meadow) is spoken of as containing a certain number of acres. In 22 cases out of the hundred that number is 60, in 8 it is 30, in 7 it is 20, in 5 it is 40, in 5 it is 15; no other number occurs more than 4 times, and yet the numbers that appear range from 100 to 2. We have tried the same experiment on two hundred cases in Norfolk; in 28 cases the number of acres was 30, in 16 cases it was 60, in 13 it was 40, in 13 it was 16, in 12 it was 20, in 10 it was 80, in 9 it was 15, though the numbers ranged from 1 to 405. Surely the explanation of this must be that 60 acres are half a carucate, that 30 acres are a quarter, that 40 acres are a third, 20 a sixth, 15 an eighth. We have made many similar experiments and always with a similar result; wherever we open the book we find plots of 60 acres and of 30 acres in rich abundance. We use another test. When land is described by the formula

Acreage of the fiscal carucate.

This land is rated at a hide, but when you come to plough it, you will find only 64 acres.

[1] D. B. i. 93 b, Dudesham; iv. 396.
[2] D. B. i. 79 b. Eyton, Dorset, 16, says that this is a clumsy way of describing 1 H. +1 A. Round, Domesday Studies, i. 213, makes some just remarks on Eyton's treatment of this passage.
[3] D. B. i. 95 b, Ecewiche; iv. 333.
[4] D. B. ii. 389 (Cratingas). In Northamptonshire also there is talk of virgates; e.g. D. B. 225 b, 226 b: 3 v. – 1 B.; 2 v. +1 B.

'*x* carucatae et *z* acrae,' what values are assigned to *z*? We find 40 very commonly, 42, 45, 50, 60 (but this is rare, for it is easier to say '*x*$\frac{1}{2}$ carucates' than '*x* carucates and 60 acres') 68, 69, 80 (at least four times), 81, and 100[1]. On the one hand, then, we have a good deal of evidence that the carucate contains more than 80 acres, some evidence that it contains more than 100 acres, and some that it does not contain many more, for no case have we seen in which *z* exceeds 100. Perhaps in Norfolk the figure 16 occurs rather more frequently than our theory would expect, but 16 is two-fifteenths of 120, and the figures 32 and 64 occur but rarely. Also it must be confessed that in Derbyshire we hear of 'eleven bovates and a half and eight acres,' also of 'twelve bovates and a half and eight acres[2].' These entries, to use an argument which we have formerly used in our own favour, seem to imply that half a bovate is more than eight acres and would therefore give us a carucate of at least 144. We can only answer that, though men do not habitually use clumsy modes of reckoning, they do this occasionally[3].

Acreage of the fiscal sulung.

Of the Kentish sulung very little can be discovered from Domesday. Apparently it was divided into 4 yokes (*iuga*)[4] and the yoke was probably divided into 4 virgates. We have indeed one statement connecting acres with sulungs which some have thought of great importance. 'In the common land of S^t. Martin [i.e. the land which belongs to the *communitas* of the canons of S^t. Martin] are 400 acres and a half which make two sulungs and a half[5].' Thence, a small quantity being neglected, the inference has been drawn that the Kentish sulung was composed of 160 acres, while some would read '400 acres and a half' to mean 450 acres and would so get 180 acres for the sulung[6]. But the entry deals with one particular case and it connects real acres with rateable units :—the canons have 400$\frac{1}{2}$ or more probably 450 acres, which

---

[1] D. B. ii. 377 b. [2] D. B. i. 276 b, 278.

[3] If I hold two and a half acres in one place and three roods in a neighbouring place and you ask me how much land I have, I may tell you that I have two and a half acres and three roods. If you ask me how much money I have in my purse, I may tell you that I have half-a-crown and three shillings. But returns to governmental inquiries would not be habitually made in this way.

[4] D. B. i. 13 : 'pro uno solin se defendit ; tria iuga sunt infra divisionem Hugonis et quartum iugum est extra.'

[5] D. B. i. 2. [6] Elton, Tenures of Kent, 133–4.

are rated at $2\frac{1}{2}$ sulungs. If we passed to another estate, we might find a different relation between the fiscal and the real units. Kent was egregiously undertaxed and as a general rule its fiscal sulung will have many real acres. Turning to the cases in which the geldability of land is expressed in terms of sulungs and acres, or yokes and acres, we can gather no more than that the sulung is greater than 60 acres, so much greater that '3 sulungs less 60 acres[1]' is a natural phrase, and that the half-sulung is greater than 40[2] and than 42 acres[3]. We may suspect that the Exchequer was reckoning 120 (fiscal) acres to the sulung but can not say that this is proved.

And now we must glance at certain theories opposed to that which has been here stated. Kemble contends that the hide contained 30 or 33 Saxon which were equal to 40 Norman acres, and that the hide of Domesday Book contains 40 Norman acres[4]. Now in so far as this doctrine deals with the time before the Conquest, we will postpone our judgment upon it. So far as it deals with the Domesday hide, it is supported by two arguments. One of these is to the effect that England has not room for all the hides that are attributed to it if the hide had many more than 30 or 40 acres; this argument also we will for a while defer. The other[5] is based on a single passage in the Exeter Domesday relating to the manor of Poleham. That entry seems to involve an equation which can only be solved if 1 virgate = 10 acres. William of Mohun has a manor which in the time of King Edward paid geld for 10 hides; he has in demesne 4 H., 1 V., 6 A. and the villeins have $5\frac{1}{2}$ H., 4 A.[6] Now three or four such entries would certainly set the matter at rest; but a single entry can not. By way of answer it will be enough to say that the very next entry seems to imply an equation of precisely the same form, but one that is plainly absurd. This same William has a manor called Ham; it paid geld for 5 hides; there were 3 H., 8 A. in demesne and the villains had 2 H. less 12 A. Shall we draw the conclusion that 5 H. = 5 H. − 4 A.? The truth we suspect to be that here, as in Middlesex, geldable units and actual areal units have already begun to perplex each other. Both Poleham

Kemble's theory.

[1] D. B. i. 12 b.   [2] D. B. i. 9 b.   [3] D. B. i. 12.
[4] Kemble, Saxons, ch. iv. and App. B.
[5] Saxons, i. 490.
[6] D. B. iv. 42. Cf. D. B. i. 81 b.

and Ham are what we call 'over-rated' manors. It is known that Poleham contains 10 hides and Ham 5 hides, but, when we come to look for the acres that will make up the due tale of hides, we can not find them ; for let King William's officers have never so clear a terminology of their own, the country folk will not for ever be distinguishing between 'acres *ad geldum*' and 'acres *ad arandum*.' But be the explanation what it may, we repeat that the one equation that Kemble could find to support his argument is found in the closest company with an equation which when similarly treated produces a nonsensical result. This is all the direct evidence that he has produced from Domesday Book in favour of the hide of 40 acres. Robertson, while holding that the hide of Mercia contained 120 acres, adopted Kemble's opinion that the hide of Wessex contained 40 without producing any witness from Domesday save only the passage about Poleham[1]. Eyton reckons 48 'gheld acres' to the 'gheld hide,' but he leaves us utterly at a loss to tell how he came by this computation[2].

The plough-land and the plough.

Another theory we must examine. It is ingenious and, were it true, would throw much light on a dark corner. It starts from the facts disclosed by the survey of the East Riding of Yorkshire[3]. In that district, it is said, the number of carucates for geld that there are in any manor (this number we will call a) is usually either equal to, or just twice the number (which we call b) of the 'lands for one plough,' or, as we say, teamlands. Further, it can be shown from maps and other modern evidences that the manors in which $a = b$ were manors with two common fields, in other words, were 'two-course manors,' while those in which $a = 2b$ were manors with three common fields, in other words were 'three-course manors.' The suggested explanation is that while the teamland or 'land for one plough' means the amount of land that one plough will till in the course of a year, the 'carucate for geld' is the amount of land which one plough tills in one field in the course of a year. Manor X, let us suppose, is a two-course manor; the whole amount of

[1] Robertson, Hist. Essays, 95, 96. He has entirely misunderstood the entry touching the hundred of Ailestebba. The equation involved in it is merely the following : 16 H. (i.e. $10 + 4\frac{1}{2} + 1\frac{1}{2}$) + 37 H. + 20 H. = 73 H.

[2] Eyton, Dorset, 15 ; Round in Domesday Studies, i. 213.

[3] Dr Isaac Taylor, The Ploughland and the Plough, in Domesday Studies, i. 143. Of this paper there is an excellent review by W. H. Stevenson in Engl. Hist. Rev. v. 142.

land which a plough will till there in a year will lie in one field; therefore in this case $a = b$. Manor Y is a three-course manor; in a given year a plough will there till a certain quantity of land, but half its work will have been done in one field, half in another; therefore in this case $a = 2b$.

Now we must own to doubting the possibility of deciding with any certainty from comparatively modern evidence which (if any) of the Yorkshire vills were under a system of three-course culture in the eleventh century. In the year 1086 many of them were lying and for long years had lain waste either in whole or in part. Thus the first group of examples that is put before us as the foundation for a theory consists of 15 manors the sum of whose carucates for geld is $91\frac{1}{4}$ while the sum of the teamlands is $91\frac{3}{4}$. What was the state of these manors in 1086? Three of them were absolutely waste. The recorded population on the others consisted of four priests, one sokemean, eighty-four villeins and twenty-six bordiers; the number of existing teams was $35\frac{1}{2}$; the total *valet* of the whole fifteen estates was £7. 1s., though they had been worth £72 in King Edward's day[1]. It is obvious enough that very little land is really being ploughed, and surely it is a most perilous inference that, when culture comes back to these deserted villages, the old state of things will be reproduced, so that we shall be able to decide which of them had three and which had two fields in the days before the devastation. Further, we can not think that, even for the East Riding of Yorkshire, the figures show as much regularity as has been attributed to them. In the first place, there are admittedly many cases in which neither of the two equations of which we have spoken ($a = b$ or $a = 2b$) is precisely true. We can only say that they are approximately true. Then there are other cases—too many, as we think, to be treated as exceptional—in which a bears to b some very simple ratio which is neither 1 : 1 nor yet 2 : 1; it is 3 : 2, or 4 : 3, or 5 : 3.

But at any rate, to extend the theory to the whole of Yorkshire, to say nothing of all England, is out of the question. No doubt as a whole Yorkshire was (in the terms that we have used) an 'over-rated' county: that is to say, as a general rule, a, if not equal to, was greater than b. But it can not be said that when a was not equal to b it normally was, or even tended to be equal to $2b$. We take by chance a page describing the

The Yorkshire carucates.

Relation between teamlands and fiscal carucates.

[1] Domesday Studies, 150; D. B. i. 324.

possessions of Count Alan[1]; it contains 20 entries; in one of these $a = b$, in one $a = 2b$, in one b is greater than a; in ten cases the proportion which a bears to b is 3 : 2, in two it is 4 : 3, in two it is 5 : 3, in one 6 : 5, in one 7 : 5, in one it is 17 : 12. In the counties of Lincoln, Nottingham and Derby an application of this doctrine would be ludicrous, for very commonly b is greater than a. What is more, the method of taxation that it presupposes is so unjust that we are loath to attribute it to any one. To tax a man in proportion to the area of the land that he treats as arable, that is a plausibly equitable method; to tax him in proportion to the area that he has ploughed in a given year, that also is a plausibly equitable method; but the present proposal could only be explained as a deliberate effort to tax the three-field system out of existence[2]. To take the figures that have been suggested to us by the author of this theory, we suppose that X is using a team of oxen in 'a two-course manor'; he has 160 acres of arable land and ploughs 80 of them in every year. Then in another village Y is using a team of oxen according to the three-course system; he has, we are told, 180 acres of arable and ploughs 120 acres in every year. This unfortunate Y is to pay double the amount of geld that is paid by X. We could understand a demand that Y should pay nine shillings when X pays eight, for Y has in all 180 acres of arable and X has 160. We could understand a demand that Y should pay three shillings when X pays two, for Y sows 120 acres a year and X sows 80. But nothing short of a settled desire to extirpate the three-field system will prompt us to exact two shillings from Y for every one that is paid by X. Lastly, we must repeat in passing our protest[3] against the introduction into this context of those figures which express the aspirations of that enthusiast of the plough, Walter of Henley. That the 'land for one team' of Domesday Book points normally or commonly to an area of arable land containing 160 or 180 acres we can not believe. If we give it on an average 120 acres we may perhaps find room for the recorded teamlands, though probably we shall often have to make our acres small; but county after county will refuse to make room for teamlands with 160 or 180 acres[4]. No doubt the regularity of the Yorkshire figures is remarkable. There are other districts

---

[1] D. B. i. 311 b.
[2] Round, Feudal England, 60.
[3] See above, p. 397.
[4] See above, pp. 402, 435.

in northern England where we may see some one relation between A and B steadily prevailing. We will call to mind,
by way of example, the symmetrical arrangement that we have
seen in one of the Rutland wapentakes, where $A = 4B$. This
we can not explain, nor will it be explained until Domesday
Book has been rearranged by hundreds and vills; we have,
however, hazarded a guess as to the quarter in which the
explanation may be found[1]. As to the Yorkshire figures, we
think that of all the figures in the record they are the least
likely to be telling us the simple truth about the amount of
cultivated land.

We may now briefly recapitulate the evidence which leads *The fiscal
hide of 120
acres.* us to the old-fashioned belief that King William's Exchequer
reckons 120 acres to the hide. There are at the least twenty
sums set before us which involve the equation: $1\text{H.} = 120\text{A.}$
or $1\text{V.} = 30\text{A.}$ We doubt whether there are two sums which
involve any one other equation. That there are sums which
involve or seem to involve other equations we fully admit; but
when a fair allowance has been made for mistranscription,
miscalculation, the loss of acres due to partitionary arrangements[2], and, above all, to a transition from the rateable to the
real, from the hidage on the roll to the strips in the fields, we
can not think that these cases are sufficiently numerous to
shake our faith. We have further seen that in Essex and East
Anglia the acres of the fiscal system lie in batches of just those
sizes which would be produced if an unit of 120 acres was
being broken into halfs, thirds, quarters and fifths. Lastly,
'the rustics' of the twelfth century 'tell us that the hide
according to its original constitution consists of a hundred
acres[3]' and probably these rustics reckon by the long hundred.

If now we are satisfied about this matter, we seem to be *Antiquity
of the large
hide.* entitled to some inferences about remoter history. The fiscal
practice of reckoning 120 acres to the hide can hardly be new.
Owing to many causes, among which we recall the partitionary
system of taxation, the influence of an equity which would
consider value as well as area, and the disturbing forces of
privilege and favouritism, the fiscal hide of the Confessor's day
has strayed far away from the fields and is no measure of land[4].

---

[1] See above, p. 471.   [2] See above, p. 480.

[3] Dial. de Scac. i. 17.

[4] The appearance in D. B. of a few 'hides' which apparently consist

At its worst it is jobbery; at its best a lame compromise between an unit of area and an unit of value. And yet, for all this, it is composed of acres, of 120 acres. The theory that is involved in this mode of calculation is so little in harmony with the existing facts that we can not but believe that it is ancient. It seems to point to a time long gone by when the typical tenement which was to serve as an unit of taxation generally had six score arable acres, little more or less.

§ 3. *Beyond Domesday.*

The hide beyond Domesday.
We have now seen a good deal of evidence which tends to prove that the hide has had for its model a tenement comprising 120 acres of arable land or thereabouts. Some slight evidence of this we have seen on the face of the Anglo-Saxon land-books[1]. A little more evidence pointing in the same direction we have seen in the manorial extents of a later day[2]. And now we have argued that the fiscal hide of the Conqueror's day is composed of 120 (fiscal) acres. From all this we are inclined to infer that the hide has, if we may so speak, started by being a tenement which, if it attained its ideal, would comprise a long-hundred of arable acre-strips, and thence to infer that in the very old days of conquest and settlement the free family or the free house-father commonly and normally possessed a tenement of this large size.

We have now to confess that this theory is open to attack, and must endeavour to defend it, or rather to explain why we think that, when all objections have been weighed, the balance of probability still inclines in its favour.

Arguments in favour of the small hide.
That all along from Bede's day downwards Englishmen have had in their minds a typical tenement and have been making this idea the framework of their scheme of government can not be doubted. Nor can we doubt that this idea has had some foundation in fact. It could not occur to any one except in a country where a large and preponderant number of tenements

altogether of wood-land (e.g. ii. 55 b) is one of the many signs that the fiscal hide has diverged from its original pattern. A block of wood-land would not be ' the land of one family.'

[1] See above, p. 389.   [2] See above, p. 393.

really, if roughly, conformed to a single type. Therefore the contest must be, and indeed has been, between the champions of different typical tenements, and in the main there are but two theories in the field. The one would give the Anglo-Saxon hide its long-hundred of acres, the other would concede to it but some thirty or forty, and would in effect equate it with the virgate rather than with the hide of later days[1]. Perhaps we may briefly state the arguments which have been urged in favour of this small hide by saying that small hides are requisite (1) if we are to find room enough within the appropriate areal boundaries for the hides that are distributed by Domesday Book and the Anglo-Saxon charters, (2) if we are to explain the large quantities of hides or family-lands which are assigned to divers districts by Bede and by that ancient document which we call The Tribal Hidage, (3) if we are to bring our own typical tenement into line with the typical tenement of Germany, (4) if we are not to overdo our family or house-father with arable acres and bushels of corn.

A 'name-shifting' must be postulated. Somehow or another, what was the hide becomes the virgate, while the name 'hide' is transferred to a much larger unit. Now in such a name-shifting there is nothing that is very improbable, if we approach the matter *a priori*. Thought has been poor and language has been poor. The term 'yard of land' may, as we have seen[2], stand for a quarter-acre or for a much larger space. But this particular name-shifting seems to us improbable in a high degree. For when did it happen? Surely it did not happen after the Norman Conquest. We have from Edward the Confessor quite enough documents to warrant our saying with certainty that the hides and manses of his charters are the hides of Domesday Book. Suppose for a moment that all these parchments were forged after the Conquest, this would only strengthen our case, for stupid indeed must the forger

Continuity in the hide of the land-books.

---

[1] Dr Stubbs, Const. Hist. i. 79, has endeavoured to find a *via media*. To me it seems that his suggestion is open to almost all the objections that can be urged against our Big Hide, for he seems prepared to give the normal household of the oldest day its 120 acres. Mr Seebohm's adhesion to the party of the Big Hide is of importance, for I can not but think that a small hide (which afterwards was called a virgate) would have assorted better with his general theory. Conversely, it is curious that Kemble, the champion of the free ceorls, was also the champion, if not the inventor, of the Little Hide.

[2] See above, p. 385.

have been who did not remember that if he was to make a
title-deed for the abbey's lands he must multiply the hides by
four or thereabouts. This argument will carry us far. We
trace the stream of land-books back from Edward to Cnut, to
Æthelred, to Edgar, to Offa, nay, to the very days of Bede;
nowhere can we see any such breach of continuity as that which
would appear had the hypothetical name-shifting taken place.
The forgers know nothing of it. Boldly they make the first
Christian kings bestow upon the church just about the number
of manses that the church has in the eleventh century if the
manse be Domesday's hide.

Examples from charters of Chertsey.

Both points might be illustrated by the Chertsey charters.
In Domesday Book S[t]. Peter of Chertsey is credited with many
hides in divers parts of Surrey[1]. A charter is forthcoming
whereby Edward the Confessor confirms the abbey's possession
of these estates[2], and in the main the number of 'manses' that
this charter locates in any village is the number of 'hides' that
the abbey will have there in the year 1086. The two lists are
not and ought not to be identical, for there have been rearrangements; but obviously the manse of the one is the hide of the
other. Then the monks have books which profess to come from
the seventh century[3] and to show how Frithwald the kingling
of Surrey endowed their monastery. These books may be
forgeries; but the scale on which they are forged is the scale
of the Confessor's charter and of Domesday Book. It has
been thought that they are as old as Edgar's day[4]; but at
any rate their makers did not suppose that in order to tell a
profitable story they must portray Frithwald bestowing four
manses for every hide that the abbey possessed.

Examples from charters of Malmesbury.

Or look we at the estates of S[t]. Aldhelm. The monks of
Malmesbury have a book from the Confessor[5] which agrees very
accurately, perhaps too accurately, with the Domesday record[6].
The latter ascribes to their house (among other lands) 10 hides
at Dauntsey, 5 at Somerford, 5 at Norton, 30 at Kemble, 35 at
Purton. The Confessor has confirmed to them (among other
lands) 10 'hides' at Dauntsey given by Æthelwulf, 5 at Somerford and 5 at Norton given by Æthelstan, 30 at Kemble and 35

[1] D. B. i. 32 b. [2] K. 812 (iv. 151).
[3] K. 986–988 (v. 14–21); B. i. 55–9, 64.
[4] Plummer, Bede, ii. 217. [5] K. 917 (iv. 165).
[6] D. B. i. 66 b, 67.

at Purton given by Ceadwealla. Then behind this book are older books. Here is one dated in 931 by which Æthelstan gives *quinque mansas* at Somerford and *quinque mansas* at Norton[1]. Here is another dated in 850 by which Æthelwulf gives *decem mansiones* at Dauntsey[2]. Here is a third by which in 796 Egfrith restores that *terram xxxv manentium* at Purton[3]. Here from 682, from the days of Aldhelm himself, is a deed of Ceadwealla bestowing *xxxii cassatos* at Kemble[4]. It is pretty; it is much too pretty; but it is good proof that the Malmesbury monks know nothing of any change in the conveyancer's unit[5].

If we examine any reputable set of land-books, those of Worcester, for example, or those of Abingdon and try to trace the history of those very hides the existence of which is chronicled by Domesday Book, we shall often fail. This was to be expected. Any one who has 'read with a conveyancer' will know that many difficulties are apt to arise when an attempt is made to identify the piece of land described in one with that described in another and much older document. In the days before the Conquest many causes were perplexing our task. We have spoken of them before, but will recall them to memory. New assessments were sometimes made, and thenceforth an estate which had formerly contained five hides might be spoken of as having only four. New villages were formed, and the hides which had been attributed to one place would thenceforth be attributed to another. Great landlords enjoyed a large power of rearranging their lands, not only for the purposes of their own economy, but also for the purposes of public finance. In some cases they had collected their estates into a few gigantic *maneria* each of which would pay a single round sum to the king[6]. Lastly, the kings gave and the kings took away. The disendowment of churches and simple spoliation were not unknown; exchanges were frequent; no series of land-books is complete. But when some allowance has been made for the effects of these causes, we shall see plainly that, if the charters are to account for the facts displayed by Domesday Book, then the manses of the charters, even of the earliest charters, can not

Permanence of the hidation.

[1] K. 355 (ii. 179).   [2] K. 263 (ii. 35). Accepted by Kemble.
[3] K. 174 (i. 209).   [4] K. 24 (i. 28).
[5] It is fair to say that the instances here given are picked instances and that the Malmesbury title to some other lands is not so exceedingly neat.
[6] See above, p. 112.

have been of much less extent than the hides of the Norman record. We know of no case in which a church, whatever its wealth of genuine and spurious parchments, could make a title to many more manses than the hides that it had in 1086[1].

Another test of continuity may be applied. In the Conqueror's day a village in the south of England will very commonly be rated at five or some low multiple of five hides, ten, fifteen or twenty[2]. Now we have argued above that the land-book of an Anglo-Saxon king generally, though not always, disposes of an integral village or several integral villages, and if we look at the land-books we shall commonly see that the manses or hides which they describe as being at a single place are in number five or some low multiple of five. We open the second volume of the Codex Diplomaticus and analyze the first hundred instances of royal gifts which do not bear a condemnatory asterisk and which are not gifts of small plots in or about the towns of Canterbury and Rochester. In date these land-books range from A.D. 840 to A.D. 956. In sixty out of a hundred cases the number of manses is 5 or a multiple of 5. In eighteen it is 5; in sixteen 10; in six 15; in thirteen 20; in three 25; in one 30; in one 80; in two 100. There are a few small gifts; one of a yokelet; six of 1 manse; four of 2 manses; five of 3. The great bulk of the gifts range from 5 to 25 manses. Only four out of 100 exceed 25; of these four, one is of 30, another of 80, while two are of 100. At this rate of progress and if the manse had no more than some 30 acres, we shall have extreme difficulty in accounting for the large territ ies which on the eve of the Conquest were held by the ies of Wessex, and by those very churches which have left us cartularies that are only too ample. This is not all. If these manses were but yard-lands, then, unless

---

[1] This is so even in the case of the Kentish churches, see above, p. 466. The Chronicle of Abingdon affords good materials for comparison with D. B. As a general rule the charters will account for just about the right number of manses, if the manses are to be the hides. There are exceptions; but not more than might be fairly explained by changes such as those recorded in the following words (Chron. Abingd. i. 270):—'Fuerunt autem Witham, Seouecurt, Henstesie, Eatun membra de Cumenora temporibus Eadgari regis Angliae, habentes cassatos xxv; nunc vero Hensteseie membrum est de Bertona; Witheham et Seouecurt militibus datae; Eatun omnimodo ablata.' See also an excellent paper by Mr C. S. Taylor, The Pre-Domesday Hide of Gloucestershire, Trans. Brist. and Glouc. Archæol. Soc. vol. xviii.

[2] Round, Feudal England, 44 ff.

we suppose that the average village was a tiny cluster, it is plain enough that the kings did not usually give away integral villages, and yet a church's lordship of integral villages and even of divers contiguous villages is one of the surest and most impressive traits that the Conqueror's record reveals.

Parenthetically we may admit that the king is not always giving away a whole village. Nasse has contended that when a land-book professes to dispose of a certain number (x) of manses at the place called X, and then sets forth the boundaries of X, we must not infer that the whole of the land that lies within those boundaries is comprised in the grant[1]. The proof of this consists of a few instances in which, to all appearance, two different tracts of land are conveyed by two different books and yet the boundaries stated in those two books are the same. We will allege one instance additional to those that have been mentioned by others. In 969 Bishop Oswald of Worcester gave to his man Æthelweard seven manses, whereof five lay in the place called Tedington. The book which effected this conveyance states the bounds of Tedington[2]. In 977 the same bishop gave to his man Eadric three manses at Tedington by a book which describes the boundaries of that place in just the same manner as that in which they were set forth by the earlier charter[3]. Some care, however, should be taken before we assume that the two deeds which deal with land at X dispose of different tracts; for book-land had a way of returning to the king who gave it; also the gift of one king was sometimes confirmed by another; and even if the one book purports to convey x and the other y manses, we must call to mind the possibility that there has been a reassessment or a clerical error. Still it seems to be fairly well proved that there are cases in which the x manses which the donor gives are but some of the manses that lie within the meres drawn by his deed of gift. This certainly deserves remark. At first sight nothing could look more foolish than that we should painfully define the limits of the village territory and yet leave undefined the limits of that part of the village territory which we are giving away. But this practice is explicable if we remember the nature of a manse in a village. It consists of many

Gifts of manses in villages.

[1] Nasse, Agricultural Community, Engl. transl., 23-5. Seebohm, Village Community, 111.
[2] K. 552 (iii. 35). [3] K. 617 (iii. 164).

scattered strips of arable land and of rights over uncultivated waste. To define the limits of the whole territory is important, for the donee should know how far his cattle can wander without trespass. To specify each acre-strip would, on the other hand, be a tedious task and would serve no profitable end. However, there can be little doubt that very generally what a charter bestows is the whole of the land of which the boundaries are described, and therefore the whole territory of a village or of several neighbouring villages.

The largest gifts

But at the moment the charters which will be the most instructive will be those which attribute to a single place some large number of hides. In these the champions of a small hide have found their stronghold. They see perhaps 100 hides ascribed to the place called X; they look for that place in modern maps and gazetteers and then tell us that in order to pack our 100 hides within the parochial boundary we must reduce the size of the hide to 30 acres at the most.

The Winchester estate at Chilcombe.

The dangers that beset this process may be well illustrated by the documents relating to one of the most interesting estates in all England, the great Chilcombe estate of the church of Winchester, which stretched for many a mile from the gates of the royal city of the West Saxon kings. Let us follow the story as the monks told it in a series of charters, few of which have escaped Kemble's asterisk. In the first days of English Christianity, Cynegils, king of the West Saxons, gave the Chilcombe valley to St. Birinus. King after king confirmed the gift, but it was never put into writing until the days of Æthelwulf. He declared by charter that this land should defend itself for one hide. This was part of that great tithing operation which puzzles the modern historian[1]. In 908 Edward the Elder confirmed this act by a charter in which he declared that the land at Chilcombe (including that at Nursling and Chilbolton) contained 100 manses, but that the whole was to be reckoned as a single manse. He also remarked that the land included many *villae*[2]. The next book comes from Æthelstan; the whole valley (*vallis illuster Ciltecumb appellata*) with all its appendages was to owe the service of a single

---

[1] Charter of Æthelwulf, K. 1057 (v. 113); T. p. 115; H. & S. 646. We should not be surprised if at least one part of the mysterious 'decimation' turned out to be an early act of 'beneficial hidation.'

[2] Charter of Edward, K. 342 (ii. 153).

manse[1]. Two charters were obtained from Edgar. However much land there might be at Chilcombe, it was to defend itself for one hide[2]. A writ of similar import, which Kemble has accepted, was issued by Æthelred the Unready[3]. It said that there were a hundred hides at Chilcombe and proceeded to allot them thus:—

Æstun	4	Easton
Afintun and Ufintun	5	Avington and Ovington
Ticceburn	25	Titchbourne
Cymestun	5	Kilmiston
Stoke	5	Bishopstoke
Brombrygce and Oterburn	5	Brambridge and Otterbourne
Twyfyrde	20	Twyford
Ceolbandingtun	20	Chilbolton
Hnutscilling	5	Nursling

This territory extends along the left-hand bank of the Itchen from Kilmiston to Titchbourne, thence past Ovington, Avington, Easton, Chilcombe, and Winchester itself, Twyford, Brambridge, Otterbourne to Bishopstoke. If we journeyed by straight lines from village to village we should find that our course was a long twenty miles. Then, to complete the 100 hides, Nursling which is near Southampton and Chilbolton which is near Andover are thrown in. But all these lands lie 'into Ciltecumbe.'

It is to be feared that these charters tell lies invented by those who wished to evade their share of national burdens. And they seem to have failed in their object, for in the Confessor's day, though a very large estate at 'Chilcombe' with nine churches upon it was rated at but one hide, several of the other villages that we have mentioned were separately assessed[4]. But to lie themselves into an immunity from taxes, this the monks might hope to do; to lie themselves into the possession of square leagues of land, this would have been an impossible feat, and the solid fact remains that their church was the lord of a spacious and continuous block of territory in the very heart of the old West Saxon realm, just outside the gates of the royal burg, along the Itchen river, the land that would be

The many hides at Chilcombe.

---

[1] Charter of Æthelstan, K. 1113 (v. 224).
[2] Charters of Edgar, K. 512 (ii. 401); K. 583 (iii. 111).
[3] Writ of Æthelred, K. 642 (iii. 203).
[4] D. B. i. 40–41.

seized and settled at the earliest moment. The best explanation that they could give of this fact was that the first Christian kings had bestowed mile after mile of land upon the minster. What better theory have we[1]?

The truth seems to be that some of the very earliest gifts of land that were made to the churches might, if we have regard to the size of the existing kingdoms, be fairly called the cession of provinces, the cession of large governmental and jurisdictional districts. The bishops want a revenue, and in the earliest days a large district must be ceded if even a modest revenue is to be produced, for all that the king has to give away is the chieftain's right to live at the expense of the folk and to receive the proceeds of justice. Therefore not only whole villages but whole hundreds were given. Chilcombe was by no means the only vast estate that the bishop of the West Saxons acquired in very early days. Domesday Book shows us how at Downton in Wiltshire the church of Winchester has had a round 100 hides[2]. For these 100 hides we have a series of charters which professes to begin in the days when the men of Wessex were accepting the new faith. They bear the names of Cenwealla[3], Egbert[4], Edward[5], Æthelstan[6], Edred[7], Edgar[8], and Æthelred[9]. Kemble has accepted the last four of them. They tell a consistent story. There were 100 manses at Downton, or, to speak more accurately, 55 at Downton itself and 45 at Ebbesborne (the modern Bishopston) on the other side of the Avon[10]. We might speak of other

---

[1] Kitchin, Winchester, 7: 'Cenwalh built the church, the parent of Winchester cathedral...The monks at once set themselves to ennoble toil, to wed tillage with culture; and it is interesting to note that the first endowment of the Church in Wessex fell to them in the form of a great grant of all the land for some leagues around the city, given for the building of the church.' Did the monks till the land for some leagues around the city? I think not. Was it all occupied by their serfs? I think not. What was given was a superiority. One last question:—Did the monks really ennoble toil by appropriating its proceeds?

[2] D. B. i. 65 b: 'Episcopus Wintoniensis tenet Duntone. T. R. E. geldavit pro 100 hidis tribus minus. Duae ex his non sunt episcopi, quia ablatae fuerunt cum aliis tribus de aecclesia et de manu episcopi tempore Cnut Regis.'

[3] K. 985 (v. 12). [4] K. 1036 (v. 80). [5] K. 342 (ii. 153).
[6] K. 1108 (v. 211). [7] K. 421 (ii. 287). [8] K. 599 (iii. 139).
[9] K. 698 (iii. 299).

[10] As to the limits of Downton, see W. H. Jones, Domesday for Wiltshire, 213.

extensive tracts, of Farnham where there have been 60 hides[1], of Alresford where there have been 51[2], of Mitcheldever where there have been 106[3], of Taunton where there have been 54 and more[4]. Whenever the West Saxons conquer new lands they cede a wide province to their bishop. But perhaps we have already said more than enough of these cessions, though in our eyes they are very important; they are among the first manifestations of incipient feudalism and feudalism brings manorialism in its train. We have recurred to them here because the Winchester charters which describe them testify strongly to the continuity of the hide and also indicate the weak point in the arguments that are urged by the advocates of little hides[5].

Kemble has argued that it is impossible for us to allow the hide of Domesday Book or the hide or manse of the charters as many as 120 acres. Take a village, discover how many hides are ascribed to it, discover how many acres it has at the present day, you will often find that the whole territory of the village will not suffice to supply the requisite number of hides if the hide is to have 120 or even 60 acres. Kemble illustrates this method by taking nine vills in Somerset and Devon. One of them is Taunton. Modern Taunton, he says, has 2730 acres, the Tantone of 1086 had 65 hides[6]; multiply 65 even by so low a figure as 40 and you will nearly exhaust all Taunton's soil[6]. This argument involves the assumption that the limits of modern Taunton include the whole land that is ascribed to 'Tantone' in the Conqueror's geld-book. Strangely different was the result to which Eyton came after a minute examination of the whole survey of Somersetshire. The 'Tantone' of

Kemble and the Taunton estate.

---

[1] D. B. i. 31; K. 1058 (v. 114); 1093 (v. 176); 605 (iii. 149).

[2] D. B. i. 40. Forty hides said to have been given by Cenwealla.. K. 997 (v. 39); 1039 (v. 85); 1086 (v. 162); 1090 (v. 162); 601 (iii. 144).

[3] D. B. i. 42 b. This belongs to the New Minster. In K. 336 (ii. 144) Edward the Elder is made to give 'quendam fundum quem indigenae Myceldefer appellant cum suo hundredo et appendicibus, habens centum cassatos et aecclesiam.' The territory has 100 hides and is a 'hundred.'

[4] D. B. i. 87 b. K. 1002 (v. 44); 1051–2 (v. 99, 101); 1084 (v. 157); 374 (ii. 209); 598 (iii. 136).

[5] They are hardly the worse witnesses about this matter for having been much 'improved.' They do not look like late forgeries. Those which bear the earliest dates seem to be treated as genuine in charters of the tenth century which are not (if anything that comes from Winchester is not) suspected.

[6] Kemble, Saxons, i. 487; D. B. i. 87 b.

Domesday covers some thirteen or fourteen villages and is now represented not by 2730 but by 24,000 acres[1]. The editor of the Anglo-Saxon charters should have guessed that many hides 'lay in' Taunton which as a matter of physical geography were far off from the walls of the bishop's burg[2]. There are counties in which the list of the places that are mentioned in Domesday is so nearly identical with the list of our modern parishes, that no very great risk would be run if we circumspectly pursued Kemble's method; but just in those counties to which he applied it the risk is immeasurably great, for it is the land where many villages are often collected into one great *manerium* and all their hides are spoken of as lying in one place. Not until we have compared the whole survey of the county with the whole of its modern map, are we entitled to make even a guess as to the amount of land that a place-name covers. Often enough in those shires where there are large and ancient ecclesiastical estates, those shires in which the feudal and manorial development began earliest and has gone furthest, hides 'are' in law where they are not in fact. They 'lie into' the hall at which they geld or the moot-stow to which they render soke, and this may be far distant from their natural bed[3].

Difficulty of identifying parcels. As we go backwards this danger is complicated by another, namely, by the growth of new villages. The village of Hamton has been a large village with 20 hides. Some of its arable

---

[1] Eyton, Somerset, ii. 34.

[2] See above, p. 499, note 4.

[3] Compare, for instance, the account of the estates of the Bishop of Wells, D. B. i. 89, with the charter ascribed to the Confessor, K. 816 (iv. 163). In the former we read of 50 hides at Wells; in the latter we see that these hides cover 24 villages or hamlets, each of which has its name. According to Eyton (Somerset, 24) this estate extends over nearly 22,000 acres. The Malmesbury charter, K. 817 (iv. 165) is another good illustration. Kemble's identifications were hasty and have fared ill at the hands of those who have made local researches. A few examples follow :—Keynsham, 50 H. = 3330 A. (Kemble), 11,138 A. and more (Eyton). Dowlish, 9 H. = 680 A. (Kemble), 1282 (Eyton). Road, 9 H. = 1010 A. (Kemble), 1664 (Eyton). Portishead, 11 H. = 1610 (Kemble), 2093 (Eyton). The instances that Kemble gives (vol. i. p. 106) from the A.-S. land-books are equally unfortunate. Thus he reads of 50 H. at Brokenborough, Wilts, and seeks for them all in a modern parish which has 2950 A.; but the Domesday manor of this name covered 'at least 6000 or perhaps 7000 acres' (W. H. Jones, Domesday for Wilts, p. xxvii.). In several instances Kemble tries to force into a single parish all the hides of a hundred which takes its name from that parish.

land has lain two or three miles from the clustered steads. A
partition of its fields is made and a new cluster of steads is
formed; for housebuilding is not a lengthy or costly process.
And so Little Hamton or 'Other' Hamton with 5 hides
splits off from the old Hamton which has 15. We must not
now try to force 20 hides into the territory of either village[1].
And as this danger increases, the other hardly diminishes, for
we come to the time when a king will sometimes give a large
jurisdictional district and call it all by one name. If the once
heathen Osric of the Hwiccas gave to a church '100 *manentes*
adjoining the city that is called the Hot Baths,' he in all
probability gave away the 'hundred' of Bath; he gave Bath
itself and a territory which in the eleventh century was the
site of a dozen villages[2]. We have the best reason for believing
that when a king of the eighth century says that he is giving
20 manses in the place called Cridie he is giving his rights
over a tract which comprises ten or twelve of our modern
parishes and more than the whole of the modern hundred of
Crediton[3].

We have given above some figures which will enable our
readers to compare the hides and the teamlands of a county
with its modern acreage. Also we have confessed to thinking
that we can hardly concede to every teamland that Domesday
mentions 120 statute acres of arable land[4]. On the other
hand, we do not think that there would in general be much
difficulty in finding 120 arable acres for every fiscal hide,
though perhaps in the south the average size of the acre would
be small[5]. However, we have admitted, or rather contended,
that before the middle of the eleventh century the hides of the
fiscal system had strayed far away from the original type, and
the sight of an over-hided vill would not disconcert us. But

[1] Hanssen, Abhandlungen, i. 499.
[2] See above, p. 229, and Mr Taylor's paper there mentioned.
[3] Napier and Stevenson, Crawford Charters, 43. Compare D. B. i. 101 b. In
the Confessor's time 'Crediton' gelded for 15 hides. There was land for 185
teams, and teams to that number existed. There were 264 villeins, 73 bordiers
and 40 serfs. Æthelheard's charter suggests either that in his day this part of
Devon was very sparsely peopled, or that already, under a system of partitionary taxation, a small number of fiscal units had been cast upon a poor
district. When at a later time Eadnoth bishop of Crediton mortgages a
yardland for 30 mancuses of gold (Ibid. p. 5), this yardland will be a fiscal
virgate of wide extent. See above, p. 467, note 2.
[4] See above, p. 445.   [5] See above, p. 400.

unfortunately we can not be content with such results as we have as yet attained. We have already seen that the hides attributed to a district show a tendency to increase their number as we trace them backwards[1], and there are certain old documents which deal out hides so lavishly that we must seriously face the question whether, notwithstanding the continuity of the land-books, we must not suppose that some large change has taken place in the character of the typical tenement.

The Burghal Hidage. We have said above that we have inherited three ancient documents which distribute hides among districts. We call them in order of date (1) The Tribal Hidage, (2) The Burghal Hidage, (3) The County Hidage. Of the youngest we have spoken. We must now attend to that which holds the middle place. It states that large round numbers of hides belong to certain places, which seem to be strongholds. The sense in which a large number of hides might belong to a *burh* will be clear to those who have read the foregoing pages[2]. This document has only come down to us in a corrupt form, but it has come from a remote time and seems to represent a scheme of West-Saxon defence which was antiquated long years before the coming of the Normans. We will give its effect, preserving the most important variants and adding within brackets some guesses of our own.

THE BURGHAL HIDAGE[3]

	Hides.
to Heorepeburan, Heorewburan[4]	324
to Hastingecestre [Hastings]	15 or 500
to Lathe, Lawe [Lewes][5]	1300
to Burhham [Burpham near Arundel]	726
to Cisseceastre [Chichester]	1500
to Portecheastre [Porchester]	650

[1] See above, p. 458.   [2] See above, p. 188.

[3] Birch, Cart. Sax. iii. 671; Munimenta Gildhallae, ii. 627; Gale, Scriptores xv., i. 748; Liebermann, Leges Anglorum, 9. 10.

[4] This we can not find. If Kent were included in the scheme, we should read of Canterbury, Rochester etc. Therefore we probably start in Sussex, but at some point east of Hastings. In any case, unless a name has dropped out, we can not make the five Sussex burgs correspond to the six rapes of a later day, which, going from east to west, are Hastings, Pevensey, Lewes, Bramber, Arundel, Chichester.

[5] See the Læwe, Læwes of K. 499, 1237.

	Hides.
to Hamtona and to Wincestre [Southampton and Winchester]	2400
to Piltone, Pistone[1], Wiltone [Wilton]	1400
to Tysanbyring [Tisbury][2]	700
to Soraflesbyring, Soraflesburieg, Sceaftesbyrig [Shaftesbury]	700
to Thoriham, Tweonham, Twenham [Twyneham][3]	470
to Weareham [Wareham]	1600
to Brydian [Bridport or more probably Bredy][4]	1760
to Excencestre [Exeter]	734
to Halganwille, Hallgan Wylla [Halwell][5]	300
to Hlidan, Hlida [Lidford]	140
to Wiltone Wisbearstaple, Piltone wið Bearstaple [Pilton[6] with Barnstaple]	360
to Weted, Weced [Watchet][7]	513
to Orenbrege, Oxenebrege, Axanbrige [Axbridge]	400
to Lenge, Lengen [Lyng][8]	100
to Langiord, Langport [Langport]	600
to Bathan, Badecan, Baderan [Bath]	3200 (?)
to Malmesberinge [Malmesbury]	1500
to Croccegelate, Croccagelada [Cricklade]	1003 or 1300
to Oxeforde and to Wallingeforde [Oxford and Wallingford]	2400
to Buckingham and to Sceaftelege, Sceafteslege, Steaftesege [Buckingham and ?][9]	600 or 1500
to Eschingum and to Suthringa geweorc [Southwark and Eashing][10]	1800

[1] A confusion of P and W is common.

[2] Tisbury lies between Wilton and Shaftesbury. See K. 104, 641. Mr Stevenson suggests that the word may be *Cysanbyrig*, thereby being meant Chiselbury Camp. This also lies in the right quarter.

[3] *Tweoxneam*, A.-S. Chron. ann. 901.

[4] See *Bridian* in K. 656. Bredy lies about eight miles west of Dorchester. It seems to contain a 'Kingston.'

[5] There is a Halwell a little to the south of Totness. Already in 1018 (Crawford Charters, pp. 9, 79) the Devonshire burgs are Exeter, Lidford, Totness and Barnstaple.

[6] Pilton lies close to Barnstaple.

[7] A.-S. Chron. ann. 915 : 'be eastan Weced.'

[8] A little to the west of Langport; close to Athelney. A.-S. Chron. ann. 878: 'And þæs on Eastron worhte Ælfred cyning lytle werede geweorc æt Æþelinga eigge.' Green, Conquest of England, 110. Observe that a very small district is assigned to Lyng.

[9] After seeing Oxford and Wallingford together, we should naturally expect Bedford with Buckingham. See A.-S. Chron. ann. 918-9. Or we might look for Hertford. Ibid. ann. 913.

[10] Eashing is a tithing in the parish of Godalming. See King Alfred's will (K. 314): 'æt Æscengum.' Eashing may have been supplanted by Guildford.

These figures having been stated, we are told that they make a total of 27,070 hides[1]. And then we read 'et triginta[2] to Astsexum [*al.* Westsexum], and to Wygraceastrum mcc. hydas. to Wæringewice [*al.* Parlingewice] feower and xxiiii. hund hyda.'

Meaning of The Burgh-al Hidage. Apparently we start at some burg in the extreme east of Sussex, go through Hastings, Lewes, Burpham, Chichester, Porchester, and then pass through Hampshire, through the south of Wiltshire, through Dorset to Devon, keeping always well to the south. Then in Devon we turn to the north and retrace our steps by moving to the east along a more northerly route than that which we followed in the first instance. In short, we make a round of Wessex and end at Southwark. This done, we cast up the number of hides and find them to be somewhat more than 27,000. Then in what may be a post-script the remark is made that to Essex and Worcester belong 1200 hides (probably 1200 apiece) and to Warwick 2404. The writer seems to know Wessex pretty thoroughly; of the rest of England he (if he added the postscript) has little to tell us. We might perhaps imagine him drawing up this state-ment under Edward the Elder[3]. He hears reports of what has been done to make Essex defensible and of two famous burgs built in Mercia; but the military system of Wessex he knows[4]. Of a military system it is that he is telling us. He does not take the counties of Wessex one by one; he visits the burgs, and his tour through them takes him twice through Wiltshire: westwards along a southerly and eastwards along a northerly line.

It is an artificial system that he discloses to us. The 324 hides allotted to 'Heorepeburan' (a place that eludes us)

---

[1] Taking in the particulars the figures which seem the more probable, we make a larger total.

[2] If Essex is meant this figure seems impossibly small. Gale gives 'Ast Saxhum et Wygeaceastrum 1200 hidas.' This may give Essex and Worcester 1200 hides *apiece*.

[3] Mr Stevenson tells me that, though the document is very corrupt, some of the verbal forms seem to speak of this date.

[4] Such a document is apt to be tampered with. Some bits of it may be older than other bits, but the reign of Edward the Elder seems the latest to which we could ascribe its core. If we compare it with the list of Domesday boroughs we shall be struck by the absence of Dorchester, Bridport, Ilchester, Totness, Hertford, Bedford and Guildford, as well as by the appearance of Burpham, Tisbury, Bredy, Halwell, Watchet, Lyng and Eashing.

may seem insufficiently round until we add it to the 726 given
to 'Burhham.' The Wiltshire burgs seem to be grouped
thus:—

$$
\left.
\begin{array}{l}
\left.
\begin{array}{ll}
\text{Wilton} & 1400 \\
\text{Tisbury} & 700 \\
\text{Shaftesbury} & 700
\end{array}
\right\} 2800 \\
\left.
\begin{array}{ll}
\text{Malmesbury} & 1500 \\
\text{Cricklade} & 1300
\end{array}
\right\} 2800
\end{array}
\right\} 5600
$$

To compare these figures with those given in Domesday *The Burgh-al Hidage* Book and in The County Hidage is not a straightforward task, *and later* for the military districts of 900 may not have been coincident *documents.* with the counties of 1086, and, for example, Bath may have been supported partly by Gloucestershire and partly by Somerset[1]. The best comparison that we can make is the following:—

	Burghal Hidage	County Hidage	Domesday Book
Sussex[2]	4350		3474
Surrey[3]	1800 (or 3600)		1830
Hampshire[4]	3520		2588
Berkshire[5]	2400		2473
Wiltshire[6]	5600	4800	4050
Dorset[7]	3360		2321
Somerset[8]	4813		2951
Devon[9]	1534		1119
Oxford	2400	2400	2412
Buckingham	1500		2074
Essex (?)	1200		2650
Worcester	1200	1200	1189
Warwick	2404	1200	1338

There is discord here, but also there is concord. According to our reckoning, the Oxfordshire and Berkshire of Domesday Book have just about 2400 hides apiece; then The County Hidage gives Oxfordshire 2400; and The Burghal Hidage gives 2400 to Oxford and 2400 to Wallingford. Both documents give

[1] See above, p. 189, note 1.
[2] 'Heorepeburan,' Hastings, Lewes, Burpham, Chichester.
[3] Eashing, Southwark.
[4] Porchester, Southampton, Winchester, Twyneham.
[5] Wallingford.
[6] Wilton, Tisbury, Shaftesbury, Malmesbury, Cricklade.
[7] Wareham, Bredy.
[8] Watchet, Axbridge, Lyng, Langport, Bath.
[9] Exeter, Halwell, Lidford, Barnstaple.

1200 to Worcester, and this is very close to the number that Domesday Book assigns. Next we see that, with hardly an exception[1], all the aberrations of our Burghal Hidage from Domesday Book lie in one direction. They all point to great reductions of hidage, which seem to have been distributed with a fairly even hand. Further, in the case of Wiltshire we see a progressive abatement. The hidage is lowered from 5600 to 4800 and then to a little over 4000, and the first reduction seems to have relieved the shire of just one-seventh of its hides.

Criticism of *The Burghal Hidage.*

Now it seems to us that, on the one hand, we must reckon with this document as with one which, however much it may have been distorted by copyists, is or once was a truthful, and possibly an official record, and that, on the other hand, we can reckon with it and yet retain that notion of the hide which we have been elaborating. In a general way it both gives support to and receives support from the evidence that has already come before us. We have seen reductions of hidage or carucatage made in Yorkshire and Leicestershire after the Domesday survey; we have seen reductions in Sussex, Surrey, Hampshire, Berkshire, Cambridge, Northamptonshire. Here we come upon earlier reductions. They are large; but still they are not of such a kind as to make us think that any great change has taken place in men's idea of a normal and typical hide. For one thing, we might be rash if we denied that during that miserable tenth century both the population and the wealth of Wessex were declining, for, despite its Æthelstan and Edgar, a miserable time it was. A real extinction of many a ' real hide ' there may have been. But our main explanation will be that, by a process which is gradual and yet catastrophic, the ancient exaggerated estimates of population and wealth are being brought into correspondence with the humbler facts.

The Tribal Hidage.

We must now turn to a more famous and yet older document, namely that which we call The Tribal Hidage[2]. It assigns large round quantities of hides to various districts, or rather to various peoples, whose very names would otherwise have been unknown to us. We are not about to add to the commentaries

---

[1] A good deal of doubt hangs over the entries touching Buckingham, Essex and Warwick.

[2] Birch, Cartularium, i. 414; Birch, Journal Brit. Archæol. Assoc. xl. 29 (1884); Earle, Land Charters, 458; Liebermann, Leges Anglorum, 8; Stevenson, Engl. Hist. Rev., 1889, 354.

that have been written upon it; but its general scheme seems to be fairly plain. It begins by allotting to Myrcna land 30,000 hides. On this follow eighteen more or less obscure names to each of which a sum of hides is assigned; 36,100 hides are distributed between them. Then a grand total of 66,100 is stated. Ten other more or less obscure names follow, and 19,000 hides are thus disposed of. Then we have more intelligible entries:—'East Engle 30,000. East Sexena 7,000. Cantwarena 15,000. South Sexena 7,000. West Sexena 100,000.' Then we are told that the complete sum is 242,700, a statement which is not true as the figures stand, for they amount to 244,100. The broad features, therefore, of this system seem to be these:—It ascribes to Wessex 100,000 hides to Sussex 7,000, to Kent 15,000, to Essex 7,000, to East Anglia 30,000, to Mercia 30,000, to the rest of England 55,100. Apparently we must look for this rest of England outside Wessex, Sussex, Kent, Essex and East Anglia and outside the Mercians' land, though this last term is probably used in an old and therefore narrow sense. The least obscure of the obscure names that are put before us, those of the dwellers in the Peak, the dwellers in Elmet and the men of Lindsey, seem to point to the same conclusion[1].

Now our first remark about this document will perhaps be either that it is wild nonsense, or that its 'hide' has for its type something very different from the model that has served for those hides of which we have hitherto been reading. Domesday will not allow the whole of England 70,000 hides (carucates, sulungs) and now we are asked to accommodate more than 240,000. Kent is to have 15,000 hides instead of 1200 sulungs. Even the gulf between The Burghal Hidage and this Tribal Hidage is enormous. The one would attribute less than 4500 hides to the Sussex burgs, the other would burden the South Saxons with 7000. In the older document Wessex has 100,000 hides, while in the younger the burgs of Surrey, Hampshire, Berkshire, Wiltshire, Dorset, Somerset and Devon have as their contributories less than a quarter of that number. The suspicion can not but cross our mind

Criticism of The Tribal Hidage.

---

[1] Unless the mention of Wessex is interpolated (and if it be interpolated then the grand total has been tampered with) it is difficult to suppose that 'Wiht gara 600' points to the Isle of Wight, 'Gifla 300' to the district round Ilchester, or the like. I owe this observation to Mr W. J. Corbett.

that the 'hides' of The Tribal Hidage are yard-lands, or, in other words have for their moulding idea rather a tenement of 30 than a tenement of 120 arable acres[1].

Bede's hidage.

Before we decide this important question we must give audience to Bede, whose testimony seems to point in the same direction. As already said, he uses one and the same unit, namely, the land of a family, whenever he speaks of a tract of soil, whether that tract be the territory of a large tribe or an estate that is granted to a monastery. He gives 7000 of these units to the South Saxons, 5000 to the South Mercians, 7000 to the North Mercians, 960 to Anglesey, 300 and more to Man, 600 to Thanet, 1200 to Wight, 600 to the Isle of Ely, 87 to the promontory of Selsey, 5 to Iona. Then he tells how Alchfrid bestowed on Wilfrid the land of 10 families at Stanford and a monastery of 30 families at Ripon, and in various other cases we hear of a prelate acquiring the land of 20, 12, 10, 8 families or of one family[2].

---

[1] It is a little curious that if we multiply the 244,100 hides by 120 we obtain 29,292,000, a figure which is not very far off from the 32,543,890 which gives the total acreage (tidal water excepted) of modern England. However, it is in the highest degree improbable that the computer of hides was aiming at pure areal measurement. Nor could his credit be saved in that way, for the area of Kent is to that of Sussex as 975 : 932, not as 15 : 7. The total of 'cultivated land' in England is less than 25 million acres, that of arable is less than 12 million.

[2] Bede, Hist. Eccl. ii. 9 (ed. Plummer, i. 97): '...Meuanias insulas... quarum prior...nongentarum lx. familiarum mensuram iuxta aestimationem Anglorum, secunda trecentarum et ultra spatium tenet.' Ibid. iii. 24 (p. 180) : '...regnum Australium Merciorum, qui sunt, ut dicunt, familiarum quinque millium...Aquilonaribus Merciis quorum terra est familiarum vii. milium.' Ibid. i. 25 (p. 45): 'Est autem ad orientalem Cantiae plagam Tanatos insula non modica, id est, magnitudinis iuxta consuetudinem aestimationis Anglorum familiarum sexcentarum (þæt is syx hund hida micel æfter Angel cynnes æhta).' Ibid. iv. 13 (p. 230): 'ad provinciam Australium Saxonum, quae post Cantuarios ad austrum et ad occidentem usque ad Occidentales Saxones pertingit, habens terram familiarum septem millium (is þæs landes seofen þusendo [hida]).' Ibid. iv. 14 (p. 237): 'Est autem mensura eiusdem insulae [Vectae] iuxta aestimationem Anglorum mille ducentarum familiarum : unde data est episcopo possessio terrae trecentarum familiarum (æfter Angel cynnes æhta twelf hund hida, and he þa þam biscop gesealde on æht þreo hund hida).' Ibid. iv. 17 (p. 246): 'Est autem Elge in provincia Orientalium Anglorum regio familiarum circiter sexcentarum (six hund hida) in similitudinem insulae.' Ibid. iii. 25 (pp. 182-3): 'donaverat monasterium quadraginta familiarum in loco qui dicitur Inrhypum.' Ibid. v. 19 : 'mox donavit terram decem familiarum in loco qui dicitur Stanford, et non multo post monasterium triginta familiarum in loco qui vocatur Inrhypum (tyn hiwisca landes on þære stowe þe is cweðon Stanford...minster xxx. hiwisca).' Ibid. iv. 13 (p. 232): 'donavit...Uilfrido

Now we must notice that in their estimates of one large province there is a certain agreement between the Eccle- siastical History and The Tribal Hidage. Both give the South Saxons 7000 hides or families[1]. What are we then to say? If we suppose that Bede is speaking to us of tenements which tend to conform to the hide of 120 arable acres his statements must fly far beyond their mark. For example, the Isle of Wight is to have 1200 hides, and yet, according to Domesday Book, the whole of Hampshire including that island will not have 3000 hides, nor 3000 'teamlands,' nor 3000 teams. Bede's Wight contains as many hides as the Worcestershire or the Herefordshire of Domesday. He allots 600 of his units to the Isle of Ely, which in 1086 had about 80 hides and 126 teamlands. He allots another 600 of his units to the Isle of Thanet, which in 1086 had about 66 sulungs and 93 teamlands[2].

We have now reached the critical point in our essay. Be- fore us lie two paths and it is hardly too much to say that our whole conception of early English history depends on the choice that we make. Either as we pursue our retrogressive course through the centuries there comes a time when the hide of 120 acres gives place to some other and much smaller typical tenement, or the men of Bede's day grossly exaggerated the number of the hides that there were in England and the various parts thereof.

We make our choice. We refuse to abandon the large hide. In the first place, we call to mind the continuity of the charters. They have begun to flow in Bede's day; they

terram lxxxvii. familiarum (seofan and hund eahtig hida landes)...vocabulo Selæseu.' Historia Abbatum (p. 380): 'terram octo familiarum iuxta fluvium Fresca ab Aldfrido rege...comparavit......terram xx. familiarum in loco qui incolarum lingua Ad villam Sambuce vocatur...accepit......Terram decem familiarum quam ab Aldfrido rege in possessionem acceperat in loco villae quae Daltun nuncupatur...' Hist. Eccl. iv. 21 (p. 253): 'accepit locum unius familiae ad septentrionalem plagam Uiuri fluminis (onfeng heo anes hiwscipes stowe to norð dæle Wire ðære ea).' Ibid. iii. 4 (p. 133): 'Neque enim magna est [Iona] sed quasi familiarum quinque, iuxta aestimationem Anglorum.' Ibid. iii. 24 (p. 178): 'Singulae vero possessiones x. erant familiarum, id est simul omnes cxx.'

[1] If the 'Wiht gara 600' of The Tribal Hidage refers to Wight, we have here a discord, for Bede gives the Island 1200. The North and South Mercians have together but 1200 according to Bede; the Mercians have 30,000 according to The Tribal Hidage: but the territory of 'the Mercians' is a variable.

[2] B. i. 4 b, 12; Elton, Tenures of Kent, 135.

never cease to flow until they debouch in Domesday Book.
They know but one tenemental unit. To describe it they
use Bede's phrase, and his translator's phrases. It is the
hiwisc, the *terra unius familiae*, the *terra unius manentis*,
the manse, the hide[1]. Between this and the acre they know
nothing except the yard of land. Of it they speak but seldom,
and it can only be explained as being a yard in every acre of
a hide. No moment can we fix when an old mode of reckoning
by reference to small tenements is superseded by references
to a fourfold larger model.

Gradual
reduction
of hidage.

In the second place, we have been prepared for exaggeration.
We have seen the hides steadily increasing in number as we
passed from Domesday Book to The County Hidage and thence
to The Burghal Hidage, and what may we not expect in the
remote age that we have now reached? Even in the days
of The Burghal Hidage there was a kingdom of England. There
was a king of the English who was trying to coordinate his
various dominions in one common scheme of national defence.
But now we have penetrated to an age when there is no
English nation. The *gens Anglorum* whose ecclesiastical history is being written is but a loose congeries of kindred folks.
Rude indeed will be the guesses made at such a time about
the strength of tribes and the wealth of countries. The South
Mercians are a folk of 5000 families, 'so they say':—that is
all that Bede can tell us about them. It is not likely that they
have underestimated their numbers. When there is a kingdom
of England, when there is a crushing tax called 'danegeld,' then
the day will have come when a county will, if it can, 'conceal'
its hides. At an earlier time the various folks will brag of
their strength and there will be none to mitigate their boasts.

Moreover we can not put our finger on the spot where the
breach of continuity occurs. In 1086 Sussex has about 3100
teamlands; it has about 3500 hides. The Burghal Hidage
would burden it with nearly 4500, and now we are required
to give it 7000. There is no place where we can see its hides
suddenly multiplied or divided by four.

Over-esti-
mates of
hidage.

Dare we set any limit to the power of exaggeration? In
much later days when England had long been strongly governed
and accurate fiscal rolls were being carefully stored in the
treasury, men believed in 60,000 knight's fees; royal ministers

[1] See above, p. 359.

believed in 32,000; and yet we now see good reason for doubting whether there were more than 5000[1]. In the reign of Edward III. the collective wisdom of the nation supposed, and acted upon the supposition, that there were more than 40,000 parishes in England, and then made the humiliating discovery that there were less than 9000[2]. We hear that the same error was current in the days of Wolsey. Men still believed in those 40,000 parishes[3]. Such numbers as these stood written in ancient manuscripts, some of which seem to have taken our Tribal Hidage as a base for calculations[4]. These traditional numbers will not be lightly abandoned, though their falsehood might be proved by a few days' labour spent among the official archives. Counting hides is repulsive work. If then these things happen in an age which is much closer to our own than to Bede's, ought we not to be surprised at the moderation of those current estimates of tribal strength that he reports?

Thirdly, when Bede speaks not of a large province, but of an estate acquired by a prelate, then his story seems to require that 'the land of one family' should be that big tenemental unit, the manse or hide of the land-books. Let us take by way of example the largest act of liberality that he records. King Oswy, going to battle, promises that if he be victorious he will devote to God his daughter with twelve estates for the endowment of monasteries. He is victorious; he fulfils his vow. He gives twelve estates, six in Deira, six in Bernicia; each consists of 'the possessions of ten families.' His daughter enters Hild's monastery at Hartlepool. Two years afterwards she acquires an estate of ten families at Streanaeshalch and founds a monastery there. According to our reading of the story, Oswy bestows twelve 'ten-hide vills'; he gives, that is, his rights, his superiority, over twelve villages of about the average size, some of which are in Deira,

[marginal note:] Size of Bede's hide.

---

[1] Round, Feudal England, 289.

[2] Stubbs, Const. Hist. ii. 422—3 ; Rot. Parl. ii. 302.

[3] Bright, Hist. Engl. ii. 386; Hall's Chronicle, ed. 1809, p. 656.

[4] Some of them seem to start from The Tribal Hidage and take the number of hides to be 303,201 (Liebermann, Leges Anglorum, 10). Divide this by 5 to find the knight's fees. You have 60,640. In MS. Camb. Univ. Ii. vi. 25, f. 108 we find 60,215 knight's fees, 45,011 parish churches, 52,080 vills. Another note, printed by Hearne, Rob. of Avesbury, 264, gives 53,215 knight's fees, 46,822 parish churches, 52,285 vills.

some in Bernicia. It is a handsome gift made on a grand
occasion and in return for a magnificent victory; but it is on
the scale of those gifts whereof we read in the West Saxon and
Mercian land-books, where the hides are given away by fives
and tens, fifteens and twenties. We feel no temptation to
make thirty-acre yard-lands of the units that Oswy distributed.
Were we to do this, we should see him bestowing not entire
villages (for a village of two-and-a-half hides would, at all·
events in later days, be abnormally small) but a few of the
tenements that lie in one village and a few of those that
lie in another, and such a gift would not be like those gifts
that the oldest land-books record. And so we think that the
unit which Bede employs is our large hide. When he speaks
of the estates given to those churches with whose affairs he
is conversant, he will state the hidage correctly; but when it
comes to the hidage of Sussex or Kent, he will report current
beliefs which are far from the truth. This is what we see in
later days. The officers at the Exchequer know perfectly
well that this man has fifty knight's fees and that man five,
but opine that there are 32,000, or, may be, 60,000 fees in
England[1].

Evidence
from Iona.

Observe how moderate Bede's estimate of hidage is when
he speaks of a small parcel of land of which he had heard
much, when he speaks of the holy island of Hii or Iona. A
Pictish king gave it to Columba, who received it as a site
for a monastery. 'Neque enim magna est, sed quasi familiarum
quinque, iuxta aestimationem Anglorum[2].' 'It is not a large
island; we might compare its size with that of one of our
English five-hide túns.' The comparison would be apt. Iona

---

[1] Bede, Hist. Eccl. iii. 24 (p. 178): 'donatis insuper xii. possessiunculis
terrarum, in quibus ablato studio militiae terrestris, ad exercendam militiam
caelestem, supplicandumque pro pace gentis eius aeterna, devotioni sedulae
monachorum locus facultasque suppeteret....Singulae vero possessiones x. erant
familiarum, id est simul omnes cxx.' In these villages there have been men who
owed military service; they are not being ousted from their homes; they are
being turned over as tenants to the church; henceforth they will no longer be
bound to fight, and in consideration of this precious immunity, they will have
to supply the monks with provender. That is how I read this passage. Others
can and will read it to mean something very different. But if Bede were speaking
of *decuriae* of slaves, how could there be talk of military service? The slaves
would not fight, and if the slaves belonged to eorls who fought, then how comes
it that Oswy can expropriate his nobles?

[2] Hist. Eccl. iii. 4 (p. 133).

has 1300 Scotch acres or thereabouts[1]. Plough 600 acres; there will be ample pasture left[2]. If, however, we interpreted his statement about the 7000 hides of Sussex in a similar fashion, the result would be ridiculous. The South Saxons had not 840,000 acres of arable; our Sussex has not 940,000 acres of any kind; their Sussex was thickly wooded. The contrast, however, is not between two measures; it is between knowledge and ignorance. Bede's name is and ought to be venerated, and to accuse him of talking nonsense may seem to some an act of sacrilege. But about these matters he could only tell what was told him, and we may be sure that his informants, were, to say the least, no better provided with statistics than were the statesmen of the fourteenth century[3].

Also there is one case in which we have what may be called a very ancient, though not a contemporary, exposition of Bede's words. He tells us that Æthelwealh king of the South Saxons gave to Wilfrid the land of 87 families called Selsey[4]. Then there comes to us from Chichester the copy of a land-book which professes to tell us more touching the whereabouts of these 87 hides[5]. Ceadwealla with the approval of Archbishop Wilfrid gives to a Bishop Wilfrid a little land for the construction of a monastery in the place called Selsey: 'that is to say 55 *tributarii* in the places that are called Seolesige, Medeminige, Wihttringes, Iccannore, Bridham and Egesauude and also Bessenheie, Brimfastun and Sidelesham with the other *villae* thereto belonging and their appurtenances; also the land named

Evidence from Selsey.

---

[1] Keith Johnston, Gazetteer.

[2] I do not suggest, nor does Bede suggest, that Hii was laid out in hides. He is speaking only of size.

[3] Bede gives to Anglesey the size of 960 families, to Man that of 300 'or more.' Anglesey has 175,836 acres; Man 145,011. Anglesey in 1895 had 'under all kinds of crops, bare fallow and grass (mountain and heath land excluded)' 152,004 acres. Man 96,098. Anglesey had 24,798 acres growing corn crops and 9,305 growing green crops, while the corresponding figures for Man were 22,666 and 11,580. Rationalistic explanation of Bede's statements would be useless. He is reporting vague guesses.

[4] Hist. Eccl. iv. 13 (p. 232): 'Quo tempore Rex Ædilualch donavit reverentissimo antistiti Vilfrido terram lxxxvii familiarum, ubi suos homines, qui exules vagabantur, recipere posset, vocabulo Selæsu, quod dicitur Latine Insula Vituli Marini.' Bede goes on to describe the Selsey peninsula and Wilfrid's foundation of a monastery. Wilfrid proceeded to convert the men who were given him. They included two hundred and fifty male and female slaves whom he set at liberty.

[5] K. 992 (v. 32); B. i. 98.

M.

Aldingburne and Lydesige 6 *cassati*, and in Geinstedisgate 6, and in Mundham 8, and in Amberla and Hohtun 8, and in Uualdham 4: that is 32 *tributarii*.' This instrument bears date 683. Another purporting to come from 957 describes the land in much the same fashion[1]. Where, let us ask, did the makers of these charters propose to locate the 87 hides? Some, though not all, of the places that they mentioned can be easily found on the map. We see Selsey itself; hard by are Medmeny or Medmerry, Wittering, Itchenor, Birdham and Siddlesham. At these and some other places that are not now to be found were 55 hides. Then we go further afield and discover Aldingbourn, Lidsey, Mundham, Amberley, Houghton and perhaps Upper Waltham. But we have travelled far. At Amberley and Houghton we are fifteen miles as the crow flies from Selsey[2]. Apparently then, the 87 hides consist of a solid block of villages at and around Selsey itself and of more distant villages that are dotted about in the neighbourhood. Be it granted that these land-books are forgeries; still in all probability they are a good deal older than Domesday Book[3]. Be it granted that the number of 87 hides was suggested to the forgers by the words of Bede[4]. Still we must ask what meaning they gave to those words. They distributed the 87 hides over a territory which is at least eighteen miles in diameter[5]. Now it is by no means unlikely that Æthelwealh's gift really included some villages that were remote from Selsey. We have seen before now that lands in one village may 'lie into' another and a distant village which is the moot-stow of a 'hundred.' But at any rate the

---

[1] K. 464 (ii. 341). The 55 hides are reduced to 42, no mention is made of Medemenige, Egesauude or Bessanheie, and the 32 hides are somewhat differently distributed.

[2] D. B. i. 17. The Bp of Chichester has 24 hides at Amberley.

[3] I infer this from the thorough discrepancy that there is between these charters and D. B. A forger at work after or soon before the Conquest would have arranged the church's estates in a manner similar to that which we see in King William's record.

[4] As a matter of fact, however, it is not very easy to reconcile the earlier charter with Bede's story. The charter makes the land proceed from the West-Saxon Ceadwealla and says nothing of Æthelwealh, who, according to Bede, was the donor. Mr Plummer, Bedae Opera, ii. 226, says that the forger betrays his hand by calling Wilfrid *arch*bishop. Really he seems to cut Wilfrid into two, making of him (1) an archbishop, and (2) a bishop of the South Saxons. See the attestations.

[5] In D. B. i. 17 the bishop's manor at Selsey has but 10 hides and but 7 teamlands.

forgers were not going to attempt the impossible task of cramming 'the land of 87 families' into the Selsey peninsula.

Therefore, in spite of Bede and The Tribal Hidage, we still remain faithful to the big hide. We have seen reason for believing that in the oldest days the real number of the 'real' hides was largely over-estimated. It would be an interesting, though perhaps an unanswerable, question whether any governmental or fiscal arrangements were ever based upon these inflated figures. A negative answer would seem the more probable. In Bede's day there was no one to tax all England or to force upon all England a scheme of national defence. So soon as anything that we could dare to call a government of England came into being, the truth, the unpleasant truth, would become apparent bit by bit. All along bits of the truth were well enough known. The number of hides in a village was known to the villagers; the kingling knew the number of hides that contributed to his maintenance. As the folks were fused together, these dispersed bits of truth would be slowly pieced into a whole, though for a long while the work of co-ordination would be hampered by old mythical estimates. Perhaps The Burghal Hidage may represent one of the first attempts to arrange for political purposes the hides of a large province. There is still exaggeration, and, unfortunately for us, new causes of perplexity are introduced as the older disappear. On the one hand, statesmen are beginning to know something about the facts; on the other hand, they are beginning to perceive that tenements of equal size are often of very unequal value, and to give the name *hide* to whatever is taxed as such. Also there is privilege to be reckoned with, and there is jobbery. It is a tangled skein. And yet they are holding fast the equation $1\text{H.} = 120\text{A.}$ *Conclusion in favour of the large hide.*

There is, however, another point of view from which the evidence should be examined, though a point to which we can not climb. How will our big hide assort with the evidence that comes to us from abroad? Only a few words about this question can we hazard. *Continental analogies.*

If we look to the villages of Germany, or at any rate of some parts of Germany, we see that the typical fully endowed peasant holds a mass of dispersed acre-strips, a *Hufe, hoba, mansus* which, while it falls far short of our hide, closely resembles our virgate. The resemblance is close. As our virgate is com- *The German Hufe.*

pounded of acres, so this *Hufe* is compounded of acres, or day's-works, or mornings (*Morgen*). When the time for accurate measurement comes, these day-work-units differ somewhat widely in extent as we pass from one district to another. The English statute acre is, as we have already said[1], an unusually large day-work-unit. It contains 40·46 *ares*, while in Germany, if there is nothing exceptional in the case, the *Morgen* will have no more than from 25 to 30 *ares*[2]. This notwithstanding, the *Hufe*, is generally supposed to contain either 30 or else 60 *Morgen*, the former reckoning being the commoner. In the one case it would resemble our virgate, in the other our half-hide.

The *Königshufe*.

Then, however, we see—and it has occurred to us that some solution of our difficulty might lie in this quarter—that in Germany there appears sporadically a unit much larger than the ordinary *Hufe*, which is known as a *Königshufe* or *mansus regalis*. This is sometimes reckoned to contain 160, but sometimes 120 *Morgen*. It seems to be an unit accurately measured by a *virga regalis* of 4·70 meters and to contain 21,600 square *virgae*. In size it would closely resemble an English hide of 120 statute acres; the one would contain 47·736, the other 48·56 hectares. To explain the appearance of these large units by the side of the ordinary *Hufen*, it has been said that as the Emperor or German king reigned over wide territories and had much land to give away, he felt the need of some accurate standard for the measurement of his own gifts, so that he might be able to dispose of 'five manses' or 'ten manses' in some distant province and yet know exactly what he was doing. This theory, however, does not tell us why the unit that was thus chosen and called a king's *Hufe* or 'royal manse' was much larger than an ordinary manse or *Hufe*, and we seem invited to suppose that at some time or another a notion had prevailed that when an allotment of land in a village was made to a king, he should have for his tenement twice or thrice or four times as many strips as would fall to the lot of the common man[3].

The English hide and the *Königshufe*.

The suggestion then might be made that the manse, *terra unius familiae, terra unius manentis*, of our English documents

[1] See above, p. 378.   [2] Meitzen, op. cit. ii. 563.

[3] Meitzen, op. cit., ii. 553–69; iii. 557–61; Lamprecht, Deutsches Wirtschaftsleben, i. 348.

is not the typical manse of the common man, but the typical king's-manse. We might construct the following story:—When England was being settled, the practice was to give the common man about 30 acres to his manse, but to give the king 120. Thus in the administration of the royal lands a 'manse' would stand for this large unit. Then this same unit was employed in the computation of the *feorm, victus* or *pastus* that was due to the king from other lands, and finally the royal reckoning got so much the upper hand that when men spoke of a 'manse' or a 'family land' they meant thereby, not the typical estate of the common man, but a four times larger unit which was thrust upon their notice by fiscal arrangements.

Some such suggestion as this may deserve consideration if all simpler theories break down. But it is not easily acceptable. It supposes that in a very early and rude age a natural use of words was utterly and tracelessly expelled by a highly technical and artificial use. This might happen in a much governed country which was full of royal officials; we can hardly conceive it happening in the England of the seventh and eighth centuries. Moreover, the continental evidence does not lie all on one side. There was, for instance, one district in Northern Germany where the term *Hufe* was given to an area that was but a trifle smaller than 120 acres of our statute measure[1]. Also there are the large Scandinavian allotments to be considered. Even in Gaul on the estates of S^t. Germain the *mansus ingenuilis* sometimes contained, if Guérard's calculations are correct, fully as much arable land as we are giving to the hide[2]. Nor, though we may dispute about the degree of difference, can it be doubted that the Germanic conquest of a Britain that the legions had deserted was catastrophic when compared with the slow process by which the Franks and other tribes gained the mastery in Gaul. Just in the matter of agrarian allotment this difference might show itself in a striking form. The more barbarous a man is, the more land he must have to feed himself withal, if corn is to be his staple food. There were

[1] Meitzen, op. cit. ii. 566. The Kalenberger *Hufe* was a measure prevalent in the district of Braunschweig-Lüneberg. It contained 180 Morgen or 47·147 hectares. A hide made of 120 statute acres would contain about 48·56 hectares. Apparently Dr Meitzen (ii. 113) has found no difficulty in accepting a hide of 120 acres as the normal share of the English settler. See also Lamprecht, Deutsches Wirtschaftsleben, i. 348.

[2] Polyptyque de l'abbaye de S. Germain des Prés, ed. Longnon, i. 102.

no ecclesiastics in England to maintain the continuity of agricultural tradition. Also the heathen Germans in England had a far better chance of providing themselves with slaves than had their cousins on the mainland. Also it seems very possible that throughout the wide and always growing realm of the Frankish king, the fiscal nomenclature would be fixed by the usages which obtained in the richest and most civilized of those lands over which he reigned, and that the 'manse' that was taken as the unit for taxation was really a much smaller tenement than supported a family in the wilder and ruder east. Besides, when in Frankland a tax is imposed which closely resembles and may have been the model for our danegeld, the *mansus ingenuilis* pays twice as much as the *mansus servilis*[1]. This suggests that the Frankish statesmen have two different typical tenements in their minds, whereas in England all the hides pay equally.

The large hide not too large. No doubt at first sight 120 arable acres seem a huge tenement for the maintenance of one family. But, though the last word on this matter can not be spoken by those ignorant alike of agriculture and physiology, still they may be able to forward the formation of a sound judgment by calling attention to some points which might otherwise be neglected. In the first place, our 'acre' is a variable whose history is not yet written. Perhaps when written it will tell us that the oldest English acres fell decidedly short of the measure that now bears that name and even that a rod of 12 feet was not very uncommon. Secondly, when our fancy is catering for thriftless barbarians, we must remember that the good years will not compensate for the bad. Every harvest, however poor, must support the race for a twelvemonth. Thirdly, we must think away that atmosphere of secure expectation in which we live. When wars and blood-feuds and marauding forays are common, men must try to raise much food if they would eat a little. Fourthly, we must not light-heartedly transport the three-course or even the two-course programme of agriculture into the days of conquest and settlement. It is not impossible that no more than one-third of the arable was sown in any year[2]. Fifthly, we may doubt whether Arthur Young was

---

[1] Pertz, Leges, i. 536; Ann. Bertin. (ed. Waitz) 81, 135; Richter, Annalen, ii. 400, 443; Dümmler, Gesch. d. Ostfränk. Reichs, i. 585.

[2] Meitzen, op. cit. ii. 592–3.

further in advance of Walter of Henley than Walter was of the
wild heathen among whom the hides were allotted; and yet
Walter, with all his learned talk of marl and manure, of second-
fallowing and additional furrows, faced the possibility of gar-
nering but six bushels from an acre[1]. Sixthly, we have to
provide for men who love to drink themselves drunk with beer[2].
Their fields of barley will be wide, for their thirst is unquench-
able. Seventhly, without speaking of 'house-communities,' we
may reasonably guess that the household was much larger in
the seventh than it was in the eleventh century. We might
expect to find married brothers or even married cousins under
one roof. Eighthly, there seems no reason why we should not
allow the free family some slaves: perhaps a couple of huts
inhabited by slaves; there had been war enough. Ninthly, the
villein of the thirteenth century will often possess a full virgate
of 30 acres, and yet will spend quite half his time in cultivating
his lord's demesne. Tenthly, in Domesday Book the case of
the *villanus* who holds an integral hide is by no means unknown[3], nor the case of the *villanus* who has a full team of
oxen. When all this has been thought over, let judgment be
given. Meanwhile we can not abandon that belief to which the
evidence has brought us, namely, that the normal tenement of
the German settler was a hide, the type of which had 120 acres
of arable, little more or less.

If we are right about this matter, then, as already said[4], some important consequences follow. We may once and for all dismiss as a dream any theory which would teach us that from the first the main and normal constitutive cell in the social structure of the English people has been the manor. To call the ceorl's tenement of 120 acres a manor, though it may have a few slaves to till it, would be a grotesque misuse of words, nor, if there is to be clear thinking, shall we call it an embryo manor, for by no gradual process can a manor be developed from it. There must be a coagulation of some three or four such tenements into a single proprietary unit before that name

The large hide and the manor.

---

[1] See above, p. 438.

[2] Tacitus, Germania, c. 15, 23. The very lenient treatment by Abp
Theodore of the monk who gets drunk upon a festival tells a curious tale:
Haddan and Stubbs, Councils, iii. 177; Robertson, Hist. Essays, 68.

[3] Thus, e.g., D. B. i. 127, Fuleham: 'ibi 5 villani, quisque 1 hidam.'

[4] See above, p. 360.

can be fairly earned. That from the first there were units which by some stretch of language might be called manors is possible. The noble man, the eorl, may have usually had at least those five hides which in later days were regarded as the proper endowment for a thegn, and these large estates may have been cultivated somewhat after the manorial fashion by the slaves and freed-men of their owners. But the language of Bede and of the charters assures us that the arrangement which has been prevalent enough to be typical has been that which gave to each free family, to each house-father, to each tax-payer (*tributarius*) one hide and no more; but no less. Such a use of words is not engendered by rarities and anomalies.

Last words. However, we would not end this essay upon a discord. Therefore a last and peaceful word. There is every reason why the explorers of ancient English history should be hopeful. We are beginning to learn that there are intricate problems to be solved and yet that they are not insoluble. A century hence the student's materials will not be in the shape in which he finds them now. In the first place, the substance of Domesday Book will have been rearranged. Those villages and hundreds which the Norman clerks tore into shreds will have been reconstituted and pictured in maps, for many men from over all England will have come within King William's spell, will have bowed themselves to him and become that man's men. Then there will be a critical edition of the Anglo-Saxon charters in which the philologist and the palæographer, the annalist and the formulist will have winnowed the grain of truth from the chaff of imposture. Instead of a few photographed village maps, there will be many; the history of land-measures and of field-systems will have been elaborated. Above all, by slow degrees the thoughts of our forefathers, their common thoughts about common things, will have become thinkable once more. There are discoveries to be made; but also there are habits to be formed.

INDEX.